FLORIDA STATE
UNIVERSITY LIBRARIES

MAY 4 1999

TALLAHASSEE, FLORIDA

THOMAS MORE

**Recent Titles in
Bibliographies and Indexes in World Literature**

Bibliographic Guide to Gabriel García Márquez, 1986–1992
Nelly Sfeir de González, compiler

The Juvenile Novels of World War II: An Annotated Bibliography
Desmond Taylor

The Spanish Civil War in Literature, Film, and Art: An International Bibliography of Secondary Literature
Peter Monteath, compiler

Africa in Literature for Children and Young Adults: An Annotated Bibliography of English-Language Books
Meena Khorana

Indigenous Literature of Oceania: A Survey of Criticism and Interpretation
Nicholas J. Goetzfridt

Boccaccio in English: A Bibliography of Editions, Adaptations, and Criticism
F. S. Stych

Cloak and Dagger Fiction: An Annotated Guide to Spy Thrillers
Myron J. Smith, Jr. and Terry White

Literature for Children and Young Adults about Oceania: Analysis and Annotated Bibliography with Additional Readings for Adults
Mary C. Austin and Esther C. Jenkins

The Contemporary Spanish Novel: An Annotated, Critical Bibliography, 1936–1994
Samuel Amell

An Annotated Bibliography of Jazz Fiction and Jazz Fiction Criticism
Richard N. Albert, compiler

Recent Work in Critical Theory, 1989–1995: An Annotated Bibliography
William Baker and Kenneth Womack

The English Novel, 1660–1700: An Annotated Bibliography
Robert Ignatius Letellier

THOMAS MORE

An Annotated Bibliography of Criticism, 1935–1997

ଓ

Compiled by
Albert J. Geritz

Bibliographies and Indexes in World Literature, Number 54

Greenwood Press
Westport, Connecticut • London

Library of Congress Cataloging-in-Publication Data

Geritz, Albert J.
   Thomas More : an annotated bibliography of criticism, 1935–1997 / compiled by Albert J. Geritz.
      p. cm.—(Bibliographies and indexes in world literature, ISSN 0742-6801 ; no. 54)
   Includes bibliographical references (p.   ) and index.
   ISBN 0-313-29391-0 (alk. paper)
   1. More, Thomas, Sir, Saint, 1478-1535—Criticism and interpretation—Bibliography.   I. Title.   II. Series.
Z8592.8.G47   1998
[DA334.M8]   98-21331

British Library Cataloguing in Publication Data is available.

Copyright © 1998 by Albert J. Geritz

All rights reserved. No portion of this book may be reproduced, by any process or technique, without the express written consent of the publisher.

Library of Congress Catalog Card Number: 98-21331
ISBN: 0-313-29391-0
ISSN: 0742-6801

First published in 1998

Greenwood Press, 88 Post Road West, Westport, CT 06881
An imprint of Greenwood Publishing Group, Inc.

Printed in the United States of America

The paper used in this book complies with the Permanent Paper Standard issued by the National Information Standards Organization (Z39.48-1984).

10 9 8 7 6 5 4 3 2 1

Contents

Preface and Acknowledgments vii
Acronyms of Journal Titles ix
Collections of Essays xv

Reference 1

Standard Editions 11

Other Editions 23

Editorial Critiques and Questions 35

Canon 39

Biography 41

General Critical Studies 111

Reception and Reputation 131

Influence 137

Religious and Philosophical Backgrounds 159

Language and Style 167

Use of Classical and Christian Sources 173

English Poems	179
Latin Poems	183
Life of Pico	191
Humanist Letter-Treatises	195
History of King Richard III	199
Utopia	215
Polemical Works	311
Devotional Works	339
Personal Correspondence	355
Other Topics	359
Index	371

Preface and Acknowledgments

Intended to be of use and interest to general readers and scholars alike, this bibliography lists and annotates major writings about Thomas More--most in English, others in French, German, Dutch, Italian, Spanish, and Portuguese--that appeared between 1935 (the year More was canonized) and August 1997. It contains over 1,649 entries. Although it does not list all references to More in encyclopedias, biographical dictionaries, and general histories of English literature or reviews of works about More, it does annotate the most important ones, and it is the *only* current bibliography in print to include so many entries in languages other than English.

Arrangement of the entries modifies that used in *Recent Studies in English Renaissance Drama* (Eds. Terence P. Logan, and Denzel S. Smith, 4 vols. [Lincoln: U of Nebraska P, 1973-78]) and in the "Recent Studies in the English Renaissance" series featured in *English Literary Renaissance*. Individual entries conform to the guidelines set forth in the *MLA Handbook for Writers of Research Papers* (Ed. Joseph Gibaldi, 4th ed. [New York: MLA, 1995]).

In order to save space and avoid repetition without sacrificing clarity, I have employed the accepted acronyms for journal titles and only the titles, not all the other publication information, of collections of essays on More in the entries. If readers need to identify a journal's title or desire the complete citation for a collection of essays, they should consult the lists following this preface.

Sections on reference works and bibliographical studies, standard editions, other editions, editorial critiques and questions, and More's canon begin the compilation. Then a segment on biography (second in length only to studies of *Utopia*) precedes chapters on general critical studies, reception and reputation, influence, religious and philosophical backgrounds, language and style, and use of classical and Christian sources. Next More's works, treated more or less in chronological order of their composition, follow the accepted divisions into humanist, polemical, and devotional writings. The bibliography ends with a section, "Other Topics," in which important studies closely related but not central to scholarship on More are considered.

Although some entries defy being placed in one category because of their diverse combination of approaches, such items are listed in the section most accurately reflecting their essential emphasis. In addition, these items are usually cross-referenced in order to give readers easy access to them.

Throughout this bibliography, objectivity and accuracy of annotation, clarity, precision, conciseness, and convenient access for readers have been my major concerns. I have taken special care to ensure the index provides efficient means to consult any entries of interest to readers.

Any bibliography of More must acknowledge the previous bibliographical efforts of Frank and Majie Padberg Sullivan, Judith P. Jones, Michael Wentworth, and others. Arthur F. Kinney, editor of *English Literary Renaissance*, and Elizabeth H. Hageman, editor of the "Recent Studies in the English Renaissance" series in that journal, provided much of the original impetus for undertaking this project by commissioning me to contribute bibliographies on More and his brother-in-law, John Rastell, to that series. Germain Marc'hadour, director of *Moreana*, Clare M. Murphy, editor of *Moreana*, and Clarence H. Miller, executive director of the Yale edition of More's complete works, served as invaluable resources.

Most research for this reference guide was completed in libraries at the University of Kansas (Lawrence), the University of Missouri (both the Columbia and Kansas City campuses), Rockhurst College (Kansas City, MO), the University of Oregon (Eugene), the University of Illinois (Urbana), the University of California (Berkeley), and Yale University. The inter-library loan service at Fort Hays State University and the cooperation of many lending libraries proved most helpful. To the courteous staffs of all these libraries, I remain greatly indebted.

I also want to thank those at Fort Hays State University who helped me complete this project: the staff of Forsyth Library, especially Phyllis Schmidt, Carolyn Hermann, and Christine Gilson, for their pleasant, prompt, professional encouragement; and Clifford Edwards, chair of the Department of English, for his encouragement and support. For granting me a sabbatical to complete research for this book, I am grateful to Fort Hays State and the Kansas Board of Regents.

In addition, I want to extend special appreciation to JoAnn Crist, a flawless secretary, without whom this bibliography would not have been completed.

Finally, I wish, once again, to thank those who are most important of all: Mom and Dad, Betty and Gunther, Laura and Robb, and Dick.

Acronyms of Journal Titles

ABR   *American Benedictine Review*
AI   *American Imago: A Psychoanalytic Journal for Culture, Science, and the Arts*
Anglia: Zeitschrift für Englische Philologie
AN&Q   *American Notes & Queries*
AR   *The Antioch Review*
Archiv für das Studium der Neuren Sprachen und Literaturen
ASch   *The American Scholar*
BC   *The Book Collector*
BHR   *Bibliothèque d'Humanisme et Renaissance*
BoundaryII   *Boundary 2: An International Journal of Literature and Culture* (Formerly *Boundary 2: A Journal of Postmodern Literature and Culture*)
BSUF   *Ball State University Forum*
CahiersE   *Cahiers Elisabéthains: Etudes sur la Pre-Renaissance et la Renaissance Anglaises*
CCRev   *Comparative Civilizations Review*
CE   *College English*
CEA Critic: An Official Journal of the College English Association
CentR   *The Centennial Review* (E. Lansing, MI)
Cithara: Essays in the Judaeo-Christian Tradition
CL   *Comparative Literature* (Eugene, OR)
ClioI   *CLIO: A Journal of Literature, History, and the Philosophy of History*
CLS   *Comparative Literature Studies*

*This list is compiled from the *MLA Bibliography* and the *Annual Bibliography of English Language & Literature*.

CollL   College Literature
Comp D   Comparative Drama
CQ   The Cambridge Quarterly
Cultura (Milan, It.)
CW   The Catholic World
Daedalus: Journal of the American Academy of Arts and Sciences
Diacritics: A Review of Contemporary Criticism
DownR   Downside Review: A Quarterly of Catholic Thought
DQR   Dutch Quarterly Review of Anglo-American Letters
EA   Etudes Anglaises: Grande-Bretagne, Etats-Unis
EAL   Early American Literature
E&S   Essays and Studies (London)
EAS   Essays in Arts and Sciences
ECr   L'Esprit Créateur
EETS   Early English Text Society
ELH   English Literary History
ElizS   Elizabethan & Renaissance Studies (Salsburg, Aus.)
ELR   English Literary Renaissance
ELWIU   Essays in Literature (Macomb, IL)
EM   English Miscellany: A Symposium of History, Literature and the Arts
ER   Etudes Rabelaisiennes
ErasmusE   Erasmus in English
ES   English Studies: A Journal of English Language and Literature (Lisse, Neth.)
Esprit
ESQ   A Journal of the American Renaissance
Extrapolation: A Journal of Science Fiction and Fantasy Folklore (London)
Genre
GRM   Germanisch-Romanische Monatsschrift
HEI   History of European Ideas
HJA&S   Hitotsubashi Journal of Arts & Sciences
HLQ   Huntington Library Quarterly: A Journal for the History and Interpretation of English and American Civilization
HTR   Harvard Theological Review
HumLov   Humanistica Lovaniensia: Journal of Neo-Latin Studies (Louvain, Belg.)
IJPP   Interpretation: A Journal of Political Philosophy
Italica
JAAR   Journal of the American Academy of Religion
JEGP   Journal of English and Germanic Philology
JHI   Journal of the History of Ideas
JMRS   Journal of Medieval and Renaissance Studies

JRMMRA   Journal of the Rocky Mountain Medieval and Renaissance Association
JWCI   Journal of the Warburg and Courtauld Institutes
KR   The Kenyon Review
Latinitas: Commentarii Linguae Latinae Excolendae
Ldprov   Il Lettore di Provincia
Library   The Library: A Quarterly Journal of Bibliography
LittPrag   Litteraria Pragensia: Studies in Literature and Culture (Amsterdam)
LJHum   Lamar Journal of the Humanities
M&H   Medievalia et Humanistica: Studies in Medieval and Renaissance Culture
Manuscripta
MLN   Modern Language Notes
MLR   The Modern Language Review
Moreana: Bulletin Thomas More
Mosaic: A Journal for the Interdisciplinary Study of Literature
MP   Modern Philology: A Journal Devoted to Research in Medieval and Modern Literature
MQ   Midwest Quarterly: A Journal of Contemporary Thought (Pittsburg, KS)
MRTS   Medieval & Renaissance Texts & Studies
MS   Mediaeval Studies (Toronto, Can.)
N&Q   Notes and Queries
Neophil   Neophilologus (Groningen, Neth.)
NLH   New Literary History: A Journal of Theory and Interpretation
NM   Neuphilologische Mitteilungen: Bulletin de la Société Néophilologique/ Bulletin of the Modern Language Society
NS   Die Neuren Sprachen
P&R   Philosophy and Rhetoric
Paragraph: A Journal of Modern Critical Theory (Formerly *Paragraph: The Journal of Modern Critical Theory Group*)
Parergon: Bulletin of the Australian and New Zealand Association for Medieval and Renaissance Studies
PBSA   Papers of the Bibliographical Society of America
PMLA   Publications of the Modern Language Association of America
PPMRC   Proceedings of the PMR Conference: Annual Publication of the International Patristic, Medieval and Renaissance Conference
PQ   Philological Quarterly (Iowa City, IA)
QQ   Queen's Quarterly
RAA   Revue anglo-americaine
RCEI   Revista Canaria de Estudios Ingleses
Ren&R   Renaissance and Reformation/Renaissance et Réforme
Renascence: Essays on Value in Literature
RenP   Renaissance Papers

RenQ Renaissance Quarterly
RenSt Renaissance Studies: Journal of the Society for Renaissance Studies
RES Review of English Studies: A Quarterly Journal of English Literature and the English Language
RHE Revue d'Histoire Ecclésiastique
RI Revista Iberoamericana
RMM Revue de Métaphysique et de Morale
RN Renaissance News
RQ Riverside Quarterly
SCJ The Sixteenth-Century Journal
SCUL Soundings: Collections of the University Library, University of California, Santa Barbara
SEL Studies in English Literature, 1500-1900
SFS Science-Fiction Studies
ShJE Shakespeare-Jahrbuch (Weimar, GDR)
SHR Southern Humanities Review
ShS Shakespeare Survey: An Annual Survey of Shakespeare Studies and Production
ShStud Shakespeare Studies (Tokyo)
SMy Studia Mystica
SN Studia Neophilologica: A Journal of Germanic and Romance Languages and Literature
Soundings: An Interdisciplinary Journal
SP Studies in Philology
SPWVSRA Selected Papers from the West Virginia Shakespeare and Renaissance Association
SR Sewanee Review
SRen Studies in the Renaissance
StHum Studies in the Humanities (Indiana, PA)
Studies: An Irish Quarterly Review (Dublin)
Studium
SubStance: A Review of Theory and Literary Criticism
TEAS   Twayne's English Authors Series
Thesaurus: Boletín del Institutio Caro y Cuervo
Thought: A Review of Culture and Idea
TLS Times Literary Supplement
Traditio: Studies in Ancient and Medieval History, Thought, and Religion
TSLL Texas Studies in Literature and Language
UMSE University of Mississippi Studies in English
UtopSt Utopian Studies: Journal of the Society for Utopian Studies
UTQ University of Toronto Quarterly: A Canadian Journal of the Humanities
Viator: Medieval and Renaissance Studies

*WB   Weimarer Beiträge: Zeitschrift für Literaturwissenschaft, Ästhetik und
          Kulturtheorie*
WisSL   Wisconsin Studies in Literature
YES   Yearbook of English Studies
YFS   Yale French Studies
YR   The Yale Review
YULG   Yale University Library Gazette

Collections of Essays

Adams, Robert M., trans. and ed. Utopia: *A New Translation, Backgrounds, Criticism*. 1975. New York: Norton, 1992.

Boventer, Hermann, ed. *Thomas Morus Jahrbuch*. Dusseldorf: Triltsch Verlag, 1981, 1982, 1983/84, 1984/85, 1985/86, 1987, 1988, 1989, 1990, 1991, 1992, 1993, 1994, 1995.

Byron, Brian, and Damian Grace, eds. *Thomas More: Essays on the Icon*. Six Essays Presented at the Thomas More Quincentenary Conference, Sydney, Australia, August 1978. Melbourne: Dove Communications, 1980.

Cousins, A.D., and Damian Grace, eds. *More's* Utopia *and the Utopian Inheritance*. Lanham, MD: UP of America, 1995.

Doyle, Charles Clay, ed. *Thomas More and the U.S.A.* Special issue of *Moreana* 51 (1976).

Fox, Alistair, and Peter Leech, eds. *Thomas More: The Rhetoric of Character*. Essays Presented at the Thomas More Quincentenary Symposium, University of Otago, 1978. Dunedin: NZ, 1978.

Gallagher, Ligeia, ed. *More's* Utopia *and Its Critics*. Chicago: Scott, Foresman, 1964.

Keen, Ralph, and Daniel Kinney, eds. *Thomas More and the Classics*. Special issue of *Moreana* 86 (1985).

Marc'hadour, Germain, and R.S. Sylvester, eds. *Essential Articles for the Study of Thomas More*. Hamden, CT: Archon, 1977.

---. *Meliora: Miscellanea de Mori* Utopia. Special issue of *Moreana* 69 (1981).

*Hereafter in this bibliography these volumes are referred to by the titles of the collection or the journal.

---. *Meliora: Miscellanea de Mori* Utopia. Special issue of *Moreana* 77 (1983).

---. *Miscellanea de Mori* Utopia: *A Festschrift on More's* Utopia *in Honour of Edward Surtz, S.J.* Special issue of *Moreana* 31-32 (1971).

McCutcheon, Elizabeth, and Clarence H. Miller, eds. Utopia *Revisited*. Special issue of *Moreana* 118-119 (1994).

Moore, Michael J., ed. *Quincentennial Essays on St. Thomas More*. Selected Papers from the Thomas More College Conference. Boone, NC: Albion, Department of History, Appalachian State U, 1978.

Murphy, Clare M., Henri Gibaud, and Mario A. Di Cesare, eds. *Miscellanea Moreana: Essays for Germain Marc'hadour*. *Moreana* 100: Volume XXVI. Melanges Marc'hadour. MRTS. 61. Binghamton: MRTS, 1989.

Nelson, William, ed. *Twentieth-Century Interpretations of* Utopia: *A Collection of Critical Essays*. Englewood Cliffs, NJ: Prentice-Hall, 1968.

Olin, John C., ed. *Interpreting Thomas More's* Utopia. New York: Fordham UP, 1989.

Sullivan, E.D.S., ed. *The Utopian Vision: Seven Essays on the Quincentennial of Sir Thomas More*. San Diego: San Diego State UP, 1983.

Sylvester, R.S., ed. *St. Thomas More: Action and Contemplation*. Proceedings of the Symposium Held at St. John's University, October 9-10, 1970. New Haven: Yale UP for St. John's University, 1972.

Reference

A001 Bertagnoni, Marialisa. "Lettera da Vicenza." *Moreana* 93 (1987): 5-28.

The first item in this survey concerns Francesco Cossiga's references to More both in Italy and abroad. *Utopia* has been often discussed from 1980-86, with a special slant in 1984, the year of Orwell. Erasmus' *Praise of Folly* has been much in the news because of two Italian translations (1982, 1984), and Shakespeare has received "clamorous" attention on account of two plays: *Richard III* and his controverted authorship of *Sir Thomas More*.

A002 Bertagnoni, Marialisa; Germain Marc'hadour, intro. "Lettera da Vicenza: Postuma." *Moreana* 104 (1990): 74-86.

This article is the last installment of a bibliographical survey of More studies in Italy, which Bertagnoni published in *Moreana* over a quarter century. She saw it as a twin of the Yale Newsletter, also an annual fixture when R.S. Sylvester was executive editor of the *Complete Works*.

A003 Bertagnoni, Marialisa. "Lettera da Vicenza: Triennio Moriano 1977-79." *Moreana* 71-72 (1981): 131-53.

Bertagnoni lists and evaluates More studies during these years.

A004 Boswell, Jackson Campbell, comp. *Sir Thomas More in the English Renaissance: An Annotated Catalogue*. Introd. Anne Lake Prescott. Binghamton, NY: MRTS, 1994.

Boswell builds on the work of earlier compilers (R.W. Gibson [A014], Frank and Majie Padberg Sullivan [A043-A048], Anne Lake Prescott [A030], and Charles Clay Doyle [A009-A012]), collects all references to More in STC books published in England and English books abroad up to 1640, arranges them alphabetically, cites their STC numbers, and annotates them. The work also features a chronological appendix and Prescott's introduction on how Boswell's catalogue can be used for literary analysis.

A005 Brouwer, Piet. "Les Pays-Bas Utopiens." *Moreana* 97 (1988): 73-76.
Brouwer lists major publications of and about More and his works in Belgium and the Netherlands from its beginnings to the present.

A006 Delcourt, Marie. "Recherches sur Thomas More, La tradition continentale et la tradition anglaise." *Humanisme et Renaissance* 3 (1937): 22-42.
This article supplies a short bibliography with historical and critical commentary on scholarship, the collected works, biographies, letters, and lucubrationes.

A007 Delendick, Patricia, and Marie-Claude Rousseau. "Utopiana in *Moreana* (Articles only. Seulement les articles)." *Moreana* 69 (1981): 163-65.
The compilers list the authors and titles of all articles on *Utopia* published in *Moreana* chronologically from the first issue to 1980--no annotations are given.

A008 Desroche, Henri. "Petite bibliothèque de l'Utopie." *Esprit* 42 (1974): 663-70.
Desroche assembles a short list of works important to study of the concept of utopia.

A009 Doyle, Charles C. "Moreana of the Late Seventeenth and Early Eighteenth Centuries." *Moreana* 45 (1975): 53-60.
The fourth and last installment of a harvest of references to and quotes from More in the literature of England and Europe begins with *Donne's Satyr* (1662, John Donne the younger) and ends with a 1746 letter from William Shenstone. One of the longer quotes is a scaffold story in English and French from Abel Boyer's *Companion* (1700).

A010 Doyle, Charles C. "Moreana, 1604-1660." *Moreana* 41 (1974): 11-18.
This article continues, from *Moreana* 34, 38, and 41, a collection of materials supplementary to R.W. Gibson's *St. Thomas More: A Preliminary Bibliography of His Works and of Moreana to the Year 1750* (A014), and Doyle brings together thirty-four items, which include references to More and his works, as well as quotations, translations, and adaptations from his writings.

A011 Doyle, Charles C. "Moreana of the Seventeenth and Eighteenth Centuries." *Moreana* 34 (1972): 47-55.
Doyle cites fifty-seven references to More, not included in R.W. Gibson's

REFERENCE 3

Sir Thomas More: A Preliminary Bibliography of His Works and of Moreana to the Year 1750 (A014). These references range in time from 1636 through 1745; most are from English works, though a few are in Latin, French, or Spanish.

A012 Doyle, Charles C. "Moreana of Tudor Times." *Moreana* 38 (1973): 13-20.

Twenty-six allusions to More supplement R.W. Gibson's *Sir Thomas More: A Preliminary Bibliography of His Works and of Moreana to the Year 1750* (A014). These additional allusions, by twenty-five writers (some well-known, some obscure), range in date from 1525 to 1602.

A013 Geritz, Albert J. "Recent Studies in More (1977-1990)." *ELR* 22 (1982): 112-40.

This survey of More's treatment in criticism continues the work of Judith P. Jones (A019) and repeats a few works Jones mentions only because of their key importance to the history of More scholarship.

A014 Gibson, R.W., comp. *Sir Thomas More: A Preliminary Bibliography of His Works and of Moreana to the Year 1750. With a Bibliography of Utopiana Compiled by R.W. Gibson and J. Max Patrick.* New Haven: Yale UP, 1961.

Beginning with a frontispiece of representative signatures by More in chronological order, the volume is divided into eleven sections, six of which provide bibliographical descriptions relating to *Utopia*, separate works, collected works, Lucian, More's translations, prayers, and lives of More. Other sections list letters to and from More, allusions to More and his works, Utopiana, fictitious publishers' imprints using Utopian addresses, and portraits of More appearing in the works described. The Utopian section is a checklist of Utopias and Utopian literature. Given the number of such works written between 1500 and 1750, it is not surprising to learn the list is selective; yet it supplies a wealth of information to any student of Utopian literature. One must remember this bibliography is preliminary and that subsequent Yale editions of More's works, books, and articles (especially those found in *Moreana*) enlarge upon invaluable information found here.

A015 Haschak, Paul G. "More [Sir] Thomas." *Utopian/Dystopian Literature: A Bibliography of Literary Criticism*. Metuchen, NJ: Scarecrow P, 1994. 174-84.

Among roughly 3,500 citations for over 375 authors of utopian/dystopian works, Haschak lists over 140 important references essential to the study of More's *Utopia*.

A016 Heilen, Hans. "Moreana Materials in Dutch." *Moreana* 97 (1988): 97-100.

Heilen provides a bibliography of books (since 1935), lectures and conferences, and articles published in the Netherlands, along with his notes.

A017 Hsia, Po-Chia R. "The *Utopia* in Chinese." *Moreana* 69 (1981): 107-09.

Hsia describes and explains the status of More studies, especially as they concern *Utopia*, in China.

A018 Hunter, David G. "Thomas More in Washington, D.C." *Moreana* 51 (1976): 74-76.

Hunter provides a list of holdings from early editions of More's works and selected items of *Moreana* in D.C. libraries.

A019 Jones, Judith P. "Recent Studies in More." *ELR* 9 (1979): 442-58.

Although Jones' bibliographical essay essentially covers More scholarship published between 1945 through 1976, she includes some items outside those dates.

A020 Kapótsy, Béla. "Recent Hungarian Writings about Saint Thomas More." *Moreana* 75-76 (1982): 39-43.

Kapótsy reviews recent published and unpublished criticism written in Hungary about More.

A021 Keen, Ralph, and Constance Smith. "Updating an Update." *Moreana* 97 (1988): 137-40.

During the seven years since Smith's updating (A039) of R.W. Gibson's *Sir Thomas More: A Preliminary Bibliography* (A014) was published, a number of new locations, revisions, and corrections have come to the authors' attention, through the Yale editions and from Marc'hadour. K.J. Wilson's review of Smith's "Updating" (*Moreana* 77 [1983]: 97-99) also offers corrections presented here.

A022 Larkin, James F. "The Status of Scholarship on St. Thomas More." *American Ecclesiastical Review* 117 (1947): 33-42.

This survey of English and American scholarship is actually a review of the Sullivans' *Moreana, 1478-1945* (A044) that includes numerous items the Sullivans omit (though it generally compliments what the Sullivans accomplished).

A023 López Estrada, Francisco. "Publications Récentes Sur Thomas More et L'Utopie en Espagne et en Amérique Espagnole." *Moreana* 126 (1966): 41-50.

López Estrada reviews recent publications about More and his works, especially *Utopia*, as they relate to Spain and Latin America; he focuses upon the scholarship of Stelio Cro and Silvio Zavala and the new journal *Brispania* published in Valladolid.

A024 MacDonald, William. "Saint Thomas More and the Historians." *ABR* 21 (1970): 425-40.

MacDonald provides a list of guides to More scholarship (including Frank and Majie Padberg Sullivan [A043-A048] and R.W. Gibson [A014]) and a list of historians and critics (including Campbell, Reed, Rogers, Kautsky, Ames, Donner, Surtz, Chambers, Hexter, Bridgett, McConica, Elton, Derrett, and others).

A025 Marc'hadour, Germain. "Thomas More aux Etats Unis." *EA* 9 (1956): 315-22.

This article reviews the state of scholarship and criticism on More in the United States and includes a selective list, complete with annotations, of books and articles published there.

A026 Marmion, John P. "Thomas More in Modern Studies." *Clergy Review* 62 (1977): 384-87.

Marmion surveys More studies (beginning with Bridgett) and then singles out the works of Chambers, Allen, Campbell, Reed, Rogers, the Yale Edition of the Complete Works project, *Moreana*, Marc'hadour, Bolt, O'Sullivan, Basset, and Morison.

A027 McConica, James K., comp. "Sir Thomas More (1478-1535)." *The New Cambridge Bibliography of English Literature*. Vol. 1, *600-1600*. Ed. George Watson. Cambridge: Cambridge UP, 1974.

This list of over 600 entries (up to the year 1972) supplements previous lists--A.W. Reed, comp., "Sir Thomas More," *The Cambridge Bibliography of English Literature*, Vol. 1, *600-1600*, Ed. F.W. Batson (Cambridge: Cambridge UP, 1941); and H.W. Husbands and H.W. Donner, comps., "Sir Thomas More," *The Cambridge Bibliography of English Literature*, Vol. 5, *Supplement: A.D. 600-1900*, Ed. George Watson (Cambridge: Cambridge UP, 1957).

A028 McNamee, M.B. "St. Thomas More at St. Louis University." *Moreana* 51 (1976): 23-25.

McNamee summarizes the amount of More scholarship produced over the years at St. Louis University.

A029 Negley, Glenn. *Utopian Literature: A Bibliography with a Supplementary Listing of Works Influential in Utopian Thought.* Lawrence: Regents P of Kansas, 1977.

This bibliography provides citations useful in the study of not only More's *Utopia* but many other utopian works.

A030 Prescott, Anne Lake. "Renaissance References to Thomas More." *Moreana* 70 (1981): 5-24.

Prescott gathers some seventy-nine Renaissance references to More in French and English from Guillaume de la Perrière's *Miroir politique* (1555) to Thomas Bancroft's *Time's out of Tune* (1658).

A031 Samaan, Angele Botros. "Utopias and Utopian Novels: 1516-1949." *Moreana* 31-32 (1971): 281-93.

Samaan supplies a preliminary bibliography upon this subject.

A032 Sargent, Lyman Tower. *British and Utopian Literature, 1516-1985: An Annotated, Chronological Bibliography.* New York: Garland, 1988.

This massive bibliography of British and American utopian literature serves not merely as a most useful tool for research but also attempts to extend the boundaries of utopia far beyond the literary utopia and communitarian experiments. Besides the widely known and accepted utopias, it includes utopian satire, treatises, discourses, reform plans, and proposals for governments. The bibliography is divided into two sections: an annotated, chronological list of utopias first published in English, or, according to the compiler, in "a very few cases, Latin," and author and title indexes, together with a list of location symbols.

A033 Sawada, Paul A. "Thomas More in Japan." *Moreana* 64 (1980): 3-27.

Sawada presents a thorough assessment of major Japanese scholars and their work on More, beginning with the first recorded mention of More in Japan in 1861 and ending with a summary of quincentennial celebrations of More's birth in Japan (1977-78).

A034 Sawada, Paul A. *Thomas More in Japan.* Renaissance Monographs. 5. Tokyo: The Renaissance Institute, Sophia U, 1978.

Sawada traces the growth of More's reputation in Japan from 1861 to 1978, beginning with the opening of Japan to the western world and the first mention of More and *Utopia* there. He also discusses Japanese translations of *Utopia* and scholarship upon it. He includes a preliminary bibliography of works by and about More published in Japan between 1861 and 1978.

A035 Schulte-Herbrüggen, Hubertus, and J.B. Trapp, comps. *"The King's Good Servant": Sir Thomas More 1477/8-1535*. Published for the exhibition held at the National Portrait Gallery 25 November 1977 to 12 March 1978. Ipswich, Eng.: Boydell; Totowa, NJ: Rowman & Littlefield, 1977.

Fine illustrations are the main feature of this scholarly catalogue of paintings, woodcuts, letters, documents, mss., books, medals, relics, and other artifacts assembled at the National Portrait Gallery to commemorate the anniversary of More's birth.

A036 Smith, Constance. "Additional Locations for Thomas More's *Utopia*." *Moreana* 31 (1971): 261-62.

Smith reports additional locations of the four editions of *Utopia* that were collated for the 1965 Yale edition (B019) and listed in R.W. Gibson's *St. Thomas More: A Preliminary Bibliography of His Works and of Moreana to the Year 1750* (A014).

A037 Smith, Constance. "More's Works in American Editions: A Summary." *Moreana* 51 (1976): 44-46.

Following the procedure in the *National Union Catalogue*, Smith lists American editions of the complete works, *Utopia*, and of separate works alphabetized by title. (The first "completely American" edition of *Utopia* appeared in 1834.)

A038 Smith, Constance. "Thomas More in America: A Census of Locations According to Gibson's *Preliminary Bibliography*." *Moreana* 51 (1976): 47-52.

Smith tabulates American locations of each published work as it is entered in Gibson's work (A014).

A039 Smith, Constance. *An Updating of R.W. Gibson's* St. Thomas More: A Preliminary Bibliography. 20. St. Louis: Center for Reformation Research, 1981.

The primary value of the *Updating* is that its map of the distribution of copies of More's works assists scholars. In addition to unearthing locations of major works, it records a number of significant lesser finds. Gibson's hope his census (A014) would serve as "a nucleus for a more complete listing" is realized in Smith's work; and *Updating*, together with Gibson, illuminates readers' understanding of More's influence in his time and thereafter.

A040 Smith, Malcolm C. "Reflections on the *Fortuna* of Thomas More." *Moreana* 65 (1980): 23-31.

Smith's note supplements R.W. Gibson's *St. Thomas More: A Preliminary Bibliography of His Works and of Moreana to the Year 1750* (A014) by adding twenty-one references. Smith also states the time has come for scholars to use the "raw materials" Gibson and others collected to study the *fortuna* of More's personality, works, and thought and their influence.

A041   Spikes, Judith Doolin. "The Thomas More Collection, College of New Rochelle." *Moreana* 51 (1976): 77-78.

Spikes discusses the origins and holdings of the collection of Moreana in the library of this New York college.

A042   Stamm, Rudolf. "Die Morus Biographie von R.W. Chambers und ihre Auswirkung." *Theologische Zeitschrift* 7 (1951): 103-14.

Stamm gives a short account of the chief publications concerning More, suggested by the fourth centenary of his death in 1935, which appeared between 1931 and 1937. Among these he singles out the biography by Chambers (F040), with its epilogue, *The Place of St. Thomas More in English Literature and History* (F038) as the most influential. Chambers' biography is now available in a German translation by J.E. Nenniger (1947). After an analysis of some main points Chambers made on controversial problems, Stamm illustrates Chambers' influence on later studies--English, American, and Continental--of More and his works between 1941 and 1951.

A043   Sullivan, Frank, comp. *Syr Thomas More: A First Bibliographical Notebook Wherein betretyd divers maters compondyd & divisyd by Frank Sullivan.* Los Angeles: Loyola U of Los Angeles, 1953.

The books described are important either as scholarly sources or illustrations of the variant artistry with which early printers presented the text, and Sullivan analyzes the conditions of More's publications during the Tudor Age, "because it is always the duty of the honest scholar to scrutinize the variant editions for real variations in the presentation of the author's ideas."

A044   Sullivan, Frank, and Majie Padberg Sullivan, comps. *Moreana, 1478-1945: A Preliminary Checklist of Material By and About Saint Thomas More.* Kansas City, MO: Rockhurst College P, 1946.

In its attempt to list all editions of More and works about him from 1478 to 1945, this book serves as an index to scholarship and criticism. This work is not annotated, as are the four volumes the Sullivans later published. Its preface states their intentions: "Following the example of More's biographers from Roper to Chambers, we intend to brood some years before publishing our *Materials for the Study of Thomas More*. In the meantime, however, it seems prudent to draw the fire of criticism to this, a preliminary study, which attempts to do nothing more than list coherently the principal publications by and about our subject, together with all related works, or parts of works, which have been formally introduced as evidence or illustration into books and articles on More." Their book is arranged alphabetically by author and subject and is thorough, although they are aware of the inevitability of errors and ask readers to call oversights to their attention.

A045 Sullivan, Frank, and Majie Padberg Sullivan, comps. *Moreana: Materials for the Study of Saint Thomas More*. 4 vols. Los Angeles: Loyola U of Los Angeles, 1964-68.

The main purpose of these volumes is to guide students of More in their choice of reading. To this end, if possible the entries have been annotated in order to give readers some evaluation of their merit. Arranged alphabetically by author, the entries cover biographical, critical, and documentary materials about More from More's own times to the early 1960s.

A046 Sullivan, Majie Padberg, comp. *Index to Moreana: Materials for the Study of Saint Thomas More*. Los Angeles: Loyola U of Los Angeles, 1971.

Sullivan provides yet another useful bibliography.

A047 Sullivan, Majie Padberg, comp. *Moreana: Materials for the Study of Saint Thomas More: Supplement and Chronology to 1800*. Los Angeles: Loyola U of Los Angeles, 1977.

Sullivan adds to the materials found in the earlier volumes.

A048 Sullivan, Majie Padberg, comp. *Moreana: Materials for the Study of Saint Thomas More, Supplement II*. Los Angeles: Loyola U of Los Angeles, 1985.

The purpose of the second supplement is to update and add to the 1977 list of works about More that Sullivan assembled.

A049 Tamura, Hideo. *"Perestroika* and Thomas More in the USSR: A Checklist." *Moreana* 110 (1992): 9-18.

Recent studies on More in the USSR exceed the limit of the traditional interpretation of "Utopian socialist More" and focus on his many-sided activities, especially in the realm of humanism. This trend, begun in the 1970s with the works of Igor N. Ossinovsky, produced conferences on More in Moscow and Leningrad, and prepared the intellectual background of *perestroika* which became more widespread after Gorbachev's 1985 declaration.

A050 Trapp, J.B., and Hubertus Schulte-Herbrüggen. "'The King's Good Servant': Catalogue of the Exhibition at the National Portrait Gallery, 1977-78: Addenda and Corrigenda." *Moreana* 61 (1979): 43-50.

The authors add to and provide corrections of their catalogue of the More exhibit (A035).

A051 Wentworth, Michael D., comp. *The Essential Sir Thomas More: An*

Annotated Bibliography of Major Modern Studies. New York: G.K. Hall, 1995.

Wentworth provides a "convenient annotated survey of twentieth-century scholarship on More published in English through the year 1991." Assembled into seven chapters, the thorough annotations are "arranged...out of a concern for simplicity, directness, taxonomic consistency, and user accessibility."

A052 Williams, Franklin B., Jr. "Some More Allusions." *Moreana* 27-28 (1970): 83-86.

Williams adds twenty allusions to More (found in works from 1525 to 1646) to those listed in R.W. Gibson's *St. Thomas More: A Preliminary Bibliography of His Works and of Moreana to the Year 1750* (A014).

A053 Zajac, Hal. "Moreana at the St. John's University Law Library." *Moreana* 51 (1976): 79-80.

Zajac lists the library's early editions of More and certain other items of "Morean" interest.

A054 Zajac, Hal. "Thomas More in *The Catholic Lawyer*." *Moreana* 51 (1976): 81-82.

Zajac cites all articles on More published in *The Catholic Lawyer* from January 1955 to May 1976.

A055 Ziegler, Georgianna M. "Recent Studies in Women Writers of Tudor England, 1485-1603 (1990 to mid-1993)." *ELR* 24 (1994): 229-42.

Section B of "Studies of Individual Writers" lists and annotates scholarly works about Margaret More Roper.

A056 Znidarsic, Lilijana. "Thomas More in Slovenia." *Moreana* 95-96 (1987): 83-88.

This article reviews publications on More in the Slovene part of Yugoslavia from 1958 to 1970.

Standard Editions

B001 Erasmus, Desiderius. *Opus Epistolarum Des Erasmi Roterodami.* Eds. P.S. Allen, H.M. Allen, and H.W. Garrod. 12 vols. Oxford: Clarendon, 1906-58.

These volumes arrange the extant Latin correspondence between Erasmus and More chronologically and supply information about each letter's source and date, along with explanatory and textual commentary. In the "General Index" (Vol. 12), Barbara Flower and Elisabeth Rosenbaum provide references to specific topics about More covered in the correspondence. For English translation of the correspondence through the year 1524, see *The Correspondence of Erasmus*, trans. R.A.B. Mynors, and D.F.S. Thompson, Vols. 1-9, and R.A.B. Mynors, and Alexander Dalzell, Vol. 10, *Collected Works of Erasmus* (Toronto: U of Toronto P, 1974-92).

B002 More, Thomas. *The Answer to a Poisoned Book.* Eds. Stephen Merriam Foley, and Clarence H. Miller. Vol. 2 of The Yale Edition of the Complete Works of St. Thomas More. New Haven: Yale UP, 1985.

More's text, based on the first edition of 1533, is reproduced in handsome Baskerville type, the topical headings on alternate pages, the original side notes now indented in the body of the text in order to guide the reader's eye and make the study of the work's content as easy as possible. The words of More's opponent, frequently cited in the course of *The Answer*, are contrasted to More's prose by means of a smaller Roman type-face, while quotations from Scripture and other works are set in italics. The introduction begins with an historical account of the eucharistic controversy as it took place in Germany, Switzerland, and England between 1524 and 1533. The introduction's second part, Foley's "The Argument of the Book," delineates the exposition and theology of Book I, in which, before defending himself, More must show how John 6 clearly presents the doctrine of the real presence in the Lord's Supper, the essential Christian nourishment the Masker's poisonous exposition would take away; what Foley calls the "return to battle" (Books II-IV); and the way More makes the Masker's title literal, thereby "reducing the Masker's often high-flown arguments to the level of common sense--where they fall apart." Appendices include the text of *The Souper of the Lorde* (1533), the book to which *Poisoned Book* responds, and "The Probable Author of *The Souper of the Lorde*, George Joye" by Michael Anderegg.

B003   More, Thomas. *The Apology of Sir Thomas More*. Ed. J.B. Trapp. Vol. 9 of The Yale Edition of the Complete Works of St. Thomas More. New Haven: Yale UP, 1979.

Trapp bases his text on the 1533 edition of William Rastell, along with the list of errata printed at the end of the Rastell publication. The introduction discusses More's activities as a controversialist, opposing and putting down heretical works and men and defending the Church. He gives extensive background on Christopher St. German, More's opponent in this controversy, and his tracts; and provides a detailed analysis of the *Apology*, in which More is defending not only "his and the church's position, but...his own integrity." More's response to dissent was sternly authoritarian and repressive; in this work, his technique is that of full quotation and lengthy, careful refutation. Although More's characteristic wit and colloquial vigor appear occasionally, in general, as the editor admits, the extended process of argument and counter-argument is tedious. The volume includes illustrations, appendices, an extensive bibliography, and a thorough glossary. Appendix A reprints the text of St. German's *Division*, to which the *Apology* responds.

B004   More, Thomas. *The Confutation of Tyndale's Answer*. Eds. Louis A. Schuster, Richard C. Marius, James P. Lusardi, and Richard J. Schoeck. Vol. 8. Pt. I: Books I-IV; Pt. II: Books V-IX, Appendices; Pt. III: Introduction, Commentary, Glossary, and Index of The Yale Edition of the Complete Works of St. Thomas More. New Haven: Yale UP, 1983.

Based on the texts of 1532 and 1533 and collated with the *English Works* (1557), this is the first edition of "More's most mountainous writing" in over four-hundred years. The text has all the substantive variants in the early editions recorded as footnotes, while appendices A-D give the texts of Robert Barnes' tract on the nature of the Church from both the 1531 and 1534 versions of his *Supplication*, list English Protestant books printed abroad between 1525-35, provide a table of corresponding pages between the earliest texts and the Yale edition, and supply a list of press-variants with facsimiles. Three editors write introductions. Schuster presents an exhaustive account of "Thomas More's Polemical Career, 1523-1533," tracing the fortunes of Lutheranism in England and the part More played in confronting it, characterizing the "labyrinthine quality of More's polemic, spun out of the legal mind night after sleepless night, alert to the nature of each bit of evidence as well as its reliability and strength under scrutiny...relentless in chipping away every prop of the opponent's position until the very possibility of rebuttal seems confounded...using each statement of Tyndale as a springboard for a mass refutation of reformist doctrine." Marius contributes a detailed essay of "Thomas More's View of the Church," setting the work in its theological and historical context and positing "More was too deeply impressed by the existence of the church through centuries of history to be able to cast it off in the name of some novelty of faith resting upon nothing more, as he thought, than the rhetoric of a vagabond monk." Lusardi discusses "The Career of Robert Barnes" and treats textual problems, arguing why the editors relied upon the 1532-33 copy rather than the *English Works*. The bibliography and commentary occupy over 250 pages; the glossary gives guidance for almost all unfamiliar forms and meanings; the index is thorough.

B005 More, Thomas. *The Correspondence of Sir Thomas More.* Ed. Elizabeth Frances Rogers. Princeton: Princeton UP, 1947.

Rogers' authoritative edition of 218 letters is the result of many years' labor. Whenever possible the letters are reproduced from original mss., many of which are in More's hand. When no ms. is available, the earliest published source is used. The majority are in Latin, but quite a few are in English, and some French. In her introductions and notes, Rogers brings together all aids--biographical, historical, bibliographical--to give the fullest possible understanding and appreciation of More's correspondence, and the chronological order of the letters is especially useful. Until the appearance of The Yale Edition of the Complete Works of St. Thomas More (B012, B014), her edition provided the definitive texts of and scholarship on the *Letter to Bugenhagen, Letter to Brixius, Letter to Martin Dorp, Letter against Frith, Letter to a Monk, Letter to the University of Oxford,* and *Letter to Edward Lee.*

B006 More, Thomas. *The Debellation of Salem and Bizance.* Eds. John A. Guy, Ralph Keen, and Clarence H. Miller. Vol. 10 of The Yale Edition of the Complete Works of St. Thomas More. New Haven: Yale UP, 1987.

Debellation, originally written in ten days in 1533 as More's response to Christopher St. German in the debate on the limits of ecclesiastical jurisdiction in England, has the usual meticulous editing and helpful introduction and commentary expected of the Yale edition. Guy's introduction deliberates upon the political context of the *Debellation*, St. German's legal and political career up to 1534, and the legal context of this controversy. Appendix B reprints the text of St. German's *Salem and Bizance*, the tract which provoked More's rebuttal.

B007 More, Thomas. *De Tristitia Christi.* Trans. and ed. Clarence H. Miller. Vol. 14 (issued in two vols.) of The Yale Edition of the Complete

Works of St. Thomas More. New Haven: Yale UP, 1976.

Part I transcribes More's autograph copy (the Valencia ms.) of the Latin text on one page with an English translation and facsimile of the Valencia ms. on the facing page and a running list of variants, canceled words, and interlineations. Miller also reproduces three pages of the Valencia ms. In Part II, Miller's introduction describes the material, assembly, binding, retouching, and transmission of the autograph copy of the Valencia ms.; compares it with other ms. versions and the 1565 edition; speculates upon its date and composition; proves why this Latin tract is not a mere continuation of More's English *Treatise upon the Passion*; discusses why More wrote it in Latin; and examines Basset's translation. This volume also contains a bibliography, notes on revision in the Valencia ms., historical and explanatory notes, and an index. Three appendices provide a reproduction and translation of Pedro de Soto's Resume of More's Opinion on Papal Primacy and his praise of More and Fisher in *Defensio Catholicae Confessionis*, Mary Basset's translation of *De Tristitia* as it appears in Rastell's 1557 *English Works*, and the gatherings of the Valencia ms.

B008 More, Thomas. *A Dialogue Concerning Heresies*. Eds. Thomas M.C. Lawler, Germain Marc'hadour, and Richard C. Marius. Vol. 6, Pts. I & II of The Yale Edition of the Complete Works of St. Thomas More. New Haven: Yale UP, 1981.

Part I contains the *Dialogue* itself, using the second edition (1531) as copy-text and printed in the original spelling and punctuation with variant readings of the three sixteenth-century editions noted in the critical apparatus. Part II consists of the editors' introductory essays, a commentary on the text in Part I, four appendices, glossary, and an index. Thirteen illustrations including facsimile reprints from the original edition (1529) enhance the volume. Seven related essays treat the historical context and theological content of the *Dialogue*. In "A General View of the *Dialogue*: An Anatomy of Heresies," Lawler analyzes the character of the speaker "More," the predicament of the Messenger, and the implications of the motif of "busyness." Marc'hadour's "The World of the *Dialogue*" examines its historical/theological context and looks at the tract's reliance upon the Church fathers and doctors, especially Aquinas. "Sources: The Contemporary Scene," by Marius, examines the role of Henry VIII's letter to the Princes of Saxony in this controversy and sketches the lives and writings of Eck and Cochlaeus, German authors from whom More may have gathered information to use in his polemical writing.

B009 More, Thomas. *A Dialogue of Comfort against Tribulation*. Eds. Louis L. Martz, and Frank Manley. Vol. 12 of The Yale Edition of the Complete Works of St. Thomas More. New Haven: Yale UP, 1976.

In the introduction, Martz provides an account of the text (transcribed from the Corpus Christi College ms.) and history of the book, together with versions

STANDARD EDITIONS   15

of his earlier discussions of the design of the *Dialogue* and other Tower works. He describes the order and method of composition of the Tower Works and explores More's "art of improvisation"--the informal, digressive, but continuous movement toward a literary goal, specifically, the complex design of the *Dialogue*, which by means of digression and postponement moves toward the climactic meditation on Christ's Passion. Manley presents an analysis of the three books in terms of the three virtues of faith, hope, and charity--faith that enables us to see suffering as a "caress of God," hope that enables us to resist temptation and long for heaven, and charity that is related to grace and associated with various aspects of the Passion. He also has a valuable essay on "The Audience," in which he deals with the historical, symbolic significance of the Turks for More's contemporaries, More's friends and family, and More himself. His analysis of More's use of scriptural quotations and allusions offers insight into More's thought during this last period, and he emphasizes the thematic, personal function of scriptural repetition. The volume includes a commentary with textual notes and glossary.

B010   More, Thomas. *English Poems, Life of Pico, The Last Things*. Eds. Anthony S.G. Edwards, Katherine Gardiner Rodgers, and Clarence H. Miller. Vol. 1 of The Yale Edition of the Complete Works of St. Thomas More. New Haven: Yale UP, 1997.

The Yale edition, "for which actual work began in 1960, now at last has reached conclusion with the publication of Volume 1"--an anomaly explained by the practice of not publishing volumes in any set order but whenever one was ready for press. In the introduction, Edwards discusses the date and occasion, sources, form and genre, literary and iconographical traditions, and critical reaction to the *English Poems*, as well as the date, occasion, circulation of Pico's works after his death, various prose and verse translations of the *Life*, More's technique as translator, the *Life*'s genre, and the reception of More's translation. Miller explores the *Life*'s Latin sources in appendix A. Rodgers expounds upon *The Last Things*--date and circumstances of composition, the medieval tradition, the ancillary traditions of *ars moriendi* and the seven deadly sins, and the style of More's treatise. The editors detail the textual history of all these works before the texts are presented; commentary, appendices, glossary, index, and an addenda and corrigenda to earlier volumes, along with illustrations, further enhance this volume.

B011   More, Thomas. *The History of King Richard III*. Ed. Richard S. Sylvester. Vol. 2 of The Yale Edition of the Complete Works of St. Thomas More. New Haven: Yale UP, 1963.

This edition includes both the English (Rastell's 1557 issue) and 1565 Latin texts, printed in parallel, full textual apparatus (including variant readings from the Chronicles of Hardyng and Hall), collation of extant ms.

versions, and the draft of the Latin text preserved in MS Arundel 43 at the College of Arms. The introduction examines the relationships among these texts; comparison of the five English printed versions with the four Latin ones, three of which are extant only in ms., points to the conclusion More wrote the *History* in both languages for the benefit of both English and continental readers, leaving both unfinished. Furthermore, the redactions have affected each text. The problem of textual variants is related to More's treatment of his theme, his object in shaping the "Richard legend," and his habit of composition *per occasionem* shown in this and other works, including *Utopia*. On the historical side, Sylvester makes no claim to have plucked out the heart of the mystery, leaving "both white and red rose to flourish in the arbors of those who best know how to tend them." The introduction also discusses More's use of sources, literary methods, and notion of history as *exemplum*.

B012 More, Thomas. *In Defense of Humanism*. Letter to Martin Dorp, Letter to the University of Oxford, Letter to Edward Lee, Letter to a Monk. *With a New Text and Translation of* Historia Richardi Tertii. Ed. and trans. Daniel Kinney. Vol. 15 of The Yale Edition of the Complete Works of St. Thomas More. New Haven: Yale UP, 1986.

This volume presents four more or less public letters in which More defends the humanist enterprise, especially the works of Erasmus. The editor's introduction explores their historical context, Christian wisdom and secular learning, positive theology and Erasmian reforms, structure and style, and More's readers. Kinney believes the intellectual and religious concerns these defenses share with *Utopia* and the polemical works make them valuable resources for readers who seek to gain a "balanced and reasonably complete understanding of More's life and works." A new translation of the Latin *Richard III*, based on a manuscript Kinney found "by accident" in the Bibliothèque Nationale, also appears in this edition, which includes a section on this text and its history.

B013 More, Thomas. *Latin Poems*. Eds. Clarence H. Miller, Leicester Bradner, Charles A. Lynch, and Revilo P. Oliver. Vol. 3, Pt. II, of The Yale Edition of the Complete Works of St. Thomas More. New Haven: Yale UP, 1984.

Incorporating and revising the work of Bradner and Lynch's 1953 edition (C014), the *Latin Poems* contains an introduction (by Bradner and Lynch) with accounts of printing history, dates of composition, sources and analogues, and the humane scope of subjects and themes. Oliver writes about the date, style, and sources of the *Progymnasmata;* he also discusses More as translator, More's Latinity and the strictures of Brixius, techniques of versification, and the subjects and themes of the "choice" poems. Because the 1518 volume in which More's poems first appeared also included some of Erasmus' poems,

Miller compares the epigrams of those two authors. In addition, he translates the poems and provides extensive notes, a bibliography, and five appendices--three (trans. and with an intro. by Stephen Merriam Foley) containing the text of *Chordigera* by Brixius, and the texts of Brixius' *Antimorus* and More's *Letters to Brixius* (ed. and trans. by Daniel Kinney). An appendix by Charles Clay Doyle lists the reprints, translations, and adaptations of More's poems in the sixteenth and seventeenth centuries and traces their reputation "as models of Latin verse."

B014 More, Thomas. *Letter to Bugenhagen, Supplication of Souls, Letter against Frith*. Eds. Frank Manley, Germain Marc'hadour, Richard C. Marius, and Clarence H. Miller. Vol. 7 of The Yale Edition of the Complete Works of St. Thomas More. New Haven: Yale UP, 1990.

This volume contains three of the lesser known polemical works, each of which represents a different stage of More's doctrinal reflection. The *Letter to Bugenhagen* (1526) looks back to *Responsio ad Lutherum* (B015) in which More prophesies that a day of violence will erupt in Germany. By the time he writes to Bugenhagen, the Peasants' War had fulfilled his prophecy. In the *Supplication* (which adopts the second edition of 1529 as copy-text), More replies to Simon Fish's *Supplication for the Beggars*, in which Fish sets out to undermine the power of the clergy and existence of purgatory. The *Letter against Frith* (1532) shows More entering a stage of argument devoted to Christ's presence in the Eucharist. Manley's introduction to the *Letter to Bugenhagen* examines the circumstances of composition and rhetorical strategies of both Bugenhagen's *Letter to the English*, in which he defends the Lutheran sect and central articles of Protestant doctrine, and More's *Letter*, a point-by-point answer to Bugenhagen employing the device of quotation-response. Marc'ha-dour's essay on the *Supplication* unfolds background to Fish's treatise to place More's response to this diatribe against indulgences, prayers for the dead, and purgatory in its political, economic, and theological context. Marius discusses the *Letter against Frith* by probing Frith's early career, Henry VIII's approach to Frith, Frith's sentence, More's defense of the real presence against Frith, in which More brings his favorite argument--"the venerable and sacred tradition of the Catholic church, the *consensus fidelium*"-- to bear against Frith's arguments, and Frith's counterattack and death. In addition, the edition features a list of variants, commentary notes, bibliography, glossary, and index; appendices reprint Bugenhagen's *Epistola ad Anglos*, Frith's *A Christen Sentence*, Fish's *Supplication for the Beggars*, and "The Story of Simon Fish" from John Foxe's *Acts and Monuments*.

B015 More, Thomas. *Responsio ad Lutherum*. Ed. John M. Headley; trans. Scholastica Mandeville. Vol. 5 (issued in two vols.) of The Yale Edition of the Complete Works of St. Thomas More. New Haven: Yale UP, 1969.

This edition, based on the text of the latter "Rosseus" version and collated with that of the earlier "Baravellus" version, features Mandeville's parallel translation from Latin into English, along with a running list of variant readings. Headley believes More may have drafted the first version independently of court influence, and that the king, who "anxiously sought to bring Erasmus into the lists against Luther," may have ordered publication to be deferred for political reasons. Comparison between the two versions shows substantial differences in character and intention. While the earlier version is mainly directed to exposing the lies, follies, and inconsistencies of Luther, in the later one, apologetics, to some degree, replace polemics, and more attention is given to ecclesiology, based on a "definition of the Church, which faced the issues and was in some ways remarkably precise and mature." Other topics the introduction covers are the fusion of northern humanism and scholasticism in the *Responsio*, evidence of More's legal training in his argumentative tactics, the form and style of his vituperation, interweaving *festivitas* with *gravitas*, and the reception of the work by continental readers, more specifically its influence on Cochlaeus. The commentary, besides clarifying textual details and allusions, includes references not only to theological works More cites but also those relevant to his tract. Consideration of Luther's writings and their background induces an impartial assessment of the case between the antagonists. As defendant, ill acquainted with Luther's activities and writings, More was necessarily at a disadvantage, and interest in the *Responsio* resides primarily in its significance as an historical document, which is also More's first major polemical tract, in substance and style an earnest of others to follow.

B016 More, Thomas. *Thomas More's Prayer Book: A Facsimile Reproduction of the Annotated Pages*. Eds. Louis L. Martz, and R.S. Sylvester. The Elizabethan Club Ser. 4. A Companion to The Yale Edition of the Complete Works of St. Thomas More. New Haven: Yale UP for the Elizabethan Club, 1969.

This edition reproduces a volume preserved in the Beineke Library, consisting of two printed books bound together, a Latin Book of Hours and Latin Psalter, with More's marginal notes. Those notes in the former, assembled together, make up the "Godly Meditation" William Rastell includes in his 1557 edition of More's *English Works*; those in the latter refer to the verses beside which they appear. Internal and external evidence, set forth in the introduction, convinces the editors More inserted the marginalia while imprisoned in the Tower, and they include a bibliographical account of the prayer book, transcriptions, and translations of More's notes. The portion of the Book of Hours containing More's prayer, in view of its historical importance and visual interest, is reproduced in full color facsimile. The marginalia in the Psalter "reflect his personal griefs and fears as he prayed his Psalter and strove to comfort his soul"; many of them reflect the central situation of *Dialogue of Comfort*.

Perused as a whole, the prayer book gives a moving impression of More's state of mind, torn between fear and hope, in the face of death. The fine quality of this volume's editing and production match its content.

B017 More, Thomas. *Translations of Lucian.* Ed. Craig R. Thompson. Vol. 3, Pt. 1 of The Yale Edition of the Complete Works of St. Thomas More. New Haven: Yale UP, 1974.

Thompson uses Froeben's 1521 edition of More and Erasmus' Latin translations of Lucian; includes Lucian's Greek originals in facsimile taken from the 1503 Aldine edition (More's probable source); and presents More's Latin versions of Lucian's dialogues *Cynicus, Menippus, Philopseudes,* and *Tyrannicida* with English translations supplied from the Loeb versions in an appendix, More's dedicatory letter to Thomas Ruthall, with his declamation in reply to the *Tyrannicida* (both with English versions the editor supplies). Printing Lucian's Greek and More's Latin on facing pages facilitates comparison; aid in reading More's Latin can be found in the appendix. The introduction sets More's translations in the context of the humanists' rediscovery of Greek writers, among whom Lucian became a favorite with some translators and imitators. Whether Erasmus or More knew Lucian first and who suggested the joint project of translating some of his dialogues is unknown; not only are the translations and reply virtually More's earliest surviving Latin writings, they are probably the first of his prose compositions to be published, and apart from his epigrams, his first writing of any kind to appear in print. In More's lifetime they seem to have been printed more frequently than any of his other works, including *Utopia.* Of special interest is More's reply to the *Tyrannicida.* By Tudor standards, "More was a careful, conscientious translator, accurate and resourceful: a man who respected his text and wanted to render it correctly." Part of Lucian's appeal was due to his range, and his satirical prose dialogue provided the ideal medium in which to express his irony, social criticism, dramatic conversation--all qualities which More admired in Lucian. Thompson minimizes More's direct debt to Lucian in later writings, regarding his influence as general and pervasive rather than specific, consisting of resemblances of conception, tone, approach, and invention. Though there is evidence to suggest More repudiated his one-time literary favorite, he never seems to have forgotten Lucian, some of whose works he was the first Englishman to translate into Latin. See also Thompson's "The Translations of Lucian by Erasmus and St. Thomas More" (*Revue belge de philologie et d'historie,* 18 [1939], 855-81; 19 [1940], 5-35) which revises parts of the author's dissertation ("Lucian and Lucianism in the English Renaissance: An Introductory Study" [Princeton U, 1937]) and explores Lucian's reputation in the fifteenth and sixteenth centuries, early translations from the Greek texts by Erasmus and More and their knowledge of Greek and enthusiasm for Greek literature, Erasmus' 1505-06 translations of Lucian; and More's translations of

Lucian's *Cynicus, Menippus,* and *Philopseudes*. Rpt., with changes and addition of an index as *The Translations of Lucian by Erasmus and St. Thomas More* (Ithaca, NY: Vail-Ballou, 1940).

B018 More, Thomas. *Treatise on the Passion, Treatise on the Blessed Body, Instructions and Prayers*. Ed. Garry E. Haupt. Vol. 13 of The Yale Edition of the Complete Works of St. Thomas More. New Haven: Yale UP, 1976.

Haupt follows the order of Rastell's 1557 edition of More's *English Works* for his edition of *Instructions and Prayers* (copy-texts based upon the Valencia ms. of *De Tristitia* for the Latin *Godly Instructions*; More's *Prayer Book* for the English "Godly Meditation"; Rastell's volume for the English "Godly Instruction"; the English translation of the Latin "Godly Instruction," "A Devout Prayer, Collected out of the Psalms of David," and "A Devout Prayer"). The introduction explores textual problems; composition, meaning, arrangement, and structure of the *Instructions and Prayers*; and the relationship between some prayers and More's *Prayer Book*. Two separate essays are included--"The Late Devotional and Exegetical Works and More the Man" relates these works and the *Instructions and Prayers* to More's spiritual life; "A Note on the Texts" examines editorial procedures. Haupt also lists variants and supplies a bibliography, commentary, glossary, and index.

B019 More, Thomas. *Utopia*. Eds. Edward Surtz, and J.H. Hexter. Trans. Edward Surtz. Vol. 4 of The Yale Edition of the Complete Works of St. Thomas More. New Haven: Yale UP, 1965.

The Latin text, following that of the third edition (1518) is printed in parallel with G.C. Richards' English version (1923). The introduction represents the editors' joint work, Hexter writing on the composition and historical milieu of *Utopia*, Surtz on its literary character, analogues, and editions. Hexter cites internal evidence to support the view he has previously advanced that the discourses on Utopia in Book II and the earlier part of Book I were written in the Netherlands, the dialogue on counsel and exordium to Book I and peroration and conclusion to Book II added after More returned to London. He surveys the work against the perspective of its age, commenting on the rise of the middle class, More's affinities with Erasmus, and his anticipation of modern radicalism--perceiving some incongruity between what was going on in the world and "the furniture of the author's mind at the time he wrote the book." Parts of Hexter's introduction and his appended essay, "More's Visit to Antwerp in 1515," were included in different form in chapter two of his *The Vision of Politics on the Eve of the Reformation: More, Machiavelli, and Seyssel* (R196), and "Thomas More: On the Margins of Modernity" (R194). In other parts of the introduction, Surtz discusses *Utopia's* literary and bibliographical aspects and deals with theme and structure, dramatic and comic elements, sources, influences, and the texts (Latin and English) used in this edition. He perceives underlying the seeming complexity of More's fantasy a basic unity, notes the significance of *festivus* on the title-page, and emphasizes the dramatic interplay of dialogue sustained by humor which ranges from gentle irony to fierce invective. The third printing (1974) of this edition adds "minor revisions" to the English translation; the fourth printing (1979) includes "significant revisions" in the translation that Clarence H. Miller offers in two reviews in *Moreana* 9 (1966): 57-64 and *ELN* 3 (1966): 303-09.

B020 More, Thomas. *Thomas More,* Utopia; *Latin Text and English Translation.* Eds. George M. Logan, Robert M. Adams, and Clarence H. Miller. Cambridge: Cambridge UP, 1995.

This bilingual edition features a revision of the English translation Adams published (C021) and a revised, expanded version of the translation Adams and Logan prepared for Cambridge Texts in the History of Political Thought (C037). Adams and Logan examined each other's contributions, and Miller subsequently examined all parts of the edition, correcting errors in the text and making suggestions for changes in the apparatus, translation, and commentary. This edition adds a redaction of the Latin text, together with a textual introduction and notes, and an appendix on the choice of copy-text. It also incorporates changes to the introductory materials and annotations of the earlier Cambridge edition, prompted by the addition of the Latin text and redirection of the edition to a partly different audience from the undergraduates to whom the earlier edition is directed.

Other Editions

C001 More, Thomas. *Conscience Decides: Letters and Prayers from Prison Written by Sir Thomas More Between April 1534 and July 1535.* Selected and arranged by Bede Foord, with preface by Rt. Rev. Trevor Huddleston and introd. by Germain Marc'hadour. Ed. Bede Foord. London: Geoffrey Chapman, 1971.

This edition consists of eight letters from More to Margaret Roper and some ten meditations and prayers, all written during his last imprisonment. Not only have the original spelling and punctuation been modernized, but modern equivalents have been substituted for More's words; even word sequence has occasionally been altered in the interests of clarity. It is, however, useful for general readers to have More's shorter writings from prison available.

C002 More, Thomas. *A Dialogue of Comfort against Tribulation.* Ed. Philip Edward Hallett. London: Burns & Oates, 1937.

This modernized edition, based on Rastell's 1557 folio edition of More's *English Works,* also adopts some readings from the 1553 edition, and provides running notes glossing archaic words and identifying scriptural allusions. Hallett's introduction discusses the circumstances under which More composed this work, its connection with his last letters, and some of its autobiographical details and stylistic elements.

C003 More, Thomas. *A Dialogue of Comfort against Tribulation.* Ed. Leland Miles. Midland Book 80. Bloomington: Indiana UP, 1965.

Miles produces a shortened, modernized version of *Dialogue,* based on Rastell's 1557 text of the *English Works* and collated with the 1553 and 1573 editions and the British Museum ms. (Royal Collection 17-D-XIV). In abridging the text, Miles deletes repetitions, Latin biblical quotations, and some minor abstract arguments, dropping altogether some less relevant chapters.

Punctuation, paragraphing, and chapter divisions have been modernized, but More's archaic words and usages have been left in their original forms. Annotations have been expanded considerably beyond those in editions by Thomas Baker (1847) and Hallett (C002). A long introduction comments on the structure and evolution of the *Dialogue*, its relation to More's other words, autobiographical features, methods of argumentation, and use of patristic sources. A synopsis of the *Dialogue*'s chief lines of argument and chronology are appended. Although the edition furnishes an extensive bibliography to facilitate further study of the *Dialogue*, it lacks an index.

C004 More, Thomas. *Sir Thomas More*: A dialogue of comfort against tribulation. 1573. English Recusant Literature: 1558-1640. Vol. 25. Menston, Eng.: Scolar Press, 1970.

Dialogue is reproduced in facsimile from a copy of the 1573 edition printed in Antwerp in the library of Downside Abbey.

C005 More, Thomas. *A Dialogue of Comfort against Tribulation*. Ed. Frank E. Manley. The Yale Selected Works of St. Thomas More. 4. New Haven: Yale UP, 1977.

Based on the text as established in Vol. 12 of The Yale Edition (B009), this modernized version contains historical and explanatory notes, glossary, bibliography, and index. The first section of its introduction discusses its levels of address, More's relationship to it, its comparison of the persecution of the faith in Hungary and England, and its scriptural references. The second section (by Martz) analyzes the work's design; the last section shows how *Dialogue*'s first book focuses on faith, its second on hope, its third on charity.

C006 More, Thomas. *English Prayers and* Treatise on the Holy Eucharist *by St. Thomas More*. Ed. Philip Edward Hallett. London: Burns & Oates, 1938.

This edition reprints English prayers and provides a modernized version of the *Treatise* (based on Rastell's 1557 *English Works*). His introduction comments on the selections included and compares More's English devotional prose favorably with that of Cranmer.

C007 More, Thomas. *The Essential Thomas More*. Eds. James J. Greene, and John P. Dolan. New York: New American Library, 1967.

Although the editors admit the title may be misleading (because they cannot convey anything remotely resembling the "essential" Thomas More), their book contains all or parts of all More's writings, a translation of *Utopia* that lacks the parerga, and explanatory notes throughout and in the appendix.

C008 More, Thomas. *A Fruitful Pleasant and Witty Work called* Utopia.

Trans. Ralph Robinson. 1556. Menston, Eng.: Scolar P, 1970.

The text of Robinson's *Utopia* follows that of the second and revision edition (1556), reproduced, in facsimile, from a copy in Cambridge University Library, except for the colophon, missing in this copy, reproduced from a copy in the BM. The editor lists earlier editions and translations of *Utopia*, including the first of Robinson's (1551), and others in German (1524), Italian (1548), French (1550), and Dutch (1553).

C009 More, Thomas. *Die Geschichte König Richards III*. Ed. Hans P. Heinrich. Thomas Morus Werke, Heraugegeben von Hubertus Schulte-Hërbruggen. Band 3. Munich: Kösel, 1984.

The first German translation of More's history features a chart of dates in More's biography, a register of names and places, an analytic table of contents, notes throwing light on the relationships of the persons in the work, illustrations, and a bibliography. Heinrich bases his translation on Richard Sylvester's version in the Yale edition (B011); Heinrich also consults the Latin text of the work. Heinrich's introduction mainly views *Utopia* as the positive design of a harmonious commonwealth, thriving on sound principles of reason, while *Richard III* describes the complementary negative example of a state delivered over to irrationality and inhumanity and thus destroyed.

C010 More, Thomas. *The Heart of Thomas More: Readings for Everyday of the Year*. Ed. E.E. Reynolds. London: Burns & Oates, 1966.

Reynolds selects daily readings drawn from the 1557 *English Works* and Roper's *Life*, designed to represent More's teachings on religion and spiritual life. Because the selection includes passages reprinted for the first time, it makes accessible purple passages hitherto unfamiliar, and reveals aspects of More's inner life, especially his profound sacramental sense, along with characteristic features of his literary style, such as command of sentences and fondness for autobiographical anecdote. Reynolds reissues this work as *A Book for All Seasons* (Springfield, IL: Templegate, 1978).

C011 More, Thomas. *The History of King Richard III. English Historians: Selected Passages*. Comp. Bertram Newman. London: Oxford UP for the English Association, 1957.

Newman collects eighty passages from works of English historians from the sixteenth century to the present, among which he includes sections from More's *Richard III*.

C012 More, Thomas. *The History of King Richard III. Tudor Prose, 1513-1570*. Ed. Edmund Creeth. Garden City, NY: Doubleday, 1969.

Creeth provides a complete, useful anthology of important prose works by More, Roper, Tyndale, Elyot, Cavendish, Starkey, Foxe, and Ascham. He includes a text of the *History of King Richard the Thirde* (based on that of Rastell's 1557 *English Works*) and Roper's *Lyfe of Sir Thomas More* (based on Elsie V. Hitchcock's edition [F273] of MS. Harleian 6254).

C013 More, Thomas. The History of King Richard III *and Selections from the English and Latin Poems*. Ed. R.S. Sylvester. The Yale Selected Works of St. Thomas More Ser. 3. New Haven: Yale UP, 1976.

Sylvester bases his modernized-spelling edition of *Richard* on Rastell's *English Works* (1557), and his notes are largely confined to glossing words with meanings that have either changed or been lost, although he does occasionally append biographical information about persons named in the history. His brief introduction covers the main issues and comments on More's style. A selection of More's English and Latin poems and a detailed bibliography complete the volume.

C014 More, Thomas. *The Latin Epigrams of Sir Thomas More*. Eds. Leicester Bradner, and Charles A. Lynch. Chicago: U of Chicago P, 1953.

Based upon the text of 1520, Bradner and Lynch's edition shows More heeded the criticisms Germanus Brixius made in his *Antimorus* (1519). In their introduction, they also note 160 of More's epigrams are original compositions and 102 derive from the Greek of the *Planudean Anthology*. More's translations contain few errors; sometimes he improves the originals. He appreciates the genius of the epigram better than such humanists as Pontanus, Marullus, and Erasmus. He eschews the Ovidian licentiousness of the Italians and the religiosity of the Dutch, realizing the epigram is most effective as a terse and pungent commentary on men and manners. Hence, his epigrams exhibit a wide, refreshing range of subjects, including kingship and government, praise of eminent men, satire of unworthy churchmen, feminine eccentricities, fabliaux humor, death, astrology, doctors, animals, and memorable moments in his own life. Kingship was a new theme for epigrams, and More's treatment of it gives strong support to the theory he was "a republican at heart." The autobiographical poems provide valuable commentary on his private life. The appendixes include ten epigrams not printed in the 1520 edition.

C015 More, Thomas. *More's* Utopia *and Its Critics*. Ed. Ligeia Gallagher. Chicago: Scott, Foresman, 1964.

This collection reprints a modernized version of Robinson's 1551 translation and a numerous, useful selection of excerpts from important critics.

C016 More, Thomas. *Prayers of St. Thomas More with A Treatise on the Holy Eucharist*. London: Catholic Truth Society, Publishers to the Holy See, 1979.

This edition contains Roper's "The Death of St. Thomas More," "A Godly

Meditation," "A Devout Prayer," "Prayers from the Treatise on the Passion," and "A Treatise on the Holy Eucharist."

C017 More, Thomas. *The Sadness of Christ: And Final Prayers and Instructions.* Ed. Gerard Wegemer. Princeton, NJ: Scepter Publishers, 1993.

Wegemer provides a paperback edition of Clarence Miller's translation and edition of *De Tristitia Christi* (B007) and three final prayers and two instructions adapted from Garry E. Haupt's edition of the *Treatise on the Passion, Treatise on the Blessed Body, Instructions and Prayers* (B018). Wegemer aims to give readers unfamiliar with More's spiritual writings enough information to understand and use them for personal meditation, and his introduction summarizes More's commentary on the Agony in the Garden, sketches his life, and makes suggestions for further reading.

C018 More, Thomas. *St. Thomas More:* The History of King Richard III *and Selections from the English and Latin Poems.* Ed. R.S. Sylvester. The Yale Selected Works of St. Thomas More Ser. 3. New Haven: Yale UP, 1976.

Sylvester presents some of More's English verse and 48 of his epigrams (translated by Bradner and Lynch [C014]) and *Richard III* (Sylvester's Yale Edition [B011]), and includes an introduction, notes, bibliography, and index.

C019 More, Thomas. *St. Thomas More: Selected Letters.* Ed. Elizabeth Frances Rogers. The Yale Selected Works of St. Thomas More Ser. 1. New Haven: Yale UP, 1961.

This edition presents in chronological sequence sixty-six letters, forty-four translated from Latin, among which is More's *Letter to Martin Dorp*, here rendered in English for the first time. Notes provide information about each correspondent and put the letter in context as part of More's extant correspondence. The selection includes letters to Colet, Erasmus, Tunstall, Fisher, Wolsey, Cromwell, Henry VIII, and members of More's family, and reflects the many-sided personality and interests of the man "born and made for friendship." Rogers' introduction categorizes the letters; explains how they were usually drafted, copied, and sent; tells why they are extant; identifies the translators of the Latin letters; and discusses her editorial method.

C020 More, Thomas. *St. Thomas More's* History of the Passion. Ed. Philip Edward Hallett; trans. Mary Basset. London: Burns & Oates, 1941.

Hallett provides a modern spelling edition of Basset's English translation of *De Tristitia*, which originally appears in Rastell's *English Works* (1557), along with the earlier English *Treatise on the Passion.* In his introduction, Hallett deals with the lives of the Rastells and Mary Basset and the features of her translation; he also discusses More's devotion to the Passion throughout his life, the relationship between the English and Latin treatises, and the early publication history of each. The edition is complete with notes.

C021 More, Thomas. *Sir Thomas More,* Utopia: *A Revised Translation, Backgrounds, Criticism.* Ed. Robert M. Adams. A Norton Critical edition. 1975. New York: Norton, 1992.

This student edition contains an excellent translation and generous selection of critical extracts--from the studies of Allen, Ames, Chambers, Hexter, Kautsky, Lewis, Morgan, Seebohm, Berger, Elliott, and McCutcheon. An essay by Adams compares *Utopia* with the *Prince*, works which he describes as having a relationship similar to that between *Candide* and *Rasselas*. In his translation, Adams aims to achieve clarity, completeness, colloquial ease, and a sense of contour in the prose; and, in his efforts, he has consulted predecessors, such as Robinson, Ogden, and Surtz. Under the heading, "Backgrounds," Adams has assembled diverse, instructive material, like extracts from Ovid, Plato, and others, and some of the parerga. Adams also provides a selected bibliography on More and *Utopia*.

C022 More, Thomas. *The Supplication of Souls.* Ed. Mary Thelca. Westminster, MD, Newman, 1950.

Thelca reproduces (except for modernized spelling and punctuation) the black-letter first edition of More's *Supplication* (1529) and provides an introduction describing More's controversy with Simon Fish and examining the style, tone, structure, and major points of More's response to Fish's *Supplication for the Beggars*.

C023 More, Thomas. *The Supplication of Souls.* Ed. Eileen Morris. London: Primary Publications, 1970.

Morris edits More's *Supplication*, together with Fish's tract. In her introduction, she assesses More's treatise as "perhaps the most surprising of all his writings." More's definition of the Catholic faith "in plain, ordinary everyday English" suggests comparison with Newman's *Apologia*. Illustrations include reproductions of a contemporary portrait of More; a false portrait, published by adversaries, representing him as a villain; and a black-letter extract from the text. A glossary is appended.

C024 More, Thomas. *Thomas More as Poet.* Ed. Martin Haley. Brisbane, Austral.: Smith and Paterson, 1974.

This is not a critical analysis as its title would seem to indicate, but a collection of Haley's translations of some of More's Latin epigrams, some of More's English poems, and some works of other poets.

C025 More, Thomas. "Thomas More's Humanistic Defenses: A New Critical Edition and Translation of Five Letter-Essays." Vols. I-III. Ed. James

Daniel Kinney. Diss. Yale U, 1983.

Kinney edits and translates More's *Letter to Dorp* (1515), *Letter to Oxford* (1518), *Letter to Lee* (1519), *Letter to a Monk* (1519), and *Letter to Brixius* (1520), and provides chapters on "Historical Contexts," "Christian Wisdom and Secular Learning," "Positive Theology and Erasmian Reform," "Structure, Style, and More's Readers," "The *Letter to Brixius*," and "Texts and Translations."

C026 More, Thomas. *Thomas More: OEuvres Choisies*. Ed. and trans. Marie Delcourt. Paris: La Renaissance du Livre, 1936.

Designed to attract French readers to More's work and proof of his growing international reputation, Delcourt supplements her edition of some of More's writings with a short life, prefaces, and notes; and she divides his work into three sections--Master More, Thomas Morus, and Sir Thomas. The first part contains translations of some English and Latin poems and portions of *Richard III*; the second an abbreviated version of *Utopia* (followed by some letters to Erasmus and others); the third selections from his religious writings.

C027 More, Thomas. *The Tower Works: Devotional Writings*. Ed. Garry E. Haupt. The Yale Selected Works of St. Thomas More Ser. 5. New Haven: Yale UP, 1980.

Haupt provides modernized texts of *A Treatise upon the Passion, A Treatise to Receive the Blessed Body of Our Lord*, and *Instructions and Prayers* (B018), and he reproduces the text of Clarence Miller's translation of the Latin *De Tristitia Christi* (B007). The introduction assesses the quality and appeal of More's Tower works, focuses on the theme of the Passion and its connection (especially the Agony in the Garden) to More's situation in prison, and stresses More's attempt to "transcend, while alluding to, his own personal peril" throughout the Tower works. Haupt devotes special attention to *De Tristitia* and More's preoccupation with martyrdom which emerges as the work's major theme, and he finds an emotional depth and understanding in it beyond anything in the treatises, hence making it "the greater work." The edition also includes a selected bibliography, glossary, index, notes, and running commentary on archaic words and biblical and patristic references.

C028 More, Thomas. *A Translation of St. Thomas More's* Responsio ad Lutherum *with an Introduction and Notes*. Ed. and trans. Gertrude Joseph Donnelly. The Catholic University of America Studies in Medieval and Renaissance Latin Language and Literature. 23. Washington, D.C.: Catholic University of America P, 1962.

Donnelly uses the 1523 first edition as the source text and translates from the Latin Book I of the *Responsio*, the introductory "Baravellus" letters, and the peroration that follows Book II. In her introduction and notes, she deals with the occasion prompting the *Responsio*, authorship problems connected with the identity of "William Ross," More's use of the dialogue form, his theological competence and style, his descent to scurrility as a polemical weapon, and the alleged inconsistency between his controversial works and *Utopia*. This version of Donnelly's doctoral dissertation (Catholic University of America, 1962) features a translation effectively capturing the popular, racy idiom at which More was aiming and renders more accessible, for modern readers, a relatively unfamiliar work of historical importance.

C029 More, Thomas. *Utopia*. Ed. Philip Edward Hallett. London: Burns, Oates & Washbourne, 1937.

Hallett, vice-postulator for More's canonization, publishes "the first Catholic edition of the *Utopia* in modern times." He uses the second edition of Robinson's translation (1556) as the text for his modern spelling version. The foreword by Lord Russell of Killowen explains More only approved of certain Utopian customs as they coincided with Catholic doctrine and practices; he also discusses More's social theories in relation to present day conditions. Hallett's preface claims *Utopia* is not a revolt against medieval Christianity but a product of Renaissance humanism and a Catholic plea on behalf of the poor. The notes, apart from explanations of verbal difficulties of classical allusions, concern themselves mainly with those subjects, as well as circumstances of composition, motives in the work, More's Latin style, sources, and the extent ideas in the book are consistent with More's personal opinions.

C030 More, Thomas. *Utopia*. Ed. and trans. H.V.S. Ogden. Crofts Classics. Arlington Heights, IL: AHM, 1949.

Although Ogden provides an "entirely new," modern translation of *Utopia*, he acknowledges he has consulted Robinson and Burnet's translations. In his introduction, he claims *Utopia* is essentially about ethics and that the work's ideas are Christian; he also discusses *Utopia*'s use of *festivitas* and Utopian religion--their notions of happiness and rejection of pride, as well as the relation between parts of the dialogue in Book I and More's decision to enter royal service. The volume includes a selective bibliography.

C031 More, Thomas. *Utopia*. Ed. J. Rawson Lumby. 1879. Cambridge: At the University P, 1956.

This often reprinted edition of Robinson's translation of *Utopia* includes Roper's *Life of More*, an introduction, notes, glossary, and index of names.

C032 More, Thomas. *Utopia*. Ed. and trans. Edward Surtz. The Yale Selected Works of St. Thomas More Ser. 2. New Haven: Yale UP, 1964.

Drawing from G.C. Richards' translation (1923) and based on the text for the fourth vol. of Yale's definitive editions (B019), this edition includes a short

OTHER EDITIONS 31

bibliography of primary and secondary works, running explanatory notes, and an index. The introduction covers the work's universal appeal, contexts, humanistic audience, use of sources, originality, Latin style, literary techniques, figurative language, comic elements, a comparison of Books I and II, Hythloday's characterization and purpose, and its early textual history.

C033 More, Thomas. *Utopia.* Trans. Peter K. Marshall. New York: Washington Square P, 1965.

Marshall translates More's Latin into modern English for American readers and provides a bibliographical survey of More's life, works, and correspondence, along with important scholarship on *Utopia* and the political-social background of early Tudor age. John Anthony Scott's introduction discusses *Utopia*'s composition, summarizes Books I and II, reviews the work's humanist background (particularly its connection to humanist ideas about education), and speculates upon its meanings, after evaluating interpretations of the Marxists, Catholics, and Hexter.

C034 More, Thomas. *Utopia.* Trans. Paul Turner. New York: Penguin, 1965.

This colloquial, racy translation of *Utopia* is a lively modern English rendering that emphasizes Lucianic elements, though it sometimes deprives names of their ambiguity. The introduction places More's book in the long tradition of fantasy states, claims the work is a "blueprint...for a perfect society," and shows elements of Utopian society that seem restrictive today should be seen in the context of more oppressive conditions when the book was composed. The volume also has notes, an appendix on More's views of communism, and a glossary.

C035 More, Thomas. *Utopia.* Ed. R.C. Alston. Scolar P Facsimiles. Leeds, Eng.: Scolar P, Ltd., 1966.

This volume reprints the 1516 Louvain edition.

C036 More, Thomas. *Utopia.* Eds. John Sheehan, and John P. Donnelly. Milwaukee: Marquette UP, 1984.

Using More's Latin as a base text, this English translation, "aimed at American college students," provides an introduction which includes a short biography, information on *Utopia*'s composition and content, an overview of problems interpreting it; places it in the "Utopian literary tradition"; and assembles a brief bibliography and selective notes to complement the clear, colloquial translation.

C037 More, Thomas. *Utopia.* 1975. Eds. George M. Logan, and Robert M. Adams. Cambridge Texts in the History of Political Thought. Cambridge:

Cambridge UP, 1989.

Designed primarily for students and general readers, this series makes available new versions, based upon recent scholarship, of important texts in the history of political thought. For this edition, Adams has recast his translation of *Utopia* (C021) and included new translations of the ancillary letters and poems. Logan wrote the introduction which discusses More's life and political and literary career, the composition and sources of *Utopia*, and the relationship between the work's two parts. Notes, a chronology of More's life, and suggestions for further reading complete this volume.

C038 More, Thomas. Utopia *and* A Dialogue of Comfort. Everyman's Library. 1910. London: J.M. Dent, 1991.

This popular edition combined two of More's works until the 1974 issue reprinted *Utopia* only. Richard Marius composed the introduction for the 1985 issue, which remains in all editions subsequent to that date.

C039 More, Thomas. Utopia *and Other Essential Writings of Thomas More*. Eds. John P. Dolan, and James J. Greene. New York: New American Library, 1984.

Dolan and Greene represent the range of More's writings with an English translation of *Utopia* and selections from other English and Latin works. They also include More's epitaph, Erasmus' letter to von Hutten, and the account of More's execution in the *Paris News Letter*. Dolan uses the March 1518 Basel edition as the basis for his translation of *Utopia*; Greene bases his selections from the English works on Rastell's 1557 edition of More's *English Works*. The general introduction discusses More's life, wit, spirit, and dialectical play of mind; and *Utopia*, which is inspired by humanist desire for reform, but hardly intended to be read literally as such a plan. In Greene's introduction to the "Selected English Writings," he disagrees with R.W. Chambers' assertion (F116) More's prose style grows almost entirely from the tradition of medieval devotional and spiritual writings, because such a view fails to account for the humanist influence (seen in *Richard* and other works). This book reprints, with a shorter general introduction, Greene and Dolan's *The Essential Thomas More* (C007).

C040 Rastell, William, ed. *The Works of Sir Thomas More Knyght, sometyme Lorde Chauncellour of England, wrytten by him in the Englysh Tonge*. 1557. 2 vols. Intro. K.J. Wilson. London: Scolar, 1978.

Wilson's introduction to this facsimile of Rastell's edition of More's *English Works* assesses its historical importance, describes its bibliographic characteristics, and discusses Rastell's editorial procedures and his work's relation to the text More produced. Generally, he praises Rastell's editorial methods, noting his folio fashions an image of More as *miles christianus*--polemicist and saint, while collections of his Latin works create the image of Erasmian humanist. He also compares Rastell's folio with the First Folio of Shakespeare.

C041   Robinson, Ralph, trans. "Ralph Robinson's Translations of More's *Utopia*: A Critical Edition." Ed. Janet Sussman Gross. Diss. U of North Carolina, Chapel Hill, 1971.

Gross modernizes the spelling and paragraph divisions of the copy-text of Robinson's translation and includes the variant readings of other editions. Her introduction discusses the French, German, and Italian translations which preceded Robinson's, and a glossary and commentary follow the text.

Editorial Critiques and Questions

D001 Billingsley, Dale B. "The Editorial Design of the 1557 *English Works*." *Moreana* 89 (1986): 39-48.

Billingsley argues that by arranging More's works, Rastell creates both an icon and a reliquary, but that the problems set by More's life, works, and death make Rastell's achievement particularly notable. Beyond the literary-historical problem common to all such collations, Rastell faced an "iconic" problem, the framing of dual images of the same figure, for More is both a confessor and martyr whose life and death testify to his sanctity as a *miles christianus*. The editorial methods to solve those problems are apparently contradictory, and the icon created by the folio is paradoxically complicated by More's public career, especially by his dramatic fall and execution.

D002 Black, J.B. "The Literary Survival of Thomas More." *Culture* 21 (1960): 186-202.

Black provides a history of the editions of More's works. Suppressed by agents of Henry VIII, More's family preserved his writings after his execution. In 1557, during a brief period of relief from religious persecutions, William Rastell published an edition of More's English works. Current scholarship, under the auspices of Yale University, is in the process of producing a new edition in order to make More's works accessible to scholars and the general public.

D003 Bullough, Geoffrey. "More in Valencia." *Tablet* 117 (21 Dec. 1961): 1379-80.

Bullough tells how the holograph ms. of More's last work, *De Tristitia Christi*, found its way to and is kept at the Royal College of Corpus Christi at Valencia.

D004 Dauglish, A.F. "Alfred Cock: His More Collection." *N&Q* 168 (1935): 341.

Cock's collection of rare editions of More's works and some mss. was purchased by his friends and presented to the Corporation of the City of London as a gift to the Guild Hall Library.

D005 Devereux, E.J. "Thomas More and His Printers." *A Festschrift for Edgar Ronald Seary: Essays in English Literature and Literature Presented by Colleagues and Former Students*. Eds. A.A. MacDonald, P.A. Flaherty, and G.M. Story. St. John's, Newfoundland: Memorial U of Newfoundland, 1975. 40-57.

Devereux explores circumstances about the printing of some of More's works, such as *Utopia*; discusses More's relationship with some of his printers; explains More's humanistic views of the art of printing; and shows why More was not easy to print for. In particular, he focuses on More's relationship with two of his printers--brother-in-law John Rastell and nephew William Rastell.

D006 Gibson, R.W. "Pursuits, Problems and Pitfalls in Sixteenth- and Seventeenth-Century Bibliography." *PBSA* 59 (1965): 355-66.

Examples drawn from Francis Bacon and More illustrate such difficulties as "bibliographic ghosts," forgeries (or restoration work), and the absence of "ideal" or "control" copies.

D007 Keen, Ralph. "More Bibliographical Notes." *Moreana* 97 (1988): 141-43.

Keen offers two notes about bibliographical problems with More's *Englysh Workes* (1557) and the date of the second edition of *Dialogue Concerning Heresies*.

D008 Kinney, Daniel. "Rewriting Thomas More: Devotional Anthology." *Manuscripta* 33 (1989): 29-35.

Kinney describes, lists, and examines the contents of MS Dd.xii.41. in the Cambridge University Library which contains four sections chiefly "by" More or borrowed from *Dialogue of Comfort*, *Treatise on the Passion*, *Dialogue Concerning Heresies*, *Confutation of Tyndale's Answer*, *Debellation*, and his brief Latin essays on perjury and on death for the faith. Kinney concludes this book "represents an attempt to provide a concise *summa* according to More and a fairly successful sustained *imitatio Mori*."

D009 Marc'hadour, Germain. "More's Folio Works, 1557; For a Census and an Anatomy." *Moreana* 13 (1967): 69-78.

Marc'hadour describes more than sixty copies of Rastell's edition of More's *English Works* he has examined on both sides of the Atlantic and names the owners of many of these volumes.

D010   Reed, A.W. "William Rastell and More's English Works." *The English Works of Sir Thomas More*. Ed. W.E. Campbell. Vol. 1. London: Eyre & Spottiswoode, 1931. 1-12. Rpt. in *Essential Articles for the Study of Thomas More*, 436-46.

This biography explores Rastell's connection with More and his Circle and discusses his work as the printer of More's polemical works, but is mainly concerned with his collection and preservation of More's writings following More's death. Reed praises the high caliber of Rastell's 1557 edition of More's *English Works* and mentions the surviving fragments of his *Life of More*.

D011   Schulte-Herbrüggen, Hubertus. "Das St. Thomas More Project der Yale University." *Archiv* 200 (1963): 194-96.

This note describes the projected Yale edition and reviews volumes already issued.

D012   Sylvester, R.S. "Editing Thomas More." *Moreana* 51 (1976): 26-37.

As executive director of the Yale edition, Sylvester outlines the history of the Yale project, the four major classes into which More's works fall (works extant only in ms. that have never been printed, English works in the 1557 folio, works extant in more than one early printed edition but not in ms., works extant both in early printed editions and in ms.), and problems "beyond and around the text."

D013   Watkins, David R. "The St. Thomas More Project." *YULG* 36 (1962): 162-68.

Watkins outlines the scope of the Yale edition, which will provide the first comprehensive modern edition of More in two series--one scholarly edition, the other of selected works in modernized spelling and punctuation.

D014   Welti, Manfred E. "A Propos des Premières Collections d'Écrits de Thomas More." *Moreana* 2 (1964): 51-54.

Early editions of his work give differing views of More. That of Nicolas Episcopius of Basel consists largely of works by More, the pre-Reformation humanist. The edition by Catholic emigrés at Louvain emphasizes More, the polemical and anti-heretical martyr.

Canon

E001 Butkie, Joseph, Sabita Sankaran, and Donald Vecchiolla. "Some Reflections on the 'Vision' Attributed to Thomas More." *Moreana* 42 (1974): 33-38.

In the seven "Vision" sonnets erroneously ascribed to More in a seventeenth-century ms., the anonymous poet creates a distinct symbology to depict personages and events during Henry VIII's reign. Analysis of the poems' historical, symbolic dimensions helps to decipher authorial intent, indicates the impossibility of assigning authorship to More, and underscores the talent displayed in the intellectual maneuvering of a writer concerned with sensitive political-religious matters.

E002 Dickens, A.G. "A New Prayer of Sir Thomas More." *Church Quarterly Review* 124 (1937): 224-37.

Dickens prints, for the first time, a prayer ("Help me dere father, help me") that appears in a ms. book compiled by Robert Parkyn, and believes Parkyn may have obtained the prayer through his possible connection with More's son, John. Because the collection includes four other prayers clearly attributed to More, Dickens thinks More was also the author of "Help me dere father" and that he wrote it near the end of his life.

E003 Meulon, Henri. "Un Poème Inédit de Thomas More?" *Moreana* 23 (1969): 66-68.

Meulon claims a twelve-line poem (attributed to More and featured in the catalogue of the Thomas More Exposition at Brussels in 1962) is not More's work.

E004 Prescott, Anne Lake. "Further Comments on 'Thomas More's Vision.'" *Moreana* 54 (1977): 5-9.

Prescott refers to a seventeenth-century ms. by John Hawkins, which contains mention of a "vision" More is said to have written while he was in prison.

E005 Smith, Constance. "A Seventeenth-Century Manuscript of 'A Vision' Attributed to Thomas More." *Moreana* 37 (1973): 5-14.

Advocates' MS. 33.7.16 in the National Library of Scotland, Edinburgh, entitled "The life, arraignment, and death of the famous and learned Sir Thomas More together with his vision," contains in the same seventeenth-century hand a dedication by John Hawkins, a life based on Roper's but in the third person, and seven sonnets (modeled on Spenser's *Visions*) which Hawkins claims More wrote when he was in the Tower. Since it is unlikely More could have written such fluent sonnets in the English form in 1534/35, Hawkins himself or someone he knew might have composed them in the seventeenth century to express Catholic sympathies or as a sort of humanist joke in the manner More helped to create. The seven sonnets and Hawkins' dedication are printed here.

E006 Sullivan, Frank. "Sir Thomas More." *TLS* 9 Jan. 1960: 19.

Sullivan discovers a hitherto unprinted writing of More's in MS. Bodley 431--an English treatise on the meaning of Neomenia.

Biography

F001 Allen, DeWitt Clinton. "Patterned Lives: Social Roles and the Self in Early English Biography." Diss. U of California-Los Angeles, 1984.

Allen argues early biography is as realistic as modern biography; "it simply conceives human identity and social realities differently than we do." Roper's *Life*, one of the texts used to support this point, presents More as a "medieval saint."

F002 Anderegg, Michael A. "The Anecdotal Tradition of Thomas More: A Note." *Moreana* 35 (1972): 55-56.

Anderegg supplements Sorlien's "Thomas More Anecdotes in an Elizabethan Diary" (I102) to show how More's anecdotal fame endured in oral tradition until well into the seventeenth century, furnishing material for early biographers, such as Cresacre More.

F003 Anderegg, Michael A. "An Edition of Cresacre More's *Life of Sir Thomas Moore*." Diss. Yale U, 1972.

Anderegg's edition places it in the tradition of English biography and early lives of More in order to "begin the process of rescuing it from continuing neglect."

F004 Anderegg, Michael A. "The Tradition of Early More Biography." *Essential Articles for the Study of Thomas More*. 3-25.

After a comparative assessment of early biographers Roper, Harpsfield, Stapleton, Ro:Ba:, and Cresacre More (including mention of the Rastell fragment), Anderegg discusses More's indirect contribution as a subject to the development of the biographical genre in Tudor/Stuart England. Although he stresses the originality and excellence of Roper's work, he believes subsequent writers also deserve credit for what they add not only to the knowledge of More but also to the development of the biography genre. He pays special attention to Cresacre More's *Life*.

F005 Anderegg, Michael A. "*Utopia* and Early More Biography: Another View." *Moreana* 33 (1972): 23-29.

Anderegg argues against James J. Greene's conclusion early Catholic biographers slighted or ignored *Utopia* by suggesting Roper also ignores most of More's other literary works, that Harpsfield's inadequacy merely reflects that of other humanists confronted with the book, and that Stapleton and Cresacre More are fuller and more significant than Greene realizes (see F096).

F006 Aveling, J.C.H. "The More Family and Yorkshire." *Essential Articles for the Study of Thomas More*. 26-48.

Aveling draws the More family's connection with Yorkshire, which began when More took Anne Cresacre into his Chelsea household and married her to his son John, and traces that line's descendants to 1795 when the death of Thomas More, S.J., ended it.

F007 Baker, Howard. "Thomas More at Oxford." *Moreana* 43 (1974): 5-11.

The two views--the university tradition More was a student at St. Mary's Hall, Oxford, and the biographical evidence he was a member of Canterbury College--are not mutually exclusive. More probably had connections with both establishments, and the effect of Oxford on More is briefly mentioned.

F008 Barker, Nicolas. "Holbein's Portrait of More: Two Unrecorded Episodes in Its History." *Moreana* 62 (1979): 69-72.

Barker constructs a complete pedigree for the primary versions of the Holbein portrait of More.

F009 Basset, Bernard. *Born for Friendship: The Spirit of Sir Thomas More*. London: Burns & Oates, 1965.

Erasmus' comment, "he seems born and made for friendship," supplies the title for this life of More, which is concerned with More's "humanity and sanctity" and "advance in holiness." Chapter headings--"Young More," "The Realist," "Licentious Priest," "At the Barge in Bucklersbury," "The School of Sir Thomas More," "The Court," "Tragedy and Triumph"--indicate the book's scope and its focus on More's "spiritual realism," vocational crisis, personal affinities and attraction to Pico, familial life, educational views and household school as they reflect his "general pattern of holiness."

F010 Beck, Egerton. "St. Thomas More and the Law." *Dublin Review* 97 (1935): 53-72.

Beck examines More's connection with the law from his training in the Inns of Court to his trial at Westminster, gives estimates of what his salary may have been, and looks into records of his trial.

F011 Bek, Lise. "Thomas More on the Double Portrait of Erasmus and Pierre Gillis: Humanist Rhetoric or Renaissance Art Theory?" *Acta Conventus Neo-Latini Guelpherbytani*. Proceedings of the Sixth International Congress of Neo-Latin Studies. Wolfenbüttel 12 August to 16 August 1985. Eds. Stella P. Revard, Fidel Rädle, and Mario A. Di Cesare. MRTS. 53. Binghamton: MRTS, 1988. 468-79.

Bek retells the story of Quentin Metsys' double portrait of Erasmus and Giles commissioned by the two as a gift to More, describes the painting, and mainly discusses More's notions of painting and the portrait in his two letters thanking his friends for it.

F012 Bell, Philip Ingress. "Lady Alice the Unknown." *Moreana* 59 (1978): 9-12.

Bell investigates the generally abused and probably much misunderstood Lady Alice and speculates on what became of her after More's death, why she is not mentioned in More's last letter to his children, and where she died and was buried.

F013 Bell, Philip Ingress. "The Trial of Thomas More." *Month* ns 23 (1960): 325-39.

Bell analyzes documents related to the trial and stresses the importance of the Act of Supremacy and the clergy's submission to it which was, for More, the point of no return.

F014 Belloc, Hilaire. "Saint Thomas More." *Characters of the Reformation*. London: Sheed & Ward, 1938. 98-110.

Belloc thinks the usual portrait of More during his final years is oversimplified and clarifies what More did, what victory he won, and how those things "explain the time."

F015 Bietenholz, Peter G. "Erasmus' View of More." *Moreana* 5 (1965): 5-16.

Bietenholz speculates upon why Erasmus' biographical sketches of More concentrate on More's humanistic achievements, such as *Utopia*, and are less concerned with his theological and political activities. He believes that, throughout his life, Erasmus admired and praised More for what he (Erasmus) was not. He also discusses Erasmus' view of More's entry into royal service, his theological views, saintliness, martyrdom, and the affinities More and Erasmus shared about the Church and reform, the authority of the Church

Fathers, and the ideas and goals of Christian humanism.

F016 Bietenholz, Peter G. "A Protestant Presentation of *More* in 1581." *Moreana* 13 (1967): 59-62.
Bietenholz examines Richard Dinoth's portrait of More in *Adversaria Historica*.

F017 Bietenholz, Peter G., and Thomas B. Deutscher, eds. *Contemporaries of Erasmus: A Biographical Register of the Renaissance and Reformation.* 3 vols. Toronto: U of Toronto P, 1985-87.
The series affords a biographical register of a number of figures connected with Erasmus, many of them great and just as many relatively obscure. Volume two (F-M) features an account of More.

F018 Birchenough, Edwyn. "More's Appointment as Chancellor and His Resignation." *Moreana* 12 (1966): 71-80.
Birchenough traces the complexities and contradictions involving this part of More's life, especially its influence on the later history of the Great Seal.

F019 Birchenough, Edwyn, and Josephine Birchenough. "Pilgrimage to More's Eltham." *Moreana* 4 (1964): 49-50.
The authors point out the sites nearby Eltham connected with More, Erasmus, and the Ropers.

F020 Bishop, R.J. "Sir Thomas More: The Duty of a Christian." *Humanities Association Bulletin* 17 (1966): 21-32.
More's letters and prose works offer answers to why he chose to die, and Bishop believes he "sacrificed himself in the hope that his death would jar his contemporaries into an awareness of their peril."

F021 Blackburn, Elizabeth Brooke. "The Second and Third Generation: Some MS. Letters of the More Circle." *WisSL* 4 (1967): 119-28.
Authorship of a long Latin letter to William Roper that constitutes the prefatory epistle to a small ms. folio of Latin translations from the Greek Church Fathers has been ascribed to John Morwen, and its content casts new light on More and his Circle.

F022 Bolt, Robert. Preface to *A Man for All Seasons: A Play in Two Acts.* London: Heinemann, 1960. v-xix.
Bolt discusses the political, social, economic, legal, and theological background to his play, especially as it concerns the divorce question and church-state relationships during Henry VIII's reign. He also gives his own notion of More's character, attitude about the law and society, refusal to swear the Oath

of Supremacy, and sense of "self." (Rpt. in *Essential Articles for the Study of Thomas More*, 92-97.)

F023 Boswell, Jackson C. "Poor Lady More." *Renaissance Papers 1991*. Eds. George Walton Williams, and Barbara J. Baines. Raleigh, NC: Published by The Southeastern Renaissance Conference, 1992. 31-41.

This account of Alice Middleton's relationship with More and his family is largely sympathetic to Lady More whom, Boswell suspects, went to her grave "without ever understanding the mocking irony of the strange and wonderful man who was her husband." He concludes "More may well have been a saint, but he certainly wasn't easy to live with--in any season."

F024 Bradshaw, Brendan. "Saint Thomas More: *Moriae Encomium*, 1478-1978." *Studies: An Irish Quarterly Review* 67 (1978): 292-305.

Bradshaw posits the result of the deference shown to More by his early biographers and in studies since his canonization in 1935 has produced a kind of Mannerist portrait. More has been bathed in a soft light; the angularities have been rounded out; the proportions have been distorted. Bradshaw suggests the saint as well as the man is likely to gain in stature from the attempt to draw an alternative portrait.

F025 Bradshaw, Jack R. "Thomas More in Two Almanacs of Oxford University." *Moreana* 111-112 (1992): 5-14.

More was an alumnus of Oxford and High Steward (1525) of that university; because of that double connection, he is featured in several almanacs, two of which are reproduced here.

F026 Brémond, Henri. *Thomas More, Lord-Kanzler, Märtyrer und Held*. Regensburg: Hubbel, 1935.

This life of More, emphasizing his place as public figure, controversialist, writer, and family man, is particularly concerned with defending More's consistency and complete orthodoxy; it also comments on his friendship with Erasmus.

F027 Brown, Brendan F. "St. Thomas More, Lawyer." *Fordham Law Review* 4 (1935): 375-90.

Brown assesses More's legal career, beginning with his legal education and early activities in and related to the profession. He spends, however, the most time recounting and evaluating More's administrative and juristic acts as chancellor. He also examines the legal questions in More's dispute with the king, resignation of the chancellorship, refusal to take the oath, trial, and execution.

F028 Bush, Douglas. "Tudor Humanism and Henry VIII." *UTQ* 7 (1938): 162-77.

Bush rejects the beliefs of J.S. Phillimore ("Blessed Thomas More and the Arrest of Humanism in England," *Dublin Review* 153 [1913]: 1-26) and R.W. Chambers (F040) that Henry VIII's execution of More arrested the growth of humanism in England; he argues Henry encouraged education and the new learning and that humanism continued to grow following More's death.

F029 Butler, Brian. "Thomas More and the Inns of Court." *Catholic Lawyer* 17 (1971): 78-87.

Butler rejects the idea More's education at Lincoln's Inn was provincial and restricted to study of English law and argues it played a major role in developing his intellect. He also maintains More became a great humanist there (not at Oxford), explores the impact of that part of his education on *Utopia*, and examines More's lifelong relationship with Lincoln's Inn.

F030 Byron, Brian. "The Fourth Count of the Indictment of St. Thomas More." *Moreana* 10 (1966): 33-46.

Byron reopens discussion on the question of the fourth count of the indictment against More, concerning his conversation with Sir Richard Rich on Henry VIII's assumed supremacy of the Church.

F031 Byron, Brian. *Loyalty in the Spirituality of St. Thomas More.* Bibliotheca Humanistica et Reformatorica. Vol. 4 Nieuwkoop: De Graaf, 1972.

Its subject being "the policy More adopted when he found himself confronted with conflicting demands on his loyalty" and its approach an exploration of the conscious part played by loyalty in More's spiritual life and writings, Byron's book studies important aspects of More's thought and personality. Defining loyalty as "a complex notion which includes the ideas of obedience, devotion to duty, fidelity," Byron examines More's concept of the law. The second chapter demonstrates how "More was acutely aware of his various duties and assiduously tried to fulfill them"; the third treats of the time when More's "hierarchy of authority was subjected to attack from without and from the society which he had been able to serve conscientiously up to that time." The grounds of More's opposition to official policies at the time of Henry's divorce are made clear, and Byron shows how "More was obedient to the laws of the English Parliament right up to, but not beyond, the point where they conflicted with the law of Christ and the law of Christendom in spiritual matters."

F032 Byron, Brian. "Through a Needle's Eye: Thomas More the Wealthy Saint." *Thomas More: Essays on the Icon.* 53-69.

Byron explores the "manner in which More came to terms with the Gospel message regarding the abandonment of wealth." More was a wealthy man for most of his life, but, while keeping the ownership of his goods, he used them wisely and shared them generously. Best of all, he was ready to part with everything rather than allow it to stand between himself and God.

F033 Cahn, Edmond, Daniel G. Collins, Albert H. Garretson, and John Noonan, Jr. "Thomas More among the Lawyers." *New York University Law Review* 38 (1963): 813-34.

Collins edits and annotates a transcript of a panel discussion (New York University School of Law, 19 March 1963) ranging over questions related to More, such as his spiritual life, criticism of the Church, interest in reform, views on the treatment of heretics while he was chancellor, attitudes toward Utopian communism, exclusion of lawyers from *Utopia*, rhetorical prowess, thoughts on the divorce question, divorce in *Utopia*, reasons for refusing to take the Oath of Supremacy, dilemma as a lawyer sworn to obey the laws of the land who disobeys laws he finds unjust, legal circumspection following his arrest, the fairness of More's trial, the nature of his conscience and loyalty to the universality of Christianity, and the question of the merit of More's portrayal in Bolt's *A Man for All Seasons* (F022, I018).

F034 Campbell, W.E. *Erasmus, Tyndale, and More.* London: Eyre & Spottiswoode, 1949.

This biography traces the lives of these men and discusses the *Encomium Moriae* and *Utopia*. Campbell's special interest is the theological debate between More and Tyndale, and he follows that controversy through several chapters.

F035 "The Canonization of a Humanist." *CW* 141 (1935): 257-62.

This article describes the events in More's life which brought about his canonization and the canonization ceremony itself.

F036 Carpinelli, Frank. "Thomas More and the Daunce Family." *Quincentennial Essays on St. Thomas More.* 1-10.

Carpinelli does detective work by looking at a small detail of More's will, by correcting the identity of William Daunce who married Elizabeth More, and by discussing the Daunce family and its dealings with the Mores.

F037 Cecil, Algernon. *A Portrait of Thomas More: Scholar, Statesman, Saint.* New York: Putnam's, 1937.

Cecil studies More's life, character, thought, and works, and deals with his vocational crisis, years at the London Charterhouse, early public career, entry into royal service, chancellorship, resignation, imprisonment, trial, and execution. He also discusses More's relationships with Cardinal Morton, Erasmus, Wolsey, and Henry VIII, along with his attraction to Pico, political career, opposition to heresy, and positions on the Hunne case and the divorce questions. He limits his discussion of More's works almost entirely to *Utopia, Dialogue Concerning Heresies,* and *Dialogue of Comfort.*

F038 Chambers, R.W. *The Place of Saint Thomas More in English Literature and History. Being a Revision of a Lecture Delivered to the Thomas More Society.* 1937. New York: Haskell House, 1964.

Because this book revises a lecture given before the Thomas More Society in Lincoln's Inn, it pays special attention to the connection of More and his family with the Inn and to lawyers' views of his career. It records the identification among the British Museum Royal MSS. of a legal *Abridgment*, with a Latin entry that the book belongs to John More, member of Lincoln's Inn, and with additional entries in the same hand, which is identical to that which entered the dates of John More's marriage and the births of his children in the ms. of Geoffrey of Monmouth's *History*, now in Trinity College, Cambridge. Facsimiles are given of the entries in the *Abridgment* and *History*, and Holbein's miniature of More is the frontispiece. In the lecture's body, Chambers summarizes his well-known views of More's career and expresses his opposition to some of his critics.

F039 Chambers, R.W. "Sir Thomas More." *The Great Tudors.* Ed. Katharine Garvin. London: Ivor Nicholson & Watson, 1935. 101-16.

Chambers says More's writings and those of early biographers offer the best answers to the "riddles" of his personality and public life. He then chooses three wishes More expressed to son-in-law and biographer Roper--universal peace in Europe, uniformity of religion, and settlement of the divorce question--and attempts to determine the degree to which each captured his attention. He also discusses More's chancellorship and *Utopia*. (Rpt. as "Martyr of the Reformation: Thomas More" in *Essential Articles for the Study of Thomas More*, 489-500; and, along with information on William Tyndale, as "Martyrs of the Reformation: More and Tyndale," in Chambers' *Man's Unconquerable Mind: Studies of English Writers, from Bede to A.E. Housman and W.P. Ker* [London: Jonathan Cape, 1939], 179-89.)

F040 Chambers, R.W. *Thomas More.* London: Jonathan Cape, 1935.

Long hailed as the definitive biography (though Marius' study [F180] supersedes it), Chambers draws a picture of More as scholar, writer, and man, and his account is complete with dates and copious notes. The work also depicts how More and the Oxford Reformers studied Greek together and later became close friends. An analysis of what humanism meant to the reformers, and especially to More, is penetrating, as is the discussion of the relationship of More and Erasmus. More's life is placed against the backdrop of England in the early days of Henry VIII's reign. Chambers insists *Utopia* must be considered in relation to its own day, and his explanation of the book's ironies has influenced many.

F041 Condren, Conal. "Dame Alice More & Xanthippe: Sisters to Mistress Quickly?" *Moreana* 64 (1980): 59-64.

Condren suggests Roper and Harpsfield based their characterizations of More's wife upon the traditional views of Xanthippe as a means of inducing an association of More with Socrates.

F042 Conrad, F.W. "Manipulating Reputations: Sir Thomas More, Sir Thomas Elyot, and the Conclusion of William Roper's *Lyfe of Sir Thomas Moore, Knighte.*" *The Rhetorics of Life-Writing in Early Modern Europe: Forms of Biography from Cassandra Fedele to Louis XIV.* Eds. Thomas F. Mayer, and D.R. Woolf. Ann Arbor: U of Michigan P, 1995. 133-61.

Conrad discusses the political, diplomatic context of Roper's reconstruction of More's life, especially his death; and suspects Roper reshaped his narrative and condensed time so as to conflate Charles V's reception of More's decision to surrender the Great Seal and the news, three years later, of More's execution.

F043 Coulton, G.G. "The Faith of St. Thomas More." *Quarterly Review* 265 (1935): 327-43.

Although Coulton concedes Chambers' biography (F040) is a "great book," he states his reservations over certain aspects of its treatment of More, such as the need to include "more prehistory" to explain More's story. Because Coulton believes the Church was no less totalitarian than Henry VIII, he posits *Utopia* is no mere *jeu d'esprit* and as much a satire on the Church as on Henry VIII's England. He believes both Chambers and More confused the reformers with the Reformation, and he explores More's ultimate problem of choosing between being loyal to the king and the Church.

F044 Cowie, L.W. "More's House in Chelsea." *History Today* 26 (1976): 118-24.

Cowie outlines More's family life at Chelsea from 1518 until his imprisonment in April 1534, includes illustrations of the house and grounds, and notes portions of the estate remain today.

F045 Crewe, Jonathan V. "The *Encomium Moriae* of William Roper." *ELH* 55 (1988): 287-307.

Crewe believes Roper, in his *Life*, sought to present a man constant in saintliness, though this is not the whole story, and that the *Life* can be read as an *encomium moriae* not only in the Erasmian sense but also in satirical, negative senses that subvert the hagiographic approach to the text.

F046 Dart, J.L.C. "Thomas Becket and Thomas More: Were They Both Martyrs?" *Church Quarterly Review* 157 (1956): 35-46.

Although Dart terms both holy men, he considers only Becket a martyr, because he supported the pope against the king during the time it was deemed good to do so. More gave his life bravely, but for a mistaken cause (a Church most of his countrymen viewed as sorely in need of reform), a conscientious, courageous act that demands respect, but not the title of martyr. Becket was canonized right after his death; whereas More was canonized four centuries after his beheading.

F047 Deakins, Roger Lee. Introduction. Il Moro. *Ellis Heywood's Dialogue in Memory of Thomas More.* Ed. and trans. Roger Lee Deakins. Cambridge, MA: Harvard UP, 1972. ix-xxxvi.

Heywood, who died an exiled Jesuit priest, wrote this work, which first appeared in Italian in Florence. The More of the dialogue entertains six friends in his Chelsea home, listens to their views on true happiness, and then provides his own speech, which Heywood directly and the book's structure indirectly, indicates as the true answer. Deakins' introduction discusses how Heywood, the son of dramatist John Heywood and More's great nephew, was working "to stimulate greater interest in the martyr and through such interest a...humanist view based on a virtuous, religiously inspired man."

F048 Delany, Selden P. "St. Thomas More." *CW* 141 (1935): 187-94.

Written in response to the canonization, Delany surveys More's adult life and pays attention to his excellent qualities as a Catholic layman, family man, humanist, and scholar.

F049 Delcourt, Joseph. "Apropos de IVe centenaire et de la Canonisation de Thomas More." *RAA* (June 1936): 416-30.

This article surmises as to the whereabouts of More's remains; considers places in London connected with More; and discusses the convent on Beaufort Street, the various writings about More throughout the years, the More relics, and the efforts to secure his canonization. It also lists exhibitions, plays, and pageants held in More's honor during 1935-36.

F050 Delcourt, Joseph. *Deux Saints Anglais: John Fisher (1459-1535) et Thomas More (1478-1535).* Paris: Bonne Presse, 1935.

This life is largely based upon Bridgett's *Life* and Chambers' biography (F040). The material on Fisher is not as extensive as that on More, and Delcourt tries to omit no important aspects of More's career.

F051 Delcourt, Joseph. "St. Thomas More." *CW* 148 (1939): 446-54.

Delcourt feels the need for more detailed treatment of More's life and court and the members of his Circle than Chambers provides in his biography (F040). He also believes a special journal devoted to new scholarly discoveries about More should be founded.

F052 Delcourt, Joseph. "Saint Thomas More and France." *Tradition* 5 (1947): 285-310.

Delcourt considers More's knowledge of French thought and politics and his personal, diplomatic, and intellectual contacts with the French, emphasizing his familiarity with the French language, French manners and culture, English relations with France, More's quarrel with Budé, and More's part in Anglo-French negotiations at Cambrai. He also surveys the growth of More's personal and literary reputation in France and discusses French translations of *Utopia*, *Utopia*'s influence on Rabelais, the treatment of More's life in French novels and plays, and the account of More's death in the *Paris News Letter*.

F053 Delcourt, Marie. "L'amitié d'Erasme et de More entre 1520 et 1535." *Bulletin G. Budé* (Jan. 1936): 7-29.

Using excerpts from their correspondence, Delcourt traces the course of their friendship during the years when the spread of heresy and their differing attitudes to it caused some decline in affection and stresses how the earliest biographers of More tend to ignore or depreciate his friendship with Erasmus.

F054 Derrett, J. Duncan M. "*Juramenta in Legem*: St. Thomas More's Crisis of Conscience and the 'Good Roman.'" *DownR* 91 (1973): 111-16.

Derrett examines More's refusal to take the oath ratifying the Act of Succession; reiterates More knew he would be deprived of his property and probably his life if he refused to swear; argues "his refusal was based on the fact that the formula adopted exceeded the scope of the Act of Succession, apart from his disagreement with the supremacy theory"; and draws attention to the classical precedent of Q. Caecilius Metellus, who refused an oath, was exiled in 100 B.C., and regarded as a citizen of supreme integrity by humanist scholars.

F055 Derrett, J. Duncan M. "More's Attainder and Dame Alice's Predicament." *Moreana* 6 (1965): 9-26.

Derrett describes Dame Alice's plight as custodian of More's property during his imprisonment and before the king's confiscation of it and how she administered it and sold parts of it to maintain the family.

F056 Derrett, J. Duncan M. "More's Conveyance of His Lands and the Law of 'Fraud.'" *Moreana* 5 (1965): 19-26.

Derrett discusses the legal technicalities of property conveyances through which More attempted to protect his family and property from what he foresaw would attend his inevitable attainder for treason.

F057 Derrett, J. Duncan M. "More's Silence and His Trial." *Moreana* 87-88 (1985): 25-27.

Derrett traces Roman law and medieval commentaries on law to explain how More's refusal to break his silence could be interpreted as treason. He shows that silence was no crime by common law. Those who developed the law of treason under Henry VIII had civil law at their disposal, whether for their consciences or contrivances. If important men, like More, were allowed to escape punishment for concealing their opinion, or their consultations with dissidents, no statutory enactment of constitutional opinions or principles could have any hope of success. Hence, More's death was a foregone conclusion, because of the international notion failure to disclose what was going on was in itself a crime.

F058 Derrett, J. Duncan M. "Neglected Versions of the Contemporary Account of the Trial of Sir Thomas More." *Bulletin of the Institute of Historical Research* 33 (1960): 202-23.

Derrett reconstructs a supposed common missing source to the extant versions, an hypothesis which goes far to explain their divergencies and inconsistencies. The author, possibly a foreigner with special immunities, would appear to have been a sympathizer with More, but one concerned with the trial mainly from its technical, juridical sides. Derrett presents a text of the "missing" version in juxtaposition with that of the *Paris News Letter*.

F059 Derrett, J. Duncan M. "The 'New' Document on Thomas More's Trial." *Moreana* 3 (1964): 5-19.

Reynolds' discovery of the record of the conversation between More and Sir Richard Rich (F266) is significant for the light it throws upon More's conduct at his trial. Reynolds is incorrect, however, in concluding More did not deny the supremacy during the interview and that Rich perjured himself at the trial. More did commit a crime within the Act of Treason at his interview with Rich. His denial took the form of an academic opinion, not a personal statement; and on this quibble, he was able to say at the trial he had not denied Henry's supremacy. An untitled list of responses by Reynolds follows Derrett's article (20-22).

F060 Derrett, J. Duncan M. "St. Thomas More and the Would-Be Suicide." *DownR* 88 (1970): 372-77.

Derrett calls attention to two records, possibly apocryphal, implying More's interest in the individual contemplating suicide. The first, traceable to Dorothy Colley, concerns a citizen of Winchester who, despairing of his life, followed More on his way to execution and entreated his prayers, which forthwith cured the man of his affliction. The second, recorded in John Strype's *Annals of the Reformation*, concerns a woman named Norton, apparently brought up as a servant or foster-child in More's household, who may have received some spiritual remedies against a death wish.

F061 Derrett, J. Duncan M. "Sir Thomas More and the Nun of Kent." *Moreana* 15-16 (1967): 267-84.

Derrett describes the complex nature of More's dealings with the Nun of Kent and decides More agreed to meet with the Nun, was aware of the personal risk involved in that meeting, and was unable to detect any fraud in her during the interview. The Nun and More did not discuss the king's matters during their conference, and More advised the Nun to quit her interference in the king's matters in his subsequent letter to her.

F062 Derrett, J. Duncan M. "Thomas More and the Legislation of the Corporation of London." *Guildhall Miscellany* 2 (1963): 175-80.

Derrett presents an argument used during More's trial that attempted to justify Parliament's passage of the Act of Supremacy without formal consent of a General Council on the basis of the traditional capacity of the City of London's legislature--the Common Council--to enact legislation without Parliament's approval. More rejected the analogy as invalid, for just as the City of London cannot enact a statute contrary to Parliament, so Parliament cannot declare the king head of the Church because it is contrary to the ancient faith and constitution of the Catholic Church. (Revised for publication in *Essential Articles for the Study of Thomas More*, 49-54.)

F063 Derrett, J. Duncan M. "The Trial of Sir Thomas More." *English Historical Review* 79 (1964): 449-77.

Derrett studies incidents which may have been overlooked in the legal technicalities of the trial and ultimate issue between More and Henry VIII, in particular Chapuys' colloquy with the king's servants a year earlier and the affair of Friar Standish.

F064 Devereux, E.J. "More, Fisher, and the Attainder Bill." *Moreana* 62 (1979): 43-50.

Devereux's "excuse" for telling this story again is the search for a better understanding of it, because reading the *Lords Journals* for the case suggests a different emphasis on the parts played by Cromwell and Cranmer, the traditional villains, who seem in the documents almost to be trying to save More from the king's wrath. The passage of the bill through the traditional stages of readings shows Roper was right as usual, and that Parliament was not willing to condemn More, even in the presence of the king, who threatened to attend and demand conviction.

F065 Dickens, A.G. *Thomas Cromwell and the English Reformation.*

London: English Universities P, 1959. 61-67, 172-73.

Among many references to More, Dickens focuses upon his imprisonment, trial, and execution; compares the loyalties of Fisher and More to pope and crown; and examines More's relationship with Cromwell. Dickens names More a genuine martyr for Catholicism as opposed to others whose motives were stained with politics.

F066 Donnelly, Dorothy. "St. Thomas More." *The Catholic Lawyer* 14 (1968): 320-25.

Donnelly deals not with More the politician, gentleman farmer, realtor, scholar, or courtier, but More the lawyer.

F067 Donnelly, Dorothy. "The 'Size' of More (On His 500th Birthday)." *Quincentennial Essays on St. Thomas More*. 11-26.

Donnelly charts stages and events in More's commitment to his vocation as a Christian; views More's life as a series of challenges; and regards his trial, imprisonment, and execution as a crucial time in his intellectual, moral, religious, and affective conversion.

F068 Donner, H.W. "The Emperor and Sir Thomas Elyot." *RES* ns 2 (1951): 55-59.

Donner claims Charles V's conversation with Elyot about More's death (which Roper reports in his *Life*) was based upon More's resignation, not his execution. He also connects the reference to Dionysius' dismissal of Plato in Elyot's *Of the Knowledge Which Maketh a Wise Man* (1533) to More's relationship with Henry VIII.

F069 Elton, G.R. "The Real Thomas More?" *Reformation Principle and Practice: Essays in Honour of Arthur Geoffrey Dickens*. Ed. Peter Newman Brooks. London: Scolar, 1980. 21-31.

After noting contradictions and paradoxes in More's life, Elton asks "Where is the real Thomas More?" To answer this question, Elton examines common elements in *Utopia, Confutation of Tyndale's Answer*, and *Dialogue of Comfort* and shows, throughout his life, More was so conscious of sin and its consequences that the result at the center of all his serious writing is "not humanism but antihumanism." Elton also discusses More's sense of guilt as a result of his inability to enter the priesthood and accept celibacy, and he depicts More's life as a struggle to gain self-control and peace. Elton believes More found the peace and balance he sought after his resignation of the chancellorship and during his imprisonment in the Tower. (Rpt. as "Thomas More" in *Studies in Tudor and Stuart Politics and Government. Papers and Reviews 1973-1981*, Vol. 3, Ed. G.R. Elton [Cambridge: Cambridge UP, 1983], 344-55.)

F070 Elton, G.R. "Sir Thomas More and the Opposition to Henry VIII." *Bulletin of the Institute of Historical Research* 41 (1968): 19-34.

In order to understand More's acceptance of the chancellorship and his role in the years 1529-1532, Elton probes his attitudes toward heresy and his relationship with the Reformation Parliament. Elton believes More involved himself because he hoped to stave off the evils of heresy and the king's break with the Church by becoming the center of an opposition party. When he failed at this effort, he decided he must resign the chancellorship, but the king and Cromwell would not let his conscience be "private to himself" for that risk was too great for them to take. (Rpt. in *Essential Articles for the Study of Thomas More*, 79-91; and, with some editorial changes, in *Studies in Tudor and Stuart Politics and Government. Papers and Reviews 1946-1972*, Vol. 1, *Tudor Politics/Tudor Government*, Ed. G.R. Elton [Cambridge: Cambridge UP, 1974], 155-72; an earlier version appeared in *Moreana* 15-16 [1967], 285-303.)

F071 Elton, G.R. "Thomas More, Councilor (1517-19)." *St. Thomas More: Action and Contemplation.* 85-122.

Elton focuses on More's role as "the king's good servant" and traces the steps by which he rose in power and royal esteem, although "his career was very far from meteoric, and his offices remain unspectacular." Nor did he fit any of the standard categories of royal officer, courtier, bureaucrat, or lawyer; More's chief roles seem to have been as an expert in foreign affairs and as a kind of "spare secretary" to the king, who saw him as his "tame Humanist." More's fate was to be called to the chancellorship when he felt the Church to be in danger, and he found himself "trying to serve at a time when his fundamental ideas stood in opposition to the fundamental desires of those in power." (Rpt. in *Studies in Tudor and Stuart Politics and Government. Papers and Reviews 1946-72*, Vol. 1, *Tudor Politics/Tudor Government*, Ed. G.R. Elton [Cambridge: Cambridge UP, 1974], 129-54.)

F072 Elton, G.R. "Victims and Victors." *Policy and Police: The Enforcement of the Reformation in the Age of Thomas Cromwell.* Cambridge: Cambridge UP, 1972. 383-425.

Elton examines the manner in which the early Reformation affected England between 1532 and 1540, investigating the conflicting views the country accepted such changes with little demur or that the king and Cromwell sanctioned a Reign of Terror in order to force their policies. Far from constituting a tyranny, Cromwell's regime was one in which the rule of law and concern for its traditional procedures prevailed. The imprisonment, interrogation, trial, and sentencing of More are reconsidered as the severest test of the legality of the government's proceedings, and Elton concludes More's treatment does not represent "a single sustained assault always intended to end on the scaffold."

F073 Emden, A.B. *A Biographical Register to the University of Oxford*. Vol. 2. Oxford: Clarendon P, 1958. 1305-08.

This list of events about More from his birth to his canonization (he was at Oxford from c. 1492 to c. 1494) provides sources for each entry and includes a bibliography of early biographies and some scholarship.

F074 Emerson, Kathy Lynn. *Wives and Daughters: The Women of Sixteenth-Century England*. Troy, NY: Whitson, 1984.

More's Circle claims a dozen of the work's 570 entries, and the More family portrait by Rowland Lockey is reproduced on p. 153.

F075 Estep, William R. *Renaissance & Reformation*. Grand Rapids, MI: William B. Eerdmans Publishing Co., 1986. 82, 86, 87, 165, 250, 251, 253, 262, 271, 307.

Estep makes general points about More's role in these movements and pays attention to his reaction to Tyndale's translation of the New Testament.

F076 Farrow, John. *The Story of Thomas More*. New York: Sheed & Ward, 1954.

This work provides basic facts about More's life for general readers.

F077 Feho, Door. *Heilige Thomas More, Staatsman, Martelaar*. Tiburg: Bergmans, 1935.

This biography in Dutch begins with the marriage of More's parents; ends with his canonization, Sunday, 19 May 1935; and includes chapters on his youth, family life, public offices, *Utopia* and other writings, and his martyrdom.

F078 Fisher, Bernard. "The Spirituality of St. Thomas More." *Life of the Spirit* 5 (1951): 515-21.

Fisher claims understanding the essential More must account for him as saint, mystic, and martyr, so he studies More's spirituality, particularly his silence and theological abilities. He believes More's vocation was "to live the...life of the monk in the world" and to combine his public and familial life with the awareness of God associated with mystics; he also examines More's special devotion to Christ's Passion and Christendom.

F079 Flegel, Kenneth M. "Thomas More: Was a Sick Man Beheaded?" *Moreana* 49 (1976): 15-27.

Evidence in More's letters, writings, biographies, and comments from his friends suggest angina pectoris caused his chest pains. Hard-working people such as More, burdened with responsibility and eating high concentrations of animal fat, eggs, and salt, frequently suffer coronary artery disease.

F080 Fletcher, Anthony. *Gender, Sex & Subordination in England 1500-1800*. New Haven: Yale UP, 1995. 209, 367.

Fletcher notes More's theories of education for his daughter were the same as those for his son.

F081 Flynn, Dennis. "Sir Thomas More and His Family." *John Donne and the Ancient Catholic Nobility*. Bloomington: Indiana UP, 1995. 19-35.

Chapter one covers the More, Rastell, and Heywood families; More is also mentioned in chapter two, "Ellis and Jasper Heywood," 36-53.

F082 Freemantle, Anne. "St. Thomas More, 1477-1535." *Saints Alive*. Garden City, NY: Doubleday, 1978. 90-113.

This chapter on More's life concludes by stressing his relevance today.

F083 Fressanges, G.A. "More and Scholarship." *Month* 165 (1935): 414-22.

Because More stands out as a champion of the unity of Christendom and the "unity of letters," Fressanges examines him as the scholar who loves and supports learning and defends the rebirth of classical learning. Fressanges also notes the influence of Pico, the special qualities of More's humanism, his household school at Chelsea, and his vision of the purpose of study in bringing the true scholar to a more perfect knowledge of God. More is the ideal Catholic scholar.

F084 Garanderie, M.M. de la. "Le feminisme de Thomas More et d'Erasme." *Moreana* 10 (1966): 23-29.

Garanderie, in order to illustrate the feminist views of More and Erasmus, quotes at length from the letter to Budé describing More's family life, especially the harmony maintained between the sexes.

F085 Garavaglia, Gian Paolo. "Cresacre and Thomas More During the English Revolution, 1640-1660." *Moreana* 42 (1974): 39-42.

Garavaglia writes about More's relative and his biography of his famous forebear.

F086 Gelman, Richard. "Sir Thomas More." *Catholic Lawyer* 1 (1955): 44-47.

Gelman concentrates on the changes More's death brought to Henry VIII and England and includes the Basle sketch and an account from *Howell's State Trials*.

F087 Geritz, Albert J. "John Aubrey's Brief Life of More: Facts, Half-Truths, or Fictions?" *Miscellanea Moreana: Essays for Germain*

Marc'hadour. *Moreana* 100. 223-31.

Geritz shows how Aubrey (in his *Brief Lives*) found or invented stories to fit the image of More as a man of wit. In assessing the authenticity of the five anecdotes Aubrey relates, Geritz points out that, although the stories range from truths, half-truths, to fictions, they add valuable information about how Aubrey and his contemporaries may have perceived More.

F088 Geritz, Albert J. "The Marriage Date of John Rastell and Elizabeth More." *Moreana* 52 (1976): 23-24.

Because Rastell's eldest son entered a guild in 1511 (and fourteen was the usual age for doing so), Geritz argues More's sister Elizabeth may have married Rastell as early as 1496.

F089 Geritz, Albert J. "More's Remarriage: Or, Dame Alice Vindicated." *Indiana Social Studies Quarterly* 37.2 (1984): 47-56.

Geritz argues Lady Alice was probably not a vain, ignorant shrew but a practical housekeeper, loving stepmother, and devoted wife. He attributes the common misperception of Alice to uncritical acceptance of Erasmus and Ammonius' statements about her, misinterpretation of the tone and manner of More's anecdotal references to her, misunderstanding of the hardships she and More's family endured as a result of his political misfortunes, and failure to consider the purposes of More's early biographers who omitted or altered details about More's remarriage to and relationship with Alice primarily because of their hagiographical intentions.

F090 Goodier, Alban. "The World-Vision of St. Thomas More." *Month* 172 (1938): 109-17.

Because More goes out of himself, seeming to forget himself, Goodier claims no other writer in English, except Shakespeare, "has more unconsciously...described himself." He also examines the failures of the three things More most desired--peace in Europe, religious unity, and settlement of the divorce question.

F091 Gottfried, Rudolf B. *A Conscience Undeflowered: A Lecture on Thomas More*. Read at Indiana University, November 7, 1957. Lunenburg, VT: Stinehour P, 1958.

Gottfried singles out three of More's decisions in order to probe the meaning of his life--to marry instead of enter the monastic life, to serve the king, and to refuse the Oath of Supremacy. As to the second decision, he believes More, in royal service, inevitably experienced some of the pessimism Hythloday voices about its efficacy; as to the third decision, he argues More was convicted not for treason, but for refusing to take the oath. Gottfried concludes by comparing More and Becket. (Rpt. in *Essential Articles for the Study of Thomas More*, 520-38.)

F092 Goulder, Laurance. "Thomas More's London." *The Critic* 24 (Dec. 1965-Jan. 1966): 42-55.

Daniel Fresnay photographs the major places in London (Lincoln's Inn, the Chelsea home, the Tower) with which More was connected, and Goulder supplies the text. (Rpt. in *The Catholic Lawyer* 13 [1967]: 8-20.)

F093 Graham, Hugh. "Saint Thomas More and Christian Education." *Thought* 11 (1936): 19-33.

Graham assesses More's place in the history of education by noting his early training, legal studies, love of the classics, achievements as a classical scholar, humanism, defense of women's education, application of his theories in educating his children, and ideas on education in *Utopia*.

F094 Green, Paul D. "Suicide, Martyrdom, and Thomas More." *SRen* 19 (1972): 135-55.

Green explores the significance of suicide for More who not only encountered instances of it in his public life and revealed a concern with it in his major works, but who ultimately had to decide whether his own refusal to acknowledge Henry VIII as England's spiritual leader was equivalent to an act of suicide. The use of voluntary euthanasia in *Utopia* has led many to conclude More favored at least one form of self-destruction, but Green points out More himself rejected every form of suicide as sinful. *A Dialogue of Comfort*, in particular, urges men to accept adversity as part of a divine scheme and "instructs Christians in the art of self-defense against the attacks of the devil," the temptation to suicide being one of the most potent. That More's martyrdom was self-inflicted is emphatically rejected.

F095 Greene, James J. "Thomas More and the More Tradition: *Utopia* and Early More Biography." *Moreana* 31-32 (1971): 199-207.

Greene shows how More's early Catholic biographers treated *Utopia* with "generalized evasiveness," because some details in its text would have been inconsistent with their hagiographical purposes.

F096 Greene, James J. "Thomas More and the More Traditions." Diss. Columbia U, 1966.

Greene explores the "context of heated partisanship" in which various More traditions arose, took shape, and grew; for instance, More's reputation during his life, early Protestant and Catholic responses to his death, early biographers' treatments, and the Catholic tradition.

F097   Guy, John A. *The Public Career of Sir Thomas More*. New Haven: Yale UP, 1980.

Guy intends to write the first "comprehensive account" of More's "public career" from its beginnings in London to his resignation as Lord Chancellor and to "discover More's career and assess his achievements." He assumes archival records provide the best window to reality; thus, "the evidence of the record" tends to preempt every other kind of evidence. The bulk of the work covers only the eighteen months of More's tenure as chancellor (late 1529 to mid 1532). Two principal chapters examine his career in the courts (property and commercial suits) and his involvement in the factional struggles the rise of Anne Boleyn's party occasioned. A brief overview of More's public service up to 1529 (principally as counselor under Wolsey) is prefaced to these chapters. The overall picture of More emerging from Guy's archival efforts is that of a tragic figure: More as a high-minded and selfless reformer hopelessly outclassed by unscrupulous men and the victim of circumstantial defeats inevitably leading to his resignation, imprisonment, and execution. Guy also challenges the myth More was dragged to court against his will, confirms More's image as an astute magistrate, disposes of two traditions about his legal career, and underlines the idea that, in any assessment "More was not only meant to be a lawyer, he was that above all else."

F098   Guy, John A. "Sir Thomas More & the Heretics." *History Today* 30 (1980): 11-15.

Guy analyzes More's attitude toward and treatment of heretics, especially during his chancellorship, and finds his persecution of heretics (very close to the totalitarianism of *Utopia*) was becoming unacceptable to many, for instance, Henry, Anne Boleyn, and Cromwell.

F099   Guy, John A. "Thomas More as Successor to Wolsey." *Thought* 52 (1977): 275-92.

Guy evaluates More's legal and administrative work in Chancery and Star Chamber to discover the direction of More's policy in the courts of equity. He compares More's judicial policy with that of Wolsey and finds More strengthened Wolsey's policy, mainly by adding practical realism to Wolsey's idealism.

F100   Hall, Noeline. "Henry Patenson--Sir Thomas More's Fool." *Moreana* 101-102 (1990): 75-86.

After Hall claims employment of a domestic fool makes More as much a man of the Middle Ages as the Renaissance, she delineates Patenson's character and status in More's household and compares accounts of him in More's early biographers.

F101   Harrison, Maurice E. *Saint Thomas More*. San Francisco: Privately printed at the Grabhorn P, 1941.

To exemplify the appeal of More's life as a layman who was able to preserve his sanctity in the secular world, Harrison discusses his loyalty to civil authority, allegiance to Rome, trial and execution; and the intellectual, instead of emotional, nature of most of his work.

F102 Hastings, Margaret. "The Ancestry of Sir Thomas More." *Guildhall Miscellany* 2.2 (1961): 47-60.

Hastings examines both sides of More's genealogy, provides a genealogical table, and reproduces John More's will (More's father). (Rpt. in *Essential Articles for the Study of Thomas More*, 92-103.)

F103 Hastings, Margaret. "Sir Thomas More: Maker of English Law?" *Essential Articles for the Study of Thomas More*. 104-18.

Hastings examines cases during More's tenure as Chancellor of the Duchy of Lancaster (September 1525 to October 1529) to assess his legal, judicial abilities and his contribution to the development of English law.

F104 Hastings, Margaret. "Sir Thomas More's Ancestry." *TLS* 12 Sept. 1952: 604.

Hastings shows legal documents prove More's great-grandmother was a certain Jane Leicester and that his grandfather, William More, was a London baker.

F105 Haussy, Nathalie. "The Execution of Thomas More: A Comparative Study of the Iconography." *Thomas Morus Jahrbuch 1995*. 149-55.

Haussy discusses the composition and symbolism of early representations of More's execution, especially Antoine Caron's painting, "La Martyre de Sir Thomas More" (1590).

F106 Haussy, Nathalie. "'La Martyre de Sir Thomas More' by Antoine Caron (c. 1590)." *Thomas More Gazette* 5 (1995): 13-18.

Haussy summarizes Caron's life and work, sketches the political context that influenced Caron's treatment of More in his painting, discusses the work's composition and use of symbolism, and includes a reproduction of the entire painting and enlargements of portions to which she draws attention.

F107 Hay, Denys. "A Note on More and the General Council." *Moreana* 15-16 (1967): 249-51.

Hay finds important More's correspondence during his last months (in which he supports regular convocation of general councils and asserts their superiority over the pope) and feels More biographers and Reformation historians have often neglected those views.

F108 Headley, John. "The New Debate on More's Political Career." *Thought* 52 (1977): 269-74.

Headley probes the questions why More entered royal service, why Henry chose him, what the nature of their relationship was, and how More used his political opportunities. He also evaluates his accomplishments as chancellor.

F109 Headley, John. "The *Nos Papistae* of Thomas More." *Moreana* 64 (1980): 89-90.

Headley asserts applying the term "papist" to More's ecclesiology is misleading; explains More's reference, "*Nos Papistae*," in *Responsio ad Lutherum* was not intended as an argument against conciliar privileges; and believes More only considered the Church papist because the pope gave it identity and continuity over time. See also Headley's comments on the subject in his edition of *Responsio ad Luterum*, (B015); Headley's "On More and the Papacy" (F110); Richard C. Marius' "More the Conciliarist" (F179); Marius' "Thomas More's View of the Church," *The Confutation of Tyndale's Answer*, (B004); and Francis Oakley's "Headley, Marius, and the Matter of Thomas More's 'Conciliarism'" (F222).

F110 Headley, John. "On More and the Papacy." *Moreana* 41 (1974): 5-10.

Headley examines More's views on papal primacy from 1523 (the second version of *Responsio ad Lutherum*) to his death in 1535 to show their consistency as they develop and that it would be a "dis-service" to see More exclusively as either a papist or a conciliarist for both aspects are inseparable in his ecclesiology. For further views on this subject, see Headley's "The *Nos Papistae* of Thomas More" (F109).

F111 Heffernan, Thomas J. *Sacred Biography: Saints and Their Biographers in the Middle Ages*. New York: Oxford UP, 1968. 64-65.

Heffernan criticizes G.R. Elton's remark calling early biographies of More hagiographical fiction.

F112 Heilen, Hans. "Martin Van Dorp (1485-1525)." *Moreana* 97 (1988): 67-71.

Heilen concentrates on the early life of Dorp, the Dutch theologian to whom More wrote at length in 1515, converting him to Erasmus' view Greek was needed for a professional knowledge of the New Testament.

F113 Helmstaedter, Gerhard. "Physicians in Thomas More's Circle: The Impact of the New Learning on Medicine." *Thomas Morus Jahrbuch 1989*. 158-63.

Helmstaedter shows how More's "friendship and generosity, educational goals, humanistic wisdom and public efforts" enabled those in medicine, especially Linacre and Elyot, to spread their ideas and "help the afflicted."

F114 Hernandez Conesa, Salvador. "Did Thomas More Have a Cervical Disc Lesion?" *Moreana* 83-84 (1984): 27-31.

The author argues not much attention has been paid to the illness from which More suffered, since it did not directly cause his resignation from the chancellorship. He believes the diagnoses previously put forward are not reliable and tries to show More probably suffered from a cervical disc lesion of the lower cervical segments.

F115 Herrero, Javier. "More and Vives: Christian Radical Thought in the Renaissance." *Spain: Church-State Relations.* Eds. Lawrence Biondi, and Mercedes M. Robles. Chicago: Loyola U of Chicago, 1983. 17-36.

Herrero believes Christian humanism and the ideals of the Christian tradition influenced More and Vives in their criticism of social ills and call for reform. He is concerned with their attitudes about injustice and poverty and their hope both could be solved through the use of reason, and he compares and contrasts their views on these subjects. He also discusses their friendship and the relationship of Vives' *De Subventione Pauperun* to *Utopia*.

F116 Hitchcock, Elsie Vaughan, ed. *The Life and Death of Sir Thomas More, Knight, Sometymes Lord High Chancellor of England.* By Nicholas Harpsfield. With an Introduction on the Continuity of English Prose from Alfred to More and His School, a Life of Harpsfield, and Historical Notes by R.W. Chambers. EETS. 186. London: Oxford UP for EETS, 1932.

The first published edition of Harpsfield's *Life* contains notes, glossary, index, and four appendices--a reproduction of the *Rastell Fragments* (MS. Arundel 152) concerned with Fisher and collected from Rastell's *Life* of More (which is not extant), the *Paris News Letter*, More's indictment, and his epitaph.

F117 Hogrefe, Pearl. "John More's Translation." *PBSA* 49 (1955): 188-89.

Hogrefe points out the scholarly accomplishments of More's son by citing his 1533 translation of Bishop Nausea's *A Sermon of the Sacrament of the Altar* (translated in defense of his father's position and printed by William Rastell) and his other academic interests.

F118 Hogrefe, Pearl. "Sir Thomas More and Doctors' Commons." *Moreana* 14 (1967): 15-21.

Hogrefe speculates More may have been a member of Doctors' Commons and believes More's knowledge of canon and Roman Law requires further research. She also looks at a letter from More to Cromwell, in which he refers to Anne Boleyn.

F119 Holden, W.H. "Margaret Roper: Her Descendants." *N&Q* 168 (1935): 191.

Holden traces the descendants of More's daughter to 1722 and lists the documents from which he obtained these facts.

F120 Holdsworth, William. "St. German, More, Ellesmore, and Bacon." Lecture V. *Some Makers of the English Law*. The Tagore Lectures 1937-38. Cambridge: Cambridge UP, 1938. 91-110.

Holdsworth asserts St. German, More, Ellesmore, and Bacon determined the place of equity in English law, the procedure by which it operated, and its relation to common law and other types of law that compose English law. He believes More's appointment as chancellor marks a turning point in this development, because More signals the shift from the administration of equity by churchmen and canon lawyers to laymen and common lawyers.

F121 Hollis, Christopher. *St. Thomas More*. 1934. London: Burns & Oates, 1961.

This account of More's life, character, thought, and works examines his early education, legal training, relationship with other humanists, domestic life, and public career.

F122 Hollis, Christopher. "Saint Thomas More, European." *Studies* 24 (1935): 379-90.

Hollis insists More's outlook was focused on all of Europe, not just England; and he demonstrates this view by referring not only to *Utopia* (which is not a precursor to British imperialism) but also to his condemnation of Lutheranism as a threat to Christian unity.

F123 House, Seymour Baker. "Sir Thomas More as Church Patron." *Journal of Ecclesiastical History* 40 (1989): 208-18.

House examines More's role as a Church patron who influences "parochial care by extending" his patronage to priests "who would be certain to maintain their cures satisfactorily."

F124 Hulse, Clark. "Dead Man's Treasure: The Cult of Thomas More." *The Production of English Renaissance Culture*. Eds. David Lee Miller, Sharon O'Dair, and Harold Weber. Ithaca: Cornell UP, 1994. 190-225.

Hulse looks at the "transformation" of More's body into a thing, and the transformation of that thing into art and the economy, as an example of the production of culture. Because this subject is filled with riches left behind by others--"financial, political, social, aesthetic abundance," Hulse calls it "dead man's treasure." As examples of the many artifacts related to More after his death, Hulse's essay features several reproductions of works by Holbein and Rowland Lockey.

F125 Jacques, J. "Le détachment à l'école de Thomas More." *Moreana* 18 (1968): 11-19.

Jacques finds detachment, which means indifference, an apt term to describe More's life, for More was able to detach himself from wealth, luxury, high position, and the king's favor and attach himself to his family, friends, and God.

F126 Janelle, Pierre. "Humanisme et unité Chrêtienne: John Fisher et Thomas More." *Etudes* 20 May 1935: 442-60.

Janelle provides sketches of the lives of More and Fisher, stressing More's rich intellectual activity, writings, household, patronage of Holbein, and education of his family.

F127 Jansen, Sharon L. *Dangerous Talk and Strange Behavior: Women and Popular Resistance to the Reforms of Henry VIII.* New York: St. Martin's, 1996. 47-48, 49-50, 65-66, 108.

Jansen discusses More and the Evil May Day riots, his involvement with Elizabeth Barton, and his interest in Anne Wentworth.

F128 Jarrott, Catherine. "The Vocation of St. Thomas More." *ABR* 12 (1961): 298-309.

Statements of More's early biographers confirm the assumption of his early vocation to the cloister, which he could not reconcile, however, with his desire to be married. But as a layman he consistently submitted himself to the discipline of asceticism, and in several works he suggests how the layman may secure for himself a contemplative life by having "some secret place in his own house to which he may withdraw." The life of More, "the King's good servant, but God's first," may be summed up as "essentially contemplative, but superabundantly active."

F129 Jenkins, Claude. *Sir Thomas More.* Canterbury: Published by the Friends of Canterbury Cathedral, 1935.

This résumé of major events of More's life comments on the *Utopia* and *Apology* and includes a memoranda of places More is known to have been. In particular, Jenkins emphasizes the comic tone he finds in *Utopia*.

F130 Kaufman, Peter Iver. "Absolute Margaret: Margaret More Roper and 'Well Learned' Men." *SCJ* 20 (1989): 443-56.

Kaufman suggests Margaret More Roper's 1534 letter to Alice Alington is an important witness to Tudor ideas of patriarchy and the history of gender identity. In 1557 William Rastell was the first of many to question not only Margaret's authorship of the letter, but also her acquiescence to authorities and opposition to her father. Evidence shows, however, Margaret was part of Erasmus' humanist network of friendship and remained so after More's refusal to swear the oath and his imprisonment and that her appeals to her father were genuine. By the time Margaret and More debated conformity, she was inside the humanist network but he had apparently stepped out. With Margaret's opposition to her father, Kaufman believes readers may have an example of what some Renaissance humanists dimly perceived or feared, an indication that inadvertently they had begun a pattern for feminists to follow.

F131   Kelley, Donald R. "The Conscience of the King's 'Good Servant.'" *Thought* 52 (1977): 293-99.

Kelley believes More failed to reconcile the conflicts between law and conscience in relation to the habits of mind he had developed from training in English law, so he turned to natural reason and his own conscience and based his "vision of politics" not on institutional traditions but private values and morality.

F132   Kendell, Angela J. "Thomas More, Richard Fox, and the Manor of Temple Guyting (in 1515)." *Moreana* 91-92 (1986): 5-10.

Kendell examines the Temple Guyting case, which occurred when More may already have been composing *Utopia*, and she speculates it may have been one of many suits causing him to ponder the issue of ownership of property. Certainly the bulk of More's work in Chancery concerned disputes over property, another reason Kendell advances for his interest in that issue in *Utopia*.

F133   Kenny, Anthony. *Thomas More*. Past Masters Ser. Oxford: Oxford UP, 1983.

The first six chapters treat More as humanist, king's councilor, polemicist, chancellor, and martyr, and rely heavily on Roper and More's own letters. Kenny's purpose is to show why More is important for "the intellectual and moral history of our culture," and part of More's legacy is the example of "homey" virtue memorialized by his son-in-law. Chapter seven takes a new direction. Having told of More's end, Kenny delves into two problems of interpretation: in what sense was More a "martyr of conscience," and what meaning should readers attach to *Utopia*.

F134   Klawiter, Randolph. "Thomas More, Erasmus and Ulrich von Hutten: Some Reflections." *Moreana* 67-68 (1980): 17-30.

Klawiter reviews the character, relationships, and careers of More, Erasmus, and von Hutten, indicating the relations between their values and their personal, social, and political situations.

F135 Knowles, David. "For What So Silently Died More? A Study of the Last Months and Motives of Sir Thomas More, Lord Chancellor and Martyr." *Ampleforth Journal* 83 (1978): 31-36.

Knowles ponders More's silence during his last fifteen months of life and argues More did not die defending his individual conscience, but the Church and God's laws, and that he let both the king and Cromwell know what he thought about the divorce and Act of Supremacy, but refused to give his reasons for his position. Knowles uses More's loyalty to Henry VIII and lack of popular resistance to the king's regime to explain his failure to protest his imprisonment and trial and possibly incite public reaction to the state's action.

F136 Küng, Hans. *Freedom in the World: St. Thomas More.* Trans. Cecily Hastings (from German). Theological Meditations. 3. London: Sheed & Ward, 1965.

Küng uses More as an example to explore the problem of living in the world and following Christ. At first sight, More appears to have abandoned poverty, celibacy, and obedience for property, family, and state; a closer look, however, shows More qualified all his attachments.

F137 Larkin, Michael J. *Saint Thomas More: Model for Lawyers and Laymen.* New York: Paulist P, 1937.

The purpose of this pamphlet is to capture the "epitome" of the life of the recently canonized saint.

F138 Lehmberg, Stanford E. *Sir Thomas Elyot: Tudor Humanist.* Austin: U of Texas P, 1960. 14-19, 108-10, 153-54.

Lehmberg demonstrates Charles V's tribute to More (in conversation with Elyot) was spoken before More's resignation, not after his execution (as Roper's *Life* claims), and examines Elyot's remark (in a letter to Cromwell after More's execution) to show that his friendship with More was not as close as one might think. He pays the most attention to More and his Circle's effect on the young Elyot.

F139 Lewi, Angela. *The Thomas More Family Group.* London: Her Majesty's Stationery Office, 1974.

Lewi describes Rowland Lockey's portrait "Sir Thomas More and Descendants" (National Portrait Gallery, London) and discusses its relationship to the Holbein portrait of More's family (no longer extant) and Holbein's pen and ink sketch of the family (which was preliminary to the portrait and does exist).

F140 Llanos y Torriglia, Felix de. *El Divorcio de Catarina de Aragón, San Juan Fisher y Santo Tomas More*. Madrid: Gráfica Universal, 1935.

The first part of the work is mainly concerned with Catherine, though it refers to More three times. The second part contains short lives of Fisher and More with accounts of their involvement in the divorce and with the maid of Kent and their eventual condemnation and execution.

F141 Loades, David. *Power in Tudor England*. British Studies Ser. New York: St. Martin's, 1997. 53, 54, 155.

More's roles as chancellor are briefly discussed.

F142 Loomie, Albert. "A Grandniece of Thomas More: Catherine Bentley ca. 1565-ca. 1625." *Moreana* 29 (1971): 13-15.

Loomie discusses a descendant of More mentioned in a letter discovered in the papers of the Council of State of Philip III of Spain. (See also F189.)

F143 Lovera di Castiglione, Carlo. *Tomasso Moro*. Rome: Casa Editrice, 1935.

This biography in Italian contains sections on More's youth, education, marriage, friendship with Erasmus, *Utopia*, relationship with Henry VIII, view of the divorce, imprisonment, execution, and canonization.

F144 MacCulloch, Diarmid, ed. *The Reign of Henry VIII: Politics, Policy, and Piety*. New York: St. Martin's, 1995. 7, 31, 32, 40, 42, 50, 108-09, 128-29, 143-44, 146, 153, 166, 172-73, 195-99, 205, 208, 271.

References to More and his roles during Henry's reign abound in this collection of essays by Eric Ives, John A. Guy, Neil Samaan, Richard Hoyle, David Potter, Virginia Murphy, MacCulloch, Seymour Baker House, and Robert Whiting.

F145 Mackey, John. "The Spirituality of Thomas More." *Thomas More: The Rhetoric of Character*. 37-63.

Mackey discusses More's father, Morton, Pico, More's vocational crises and decisions to marry and to enter royal service, his application of his spiritual values to everyday life, and his last years to "show how theology, the culture of the time and his social circumstances uniquely filtered through More's personality, came to determine his spirituality."

F146 MacNalty, Arthur S. "Sir Thomas More as Public Health Reformer." *Journal of the Royal Institute of Public Health & Hygiene* 10 (1947): 7-23.

MacNalty outlines More's views on health and hygiene, shows how they are illustrated in *Utopia*, and "marvels" at More's outlook. More gained some of these notions from the physician and scholar Linacre.

F147 MacNalty, Arthur S. "Sir Thomas More as Student of Medicine and Public Health Reformer." *Science, Medicine and History. Essays on the Evolution of Scientific Thought and Medical Practice Written in Honour of Charles Singer.* Ed. E. Ashworth Underwood. Vol. 1. London: Oxford UP, 1953. 418-36.

MacNalty shows More probably learned much from Linacre and the best physicians of his day, because many images and references in his works bear witness to his accurate knowledge of medicine. More became one of the Commissioners of Sewers in 1514, and the problem of improving London's water supply was evidently in his mind when he described the provisions made to secure clean water in the chief city of Utopia. Passages in *Utopia* on hospitals, abattoirs, communal meals, municipal nurses, eugenic mating, nursery schools, and industrial welfare also attest to his deep interest in medicine and hygiene. (Rpt. as "Sir Thomas More as Public Health Reformer" in *Essential Articles for the Study of Thomas More*, 119-35.)

F148 Maguire, John. "The Development of Sixteenth-Century English Biography in the Tradition of Erasmus and Thomas More." Diss. Stanford U, 1970.

Maguire studies not only the biographical writings of Erasmus and More (*Pico* and *Richard III*) against the "life-writing landscape" of early sixteenth-century England (saints' life, chronicle, rediscovered classical theory) but also sixteenth-century biographies of More, which demonstrate how those authors often followed More's methods in composing such works.

F149 Maguire, John. "William Roper's *Life of More*: The Working Methods of a Tudor Biographer." *Moreana* 23 (1969): 59-65.

Maguire compares the unusually sophisticated dialogue of Roper's *Life* with selected passages from More's correspondence to demonstrate how Roper employed artistic methods to shape his work, thereby overturning notions Roper largely based his *Life* on random memories.

F150 Maier, Hans. "Der Humanist und der Ernstfall: Thomas Morus 1478-1978." *Thomas More as Humanist: Zwei Essays.* Ed. Dieter Wuttke. Bamberg: H. Kaiser, 1982. 39-58.

Maier includes biographical information in this study about More's relationship to humanism.

F151 Marc'hadour, Germain. "Additions et Corrections à *L'Univers de Thomas More*." *Moreana* 4 (1964): 57-68.

A number of corrections and additions to Marc'hadour's history of More and his times (F174) are listed.

F152 Marc'hadour, Germain. "Additions et Corrections à *L'Univers de Thomas More*." *Moreana* 5 (1965): 41-52.

Marc'hadour lists corrections and additions to his study of More and his times (F174).

F153 Marc'hadour, Germain. "Budé of Paris and More of London." *Moreana* 19-20 (1968): 157-64.

Marc'hadour attributes the friendship of Budé and More to their shared concern for reform of Christendom.

F154 Marc'hadour, Germain. "The Death-Year of Thomas More's Mother." *Moreana* 63 (1979): 13-16.

This note attempts to close the date of Agnes Graunger's death by quoting the inscription which appears to have been carved on her tomb in the Church of St. Michael, Bassingshall, London, and published by John Weever in his *Funeral Monuments*. If she died in 1499, her eldest son Thomas was 21 or 22 and skilled enough to compose her Latin epitaph. R.S. Sylvester and Marc'hadour agree that epitaph could well represent an addition to the corpus of More's Latin verse.

F155 Marc'hadour, Germain. "Fuitne Thomas Morus in Aulam pertractus?" *Acta Conventus Neo-Latini Sanctandreani*. Proceedings of the Fifth International Congress of Neo-Latin Studies. University of St. Andrews, Scotland, 14 August to 1 September 1982. Ed. I.D. McFarlane. MRTS. 38. Binghamton, NY: MRTS, 1986. 441-48.

Marc'hadour considers the apparent reluctance with which More entered the royal service (suggested in Erasmus' letter of 1519) through an analysis of the meaning of the verb *pertraho* as it was used not only in the letter but also in *Utopia* and other Latin writings by More's Circle of humanists. Marc'hadour believes that, although More's reluctance was genuine, Wolsey and Henry VIII did not force him to enter royal service, and that whatever More's reluctance, he was determined to remain "his own master."

F156 Marc'hadour, Germain. "*Funiculus Triplex*: Margaret Roper and Thomas More." *Moreana* 78 (1983): 93-97.

Marc'hadour examines the parting scene between More and eldest daughter as Roper and Stapleton record it.

F157 Marc'hadour, Germain. "Gardener in the Spring of Scriptural Humanism: Jacques Lefèvre d'Étaples." *Moreana* 85 (1985): 85-92.

Marc'hadour cites Erasmus' protracted quarrel with Lefèvre over Hebrews 2:9 and his complaint to More that his exegesis of that verse was attacked in Lefèvre's second edition of St. Paul's Epistles as means to begin a discussion of

Lefèvre's work and More's estimate of it. Although More humored his friend's annoyance, regretting that the good old master, pious and modest as he was, allowed himself to be carried away by his fervor into a show of force, More's final judgment of Lefèvre remained that "for centuries no man had proved more venerable through learning and virtue."

F158 Marc'hadour, Germain. "How A Christian Lives in an Affluent Society." *Franciscan Herald and Forum* 42 (1964): 332-40.

Marc'hadour heralds More as the model for affluent Catholic laity today and examines More's attitudes and practices toward poverty and the poor, his ability to make money and yet detach himself from it and material things, and his spirit of resignation in the face of material loss. He also observes St. Francis of Assisi inspired More's voluntary poverty and that the Franciscan order influenced the communism *Utopia* describes.

F159 Marc'hadour, Germain. "Hugh Latimer (c. 1492-1555) and Thomas More." *Moreana* 18 (1968): 29-48.

Though Latimer and More were both at court and were hardly close personal friends, Marc'hadour connects them as professional associates and comments upon their similarities and differences, particularly in theology.

F160 Marc'hadour, Germain. "The Likeness of Thomas More: Two Additions to Morison." *Moreana* 35 (1972): 85-89.

The classic tool in the realm of Morean iconography--*The Likeness of Thomas More* (F213)--does not claim exhaustiveness. This article reproduces and comments on two items Morison does not include. One, in the Uffizi, Florence, derives from Paolo Giovio's famous collection. Another painting at the Museé des Beaux-Arts, Bayeux, is further from that unique source; like many other portraits in recent decades, it will soon cease to be captioned and catalogued as "of More" or as "by Holbein."

F161 Marc'hadour, Germain. "More's First Wife...Jane? or Joan?" *Moreana* 109 (1992): 3-22.

More's epitaph for his first wife calls her Ioanna, which, in his *English Works* (1557), is Englished as Ione (Joan). It remains Joan in Ro:Ba:'s Elizabethan *Life of More*. The rival Jane appears in a seventeenth-century biography, becomes dominant in the nineteenth, and is practically taken for granted in the twentieth. To explain this shift, Marc'hadour uses the precedent of Edward IV's mistress: she is Mistress Shore, or Shore's wife, in the *Richard III* of both More and Shakespeare, who give her no Christian name. Though she was named Elizabeth, legend and myth, ballad and play, have made her Jane; this name had an urban and even courtly ring, due above all to the glamour of Jane Seymour and Lady Jane Grey. Because Joan, the by-name for a female rustic, was felt to be improper for "the little wife" of Thomas More, Jane has taken over.

F162 Marc'hadour, Germain. "A Name for All Seasons." *Essential Articles for the Study of Thomas More.* 539-62.

Marc'hadour explores the etymology of variants of More (fool, mulberry, moor, and so on), relating them to More's coat of arms and the mulberry tree he planted with his own hands at Chelsea. He also discusses More's delight in playing with words and names; Erasmus, Budé, and Vives' puns on More's surname; and the fact Thomas (perhaps because of Becket) was second only to John as a favorite name in England. This article translates and revises Marc'hadour's "Les arcanes d'un nom," *Moreana* 2 (1964): 55-70; 3 (1964): 71-80; and 5 (1965): 73-88.

F163 Marc'hadour, Germain. "Obedient Unto Death: A Key to St. Thomas More." *Spiritual Life* 7 (1961): 205-21.

Marc'hadour claims Christian obedience was More's most characteristic virtue, which "shaped and determined his whole intellectual, social, and political career." More never, however, equated this obedience with surrender to what others dictated but held to the individual soul's independence and responsibility to God alone--traits More admired in Abraham (his favorite Old Testament hero) and St. Peter.

F164 Marc'hadour, Germain. "Saint Thomas More and Conscience." *Moreana* 113 (1993): 55-64.

Not content to follow the dictates of his conscience, More justified the most controversial of his decisions--his refusal to take an oath which most of his fellow citizens had taken without any qualms. For them as for him and for all believers, conscience is God's voice interpreting God's law in the depths of the human soul. Though its choices must conform to an objective order, the bearing of that order on concrete situations is perceived differently by different persons--hence More's insistence on the freedom of every individual, his care to exert no pressure even on his children, and his resistance to pressure.

F165 Marc'hadour, Germain. "Supplique de Dame Alice More au Chancelier Audley (1538?)." *Moreana* 4 (1964): 69-75.

A petition from Dame Alice to Audley about the failure of John Lane to meet his financial obligations to her has been discovered in the Public Record Office.

F166 Marc'hadour, Germain. "Thomas More and Thomas Linacre." *Moreana* 13 (1967): 63-67.

Marc'hadour notes the admiration both men repeatedly expressed for one another, but distinguishes their friendship from that of More and Colet, Grocyn, Tunstall, Fisher, and Erasmus, with all of whom More shared not only the ideals of humanism but also deeper spiritual concerns. Interest in knowledge of classical culture, Latin and Greek, and human anatomy formed the basis of Linacre's relationship with More, but these concerns were not as central to More as they were to Linacre.

F167 Marc'hadour, Germain. "Thomas More dans l'histoire de Bruges." *Moreana* 97 (1988): 105-10.

This article begins with the English Convent which had Mary More, a direct descendant of the martyr, for its Prioress during forty years spanning the French Revolution and a crossing to Britain for safety. The Louvain Convent from which that of Bruges was founded had More connections from 1548 on. More himself sojourned in Bruges on three diplomatic missions in 1515, 1520, and 1521. The Flemish city looms large in *Utopia*, his correspondence, and even the *Confutation*.

F168 Marc'hadour, Germain. "Thomas More Homme de Loi." *Moreana* 126 (1996): 55-66.

The fifth centennial of More's admission into Lincoln's Inn (12 February 1496) prompts Marc'hadour to focus on More's legal training and its effects upon his career.

F169 Marc'hadour, Germain. "Thomas More in Emulation and Defense of Erasmus." *Erasmus of Rotterdam, the Man and the Scholar*. Proceedings of the Symposium Held at the Erasmus University, Rotterdam, 9-11 November 1986. Eds. J. Sperna Weiland, and W. Th. M. Frijhoff. Leiden: Brill, 1988. 203-14.

Marc'hadour explores the relationship of More and Erasmus over thirty-six years, with special emphasis on the early days of their friendship and More's defense of Erasmus' writings and plans for reformation in his humanist letters to Dorp, Lee, and a Monk. Marc'hadour believes More admired and emulated Erasmus from the time of their introduction throughout his life.

F170 Marc'hadour, Germain. "Thomas More, Parishioner and Champion of the Universal Church." *Thomas Morus Jahrbuch 1989*. 165-76.

Marc'hadour depicts the More who was the "ordi-nary lay Catholic playing his part in the daily life of the local Church" in addition to his role as an apologist and martyr who fought and suffered for what he called "the common corps of Christendom."

F171 Marc'hadour, Germain. "Thomas More's Birth: 1477 or 1478?" *Moreana* 53 (1977): 5-10.

Marc'hadour's preference for 1477 rests on Erasmus' letter to Hutten of 23 July 1519 and consideration of a "number of advantages presented by that earlier year."

F172 Marc'hadour, Germain. "Thomas More's Early Traumas and Complexes." *Moreana* 45 (1975): 49-52.

William Saffady's diagnosis of More in "The Effects of Childhood Bereavement and Parental Remarriage in Sixteenth-Century England: The Case of Thomas More" (F279) is distorted by Freudian perspective. Aside from a spurious document--a prayer written by Fisher but attributed to More--there is in Saffady's article a reliance upon hypothesis, frequent neglect of historical context, evidence of hasty reading, and equal evaluation of More's translations, "earnest statements," and even *Utopia*, all of which lead to questionable assertions. More's refusal to accept death's finality, his belief in Christ's submission to Divine Will, his "eucharistic eating of Christ's flesh," and his willingness to ponder death's reality are traditionally Catholic rather than idiosyncratic.

F173 Marc'hadour, Germain. "Thomas Stapleton's Use of More's *English Works* (1557) in his *Vita Thomae Mori* (1588)." *Acta Coventus Neo-Latini Torontonensis*. Proceedings of the Seventh International Congress of Neo-Latin Studies, Toronto, 8 August to 13 August 1988. Eds. Alexander Dalzell, Charles Fantazzi, and R.J. Schoeck. MRTS. 86. Binghamton, NY: MRTS, 1991. 83-90.

A comparison of references to More's *English Works* in Stapleton's *Vita* shows how carefully he read the *English Works* in preparation to write his biography.

F174 Marc'hadour, Germain. *L'Univers de Thomas More: Chronologie Critique de More, Erasme, et leur Époque (1477-1536)*. Paris: Librairie Philosophique, 1963.

This chronological compilation falls into three phases: More's birth to 1500, 1500 to 1536, and 1537 to 1559. The first part consists of a detailed inventory of events happening in the world and in More's life. In the second and longest part are chronological accounts of world events and those of More and Erasmus' lives. The third section traces world history and events in the lives of members of More's Circle to 1559. This valuable work is essential to the study of More's biography.

F175 Marc'hadour, Germain, Edwyn Birchenough, and Josephine Birchenough. "More's Appointment as Chancellor and His Resignation." *Moreana* 12 (1966): 71-80.

On the basis of information in the Close Rolls, the authors examine the dates and procedures in More's appointment and resignation of the chancellorship. They transcribe and translate (into English) Close Roll 24 Henry VIII m.24.d, which presents details of More's delivery of the Great Seal.

F176 Margolin, Jean Claude. "Thomas More et l'Education des Filles." *Revue Philosophiques* 146 (1956): 539-47.

Margolin notes Vives' contributions to ideas about women's education and shows how More utilized those notions in his household school.

F177 Marius, Richard C. "Henry VIII, Thomas More, and the Bishop of Rome." *Quincentennial Essays on St. Thomas More*. 89-107.

Marius defines More's part in the *Assertio* and the actual doctrine, as it concerns the papacy, held by its author or authors. He argues that, although More may have believed in the divine institution of the papacy, he did not necessarily believe in papal supremacy. Because he wanted a pope with limited authority, he concludes More was a conciliarist.

F178 Marius, Richard C. "Many an Extravagant Prank and Mummery: Wilson, Race, and the Brahmin Historians." *SCUL* 76 (1993): 439-65.

Marius speculates on writing about More's life as he lays the foundations for his study about some realities of Wilson's life and thought that break commonly accepted images, and he observes that even the most objective historians have prejudices they themselves might not recognize as such and that, in shaping history, historians "inevitably create an image of themselves." He then briefly discusses these two ideas as they relate to studies of More's life.

F179 Marius, Richard C. "More the Conciliarist." *Moreana* 64 (1980): 91-99.

Marius responds to John Headley ("The *Nos Papistae* of Thomas More" [F109]) and Francis Oakley ("Headley, Marius and the Matter of Thomas More's 'Conciliarism'" [F222]) and argues that a general council of the Church carried greater authority than the pope for More and that, as for any conciliarist, More's problem was to define the relationship between the council's authority and that of the pope.

F180 Marius, Richard C. *Thomas More*. London: J.M. Dent, 1984.

This revisionist biography takes issue with many assumptions of previous biographers and supersedes the work of R.W. Chambers (F040), which was long hailed as the most authoritative biography. After Marius expresses his reservations about the "More of history buried under the pyramid of praise" he sees in the major biographers who created More's image, he qualifies and repudiates many of those notions. He claims, for instance, that More's friendship with Erasmus was never intimate; that, throughout life, More self-consciously performed roles others would admire; that, while More did not exactly lie, he willingly distorted the truth; that More fought a battle between a powerful sexual desire and a conscience guilty about sexuality; and that More revealed in his attacks on heretics a fury that was "almost the essence of the man."

F181 Marius, Richard C. "What Kind of Man Was Thomas More?" *Moreana* 4 (1964): 115-17.

Marius uses More's speech to Parliament after Wolsey's fall to investigate what kind of man More was.

F182 Marmion, John P. "Learning Joined with Virtue: St. Thomas More's View on Education." *Ampleforth Journal* 83 (1978): 37-47.

After discussing More's education, Marmion focuses on his views on pagan learning (in *Letter to Dorp* and *Letter to a Monk*) and on Greek and Latin (in *Letter to Oxford*) to demonstrate that, though More's learning is extensive, nothing is "especially unique" in his defense of the classics. What is unique are his views of women's education and the education of his own children (his daughter Margaret is a testament to both). Marmion also looks at the influence of More's ideas about education and his household school on Erasmus, Vives, and Elyot.

F183 Martz, Louis L. "Thomas More: The Search for the Inner Man." *Miscellanea Moreana: Essays for Germain Marc'hadour. Moreana* 100. 397-416.

Martz uses More's family life and the spirit he finds captured in the Holbein portraits and drawings to initiate a defense of More against charges of asceticism, cruelty to heretics, intemperance, and vituperation, especially as seen in More's disputation.

F184 Martz, Louis L. *Thomas More: The Search for the Inner Man*. New Haven: Yale UP, 1990.

Martz counteracts the views set forth in some revisionist biographies, especially those of Marius (F180), and argues the controversial works cannot be the key to the "real" More. Martz' opening chapter largely rejects the image of the "outer" man in More as revisionist studies have reshaped it; the rest of the book uses the Tower Works and Holbein's drawings and portraits of More and his family to initiate a discussion of More's essential being, which is found in those writings and the familial, devotional atmosphere Holbein captured so well.

F185 Massingham, K.R. "Thomas More, 'Lacius,' gent." *Moreana* 87-88 (1985): 29-35.

Massingham draws attention to the appearance of the first recorded subscriptions of a lay member (More, 3 December 1514) of the College of Advocates (to give Doctors' Commons its later and more formal title) and suggests it indicates More's decision not to be a common law judge, but to attempt to progress in the royal service.

F186 Maynard, Theodore. *Humanist as Hero: The Life of Thomas More.* New York: Macmillan, 1947.

Maynard supports his life of More with scholarly discoveries, quotes both contemporary and modern authorities, and includes sections on humanism, More's character and antipathy to heresy, and Henry VIII's temperament.

F187 Maynard, Theodore. "Saint Thomas More." *Pillars of the Church.* New York: Longmans, Green, 1945. 121-44.

Maynard discusses More's life, character, and personality, with attention to his dispute with Henry VIII. He also presents a lengthy analysis of *Utopia* that emphasizes the Utopians' religion, communism, and the attack on greed and pride and description of social-economic conditions in England at that time; he concludes the work should not be taken as a *jeu d'esprit*, but a call for reform.

F188 McAleer, John. "More and His Detractors." *Month* ns 26 (1961): 14-23.

McAleer refutes charges More persecuted heretics and justified his actions. The allegation More suffered heretics to be beaten, tortured, and martyred in his own house is shown to be a fiction, first disseminated by Foxe, but based on nothing beyond garbled report and hearsay. There is no reason to doubt Erasmus' statement no man was put to death for heresy during More's chancellorship or More's assertion no one who came into his hand had "any stripe or stroke given them." The legend of More's violence toward heretics was maintained, to some degree, even by reputable historians, at least until the date of his canonization, 1935.

F189 McCann, Timothy J. "Catherine Bentley, Great Grand-daughter of St. Thomas More, and Her Catholic Connections in Sussex." *Moreana* 43 (1974): 41-45.

McCann adds to Albert Loomie's "A Grandniece of Thomas More: Catherine Bentley ca. 1565-ca. 1625" (F142) by outlining the lives and fortunes of More's other descendants in Sussex.

F190 McConica, James Kelsey. "The Patrimony of Thomas More." *History and Imagination: Essays in Honor of H.R. Trevor-Roper.* Eds. Lloyd Jones-Hugh, Valerie Pearl, and Blair Worden. New York: Holmes & Meier, 1982. 56-71.

McConica describes aspects of More's upbringing to gain insight into the formation of his humanism and to explain how and why it differs from that of Erasmus.

F191 McConica, James Kelsey. *Thomas More: A Short Biography*. London: Her Majesty's Stationery Office, 1977.

McConica attends to turning points in More's life--his vocational crisis and decision to marry, his entrance into royal service, his acceptance and resignation of the chancellorship. He also explores the tension between More's devotion to the Christian ideals of the later Middle Ages and his desire for secular reform, his public career and familial life, his part in the continental humanist community, his attitude toward and treatment of heretics, and his imprisonment, trial, and execution. A chapter on *Utopia* centers on its development of the subject of counsel and how that discussion relates to More's life; in other sections, McConica discusses other works, especially the translations of Lucian and *Richard III*.

F192 McCutcheon, Elizabeth. "The Education of Thomas More's Daughters: Concepts and Praxis." *East Meets West: Homage to Edgar C. Knowlton*. Eds. Roger L. Hadlich, and J.D. Ellsworth. Honolulu: U of Hawaii P, 1988. 193-207.

Noting early on that the "learned woman remained an anomaly throughout the Renaissance," McCutcheon argues the example of More in the education of his daughters produced a kind of "ripple effect," first within his circle of humanist friends and later in ever-widening circles. The published work of Margaret More Roper and the More family's reputation for virtue and learning in the sixteenth century were seen as tangible results of More's humanist approach to the education of children.

F193 McCutcheon, Elizabeth. "Featured Review." *Biography* 8.1 (1985): 83-92.

McCutcheon provides penetrating evaluation of Jasper Ridley's *Statesman and Saint: Cardinal Wolsey, Sir Thomas More, and the Politics of Henry VIII* (F269); John A. Guy's *The Public Career of Sir Thomas More* (F097); and Alistair Fox's *Thomas More: History and Providence* (G027).

F194 McCutcheon, Elizabeth. "Margaret More Roper: The Learned Woman in Tudor England." *Women Writers of the Renaissance and Reformation*. Ed. Katharina M. Wilson. Athens: U of Georgia P, 1987. 449-80.

McCutcheon assesses Margaret Roper's learning and scholastic accomplishments on the basis of her education and relationship with her father. She first discusses More's school in his household and its curriculum, methods, and goals; then she shows how her learning not only embodied her father's ideals for women's education but also expressed her love for him. The essay includes a lengthy bibliography and reproduces some of Margaret's letters to her father, the "Tower Dialogue" between father and daughter, and Margaret's translation of Erasmus' commentary on the Lord's Prayer. McCutcheon's "The Education of Thomas More's Daughters: Concepts and Praxis" (F192) adds to this study.

F195 McDonald, Miles. "Thomas More, Lawyer and Politician." *Catholic Lawyer* 1 (1955): 121-27.

McDonald stresses the political and moral lessons laypersons can learn from More's life.

F196 Meagher, R.W. "B[lessed] Thomas More and the Papacy." *Clergy Review* 9 (1935): 392-407.

Meagher decided that, though More may have once thought the Church established the papacy, he was convinced of its divine origin by the time he wrote *Responsio ad Lutherum*. In addition, he finds support for More's belief the papacy was divinely ordained in his *Dialogue Concerning Heresies, Confutation of Tyndale's Answer*, and his choice to die.

F197 Mermel, Jerry. "Preparations for a Public Life: Sir Thomas More's Entry into the King's Service." *JMRS* 7 (1977): 53-66.

Mermel claims that early in his career More had committed himself to an active public life (contrary to the assumption he had little interest in royal service). To support his claim, Mermel cites More's interest in politics and government not only in *Utopia* and *Richard III* but also in many epigrams. He sees his education at St. Anthony's, Morton's houschold, Oxford, and the Inns of Court as further preparation for public service; he also discusses More's interest in international law, 1514 entry to Doctors' Commons, involvement in public affairs during the early years of Henry VIII's reign, and believes More decided to join Henry's government in 1516 rather than 1518.

F198 Merriam, Thomas. "John Clement: His Identity, and His Marshfoot House in Essex." *Moreana* 25 (1988): 145-52.

Merriam provides a biography of this member of More's household. In More's house Clement met his future wife, More's "adopted" daughter, Margaret Giggs, whose age in 1527, according to the sketch of the More family portrait in Basel, was 22, exactly the same as her *cognatu*, Margaret More Roper.

F199 Meulon, Henri. "La Dévotion chez Thomas More." *Moreana* 19 (1968): 5-10.

Meulon uses Roper's *Life*, parts of the Tower Works, the opinions of some of More's contemporaries, and More's way of life to discuss his spirituality.

F200 Meulon, Henri. "La Docilité chez Thomas More." *Moreana* 12

(1966): 11-28.

Meulon investigates More's "docility," which was not merely obedience, but tractability, cooperation, affability that came from the greatness of his heart and the integrity of his spirit.

F201 Meulon, Henri. "La Pensée du Ciel chez Thomas More." *Moreana* 27 (1970): 5-13.

Meulon examines the dialogue between More and Margaret More Roper in the Tower (as reported in Margaret's letter to Alice Alington), and he believes More's reason for not recanting can be found in his meditation on heaven and his sense of God's presence.

F202 Meulon, Henri. "Présence de Thomas More." *Moreana* 4 (1964): 23-25.

Meulon cites passages from More and Erasmus' letters and Holbein's portraits to illustrate his ideas about More's "presence."

F203 Meulon, Henri. "Un Sermon Entendu par More: l'*Oraison de la paix* de Robert Ceneau à Cambrai (1529)." *Moreana* 25 (1970): 31-40.

Meulon comments on a sermon preached before Tunstall and More in the cathedral in Cambrai in the summer of 1529.

F204 Meulon, Henri. "Thomas More à la Paix des Dames (1529)." *Moreana* 15-16 (1967): 225-40; 17 *Moreana* (1967): 5-14.

Meulon discusses More's role in the negotiations (named for Louise of Savoy and Margaret of Austria in 1529) for the peace of Cambrai as More's longest time away from his family and possibly his most important diplomatic service.

F205 Meulon, Henri. "Thomas More et la Souffrance." *Moreana* 37 (1973): 53-60.

Meulon examines More's physical and mental sufferings during imprisonment as reasons for More's sanctity.

F206 Meulon, Henri. "Thomas More, homme d'action: Le defenseur de la Cité." *Moreana* 21 (1969): 89-97.

Meulon traces More's life as a model citizen, points out the influence of Augustine's *City of God* upon that role, and discusses More's view on citizenship and urban life in *Utopia* (some of which, Meulon believes, More derived from his visits to the continent).

F207 Miles, Leland. "Thomas More: Disenchanted Saint." *Literature and Society*. A Selection of Papers Delivered at the Joint Meeting of the Midwest

Modern Language Association and the Central Renaissance Conference, 1963. Ed. Bernice Slote. Lincoln: U of Nebraska P, 1964. 65-84.

Miles traces More's "gradual disenchantment" in his belief in human nature, the capacity for knowledge and mystical union, extent of free will, and the world's metaphysical nature. He argues More's rejection of the idealism he "appended to his hero-worshipping biography" of Pico can be seen in his reaction to Buckingham's execution, his entanglement in the conditions of royal service, and the disillusionment that comes with maturity. However, More's idealism is not entirely confined to his earlier works, and a steady progression toward disenchantment cannot be discerned, be-cause Miles finds skepticism always part of More's nature.

F208 Miller, Clarence H. "A Seventeenth-Century German Life of Thomas More." *Moreana* 71-72 (1981): 29-36.

Miller presents an outline of the contents and a translation of a portion of a brief life of More (taken mainly from Stapleton's *Tres Thomae*) in a collection of biographies assembled by Erasmus Francisci and published at Nürnberg in 1665: *Der Hohe Traur-Saal oder Steigen und Fallen grosser Herren*.

F209 More, Cresacre. *Life of Sir Thomas More*. Ed. James L. Kennedy. Greensburg, PA: J.L. Kennedy, 1941.

Originally attributed to Father Thomas More, Joseph Hunter later assigned this work to Cresacre More; subsequent scholars have retained this ascription. Another of the important early lives of More, this work includes crucial, though not always factual, details, such as the Duke of Norfolk's speech at More's installation as chancellor. Because its author wrote it so More's memory might be preserved for his children, it is a glowing tribute, which also displays stylistic devices common to Renaissance biographers. Scholars do not hold Kennedy's edition in high esteem.

F210 More, Cresacre. *The Life and Death of Sir Thomas More*. 1630. English Recusant Literature. Vol. 66. Menston: Scolar P, 1971.

Cresacre More's biography has been issued in this facsimile version reproduced from a copy in the library of Ampleforth Abbey.

F211 More, David. "Thomas More as Lawyer." *Thomas More: The Rhetoric of Character*. 83-99.

One cannot separate those qualities which made More a good lawyer from the character of the total man, and the author reviews More's legal training and achievements in his legal and public career and examines how they affected his life, with special emphasis on his relationship with Thomas Wolsey, Bishop of Lincoln.

F212 "The More Family in Hertfordshire." *Essex Recusant* 6 (1964): 112-17.

Along with other points, this article includes the pardon granted to Cresacre More by Charles I, 10 February 1626.

F213 Morison, Stanley. *The Likeness of Sir Thomas More*. Ed. Nicholas Barker. London: Burns & Oates, 1963.

Morison presents a detailed survey, with illustrations of More's portraits over three centuries, composed of the single and group portraits of Holbein and later schools, drawings, engravings, miniatures, the bronze medallion, and representations which are likenesses. Two striking conclusions emerging from it are the abundance and variety of likenesses preserved and the growth of an ideal to portray More as he was rather than as a representative figure of his age. In the introduction, Morison describes the background of Holbein's acquaintance with More and his collaboration with his brother Ambrosius in providing decorations for *Utopia*. The permanence and vitality of Holbein's image constitutes "one of the most astonishing features in this iconography of a man whose features were so frequently represented."

F214 Morison, Stanley. *The Portraiture of Thomas More, by Hans Holbein and After; An Iconographical Consultation Illustrated by the Paintings, Miniatures, Drawings, and Engravings by Artists of Four Centuries*. Read to the Thomas More Society in the Library of the Inner Temple on 18 October 1957. Cambridge: Cambridge UP, 1958.

Morison's *The Likeness of Thomas More* (F213) revises and expands this work.

F215 Murray, Francis G. "Feminine Spirituality in the More Household." *Moreana* 27-28 (1970): 92-102.

Murray believes More, after Jane Colt died and he married Dame Alice, changed his ideas about the education of wives--largely because of Alice's temperament and independence. He discusses More's ideas about learning, women's education, and his children's education--with some mention of the excellence of his household school and the achievements of two of its students--his daughter Margaret and Margaret Clement.

F216 Neame, Alan. *The Holy Maid of Kent: The Life of Elizabeth Barton, 1506-1534*. London: Hodder and Stoughton, 1971.

More is featured in Neame's biography of Barton whose prophecies and denunciations of Henry VIII led to her death for high treason in April 1534 and inaugurated a period of state trials and executions which culminated in the deaths of Fisher and More the following year.

F217 Nelson, William. "The Friendship of Thomas More and John Colet." *MLQ* 1 (1940): 459-60.

Nelson draws attention to a document among the Westminster Abbey muniments recording Colet's resignation from his prebend of Goodeaster in St. Martin's le Grand Church. The document, dated 26 January 1503, asks More to witness the resignation, thereby making it clear More and Colet were already intimate friends by this time.

F218 Nelson, William. "Thomas More, Grammarian and Orator." *PMLA* 58 (1943): 337-52.

Nelson points out aspects of More's earlier career Reed, Chambers, Delcourt, and others neglected, and argues that, in his early writings and connections with grammarians (such as Grocyn, Linacre, William Lily, and John Holt), More appears as a typical humanist grammarian devoted to the study and teaching of eloquence, and that his oratorical powers opened a political career to him. (Revised and rpt. in *Essential Articles for the Study of Thomas More*, 150-60.)

F219 Nolan, Fergal. "Henry's Case Against More." *Thomas Morus Jahrbuch 1989*. 153-57.

Although Henry had a case against More, prosecuted it relentlessly, "gave no quarter," and won, Nolan asserts Henry's case against More was ultimately More himself--his character and reputation.

F220 Norrington, Ruth. *The Household of Sir Thomas More, A Portrait Described by Ruth Norrington*. Waddesdon, Buckinghamshire, Eng.: Kylin P, 1984.

The More family portrait Holbein painted at the Great House in Chelsea inspired Norrington to publish this 26-page booklet describing the painting itself, as well as each household member represented. Three separate, mounted illustrations accompany the descriptions.

F221 Norrington, Ruth. *In the Shadow of a Saint: Lady Alice More*. Waddesdon, Buckinghamshire, Eng.: Kylin P, 1983.

Norrington provides a full life of Dame Alice More. From her narrative emerges a portrait of the Mores' life in the city and Chelsea that can only be described as "merry." Norrington does credit to More's judgment by showing that far from choosing a mere stepmother-housekeeper for his children and wards, "and an additional hair-shirt for himself," he selected a woman capable of building with him a rare family community.

F222 Oakley, Francis. "Headley, Marius and the Matter of Thomas More's 'Conciliarism.'" *Moreana* 64 (1980): 82-88.

Oakley compares the opposing positions of Headley and Marius on More's ideas about papal primacy and the relationship between popes and general councils and determines both scholars are at their best when they argue More's most compelling interests in ecclesiology were not in the old papal-conciliarist question but elsewhere. For background to this question, see Headley's "The *Nos Papistae* of Thomas More" (F109) and all references listed there.

F223 O'Connell, John R. *St. Thomas More*. London: Duckworth, 1935.

This biography focuses upon More's connection with London and his so-called English characteristics, including his love of home life. It also discusses Holbein's portraits of More's family.

F224 O'Connell, John R. "St. Thomas More as Citizen." *Dublin Review* 197 (1935): 37-52.

Through an examination of documents at the Public Record Office, O'Connell adds to what is known about More's official and unofficial connections with the City of London, as he traces More's career from his appointment as sub-sheriff on 3 September 1516 to his execution.

F225 O'Leary, John. "Sir Thomas More's School Days." *TLS* 4 Dec. 1953: 781.

After examining numerous records, O'Leary can find no evidence for Leslie Paul (F240) and R.W. Chambers' (F040) claim Nicholas Holt was More's schoolmaster at St. Anthony's.

F226 O'Leary, John, and R.S. Stanier. "Sir Thomas More's School Days." *TLS* 1 Jan. 1954: 9.

Still trying to find evidence Nicholas Holt taught More, they admit their search through Tudor records has yet to yield support for their claim.

F227 O'Neill, Mary. "Lady Alice: Out from the Shadows." *Moreana* 83-84 (1984): 83-86.

O'Neill lists excerpts of the reviews of Ruth Norrington's *In the Shadow of a Saint: Lady Alice More* (F221) and provides additional biographical information about More's second wife.

F228 O'Neill, Mary. "Marius on More: A Survey of Reviews." *Moreana* 87-88 (1985): 75-82.

O'Neill provides quotes from and summaries of numerous reviews of Richard Marius' biography, *Thomas More* (F180).

F229 O'Sullivan, Richard. "Changing Tides in English Law and History." *The King's Good Servant*. Papers read to the Thomas More Society of London.

1st ser. Ed. Richard O'Sullivan. Oxford: Basil Blackwell, 1948. 7-25.

O'Sullivan discusses More's indictment and his protest to the first count about his silence; he believes More's trial and execution epitomize the destruction of the balance of Church and state, the related destruction of schools of canon and common law, and the changing scope of Parliamentary jurisprudence.

F230 O'Sullivan, Richard. "The Christian Spirit of the Common Law." Introduction. *Under God and the Law*. Papers read to the Thomas More Society of London. 2nd ser. Ed. Richard O'Sullivan. Oxford: Basil Blackwell, 1949. vii-xxviii.

O'Sullivan sees More's trial as a turning point in English history, marking the birth of English law and equity and the distribution and balance of power between Church and state.

F231 O'Sullivan, Richard. "St. Thomas More and Lincoln's Inn." *Catholic Lawyer* 3 (1957): 71-80.

O'Sullivan places More's connection with Lincoln's Inn (from his entrance as a student in 1496 to his election as Lent Reader in 1515) and his legal activities outside the Inn within the context of the legal curriculum at the Inns of Court prior to and during More's time. He also describes the foundation and history of Lincoln's Inn. (Rpt. in *Essential Articles for the Study of Thomas More*, 161-68.)

F232 O'Sullivan, Richard. "Sir Thomas More the Lawyer." *The Spirit of the Common Law*. A Representative Collection of the Papers of Richard O'Sullivan. Ed. B.A. Wortley. Tenbury Wells, Eng.: Fowler Wright, 1965. 19-39.

In his evaluation of More's legal and judicial career, O'Sullivan examines More's legal training, apprenticeship, and activities in the City of London; then moves on to his actions in the king's service; and finally analyzes More's resignation as chancellor, imprisonment, trial, and execution--especially the four counts in More's indictment and his protest. (This essay appeared previously in *Law Times* 213 [1952]: 30-31, 57-59, 103-05.)

F233 Ozment, Steven. *The Age of Reform, 1250-1550: An Intellectual and Religious History of Late Medieval and Reformation Europe*. New Haven: Yale UP, 1980. 254, 304, 404.

Ozment treats More's roles in major issues of the times.

F234 Parmiter, Geoffrey de C. "The Indictment of Saint Thomas More." *DownR* 75 (1957): 149-66.

Parmiter believes accounts of More's trial are often inaccurate due to a lack of understanding of both exactly what he was charged with and the rules governing how indictments were drafted in the sixteenth century. To clarify these matters, he examines More's indictment, the Treason Act of 1534, the Act of Supremacy, and the rules applied to indictments at that time, and he shows More was charged only with treason in his refusal to take the oath and that his indictment does not contain other charges as most accounts of the trial attest. Because some biographers have assumed there were more charges, they have mistakenly asserted More's defense at his trial was inadequate, for they fail to see he is mainly concerned to defend himself against only the charge of treason.

F235 Parmiter, Geoffrey de C. "A Note on Some Aspects of the Royal Supremacy of Henry VIII." *Recusant History* 10 (1970): 183-92.

Parmiter scrutinizes More's argument against the Act of Supremacy in which he claimed it was impossible for part of Christendom to alter a law applicable to all Christendom just as it was impossible for London to alter a law governing all England. Although Parmiter says More's argument was reasonable, it failed because, by the time of his sentence, the forces limiting Parliament's power had diminished.

F236 Parmiter, Geoffrey de C. "Saint Thomas More and the Oath." *DownR* 78 (1960): 1-13.

Parmiter examines the legal technicalities of the oath which More refused to take and his plea both as churchman and lawyer that the oath was "not agreeable with the Statute Oath, nor warranted beyond the Act of Succession."

F237 Parmiter, Geoffrey de C. "Tudor Indictments Illustrated by the Indictment of St. Thomas More." *Recusant History* 6 (1961): 141-56.

This highly technical essay examines the rules of indictments, particularly indictment for treason, as shown by More's case. Although More's indictment set down various acts he had done, he was charged with only one crime (not several as modern biographers often claim)--denial of royal supremacy--treason.

F238 Paul, Frances. "The Daughters of Sir Thomas More." *Fortnightly* 161 (1948): 289-95.

Paul supports her findings on More's views on the education of women and his education of his daughters with quotes from Erasmus on More's home life, from Heywood's *Il Moro* about evening gatherings at More's house, and from More's letter to Gonnell, the tutor.

F239 Paul, John E. *Catherine of Aragon and Her Friends*. London: Burns & Oates, 1966. 9, 17, 32, 35, 41, 65-68, 113, 172, 174-76, 191-99.

Paul claims not to write a life of the queen, but rather "a valid appreciation on the activities of her friends in relation to Catherine herself." The story begins with Catherine's arrival in England at the age of fifteen and her introduction to a circle of friends, all of whom were destined to play an active part in her unhappy life. Interest is sustained through selection of material relating to characters of great diversity in temperament, taste, and objective, to their fortunes and the intrigues in which they were involved: the formidable Doña Elvira, Mary of France, Margaret Pole, Vives, More, and Fisher. More "never ceased to be devoted to Catherine."

F240 Paul, Leslie. *Sir Thomas More*. London: Faber, 1953.

Paul places More's life against the background of conditions prevailing as the fifteenth century merged into the sixteenth, which he parallels with those of the nineteenth century merging into the twentieth. Although he repeats statements made by earlier biographers and acknowledges much of what he says (especially on *Utopia*) comes from Chambers (F040), his biography presents a well-balanced introduction to More, along with some fresh insights about him and Erasmus. (See F225.)

F241 Petrilli, Giuseppe. *San Tomasso Moro*. Milan: Aldo Martello, 1972.
Petrilli writes a life of More in Italian.

F242 Phillips, Margaret Mann. "Omnium Horarum Homo: 'A Man For All Seasons.'" *Moreana* 50 (1976): 13-14.

Phillips returns to the theme of "a man for all seasons" when discussing Erasmus' description of More (*omnium horarum homo*) in the preface of *Moriae Encomium* in the light of its earlier appearance in *Adagia I* where "it is the subject of a short commentary." She suggests Erasmus "interprets it as meaning a man equally ready to share jokes and serious talk, one whom it is a pleasure to live with."

F243 Pineas, Rainer. "Erasmus and More: Some Contrasting Theological Opinions." *RN* 13 (1960): 289-300.

Pineas takes up More's answer to Tyndale's question why he had said nothing against the translation of his "derelyng" Erasmus by detailing the theological differences between the two friends, which were so fundamental as to suggest that "but for the evidence of the correspondence which has survived, it would scarcely be credible that More and Erasmus did retain their regard for each other."

F244 Pineas, Rainer. "George Joye's *Exposicion of Daniel*." *RQ* 28 (1975): 332-42.

The expositor of *Daniel the Prophete* (1545--ten years after More's execution) continues to harp on a stale but politically shrewd accusation against

More for attempting to arrest Barnes while he was in England under Henry VIII's safe conduct.

F245 Pinnard, Pierre. *St. Thomas More, Humaniste, Chancelier et Martyr*. Paris: Lethielleux, 1946.

Pinnard draws an accurate portrait of More the humanist but follows the popular prejudice of continental opinion in stressing the less pleasant features of Erasmus' character, thereby making him what he probably never was entirely--an anti-social bookworm.

F246 Piper, David. "Holbein the Younger in England." *The Journal of the Royal Society of Arts* 3 (1963): 736-55.

Piper describes how Holbein's famous portrait of More and the sketch of his family were composed and compares Holbein's sketch to Rowland Lockey's copy of the no longer extant Holbein portrait of More's family. He praises Holbein's informal arrangement of the family group and says the portraits can justly be compared to any like them produced in Italy during the High Renaissance.

F247 Plant, Raymond M. "Thomas More and the Rule of Law." *Thomas Morus Jahrbuch 1989*. 118-28.

Plant considers the conflicts between common and canon law and the Common Law Courts and Equity Courts, the principles by which they functioned, the influence of the praemunire and provisor statutes, and how these issues affected More and how he reacted to them.

F248 Pope-Hennessy, John. *The Portrait in the Renaissance*. Bolligen ser. 35. New York: Bolligen Foundation, distributed by Pantheon Books, 1966.

Of interest to More scholars are references to Erasmus, whose "abiding interest in his own appearance" and in portraiture generally is indicated in his correspondence with More over the diptych of himself and Aegidius, designed as a gift to More. At the instigation of Erasmus, Pope-Hennessy suggests, Holbein lodged with More during the winter of 1526, Erasmus having already expressed the view, as early as 1519, that it was "no less a task to portray More than it would be to portray Alexander the Great or Achilles." The author gives a full account of the drawing and painting of the More family group, with comments on origins and analogues of these portraits.

F249 Potter, George Richard. "The English Renaissance: Sir Thomas More." *Renaissance Men and Ideas*. Ed. Robert Schwoebel. New York: St. Martin's, 1971. 39-51.

Potter's essay is mainly biographical, setting More's scholarly interests and public service against an intellectual and political backdrop.

F250 Prada, Andres Vasquez de. *Sir Thomas Moro*. Madrid: Ediciones Rialp, 1962.

This detailed biography in Spanish contains illustrations, appendices, and indices.

F251 Prévost, André. "Conscience the Ultimate Court of Appeal." *Essential Articles for the Study of Thomas More*. 563-68.

Through a close reading of the Tower letters, Prévost focuses upon More's preparation for death and belief in the rights of his conscience and explains More's notion of conscience was not just tied to himself but related to reality outside himself that imposed itself upon him; hence, his death also testifies to his loyalty to the Church and humanism. This article is translated from French and part of Prévost's *Thomas More, 1477-1535, et la crise de la pensée européenne*, 343-54 (G072).

F252 Privat, Edmond. *Le chancelier decapilé, St. Thomas More, Henri VIII et la Republique des Utopiens*. Paris: Attinger, 1938.

This biography, grounded on standard authorities such as Roper and the *English Works*, is couched in clear, simple French and consists of twenty-three short chapters beginning with the king's visit to the French castle, then reverting to the earliest years, and proceeding with some chronological discrepancies to the end.

F253 Quenneville, Jean-Guy. "Public Policy and Personal Conscience: Thomas More, Judge in the King's Court of Equity and Christian Fool." *Thomas Morus Jahrbuch 1989*. 129-38.

More's life goes beyond his conduct and pursuit of good; it is the Christian humanist's assertion of the person as a source of goodness; and, "in this his behaviour is that of the Christian fool, in the true imitation of Christ."

F254 Ramsey, G.D. "A Saint in the City: Thomas More at Mercers' Hall, London." *English Historical Review* 97 (1982): 269-88.

Ramsey uses the *Acts of Court of the Mercers' Company* to detail More's career in the city, starting with his admission into the Mercers' Company in 1509 and closing with his resignation of under-sheriff in 1518. He is mainly concerned with More's successful activity in commercial negotiation for the London Adventurers and his gaining the support of London merchants. Although More had reservations about the Mercers making money, they made it possible for More to enter Parliament in 1510, which enabled him to help shape economic policy advantageous to them.

F255 Rawlinson of Ewell, Lord. "Public Duty and Personal Faith--the Example of Sir Thomas More." *Australian Law Journal* 53 (1979): 9-18.

Rawlinson examines More as a lawyer in politics. After discussing More's legal training and early public career, he concentrates on his chancellorship and its judicial successes and political failures; he also focuses upon his resignation, imprisonment, trial, and execution (viewing his condemnation as a "foregone conclusion"). Some material here can also be found in Rawlinson's "Thomas More as a Public Figure" (F256).

F256 Rawlinson, Peter. "Thomas More as a Public Figure." *Moreana* 54 (1977): 41-55.

Rawlinson, a lawyer and member of Parliament, discusses personal and professional aspects of More as a public figure, and pays tribute to him as "the first in modern times to shew the way...that the State is not all."

F257 Reed, A.W. "Young More." *Under God and the Law*. Papers read to the Thomas More Society of London. 2nd ser. Ed. Richard O'Sullivan. Oxford: Basil Blackwell, 1949. 1-27.

Reed follows More's career from his school days to about his fortieth year, supplies biographical details that correct some notions previous scholars held, and has much to say on More's relationship with John Holt of Magdalen College (see F225 and F226), William Lily, and Richard Whitford.

F258 Rex, Richard. *Henry VIII and the English Reformation*. New York: St. Martin's, 1993. 16, 17, 20, 21, 22, 23, 37, 53, 85, 107, 114, 116, 118, 120, 131, 135, 142.

Rex covers More's important actions during the Reformation.

F259 Reynolds, E.E. "The Fame of Saint Thomas More." *Moreana* 62 (1979): 31-41.

Intended as an additional chapter for a revised, augmented edition of *The Field is Won* (F259) but never printed because the publishers decided to reprint the original text, this essay sums up Reynolds' thoughts after years of studying More. Reynolds epitomizes More as one "exceptional in combining a full active life in the world with an inner life of prayer and meditation of an intensity rarely achieved outside a cloister."

F260 Reynolds, E.E. *The Field is Won: The Life and Death of Saint Thomas More*. Milwaukee: Bruce, 1968.

This work is not a revision of Reynolds' *Saint Thomas More* (F263), but substantially a new biography, written in the light of much recent work on More as well as the Renaissance and Reformation. The fruit of long and devoted research, it takes account of the Yale edition of More, bibliographies and articles by Marc'hadour, contributions to *Moreana*, Schulte-Herbrüggen's collection of More's official letters (U010), and Reynolds' discovery of the draft record of the conversation between More and Rich in the Tower shortly before More's execution (F266). The character and personality that emerge are those of a gracious, yet commanding, protagonist, moving within circles of public figures and intimate friends, portrayed from the evidence of correspondence and recorded conversations. Sidelights on More's household include an account of the private school he established for his children's benefit. The chapter on *Utopia* adds nothing substantially new by way of information, but it carefully assesses More's views on religious toleration and his contribution to English prose.

F261 Reynolds, E.E. "Hagiographers?" *Moreana* 57 (1978): 9-12.

Reynolds takes issue with the pejorative sense G.R. Elton, in his *Reform and Reformation* (1977), gives the word, hagiography, when Elton calls R.W. Chambers' *Thomas More* (F040) a hagiographical biography. Although Reynolds disagrees with Elton on other points, he says Elton's book is important and will not be harmed by his criticism.

F262 Reynolds, E.E. *Margaret Roper: Eldest Daughter of St. Thomas More*. London: Burns & Oates, 1960.

Reynolds refers almost as much to More as to his daughter in this book which draws freely on the correspondence between them and quotes in full Margaret's letter to Lady Alice Alington reproducing the dialogue between herself and her father shortly before his death. Considerable space is given to an account of the education of More's children and of his liberal ideas, shared by Vives and Erasmus, on the education of women.

F263 Reynolds, E.E. "The Mores and Hatfield." *Moreana* 23 (1969): 31-33.

Reynolds lists references made to the More family in or near Hatfield, such as John More's transfer of lands to son Thomas.

F264 Reynolds, E.E. *Saint Thomas More*. London: Burns & Oates, 1953.

After reviewing previous biographers of More (with emphasis on T.E. Bridgett's *Life and Writings of Sir Thomas More* [1891]), this study provides a Catholic interpretation of More's life and works which takes stock of materials un-earthed since Bridgett's work. Seventeen reproductions of contemporary drawings and paintings enhance Reynolds' lucid style and fluent chronicle of More's activities. Numerous quotations from first-hand sources grace his chapters on More's enlightened education of his family and the genial patriarchy of his Chelsea household. He also pays special attention to More's conflict with Henry VIII, his humanist interests and associates, his two marriages, and provides an analysis of *Richard III, Utopia, Dialogue of Comfort*, and some other works.

F265 Reynolds, E.E. *Thomas More and Erasmus.* New York: Fordham UP, 1965.

A companion to *Saint Thomas More* (F263), *Margaret Roper* (F261), and *The Trial of St. Thomas More* (F265), this study assesses the mutual influence and friendship of the two great companion humanists and claims these outstanding personalities cannot be treated in isolation. Reynolds sees More and Erasmus as a vital link in his discussion of other members of their Circle and their views on the study of Greek, education, war, politics, public service, crime and punishment, reform of the Church, papal authority, and other topics.

F266 Reynolds, E.E. *The Trial of St. Thomas More.* New York: P.J. Kenedy, 1964.

Reynolds studies the records relating to the arraignment, trial, and execution, and analyzes the Acts of Succession, Supremacy, and Treason, and the four counts in the charge. These records throw light both upon the political setting of the trial and the fundamental principles directing More's faith, character, and conduct, his horror of heresy, and his preference of Church to Parliament finally outweighing his regard for legality and the prestige of monarchy, a conflict of motives reflected in his self-imposed silence. In the course of his book, Reynolds takes occasion to correct or amplify some statements in his *Saint Thomas More* (F263) and *Margaret Roper* (F261).

F267 Reynolds, E.E. "An Unnoticed Document." *Moreana* 1 (1963): 12-17.

In the *Letters and State Papers of Henry VIII* is the primary account of the conversation between More and Sir Richard Rich on 12 June 1535 in the Tower, which reveals More did not speak the words denying Henry his new title. Thus, Roper's charge Rich perjured himself at More's trial is confirmed.

F268 Reynolds, E.E., ed. *William Roper and Nicholas Harpsfield: Lives of St. Thomas More.* London: Dent, 1963.

This edition places the two *Lives* in one volume for readers' convenience, thereby enabling scholars to compare these early biographers.

F269 Ridley, Jasper. *The Statesman and the Fanatic: Thomas Wolsey and Thomas More.* London: Constable, 1982. (Published in the United States as *Statesman and Saint: Cardinal Wolsey, Sir Thomas More, and the Politics of Henry VIII* [New York: Viking P, 1983].)

The purpose of Ridley's iconoclastic study is to overturn the stereotypes of Wolsey the unscrupulous politician and More the saint by paying notice to More's attitude toward heresy and treatment of heretics, because More was "far more zealous" about such matters than Wolsey. In contrast to Wolsey who was a "rogue" faithful only to his king and who met his death with dignity, More was a liar, forger, sycophant, paranoid, bigot, and fanatic who unaccountably found steadiness and "redeems" himself *only* at the end of a life animated by heretic-hating and foul, slanderous abuse of Lutherans.

F270 Rimmel, Lesley A. "Was Thomas Cromwell a Morean?" *Moreana* 75-76 (1982): 5-24.

Although progress has been made in revising the traditional views of More the Catholic martyr and Cromwell the strict adherent of Machiavelli, the two statesmen are still considered to represent two conflicting ideologies. Rimmel qualifies this view and demonstrates how the two men shared a belief in the possibility of improving the social and economic life of the world, through public institutions guided by human intelligence and reason. In philosophy of reform, theories of justice and law, and specific plans for social and economic reform, the two men were much more in agreement than is generally believed. The last years of More's life notwithstanding, both men believed in the necessity and feasibility of improving, through law, their world, Cromwell attempting to translate into action some of More's ideas.

F271 Ro:Ba:. *The Lyfe of Syr Thomas More, Sometymes Lord Chancellor of England.* Eds. Elsie Vaughan Hitchcock, and Philip E. Hallett (with additional notes and appendices by A.W. Reed). EETS. os 222. London: Oxford UP, 1950.

Hitchcock and Hallett died before their labors on this authoritative edition were completed, so Mabel Day saw it through to press. Hitchcock collated the eight variant mss. of the early biography and offers notes on those readings; Hallett supplies the introduction, notes, glossary, and index. The date and place of composition, purpose, content, style, and author are discussed, along with a comparison of textual problems in the three Tudor *Lives* of More.

F272 Rope, H.E.G. *Fisher and More.* London: Herder, 1935.

This short biography repeats Foxe's charge that More as chancellor had Frith arrested despite the fact it has been established that he resigned the office before Frith returned to England. In addition to tracing some of More's ancestors, Rope maintains that More's life is full of seeming anomalies "that are at times difficult to reconcile."

F273 Roper, William. *The Lyfe of Sir Thomas Moore, Knighte.* Ed. Elsie Vaughan Hitchcock. EETS. os 197. London: Oxford UP, 1935.

This scholarly edition of Roper's biography provides extensive notes on the collations of mss. and editions of the work, facts about Roper, dates and circumstances of composition, and other information. The text is complete with numerous glosses to help readers through obscure passages.

F274 Roper, William. *The Lyfe of Sir Thomas Moore, Knighte, written by William Roper, Esquire, Whiche Maried Margreat daughter of Sayed Thomas Moore.* Ed. James Mason Cline. New York: Swallow P & William Morrow, 1950.

This is a less scholarly edition than that of Elsie Vaughan Hitchcock (F273).

R275 Roper, William. *The Lyf of Syr Thomas More.* 1626. English Recusant Literature 1558-1640. Vol. 4. Menston: Scolar, 1970.

A volume in the library of Downside Abbey supplies copy for a facsimile of Roper's *Lyf.*

F276 Rousseau, Marie-Claude. "Thomas More, énigme et paradoxe: 'Non sum Oedipus, sed Morus.'" *Le Paradoxe au temps de la Renaissance.* Ed. Marie-Thérèse Jones-Davies. Paris: Touzot, 1982. 87-103.

Rousseau's title uses a line from More's 1534 letter to his daughter Margaret as a point of departure for a study of the paradoxes, enigmas, "incomprehensible riddle" of More's personality throughout his life, but especially during his imprisonment. (Rpt. as "Non sum Oedipus, sed Morus," *Moreana* 91-92 [1968]: 173-87.)

F277 Routh, E.M.G. *Sir Thomas More and His Friends, 1477-1535.* 1934. New York: Russell, 1963.

Routh wants to depict More as he appears in his own letters and those written to him, and he is interested in More's earlier life, friendship with humanists, appointments to office, and services for education. Of More's writings he is most concerned with *Utopia*, and he largely views More as a link between the Middle Ages and the Renaissance.

F278 Rupp, Gordon. *Thomas More: The King's Good Servant.* London: Collins, 1978.

This beautiful pictorial biography includes basic information on More's literary and political career.

F279 Saffady, William. "The Effects of Childhood Bereavement and Parental Remarriage in Sixteenth-Century England: The Case of Thomas More." *History of Childhood Quarterly: The Journal of Psychohistory* 1 (1973): 310-36.

Using biographies and More's own writings, Saffady presents a psychoanalytical reading of More's reactions to his mother's death and father's remarriages, theorizing the loss of his mother created unresolved Oedipal problems and a confusion of sexuality and death while his father's survival and remarriages caused repressed hostility directed toward heretics, especially Luther, and the divorce and remarriage of Henry VIII.

F280 Sargent, Daniel. *Thomas More.* 1933. Freeport, NY: Books for Libraries P, 1970.

Sargent covers More's vocational crisis, friendship with Erasmus, humanism, *Utopia*, family life and educational views, spirituality, service to the state, involvement in religious controversy, Wolsey's downfall, years as chancellor, attitude toward the divorce question, treatment of heretics, resignation as chancellor, retirement to private life, refusal to acknowledge the king as supreme head of the English church, imprisonment, *Dialogue of Comfort*, trial, and execution.

F281 Sargent, Daniel. "The Trial of Saint Thomas More." *Catholic Historical Review* 22 (1936): 1-11.

Sargent suggests More thought the Act of Treason of 1535 endangered harmless lives, because it completely disregarded the Statute of Treason of 1350 which defined treason as an act plotting or executing the king's death only. More thought the 1535 law showed no sense of justice in making mere words spoken casually against a half dozen of Henry's titles treasonous. More's trial proved his innocence according to the 1350 law, and the fatal results that trial had for More underlined Henry's tyranny.

F282 Scarisbrick, John J. "Thomas More: The King's Good Servant." *Thought* 52 (1977): 249-68.

Scarisbrick discusses More's political motivation and unique relationship with the king as a royal councilor, secretary, diplomat, and chancellor in great detail.

F283 Schoeck, R.J. "Another Renaissance Biography of Sir Thomas More." *ES* 34 (1953): 115-17.

This note draws attention to Graziani's account of More in *De Casibus Virorum Illustrium* (Paris, 1680), which describes More as one of the mighty fallen rather than as a saint and stresses the legal interest of *Utopia*.

F284 Schoeck, R.J. "Anthony Bonvisi, the Heywoods and the Ropers." *N&Q* 197 (1952): 178-79.

Bonvisi was a life-long friend of More to whom More sold Crosby Place in 1524. In 1547 Bonvisi made over its deed to William Roper and William Rastell for ninety years, and in the same year obtained a license to convey the property to Richard Heywood and John Webb in trust for him for life. In 1549 Bonvisi withdrew himself "without and departed out of England unto the places beyond the sea without lycence of his soverayne lord." Crosby Place was then seized by the sheriffs of London, but given back to Bonvisi in 1554 by Queen

Mary. Bonvisi died 7 December 1558.

F285 Schoeck, R.J. "Canon Law in England on the Eve of the Reformation." *MS* 25 (1963): 125-47.

Schoeck shows More was "interested and competent" in canon law by pointing to his admission into Doctors' Commons in 1514, his administrative positions (the chancellorship included) that would demand knowledge of canon law, his involvement in the Hunne case, and some of his controversial tracts which evidence his familiarity with canon law.

F286 Schoeck, R.J. "A Lawyer with a Conscience (Luncheon Address to the Thomas More Society, Washington, D.C., 17 May 1973)." *Moreana* 39 (1973): 25-32.

Schoeck emphasizes More's dedication to his profession and suggests what emerges from Roper's *Life* is the "carefully constructed picture of a lawyer with a superlatively developed sense of conscience," and "what makes him a man for all our seasons of moral crisis is his 'clear unspotted conscience.'"

F287 Schoeck, R.J. "More, Erasmus, and the Devil." *N&Q* 196 (1951): 313.

Schoeck discusses the repartee attributed to the two men on their first meeting, which may have involved an allusion to the identification of "morus" (mulberry tree) with the devil in the *Allegoriae in Sacrum Scripturam*.

F288 Schoeck, R.J. "Neo-Latin Resources for Biography: A Preliminary View." *Acta Conventus Neo-Latini Torontonensis*. Proceedings of the Seventh International Congress of Neo-Latin Studies, Toronto, 8 August to 13 August 1988. Eds. Alexander Dalzell, Charles Fantazzi, R.J. Schoeck. MRTS. 86. Binghamton, NY: MRTS, 1991. 101-10.

Schoeck uses sixteenth-century biographies of More to identify and comment upon some of the models, *topoi*, and lore from which their authors drew.

F289 Schoeck, R.J. "On the Spiritual Life of St. Thomas More." *Thought* 52 (1977): 324-27.

Schoeck believes any examination of More's spirituality must consider the daily and weekly devotional practices his early biographers describe. He suggests one view of his spirituality is vertical--from love of humankind up to love of God with mysticism at its apex. More's realism and earthiness, however, did not lessen the spirituality learned in the Charterhouse and reaching its summit in the months of devotion and contemplation recorded in the Tower Works.

F290 Schoeck, R.J. "The Place of Sir Thomas More in Legal History and Tradition: Some Notes and Observations." *American Journal of Jurisprudence*

23 (1978): 212-23.

Although he was not involved in a leading case, authored no texts, and published no legal literature, More was influential as an administrator of the law, and his exemplary character which "subsumed the spirit of common law" was of great importance to the legal tradition. His service as under-sheriff and sheriff of London (1510-17), his chancellorship of the Duchy of Lancaster (1525-29), and his Lord Chancellorship (1529-32) created his reputation as a skillful arbitrator of "utter scrupulosity and strict impartiality." More's appointment to the chancery in 1529 brought "immense prestige" to that office, and his unblemished character "had much to do with the high place of the judiciary in English traditions." (This essay revises and expands upon "The Place of Sir Thomas More in Legal History and Tradition: A Sketch with Some Observations," *Moreana* 51 [1976]: 83-94.)

F291 Schoeck, R.J. "Sir Thomas More and the Lincoln's Inn Revels." *PQ* 29 (1950): 426-30.

Schoeck recounts More was elected Butler of the Inn Michaelmas Term 1507 to serve with the Steward at Christmas under the Master of the Revels. He was elected Marshall for 1510-11 to be responsible to the Master of the Revels during the Christmas festivities; but having recently been appointed one of the under-sheriffs of the City of London, he paid a fine instead of serving. Even when he became chancellor in 1529, he continued his interest in the affairs of the Inn.

F292 Schoeck, R.J. "Sir Thomas More, Humanist and Lawyer." *UTQ* 34 (1964): 1-14.

Schoeck opposes the view, first promulgated by Erasmus, that More's father dragooned him into the legal profession, noting that many humanists were lawyers in accord with early humanistic traditions at the Inns of Court, which survived throughout the sixteenth century in Elyot, Coke, Bacon, and others. More should not be considered a humanist in spite of being a lawyer, but rather as a humanist and lawyer. The "legal strands of More's thought run steadily through his life," and the picture of More as a humanist who was a reluctant prisoner at law is misleading. (Rpt. in *Essential Articles for the Study of Thomas More*, 569-79.)

F293 Schoeck, R.J. "Sir Thomas More's School Days." *TLS* 18 Dec. 1953: 817.

Roper and Harpsfield claim More went to St. Anthony's School; Ro:Ba: is the first to state he was enrolled under Nicholas Holt; Stapleton also says Holt taught More. Although no record of Holt exists, Ro:Ba: and Stapleton's assertions are not necessarily untrue.

F294 Schoeck, R.J. "Telling More from Erasmus: An *Essai* in Renaissance Humanism." *Moreana* 91-92 (1986): 11-19.

Schoeck examines the "new statement of the non-friendship thesis lest it harden into dogma," because the question of More and Erasmus' friendship bears upon the larger question of their humanism and on the closeness of their collaboration and "has therefore implications for the story of humanism in England and on the Continent." Schoeck concludes the relationship was indeed complex, for at every level there are likenesses as remarkable as the differences, and he cautions that friendship among humanists was not merely a rhetorical *topos* handed down from Cicero and popularized by numerous intermediary writers, but also a *habitus* developed over time from close study, as in the case of Petrarch and Ficino.

F295 Schoeck, R.J. "Thomas Gygges, Tudor Lawyer." *N&Q* 195 (1950): 269-71.

This note presents further evidence which does not support Gygges' conjectured relationship with More's foster daughter.

F296 Schoeck, R.J. "Thomas More and the Italian Heritage of Early Tudor Humanism." *Arts libéraux et philosophie au Moyen Âge*. Actes du quartrième Congrès international de philosophie médiévale. Université de Montréal, Montréal, Canada, 27 aôut-2 Septembre 1967. Vol. 1. Montréal: Institut d'Études Médiévales; Paris: Vrin, 1969. 1191-97.

Schoeck argues that, while the Italian heritage of More's humanism is dominant and Colet was the bridge between More and Italian humanism generally and Florentine humanism in particular, More's Italian humanism was "ultimately (if not directly) inspired by Pico," and he discusses the *Life of Pico* and considers factors outside Italian humanism that contributed to More's sense of humanism.

F297 Schoeck, R.J. "Thomas More and the Printing Press." *Thomas Morus Jahrbuch 1995*. 104-13.

Schoeck examines More and Erasmus' attitudes toward the new craft of printing and studies how More adapted himself to the print culture through the "textual community of judges and lawyers" and publication of his own works.

F298 Schoeck, R.J. "The Two Laws in Thomas More: A Preliminary Reading of the Canon and Common Law in His Career and Writing." *Catholic Lawyer* 16 (1970): 277-95.

Schoeck reviews More's legal career, emphasizing the affair of the pope's ship which brought him to the court's attention from which he eventually moved to the highest office in England. Schoeck also discusses two books which influenced common law principles--St. German's *Doctor and Student* and John Parkins' *Profitable Nook*--the Hunne case, Standish, and More's trial.

F299 Schoeck, R.J. "Two Notes on Margaret Giggs Clement, Foster-Daughter of Sir Thomas More." *N&Q* 194 (1949): 532-33.

Schoeck tries to determine who Margaret's father may have been and why she was More's ward.

F300 Schoeck, R.J. "Was Sir Thomas More a 'Roman Lawyer'?" *N&Q* 194 (1949): 203.

Schoeck doubts the T. Morus admitted to Doctors' Commons in 1514 is the author of *Utopia*, because he maintains *Utopia*'s author did not have the degree qualifications for admission to the Commons or sufficient leisure for study of civil law.

F301 Schroeder, Karl G. "Jerome de Busleyden and Thomas More." *Moreana* 121 (1995): 3-10.

Schroeder outlines the life of Busleyden from his birth in Luxembourg about 1470 until his death in Bordeaux in 1517. He describes the relationship of Busleyden, More, and Erasmus, and the significance of Busleyden's role in three of More's works: the *Lucianica*, the Epigrams, and the parerga to *Utopia*.

F302 Schulte-Herbrüggen, Hubertus. "Erasmus und England: Erasmus und Morus." *Erasmus und Europa*. Ed. August Buck. Wiesbaden: Harrassowitz, 1988. 91-110.

Schulte-Herbrüggen explores the relationship of Erasmus and More.

F303 Schulte-Herbrüggen, Hubertus. *Das Haupt des Thomas Morus in der St. Dunstan-Kirche zu Canterbury*. Forschungsberichte des Landes Nordrhein-Westfalen, No. 3083. Fachgruppe Geisteswissenschaften. Opladen: Westdeutscher Verlag, 1982.

Schulte-Herbrüggen, by minute exposure and meticulous sifting of all evidence, investigates the question of whether the skull behind the iron grill on the north wall of the sepulchral vault of the Roper family in St. Dunstan's Church is More's skull.

F304 Schulte-Herbrüggen, Hubertus. "More's Dates." *TLS* 20 Jan. 1966: 48.

Through examination of *Warrants for the Great Seal* for 1529, Schulte-Herbrüggen discovers evidence More may have received the office of chancellor as much as a month earlier than 25 October 1529--the generally accepted date.

F305 Schulte-Herbrüggen, Hubertus. "More's Genealogy." *TLS* 18 June 1970: 662.

This note points out some of the difficulties in tracing More's ancestors and descendants.

F306 Schulte-Herbrüggen, Hubertus. "The Process against Sir Thomas More." *The Law Quarterly Review* 99 (1983): 113-36.

Schulte-Herbrüggen defines seven stages in the criminal process against More from historical, constitutional, and legal precedents and preliminary procedures to committal and criminal proceedings in the trial, judgment, and execution. From Cromwell's personal papers, he determines Henry decided and Cromwell implemented More's condemnation and execution about a week before the judicial court was assigned and about two weeks before More's trial. The author also discusses More's defense of himself during the trial.

F307 Schütt, Marie. "Die englische Biographik der frühen Stuartzeit (1603-1640)." *Anglia* 81 (1963): 129-41.

The *Vita* of More in its various reworkings indicates approaches to biography in these decades. From a laudatory memorial in one biography, More's life becomes the ideal of the proto-martyr for English laymen in another. Other biographies of the period use conversion from Protestantism to Catholicism or vice versa as works of propaganda, and the status of Catholicism at varying periods can be deduced from them. There is increasing concern for using primary materials, documentation, and biography to show historical trends and psychological motivation.

F308 Shanahan, D. "The Death of Thomas More, Secular Priest, Great Grandson to St. Thomas More." *Recusant History* 7 (1963): 23-32.

Shanahan relates the death of this descendant of More and speculates he may have begun a life of More that Cresacre More put together and published. Shanahan provides further information on this descendant in "Thomas More IV, Secular Priest," *Recusant History* 8 (1965): 88-91, 105-14.

F309 Shanahan, D. "The Family of St. Thomas More in Essex, 1581-1640." *Recusant History* 1 (1959): 62-72, 95-103; 2 (1960): 44-45, 76-85; 5 (1963): 49-57; 6 (1964): 96-98.

Shanahan tells the story of the More family in Essex to show they were joined by blood or marriage to the major recusant families of the time and that many of them were prominent in law, printing, and writing.

F310 Smith, Lacey Baldwin. "English Treason Trials and the Confessions of the 16th Century." *JHI* 15 (1954): 471-98.

Although much of this essay deals with Anne Boleyn's trial and others, Smith comments on More's conviction for remaining silent, because silence might be construed as having evil intentions and once the government decided the state's safety required More's death, even silence could not save him.

F311 Smith, Richard Lawrence. *John Fisher and Thomas More: Two English Saints*. London: Sheed & Ward, 1935.

This "study primarily of their sanctity, of their characters as supernaturalized by grace, and of their martyrdom" is the English translation of the Italian account presented to the pope and other ecclesiastical dignitaries after the canonizations of Fisher and More on 19 May 1935.

F312 Sorlien, Robert P. "Henry Howard on Cromwell to More (an Augmentation)." *Moreana* 42 (1974): 43-44.

Sorlien traces a reference to More (made by Cromwell) in Howard's work.

F313 Sowards, J.K. "Thomas More, Erasmus, and Julius II: A Case of Advocacy." *Moreana* 24 (1969): 81-99.

Sowards discuses More's role in connection with Erasmus' *Julius Exclusus* (a satiric attack on Pope Julius II) and suggests, as possible reasons for More's falsification of facts concerning the tract's authorship, his sense of loyalty and friendship, hatred of tyranny, innate pacifism, and love of a jest.

F314 Stapleton, Thomas. *The Life and Illustrious Martyrdom of Sir Thomas More*. 1928. Trans. Philip E. Hallett. New York: Fordham UP, 1966.

Essentially a reprint of Hallett's translation, this edition has the advantage of E.E. Reynolds' notes.

F315 Stapleton, Thomas. *The Life and Illustrious Martyrdom of Sir Thomas More*. Trans. Philip E. Hallett. 1928. Ed. E.E. Reynolds. New York: Fordham UP, 1984.

Reynolds annotates this paperback reprint of Hallett's translation of Stapleton's biography.

F316 Stapleton, Thomas. *Vita Thomae Mori*. Frankfurt: Unveranderter Nachdruck, n.d.

A facsimile of the 1689 Francofurti and Moenum edition of Stapleton's Latin biography.

F317 Sullivan, Frank. "The Author of Ro:Ba:'s Life of St. Thomas More." *Los Angeles Tidings* 10 Dec. 1948: 15.

Sullivan suggests More's anonymous biographer, Ro:Ba:, is the Venerable Bartholomew Roe, since he wrote the preface to Rose R. whom he calls his "dear and thrice dear friend." Sullivan acknowledges his case is weak, but he intends to abandon the usual idea of attributing the *Life* to Robert Barnstable.

F318 Sullivan, Frank. "A Lesson from Thomas More." *Historical Bulletin* 20 (1941): 33-35.

This article emphasizes the difficulty of More's decision in the face of the terrible death meted out to so-called traitors, with prescience before the fact, not knowledge after it, of the debacle that was to be the consequence of Henry's break with Rome.

F319 Sullivan, Frank. "The Letter of the Law of a Christian Socrates." *Moreana* 15-16 (1967): 304-10.

Sullivan qualifies Harpsfield's reference to More as a Christian Socrates by listing their differences on physical pleasure, consolation, death, and advocacy of personal convictions. He believes their most basic difference, however, is their attitude toward others--More is a social being, Socrates an aloft "intellect."

F320 Sullivan, Frank. "Sir Thomas More." *TLS* 26 Dec. 1958: 751.

This note includes three facts: (1) More was a member of Parliament in January 1510 with John Bregis; (2) while at the university he spent "some time at Culham to escape the plague" (c. 1492-94); (3) some unprinted writings of More may be found in MS. Bodley 431, which contains a Latin version of *Treatise on the Passion*.

F321 Surtz, Edward. "More's Friendship with Fisher." *Moreana* 15-16 (1967): 115-33.

Surtz recounts all known contacts between More and Fisher and their relationships with mutual acquaintances, compares their intellectual and spiritual values, and concludes they "were on good, familiar and respectful terms" but did not "constantly" seek "each other's company out of deep and unreserved affection." (Rpt. in *Essential Articles for the Study of Thomas More*, 169-79.)

F322 Surtz, Edward L. "Richard Pace's Sketch of More." *JEGP* 57 (1958): 36-50.

Since Pace left England in 1517, his sketch of More in his widely read *De Fructu Qui ex Doctrina Percipitur Liber* (published in Basle in October 1517) antedates that which Erasmus sent to Ulrich von Hutten in July 1519. By comparing the two descriptions, Surtz concludes that, although Pace's sketch is not as carefully balanced as that of Erasmus, yet because of its brevity, it hits off the main features of More's character. Pace tends to exaggerate More's merriness. Despite Pace's eclecticism, More is presented as "another Democritus, another Laughing Philosopher." Surtz then suggests *Utopia* should be interpreted "much more than hitherto in the spirit of humor and wit" in order to throw light on More's complex attitude to the world of Utopia and toward radical and universal reform in Europe. In an appendix to his article, Surtz transcribes

Pace's *De Moro*. (Rpt. in *Essential Articles for the Study of Thomas More*, 180-88.)

F323 Surtz, Edward L., and Virginia Murphy, eds. *The Divorce Tracts of Henry VIII*. Angers, Fr.: Moreana, 1988.

The king's books clearly demonstrate that from the first (1527) Henry consciously advocated a constant and implicit challenge to papal secular power. While not generally credited with consistency in so important a matter as this, Henry defies his standard caricature. Not content with an occasional supervision of this polemic, in at least one tract Henry did the writing; in the rest, he clearly was on top of the matter. Anyone seriously concerned with early Tudor history must consult this source.

F324 Suzuki, Yoshinori. "Thomas More on Politics as a Profession." *Moreana* 97 (1988): 125-32.

Suzuki argues More neither entered into Henry VIII's service unwillingly nor willingly to make a career, but did so to try to bring his special talents to the creation of the ideal statesman urged by his sense of duty. After satisfying himself he fulfilled the conditions necessary to be a statesman, he was solicited by the king with the guarantee of a reasonable stipend, and hoped he could do something good for the commonweal, at least by making matters as little bad as possible.

F325 Sylvester, R.S. "More's Discussion of Perjury." *Moreana* 55-56 (1977): 73-77.

Sylvester reprints British Library MS. Royal 17.D.XIV, in which More discusses perjury; compares it with two other versions in British Library MS. Arundel 152; and believes More composed it as a kind of briefing while imprisoned in the Tower. He also likens it to other pieces in which More wrote about perjury and decides More's "deepest feelings" about the subject can be found in the Tower letters.

F326 Sylvester, R.S. "Roper's *Life of More*." *Moreana* 36 (1972): 47-59.

Roper's *Life* has usually been regarded as a valuable, if sometimes erroneous, historical memoir. Its literary merits, however, outweigh its strictly historical virtues. Roper's adoption, as narrator and character, of a naive persona both contrasts with and complements the role-playing characteristic of More himself. As Roper acts out his role of a simple reporter, so too does More emerge as a complete Renaissance man, a player of many parts who consistently manages to achieve an admirable, controlled balance between the moral implications of role-playing and the aesthetic satisfaction it offers. The manner in which Roper structures his *Life* around a series of carefully chosen and carefully placed anecdotes reflects More's own staging of his career, right down to his trial and death, where, as always, he played the part he had deliberately chosen for himself. (With minor revisions, rpt. in *Essential Articles for the Study of Thomas More*, 189-97.)

F327 Sylvester, R.S. "Thomas More: New Buildings and Old." *Moreana* 4 (1964): 5-17.

Sylvester clarifies the paradoxical nature of More's personality, character, and writings by claiming he possessed a kind of "double vision" that enabled him to participate in events and to observe himself participating in them. This is evident in his bookishness--both in his reading and writing.

F328 Sylvester, R.S., and David P. Harding, eds. *Two Early Tudor Lives*. The Life and Death of Cardinal Wolsey, *by George Cavendish*. The Life of Sir Thomas More, *by William Roper*. New Haven: Yale UP, 1962.

The text of Roper's biography is based on Hitchcock's edition (F273), and these biographies have been reprinted together on the ground the two complement each other and "exhibit a remarkably similar structural development," though rooted in different literary traditions.

F329 Thompson, Craig R. "Erasmus, More, and the Conjuration of Spirits: A Possible Source of a Practical Joke." *Moreana* 24 (1969): 45-50.

This article refers to Erasmus' colloquy *Exorcismus sive spectrum*, describing a practical joke, in which More is involved.

F330 Tournoy, Gilbert. "La Poésie de William Lily pour le diptyque de Quentin Metsijs." *Moreana* 97 (1988): 63-66.

Tournoy introduces an eight-line Latin poem by More's friend Lily about the joint portrait of Erasmus and Peter Giles painted by Metsijs in 1517 and brought to More by the Dutchman Peter Meghen; Lily singles out for attention the golden ring on Erasmus' finger, because it was a gift from More.

F331 Tsukada, Tomiharu. "Thomas More as a Political Thinker and Actor for Reform." *HJA&S* 22.1 (1981): 17-30.

Tsukada charts More's development as a political thinker and how changes in it affect his plans and actions for social reform. Although Tsukada believes More's early political ideas were optimistic when Henry VIII ascended the throne, he became increasingly disillusioned as he became more aware of some abuses of power--some of which found its expression in *Richard III* and *Utopia*.

F332 Tucker, M.J. "The More-Norfolk Connection." *Moreana* 33 (1972): 5-13.

More's friendship with Thomas Howard, third Duke of Norfolk (d. 1554), has been distorted by Bolt's play, *A Man for All Seasons* (F022, I018). Norfolk, far from being Bolt's intellectual cipher, was a man with Renaissance tastes, interests, and aspirations. Thus, the historical background and association of More and Norfolk, which commenced as a consequence of royal service for both in the Exchequer, is drawn against the rising tide of the Reformation. Despite Norfolk's urgings, More denied Henry VIII's supremacy and lost his life; Norfolk clung to his king and life, but lost a friend.

F333 Tucker, M.J. "Skelton's More-Howard Connections." *Moreana* 37 (1973): 15-23.

Tucker speculates on the relationship between the poet and More: "though the two men represented opposite poles of the humanistic spectrum, they shared certain affinities. Both sought royal favor; both used Chaucer's seven line rhyme-royal; both wrote major satires. In addition each produced anti-Lutheran tracts and became in their own lifetimes central characters of 'merie' jests." But Tucker is forced to conclude that "More's estimate of Skelton, like so much of Skelton's life, must always remain conjectural."

F334 Tucker, M.J. "Thomas More and the Wentworths." *Moreana* 34 (1972): 57-60.

The family connections of Margaret Wentworth, one of the ladies who wove the Tudor poet John Skelton's *A Garland of Laurel*, are traced in relation to Sir Roger Wentworth, "The worshipful knight," cited in More's *The Dialogue Concerning Heresies*. Commentary is provided on Sir Roger's daughter Margaret whom More noted as being cured of possession by a devil and of Roger's other daughter, the adulterous Laura.

F335 Vocht, Henry de., ed. *Acta Thomae Mori: History of the Reports of His Trial and Death with an Unedited Contemporary Narrative*. 1947. Nendeln, Liechtenstein: Kraus Reprint, 1966.

Vocht's discussion of an early Latin translation of the English account of More's trial and execution (the *Ordo Condemnationis Mori*) casts new light on More's last days, and his introduction provides a detailed account of its text, authorship, date of composition, source report, content, and historical significance.

F336 Vrljicak, Kazimir. "La Batalla Está Ganada, Master Roper: La personalidad y el carácter de Tomás Moro." *Moreana* 91-92 (1986): 111-12.

For the author, "the field is won," words More addressed to Roper (April 13, 1534), crystallize the personality and character of a man whose inner struggle had reached a dramatic climax.

F337 Walker, Greg. *John Skelton and the Politics of the 1520s*. Cambridge Studies in Early Modern British History. Cambridge: Cambridge UP, 1988.

43, 64, 76, 139, 151, 173, 176-77, 179-80, 183, 220.

More is given special importance in chapter five which deals with Wolsey's relationship to Henry's court.

F338 Warnicke, Retha. "The Harpy in More's Household: Was It Lady Alice?" *Moreana* 87-88 (1985): 5-13.

In order to revise the traditional view of Alice Middleton, More's second wife, as a shrew, Warnicke surmises about the identification of the harpy (often taken to refer to Lady Alice) in Erasmus' correspondence, and she believes it and other phrases from Erasmus' letters, which have been used to buttress the view of her as a loquacious woman, could be interpreted in more positive ways and should be recognized as incorrect and no longer used as evidence of her character.

F339 Warnicke, Retha M. "The Making of a Shrew: The Legendary History of Alice More." *Rendezvous* 15 (1980): 25-36.

Biographers Roper, Harpsfield, and Stapleton vilify More's second wife Alice as a shrew who fails to understand or appreciate her husband. Modern biographer Chambers (F040) largely accepts this unfair characterization, and Bolt (F022, I018) follows it in his play. A more truthful picture might be of an Alice who was a good housekeeper and enforced upon the household the rules her devout husband prescribed. Alice raised More's four young children, and when More's quarrel with Henry VIII erupted, she was left to manage the material and financial affairs of More's household. In his few allusions to his second wife, More gives witness to his respect and admiration for her.

F340 Warnicke, Retha. "The Restive Wife in Erasmus' Colloquy: Mistress More or Lady Mountjoy?" *Moreana* 79-80 (1983): 5-14.

Warnicke recommends that, while Erasmus did sometimes include autobiographical material in his work, any attempt to identify his acquaintances as the characters of his anecdotes should be done with extreme caution. In this case, Percy S. Allen's argument (*Selections from Erasmus*, 1908), that Jane Colt was the prototype of the fictitious woman in Erasmus' colloquy entitled "Marriage" is questionable, as can be proved by pointing to dissimilarities as well as similarities between the two women, by rehearsing the known facts about Jane, by presenting the story of the anonymous woman, and by comparing and contrasting them and their families. Warnicke offers the best possible challenge to Allen's claim and argues that Elizabeth Say, the first wife of Sir William Blount, fourth Baron Mountjoy, is a better model than Jane for the uncooperative wife of the anecdote.

F341 Warren, James Perrin. "The Canonization of John Fisher and Thomas More." *Moreana* 63.2 (1979): 49-52.

Warren gives the history of the process that led to their canonization and describes the ceremonies for canonization which began at 7:45 a.m. on 19 May 1935 in St. Peter's, Rome.

F342 Wegemer, Gerard. *Thomas More: A Portrait of Courage.* Princeton: Scepter Pub., 1995.

This biography emphasizes More's spiritual development without ignoring his faults, the "most obvious" of which "went hand in hand with his most obvious strengths," and Wegemer examines how More courageously conquered his weaknesses throughout his life "in the heart of London."

F343 Wells, Kathleen. "The Iconography of Saint Thomas More." *Studies* 70 (1981): 55-71.

Wells describes and discusses motifs within the portraits of More from Holbein (the source of those motifs) through the nineteenth century. She also emphasizes artists' treatment of More as a devotional figure and their attraction to his personal and familial rather than his public life.

F344 Wheeler, Thomas. "An Italian Account of Thomas More's Trial and Execution." *Moreana* 26 (1970): 33-39.

Wheeler duplicates the text of Cardinal Nicolo Scombargo's letter (which contains an account of More's trial and death), speculates upon Scombargo's sources, and suggests More and Scombargo may have met in London in 1524.

F345 White, Thomas I. "Legend and Reality: The Friendship Between More and Erasmus." *Supplementum Festivum: Studies in Honor of Paul Oskar Kristeller.* Eds. James Hankins, John Monfasani, and Frederick Purnell, Jr. MRTS. 49. Binghamton, NY: MRTS, 1987. 489-504.

White examines the friendship between More and Erasmus as presented in their correspondence and argues the rules of oratorical and epistolary rhetoric affect the presentation of reality in them. Disregard of these conventions and their rhetorical colors have in the past led to doubtful interpretations of monastic love, and in Erasmus' case there is evidence his broadcasting of friendships served his ambitions for reputation and position.

F346 Whiting, M.B. "Sir Thomas More, 1478-1535." *Catholic Review* 148 (1935): 55-64.

Largely based on Roper's biography (from which it quotes quite freely), Whiting includes an appreciation of *Utopia*, emphasizing its humanity and modernity.

F347 Wilby, Noel McDonald. "Sir Thomas More and the Refugees in Flanders." *Dublin Review* 194 (1938): 315-29.

This article is concerned with stories about the descendants of John and Margaret Giggs Clement, who spent many happy years in More's household-- Margaret as his ward, John as his protege and tutor to his children. They left England for Flanders, probably because of the many friends More had there.

F348 Wilson, K.J. "*Usque ad aras*: Thomas Elyot's Friendship with Thomas More." *Acta Conventus Neo-Latini Sanctandreani*. Proceedings of the Fifth International Conference of Neo-Latin Studies. University of St. Andrews, Scotland, 24 August to 1 September 1982. Ed. I.D. McFarlane. MRTS. 38. Binghamton, NY: MRTS, 1986. 531-35.

In order to comment upon the extent of Elyot and More's friendship, Wilson uses an allusion to Gellius and Plutarch as indicated by the phrase "*usque ad aras*" to clarify how Elyot employs it in a letter to Cromwell. Elyot clearly intends the phrase to mean his friendship with More ended when More refused to swear the Oath of Supremacy, because the phrase refers to the moral limits of friendship that More exceeded when he refused to place the welfare of England above that of Catholic unity. Wilson concludes that More and others were aware of this usage and that it illustrates the dilemma More's decision caused some of his friends.

F349 Wooden, Warren W. "Structural Patterning in William Roper's *Life of More*." *Moreana* 64 (1980): 100-06.

Wooden argues Roper's *Life* is organized on the principles of medieval hagiography, with the *capitula generalia* biography, required as part of the canonization process, particularly in mind.

F350 Wright, John. "Saint Thomas More, Patron of Lawyers and Model for our Changing Times." *Moreana* 51 (1976): 95-101.

Wright emphasizes the fact More as a lawyer is a member of a learned profession, a man in public life, who remains a family man.

F351 Zapatka, Francis E. "Thomas More and Thomas Darcy." *Moreana* 71-72 (1981): 15-27.

Zapatka draws connections between More and Darcy: indirect, direct, parallel. The indirect involve people with whom both had significant, repeated contact, such as Chapuys. Direct connections are found in official and family documents in which More and Darcy are mentioned together, implicitly or explicitly. Certain parallels between their lives and deaths establish the last kind of connection. Though Darcy is no More, Zapatka claims he sees More in Darcy "as through a glass darkly."

F352 Zeeveld, W. Gordon. "Apology for an Execution." *Moreana* 15-16 (1967): 353-71.

Zeeveld discusses the strategy Henry VIII and his ministers developed to justify More and Fisher's executions (both in England and on the Continent) and concentrates on Richard Morison's tract, *Apomaxis*, a defense of the government's position and a response to Cochlaeus' *Defensio Clarissimorum Virorum Joannis Fyscheri Episcopi Roffensis et Thomae Mori* (1536). (Rpt. in *Essential Articles for the Study of Thomas More*, 198-211.)

General Critical Studies

G001 Adams, Robert P. *The Better Part of Valor: More, Erasmus, Colet, and Vives on Humanism, War, and Peace, 1496-1535.* Seattle: U of Washington P, 1962.

Adams studies humanistic pacifism in the reactions of Colet, Erasmus, Vives, and More against the "open manslaughter" applauded in chivalric literature and the increasing belligerency of contemporary monarchs. These London reformers, bound together by friendship and a common ideal of Christian humanism, saw the "goal of social change as rightly the creation of a peaceful good life," a "utopia" based on reason or nature and derived from a continuous tradition, dating from the ancient myth of the Golden Age, and maintained, under different aspects, in Latin Stoicism and the medieval concept of *Pax Ecclesiae*.

G002 Adams, Robert P. "Bold Bawdry and Open Manslaughter: The English New Humanist Attack on Medieval Romance." *HLQ* 23 (1959): 33-48.

More's *Utopia*, Erasmus' *Christian Prince*, and Vives' *Christen Woman* show the humanist attack on medieval romance stemmed from new humanist ideas about tyrants vs. just kings, a war-ridden and disintegrating late-medieval society vs. a desired Renaissance social order of peace and Christian justice, a conflict between two opposed codes of value, and opposed ideas of woman's nature and potential role in society.

G003 Adams, Robert P. "Erasmus' Ideas of his Role as a Social Critic c. 1480-1500." *RN* 11 (1958): 11-16.

Adams has a double aim: (1) to consider Erasmus' attitude toward war and social criticism before he met Colet and More between October 1499 and January 1500, and (2) to determine the extent of their influence upon him. Before his meeting with Colet and More, Erasmus thought about man's inhumanity to man, but had limited himself to conditions in the Netherlands and had not found his sense of vocation as social satirist and critic. After his work on Lucian with More (1505-06), Erasmus found his vocation as social critic. Adams finds it unlikely Erasmus influenced Colet and More who, before they met him, had been engaged in "a daring effort to help build, on Christian humanist lines, a new and workable social order in England."

G004 Barnett, Mary Jane. "The Hermeneutics of Proteus: Linguistic Praxis and Sixteenth-Century English Humanism." Diss. U of Maryland-College Park, 1995.

Barnett argues the confidence in discourse in sixteenth-century England is "persistently troubled by practical intimations" there may be something potentially uncontrollable as well as instrumental about language, and makes the case Erasmus, with his relation to More's Circle, brought this awareness to England.

G005 Baumann, Uwe, and Hans Peter Heinrich. *Thomas Morus: Humanistische Schriften, Mit einer Einführung von Hubertus Schulte Herbrüggen. Erträge der Forschung.* 243. Darmstadt: Wissenschaftliche Buchgesellschaft, 1986.

After an essay by Schulte Herbrüggen on More's life, works, and humanism, this study considers the dates of composition and texts of the humanistic works--*Life of Picus*, the epigrams, *History of King Richard III*, and *Utopia*--and provides various interpretations of each, along with a bibliography.

G006 Beringause, Arthur F. "The Religious Writings of Thomas More." *Cresset* 27 (1964): 11-15.

More's religious pieces show that in youth he was liberal; in maturity, conservative. At first he agitated for reforms within the Church, but (as the Reformation progressed) he turned to religion to preserve order. The bold speculations of his early manhood yielded place to a desire for order, peace, and preservation of the status quo.

G007 Bertagnoni, Marialisa. "Discordia Concors: *Utopia e Il dialogo del Conforto*." *Moreana* 31-32 (1971): 183-88.

Two dialogues, some twenty years apart, dramatize More's spiritual conflicts--about 1515 the question whether he could ameliorate society via political position; in 1534 the question whether he could accept the King's divorce. More projected these dilemmas into art, and *Utopia* and *Dialogue* have qualities in common. Before death, the brave Hungarian-Christian agrees with the Utopians. In both situations, salvation--both individual and societal--firmly links with an interior conversation, liberating the soul from cupidity and pride.

G008 Billingsley, Dale B. "Reading and the Dangers of Reading in More's Works." *Moreana* 115-116 (1993): 5-18.

More's surviving Latin letters to his children train them in humanist conventions of literary representation, including the use of artful fiction as a medium for truth, which in the Latin version of *Richard III* implies an audience that shared More's conventions. After *Utopia*, More's strategies changed when he faced an audience that did not share these conventions. Although the controversial works in Latin show some of the same formal characteristics, those in English abandon artful form for direct confrontation, with damaging effects. In *Dialogue Concerning Heresies* and later works, the representation of face-to-face conversation becomes an icon of ideal communication and of the best means of combating heresy.

G009 Bridgett, T.E. "The Wit of Thomas More." *The Wisdom and Wit of Blessed Thomas More*. 1892. *Essential Articles for the Study of Thomas More*. 481-88.

This excerpt from Bridgett's biography focuses upon More's wit and humor as the most distinctive quality of his work and his life.

G010 Burns, John Lanier. "Justice in Thomas More." Diss. U of Texas-Dallas, 1993.

Burns examines the concept of justice in the commonwealth in More's life and works that manifest an Augustinian awareness of pride's destructiveness, Lucianic skill in ironic and satiric writing, and humanist hope in an enlightened monarch.

G011 Butler, Mary Basil. "Religious Satire in the Works of Medwall, Rastell, Heywood, and More: A Spirit of Devotion to the Ideal of the Church Rather than that of the Reformation." Diss. St. John's U, 1945.

Butler examines religious satire in the works of these authors and shows how they employ it to defend Catholicism.

G012 Carey, John. "Sixteenth and Seventeenth-Century Prose." *History of Literature in the English Language*. Vol. 2. *English Poetry and Prose, 1540-1674*. Ed. Christopher Ricks. London: Barrie & Jenkins, 1970. 339-58.

Carey divides More's works into three distinct groups chronologically: (1) humanist (*Pico, Utopia, Richard*), (2) polemical, and (3) devotional. For the humanist writings, he focuses largely on *Richard* and argues it is far better than More's other English works; he finds little to praise in either the polemical or devotional writings.

G013 Carpenter, Nan C. "A Song for All Seasons: Sir Thomas More and Music." *CL* 33 (1981): 113-36.

Carpenter examines the concept, *musica reservata* (the relationship between words and music, a new art of expression and symbolism, with resulting effects on listeners), in *Utopia* and *Dialogue of Comfort*. She also notes More's interest in drama, especially interludes, which developed from the fusion of music with literary elements and started the tradition of including songs with drama and lasted throughout the Elizabethan period.

G014 Caspari, Fritz. "Sir Thomas More." *Humanism and the Social Order in Tudor England*. Classics in Education. 34. 1954. New York: Teachers College P, 1968. 90-144.

Caspari's thesis is that knights and squires became the dominant social class in Tudor England and that the best of them were influenced by a new humanistic ideal which combined learning with a life of action. Though such humanists and poets as Erasmus, More, Elyot, Starkey, Sidney, and Spenser favored a hierarchical form of society, they emphasized the value of ability as well as noble birth and thus aided the rise of the Tudor gentry to power. Elyot's *The Governor* occupies a central place in Caspari's argument, because it shows how Erasmus' ideal of the reasonable and More's Utopian order of the learned were adapted to English conditions.

G015 Castelli, Alberto. *Note sull' Umanesimo in Inghilterra*. Milan: Editrica Vita e Pensiero, 1949.

Castelli focuses upon Margaret More, the *Dialogue of Comfort*, More and Oxford University, Erasmus' treatment in England, and More's defense of *The Praise of Folly*. The work provides useful notes and a bibliography.

G016 Checksfield, Muriel May. "Thomas More." *Portraits of Renaissance Life and Thought*. New York: Barnes & Noble, 1964. 27-45.

Erasmus and More both figure in company with the Medicis, Columbus, Francis I, Bodin, Montaigne, William the Silent, Sidney, and Cervantes in Checksfield's study, which illustrates aspects and features of the movement through the lives and works of some of its leading protagonists. Checksfield claims More's biography has three strands--his family life, service to his king and country, and his writings--and contends More probably never took *Utopia* as seriously as most readers have done, and that therefore the problem of reconciling some Utopian views with those advanced in his other writings, as well as with his actual conduct, is largely an artificial one. Other references to More can be found in the chapter on Erasmus.

G017 Delcourt, Joseph. "Some Aspects of Sir Thomas More's English." *E&S* 21 (1936): 7-31.

Based on his more detailed doctoral dissertation, "Esai sur la Langue de Sir Thomas More d'après ses oeuvres anglaises" [1913; published with the same title (Paris: Didier, 1914)], Delcourt attempts to determine More's contribution to modern English by examining his syntax and pronunciation, and he shows More's language to be modern rather than medieval to the extent it is individualized and precise. (Rpt. in *Essential Articles for the Study of Thomas More*, 326-42.)

G018 Diamond, Jeff Barja. "Politics and 'Play-Acting' in the European Renaissance." Diss. McGill U (Can.), 1992.

Diamond examines the works of Machiavelli, Erasmus, More, and Montagne for the dilemma humanists faced as they drew upon the teachings of classical antiquity and reinterpreted them to suit their own intellectual, ethical purposes--a process sometimes resulting in contradictions in their lives and writings.

G019 Dolan, Patrick Anthony, Jr. "Execution and the Body in the Works of Thomas More." Diss. U of Iowa, 1994.

Dolan explores interrelations of pain, power, and violence, rhetoric and writing in early modern culture, and shows how More aims "to appropriate violence for power by reading injured bodies as realizing cultural fictions." Dolan also examines More's writings to delineate how More forms his culture as he forms himself.

G020 Dowling, Maria. *Humanism in the Age of Henry VIII*. London: Croom Helm, 1986.

Dowling traces the fortunes of humanists and humanism as they interacted with the changing religious and political policies of Henry's long reign. Colet, Erasmus, and More believed religious abuses could be countered by placing the pure, original Scriptures before the people, uncluttered by the allegory and superstition of the Schoolmen. Luther's extremism, however, threatened their hopes for a gradual reform, and the writings and actions of Fisher, Fox, More, Erasmus, Wolsey, and Queen Catherine solidly supported Henry's *Assertio* against Luther. The "King's Great Matter" shattered the unanimity of the humanists and altered the course of the new learning and eventually resulted in conservative humanist silence in debate and doctrinal speculation.

G021 Doyle-Davidson, W.A.G. "The Earlier English Works of Sir Thomas More." *English Studies: A Journal of English Letters & Philology* 17 (1935): 50-70.

After evaluating much late nineteenth- and early twentieth-century More scholarship, Doyle-Davidson provides his interpretation and appreciation of the English works in Rastell's 1557 edition.

G022 Dust, Philip C. *Three Renaissance Pacifists: Essays in the Theories of*

Erasmus, More, and Vives. American University Studies, Ser. 9. History. Vol. 23. New York: Peter Lang, 1987.

Dust introduces his study by observing the Renaissance, a time of great wars, was therefore also a time of great pacifist ideas. More the Englishman was the link between Erasmus the Dutchman and Vives the Spaniard, whose shared ground was their Christian humanism. In Henry VIII, they thought they had found a fellow humanist interested in the reform of letters and of society; but by going to war against France in 1513, he betrayed these ideals, and "the only alternative was to turn to letters as a recourse of protest."

G023 Fenlon, Dermot. "Thomas More and Tyranny." *Journal of Ecclesiastical History* 32 (1981): 453-76.

Fenlon explores More's "recurrent preoccupation" with tyranny and argues his understanding of the place of martyrdom in the Christian life (as shown in *Dialogue of Comfort*) can be likened to his understanding of the place of tyranny in politics (as shown in *Richard* and *Utopia*). Fenlon believes More thought the events causing the Reformation signaled the collapse of his country into tyranny and that true Christians were called upon to prevent such events from happening. (This essay revises one previously published [in Italian] in *Cultura* 4 [1980].)

G024 Ferguson, Arthur B. *The Articulate Citizen and the English Renaissance.* Durham, NC: Duke UP, 1965. 177-80, 182-84, 191-92, 207-20, 228-31, 280-83, 307-08, 318-21, 330-31, 335-36, 340-42, 364-66, 394-95.

Ferguson surveys the development of self-conscious citizenship with "the shifting responsibility for man's welfare from the unaided, unqualified moral nature of man to his intellectual potentialities," a new spirit encouraged through the growth of humanism, suggesting a foretaste of modern public discussion; and he views More as an ideal figure to bridge the gap separating the medieval critic of society to the articulate citizen of the Renaissance.

G025 Ferguson, Arthur B. "By little and little: The early Tudor humanists on the development of man." *Florilegium Historiale: Essays Presented to Wallace K. Ferguson.* Eds. J.G. Rowe, and W.H. Stockdale. Toronto: U of Toronto P, 1971. 125-50.

Ferguson discusses the use English humanists made of classical speculation on the early career of man on earth and the way in which these accounts were utilized to support the notion of human progress. The classical tradition "implied that man's rise to civilized status was a natural process" which sustained humanist reformers in their "deep and stubborn faith in the educability of man." Ferguson analyzes how this idea is treated in Starkey, Vives, Erasmus, Colet, and More's *Utopia*.

G026 Ferguson, Arthur B. *The Indian Summer of English Chivalry: Studies in the Decline and Transformation of Chivalric Idealism.* Durham, NC: Duke UP, 1960. 25, 93, 169-72.

The complex process of transition from the waning Middle Ages to the Renaissance provides the background to this survey of the decline of chivalry from an active rule of conduct to a romantic, evocative memory, as intimated in the works of Sidney and Spenser. This change of outlook is traceable through the works of successive historians of the period and of humanists like Erasmus, More, and Ascham, all of whom, from different angles, distrust the chivalric ideal, for this last refuge of an aristocracy giving way to a new society of bourgeoisie is incompatible with the new political, social, and cultural order of the Renaissance.

G027 Fox, Alistair. *Thomas More: History and Providence.* Oxford: Basil Blackwell, 1982.

Arranged in three sections partitioning More's literary career into humanistic, polemical, and devotional periods, Foxe's study abandons portraits of More as the benign, even-tempered humanist or the pure-minded defender of the Church to create a third new More, a modern Christian intellect in the process of discovering himself. More's prolific writings and the regularity with which they appeared testify to a steady progression in the evolution of his thought, and Foxe links all of them with one intellectual preoccupation: "his attempt to discover the precise nature of the divine providence by which he believed the world must be ruled."

G028 Fredericks, Daniel David. "Drama in the Life and Works of Thomas More." Diss. U of North Carolina at Greensboro, 1988.

Because the record of More's experience with drama has been scattered throughout biographies and critical literature, Fredericks attempts to give a coherent picture of this aspect of More's life. Another dimension of More's fascination with drama manifests itself in his own role playing. More attempts to find the voice for the role of counselor in "Coronation Poem," *Richard III*, and *Utopia*; the imprisoned More plays the role of martyr. At each stage of his role playing, More was the author of the script he was following.

G029 Fritze, Ronald H., Geoffrey Elton, and Walter Sutton, eds. *Historical Dictionary of Tudor England, 1485-1603.* New York: Greenwood P, 1991.

This volume sets out to provide a compendium of knowledge for students and nonspecialists and includes important references to More.

G030 Gabrieli, Vittorio. "The Merry Tales of Sir Thomas More." *Cultura* 12 (1974): 23-46.

In order to emphasize More's wit, playfulness, and sense of humor,

Gabrieli analyzes More's merry tales, especially those found in his polemical works. She also discusses the tradition of More as jester and wit; More's notion of himself as a jester; sources and analogues of the merry tales; and their values as comic diversion, comic relief, and vehicles for popular moral instruction; as well as their literary attributes, use of language, and comic characters. (An enlarged version of this article appears as the introduction to Vittorio Gabrieli, ed., *Thomas More: Fancies, Sports and Merry Tales* [Bari: Adriatrice Editrice, 1974].)

G031 Gentrup, William Frederick. "Political Applications of Classical Friendship in Renaissance Literature." Diss. Arizona State U, 1987.

Gentrup investigates Renaissance literary expressions of the friendship *topoi* applied to social and political issues, and the study first focuses on "how friendship conventions figure in the utopian idealism" of Erasmus and More.

G032 Gleckman, Jason. "Sixteenth-Century Parody." Diss. U of Wisconsin-Madison, 1994.

Gleckman defines parody as exaggerated imitation, discusses this definition's implications, and elaborates upon its use in the writings of Wyatt, Gascoigne, and More (specifically parody of travel literature in *Utopia*).

G033 Glunz, Hans Hermann. *Shakespeare und More*. Bochum-Langendreer: Heinrich Poppinghaus, 1938.

This book's theme is the relationship between More's *Richard III* and Shakespeare's play, along with other Shakespearean criticism which occupies 267 pages. In addition, there is an eight-page life of More based on Roper, Harpsfield, Erasmus' letter to von Hutten, and More's letter to Gunnell; and a fifteen-page chapter on *Utopia*.

G034 Gordon, Walter M. "*Maiestas* in Thomas More's Political Thought." *Moreana* 129 (1997): 5-20.

Maiestas has special importance in More's reflection on humankind's relation to God within the community. More alters the term's meaning as once applied to the greatness of the Roman people and then attached to their emperor who assumed divine stature. More links its meaning to the populace's mind, so majesty ceases to function when the ruler loses the respect of those he is supposed to serve.

G035 Gordon, Walter M. "The Religious Edifice and Its Symbolism in the Writings of Erasmus, Colet, and More." *Moreana* 87-88 (1985): 15-23.

Gordon shows that, in all three writers, there is a strong sensitivity to the church edifice as what Mircea Eliade calls "sacred space, an absolute reality, opposed to the nonreality of the vast surrounding expanse." For Erasmus, the church is a place of orientation where physical reality is directed toward spiritual mystery. For Colet, the liturgical act and its situs involve divinity's special presence on earth and man's ascent to God. For More, the sanctuary is the realm removed from the secular eon because it is hallowed by divine visitation, and Gordon cites passages from *Richard III* to support this assertion.

G036 Grace, Damian. "*Utopia* and Academic Scepticism." *More's* Utopia *and the Utopian Inheritance*. 1-21.

Grace examines skeptical affinities in More's intellectual context and identifies them in some of his works, especially *Utopia* and *Letter to Dorp*.

G037 Greenblatt, Stephen. "At the Table of the Great: More's Self-Fashioning and Self-Cancellation." *Renaissance Self-Fashioning: From More to Shakespeare*. Chicago: U of Chicago P, 1980. 11-73.

Greenblatt sees the literature of More, Tyndale, Wyatt, Marlowe, Spenser, and Shakespeare as a cultural product, expressing the cultural codes that govern the consciousness and behavior of these authors. Where Burckhardt invented Renaissance man on the model of nineteenth-century individualism, Greenblatt presents more insecure characters, subject to fundamental instability, creating themselves through improvisation and role-playing. He describes the complex interplay in More's life and writings of crafting a public role and the desire to escape it. In most of his writings, More returns to unsettling man's sense of reality; what unites *Utopia*--"enigmatic in its relation to the ultimate authority of the Church"--and *Dialogue of Comfort*--"unambiguously committed to authority"--is More's lifelong interest in the ironies arising from man's confident belief in illusions. More's self-fashioning often amounts to self-annihilation.

G038 Greene, Thomas. "The Flexibility of Self in Renaissance Literature." *The Discipline of Criticism: Essays in Literary Theory, Interpretation, and History*. Eds. Peter Demetz, Thomas Greene, and Lowry Nelson, Jr. New Haven: Yale UP, 1968. 241-64.

Greene focuses on the humanistic concept of "willed metamorphosis," voiced in Erasmus' pronouncement, "Men are fashioned rather than born." Acceptance of this belief is intimated in the rebirth of the "Institute" as a literary genre and the tendency to confuse formation with transformation, which would account partly for renewed interest in magic and hermetic philosophy. More, like Pico, overestimated the flexibility of the human creature, and "by assuming so much human mobility he produced the Immobile State."

G039 Harvey, F. Brompton. "Thomas More: Scholar, Statesman, Saint." *Lawyers Quarterly Review* 162 (1937): 233-36.

Harvey reviews Cecil's *A Portrait of Thomas More* (F037) and adds comments concerning More's place in English literature and history.

G040 Hauerwas, Stanley, and Thomas L. Shaffer. "Hope Faces Power: Thomas More and the King of England." *Soundings* 61 (1978): 456-79.

The authors use the More familiar to contemporary audiences in Bolt's play (F022, I018) to discuss the themes of hope and power and the interrelationship of the two in their consideration of More's character. (Rpt. as "Hope in the Life of Thomas More," *Notre Dame Lawyer* 54 [1979]: 569-86.)

G041 Heckscher, William S. *The Princeton Alciati Companion, A Glossary of Neo-Latin Words and Phrases Used by Andrea Alciati and the Emblem Book Writers of the Time, including a Bibliography of Secondary Sources Relevant to the Study of Alciati's Emblems.* New York: Garland, 1989.

Every More scholar needs this book, which should have featured a more expansive secondary title--*A Neo-Latin Guide to Renaissance Culture*. Heckscher clarifies Latin as the humanists used it, and he reflects upon the cultural life of the age.

G042 Helm, P.J. *England Under the Yorkists and Tudors, 1471-1603.* New York: Humanist P, 1968.

Helm covers the period during which England was transformed from a medieval to a modern state and dates this from the consolidation of the kingdom by Edward IV. One chapter is devoted to the artistic and intellectual scene, and the historical record comes to life through quotations from the *Paston Letters, Utopia,* Cavendish's *Life of Wolsey*, and Harrison's *Description of England*. Among many passages involving More, Helm calls the happy union of York and Lancaster a myth More, Polydore Vergil, and Hall created.

G043 Hexter, J.H. "Thomas More: On the Margins of Modernity." *Journal of British Studies* 1 (1961): 20-37.

More was neither medieval nor modern; generally a Renaissance humanist, More proves himself a radical modern in one instance only--his views on the right ordering of society as expressed in *Utopia*. Parts of this essay are revised and incorporated in Hexter's "*Utopia* and Its Historical Milieu" (introduction to the Yale edition [B019]).

G044 Hibbard, G.R. "Erasmus and More in the Age of Shakespeare." *ErasmusE* 12 (1983): 2-10.

Hibbard studies the intellectual relationship of Erasmus and More, with particular emphasis on *Utopia*.

G045 Hogrefe, Pearl. *The Sir Thomas More Circle: A Program of Ideas and Their Impact on Secular Drama.* Urbana: U of Illinois P, 1959.

The first part of this study presents the program of humanist reform--ideas concerned with nature and the law of nature, the basis of true nobility, the need for religious reform, the essential role of education, the education of women, love, and marriage. The second part supports her conclusion "secular drama in England was largely developed by men who were connected with the More circle." Numerous pages discuss More's canon and its ideas, and Hogrefe examines many interludes in search of these same ideas. She also supplies a great deal of critical commentary on More's works and those of other members of his Circle.

G046 House, Seymour Baker. "Thomas More and Holy Orders: More's Views of the English Clergy, Both Secular and Regular." Diss. U of St. Andrews (UK), 1987.

House presents More's views on the sacrament of Holy Orders with particular reference to the English clergy and uses More's writings and relevant ms. material and other contemporary sources as evidence.

G047 Hurstfield, Joel. "Tradition and Change: English Society Under the Tudors." *The Age of the Renaissance*. Ed. Denys Hay. London: Thames and Hudson, 1967. 249-78.

While Hurstfield exaggerates the "built-in resistance to alien influences," the strength of native tradition in the blending of old and new cultures is indisputable and illustrated in the essentially Christian context of early English humanism, and the life and work of More may show an unworkable attempt at compromise between Christian ideals and Renaissance politics. Other topics discussed include the English gentleman, the flowering of the English language in writings of all sorts, patronage, royal progresses, the City of London, and the emergence of a new society; he briefly analyzes *Utopia* in a section, "Intellectuals and Utopians."

G048 Jones, Judith P. *Thomas More*. TEAS. 247. Boston: Twayne, 1979.

This overview of More's literary and political career, early humanistic writings, controversial tracts, and Tower works enlists chronological analysis to show More in the process of "creating himself."

G049 Jones, Judith P., and Sherianne Sellers Seibel. "Thomas More's Feminism: To Reform or Re-form." *Quincentennial Essays on St. Thomas More*. 67-77.

The authors force More's ideas, beliefs, and values into a simple fidelity to the "medieval heritage" of male chauvinism; contrast *Utopia*'s liberalism toward women with the tone of his polemical works; and find there are few pages written after *Utopia* in which More does not suggest the fatuousness and general intellectual inferiority of women.

G050 Jones, Whitney R.D. *The Tudor Commonwealth, 1529-1559.* London: Athlone P, 1970.

Jones traces the development of ideas of the Commonwealth from the first session of the Reformation Parliament to the accession of Elizabeth I. Documentary material is drawn from widely diverse contemporary sources including works by More, Tyndale, Starkey, Hales, Cheke, Skelton, and Heywood, classified as the "More" or "Erasmian" group, adapting medieval concepts to humanism; the "Cromwell" group, advocating national sovereignty based upon practical education; and the "Edwardian commonwealth" group, sponsored by Protector Somerset, planning a program of religious and socio-economic reform.

G051 Khanna, Lee Cullen. "Images of Women in Thomas More's Poetry." *Quincentennial Essays on St. Thomas More.* 78-88.

Khanna finds More going well beyond feminine stereotypes, showing respect for women's mental, moral, and religious qualities. The result is to put scattered Utopian ideas into a context in which the satiric remarks found elsewhere cannot be taken to contain More's personal values, because the English texts in which they stand lack the weight of the more favorable texts, including More's Latin and English poetry.

G052 Khanna, Lee Cullen. "No Less Real than Ideal: Images of Women in More's Work." *Moreana* 55-56 (1977): 35-51.

Khanna emphasizes the sympathetic presentation of intelligent, virtuous women and the implicit or explicit criticism of anti-feminist values and prejudices in *Utopia, Richard III*, and *Dialogue of Comfort*. Richard's character, for instance, is developed in terms of the women in the book. More's "non-medieval" jokes about women are not discussed.

G053 Krapp, George Philip. *The Rise of English Literary Prose.* 1915. New York: Ungar, 1963. 79-102.

Chapter 3, "Controversy and Free Speech," assesses More's prose style with emphasis on his polemical works, and Krapp judges *Dialogue Concerning Heresies* the best of More's English controversial works and *Confutation of Tyndale's Answer* his weakest. In general, Krapp regards More as the first modern English writer "to develop and to maintain a dignified literary style."

G054 Lewis, C.S. *English Literature in the Sixteenth Century Excluding Drama.* Vol. 3. *The Oxford History of English Literature.* Oxford: Clarendon P, 1954. 133, 164-81, 191-92.

Lewis assesses More's writing in the context of the early English Renaissance, viewing More as both medieval and humanistic, but at his best when he is most English, most comic, and most down-to-earth. Lewis advances the view *Utopia* is primarily a satire and should be read as a *jeu d'esprit*, a "holiday work," rather than as a serious philosophical treatise. (Some of this material is rpt. as "Thomas More" in *Essential Articles for the Study of Thomas More*, 388-401.)

G055 Major, John M. "Sir Thomas More." *Sir Thomas Elyot and Renaissance Humanism*. Lincoln: U of Nebraska P, 1964. 89-139.

Major considers Elyot's friendship with More in detail, traces the similarities in their careers, discusses the connection between *The Governor* and *Utopia*, and concludes Elyot and More were closely tied in their religious beliefs, opposition to heresy, and dedication to education, despite their differences in politics and social theory.

G056 Malhomme, Florence. "Castiglione, More et Érasme: Trois Contributions à la Pensée Musicale de la Renaissance." *Moreana* 125 (1996): 31-48.

Malhomme discusses Castiglione's *Courtier, Utopia*, and a few pieces from Erasmus to show the influence of these humanists on four features that transformed music during the Renaissance: (1) secularization of music prompted by the value given to musical education and its effects in creating new spaces, a new public, and new activities; (2) changes in conception and function of musical works; (3) new musical expression formed by joining words and sounds; and (4) separation of instrumental and vocal music.

G057 Marc'hadour, Germain. *Thomas More ou la Sage Folie*. Philosophes de Tous Temps. 76. Paris: Seghers, 1971.

This monograph makes no claim to being a complete study of More's life or an exhaustive survey of his works (which are only considered when they impinge on his political career and his Christianity or illuminate his point of view). Instead Marc'hadour devotes his attentions to More's formative years, friendships with humanists, and his times of meditation. More's debts to classical philosophy, along with his theological beliefs, professionalism, fondness for theatrical imagery, and his attitudes toward death and after-life, are also discussed. The last chapter offers an impression of More's spiritual and personal qualities. Nearly fifty pages of extracts from the works of leading French scholars and More's letters, the *Dialogue Concerning Heresies*, prayers, and letters from prison are included, and a biographical table and chronological list of More's writings complete this introduction to a complex, enigmatic writer.

G058 Marc'hadour, Germain. "Thomas More's Spirituality." *St. Thomas More: Action and Contemplation*. 123-59.

Marc'hadour deals with More's principles, the maxims which underlie his conduct or express his ideals, and limits himself to More's writings before he met the challenge of Luther. Of special importance is the *Life of Picus*, "a spiritual nosegay," but the early verse also has spiritual relevance, even when More is translating from the atheist Lucian. More's somewhat elastic attitude to the problem of truth and lying is investigated, together with the *Letter to a Monk*, "an essay in spirituality." Marc'hadour claims key elements found in the works he considers reappear in later works, such as *Utopia* and the *Dialogue of Comfort*.

G059 Marius, Richard. "Thomas More, Martin Luther, Hamlet and the Fear of Death in the Renaissance." *Thomas Morus Jahrbuch 1995*. 25-32.

Marius probes the "ambiguities, fears, and doubts" More, Luther, and Hamlet express concerning the question of existence "after death."

G060 Mason, H.A. *Humanism and Poetry in the Early Tudor Period: An Essay*. London: Routledge & Kegan Paul, 1959.

Mason argues "the significant activity of the age is *translation*," by which he means a "critical-creative activity in which the native digestive system is as important as the foreign matter assimilated." "Part One: Humanism in the Early Tudor Period" consists of three chapters. In the first, he examines More's Latin epigrams to illustrate their relationship to his notion of translation. In the second, he finds a complete identity of spirit between More and Erasmus in their translations of Lucian, *Praise of Folly*, and *Utopia*; and, in accord with his translation theory, he believes More's strength lies in maintaining a precarious balance and state of tension through which he holds asceticism and sensual pleasure together without resolution. In the third, "More's *Utopia*: The Vindication of Christian Humanism," he declares *Utopia* the most important document of Christian humanism and "one of the finest expressions" of humanist ideals.

G061 Mason, H.A. "'They Haven't Got No Noses.'" *CQ* 18 (1989): 129-59.

Mason reaffirms his position in his *Humanism and Poetry in the Early Tudor Period: An Essay* (G060) that More's major achievement in *Utopia* and that of Erasmus in *Praise of Folly* is applying Lucian's wit to important humanist issues. He also disagrees with Daniel Kinney's estimate of More's *Letter to Dorp* in Kinney's *In Defense of Humanism* (B012). He believes More's greatest quality as a writer can be found in his Erasmian wit.

G062 Maxcey, Carl E. "Justice and Order: Martin Luther and Thomas More on the Death Penalty and Retribution." *Moreana* 79-80 (1983): 17-33.

Maxcey posits Luther and More are interesting models for examining the question that the developing theologies of the sixteenth century provides for judging the morality of capital punishment. By following their respective theological positions, each was confronted by secular authorities and even threatened with death because of those positions. Two men from different backgrounds, with different theologies, were forced to deal with the same moral issue, and Maxcey utilizes selections from their writings in order to probe the impact of theology on capital punishment.

G063 McCarthy, John, and Anthony Reynolds, eds. *Thomas More: The Saint and the Society.* Sydney: Austral.: St. Thomas More Society, 1995.

A guild of Catholic lawyers, the St. Thomas More Society (founded in 1945), published this collection of thirteen essays by Germain Marc'hadour, John A. Guy, Brian Byron, and others that were generally written as public addresses to celebrate More as a practicing lawyer keenly aware of the moral ambiguities Christians in the legal profession face.

G064 McConica, James Kelsey. *English Humanists and Reformation Politics under Henry VIII and Edward VI.* Oxford: Clarendon P, 1965.

McConica corrects and supplements Seebohm's *Oxford Reformers* in assessing the achievement of early English humanists over a wider perspective and more precisely in relation to religious movements. As formative influences on English humanism, the author notes patterns of scholarly patronage, conditions in the universities, the work of Thomas Cromwell, the roles of Catherine Parr and her circle, contact with continental scholars and reformers, more specifically with the Erasmian counsel of the "middle way." The common tenets of Colet, More, Fisher, and their associates are represented as generous and undogmatic, infusing humanist values into the aridities of religious controversy.

G065 McCutcheon, Elizabeth. "'This Prison of the Yerth': The Topos of Immurement in the Writings of St. Thomas More." *Cithara* 25 (1985): 35-46.

McCutcheon assembles the meanings of the prison metaphor as More uses it and speculates this perception of the world "accounts for some part of More's pervasive sense of transiency and...detachment from the things of the world." Although she concentrates upon the metaphor's use in *Dialogue of Comfort*, she notes where it appears elsewhere in his work.

G066 Metzner, Patricia. "Hope in the Life of Thomas More." *Moreana* 70 (1981): 77-79.

Metzner reviews an article by Stanley Hauerwas and Thomas L. Shaffer (G040) in which they discuss the points most germane to More's practical world as a lawyer--the message of hope and the paradox of being both a Christian and a wielder of power.

G067 Musto, Ronald C. "Just Wars and Evil Empires: Erasmus and the Turks." *Renaissance Society and Culture: Essays in Honor of Eugene F. Rice, Jr.* Eds. John Monfasani, and Ronald C. Musto. New York: Ithaca P, 1991. 197-216.

In this examination of Erasmus' attention to the question of the "crusade" against the Turk and the Christian response to Turkish aggression, Musto refers to the works of two other Renaissance humanists who spoke to this issue--More (*Utopia, Dialogue Concerning Heresies*, and *Dialogue of Comfort*) and Vives.

G068 Norland, Howard B. "More." *Drama in Early Tudor Britain: 1485-1558*. Lincoln: U of Nebraska P, 1995. 111-27.

Norland notes More's knowledge and use of drama in his life and writing, and shows, from his boyhood to his death, drama played a major role in More's career.

G069 Norland, Howard B. "The Role of Drama in More's Literary Career." *SCJ* 13 (1982): 59-75.

More's early involvement with the stage, both as actor and as author of lost comedies, led to his fascination with dramatic forms and techniques. His translation of Lucian acquainted him with the dialogue, an essentially dramatic form. *Richard III, Utopia*, and the late polemical works reveal dramatic presentation of character, situation, and dialogue.

G070 O'Sullivan, Richard, ed. *The King's Good Servant*. Papers Read to the Thomas More Society of London. Oxford: Basil Blackwell, 1948.

This collection of essays by George Andrew Beck, W.E. Campbell, J.B. Hawkins, Jacques Maritain, Ivo Thomas, Lewis Watt, and others begin with O'Sullivan's introduction.

G071 Phillips, Elias H. "*Humanitas* in Tudor Literature." Diss. U of Pennsylvania, 1949.

Phillips discusses the expression of Ciceronian *humanitas* with its philosophy of world order, belief in *paideia*, and conception of human dignity in Caxton's *Prefaces* and *Epilogues*, More's *Utopia*, Elyot's *Governor*, Starkey's *Dialogue*, Baldwin's *Mirror for Magistrates*, Hoby's translation of Castiglione's *Courtier*, and Ascham's *Schoolmaster*.

G072 Prévost, André. *Thomas More 1477-1535 et la crise de la pensée européenne*. Lille: Mame, 1969.

This study of More's thought places him against the perspective of contemporary disruptive forces in religion, politics, and society. The central argument develops from the premise the essential significance of More's achievement resides in identifying his thought with that of the English society to which he belonged and English culture which he assimilated. His life and works bear witness to a singleness of purpose in defending traditional values and systematic form as safeguarded by the Church against cataclysmic changes and new ideologies. The evolution of More's thought is traced through a chronological and critical account of his early studies, theological and philosophical, and their influence upon his *juvenalia*, his contact with humanism and humanists as reflected in *Utopia*, his involvement in the universal religious crisis, particularly as it affected the Church of England. The later chapters discuss the issues in question between More and Tyndale and evaluate their arguments. Finally, More emerges as the "Christian sage," freed from the burden of public life and religious conflict, bearing witness to the Christian humanism which consistently had been the basis of his "positive theology." Prévost's outline of More's intellectual and religious milieu and discussion of More's humanism and theology within the context of the Reformation throw new light upon More as an outstanding figure of his age.

G073 Reynolds, E.E. *Sir Thomas More*. Bibliographical Series of Supplements to *British Book News* on Writers and Their Works. 178. London: Longmans, Green, for the British Council and the National Book League, 1965.

This pamphlet emphasizes More's literary accomplishments rather than his political and religious life and discusses his humanist, polemical, and devotional works, along with his letters and place in the history of the development of English prose. Reynolds also includes a selective bibliography of primary and secondary works.

G074 Ritter, Gerhard. *The Corrupting Influence of Power*. Trans. F.W. Pick. Hadleigh, Essex (Eng.): Tower Bridge, 1952.

Geography and politics are linked in this study of the origins of the problems of modern Europe, which Ritter explains by contrasting Machiavelli and More. Machiavelli, "the first nationalist and militarist of modern Europe," laid down the key policies of the major continental powers when he subordinated conscience and religion to the state, exalted the virtues of the warlike nation, and claimed it was natural for states to extend rule by conquest. More, on the other hand, was the "ideologist of the island welfare state," because a series of ideas in *Utopia* forecast the shape of English policy. (Chapter 3, "More: Ideologist of the Island Welfare State," is partially rpt. as "*Utopia* and Power Politics" in *Twentieth-Century Interpretations of* Utopia: *A Collection of Critical Essays*, 40-52.)

G075 Schoeck, R.J. *The Achievement of Thomas More: Aspects of His Life and Works*. English Literary Studies Monograph Ser. 7. Victoria, BC: English Literary Studies, U of Victoria, 1976.

This collection of essays, mainly intended for general readers, aims to "describe and evaluate some aspects" of More's achievements and includes chapters on "Sir Thomas More, Humanist and Lawyer"; "More's Letters and the Epistolary Defense of Renaissance Humanism"; "More's *Life of Pico* and

History of King Richard III"; "*Utopia* as a Humanistic Masterpiece"; "The Controversial Works"; and "The Tower Works: Death and Immortality." He concludes with an estimate of More's enduring reputation and includes a selective bibliography. Chapter 1 revises Schoeck's "Sir Thomas More, Humanist and Lawyer" (F292); chapter 2 employs material from his "On the Letters of Thomas More" (P006).

G076 Sheldrake, Philip. "Thomas More and Authority." *Month* 10 (1977): 122-25, 134.

Sheldrake examines what More said about authority in the Catholic Church in some polemical works and letters.

G077 Slavin, Arthur, ed. *Humanism, Reform, and Reformation in England*. New York: Wiley, 1969.

Slavin combines excerpts from primary sources during the period represented by the activities of humanists associated with More and Erasmus, propaganda by "more ominous voices," demanding more radical reforms in religion during the 1520s and the establishment of "official Reformation." The provision and selection of sources in each section include letters of More and Erasmus, and colloquies of the latter; Colet's lectures and his sermon to the 1511 Convocation; documents relating to the case of Richard Hunne; Latimer's account of his first conversion; polemical tracts of More, Fisher, Tyndale, and Fish; Starkey's *Dialogues*, statutes, and other relevant Reformation documents. The commentators include J.K. McConica, A.G. Dickens, A.B. Ferguson, and W.A. Clebsch. Source references and notes accompany each excerpt, and a brief general bibliography is appended, but there is no index. Intended primarily for college students, the book offers plenty to general readers in respect to both primary sources and scholarly commentary.

G078 Strauss, Paul E. "In Hope of Heaven: English Recusant Prison Writings of the Sixteenth Century." Diss. U of Nevada-Las Vegas, 1991.

Strauss focuses on the prison writings of four Catholics--Fisher, More (with emphasis on *Dialogue of Comfort*), Southwell, and Benedict Canfield.

G079 Strauss, Paul E. *In Hope of Heaven: English Recusant Prison Writings of the Sixteenth Century*. New York: Peter Lang, 1995.

Strauss places Fisher, More, Southwell, and Benedict Canfield in the tradition of persecution literature and late medieval devotional handbooks.

G080 Sylvester, R.S. "A Part of His Own: Thomas More's Literary Personality in His Early Works." *Moreana* 15-16 (1967): 29-42.

Sylvester traces the literary personality More casts on his early works by discussing Roper's story of More's participation in dramatic entertainments and proposing these activities influence his tendency toward role-playing in his English and Latin verses, "Pageant Verses," translation of Lucian, and *Life of Pico*. Sylvester concludes More's greatest literary accomplishments, like *Utopia*, *Dialogue Concerning Heresies*, and *Dialogue of Comfort*, occur as this "dramatization of himself achieves an objective form."

G081 Thelca, Mary. "St. Thomas More's 'Merye Laughing Harvest.'" *If By Your Art: Testament to Percival Hunt*. Ed. Agnes Lynch Starrett. Pittsburgh: U of Pittsburgh P, 1948. 161-73.

Thelca contends too few readers are aware of More's other works (besides *Utopia*) and underlines the fact More was always "mingling the grave with the gay." Thus, he alone among the circumspect Tudor humanists was endowed with literary charm along with learning and piety. Thelca in-cludes numerous examples of More's humor.

G082 Thompson, Craig R. "The Humanism of More Reappraised." *Thought* 52 (1977): 231-48.

Thompson reviews the historical significance and subsequent ambiguities of the concept "humanism" before turning to More's life, beliefs, and writings, which he classifies as products of northern and Christian humanism.

G083 Trinkaus, Charles. "Thomas More and the Humanist Tradition: Martyrdom and Ambiguity." *The Scope of Renaissance Humanism*. Ann Arbor: U of Michigan P, 1983. 422-36.

Trinkaus examines two elements of the humanist tradition found in More's thought and character--martyrdom and ambiguity. He finds parallels between More's life and those of Plato, Cicero, and Seneca and then investigates the ambiguity of the humanist tradition on faith and knowledge and the methods of gaining them and the relationship of will and intellect, reason and affect, action and contemplation. (Rpt. in *CCRev* 10-11 [1983-84]: 89-104.)

G084 Ziemer, Penny Benson. "Humor and Faith in the Works of St. Thomas More." Diss. Emory U, 1984.

At the center of More's humor and faith is the paradox serious truths often come to a reader masked in comedy. Throughout More's writings, this important incongruity unifies several of Lucian's dialogues More translated, some humanist letters he wrote, *Utopia*, many polemical works, and the *Dialogue of Comfort*.

Reception and Reputation

H001 Brouwer, Piet. "Thomas More dans le paysage social des Pays-Bas." *Moreana* 97 (1988): 101-04.
Brouwer lists the non-literary forms of More's presence in Belgium and the Netherlands.

H002 Butler, Johanna M. "More in Sixteenth-Century France." *Moreana* 42 (1974): 21-22.
An allusion to More's execution and the Anglican schism appears in Diz. 147 of Maurice Scève's *Délie*, a Petrarchan sequence of love poems published in Lyon in 1544. No definitive answer has been given to the question--to what extent was the cultured public of the sixteenth century aware of contemporary events and figures. Studies of sixteenth-century French private libraries show a striking lack of contemporary materials. Such a reference to More by Scève, a provincial poet in a city with neither a royal court nor a university to serve as a distribution center for international news, may be a significant indication of the degree of familiarity with contemporary events in England which could be expected of educated French society.

H003 Carver, George. "Nicholas Harpsfield and 'Sir Thomas More.'" *Alms for Oblivion: Books, Men, and Biography.* Milwaukee: Bruce, 1946. 39-49.
Carver examines Harpsfield's *Life and Death of Sir Thomas More* to demonstrate how its use of drama and careful selection and arrangement of materials available make it transcend the hagiographical tradition to which it belongs and contribute an important chapter in the history of the growth of More's reputation.

H004 Dethloff, Uwe. "Die Rezeption von Thomas Mores *Utopia* in der französischen Renaissance." *GRM* 43.2 (1993): 209-13.

Dethloff traces the reception of *Utopia* in France during the Renaissance.

H005 Friederich, Werner P. "Some Aspects of Switzerland's Literary Significance During the Renaissance." *ES* 43 (1962): 319-22.

Apart from Zwingli, sixteenth-century Switzerland was relatively unproductive of literary masterpieces. Yet it became a significant center of the Reformation and of humanism. Thus, John Knox and William Whittingham sought refuge in Geneva, John Foxe and John Bale in Basel, and many other Englishmen in Zürich. The second edition of *Utopia* and the first complete edition of More's Latin works were published in Basel, Coverdale's Bible in Zürich.

H006 Gury, Jacques. "Thomas More en France, de Voltaire à Hugo." *Moreana* 95-96 (1987): 119-24.

Gury illustrates the images of More which recur in French literature from Voltaire to Hugo: the noble victim of tyranny; the wise-foolish dreamer of an ideal commonwealth; the English Socrates, serene enough to jest on the scaffold and whose death branded forever tyrannical Henry.

H007 Marc'hadour, Germain. "A Man for All States: New-World Notes of an Old-World Pilgrim." *Moreana* 51 (1976): 53-66.

Marc'hadour catalogs and discusses the interest in More throughout the United States.

H008 Martins, Jose V. de Pina. "L'*Utopie* de Thomas More au Portugal (au 16e et au début du 17e siècle)." *Moreana* 69 (1981): 137-56.

Martins elaborates upon the reception of *Utopia* in Portugal between 1536 and 1624.

H009 McConica, James K. "The Recusant Reputation of Thomas More." *Reports of the Canada Catholic Historical Association* 30 (1964): 47-61.

McConica traces the creation and development of More's recusant reputation by examining the influence of not only recusant scholars and biographers but also the Latin and English editions of his works. He notes how the recusants were mainly interested in More as the martyr-statesman rather than the polemicist and sometimes distorted details about his life and personality and attempted to dissociate More from Erasmus. (See also H010.)

H010 McConica, James K. "The Recusant Reputation of Thomas More." *Essential Articles for the Study of Thomas More*. 136-49.

McConica discusses the creation of More's recusant reputation. Among important contributions to More's recusant reputation are the biographies of Roper, Harpsfield, Stapleton, and Ro:Ba:, and editions of More's Latin and

English works. Since the recusants generally viewed More as martyr-statesman instead of reformer, neglected his early involvement in Church reform, and separated him from Erasmus (because of their common cause--Church reform), they ignored some details about him; such omissions do not, however, distort his life that seriously. (This essay revises one with the same title [H009].)

H011 Minerva, Nadia. "D'une définition à l'autre: sur quelques préfaciers français d'*Utopia* de Thomas More." *Per una definizione dell'utopie: Metodologie e discipline a confronto*. Atti del Convengo Internazionale di Bagni di Lucca, 12-14 Settembre 1990. Ravenna: Longo, 1992. 51-59.

Minerva examines the prefaces to French translations of *Utopia* from 1550 to 1789 in order to trace the reception of the work and its ideas in France.

H012 Morris, Joseph A. "On the Legacy of Thomas More." *Moreana* 83-84 (1984): 45-46.

Arthur F. Kinney provides excerpts from a speech delivered to the U.S. Office of Personnel Management in Washington, D.C., by Morris, to mark the 504th anniversary of More's birth.

H013 Moser, Fernando de Mello. "More's Early Reputation in Portugal." *Moreana* 57 (1978): 25-30.

By presenting references to More that were written by Portuguese authors or found their way into that country the first hundred years after his execution, Moser proves More was known and admired in Portugal.

H014 Ossinovsky, Igor N. "Thomas More's *Utopia* in Russia." (Trans. into English by I.V. Victorov) *Moreana* 22 (1969): 33-38.

Ossinovsky traces the critical reception of *Utopia* in Russia in the nineteenth and twentieth centuries and comments on translations from the original Latin into Russian.

H015 Rude, Donald W. "References to More in John Jones (1579)." *Moreana* 83-84 (1984): 33-37.

Rude shows that, while Tudor literature abounds in references to More the man, treating him variously as martyr, traitor, persecutor of Protestants, author and wit; Jones, in *The Arte and Science of Preserving Bodie and Soule in Helthe, Wisdome, and Catholike Religion*, is apparently the first English writer to regard More as an authority on matters of science and philosophy and to cite him in order to substantiate his own views. Thus, the citations of More in Jones' book occupy a position of importance in the study of More's literary reputation.

H016 Rude, Donald W. "Some Unreported Seventeenth Century References to Sir Thomas More and *Utopia."* *Moreana* 101-102 (1990): 150-52.

Rude identifies unreported references to More and his work which use the word *utopia* in a slightly different sense, associating Utopia with the world of heroic action and romantic love.

H017 Rude, Donald W. "Some Unreported Sixteenth and Seventeenth Century References to Sir Thomas More." *Moreana* 101-102 (1990): 147-49.

Rude notes unreported references to More and his works in books produced in the sixteenth and seventeenth centuries. Such citations suggest the continuing vitality of More's reputation in a variety of contexts and add to understanding how he was regarded as writer, scholar, early champion of education for women, and martyr during that period.

H018 Schoeck, R.J. "The Place of Sir Thomas More: A Case for Tudor Studies." *Revue de l'Université d'Ottawa* 34 (1964): 176-90.

Schoeck explores More's place within the context of the culture of his own times, our times, and the English curriculum of today's universities. He laments the neglect of More in schools and universities, emphasizing the need for closer reading of *Utopia*, along with greater attention to More's other works and contextual criticism of More.

H019 Smith, C.N. "George Hardinge's Imitation of More's Verses on Quentin Metsys' Double Portrait of Erasmus and Peter Gilles." *Moreana* 77 (1983): 39-41.

Hardinge's imitation of More's verses towards the end of the eighteenth century supplies another piece of valuable evidence about the survival and evolution of More's reputation over the ages.

H020 Tokarczyk, Roman A. "The Reception of Thomas More's *Utopia* in Poland." *Moreana* 118-119 (1994): 169-201.

Although the translation of *Utopia* into Polish in 1947 inspired a livelier and more extensive reception of the text in Poland, almost every century from the sixteenth on has brought with it a new approach to More's personality and his achievement. Of many distinguished Poles, only Jan Dantyszek seems to have had the honor of meeting More in person. The seventeenth century marks the beginning of controversies in the reception of *Utopia* in Poland according to different religious, political, and ideological orientations. The Age of Enlightenment witnessed the first major attempts by Polish writers to imitate *Utopia*. The Catholic approach, which has evolved in the course of four centuries, seems to have been the most permanent. In the nineteenth and twentieth centuries, the socialist aspects of *Utopia* came to fore. After World War II, with the imposition of the socialist system in Poland, the reception of More's work became an instrument of political propaganda. There have been other modes of interpretation of More's work in Poland, and the conception that calls for a differentiation of the homophonic and polyphonic readings of *Utopia* is given special mention.

H021 Wheeler, Thomas. "Thomas More in Italy: 1535-1700." *Moreana* 27-28 (1970): 15-23.

Wheeler considers the respect and admiration characterizing Italian response to More during the two centuries following his death and discusses early Italian translations of *Utopia* and More's friendship with Antonio Bonvisi.

H022 White, Helen C. "The Catholic Martyrs under Henry." *Tudor Books of Saints and Martyrs*. Madison: U of Wisconsin P, 1963. 96-131.

The writings included under this title are given added meaning through being grouped as a distinctive literary genre, set against the historical background of Christian hagiography. In the development of the More legend, it is possible to recapitulate "the development of the whole of the preceding martyrological traditions," and his public status as chancellor and his reputation among continental humanists make "the history of the accounts of his life and death particularly illuminating for the possibilities of Catholic martyrology under Henry."

H023 Williams, Franklin B., Jr. "Joe Miller on Thomas More." *Moreana* 38 (1973): 59-61.

The survival of More's reputation for wit into the Age of the Enlightenment is shown by the presence of four anecdotes in the 1739 first edition of *Joe Miller's Jests*, the best being the More-Mores-Manners double-pun first recorded in 1652.

H024 Wooden, Warren W. "Thomas More in Hostile Hands: The English Image of More in Protestant Literature of the Renaissance." *Moreana* 75-76 (1982): 77-87.

Wooden ranges widely in reviewing the English image of More in the Protestant literature of the Renaissance, specifically in the chronicles. Polydore Vergil's sympathetic but foreign view had little influence; Hall dismisses More, though "coumpted learned," as essentially frivolous, a view substantially continued by Holinshed. Foxe, however, is more complex, recognizing More as author, thinker, and statesman, but condemning him for prostituting his talents and integrity to the Catholic cause. Primarily to Foxe the English anti-More tradition may be traced.

H025 Wyland, Russell M. "Thomas More's Reputation in Nineteenth-Century England." *Moreana* 127-128 (1996): 37-56.

Of the more than 230 treatments of More the Sullivans mention (A043-

A048), Wyland examines a few of them to outline More's image in nineteenth-century England as a man of letters, politics, and religion. From the political-religious debate over the "Catholic Question" early in the century came oversimplifications of More's life and times. During the century's middle years, historians corrected some of those earlier views as they examined archival materials. As More's beatification drew near, treatments of his life and thoughts focused on his attempts at social reform and tolerance. Wyland traces More's fortunes through this century to reveal what could be called the birth of "Thomas More Studies."

H026 Znidarsic, Lilijana. "Thomas More: A Christian Humanist in Independent Slovenia." *Moreana* 122 (1995): 57-61.

The publication in April 1992 of the first Slovene anthology of More's writings, *Thomas More, Christian Socialist*, has invited various reactions. Reviewers in the secular press have discussed More's social and political thinking, his attitude toward heretics, his practice of Christianity as a unifying force in both his life and works. A university student group discussed *Utopia*, a book previously presented only with a communist interpretation. The Catholic press has explored More as a martyr and a model. Finally, inspired by the appearance of the anthology, its author's friends have begun to unearth Slovene references to More dating back to 1865.

Influence

I001   Albanese, Denise. "The *New Atlantis* and the Uses of Utopia." *ELH* 57 (1990): 503-28.

Albanese believes of all Bacon's texts, *New Atlantis* can most readily be categorized as fictional. Despite its romantic aspects, however, it seeks alignment with More's *Utopia* rather than with *Amadis de Gaule*, which is to say with a political fiction that is also politic in its fictionality.

I002   Albery, Peter. *Anne Boleyn: A Tragedy in Four Acts*. London: Elgin Books, 1956.

More appears in four scenes in this play--a dialogue with Queen Catherine, a brief exchange with Anne Boleyn, a passage in which he pleads for Catherine and advises Henry on choosing a wife, and a segment in which George (Anne's brother) accuses her of causing More's death.

I003   Albin, Hugh O. "Canterbury: More's Head and a More Window." *Moreana* 37 (1973): 51-52.

Albin, the Vicar of St. Dunstan's Church (Canterbury), writes Marc'hadour about the organization of a group, the Friends of St. Dunstan's, to encourage the study of More's life and works. A new More window (above the Roper vault where More's head rests in St. Dunstan's) was dedicated to mark the group's beginnings.

I004   Allen, Ward. "Hooker and the Utopians." *ES* 51 (1970): 37-39.

Allen discovers evidence of Hooker's sympathy with the opinions of the fictional "More" in *Utopia* in certain passages of the *Lawes of Ecclesiasticall Polite*, Book V, in which Puritan arguments against formal prayers and other liturgical usages are refuted as resting on impossible premises and "subtle opinions."

I005 Anderegg, Michael A. "A Myth for All Seasons: Thomas More." *Colorado Quarterly* 23 (1975): 293-306.

Anderegg explores the ways Bolt's play (I018) and Zinneman's film (I066) have created images of More that have captured the popular imagination. He also considers the differences between the historical characters and events and the fictional adaptations thereof.

I006 Argent, Joseph Edward. "'No More Existence than the Inhabitants of Utopia': Utopian Satire in *Gulliver's Travels*." Diss. U of North Carolina-Greensboro, 1995.

Argent provides the first book-length study of *Gulliver's Travels* as a utopian work by examining the connection between satire and the utopian tradition More established.

I007 Baker-Smith, Dominic. "More, Buchanan and Florence Wilson." *Moreana* 7 (1965): 106-08.

Baker-Smith translates two epigrams about More--one by Antonio Gouveia, a friend of George Buchanan; the other by Simon Vallembert. He also notes a reference to More in a work of Buchanan's fellow Scot, Florence Wilson.

I008 Bataillon, Marcel. "L'ostension prénuptiale utopienne et 'L'antique habit des Espagnes.'" *Moreana* 35 (1972): 57-58.

Bataillon cites a reference to Utopian courtship in Andrés de Poca's *De la antiqua lingua, poblacionse y comarcos de las Espanas* (1587).

I009 Berrigan, J.R. "An Explosion of Utopias." *Moreana* 38 (1973): 21-26.

Berrigan summarizes rather than reviews Walker Percy's satirical Utopian novel *Love in the Ruins* (1971).

I010 Berrong, Richard M. "On the Possible Origin of the Name 'Nephelibates' (*Quart Livre*, Ch. 56)." *ER* 17 (1983): 93-94.

Berrong notes this possible influence of *Utopia* on Rabelais and investigates the etymology of the name.

I011 Bertagnoni, Marialisa. "*Ironia e* pietas: *Alcuna coincidenze fra* Utopia *e* I promessi sposi." *Miscellanea Moreana: Essays for Germain Marc'hadour*. *Moreana* 100. 235-43.

Although More and Alessandro Manzoni wrote voluminously, single works (*Utopia* and *I promessi sposi* [*The Betrothed*]), which bear some similarities, made both authors known. Each work blends pseudo-historical real and fictional characters and places; each develops a narrator demanding the reader's complicity.

I012 Beuchot, Mauricio. "Promoción Humana y Utopia en Don Vasco de Quiroga." *Moreana* 105 (1991): 43-54.

After a biography of Quirogo, Beuchot examines the social and philosophical ideas which the Bishop of Michoacán (Mexico) develops in his *Información en derecho*, a treatise he wrote for the defense of Indians whose way of life he viewed as "a golden age," not unlike that described by Lucian in his *Saturnalia*. With More's *Utopia* in mind, Quiroga advocated a communal political system for the Indians.

I013 Biot, Brigitte. "Barthelémy Aneau, lecteur de l'*Utopie*." *Moreana* 121 (1995): 11-28.

Critics are rediscovering Aneau, one of the lesser known Renaissance writers of Lyon. Principal of the Collège de la Trinité in that city, a scholar of Greek and Latin, acquainted with the neo-Latin humanists and the most brilliant and bold minds of that time, he wrote works which lie half-way between tradition and innovation. Several were influenced by More. *Utopia* and its author are mentioned in Aneau's play *Lyon Marchant* (1541) and in his hymn *Juris Prudentia* (1554). Aneau later cooperated in the second edition of Jean Leblond's translation of *Utopia*; and, in 1560, he imitated More by describing an ideal city, Orbe, in his *Alector, Histoire fabuleuse*.

I014 Black, Ben W. "*The Booke of Sir Thomas More*: A Critical Edition." Diss. U of Michigan, 1953.

This edition is designed primarily for modern readers and includes textual and explanatory notes. The introduction surveys criticism and discusses the ms., authorship, Tilney's censorship of the play, and the date upon which and the company by which it may first have been produced.

I015 Blanchard, André. "Jean Second et ses poèmes sur exécution de Thomas More." *Moreana* 36 (1972): 1-32.

This article concerns the family of this poet and his expression of all Europe's distress at the execution of More, and it includes the Latin texts of the poems with the French versions alongside them.

I016 Blanchard, André. "Poèmes du xvie siècle à la mémoire de Thomas More et de Jean Fisher." *Moreana* 41 (1974): 93-99.

Blanchard prints poems about More and Fisher from the sixteenth century, complete with prose translations.

I017 Boardman, Brigid M. "'Dear Jester in the Courts of God': Francis

Thompson's Tribute to St. Thomas More." *Moreana* 27 (1990): 87-92.

In his "Ode to the English Martyrs," Thompson (1859-1907) devotes 28 lines to More, celebrating More's life and death with wit and imagery such as More would have relished.

I018   Bolt, Robert. *A Man for All Seasons*. New York, Random, 1960.

This well-known play, adapted into an equally well-known movie (I066), has done much to shape popular notions of More's character and life.

I019   Britnell, Jennifer. "Jean Bouchet's Epitaphs for Thomas More and John Fisher, 1545." *Moreana* 85 (1985): 45-55.

Britnell compares the epitaphs for More and Fisher in Bouchet's *Annales* (1545). In one epitaph he makes More speak with caution and modesty, but by following it with the epitaph on the Bishop of Rochester, he can assert directly the injustice of Henry VIII and the innocence, honesty, and probable sanctity of Fisher and More.

I020   Brouwer, Piet.   "Le *Thomas More* de Henriette Roland Holst." *Moreana* 97 (1988): 9-20.

The best-known Dutch play about More was written in 1912 by a distinguished poet and militant socialist. Holst dedicated the work "to Karl Kautsky, who taught me to know and love the first modern Communist," namely the author of *Utopia*. Her sources--Anne Manning's *The Household of Sir Thomas More* and Roper's life--are used with great freedom.

I021   Brown, Dorothy Harrell. "Humanistic Doctrine in Some 'Belated Moralities.'" Diss. U of Southwestern Louisiana, 1975.

Brown seeks evidence of the continued spread of humanistic ideas long after the "first impulse" of the More Circle as she investigates English morality plays believed performed between 1535 and 1600.

I022   Chambers, R.W. "Shakespeare and More." *TLS* 3 June 1939: 327.

Chambers attributes the play to Shakespeare and employs similarities between other Shakespearean plays and *The Booke of Sir Thomas More* to support the validity of his claim.

I023   Condren, Conal. "The Image of *Utopia* in the Political Writings of George Lawson (1657): A Note on the Manipulation of Authority." *Moreana* 69 (1981): 101-05.

Condren studies how Lawson utilizes the recusant image of More, plays down More's loyalty to the authority of the Church in Rome, and refers to *Utopia* to intimate "an alternative and deeper-rooted cause for More's execution than his adherence to the Pope."

I024 Corrigan, Beatrice. "Sir Thomas More: Personage and Symbol on the Italian Stage." *Studies in the Continental Background of English Literature: Presented to John L. Lievsay*. Eds. Dale B.J. Randall, and George W. Williams. Durham: Duke UP, 1977. 91-108.

Corrigan notices how the rift between the Church and Italian nationalism widened as the nineteenth century proceeded and that new writers became increasingly anticlerical. For nearly three-hundred years dramatists had been able to relate the story of More's conscientious resistance and his death to the prerogatives of Church and state in Italy as well as England. Only when persecution became overtly political, as it had already done in Pellico's time, did the figure of the English martyr recede. The cause for which he had given his life lost its urgency, and the Italian stage looked elsewhere for its heroes.

I025 Cro, Stelio. *Realidad y utopía en el descubrimiento y conquista de la América Hispana (1492-1682)*. Pref. Francisco López Estrada. Troy, MI: International Book Pubs., 1983.

Cro discusses the influence of the concept of utopia in general and More's work in particular on Spanish exploration and colonization of the New World and on Spanish and Spanish American literature.

I026 Davis, Herbert et al., eds. *The Prose Works of Jonathan Swift*. 13 vols. London: Basil Blackwell, 1939-59. See Vol. 4, *A Proposal for Correcting the English Tongue. Polite Conversation, Etc.*, 71; Vol. 5, *Miscellaneous and Autobiographical Pieces, Fragments and Marginalia*, xi, 84, 247-48; Vol. 11, *Gulliver's Travels 1726*, 8, 196.

These volumes contain Swift's remarks on More, such as those found in the margins of the *Life and Raigne of Henry VIII*, in which he observes More was "the only Man of true Virtue tha[t] ever Engld produced."

I027 Desroche, Henri. "De Thomas More à Etienne Cabet." *Moreana* 31-32 (1971): 215-19.

Desroche discusses More's influence on Cabet's *Voyage en Icarie* (1842).

I028 Donno, Elizabeth Story. "Duo Thomas: A More Allusion." *Moreana* 7 (1965): 102-03.

When Wills, the 1577 editor of Eden's translation of Martyr's *De orbe novo decades*, accepts More's English prose style as one to be emulated, he is referring to the *Life of Picus* and just possibly accepting *Richard III* as a translation.

I029 Doyle, Charles Clay. "Echoes of More in American Folk Humor." *Moreana* 51 (1976): 145-47.

Although some boisterous wit of American folk humor might seem alien to the "subtle, scholarly, and saintly temperament" of More, Doyle compares samples of both to show "More's wit was not so delicate, nor American humor so raucous, as to preclude overlap."

I030 Doyle, Charles Clay. "The Hair and Beard of Thomas More (With Special Reference to the Play *Sir Thomas More* and an Epigram by John Owen)." *Moreana* 71-72 (1981): 5-14.

The allusion to hair in a poem by Owen about More's death prompts Doyle to examine the anecdotes concerning More's hair and beard and to show in particular how they figure in *Sir Thomas More*.

I031 Doyle, Charles Clay. "John Webster's Echoes of More." *Moreana* 70 (1981): 49-52.

Although Doyle cautions More and Webster might have been following common sources, he posits with "some likelihood" that some of Webster's plays were influenced by More or "some intermediate *amicus Mori*."

I032 Doyle, Charles Clay. "J.V. Cunningham and More's Cuckolded Astrologer." *Moreana* 75-76 (1982): 35-37.

Doyle notes the influence of More's martyrdom and his Latin Epigram 45 ("Aliud in Eundem [Astrologum Uxoris Impudicae Maritum]") upon Cunningham's *Collected Poems* (1971).

I033 Doyle, Charles Clay. "Thomas More and the Epigrams of John Owen: A Reference and an Analog." *Moreana* 67-68 (1980): 39-41.

Doyle notes one of the Cambro-Latin poet Owen's epigrams, playing on "medicus/mendicus," is derived from More.

I034 Dust, Philip. "A Reference to More in Philemon Holland's Translation of Suetonius's *Vitae Caesarum*." *Moreana* 29 (1971): 17-21.

Dust expands upon this reference of 1606 by citing More's Latin epigram 189, "Ad Sabinvm," indebted to Martial.

I035 Egretier, Noëlle-Marie. "'Thomas More, le meilleur des Anglais.'" *Moreana* 3 (1964): 23-35.

The deaths of Fisher and More marked a turning point in the life of Reginald Pole, the scholar and cousin of Henry VIII. Henceforth, Pole chose the course of Christian humanism, truth, and justice.

I036 Evans, John X. "*Utopia* on Prospero's Island." *Moreana* 69 (1981): 81-83.

Evans believes Alonso in Shakespeare's *Tempest* (2.1.165) may be "fooling" around with a play on More's name and *Utopia*; he finds other instances of similar word plays in *King Lear, Titus Andronicus*, and the sections of *The Book of Sir Thomas More* ascribed to Shakespeare.

I037 Evans, Robert C. "More's *Richard III* and Jonson's *Richard Crookback* and *Sejanus*." *CompD* 24.2 (1990): 97-132.

Discovery of Jonson's marked copy of More's Latin version of *Richard III* (in the 1565 Louvain edition of More's Latin works) allows scholars to speculate about the nature of Jonson's *Richard Crookback* and the influence More's history may have had upon it.

I038 Evans, Scott D. "A 'Divine Consideration': *Utopia* in Sidney's *Defence of Poetry*." *Moreana* 125 (1996): 7-29.

Evans discusses how Sidney commends *Utopia* in his *Defence* because of More's "way of patterning" that fictional society--a way that corresponds with Sidney's notions about the artistic method of the "right poet," the ideal literary artist he describes in his treatise. Sidney's argument suggests *Utopia*'s greatness is its power over the imagination; though More's imaginary commonweal is not a practical model, it may attract readers to virtue through its satire, comedy, and seriousness. Hence, *Utopia* achieves the highest goals Sidney ascribes to the best literature.

I039 Fellheimer, J. "Silvio Pellico's *Thomas More*." *MLR* 43 (1948): 483-91.

This article analyzes the Italian play (published in 1833), which portrays Anne Boleyn as an intercessor for More, a role not based on history or any previous creative work about More.

I040 Fleissner, Robert F. "The Editing Out of 'With Just Cause': Dispensing with an Ironic Resonance of *Utopia* in *Julius Caesar*." *NM* 95 (1994): 459-65.

In examining the readings of a crux in Shakespeare's *Julius Caesar*, Fleissner explores not only its possible source in More's *Utopia* but also refers to Shakespeare's possible uses of *Utopia* and other works by More in his other plays.

I041 Gabel, John Butler. "The Year of Robert Whittington's Death." *HLQ* 28 (1965): 77-78.

Whittington, known for his verse to More, died not in 1548, but in 1533.

I042 Gabrieli, Vittorio. "From Italy: Some Tentative Notes on More and Cervantes." *Moreana* 126 (1996): 83-87.

A passage in chapter 18 of Part I of *Don Quixote* causes Gabrieli to wonder if Cervantes had read *Utopia* and to speculate upon correspondences between More and Cervantes.

I043 Gabrieli, Vittorio. "*Sir Thomas More*: Sources, Characters, Ideas." *Moreana* 90 (1986): 17-43.

Gabrieli divides the printed sources of *Sir Thomas More* into four groups: historical, biographical, dramatic, and literary. Those available at the presumable time of the play's composition and used by the dramatists in the first seven scenes may include More's *Apology* (1533), reprinted in William Roper's 1557 edition of the *English Works*. There is little doubt in Gabrieli's mind the playwrights drew heavily from materials in the *English Works*.

I044 Garavaglia, Gian Paolo. "I Livellatori e L'*Utopia*." *Moreana* 31-32 (1971): 191-96.

Garavaglia discusses some of the Utopian schemes proposed in England during the Civil War and Commonwealth period.

I045 Geritz, Albert J. "*Sir Thomas More: A Tragedy* by James Hurdis." *Moreana* 113 (1993): 5-16.

An overview of Hurdis' life and a more detailed look at the history of his work's composition provide the background necessary for this article's analysis of one of the forty-one plays about More composed in English and the only known drama written about More during the eighteenth century in England.

I046 Gibaud, Henri. "Thomas Morus en Icarie." *Moreana* 43-44 (1974): 71-80.

Gibaud is concerned with the role assigned to More in Etienne Dolet's *Voyage en Icarie*.

I047 Gleason, John B. "Dr. Donne in the Courts of Kings: A Glimpse from Marginalia." *JEGP* 69 (1970): 599-612.

Donne's copy of More's *Lucubrationes*, housed in the University of San Francisco Library, is remarkable for certain notes on *Utopia*, which are presumably Donne's comments.

I048 Gury, Jacques. "Thomas More in Thomson's *Seasons*." *Moreana* 50 (1976): 97-100.

Gury comments on More's appearance in the *Seasons*, principally on the two-line expansion of the 1746 edition over the 1730 Quarto.

I049 Hewitt, Janice L. "More to Orwell: An Easy Leap from *Utopia* to *Nineteen Eighty-Four*." *George Orwell*. Eds. Courtney T. Wemyss, and Alexej Ugrinsky. Westport, CT: Greenwood, 1987. 127-33.

Hewitt notes *Nineteen Eighty-Four* "is not so much an anti-utopia as it is More's *Utopia* carried to the extreme," and that both men see the evils resulting from the "logical extension of authoritarian methods."

I050 Hibbert, Eleanor. *St. Thomas's Eve*. New York: Putnam's, 1970.
This novel is based on More's life.

I051 Hoeniger, F. David. "Three Amusing References to More in Peter Heylyn." *Moreana* 11 (1966): 39-42.
Hoeniger points out three references to More in Heylyn's *Microcosmos*.

I052 Honigmann, E.A.J. "The Play of *Sir Thomas More* and Some Contemporary Events." *ShS* 42. Ed. Stanley Wells. Cambridge: Cambridge UP, 1990. 77-84.
Honigmann not only looks at *Sir Thomas More* in general to explore what kind of play it is, but also speculates upon specific connections between it and More's grandson (Thomas More II) who "commissioned at least three versions" of Hans Holbein's now lost canvas of More and his household.

I053 Jones, Rayston. "Some Notes on More's *Utopia* in Spain." *MLR* 45 (1950): 478-82.
Jones finds a Spanish text of *Utopia* (a translation by Medimilla y Porres) interesting because it omits the first book along with the epistle of dedication to Peter Giles. Jones believes the Inquisitors censored the first book because they feared its misinterpretation might be harmful to the Church. Other Latin works of More, however, were read and respected in Spain during the first half of the sixteenth century.

I054 Kennedy, Richard F. "Additional References to More in Renaissance England." *Moreana* 82 (1984): 19-23.
This note records undetected references and allusions to More in nine English authors, including Thomas Fuller, all of which testify to the widespread fame of More and his writings.

I055 Konecsni, Johnemery. "A Kantian Reference to Thomas More?" *Moreana* 38 (1973): 55-57.
In the *Critique of Practical Reason*, Kant refers to an incorruptible personage who sounds like More. Detailed consideration is given to these lines of Kant's text by comparing them to More's life. The conclusion questions the existence of a more accurate model than More, given Kant's Anglophilic tendencies.

I056 Konecsni, Johnemery. "Sir Humfrey Gilbert, *Utopia*, and America."

Moreana 51 (1976): 124-25.
Konecsni finds parallels between *Utopia* and Gilbert's last voyage.

I057 Lacas, M.M. "A Social Welfare Organizer in Sixteenth-Century New Spain: Don Vasco de Quiroga, First Bishop of Michoacán." *Americas: A Quarterly Review of InterAmerican Cultural History* 14 (1957): 57-86.

Lacas expounds upon the influence of the social and economic organization of *Utopia* on the foundation of Quiroga's hospital-villages in Mexico in the 1530s.

I058 Lietz, Paul S. "More's *Utopia* in America." *Catholic Lawyer* 2 (1956): 340-49.

Lietz examines Vasco de Quiroga's *Informacion de Derecho* (1535) and its use of *Utopia* as one source of the principles upon which he founded his ideal Christian commonwealth in Mexico.

I059 Lloyd-Jones, Kenneth. "Thomas More and Maurice Scève's *Délie*." *Moreana* 42 (1974): 23-32.

Scève mentions More's death once in *Délie*. Many important contemporary personages and events are also referred to, but More's death is specifically related to Scève's spiritual and sensual rebirth through his love for Délie. Scève's special treatment of More--no other figure is so intimately or so intricately bound to the poet's situation--suggests a particular sympathy for aspects of the Utopian ideal. More's concepts for the necessary equilibrium of society and the nature and function of virtue are echoed in *Délie*. One may conclude *Utopia* played a seminal role in Scève's development.

I060 Logan, John Frederick. "Gilbert Burnet and His Whiggish *Utopia*." *Moreana* 46 (1975): 13-20.

Burnet, Whiggish in politics and latitudinarian in theology, translated *Utopia* chiefly to propagate his own views. His preface portrays a More acceptable to both Protestant and Catholic readers. Much later, in Part 3 of *History of the Reformation of the Church of England*, he returns to *Utopia*, in which he finds "some of the most essential parts of the reformation."

I061 López Estrada, Francisco. "Santo Tomás Moro en España y en la America Hispana." *Moreana* 5 (1965): 27-40.

In a survey of More's influence in Spain and Spanish America, López Estrada notes references to his political activities and martyrdom after the final breach between Rome and England, Zumarraga's use of *Utopia*, its influence on *Don Quixote*, and Spanish translations of it since the seventeenth century.

I062 López Estrada, Francisco. "Tomás Moro en un Libro de Fray Alonso de la Torre, cartujo sevillano." *Miscellanea Moreana: Essays for Germain Marc'hadour. Moreana* 100. 517-31.

López Estrada adds to the evidence of More's presence in Spain with the discovery of a ms. of Fray Alonso de la Torre in the University of Seville Library, *Historia de Mártires de la Cartuxa de Inglaterra*, a section of which deals with More's trial and execution.

I063 López Estrada, Francisco. *Tomas Moro Y España: Sus Relaciones Hasta El Siglo XVIII.* Madrid: Editorial de la Universidad Complutense, 1980.

López Estrada surveys the extent of More's influence in Spain until the eighteenth century.

I064 Lynch, Arthur, and Leicester Bradner. "On St. Thomas More, an Epitaph of Uncertain Origin." *RN* 15 (1962): 1-2.

The authors reproduce an epitaph of which More is the subject that was written "as early as March 23, 1535, 105 days" before his execution.

I065 MacNalty, Arthur S. "Shakespeare and Sir Thomas More." *E&S* ns 12 (1959): 36-57.

MacNalty discusses the Shakespearean additions to *The Booke of Sir Thomas More* and marshals considerable evidence Shakespeare was familiar with More's writings in *Richard III*, in developing characters like Falstaff and Mistress Quickly, and in passages of other plays.

I066 *Man for All Seasons.* By Robert Bolt. Dir. Fred Zinnemann. Perf. Paul Scofield, Robert Shaw, Wendy Hiller, Orson Welles, Vanessa Redgrave. Highland Films, Ltd., 1966.

Bolt's play makes a smooth translation to the screen with Zinnemann's eye for characterization rather than spectacle, and the result is a superior drama with excellent performances. Oscars for best picture, best director, best color cinematography, best screenplay (by Bolt), best color costume design all contributed to its worldwide reception, and the film's impact is multiplied by videocassettes.

I067 Marc'hadour, Germain. "Educateur, Journaliste, Martyr: Titus Brandsma." *Moreana* 97 (1988): 81-86.

A similar combination of intellectual curiosity, spiritual fervor, and vigorous involvement in the affairs of the day constitutes a parallel between More and a Frisian Carmelite who taught at the Catholic University of Nijmegen, becoming its rector for a year. It was chiefly as ecclesiastical counselor to the Catholic Press that Brandsma opposed the Nazi occupation government. Arrested by the Gestapo in January 1942, he was an inspiration to his fellow prisoners until his death at Dachau on 26 July 1942. He was beatified in 1985.

I068 Marc'hadour, Germain. "Poems About Thomas More." *Moreana* 12 (1966): 87-89.

Marc'hadour examines poems written about More--three by Johannes Secundus (Jan Everaerts), a sonnet by Faustina degli Azzi, and several anonymous pieces.

I069 Marc'hadour, Germain. "Une Dette de Shakespeare envers le Père de Thomas Morre." *Moreana* 4 (1964): 76-87.

Shakespeare's literary source for the false miracle of St. Albans (*I Henry VI*, 2.2) is More's *Dialogue Concerning Heresies*. Other mutually shared puns also suggest Shakespeare knew More's works.

I070 Martyn, John R.C. "John Owen on Thomas More." *Moreana* 50 (1976): 73-77.

Owen's ten books of epigrams contain three poems about More, which despite their sometimes morbid fascination with his death, nevertheless capture More's noble character, lively intelligence and learning, and good looks.

I071 McCutcheon, Elizabeth. "A Mid-Tudor Owner of More's *Utopia*: Sir William More." *Moreana* 70 (1981): 32-35.

McCutcheon shows how Sir William More epitomizes the first generation to read and own the *Englished Utopia* and other works of northern humanism.

I072 McCutcheon, Elizabeth. "More's *Utopia* as Commonplaced in Edward Pudsey's 'Booke' (Circa 1600)." *Moreana* 103 (1990): 33-40.

The Pudsey notebook (MS. Eng. poet.d.3 in the Bodleian) is an early seventeenth-century notebook miscellany that includes a commonplaced selection of material from *Utopia*. These entries are doubly important: they call attention to the emblematic and sententious elements in *Utopia*, and they suggest a distinctive response to the text on the part of the compiler, Edward Pudsey (1573-1613).

I073 McCutcheon, Elizabeth. "Sir Dudley Digges and More's *Utopia*." *Moreana* 69 (1981): 79-80.

In the second of his *Foure Paradoxes, or Politique Discourses* (1604), Digges sees *Utopia* as the pattern of an idealized, completely imaginary state.

I074 McCutcheon, Elizabeth. "Sir Thomas Egerton, Lord Ellesmere on More's *Utopia*." *Moreana* 79-80 (1983): 15-16.

McCutcheon presents Egerton's rejection of *Utopia* in a speech which he delivered in 1608 when he was chancellor.

I075 McCutcheon, James M. "To Build a Christian Utopia in the Pacific:

The Sandwich Islands in Early American Protestant Missionary Activity." *More's* Utopia *and the Utopian Inheritance.* 89-98.

McCutcheon considers English and American missionary endeavors in the Sandwich Islands in the light of some ideas from More's *Utopia* and other works.

I076 Meany, John W. "The Bishop of Utopia." *American Catholic Historical Society* 9 (1949): 197-212.

Meany believes *Utopia* served as a model for Vasco de Quiroga's communities founded in Mexico in the 1530s, demonstrates Quiroga's friend (Bishop Zumarraga of Mexico City) referred him to *Utopia*, and examines the similarities between More's work and the ordinances Quiroga drew up for these communities.

I077 Merriam, Thomas. "Did Shakespeare Model Camillo in *The Winter's Tale* on Sir Thomas More?" *Moreana* 75-76 (1982): 91-101.

Merriam brings forward evidence Shakespeare had More in mind, consciously and deliberately, when he wrote the part of Camillo. "To prove that he did not is patently impossible."

I078 Mezciems, Jenny. "Swift's Praise of Gulliver: Some Renaissance Background to the Travels." *The Character of Swift's Satire: A Revised Focus.* Ed. Claude Rawson. Newark: U of Delaware P, 1983. 245-81.

Mezciems connects *Gulliver's Travels* to the tradition of Renaissance humanist satire found in More's *Utopia*, Erasmus' *Praise of Folly*, and Rabelais' writings. She compares the relation of Swift to Gulliver and More to Hythloday, the rationality of both the Houynhnms and Utopians, the emphasis on war in both, and their satiric methods and intentions.

I079 Miller, Clarence H. "Thomas More, A Man for All Seasons: Robert Bolt's Play and the Elizabethan Play of *Sir Thomas More*." *Moreana* 104 (1990): 101-10.

Bolt borrowed the title for his play (I018) from an English translation of "omnium horarum homo" in the textbook *Vulgaria* (1520) by Robert Whittington, who had himself borrowed the phrase from Erasmus' dedication of *The Praise of Folly* (or *Moria*) to More. From Erasmus' explanation of the saying in his *Adagia*, one learns it could be applied not only to men of admirable flexibility but also to hedonists and opportunists, such as Henry VIII, Cromwell, Rich, and Wolsey in Bolt's play. Plays tend to limit More's complex character according to the requirements of the times and audiences. While it is not surprising Latin school plays on the Continent glorified More and vilified Henry and Anne, it is remarkable in the 1590s an English play on More was written for the Lord Strange's Men. Written by six playwrights, it survives in a single ms. which became famous in the late nineteenth century because it was thought one scene was written in Shakespeare's hand. Since the reasons for More's stand against Henry could not be specified, as the censor's notes made clear, the play cannot explore the motives of More's martyrdom and falls back on his roles as orator, London citizen, family man, and jokester, though it does make clear he looks forward to being merry in heaven. In Bolt's existentialist play, the absence of a true religious dimension makes it impossible for him to explore the real reasons for More's attempt to avoid death by keeping silent. The true grounds of More's martyrdom, his love for Christ in His Church, can be seen best in the last works he wrote in the Tower.

I080 Milward, Peter. "The Morean Counsellor in Shakespeare's Last Plays." *Moreana* 103 (1990): 25-32.

It is not usually realized how close is the connection between More and Shakespeare, because attention is mostly directed to the text of the plays. Between the lines of the text, however, one may find remarkable analogies between More and certain characters of the later plays, converging on the figure of a wise, holy counsellor.

I081 Moser, Fernando de Mello. "Had Lord Byron Read *Utopia*?" *Moreana* 49 (1976): 49-50.

Moser cites the similarity between a passage from the author of *The Prisoner of Chillon's* speech in the House of Lords, on 27 February 1812, with the passage in *Utopia* in which Hythloday attacks capital punishment.

I082 Murphy, Clare M. "The Island of Utopia and Voltaire's Country of Eldorado." *More's* Utopia *and the Utopian Inheritance*. 109-17.

Murphy explores the influence of More's "theme of discovery" in *Utopia* upon Rabelais, mainly Voltaire, and others.

I083 Noakes, Aubrey. "Lord Curzon on the *Utopia*: The Background Story of a Literary Find: Lord Curzon's Arnold Prize Essay of 1884 on Sir Thomas More." *Moreana* 31-32 (1971): 221-50.

Noakes discusses and reprints part of Lord Curzon's discourse on *Utopia* from his essay.

I084 Panofsky, Richard J. "An Unknown Sixteenth-Century Reference to More's *Utopia*." *Moreana* 75-76 (1982): 38.

Hugh Plat included "A merrie tale of master Mendax to his friends Credulus" among the poetic *juvenalia* appended as "The Pleasure of Poetrie" to his *Floures of Philosophie* (1572, 1581), in which Mendax refers to More's *Utopia* as he names the country in which his house is located.

I085 Peters, Christoph. "The Image of Thomas More in 20th Century Plays--A Presentation of Five More Dramas." *Moreana* 109 (1992): 23-46.

Peters discusses the plays about More (written for the stage or the screen) of Jean Anouilh, Morna Stuart, Felix Doherty, Thomas Regau, and Caspar Willeke.

I086 Pineas, Rainer. "More's *Utopia* and the 'Tragedy' of Polonius." *Moreana* 78 (1983): 23-24.

Although Pineas concedes scholars cannot be certain Shakespeare read *Utopia*, it "seems as if the fortunes of Polonius in *Hamlet* are almost a dramatization of the error against which More warned" in a passage in Book II of *Utopia* about decision-making in the Utopian senate.

I087 Pineas, Rainer. "Thomas More as an Anti-Catholic Weapon in Protestant Polemics." *Moreana* 70 (1981): 45-48.

Pineas demonstrates how, after More's death, Protestant polemicists forged from his motives, actions, and writings what they considered effective weapons of religious controversy.

I088 Prescott, Anne Lake. "Crime and Carnival at Chelsea: Widow Edith and Thomas More's Household." *Miscellanea Moreana: Essays for Germain Marc'hadour. Moreana* 100. 247-64.

Prescott argues the verse jests told by More's servant Walter Smith of the false "widow" Edith, a wandering thief and con artist, have ingenuity and some depth underneath their tumbling and pseudo-Chaucerian surface, for Smith attends to pattern and telling of ironic detail.

I089 Prescott, Anne Lake. "Thomas Nash (1588-1648) and Thomas More." *Moreana* 59-60 (1978): 35-41.

Prescott discusses Nash's *Quaternio* (1633), a dialogue on ways of pursuing a happy and useful life: Nash defends his use of dialogue, jokes, and merry tales by reference to More, from whom he quotes, though the extent of More's influence does not seem great.

I090 Reynolds, E.E. "At Chelchith, 1526." *Moreana* 49 (1976): 5-14.

Reynolds publishes this excerpt, a fictional summary of life at More's household in 1526, from his unpublished work about William Rastell entitled *Tudor Printer*.

I091 Reynolds, E.E. "Sir James Mackintosh and Sir Thomas More." *Moreana* 34 (1972): 5-16.

Reynolds focuses on this Scottish barrister and politician (1765-1832), whose life of More (1830) is a sound early appreciation of its subject.

I092 Rose, Eliot. "Too good to be true: Thomas Lupton's Golden Rule." *Tudor Rule and Revolution: Essays for G.R. Elton from his American Friends.* Eds. Delloyd J. Guth, and John W. McKenna. Cambridge: Cambridge UP, 1982. 183-200.

Rose discusses Lupton's *Too Good to be True* (1580-81) as the first English imitation of More's *Utopia* and compares More's work, Thomas Smith's *De Republica Anglorum* (1583), John Lyly's *Euphues,* and Lupton's book on the laws of England.

I093 Roussel, Jean. "L'Emploi du Mot Utopia chez George Sand." *Moreana* 58 (1978): 13-17.

Because Sand refers to *Utopia* in a letter of August 1840 to Abbe Rochet, Roussel speculates about the degree of her familiarity with More's work.

I094 Roussel, Jean. "Rousseau, l'Utopie et Thomas More." *Moreana* 59-60 (1978): 47-53.

Roussel notes that in his earlier years, Rousseau dismissed *Utopia* as merely impracticable in this world, but in his later years saw man's need to prepare for another world.

I095 Rude, Donald W. "Two Unreported References to Sir Thomas More." *Moreana* 91-92 (1986): 83-84.

Rude notes the pair of references to More in Giovanni Botero's *Le relazioni universali* (Rome, 1592).

I096 Sander-Regier, Raymond. "A 1751 Citation from *Utopia.*" *Moreana* 87-88 (1985): 68.

Sander-Regier notes that, in the appendix to *The Right Method of Maintaining Security in Person and Property* (1751), the author, Philonomous, cites an extended passage from Book I of *Utopia* in support of the deliberation on security of person and property which appears in the main body of the book. Although no source is given for the citation, Sander-Regier demonstrates it is from Gilbert Burnet's translation (first published in 1654).

I097 Sandgathe, Mechtild. "Tracing the Connection Between Goethe and Thomas More." *Moreana* 109 (1992): 53-57.

Sandgathe examines the question why Goethe would hang an engraving of More in the living room of his summer house.

I098 Schoeck, R.J. "Lord Acton's Views on St. Thomas More." *Moreana* 12 (1966): 47-52.

Acton, in one of his lectures delivered at Cambridge in his later years, when presumably his opinions had mellowed and finalized, called More, "the most modern and original mind among the men of his time." Schoeck quotes this judgment and maintains it is "probably the most considered opinion we have by Acton on More and the great problems of his time."

I099 Schroeder, Karl. "George Gilbert and the More Fresco of 1583." *Moreana* 42 (1974): 49-58.

Schroeder comments on this issue's cover illustration of the executions of More, Fisher, and Margaret Pole by tracing the career of Gilbert (1555-1583), founder and organizer of the Catholic Association, who financed a secret press in England and paid for Pomerancio's paintings of English confessors and martyrs in the English College chapel at Rome.

I100 Searle, William. "More and Cervantes: The Utopian 'Isle' of Barataria." *An&Q* 19 (1981): 141-44.

All the qualities Sancho exhibits in his role as governor are adequately displayed in the governance of More's Utopian community.

I101 Smith, Christopher. "Thomas More in the Works of Urbain Chevreau." *Moreana* 95-96 (1987): 89-92.

Smith discusses three references to More in the works of Chevreau which he finds interesting not only for what they tell about More's image in seventeenth-century France but also because they enable scholars to trace one of the routes for the transmission of information about More.

I102 Sorlien, Robert P. "Thomas More Anecdotes in an Elizabethan Diary." *Moreana* 34 (1972): 81-82.

Sorlien records two anecdotes of John Manningham (BM. MS. Harl. 5353), whose informant appears to have been a Lincoln Inn lawyer, Thomas Foster. Anderegg supplements Sorlien's note in "The Anecdotal Tradition of Thomas More: A Note" (F002).

I103 Standley, Fred. "Ever 'More': Utopian and Dystopian Visions of the Future 1890-1990." *More's* Utopia *and the Utopian Inheritance*. 119-36.

Standley establishes the extent of *Utopia*'s influence by examining scholarly commentaries about and interpretations of it and noting its impact on creative works of a similar nature.

I104 Stanwood, P.G., and Laetitia Yeandle. "Richard Hooker's Use of Thomas More." *Moreana* 35 (1972): 5-16.

The authors expand upon two explicit allusions in Book VIII of the *Laws of Ecclesiastical Polity* and in the *Tractate of Justification*.

I105 Stewart, Patricia L. "The Influence of Thomas More on the Early

American Stage." *Moreana* 51 (1976): 132-38.

More's influence on early American drama is twofold: indirectly through his authorship of one of Shakespeare's sources for *Richard III* and directly by references in Boker's play, *Anne Boleyn*. The first Shakespearean play produced in America and a favorite of famous actors in American history, *Richard III*, in its various versions, retained More's conception of an evil Richard. In Boker's play, Anne expresses "fear, guilt, and horror" for actions in More's execution, and Wyatt, the play's most admirable character, becomes "subtly identified" with More.

I106 Sylvester, R.S. "John Constable's Poems to Thomas More." *PQ* 42 (1963): 525-31.

Among his trifling verses, Constable leaves two addressed to More. They are probably attacks on Robert Whittington, who had attacked Constable's teacher and More's friend, William Lily; Constable mocks Whittington's poems to More and implies More, an "all-powerful Hercules," will soon destroy such monsters as Whittington.

I107 Sylvester, R.S. "The 'Man for All Seasons' Again: Robert Whittington's Verses to Sir Thomas More." *HLQ* 26 (1963): 147-54.

This article concerns two poems addressed to More by Whittington, the author of the descriptive cognomen recently popularized, which echoes a phrase in *The Praise of Folly*. The first extols More's poetic gift, his knowledge of ancient languages, law, and history, and the power of his oratory, controlled by wisdom and tempered by humor. The second is less ostentatiously poetic, its interest stemming mainly from an early reference to *Utopia*. Both poems imply a personal knowledge of More and seem to be products of the "grammarians" war.

I108 Szendrey, Thomas. *St. Thomas and East Central Europe: The Impact of his Christian Humanism*. 1981. Pittsburgh: Duquesne UP, 1985.

Szendrey points out More was an outstanding representative of Christian humanism, a "Europe-wide phenomenon," which was not limited to the western part of Europe. He presents the role of the northern or Trans-Alpine Renaissance and its Christian humanism, which spread to East Central Europe mainly through the activities of German humanists and German universities. The impact of More was mediated through Erasmus and "not direct." Nevertheless, two of More's works show the common consciousness of a united Europe at that time: *Utopia*, known to humanists of this part of the world in Latin, and *Dialogue of Comfort*, wherein the historical background of the Turkish invasion of Hungary is used as allegory.

I109 Tamura, Hideo. "Utopia in Seventeenth-Century England." *Moreana*

64 (1980): 37-49.
Tamura traces various seventeenth-century usages of the word "utopia," ranging from ideal scheme to absurd fantasy, and indicates various seventeenth-century works more or less influenced by *Utopia*.

I110   Telle, Emile V. "Edmund Lodge on John and Thomas More (1795)." *Moreana* 89 (1986): 93-96.
Telle cites the biographical sketches of More, his father, and his son found in Lodge's *Imitations of Original Drawings by Hans Holbein in the Collection of His Majesty*.

I111   Telle, Emile V. "Eloge de Thomas More par Richard Dinot." *Moreana* 42 (1974): 17-20.
Telle reprints the eulogy Dinot wrote for More, which has special interest because Dinot was a Protestant pastor who died c. 1590.

I112   Telle, Emile V. "Etienne Dolet et Thomas More." *Moreana* 36 (1972): 33-38.
Telle notes citations of More or his works in three works by this French Renaissance scholar.

I113   Teunissen, John J., and Evelyn J. Hinz. "Roger Williams, Thomas More and the Naragansett Utopia." *EAL* 2 (1976-77): 281-95.
Though the authors caution Williams may not have read *Utopia*, he was almost certainly familiar with its ideas, and they explore a number of similarities in tone, structure, and sentiment between Williams' *A Key into the Language of America* (his first and only book about America and Indians) and the Utopian tradition More's *Utopia* established in the early Renaissance.

I114   Toups, Noel Joseph. "Sir Thomas More, Humanist and Hero: A Man for Ages." Diss. Louisiana State U and Agricultural and Mechanical Coll., 1980.
Toups traces the ways More has been portrayed in diverse works from the sixteenth to twentieth century.

I115   Unterweg, Friedrich-K. "A Man for All Stages: Five Centuries of Thomas More Dramas." *Moreana* 108 (1991): 5-32.
Unterweg shows More's rise and fall treated with remarkable continuity in different dramatic forms in many countries over the last 500 years. The many-faceted image and lasting popularity of More as a stage hero direct attention to him as a literary character. Unterweg divides the plays into four groups: (1) some forty Latin plays written in the Jesuit collection between 1612 and 1764; (2) twenty-five vernacular plays written for professional stages from 1595 to

1959; (3) twenty-two vernacular or Latin dramas by non-professional authors and all but one published after 1863; and (4) fifteen plays for the professional stage written between 1931 and 1987.

I116 Unterweg, Friedrich-K. "Thomas More in Dutch Drama." *Moreana* 97 (1988): 23-40.

Unterweg discusses fourteen Dutch dramas in which More is the main character, eleven of which were written in 120 years in the seventeenth and eighteenth centuries and three which were published within sixty years in the twentieth century. He divides the plays into Latin plays written for performance in colleges and vernacular dramas written for the professional stage.

I117 Unterweg, Friedrich-K. "Thomas Morus, Tragoedia." *Acta Conventus Neo-Latini Guelpherbytani*. Proceedings of the Sixth International Congress of Neo-Latin Studies. Wolfenbüttel 12 August to 16 August 1985. Eds. Stella P. Revard, Fidel Rädle, and Mario A. Di Cesare. MRTS. 53. Binghamton: MRTS, 1988. 365-74.

Unterweg examines More in drama, especially Dutch drama and the play *Thomas Morus, Tragoedia*; and lists Jesuit plays about More from 1612 to 1764.

I118 Vickers, Brian. "The Satiric Structure of *Gulliver's Travels* and More's *Utopia*." *The World of Jonathan Swift: Essays for the Tercentenary*. Ed. Brian Vickers. Cambridge, MA: Harvard UP, 1968. 233-57.

Vickers demonstrates More's *Utopia* provided a model for more parts of *Gulliver's Travels* than is ordinarily assumed as he points out similarities in satiric devices, viewpoints, and use of a *persona*. In spite of likenesses between the works, there are also "great divergences."

I119 Vogel, Paula A. *Meg: A Play in Three Acts*. New York: Samuel French, 1977.

This historical drama depicts key moments in the lives of More and his daughter Margaret.

I120 Wands, John M. "Antipodal Imperfection: Hall's *Mundus Alter et Idem* and Its Debt to More's *Utopia*." *Moreana* 69 (1981): 85-100.

Wands indicates debts Hall's work (1605); which provides an elaborate Latin apparatus, begins with a debate, has an "angelic" narrator, Mercury, who as teacher-messenger, indicts contemporary Europe through a traveler's tale; owes to *Utopia*, though the satiric and grotesque elements are more extreme in Hall than More.

I121 Warnicke, Retha M. "Women and Humanism in Early Tudor England." *Women of the English Renaissance and Reformation.* Contributions in Women's Studies. 38. Westport, CT: Greenwood, 1983. 16-30.

Warnicke charts the accomplishments of learned women over four generations beginning with the time of More, describes the diminishing effects of Christian humanism on women's education after its initial impetus, and traces the degree to which English society adopted the classical education More advocated for women. In summarizing the impact of humanism in women's education, Warnicke says, "It is indicative of the failure of Thomas More to popularize his ideas that in the fourth generation, the Protestants came to view education as a marital handicap and a majority of women classicists of the Catholic faith remained unmarried."

I122 Warren, Fintan B. *Vasco de Quiroga and His Pueblo-Hospitals of Santa Fe.* Washington, D.C.: Academy of American Franciscan History, 1963.

References to More's *Utopia* and its influences on Quiroga compose the basis for a study of the way he adopted and adapted Utopian ideas to the pueblo-hospitals in Santa Fe.

I123 White, Olive B. *The King's Good Servant.* New York: Macmillan, 1936.

This historical novel covering the last six years of More's life fictionalizes enough to warrant classification as a novel but also adheres strictly to the facts of the standard lives.

I124 Wooden, Warren W. "An Unnoticed Sixteenth Century Reference to More's *Utopia.*" *Moreana* 59-60 (1978): 91.

Wooden notes John Foxe suggesting in a sermon of 1570 that gossips and "such stoicall stomackes" should be sent to Utopia as a "no-place" suitable for social misfits.

I125 Zapatka, F.E. "Moreana in the Poetry of Robert Lowell." *Moreana* 51 (1976): 148-52.

Zapatka analyzes Lowell's poems which give More and some of his associates significant places.

I126 Zavala, Silvio. "Noticias de Literatura Utópica en España e Hispanoamérica." *Thesaurus* 42.2 (1987): 362-69.

Zavala notes the influence of More's *Utopia* on Spanish and Spanish American literature and refers extensively to studies of this subject by Demetrio Ramos Pérez, Isaac J. Pardo, Arturo A. Roig, and others.

I127 Zavala, Silvio. "St. Thomas More in New Spain." *Essential Articles for the Study of St. Thomas More.* 302-11.

Zavala demonstrates *Utopia* had a concrete impact on life in the New World and shows that royal ordinances dealing with the Spanish colonization of Mexico were lifted directly off the pages of More's book.

I128   Zavala, Silvio. *Sir Thomas More in New Spain: A Utopian Adventure of the Renaissance*. London: The Hispanic & Luso-Brazilian Councils, 1955.

Zavala seeks to uncover a "network of links between the thought of the European Renaissance and Spanish colonial endeavor in the New World" by concentrating on the influence of *Utopia* on the ordinances of Don Vasco de Quiroga in Mexico. (This essay expands and revises Zavala's ideas in "The American Utopia of the Sixteenth Century," *HLQ* 10 [1947]: 337-47.)

I129   Zavala, Silvio. "La Utopia de Thomas More en la Nueva España y otros estudios." México: Porrua e Hijos, 1937.

Zavala describes the laws laid down by Vasco de Quiroga, Bishop of Michuacán, which *Utopia* influenced and would have provided for agrarian communism with a supervised six hour work day.

I130   Zavala, Silvio.   "Vasco de Quiroga, Traducteur de l'*Utopia*." *Moreana* 69 (1981): 115-17.

Zavala refers to Quiroga's interests in *Utopia* and his intentions to translate part of it into Spanish.

Religious and Philosophical Backgrounds

J001 Adams, Robert P. "Pacifism in the English Renaissance, 1497-1530: John Colet, Erasmus, Thomas More, and J.L. Vives." Diss. U of Chicago, 1937.

Adams assembles a compendium of thought on war and peace that he focuses upon four humanists of the early Renaissance. He presents considerable information on More's life and thought.

J002 Allen, Ward. "St. Augustine, Wycliffe, More and the Bible." *Moreana* 30 (1971): 45-46.

Allen notes similarities in More's use of others' writings, especially those of St. Augustine and perhaps even Wyclif, in his biblical studies.

J003 Baumann, Eduard H.L. "Thomas More's *Philosophia Christiana*." *Moreana* 98-99 (1988): 37-43.

Baumann utilizes three essays by Gerhard Winkler to deal with More's *philosophia christiana*: (1) More's attempt to reconcile reason and revelation in *Utopia*, the grounds for religious tolerance in *Utopia*, and the ideal "combination of monk and man of the world" More himself tried to follow; (2) his idea of the priest; and (3) his endeavor to achieve a concensus between *humanitas* and *pietas*, between reason and pleasure, and finally his decision upon conscience against "pragmatism and propheticism."

J004 Bayne, Diane Valeri. "*The Instruction of a Christian Woman*: Richard Hyrde and the Thomas More Circle." *Moreana* 45 (1975): 5-15.

Bayne focuses upon Hyrde's educational ideals and his views on women and their education. The discussion centers on Hyrde's introduction to a translation by Margaret Roper in 1524 of Erasmus' *Precatio dominica* and his own translation of Vives' *Instruction of a Christian Woman*. She indicates the extent to which More's own views on the education of women influenced others.

J005 Bork, Robert H. "Law, Morality, and Thomas More." *Moreana* 91-92 (1986): 85-87.
This article excerpts remarks from Bork's after-dinner talk to the Thomas More Society of America (Washington, D.C., 26 September 1985) in which the speaker notes "law *was* morality" for More.

J006 Brugmans, Henri. "Thomas More: humaniste european." *La Revue Nouvelle* 44 (1966): 3-20.
More is the perfect example of Europe in rebirth, the first world view of a capitalist society, the first author of an ideal social vision, but at the same time defender of the last spiritual liberty upon which, from that time on, the world would encroach.

J007 Cavanaugh, John R. "The St. Stephen Motif in St. Thomas More's Thought." *Moreana* 8 (1965): 59-66.
St. Stephen's martyrdom, a favorite motif in More's writing, indicates Christian typology was a habitual way of thinking for him and that he was attracted to Stephen's forgiveness of his persecutors.

J008 Dannenfeldt, Karl H. "The Renaissance and the Pre-Classical Civilisations." *JHI* 13 (1952): 435-49.
The debt of Greece to earlier civilizations was discussed more thoroughly during the Renaissance than in medieval times. More's writings provide evidence of this fact, for More appreciated ancient Egyptian civilization and believed "in an ancient tradition of religious philosophy which began with Moses and Zoroaster and of which Socrates, Christ, Hermes Trismegistus and others were a part."

J009 Ebert, Kenneth Bryan. "The Humanist Education of Women in Tudor England: Historical Influences and Perspectives." Diss. Michigan State U, 1983.
Ebert focuses on More (especially his education of his daughters), Vives, and others and their ideas about humanist educational programs for women to discern the historical background which influenced these programs and to examine them in relation to such programs for men.

J010 Fasan, Vada Belshaw. "John Colet's Christian Humanist Spirituality and the English Contemplative Tradition." Diss. U of Nebraska-Lincoln, 1984.
Fasan discovers the inspiration for Colet's "complex personality" by examining his relationship to traditional English spirituality by Hilton, Julian of

Norwich, and the unknown author of *Cloud of Unknowing* and then compares Colet's thoughts with those of More and Erasmus to demonstrate all three share a "purgative and illuminative piety" English mystics deemed appropriate for priests and laypersons with secular duties.

J011 Grace, Damian. "The Political Theory of St. Thomas More, 1509-1520." Diss. U of New South Wales (Austral.), 1981.

Grace shows that More's theoretical interest in politics extends beyond *Utopia* to companion works, the *Epigrammata* and *Richard III*. Each of these works is not only a diagnosis of the ills of the commonwealth, however, but an attempt to provide in a literary way a remedy for bad judgment. This study concludes that, in theorizing about politics, More used typical humanist forms to move his audience to a re-evaluation of accepted values and judgments in political life.

J012 Jones, Judith P. "'Thy Grace to Set the World at Nought': The Mystical Element in the Works of Thomas More." *SMy* 3 (1980): 61-71.

Jones locates the influence of Christian mysticism in More's early writings, such as *The Life of John Picus* and *Four Last Things*, in order to delineate how it pervades other works, especially those written in the Tower.

J013 Kaiser, Walter Jacob. *Praisers of Folly: Erasmus, Rabelais, Shakespeare*. Harvard Studies in Comparative Literature. 25. Cambridge, MA: Harvard UP, 1963. 6, 24, 26, 27-34, 43, 103-04, 144.

The cult of the fool and folly, popularized by Erasmus, and reappearing in different guises in the characters of Rabelais and Shakespeare, developed from the premise the Renaissance "brought the fool into the limelight on the stage of literature," his role representing "humanism on holiday." Erasmus' *Encomium Moriae* was misconstrued by contemporary readers, with the almost solitary exception of More, whose natural affinity with Erasmus was strengthened through their common indebtedness to Lucian. The cult is conceived as a game, based on the premise a fool persisting in folly becomes wise, a reversal of values in which Epicurianism is preferred to Stoicism.

J014 Knafla, Louis. "The Influences of Continental Humanists and Jurists on English Common Law in the Renaissance." *Acta Conventus Neo-Latini Bononiensis*. Proceedings of the Fourth International Congress of Neo-Latin Studies. Bologna, 26 August to 1 September 1979. Ed. R.J. Schoeck. MRTS. 37. Binghamton: MRTS, 1985. 60-71.

Knafla calls More the "greatest humanist lawyer of the period." Other Englishmen with an interest in law, such as John Selden, Thomas Starkey, and even More's sometime opponent Christopher St. German, show his humanist influence in their writings.

J015 Kristeller, Paul Oskar. "Thomas More as a Renaissance Humanist." *Moreana* 65-66 (1980): 5-22.

Kristeller does not claim humanism is the only or even the most important aspect of More's life, but that it constitutes a "significant" aspect of it. He notes More's activities as translator, rhetorician, historian, and moral and political philosopher, especially in *Utopia*. More's Christian humanism comes out not merely in the reservation of major offices in *Utopia* for trained scholars, but in the centrality there of belief in God and the soul's immortality--a rational and religious philosophy in fundamental agreement with Christian religion and Greek philosophy. Kristeller also emphasizes the value of *Richard III* and the *Dialogue of Comfort* and More's continuing importance.

J016 Levin, Harry. *The Myth of the Golden Age in the Renaissance.* Bloomington: Indiana UP, 1969.

Levin's point of departure is the ambiguity common to "myth," "golden age," and "Renaissance." The ancient myth promulgated by writers from Hesiod to Ovid, "buried" by medieval Christendom "under the conception of Eden," reappears in the Renaissance but with new implications. "The ethos of More's *Utopia* is premised upon what Freud would call the pleasure principle"; the fantasy is grounded on Plato and the myth of Atlantis, but quickened through recent authentic accounts of Atlantic voyagers.

J017 Marc'hadour, Germain. "Saint Thomas More et les Auteurs Spirituels." *Moreana* 130 (1997): 27-66.

Marc'hadour looks at the spiritual writers with whom More was familiar and invited his public to read--Hildegard, Bonaventure, Gerson, Hilton, Richard Whitford, some publications about the Carthusians of St. Bruno, and an English translation of Catherine of Siena.

J018 Mesnard, Pierre. "Thomas Morus ou l'Utopie d'un Humaniste." *L'Essor de la philosophie politique au XVIe siècle.* Paris: Boivin & cie, 1936. 141-77.

The theses of this study of sixteenth-century political thought are that idealists, like Erasmus and Postel, are more significant than realists, like Machiavelli, and that valuable theories of sovereignty, state, and international collaboration formulated during this period owe much to jurists like Bodin and Suarez. More is the only English humanist discussed at length, and his writings play an important part in Mesnard's argument. Like Erasmus, More was a Christian humanist, but he was a more concrete, practical thinker, because he was also an Englishman and a jurist. More's nationalism is apparent in his treatment of the problems of enclosure and monarchical power in *Utopia*. Mesnard's praise of *Utopia*, however, is qualified by his opinion of its foreign policy, which he stigmatizes as Machiavellian and cynical. Thus, he places

More as a political thinker between Erasmus and Machiavelli, because he believes More's Christian ideas of justice and social equality are curiously linked to pagan notions of imperialism and state supremacy.

J019 Nugent, Donald Christopher. "Is the Mystery of Thomas More Mystical?" *Moreana* 101-102 (1990): 25-35.

Nugent believes traditional sources as well as contemporary critiques, especially that of Alistair Fox (G027), can inspire a mystical interpretation of More. *The Cloud of Unknowing* may have inspired the very title of *Utopia*; the quality of the life and certainly More's martyrdom are evident; the result may be a broader view of mysticism and a more unified view of More.

J020 Sawada, Paul. "Was More a Utopian or a Realpolitiker?" *Moreana* 91-92 (1986): 21-29.

Sawada believes More was a realist rather than a utopian in the ordinarily accepted sense of the word, yet he was not a realist in the vulgar sense, for "his was a realism not cynical, not relativistic, not opportunistic, never totally immersed in political realities."

J021 Schoeck, R.J. "Common Law and Canon Law in Their Relation to Thomas More." *St. Thomas More: Action and Contemplation*. 15-55.

After describing More's distinguished legal career, Schoeck moves on to the important, complex case of Richard Hunne and the light it sheds on the conflict of common and canon law in early Tudor England. Schoeck believes More did not accept the dominant Commons' view Parliament could solve disputed points of canon law; and, after drawing attention to certain aspects of More's own trial, he concludes More did not question the "organic notion of the two arms of the law" but was a "legal amphibian, who could move and did work within the two systems," and, believing in the necessity of the two systems working together, could not accept subordination of one to the other.

J022 Siegel, Paul N. "English Humanism and the New Tudor Aristocracy." *JHI* 13 (1952): 450-68.

Siegel shows humanist ideas concerning man, society, and the universe arose from their social position and relation to members of the new Tudor aristocracy, who were their principal patrons. Though the application of this assumption may be questionable, the article contains valuable passages on the middle-class origins of leading humanists, their elevation of the monarch in the social hierarchy, their conceptions of the duties of kings and counselors, their interpretation of natural law to justify obedience to the state, the sanctity of private property, and the activities of tradesmen and merchants.

J023 Sowards, J.K. "On Education: More's Debt to Erasmus." *Miscellanea*

Moreana: Essays for Germain Marc'hadour. *Moreana* 100. 103-23.

Mainly through references to their correspondence, Sowards demonstrates the close association between Erasmus' ideas on education and More's educational ideas and practices. "In this area, as in so many others, the two friends who shared 'one soul between...[them],' shared also their convictions about the ideals, the means, and the ends of education."

J024 Surtz, Edward. "John Fisher and the Scholastics." *SP* 55 (1958): 136-53.

A companion study to his "Oxford Reformers and Scholasticism" (J025), Surtz analyzes Fisher's handling of four questions: the single Magdalen, the confutation of Luther, the defense of the king's assertion against "The Babylonian Captivity," and the real presence of Christ's body and blood in the Eucharist. Surtz claims the attitude of Erasmus, More, and Fisher towards Scholasticism is one of qualified approval and varying degrees of compromise. Erasmus is the least sympathetic, More is very active to defend the holy ones (especially Aquinas), while Fisher (who objects strongly to their apparent crudeness and coldness of style) approves of them more than either Erasmus or More.

J025 Surtz, Edward. "Oxford Reformers and Scholasticism." *SP* 47 (1951): 547-56.

A primary objective of the humanists was to mend the divorce between head and heart, intellect and emotions. To achieve this goal, More and other humanists eschewed the philosophy of the Schoolmen and looked to the ancient classics, especially those of Greece, for these works would make a better man in private and public life.

J026 Surtz, Edward. "Thomas More and Communism." *PMLA* 64 (1949): 549-64.

Surtz uses *Letter to a Monk, Responsio ad Lutherum, Dialogue of Comfort*, and *Utopia* to ascertain More's "real attitude" toward communism. Though Surtz believes More thought a Christian communist state was an ideal, he asserts More realized private property was the most practical system for preserving peace and order.

J027 Suzuki, Yoshinori. "The Social Ideas of the Younger More." *Moreana* 83-84 (1984): 61-71.

Suzuki aims to clarify (1) the basic structure of More's thought as expressed in his early writings (except for his political ideas in a strict sense, in which his standpoint is clear), (2) the relationships among the different expressions of More's ideas, and (3) the originality of the social ideas of the younger More.

J028 Suzuki, Yoshinori. "Thomas More's View of Politics as a Profession." *Moreana* 93 (1987): 29-40.

Suzuki defines More's image of the ideal statesman, speculates upon the main reasons he entered royal service, and explores the relationship between his ideal and his attempt to realize it.

J029 Thompson, Craig R. "Erasmian Humanism." *Society and History in the Renaissance.* Washington, D.C.: Folger, Library, 1960. 20-26.

Thompson surveys the many-sided humanism of Erasmus, who "states better than any other the aims and methods of humanistic education." He also recommends reliable reprints of the major works of Colet and Erasmus and further research on both the medieval background to Erasmus' work and on his relation with Colet and More.

J030 Thompson, Craig R. "The Humanism of More Reappraised." *Thought* 52 (1977): 231-48.

For the Renaissance, humanism means study or cultivation of classical letters. For More, moral judgments and religious considerations stem from and enrich classical studies. Humanism must also leave its mark on practical affairs. *Utopia* offers his most inclusive humanistic thought.

J031 Tinkler, John F. "Humanism and Discourse: Studies in the Rhetorical Culture of Renaissance Humanism, Petrarch to Bacon." Diss. Queen's U at Kingston (Can.), 1983.

Tinkler combines Kristeller's definition of humanism (J015) with other approaches to the subject to delineate features that constitute "humanism as a discourse or coherent tradition of writings." His premise is humanists regarded themselves as disciplinary colleagues of the ancients whose writings formed the paradigm for their discourse, and that they carried on the methods and concerns of classical rhetorical culture for their times. He isolates characteristics that fit his definition in Petrarch, Valla, Erasmus, Machiavelli, More, and Bacon.

J032 Trevor-Roper, Hugh. "The Intellectual World of Thomas More." *ASch* 48 (1978-79): 19-32.

Trevor-Roper looks at More in his own intellectual context to identify the tradition to which More attached himself and to watch the formation of his mind. Because this cannot be done from purely biographical evidence, Trevor-Roper relies largely on deduction, implication, and association to chart the influence of Erasmus; the humanists Grocyn, Linacre, and Colet; Greek studies, Plato and the Platonists upon More and his works.

J033 Weinberg, Carole. "Thomas More and the Use of English in Early

Tudor Education." *Moreana* 59-60 (1978): 21-30.

Weinberg notes More's regard for and fluency in the English language and suggests the influence of teachers at Magdalen College School.

J034 Wooden, Warren W. "The Topos of Childhood in Marian England." *JMRS* 12 (1982): 179-94.

The educational theories of More, Erasmus, and Vives constitute one element in the renewed interest "on the child as creature and symbol" during the time of Cardinal Pole who labored during Queen Mary's reign to bring the English back to Catholicism.

Language and Style

K001 Crane, Mary Thomas. "Proverbial and Aphoristic Sayings: Sources of Authority in the English Renaissance." Diss. Harvard U, 1986.

Crane examines rhetorical texts, biblical exegesis, and educational treatises from Aristotle to Bacon to trace the ways they provide sources of authority in speech and writing, and then discusses their use in the development of sententious epigrams and lyrics by More, Wyatt, Jonson, and Herrick.

K002 Deakins, Roger. "The Tudor Prose Dialogue: Genre and Anti-Genre." *SEL* 20 (1980): 5-23.

Deakin shows how many extant Tudor dialogues, including *Utopia*, embody theories about the form current in Tudor England. Rudolf Agricola's *De Inventione Dialectica* (1515) is critical for sixteenth-century dialogue theory, in simplifying the Scholastics' elaborate logical machinery and placing more emphasis on the importance of effective persuasion than on correct argument. The characteristics of the true "genre" dialogue are presented in Carlo Sigonio's *De Dialogo* (1561); Deakin finds only five sixteenth-century English genre-dialogues, by More, Elyot, Starkey, Ellis Heywood, and Buchanan. Thus, Book I of *Utopia* is the "vestibule," establishing the "real" characters and situation, Book II, the "contention," where general propositions are debated; the "characterizations" of More and Raphael derive not from More's personal situation, but from literary requirements. The remaining 220-odd Tudor dialogues are "anti-genre."

K003 Doyle-Davidson, W.A.G. "The Earlier English Works of Sir Thomas More." *ES* 17 (1935): 49-70.

Doyle-Davidson analyzes More's style in *Pico, Richard III, Four Last Things*, and his early poems, and concludes More's style provides the bridge between Old English writers and those of the early Elizabethan age without "whom Shakespeare and Spenser would seem to have emerged almost as a phenomenon without previous backgrounds or traditions in English letters." (Rpt. in *Essential Articles for the Study of Thomas More*, 356-74.)

K004 Gordon, Walter M. "The Platonic Dramaturgy of Thomas More's Dialogues." *JMRS* 8 (1978): 193-215.

Gordon notices, through a contrast of More's dialogues with those of Plato and Lucian, that *Utopia*, *Dialogue Concerning Heresies*, and *Dialogue of Comfort* in particular are endowed with carefully sustained, internal conflicts that convey the dramatic force and essence of More's works.

K005 Haynes, Robert William. "The Dramaturgy of the Early Tudor Dialogue." Diss. U of Georgia, 1991.

Haynes examines dramaturgic techniques used in More's *Utopia*, Starkey's *Dialogue*, Elyot's *Of the Knowledge which Maketh a Wise Man*, and Lupset's *A Treatise of Charitie*--all of which are discussed as dialogues. Classical dialogues contributing to Renaissance humanists' conception of this genre are also discussed in detail.

K006 Kinney, Arthur F. *Humanist Poetics: Thought, Rhetoric, and Fiction in Sixteenth-Century England.* Amherst: U of Massachusetts P, 1986.

Kinney provides an encyclopedic discussion of the nature and application of rhetorical strategies in sixteenth-century England. Illustrating this overview with close readings from More, Erasmus, Lyly, Greene, Sidney, Nashe, and Lodge, Kinney suggests a rhetorical perspective whereby the art of speech and persuasion ultimately leads to writing fiction. Such fictions must be read in a sort of triangular interaction: the text is read against a prototype; then it is read outward against the reader's own experience (which may explain why most humanist fiction that still participates in a predominantly religious frame of reference functions as a collection of *exempla*). A good example is the network established among readers, Morus and Hythlodaeus in *Utopia*, in which, as Greenblatt has noted in *Renaissance Self-Fashioning* (G037), the two characters are two aspects of the authorial personality, and the reader is called up to determine the weight of their respective discourses.

K007 Lakowski, Romuald Ian. "Sir Thomas More and the Art of Dialogue." Diss. U of British Columbia (Can.), 1993.

Lakowski analyzes *Richard III*, "Dialogue of Counsel" in Book I of *Utopia*, *Dialogue Concerning Heresies*, and *Dialogue of Comfort* for the highly coherent, tightly organized, "deep structures" beneath the "often apparently rambling," digressive surface of each to trace More's development as a writer using the dialogue form.

K008 Marc'hadour, Germain. "Here I Sit: Thomas More's Genius for Dialogue." *Thomas More: Essays on the Icon.* 9-42.

Marc'hadour analyzes More's development as a writer of dialogues by referring to *Utopia, Dialogue Concerning Heresies,* and *Dialogue of Comfort,* each of which demonstrates More's "genius for dialogue" in its own way. These literary dialogues are conversations reported and stylized, and with More, conversation was an art to be possessed, a skill to be developed, a gift to be enjoyed and used.

K009 Marc'hadour, Germain. "Thomas More: De la conversation au dialogue." *Le Dialogue au temps de la Renaissance.* Ed. M.T. Jones-Davies. Paris: Touzot, 1984. 35-57.

Marc'hadour relates More's use of the dialogue form to his love of conversation. Concentrating on More's directness, he notes More's simple speech-indications in *Utopia* and *Dialogue Concerning Heresies* and the quasi-dramatic script presentation of the speakers in the *Dialogue of Comfort.*

K010 McCutcheon, R.R. "Thomas More and the Limits of Dialogue." Diss. Stanford U, 1991.

McCutcheon examines two problems the choice of a literary genre--dialogue--poses for an "orthodox Christian and Renaissance humanist" like More: (1) traditional academic dialogue would imply Christian truth a matter of reason rather than revelation to be arrived at by careful dialectic; (2) the dialogue would seem to concede some legitimacy to the opposition.

K011 Ong, Walter. "Latin Language Study as a Renaissance Puberty Rite." *SP* 56 (1959): 103-34.

Ong singles out patterns in the Renaissance teaching of Latin as echoes of "what anthropologists, treating of more primitive peoples, call puberty rites." He shows the embarrassment of Erasmus, More, and Ascham who wished to rear youngsters at home and in the proper use of the Latin language, and he discusses the close relationship between flogging and this kind of Latin teaching. Ong then connects the association of violence with teaching Latin, and the teachers' hopes of developing courage in their pupils, along with the Renaissance cult of glory.

K012 Ong, Walter J. "Oral Residue in Tudor Prose Style." *PMLA* 80 (1965): 145-54.

Tudor prose contains a larger concentration of oral residue than one can find in any other period. This use of essentially oratorical rather than written rhetorical devices was caused by the humanists' emphasis on oral rather than written speech. The use of formulas, commonplaces, adages, synonyms, and episodic style is widespread in writers extending from the time of Erasmus and

More to that of John Lyly. More's *Richard III* exemplifies these characteristics.

K013 Raumolin-Brunberg, Helena. "The Noun Phrase in Early Sixteenth-Century English: A Study Based on Sir Thomas More's Writings." Diss. Helsingin Yliopisto (Finland), 1991.

Raumolin-Brunberg uses 2,651 "noun phrase structures" collected from More's writings to make an inventory of such phrases at the beginning of the Early Modern period and discover which "linguistic and extralinguistic factors covary with different structures."

K014 Rydén, Mats. *Relative Constructions in Early Sixteenth-Century English, With Special Reference of Syr Thomas Elyot.* Acta Universitatis Upsaliensis. Studia Anglistica Upsaliensia. 3. Uppsala: Almquist and Wiksell, 1966.

This work stems from the postulates Elyot is a "fairly true exponent of the literary language of his time" in respect to both his original works and translations, and that his position in the evolution of English justifies systematic study of his linguistic usage. Besides Elyot's works, texts referred to include those of Lord Berners, More, Fisher, Tyndale, Cavendish, and Ascham. This close, erudite analysis is useful in supplying statistical data on a basic element in Elizabethan literary English.

K015 Schoeck, R.J. "More, the Devil, and Cardinal Morton: A Note on Sixteenth-Century Names Devices." *N&Q* ns 1 (1954): 193-94.

Schoeck calls attention to puns in general during the Renaissance and in particular to those More made with Morton's name--"mor," "tun," and "morus." More used another pun on Erasmus' name, and his use of this device reveals much about his sense of humor.

K016 Sodeman, Nancy Ruthford. "More's Use of Amplification in Two Dialogues." Diss. Georgia State U, 1976.

Sodeman shows rhetorical devices of amplification strengthen arguments in *Dialogue Concerning Heresies* and *Dialogue of Comfort* by their use in fallacies, topics of arguments, and figures, such as schemes, tropes, figures of thought.

K017 Sullivan, M. Rosenda. "The Cursus in the Prose of St. Thomas More." Diss. Catholic U of America, 1943.

Sullivan studies the terminal prose rhythms of More's English writings and bases her analysis on ten-thousand syllable groups from his earliest to latest works. The cadence, cursus, or falling inflection before the pause is listed and charted, and Sullivan discovers the cursus occurs more often in his literary works than it does in his ascetical writings.

LANGUAGE AND STYLE

K018 Sylvester, R.S. "Keynote Address of 22 June 1978 at the Thomas More Conference, Georgetown University, Washington, D.C.: 'Thomas More and His Age.'" *Moreana* 62 (1979): 95-103.

Sylvester divides More's style into three types--rational mildly tempered discourse that is humanistic, balanced, detached, "self-analytic at the same time it struggles to maintain its experimental qualities"; declamation; and polemic.

K019 Sylvester, R.S. "Three Dialogues." *Moreana* 64 (1980): 65-78.

Sylvester reviews More's progress in dealing with the dramatization of the conflict of ideas, through discussions of *Utopia, Dialogues Concerning Heresies,* and *Dialogue of Comfort*, in which he considers structure, the dialogic method, and self-presentation. *Dialogue of Comfort* is seen as the most finished of More's works, enshrining his deepest thoughts.

K020 Visser, F. Th. *A Syntax of the English Language of St. Thomas More.* 3 vols. Materials for the Study of Old English Drama. Ser. 2. Vols. 19, 24, 26. 1946-56. Rpt. Vaduz: Kraus reprint, 1963.

Visser's study of the meaning and function of verbs in More's English Works points up the vitality and energy of his vernacular style as compared to that of earlier and later writers. An introduction assesses More's stature as an English prose stylist and defines the book's scope.

K021 Wilson, K.J. "Thomas More: The Transformation of Dialogue." *Incomplete Fictions: The Formation of English Renaissance Dialogue.* Washington, D.C.: Catholic U of America P, 1985. 137-75.

The thesis of Wilson's study, that the Tudor dialogue evolved into a mode for the imitation of the interior world of thought and emotion, is illustrated by the transformed relationship between the *Dialogue Concerning Heresies* and *Dialogue of Comfort*: both control "abominable thoughts"--heresy by means of dialectic and reason, fear and temptation by means of meditation and faith. Wilson also discusses the uses of dialogue in *Utopia*.

K022 Young, Archibald Morrison. "Thomas More and the Humanist Dialogue." Diss. U of Toronto, 1973.

Young contends the creation of a suitable rhetorical form for dialogue was "one of the most conspicuous features" of More's entire literary career, and that to understand More's humanist dialogue readers must examine his philosophical and theological interests, public pursuits, and private attitudes. Young compares works by both Erasmus and More to demonstrate his thesis.

Use of Classical and Christian Sources

L001   Baumann, Uwe. *Die Antike in den Epigrammen und Briefen Sir Thomas Mores*. Beiträge zur englischen und amerikanischen Literatur. Vol. 1. Paderborn: Ferdinand Schöningh, 1984.

Baumann examines the relation of the epigrams and letters to classical texts. The poems and letters do not form one unified corpus, nor are they bound to each other by falling within one thematic division of More's works--devotional, humanistic, polemical, and so on. But the very disparity of these works, with little in common except their authorship, furnishes a sort of portfolio of More in various guises, so Baumann's account of the role of the classics in these texts shows something of how More regarded the classics throughout his career.

L002   Baumann, Uwe. "Thomas More and the Classical Tyrant." *Moreana* 86 (1985): 108-27.

Baumann uses the etymology of the word "tyrant" and the characteristics of the classical tyrant figure to illustrate the fundamental qualities of the tyrant images in *Epigrammata, Utopia,* and *Richard III*. He concludes that, like most of his contemporaries, More (especially in *Richard III*) based his notion of the tyrant on what he found in classical literature.

L003   Bradshaw, David. "St. Maximus and Thomas More." *Moreana* 89 (1986): 14.

Bradshaw notes the surprising similarities of thought between More and Maximus.

L004   Chomarat, Jacques. "More, Erasme et les Historiens Latins." *Moreana* 86 (1985): 71-105.

With great detail, Chomarat compares More's historiography to that of

Erasmus and explores their piecemeal use of Roman historians, especially Livy, Sallust, Herodotus, Plutarch, and others.

L005 Condren, Conal, and A.C. Condren. "More and Sokrates: The Limits of Comparison and Symbolic Potency." *Thomas More: Essays on the Icon.* 109-29.

The authors tread a path between two extremes--at one, comparisons may easily enough become too general to have any substance; at the other, by a covert process of translation, one can easily present as a specific and direct point of comparison that which has been prejudiced or even manufactured by the terms they choose to use. They concentrate on similarities between the political attitudes, moral absolutism, and meanings and issues of their deaths, and conclude a synthesis of Socrates and More would produce a figure of the potency of Christ, in whose shadow, in their different ways, both stand, for both share the same supreme sacrifice.

L006 Coogan, Robert. "Petrarch and More's Conception of Fortune." *Italica* 46 (1969): 167-75.

Coogan demonstrates correspondences between Petrarch's *De Remediis* and passages in More, noting in both the humanistic sense of capricious fortune as contrasted with the Dantesque acceptance of fortune, the "Lord's handmaid," and believes Petrarch may have provided More with historical allusions, like the account of Hastings' death in *Richard III* or Hythloday's description in *Utopia*.

L007 Duncan, Douglas. "More." *Ben Jonson and the Lucianic Tradition.* Cambridge: Cambridge UP, 1979. 52-76.

Duncan investigates the ludic method of *Utopia* and other works and events in More's life that partake of the Lucianic spirit.

L008 Gordon, Walter M. "The Ominous Play of Children: Thomas More's Adaptation of an Image from Antiquity." *JWCI* 47 (1984): 204-05.

Gordon explores the image of the serious reference to the adult world in children's play in *Richard III* and *Dialogue of Comfort* and determines Plutarch "was most probably More's source."

L009 Harbison, E. Harris. "The Intellectual as Social Reformer: Machiavelli and Thomas More." *Rice Institute Pamphlets* 44 (1957): iii, 1-46.

Harbison credits the two men with inaugurating modern political thinking in a period of immense social change, but stresses the inherent conflict between More, the moralist, and Machiavelli, the realist.

L010 Jarrott, Catherine. "Erasmus's *In Principio erat sermo:* A Controversial Translation." *SP* 61 (1964): 35-40.

Jarrott examines Erasmus' rendering of *logos* at the beginning of St. John's Gospel, as *sermo*, in preferences to the orthodox *verbum*. Jarrott relates this idea to the humanists' faith in the power of speech and oratory as not merely an art but a habit of mind, a Ciceronian notion basic to the educational systems of both Erasmus and Colet and illustrated in More's use of the dialogue.

L011 Marc'hadour, Germain. *The Bible in the Works of St. Thomas More.* 5 vols. Nieuwkoop: B. de Graaf, 1969-72.

The first three volumes catalogue More's translating and paraphrasing of Scripture; the final two provide informal, discursive treatment of More's spirituality and uses of the Bible. Designed as a "reference book, a repertory, and something of a concordance," they are a useful appendage to *Thomas More et la Bible* (L015). They compile biblical references in More's writings, classified in the order of biblical books, chapters, and verses. Comments, where necessary, as particularly in connection with the controversial works, show the relevance of each reference to its context, and brief introductions to the sections on the Pentateuch and Psalter are included for those who may wish to do similar research in connection with other Scriptural texts.

L012 Marc'hadour, Germain. "Saint Basil and Thomas More." *Moreana* 111-112 (1992): 43-54.

Basil the Great, Bishop of Cesaraea, is far less present in More's work than Augustine, Jerome, and Gregory the Great. His *Opera Omnia* were not available in the Greek original until 1532, when Erasmus published them in Basel, and that was only three years before More's execution. The Cappadocian father and educator put the humanist movement in his debt through a most influential essay urging Christian students not to shun the commerce of pagan classics. For special recommendation, Basil singles out the historians, orators, and poets, and these are precisely the writers More twice--in Latin (1518) and in English (1529)--lists as most suited for the knowledge of man and the ripening of judgment. More, being a jurist, adds the study of law.

L013 Marc'hadour, Germain. "Saint Jérôme dans l'oeuvre et dans l'univers de Thomas More." *Moreana* 101-102 (1990): 93-124.

Marc'hadour traces the influences of St. Jerome upon More's works.

L014 Marc'hadour, Germain. "Saint Thomas More (1477-1535) and Saint Francis of Assisi (1182-1226)." *Cithara* 25 (1985): 5-18.

Despite their surface differences, the two saints are very similar in their spirituality. More began his career in the "most Franciscan school in Christendom," dedicated his first book, *The Life of John Picus*, to a "Poor Clare" and thus to the "second Order of St. Francis," based his commonwealth in *Utopia* on the Franciscan monastic ideal of shared Christian "gladness and simplicity," and was remembered in Elizabethan London as "the best friend that the poor e'er had." Like St. Francis, More was a crusader "marked by the cross" who died gladly "in" and "for" the faith of the Catholic Church.

L015 Marc'hadour, Germain. *Thomas More et la Bible: La place des livres dans son apologétique et sa spiritualité.* Paris: Vrin, 1969.

This study supplements *L'Univers de Thomas More* (F174), the man of his age, by tracing the influence of the Bible in More's spiritual life as revealed in his works. Three chapters are devoted to an account of More's career as scholar, humanist, statesman, and martyr; an extensive middle section to his use of the Bible in controversial and devotional works; four chapters to biblical books and characters that appear to have attracted More's particular attention and devotion; and, in conclusion, a commentary on his attitude towards the dichotomy of Scripture and tradition. Copious examples, systematically assembled, of citation and reminiscence from the Vulgate throughout More's writings show the impact upon More's spiritual being both of the original texts and uses made of them as sources of tales, proverbs, adages, and imagery by Schoolmen, poets, homilists, and preachers. Marc'hadour also assesses More's achievement as biblical scholar and exegete, comparing his renderings of Scripture with his *Life of Pico* and version of Lucian's *Dialogues*, and attributing the permanence of his vernacular prose style to the fact it is "nourished simultaneously by the Bible and the classics."

L016 Marc'hadour, Germain. "Virgile dans l'Angleterre de Thomas More." *Presence de Virgile.* Ed. R. Chevallier. Paris: Belles Lettres, 1978. 305-12.

Marc'hadour discusses the regard with which Virgil's works were held in England during More's life.

L017 Massaut, Jean Pierre. "L'humanisme chretienne et la Bible: le cas de Thomas More." *RHE* 57 (1972): 92-112.

Massaut examines More's treatment of the Bible, especially his use of sections about Christ's Passion. He also discusses the works of other scholars interested in More and the Bible, such as Marc'hadour (L011, L015).

L018 Mercanti, G.C. "More's Gay Genius." *Moreana* 4 (1964): 104-07.

More knew the tales of Poggio Bracciolini, but More's humor is never solely erotic as Bracciolini's is, because decorum always guides More.

L019 Miller, Clarence H. "More and MS Palatine 23 of the Greek Anthology." *Moreana* 98-99 (1988): 263-64.

Miller believes that, although scholars should be grateful for Alan

Cameron's thorough, learned, and lucid investigation of More's connection with MS Palatine (N004), Cameron would probably be the first to admit it is clearly possible, perhaps probable, but uncertain More ever owned it.

L020 Patrides, C.A. "Erasmus and More: Dialogues with Reality." *KR* ns 8 (1986): 34-48.

Patrides notes More and Erasmus' familiarity with Lucian's playfulness; points to differences in the spirit of More and Erasmus' dialogues; and traces More's qualified use of Lucian's playful spirit in *Utopia*, its loss in the polemical works, and its "recovery" in the "highly praised *Dialogue of Comfort*."

L021 Phillips, Margaret Mann. *The Adages of Erasmus: A Study with Translations*. Cambridge: Cambridge UP, 1964.

Phillips examines the *Adages* in an introductory essay on their background, content, and growth; followed by examples in translation from each of the principal editions and appendices of references to Christianity, lists of contemporaries mentioned, and analyses of sources. Of all Erasmus' works, apart from the New Testament translation, the *Adages* has the most association with England. This contact is most clearly indicated in the "Utopian" edition of 1515, which includes "all the main topics," such as attacks on tyranny, satire on courts and courtiers, condemnation of war, praise of agricultural workers, and defense of elective rule. Thus, "the essential idea of *Utopia*, community of wealth, stands at the head of the *Adages*."

L022 Ryan, Francis X. "Sir Thomas More's Use of Chaucer." *SEL* 35 (1995): 1-17.

Ryan inspects Chaucerian elements in More's canon to show he makes fifteen references to *Canterbury Tales*, three to *Troilus and Criseyde*, one to *An ABC*, and probably one to *Parliament of Fowles*. He adopts the *Clerk's Tale* as a subtext to his portraits of Elizabeth Woodville and Mistress Shore in *Richard III*.

L023 Schmidt, Mary T. "S. Augustine's Influence on S. Thomas More's English Works." Diss. Yale U, 1943.

Schmidt shows how, throughout his English Works, no other author is cited so frequently nor with such consistent admiration as "the noble doctor and glorious confessor," St. Augustine.

L024 Schoeck, R.J. "The 'Cronica Cronicarum' of Sir Thomas More and Tudor Historians." *Bul. Inst. Hist. Research* 35 (1963): 84-86.

In a letter to Frith, More refers to "Cronica Cronicarum" as his authority. Schoeck attempts to identify this work as Fabyan's history, a chronicle Polydore Vergil used.

L025 Schoeck, R.J. "More's Attic Nights: Sir Thomas More's Use of Aulus Gellius' 'Noctes Atticae.'" *RN* 13 (1960): 127-29.

Schoeck cites passages from *Richard III* and *Debellation* which suggest More may have been familiar with "Noctes Atticae."

L026 Sowards, J.K. "Thomas More and the Friendship of Erasmus, 1499-1517: A Study in Northern Humanism." Diss. U of Michigan, 1952.

Sowards examines Erasmus' influence upon More during the years their association was "most intimate," studies More's humanist ideas and works with a "humanistic character," and concludes Erasmus "exerted a constant and profound influence" upon More's development as a humanist. Particularly evident is More's debt to Erasmus in *Utopia*.

English Poems

M001 Coogan, Robert. "Petrarch and Thomas More." *Moreana* 21 (1969): 19-30.

Coogan believes More's pageant verses have a Petrarchan flavor; ponders how, where, and by whom More was exposed to Petrarch; and compares More and Petrarch's poems, especially those concerned with true honor and nobility and fortune. He also examines the humanist ideals shared by Petrarch, Pico, and More.

M002 Coogan, Robert. "Petrarch's *Trionfi* and the English Renaissance." *SP* 67 (1970): 306-27.

Two factors contributed to the popularity of the *Trionfi* in Tudor England: on one hand, Petrarch's role throughout the series as a moralist, the motif of *contemptus mundi* finding a responsive echo in English Stoicism; on the other, the association in the *Trionfi* of poetry with emblematic imagery. More is cited as possibly the first to imitate the *Trionfi*, an influence clearly evident in More's pageant verse on the ages of man.

M003 Cousins, A.C. "St. Thomas More as English Poet." *Thomas More: Essays on the Icon*. 43-52.

Cousins delineates the English poems as not only essential to an introduction to the concerns of the prose writings, but also as proof More wrote a "small but highly sophisticated collection of poems...[that] sums up a tradition of writing and does something entirely new at the same time." The themes of Fortune and the precarious nature of order and the poems' use of rime royal support the view More deserves a place of some importance as an early Tudor poet.

M004 Cousins, A.D. "More and the Refiguring of Stoicism: The Prefatory

Poems to *The Boke of Fortune*." *Moreana* 115-116 (1993): 19-32.

The three longest of More's prefatory poems to *The Boke of Fortune* make up the main body of his English poems. Expressing a refigured rather than a merely iterated Stoicism, they unorthodoxly develop ideas central to Boethius' *Consolation of Philosophy*. Thus, they indicate something of the relations between More's writings and those of the Stoics. They also prefigure the way in which More's personae are created.

M005 Duffy, Robert A. "Thomas More's 'Nine Pageants.'" *Moreana* 50 (1976): 15-32.

Duffy examines the "Nine Pageants" to illustrate the character and skill of More's dramatic and irony technique, by which means More draws "his audience further into a complex commixture of aesthetic delight and moral instruction." Having outlined the principal features of the influence of Petrarch's *Trionfi* and *De Remediis* on the themes and structure of More's work, Duffy argues for the influence of Horace's *Ars Poetica*. From direct influences, he passes on to some conjectural and indirect ones arising from certain features of public pageantry and argues that "The tradition of early Tudor pageantry...offers rich possibilities of source study." He closes with the observation that the poem "deserves more attentive regard than it has so far received."

M006 Edwards, A.S.G. "Middle English *Pageant* 'Picture'?" *N&Q* ns 39.1 (Mar. 1992): 25-26.

Edwards believes More's use of the word *pageauntes* (in connection with a forthcoming edition of his English poems) may have been synonymous with "picture" or "illustration."

M007 Howorth, R.G. "Hopkins and Sir Thomas More." *N&Q* 92 (1949): 389.

This note points out that the "original" for the last three lines in More's short address to Fortune is Psalm 107, 28-30.

M008 Kozikowski, Stanley J. "Lydgate, Machiavelli, More and Skelton's *Bowge of Courte*." *AN&Q* 15 (1977): 66-67.

Kozikowski points out that the image of Fortune followed by a train of personifications occurs not only in Skelton's poem but also in Lydgate's *Mumming at London*, Machiavelli's *Capitolo di Fortuna*, and More's "Fortune." All the poems use Skelton's style, and both More and Skelton use the image to enliven the arbitrary nature of worldly favor.

M009 McCutcheon, Elizabeth. "Number Symbolism in St. Thomas More's 'Pageant Verses.'" *Moreana* 70 (1981): 29-32.

McCutcheon notes how in More's nine "Pageant Verses" seven seven-lined stanzas (each on its respective quality or condition) are followed by an eighth eight-lined stanza, on Eternity, and links this with the number symbolism (that in fact predates the Middle Ages--to be found in Mark's Gospel, for example) by which eight after seven signifies eternity (and renewal and regeneration) after mutability.

M010   Pyle, Fitzroy. "Sir Thomas More's Verse Rhythms." *TLS* 30 Jan. 1937: 76.
Pyle provides examples of More's verse and maintains More had mastery of verse rhythms and meters far superior to many of his contemporaries. (Rpt. in *Essential Articles for the Study of Thomas More*, 432-35.)

M011   Schoeck, R.J. "More, Sallust, and Fortune." *Moreana* 65 (1980): 107-10.
Schoeck notes the significance of the Sallustian motto on Fortune found in the lawyer's ring of Sir John Fineux and the connections between Fineux and More. More read Sallust, used that reading in his own writing, and had thought much about Fortune, especially in his youth, as his English verses reveal.

M012   Schulte-Herbrüggen, Hubertus. "Sir Thomas More's Fortuna-Verse." *Lebende Antike Symposion for Rudolf Sühnel*. Eds. Horst Meller, and Hans-Joachim Zimmerman. Berlin: Erich Schmidt Verlag, 1967. 155-72.
Schulte-Herbrüggen relates More's lines on Fortune to other Renaissance treatments of that theme and uses 1503 as their date of composition.

M013   Tromly, Frederic B. "'A Ruful Lamentacion' of Elizabeth: Thomas More's Transformation of Didactic Lament." *Moreana* 53 (1977): 45-56.
Tromly suggests More, by means of dramatizing the speaking voice (speaking as from the tomb) of the dead Elizabeth York, Henry VII's queen, extends the didactic convention of contemporary elegies, so that the poem transforms *contemptus mundi* themes into an elegy that combines pathos with an implicit celebration of the subject's virtue, producing an exhortation not merely to die well, but to live well. Tromly believes this poem marks the beginning of new approaches to writing such elegies.

M014   Willow, Mary Edith. *An Analysis of the English Poems of St. Thomas More*. Bibliotheca Humanistica & Reformatorica. 8. Nieuwkoop: DeGraaf, 1974.
Willow's prosodic and thematic analysis of More's English poems stresses his poetic skills, predominant use of rime royal, and other medieval features in his twelve English poems that total less than 1,500 lines, and investigates each poem's subject, theme, technique, sound, tone, imagery, sources, and

biographical references. Although she claims all his English poetry is excellent, she regards the three poems on Fortune as his most successful. In the final chapter, she surveys More's status as a poet, the popularity of his English poems during his lifetime, and the influences seen in his English poems. She also categorizes the themes of More's English poems into four groups, mentions poems and interludes attributed to More, and analyzes More's "A Godly Meditation" as a "fitting finale" to his poetic achievements.

Latin Poems

N001 Blanchard, André. "Epigrammes de Thomas More dans une Anthologie de 1539." *Moreana* 50 (1976): 66-72.
This article thoroughly discusses over thirty of More's epigrams.

N002 Bradner, Leicester. "More's Epigrams on Death." *Moreana* 50 (1976): 33-36.
Despite More's reputation as a wit, his poems on death reveal a seriousness in his *Epigrammata*. More's translations from the Greek Anthology, dealing with the theme of death liberating people from slavery, poverty, diseases, or fear of the future, introduce the idea of death that informs his other poems on death. In Epigram 243, death liberates people from future pain; in 101, it liberates and avenges the oppressed. The only epigram More does not use death for rather grim satire is on the death of his first wife Jane; death becomes a "gift giver," bestowing what "life could not."

N003 Callahan, Virginia Woods. "Uses of the Planudean Anthology: Thomas More and Andrea Alciati." *Acta Conventus Neo-Latini Bononiensis*. Proceedings of the Fourth International Congress of Neo-Latin Studies. Bologna, 26 August to 1 September 1979. Ed. R.J. Schoeck. MRTS. 37. Binghamton: MRTS, 1985. 399-412.
Callahan examines the two authors' treatment of two themes from the *Planudean Anthology* in their poems: the reciprocal aid of the blind and lame and Lais' dedication of her mirror to Aphrodite.

N004 Cameron, Alan. "Sir Thomas More and the Greek Anthology." *Florilegium Columbianum: Essays in Honor of Paul Oskar Kristeller*. Eds. Karl-Ludwig Selig, Robert Somerville, Gillian Lindt. New York: Italica, 1987. 187-98.

Cameron details the history of the major source of More's epigrams, the Greek Anthology (*Planudean Anthology*), and postulates More may have owned a copy.

N005 Carlson, David R. "Formal Translation: Thomas More's Epigrams before and after 1518." *English Humanist Books: Writers and Patrons, Manuscript and Print, 1475-1525*. Toronto: U of Toronto P, 1993. 142-62.

The history of More's epigrams and their transformation into the *Epigrammata* confirm modes of publication were themselves meaningful in historically predetermined ways, and these poems offer striking instances of alteration of meaning as they move from one bibliographical context to another.

N006 Carlson, David R. "Reputation and Duplicity: The Texts and Contexts of Thomas More's Epigram on Bernard André." *ELH* 58 (1991): 261-81.

Carlson provides a detailed history of the 1518 publication of More's collected *Epigrammata* and focuses upon the titles and placement of the epigram on André's *Hymni Christiani* (1517) to illustrate how the poem is a "masterly bit of measured, irreproachable ambiguity" characterized by an intent to deceive--to pass off as praise something that also castigates. Carlson uses this episode and others to understand the state of literary institutions in early Tudor England, in which it was necessary to cultivate reputation, even when that was contrary to humanist notions of learned disinterest, even when that was duplicitous or deceptive.

N007 Carpenter, Nan C. "Note on Two Epigrams of More." *Moreana* 50 (1976): 11-12.

Carpenter focuses on More's Epigram 64, "A Jesting Poem to a Faithless Mistress," and Epigram 115, "Joke About a Helpful Fellow."

N008 Carpenter, Nan C. "Thomas More and Music: Stanyhurst's Translation of the Abyngdon Epitaph." *Moreana* 62 (1979): 63-68.

Carpenter discusses More's epigrams concerned with music, adding Richard Stanyhurst's translation, in leonine hexameters, of More's jocose epitaph on Henry Abyngdon.

N009 Carpenter, Nan C. "St. Thomas More and Music: The Epigrams." *RQ* 30 (1977): 24-28.

Carpenter discusses three of More's epigrams paying tribute to musician Henry Abyngdon and musical allusions and sources for some other epigrams.

N010 Day, R. Morris. "Sir Thomas More and the Defense of the Royal Navy." *Personalities and Policies: Essays on English and European History Presented in Honor of Dr. Marguerite Potter*. Ed. E. Deanne Malpass. Fort

Worth, TX: Texas Christian UP, 1977. 1-12.

Day describes the incidents behind the controversy of More and Brixius on the subject of the ship *Cordeliere*. In the heat of the war, and it grew even hotter in 1513, More, then undersheriff of London, his ability as a lawyer already established and his literary and political stars on the rise, replied to Brixius' poem (about a French/English battle in the War of the Holy League) in a series of Latin epigrams. Day shows how More's attack was no more just than Brixius' rendering of history.

N011 Dean, William. "Kendall's Translation of a Morean Epigram." *Moreana* 101-102 (1990): 139-45.

The first translation of More's epigrams into English is generally credited to Timothe Kendall in 1577, but the fact at least one of his versions is almost identical to that of James Sanford, published in 1569, raises the probability he improved already existing translations rather than produce his own.

N012 De Graaf, Bob. "Thomas More in a German Best-Seller (1600-1643): A Noteworthy Moreanum." *Moreana* 45 (1975): 29-36.

A Latin collection in two volumes, by Dyonisius Melander and his son Otto, printed in stages by German printers, under the title *Jocoseria* (a mixture of serious and jocular) includes 55 of More's epigrams and an excerpt from Calvin's Isaiah Commentary comparing More to Shebna.

N013 Doyle, Charles Clay. "The Background of More's Epigrams." *Moreana* 55-56 (1977): 61-64.

Doyle discusses the Aesopic background of More's epigrams, relating them to versions in de Vitry's *Exempla*, Gobius' *Scala Celi*, and the *Mensa Philosophica*. As he indicates, these Aesopic fables were the common property of sixteenth-century Europe.

N014 Doyle, Charles Clay. "Bourbon's *Nugae* and More's *Epigrammata*." *Moreana* 123-124 (1995): 3-12.

Of the 1300 Latin epigrams by Nicolas Bourbon the Elder (c. 1500-c. 1550), eight translate, adapt, or bear close relationships to More's epigrams.

N015 Doyle, Charles Clay. "More's Epigrams in the Sixteenth and Seventeenth Centuries: A Supplement to *CW* 3/II." *Moreana* 117 (1994): 85-94.

In the standard modern edition of More's *Latin Poems* (B013), Appendix D lists "Reprints, Translations, and Adaptations of More's Latin Poems in the Sixteenth and Seventeenth Centuries." Doyle supplements the 184 publications cited there, adding twenty-two new ones, as well as making addenda to six previously listed.

N016 Doyle, Charles Clay. "On Neglected Sources of Some Epigrams by Thomas More." *Moreana* 46 (1975): 5-11.

The source of Epigram 221 is a widely known Renaissance jest, a version of which is found in Bebel's *Facetiae*; the source of Epigram 206 is an Aesopic narrative. Epigrams 43 and 44, which describe a prophetic and preoccupied astrologer ignorant of his own cuckolding, are analogous to an Aesopic story depicting the robbery of a soothsayer's home. Though no "close counterpart in Aesop's fables" to Epigram 162 is known, there is an interesting analogue--actually a partial inversion of the situation which More presents in the Aesopic chorus, where, as in the epigram, a "fox triumphs with a verbal retort."

N017 Doyle, Charles Clay. "The Popular Aspects of Sir Thomas More's Latin Epigrams." *Southern Folklore Quarterly* 37 (1973): 87-89.

Doyle demonstrates how several of More's epigrams "overlap the realm of popular literature" despite the form's apparent failure to accord with traditional notions of folk literature. Doyle's main concern is with those epigrams which are versified jests, "miniature narratives involving some humorous situation, act, or repartee," of which Doyle provides an entertaining selection of examples, indicating the recognized motifs of folk literature present. Even when More translates from Greek and Latin, he has a fondness for jests of a popular kind. The fact many of More's epigrams found their way later into jestbooks suggests they possessed an essentially popular quality.

N018 Dust, Philip. "Thomas More's Influence on Erasmus' Epigram against Julius II." *Moreana* 65-66 (1980): 99-106.

Dust believes Erasmus was thinking of More not only in his dedication of the epigram but also in its composition. Erasmus consciously echoes More's epigrams in his poem against Julius, and later More will remember Erasmus' poem. From study of the cross-fertilization in the art of these two humanists emerges a clearer glimpse of their literary relations between 1510 and 1516.

N019 Eldridge, Laurence. "Latin Poetry of the Renaissance." *AR* 24 (1964): 83-87.

Eldridge features a section, "Sir Thomas More, 1478-1535," in which he translates seven of More's epigrams, discusses how Erasmus and More regarded the epigram, and calls their engagement in writing epigrams "Wits Recreation."

N020 Fletcher, Harris. "The Earliest (?) Printing of Sir Thomas More's Two Epigrams on John Holt." *Studies in Honor of T.W. Baldwin.* Ed. Don Cameron Allen. Urbana: U of Illinois P, 1958. 53-65.

Fletcher duplicates and discusses the text of two epigrams to Holt as they appear in the U of Illinois copy of Holt's *Lac Puerorum*. He describes More's association with Holt, summarizes the content of the epigrams (which address school boys about the study of grammar), and concludes both are "perhaps more personal than they are great poetic efforts," because they concern More's relationship with Holt and his interest in education.

N021 Grace, Damian. "Subjects or Citizens? *Populi* and *Cives* in More's *Epigrammata*." *Moreana* 97 (1988): 133-36.

Grace makes two points about *populus* and *cives* in More's epigrams: (1) these terms imply a political community and not merely a multitude which gains its corporate being from monarchical rule; and (2) the nascent civic consciousness of Tudor writers is not only to be found in discursive works like *Utopia*, but also in the vocabulary and usage of even so slight a poetic adventure as an epigram.

N022 Grace, Damian. "Thomas More's *Epigrammata*: Political Theory in a Poetic Idiom." *Parergon* ns 3 (1985): 115-29.

Grace finds these poems display the same kind of indirection, ambiguity, and criticism of pride, pretension, and the social elite as *Utopia* or *Richard III*; determines they should not be read "merely as exercises in witty versification"; and believes that politically they share much with "their cousin, the graffito."

N023 Holahan, Susan L. "More's Epigrams on Henry Abyngdon." *Moreana* 17 (1968): 21-26.

Holahan traces, in the epigrams on Abyngdon, a sequence of statement, affirmation, and reversal, deduced from the contrast between the artist and the pretender--a pattern characteristic of More's other epigrams.

N024 Hudson, Hoyt Hopewell. "The Epigrams of Sir Thomas More." *The Epigram in the English Renaissance*. Princeton: Princeton UP, 1947. 23-79.

Hudson assesses epigram writing in Renaissance England with More and places More's epigrams in popular and humanist traditions. He examines early editions of the *Epigrammata*; considers a number of the poems in detail; discusses themes and sources; and shows how the epigrams were reprinted, translated, and incorporated into later collections. Because he finds More's epigrams "fairly typical" of the times, he believes knowing More's epigrams is important in understanding that form during the period.

N025 Hutton, James. "A Speculation on Two Passages in the Latin Poems of Thomas More." *Essays on Renaissance Poetry* (by James Hutton). Ed. Rita Guerlac. Ithaca, NY: Cornell UP, 1980. 330-38.

Hutton speculates the "unique maiden" of Epigram 125 may be Catherine of Aragon and the imaginary "Candidus" to whom the poem is addressed may be Henry VIII's older brother Arthur. He believes the poem was most likely written shortly before Catherine's arrival in England in the autumn of 1501.

N026 Kinney, Daniel. "More's Epigram on Brixius' Plagiarism: One Poem or Two?" *Moreana* (1981): 37-44.
Kinney delves further into the significance of the episodes with Brixius and demonstrates that the one epigram on Brixius' plagiarism represents a conflation of two poems which contribute to the humanist debate on the nature of apt *imitatio*.

N027 Meijer, Marianne S. "Les Aventures de deux epigrammes de Thomas More." *Moreana* 50 (1976): 5-10.
Meijer discusses the translations and "fortunes" of two of More's epigrams ("To thee thou arie Prophet all" and "But no Starres").

N028 Meijer, Marianne S. "Thomas More, Lodovico Domenichi e 'L'honneur du sexe féminin.'" *Moreana* 38 (1973): 37-42.
Meijer links Francois de Billon's *Le Fort inexpugnable de l'Honneur du sexe femenin* (Paris, 1555), *La Nobilità delle donne* by Lodovico Domenichi, the fame of the intellectual capacity of More's daughters, and Domenichi's knowledge of More's epigrams.

N029 Nichols, Fred J. "More and Martial." *Moreana* 86 (1985): 61-70.
Nichols scans More's Latin epigrams to reveal an important convergence with Martial whose presence, though it does not often find its way into the verbal fabric of More's poetry, looms large as an implied point of reference.

N030 Perry, Kathleen. "Blind Saturn: The Astrological Epigrams as Records of More's Cultural Conservatism." *Moreana* 86 (1985): 44-60.
Perry scrutinizes More's closely linked poems on the fragile but vital alliance of the lame, blind beggars and his more varied poems on the self-blinded astrologers and uses them to explain how More constructs monuments to "cultural conservatism" from both classical and medieval materials. She also comments upon what More implies about the precarious relationship of reality, language, and fiction as she observes the astrologers' fictions, which they proclaim as truths, in More's self-proclaimed fictions which condemn the astrologers' fictions.

N031 Rizzi, Marius. "Thomae Mori Epigrammata Selecta." *Latinitas* 27 (1979): 187-92; 28.1 (1980): 37-40; 28.3 (1980): 192-203.
These three articles reprint selected Latin epigrams.

N032 Rundle, David. "A New Golden Age? More, Skelton and the accession verses of 1509." *RenSt* 9 (1995): 58-76.

Rundle compares More's coronation verses with those of Andrea Ammonio, John Skelton, and Stephen Hawes to demonstrate none of these works, "replete with familiar topoi, can be dismissed as merely conventional." His main point, however, counters the usually accepted view More's Latin poems on Henry VIII's coronation do not contain his characteristic ambivalence and cynicism and that More was momentarily taken in "by the splendid appearance of painted garments." Rundle suggests, on the contrary, More's poems display a more equivocal reaction to Henry's accession.

N033 Ryan, Lawrence. "The Shorter Latin Poem in Tudor England." *HumLov* 26 (1977): 101-31.

Ryan claims the Neo-Latin epigrammatic and lyric tradition in England begins with More and that he is the only English epigrammatist to earn a continental reputation before the seventeenth century. He focuses mainly on the *Epigrammata*--its use of Greek sources (mainly the *Planudean Anthology*), the poems' tones (especially those that are satiric) and their subjects.

N034 Sabol, Andrew J. "An English Source for One of More's Latin Epigrams." *MLN* 63 (1948): 542.

A contemporary and anonymous English version of More's Latin epigram, entitled "In amicam foedifragam iocosvm, versum e cantione anglica," appears in a Tudor manuscript song book, *The Fairfax MS* (Br. Mus. Add. MS. 5654).

N035 Schoeck, R.J. "Further Adventures of Two Epigrams of Thomas More: A 1573 Translation by Antoine de Verdier." *Moreana* 73 (1982): 67.

Schoeck notes Verdier, in his *Prosopographie*, translates More's Epigrams 43 and 47.

N036 Sullivan, Frank. "Sir Thomas More." *TLS* 9 Jan. 1959: 19.

Sullivan adds information about the second edition of More's collected Latin verse which "appeared with varying titles, typographical devices, imprimaturs, and dates (1565 and 1566), with two different printers, two different imprints, and three different terms of what might be called copyright."

Life of Pico

O001 Bowers, Fredson. "Printing Evidence in Wynkyn de Worde's Edition of *The Life of John Picus* by St. Thomas More." *PBSA* 43 (1949): 398-99.

Bowers notes that from the printing of the work it is apparent Worde used not the efficient method of single half-sheet imposition but printed half sheets in the gathering by the twin half-sheet system, a method requiring considerably more standing type.

O002 Craven, William G. *Pico della Mirandola, Symbol of His Age*. Genève: Librairie Droz, 1981.

Craven undertakes a critical examination of what modern historians have written about Pico, and these accounts provide reasons why More (who is listed in the bibliography) might have found Pico of such interest.

O003 Edwards, A.S.G. "More's *Life of Pico* in the Early 17th Century." *Moreana* 110 (1992): 5-7.

An account of one seventeenth-century reader's reaction to More's translation of Pico gives some ideas about its reception.

O004 Edwards, A.S.G. "More's *Lyfe of Picus* and Blacman's *Collectarium*." *N&Q* ns 40.3 (Sept. 1993): 307-08.

Edwards argues Blacman's *Collectarium Mansuetudinem et bonorum morum regis Henrici .VI.* (an account of Henry VI seemingly compiled in the early 1480s) may have influenced More's *Lyfe of Picus* (c. 1510).

O005 Edwards, A.S.G. "Robert Parkyn's Transcript of More's 'Prayer of Picus Mirandula vnto God.'" *Moreana* 101-102 (1990): 133-38.

Edwards duplicates Parkyn's transcription of More's "Prayer" found in Parkyn's commonplace book which provides variant readings of the "Prayer" as it appeared in the editions of the *Life of Pico* by John Rastell (1510?), Wynkyn de Worde (c. 1525), and William Rastell (1557). Edwards believes Parkyn's text "represents not simply a different textual tradition," but one More editors should consider seriously.

O006   Esmonde, Margaret Powell. "'A Pattern of Life': A Critical Analysis of St. Thomas More's *Life of John Picus.*" Diss. U of Miami, 1971.

Esmonde provides autobiographical details, Pico's background, discussion of relevant traditions, and analysis of theme and style. She assesses More's style as a translator of Latin; stresses More's closeness to medieval sermons, oral traditions, and the genres of the *poems morale* and saints' life; and considers the effects of his legal training, concluding that although the translation is sometimes marred by excessive parenthetical clauses and awkward syntax, it reveals More's conscious attention to prose style in its effective use of repetition and careful balancing of phrases and clauses.

O007   Gabrieli, Vittorio. "Giovanni Pico and Thomas More." *Moreana* 15-16 (1967): 43-57.

Gabrieli studies Pico's influence on More, posits their affinity was essentially spiritual rather than intellectual, points out and discusses parallel passages in More's translation of the *Life of Pico* and *Dialogue of Comfort* and *Four Last Things* to exemplify some of Pico's influence, and explores changes More made in his translations of the *Life* and other works by Pico.

O008   Gilmore, Myron. "More's Translation of Gianfrancesco Pico's Biography." *L'Opera e il pensiero di Giovanni della Mirandola nella storia dell'umanesimo. Convegno internazionale (Mirandola: 15-18 Settembre 1963).* Convegno internazionale per il v centenario della nascita di Giovanni Pico della Mirandola promosso dal comune di Mirandola e dallo Istituto nazionale di studi sul Rinascimento. Firenze: Nella sede dell'Istituto, 1965. 301-04.

Gilmore notes omissions and additions in More's translation of Pico's *Life* and explains the presentation of the translation to Joyce Leigh does not necessarily mean it was written for her. Gilmore thinks More probably translated the work, because he saw his decision against a monastic vocation reflected in Pico.

O009   Hamm, V. Michael. *Pico Della Mirandola, Of Being and Unity*. Milwaukee: Marquette P, 1943.

Hamm's study of Pico uses Christian asceticism to account for More's attraction to Pico's character and career.

O010   Lehmberg, Stanford. "Sir Thomas More's *Life of Pico della Mirandola.*" *SRen* 3 (1956): 61-74.

This study of More's translation reveals much about the so-called psychological crisis More supposedly underwent in 1504. Biographers have often considered 1504 an important year in More's life, and Lehmberg feels Pico's life as a layman who lived and died without taking monastic orders seems to have influenced More in deciding to marry and be a faithful husband instead of a lecherous priest.

O011 Maskell, David. "Robert Gaguin and Thomas More, Translators of Pico della Mirandola." *BHR* 37 (1975): 63-66.

Maskell compares the translations of Gaguin (French chronicler, professor of rhetoric, ambassador, c. 1452-1502) and More and concludes More's superior work corrects, adds, and adheres more closely to Pico than that of Gaguin.

O012 Parks, George B. "Pico della Mirandola in Tudor Translation." *Philosophy and Humanism: Renaissance Essays in Honor of Paul Oskar Kristeller.* Ed. Edward P. Mahoney. New York: Columbia UP, 1976. 352-69.

Parks divides More's translations of Pico into two parts: the prose dealing with Pico's life as a scholar, the verse dealing with his virtue and love of God. He believes these parts are not connected and may have been done at different times--the prose, for instance, during More's vocational crisis (1499-1503/04). He also discusses Joyce Leigh and her connection with More. Parks feels the verse translations are more interesting than the prose and show promise of More's abilities in English verse.

O013 Valcke, Louis. "Jean Pico de la Mirandole lu par Thomas More." *Miscellanea Moreana: Essays for Germain Marc'hadour. Moreana* 100. 77-98.

Valcke points to the choice of short "edifying" tracts Pico wrote, which More appended to the *Life*, to illustrate the types of spirituality that separate More and Pico.

O014 Zapatka, Francis E. "Prose Apothegms into Rime Royal: Thomas More's Translation of Pico della Mirandola's 'Twelve Rules.'" *Acta Conventus Neo-Latini Guelpherbytani.* Proceedings of the Sixth International Congress of Neo-Latin Studies. Wolfenbüttel 12 August to 16 August 1985. Eds. Stella P. Revard, Fidel Rädle, and Mario A. Di Cesare. MRTS. 53. Binghamton, NY: MRTS, 1988. 395-400.

Zapatka seeks to defend More's translation of Pico's "Twelve Rules" from the charge of being "appalling doggerel" by examining differences in imagery, prosody, and figurative devices and showing More's verse is as "effective, rhetorically" as Pico's prose.

Humanist Letter-Treatises

P001 Cooper, M. Scholastica. "More and the Letter to Martin Dorp." *Moreana* 6 (1965): 37-44.

On the basis of More's letter to Dorp in which he defends Erasmus against Dorp's criticism of *Praise of Folly*, Erasmus's edition of St. Jerome, and Erasmus's proposed Greek New Testament, Cooper connects More's reproof of this young rhetorician-playwright both with his recognition of Erasmus's ability and his own view of the nature of true rhetoric. Cooper also examines Dorp's scholarly career and provincial background to explain More's ironic tone and reference to Dorp as hardly a skilled enough theologian to take Erasmus to task.

P002 Guerlac, Rita, ed. *Juan Luis Vives against the Pseudodialecticians: A Humanist Attack on Medieval Logic*. "The Attack on the Pseudodialecticians" and "On Dialectic," Book III, v, vi, vii from "The Causes of the Corruption of the Arts," with an Appendix of Related Passages by Thomas More. Texts, with translation, introduction, and notes by Rita Guerlac. Synthese Historical Library. Texts and Studies in the History of Logic and Philosophy. 18. Dordecht, Holland: Reidel, 1979.

In appendix I, Guerlac discusses More's *Letter to Martin Dorp* and the influence of its attack on medieval logic on Vives's *Adversus psuedodialecticos*; provides an English translation, together with the Latin, of More's *Letter*; and reprints More's letter to Erasmus (26 May 1526) in which More expresses his admiration of Vives.

P003 Kinney, Daniel. "More's *Letter to Dorp*: Remapping the Trivium." *RenQ* 34 (1981): 179-210.

Kinney labels this letter as one of the first systematic defenses of humanistic method and shows how it encompasses a critique of Scholastic grammar and dialectic, a proper understanding of which forms the basis of More's plan for remapping the medieval trivium. Kinney then analyzes the letter's rhetorical features to demonstrate how it is a tightly argued defense with "rhetorical balance, thematic consistency, and stylistic tact." Finally, he places More's letter in the context of humanistic apologetics by pointing out its similarities to writings on the subject by Vives, Valla, and Agricola; More's views on the issues in this letter put him in line with continental humanists.

P004 Lytle, Guy. "The Church Fathers and Oxford Professors in the Late Middle Ages, Renaissance, and Reformation." *Acta Conventus Neo-Latini Bononiensis*. Proceedings of the Fourth International Congress of Neo-Latin Studies. Bologna, 26 August to 1 September 1979. Ed. R.J. Schoeck. MRTS. 37. Binghamton: MRTS, 1985. 101-15.

Lytle quotes More's letter to Oxford, which urged a study of biblical languages and especially the Fathers, thereby articulating "most of the Christian humanist case against the professional theologians of the time." Despite some heated debates involving More and others, most Oxford dons still appreciated the value of Patristic studies, though they practiced them less than their medieval predecessors. Lytle feels More's "qualifications to speak on theological matters were...suspect," but More's plea for a return to the original documents is a matter of common sense rather than theology.

P005 Murphy, Clare M. "An Epistolary Defense of Erasmus: Thomas More and an English Carthusian." *Acta Conventus Neo-Latini Turonensis*. Troisième Congrès International d'Études Néo-Latines, Tours. Université Francois-Rabelais 6-10 Septembre 1976. Ed. Jean-Claude Margolin. Vol. 1. Paris: Vrin, 1980. 329-47.

Murphy begins with More's answer in his *Letter to Edward Lee* to Lee's negative reaction to Erasmus's New Testament. Next she mainly analyzes the content and style of More's *Letter to a Monk* (known to be the Carthusian John Batmanson, an ally of Lee) in which More spends most of his time answering attacks of heresy, impiety, and vagrancy on Erasmus and on his edition of the New Testament. In addition, she discusses Batmanson's life and relationship with More, the occasion for this *Letter*, its date of composition, and the circumstances of its publication.

P006 Schoeck, R.J. "On the Letters of Thomas More." *Moreana* 15-16 (1967): 193-203.

Schoeck surveys features and structure in More's letters (especially those to Dorp, the University of Oxford, and a monk) against the background of rhetoric and epistolary convention, suggesting lines for further research.

P007 Scott-Craig, T.S.K., trans. "Thomas More's 1518 Letter to the University of Oxford." *RN* 1 (1948): 17-24.

Scott-Craig reprints a letter More wrote after he was in Abingdon near Oxford, in which More draws Henry VIII's attention to the attack on Hellenism at Oxford. The letter's tone reflects the early Tudor situation at its best, as it presents a "humanistic critique" of a Church-dominated and intellectually backward society combined with a sense of the interests of the state, through the monarch and his advisors, in a sound humanistic education for its future scholars, lawyers, and statesmen.

P008 Silva, Álvaro de. "Sir Thomas More y la Teología: El Quehacer Teológico según la Carta a Martin van Dorp." *Studium* 17 (1977): 513-27.

Silva's study of "The Mission of Theology according to More's *Letter to Dorp*" explores how far More's advocacy of *theologia positiva*, or philological and Patristic theology, preclude his tolerance for *theologia speculativa* and its most distinguished practitioner Aquinas. With this question Silva associates the problem of how far the reform of theological method humanists like More and Erasmus advocated actually coincides with the general reform of the Church Luther advocated.

P009 Sylvester, R.S. "Thomas More: Humanist in Action." *Medieval & Renaissance Studies* 1 (1966): 125-37.

Sylvester uses the phrase "humanist in action" to describe his study of More's Latin letters--*Letter to Dorp, Letter to the University of Oxford, Letter to a Monk*, and *Letter to Brixius*--which not only represent More's position on humanism and defend Erasmian humanism but also put its principles in action. (Rpt. in *Essential Articles for the Study of Thomas More*, 462-69.)

History of King Richard III

Q001 Anderson, Judith H. "More's Richard III: History and Biography." *Biographical Truth: The Representation of Historical Persons in Tudor-Stuart Writings*. New Haven: Yale UP, 1984. 75-109.

Anderson analyzes Cavendish's *Wolsey*, Roper's *More*, and Walton's *Donne*, together with more detailed study of More's *Richard III*, Shakespeare's *Richard III* and *Henry VIII*, and Bacon's *Henry VII*, to demonstrate their author's skillful manipulation of material, whether by selection, ordering, stylistic presentation, or even invention, to bring out the essential significance of the subject. For these writers, truth and fiction are by no means opposites: "fiction and history, creative invention and objective truth, are presumed to be complementary and even inseparable"; these artfully "made-up" biographies reflect a sense of the "made-up" or fictive in the concept of self, selfhood, and subjectivity. In chapter six, she reviews problems of genre and form related to More's *Richard III* and shows how it most clearly fits the tradition of "life-writing" she describes.

Q002 Armstrong, C.A.J. *The Usurpation of Richard the Third: Dominicus Mancinus ad Angelum Catonem de Occupatione Regni Angliae Ricardum Tercium Libellus*. Oxford: Humphrey Milford, 1936. 69-129.

This edition of the text and translation of Mancini's account (written at Beaugency, December 1483) contains references to More's *Richard III* in the notes.

Q003 Beith-Halahmi, Esther Yael. "Too Slight a Thing To Be Written Of?" *Angell Fayre or Strumpet Lewd: Jane Shore as an Example of Erring Beauty in Sixteenth-Century Literature*. ElizS 26-27 (1974). 2 vols. Salzburg: Universität Salzburg, Institut für Englische Sprache und Literatur, 1974. 6-59.

Beith-Halahmi employs the first chapter to explain how More uses his sympathetic portrayal of Jane Shore's character in *Richard III* for thematic and structural purposes, and she maintains More makes Queen Elizabeth and Shore foils to each other and both foils to Richard. She also compares More's *Richard III* with some historical works by Polydore Vergil, Dominic Mancini, and Plutarch.

Q004 Brown, Barbara. "Sir Thomas More and Thomas Churchyard's *Shore's Wife*." *YES* 2 (1972): 41-48.

Brown maintains *Shore's Wife* is largely derivative, with Churchyard drawing on not only biographical details from More's account, but also on his intelligent and sympathetic insight into the psychological motivation of the character of Jane Shore. Comparisons between Churchyard's presentation of his heroine and More's account support the claim Churchyard's "personal emphasis and sympathetic attitude of author to heroine...are but a pale reflection of More's compassionate and imaginative telling of her story."

Q005 Candido, Joseph. "Thomas More, the Tudor Chroniclers, and Shakespeare's Altered Richard." *ES* 68 (1987): 137-42.

Candido approaches Shakespeare's sources not, as is customary, with an eye toward how the dramatist shaped these materials, but rather how they may have shaped him. One important compositional fact bears keeping in mind: whether Shakespeare relied on Hall or Holinshed (or both) as his sources for the play, he was actually using More's history for the events preceding Richard's accession and the Hall-Holinshed's account (heavily indebted to Polydore Vergil) for the events thereafter.

Q006 Carver, George. "Saint Thomas More and King Richard III." *Alms for Oblivion: Books, Men and Biography*. Milwaukee: Bruce, 1946. 29-38.

Carver believes Cardinal Morton's influence on More caused his negative portrayal of Richard in the *History*, though he does not think the work was conceived as a Lancastrian propaganda piece but meant to be "a moral treatise" on "the immorality of power derived from force." Carver wonders if More failed to finish the work, because he found *Utopia* a better means of conveying ideas about tyranny; he also refutes the notion Morton wrote it and declares More the author of both the Latin and English versions.

Q007 Champion, Larry S. "Myth and Counter-Myth: The Many Faces of Richard III." *A Fair Day in the Affections: Literary Essays in Honor of Robert B. White, Jr.* Eds. Jack M. Durant, and M. Thomas Hester. Raleigh, NC: Winston, 1980. 37-53.

Champion brings together views of *Richard III* and concludes, whether More envisioned the *History* as intentionally ironic (a muted attack not upon Richard or fifteenth-century politics but upon Henry and his policies), as a parody of the chronicle writing form itself, or as a kind of literary exercise for circulation among his closest friends, it stands as a landmark in the development of sixteenth-century prose and as a remarkable witness to what the new humanist history could accomplish.

Q008 Condren, Conal. "Cornwallis' Paradoxical Defence of Richard III: A Machiavellian Discourse on Morean Mythology?" *Moreana* 94 (1987): 5-24.

In 1617, Cornwallis, a friend of Ben Jonson and John Donne, published a volume of essays, or paradoxes, expanded from a collection published in the previous year. Among the new material was a paradox praising Richard III, followed by another praising venereal disease ("The French Pocks"). Once cast in the paradox mode and in the context of a paradoxical counterpart, Richard's praise, which reads as an attack on More's *History*, can be seen as fundamentally one with it. In order to see how this is so, Condren turns to Machiavelli, who is so easily contrasted with More.

Q009 Cornell, Christine Anne. "Unparadised Women: Royal Mistresses in Early Modern English Literature." Diss. Dalhousie U (Can.), 1994.

Cornell focuses upon two mistresses appearing repeatedly in this period's literature--Rosamond Clifford and Jane Shore; chapter four considers More and Thomas Churchyard's representations of Shore as a "powerful and responsible courtier."

Q010 Costain, Thomas. *The Last Plantagenets.* Garden City, NY: Doubleday, 1962. 338-39.

Costain discusses the versions of the history of Richard III written by More and Polydore Vergil and speculates More did not finish his work, because he came to doubt the validity of some information he had learned from Cardinal Morton.

Q011 Cross, Gustav. "More's *Historie of Kyng Richarde the Third* and *Lust's Dominion.*" *N&Q* ns 4.5 (May 1957): 198-99.

Cross suggests that during the composition of Acts II and III of *Lust's Dominion*, and in particular the scene in which Friars Crab and Cole proclaim Philip's bastardy in the marketplace of Seville, the author seems to have had in mind the public declaration of the illegitimacy of an heir to the throne as it appears in More's *Richard III*.

Q012 Dean, Leonard F. "Literary Problems in More's *Richard III*." *PMLA* 58 (1943): 22-41.

Dean maintains this work has been adequately studied as an historical document, so his study examines some literary problems it presents. He argues it conforms to classical theories of history writing and to the "fall-of-princes" pattern. *Richard III* differs from classical histories in More's use of irony and in that More was a Christian humanist.

Q013 Dean, Paul. "Tudor Humanism and the Roman Past: A Background to Shakespeare." *RenQ* 41 (1988): 84-111.

In his survey of the effect of the Renaissance discovery of time on the concept of the Roman past, which was closely bound up with the perception of the English past, Dean focuses on More's *Richard III* for its superb sense of drama and pervasive yet elusive debt to the Roman historians.

Q014 Donno, Elizabeth Story. "Thomas More and *Richard III*." *RenQ* 35 (1982): 401-47.

Donno summarizes scholarship on the history's authorship, date of composition, and genre; and then suggests a different motive of conception for it. Given More's knowledge of classical rhetoric, his humanist interests, and his eloquence "characterized by mocking, even derisive, tendencies," Donno believes More was not writing history with a medieval cast or with a Tudor bias; rather, he was composing a historical narrative in the epideictic vein--in this case, a denunciation (*vituperatio*).

Q015 Fox, Alistair. "Richard III's Pauline Oath: Shakespeare's Response to Thomas More." *Moreana* 57 (1978): 13-23.

Fox fulfills the need to assess the contribution of the Pauline oath to the development of Richard's mock-Puritan piety or "positively impersonating, with mischievous exhilaration, the unscrupulous Apostle of the Gentiles," and to appraise Richard's character in terms of it. Neither can be done, claims Fox, until Shakespeare's debt to More's *Richard III* is recognized.

Q016 Fox, Alistair. "Thomas More and Tudor Historiography: *The History of King Richard III*." *Politics and Literature in the Reigns of Henry VII and Henry VIII*. Oxford: Basil Blackwell, 1989. 108-27.

Chapter seven analyzes *Richard III* against the background of Tudor historiography, argues More was "fully conscious of the power of humanist history to distort," and shows how the work embodies More's "intense hatred of tyrants" and "deep misgivings about the institution of kingship itself." Fox believes *Richard III* results from More's personal, political, and intellectual concerns around 1513 and his awareness of the new type of historiography Polydore Vergil was practicing, and that More's "doubleness" of vision in it generates a profound anamorphism presenting "two different appearances" existing "simultaneously."

Q017 Fussner, F. Smith. *The Historical Revolution, English Historical Writing and Thought, 1580-1640*. London: Routledge and Paul, 1962. 230.

Fussner maintains More's *Richard III* is a masterful literary portrait that lacks historical validity.

Q018 Gilmore, Myron Piper. "Freedom and Determinism in Renaissance Historians." *SRen* 3 (1956): 49-60.

Gilmore mentions More's *Richard III* as an example of how history is made by an individual's character which is basically incapable of being changed. Hence, according to psychological determinism, Richard is born evil and unnatural and remains evil throughout his life.

Q019 Gordon, Walter M. "Exemplum Narrative and Thomas More's *History of King Richard III*." *ClioI* 9 (1979): 75-88.

More's *Richard III* is a decisive stage in the evolution of tragedy out of narrative records, because it undermines exemplum patterns in the tragic, individualized sufferings of Mistress Shore and Hastings and parodies them in comic contrasts between ethical ideals and Richard's unethical conduct.

Q020 Grace, Damian. "More's *Richard III*: A 'Satirical Drama'?" *Moreana* 57 (1978): 31-37.

Grace responds to and elaborates upon Alison Hanham's *Richard III and His Early Historians* (Q027). If, as Hanham claims, More's achievement in *Richard III* has been misunderstood and underevaluated, her own interpretation does little to redress those matters. Her work is punctuated with inconsistencies and equivocations--More is not to be used as a source, but she uses his *History* as one. A suggestive metaphor leads her to analyze the work's style only and neglect a thorough investigation of More's intentions. Anachronism flaws her arguments as they develop: she is unable to free herself of her own canons of scholarly approval to evaluate her authors on their own terms. In short, if More's *Richard* is to be understood properly, it requires a more penetrating and historically informed elucidation than Hanham provides under the pseudo-classification of satirical drama.

Q021 Grace, Damian. "On Interpreting St. Thomas More's *History of King Richard the Third*." *European History and Its Historians*. Selected Papers from the Conference of Australian Historians of Medieval and Early Modern Europe, Adelaide, 18-21 May 1976. Eds. Frank McGregor, and Nicholas Wright. Adelaide: Adelaide U Union P, 1977. 11-22.

In examining the historical rather than literary nature of More's *Richard III*, Grace concentrates on the humanist's notions of the purpose and method of writing history and finds More's *History*, like other humanist histories, was shaped by political concerns that affect the selection, arrangement, distortion, and invention of historical materials to serve the author's ideas. More's work uses the past to write about the present, and its audience would assume its instructive value as a lesson to princes. The work's irony is that it is so well written for its type, it is often viewed as literature.

Q022 Grant, Patrick. "Thomas More's *Richard III*: Moral Narration and Humanist Method." *Ren&R* ns 7 (1983): 157-72.

Grant explains how the history presents a lesson as a medieval morality; an exemplum against tyranny; a story of the rise and fall of a prince on Fortune's wheel; a humanist history eclectically modeled on Sallust, Tacitus, and Suetonius; and shows how, with surprising economy, More transforms that lesson into literature by capturing readers unwittingly in complex circumstances that only Richard understands and turns to his sinister advantage.

Q023 Gresham, Stephen. "The Dramaturgy of Tyranny: More's *Richard III* and Sackville's *Complaint of Buckingham*." *Quincentennial Essays on St. Thomas More*. 34-42.

Gresham outlines biographical similarities in the lives of More and Sackville and believes both *Richard III* and the *Complaint* spring from their authors' practical understanding of the treacheries of politics. In comparing the two works, he finds similarities in themes of tyranny and civil disorder, characterization, plot, and language, and he suggests More's *Richard* may have influenced Sackville's *Complaint*.

Q024 Hall, Anne Drury. "Early Tudor Prose and Civil History in Thomas More's *History of King Richard III*." *Ceremony and Civility in English Renaissance Prose*. University Park: Pennsylvania State UP, 1991. 53-100.

Hall outlines the early modern transition between the "pathos and exaltation" of prose reflecting a relatively stable medieval religious and social world view ("ceremonial prose") and the "circumspections, hesitations, and ironic deflections" of prose associated with the recovery of classical philosophy and the rise of secularism ("civil prose"). Hall concludes More would have been more of a "civilist" had he been born into the civil culture and that the alternate conclusion has to be considered: "More failed to write a fully civil history not only because he *could* not but because he did not *want* to."

Q025 Hanham, Alison. "Fact and Fantasy: Thomas More as Historian." *Thomas More: The Rhetoric of Character*. 65-81.

Hanham discusses *Richard III* in the context of More's literary career and the stream of English historical writing. Through parallels between *Richard* and *Utopia*, Hanham concludes More's concept of history writing aims at artistic truth, realism, not reality, and that the force of *Richard* comes from the author's deep involvement with his subject.

Q026 Hanham, Alison. "Renaissance Historians and the 'Tudor Myth' of

Richard III." *Parergon* 11 (1975): 33-40.

Hanham examines notions about how Tudor writers, especially More, and later writers of the English Renaissance developed portraits of Richard that create distortions through omissions and additions to what is known. Hanham ascribes the distortions in More's *Richard* to the author's sense he is modeling his work on patterns found in classical literature and his sense of humor and fondness for satire. Hanham also believes More's work exhibits a "Lucianic vein of parody" of other historians, for example Polydore Vergil, and that *Richard* is neither history nor propaganda but a "unique blend" of the dramatic and comic.

Q027 Hanham, Alison. "Sir Thomas More's Satirical Drama." *Richard III and His Early Historians, 1483-1535*. Oxford: Claredon, 1975. 152-90.

In chapter seven, Hanham shows *Richard* is closer to satire, drama, and fiction than to history and that More uses a Lucianic approach to parody other historians and scholars in her analysis of the English version as a five-act play. An appendix, "The Texts of More's *History of King Richard III*" (198-219) studies the Latin and English texts and the relationship between various sixteenth-century versions, assesses their authenticity in terms of More's intentions, speculates on the process of composition, and posits More may have been working on a draft as late as the 1530s.

Q028 Harner, James L. "The Place of Shore's Wife in More's *The History of King Richard III*." *Moreana* 74 (1982): 69-76.

Although Harner acknowledges readers of *Richard III* have consistently singled out the description of Shore "for acclaim," his purpose is to examine thoroughly its importance to the work as a whole, its intrinsic appeal, and More's "attitude" toward Shore (as well as the inextricable relationship among these elements). Harner concludes More intends Shore's wife to function as an integral, important part of his illustration of Richard's dissimulation and cruelty, the great unifying themes of the *History*.

Q029 Harris, Muriel Sheila. "Sir Thomas More's *History of Richard III* as Humanist Historiography." Diss. Columbia U, 1972.

Harris reviews historiographical principles fifteenth-century Italian humanists discussed and practiced to set up the context which guided More as he wrote *Richard III*.

Q030 Heath, T.G. "Another Look at Thomas More's *Richard*." *Moreana* 19-20 (1968): 11-19.

Heath examines *Richard III*'s structure and concludes that "at least on one level," it is a complete composition, especially in the Latin version. He also sees the survival of More's portrayal of Richard in the English chronicles, and, from the comparison of the Latin with the English version, surmises that, for More, "the conflict is between the King and his subjects."

Q031 Heinrich, Hans P. *Sir Thomas Mores* Geschichte König Richards III, *im Lichte humanistischer Historiographie und Geschichtstheorie*. Beiträge zur Englischen und Amerikanischen Literatur. Band 5. Paderborn: Ferdinand Schöningh, 1987.

This study elaborates on Heinrich's introduction to his German translation of *Richard III* (C009), and discusses authorship, dating, the English and Latin versions, More's oral and written sources, and the question of genre. Heinrich examines the theory of humanist history and historical techniques and concludes *Richard III* is the first example in England of humanist history. He investigates More's use of classical rhetorical techniques in the work and its exploration of rhetoric itself, particularly the limits of political speech. He also compares and contrasts More and Machiavelli, discusses the place of history in More's humanist writings and in his life, and the relationship between *Richard III* and *Utopia*.

Q032 Jones, Emyr Wyn. "Richard III's Disfigurement: A Medical Postscript." *Folklore* 91 (1980): 211-27.

Jones traces the development of stories about Richard III's deformities, such as his crooked back and teeth. While he praises their power in the works of Polydore Vergil, More, Hall, and Shakespeare, he laments what these treatments have done to the ability to ascertain the truth about the king's actual physical deformities.

Q033 Kendall, Paul Murray. *Richard the Third*. New York: Norton, 1955.

Kendall's biography attempts to recreate the historical figure. Appendix I, "Who Murdered the Princes" (465-95), questions More's account of the death of Edward IV's sons; appendix II, "Richard's Reputation" (495-514), attacks More's portrait as inaccurate, distorted, and virulent.

Q034 Kendall, Paul Murray, ed. *Richard III: The Great Debate: Sir Thomas More's* History of King Richard III, *Horace Walpole's* Historic Doubts on the Life and Reign of King Richard III. New York: Norton, 1965.

This edition of the two works includes Kendall's "An introduction to [More's] *History of Richard III*," which discusses the work's date, circumstances of composition, the authorship question, the relationship between the Latin and English versions, and the largely oral sources of More's information about Richard. In the general introduction, Kendall reviews the "Great Debate" about the "real" Richard and the nature of his rule and the ways he has been characterized in mainly literary work--his emphasis falls on the extent of the influence of More's negative portrait.

Q035 Kendall, Paul Murray. *The Yorkist Age.* New York: Norton, 1962. 193, 417.

Kendall quotes a description of Edward IV and his delight in Jane Shore from More's *Richard III* which he values because More was not only a good judge of character but also closer to these times than modern historians.

Q036 Kincaid, Arthur Noel. "The Dramatic Structure of Sir Thomas More's *History of King Richard III*." *SEL* 12 (1972): 223-42.

Kincaid claims More was drawn to the theatrical mode of expression, the theater being bound up with his whole view of life; hence, he portrays Richard as an actor, manipulating others to achieve the crown. However, the principal theme is the destruction and re-establishment of the natural order, and Richard's success is seen to be only apparent and temporary. The metaphor of the stage is important, "since it defines Richard's position relative to the reader and also to the populace."

Q037 Kinney, Daniel. "Kings' Tragicomedies: Generic Misrule in More's *History of Richard III*." *Moreana* 86 (1985): 128-50.

Although Kinney acknowledges the value of work done on the genre of *Richard III*, he warns it will always be risky to use single generic affinities to account for the text as a whole, and he considers the history's unstable command of genres a "deliberately unsettling display of genre misrule." Following a discussion of the ms. of the Latin history and how it helps to clarify relations between all extant versions of the text, Kinney argues More's paradoxical scrutiny of usurpation and the rhetoric of history finds its "richest, most thorough, and most challenging expression in the least-studied version of the text."

Q038 Leslau, Jack. "The Princes in the Tower." *Moreana* 98-99 (1988): 17-36.

The princes disappeared in 1483, aged thirteen and ten years. In *Richard III*, More curiously repeats what "men say," that they were murdered by their ambitious uncle, Richard. Why does a man of truth take on board a rumor from a previous century--not to be printed during his lifetime? Why does not the mother of the princes, Elizabeth Woodville, claim her children are either missing or dead? Could the children have reappeared under false names and identities, the elder as Sir Edward Guildford, the younger as John Clement, the latter in the More family and in the Holbein portrait of that family? Leslau argues these speculations merit investigation.

Q039 Levy, F.J. *Tudor Historical Thought.* San Marino, CA: Huntington Library, 1967. 68-73, 170-71.

Because the book is concerned with historical thought, most references to

More focus on *Richard III*--its classical sources, style, Latin and English versions. Levy regards the work less as a history of a reign and more as a biography of a monarch, and he speculates on More's reason for writing it. He also notes all the major chroniclers, Shakespeare, and many today are drawn to More's portrait, in spite of the fact it often resembles a caricature.

Q040 Littleton, Taylor, and Robert P. Rea. *To Prove a Villain*. New York: MacMillan, 1964.

The editors bring together excerpts about Richard III from More's *Richard III*, Polydore Vergil, the *Croyland Chronicle, Mirror for Magistrates*, Holinshed, Shakespeare, Bacon's *Henry VII*, Markham's *Richard III, His Life and Character Reviewed in the Light of Recent Research*, and others.

Q041 Myers, A.R. "The Character of Richard III." *History Today* 4 (1954): 511-21.

Myers declares More and Polydore Vergil's histories created many Elizabethan notions about Richard, most of which exist in the popular mind today. He also considers the nature and reliability of More's sources and sees the *History* as a kind of drama, a morality play in which Richard is a Vice.

Q042 Myers, A.R. *England in the Late Middle Ages, 1307-1536*. Hammondsworth, Middlesex, Eng.: Penguin, 1952. 235.

Myers praises More's prose style for the new spirit of humanism it embodies and *Richard III* as the "first history in the English language which is not merely an artless collection of facts, but a deliberately designed and carefully executed composition."

Q043 Pollard, A.F. "The Making of Sir Thomas More's *Richard III*." *Historical Essays in Honour of James Tait*. Eds. J.G. Edwards, V.H. Galbraith, and E.F. Jacob. Manchester: Printed for subscribers only, 1933. (Rpt. in *Essential Articles for the Study of Thomas More*, 421-31.)

Pollard describes problems about *Richard III*, establishes More's authorship of both the Latin and English texts, believes they were composed before May 1515, and posits that, in addition to Cardinal Morton, More relied on various oral sources. He believes the work is mainly dramatic and, like Shakespeare's *Richard III*, should be regarded as "legitimate drama, but illegitimate history." Pollard speculates political expediency on More's part might have caused the work's "abrupt termination" and lack of revision or publication until after More's death.

Q044 Pollard, A.F. *Richard III and the Princes in the Tower*. New York: St. Martin's, 1991. 2, 3, 5, 7, 10, 11-12, 14-15, 23, 55, 83, 90, 115, 119, 120, 124-25, 131, 140, 158, 205, 227.

This illustrated book contains many references to More and his *Richard III*, along with a brief summary of scholarly views of *Richard III*.

Q045 Potter, Jeremy. *Good King Richard? An Account of Richard III and His Reputation, 1483-1983*. London: Constable, 1983. 110-25, 192-93, 239-40.

Potter argues the inaccuracies and absurdities of More's *Richard* disqualify it as history or biography and that it is best read as a "dramatic representation of villainy." He proposes Henry VII rather than Richard may be the work's "real target" and investigates More's authorship, sources, style, early editions, and More's representation and distortion of Richard.

Q046 Reiter, Robert E. "On the Genre of Thomas More's *Richard III*." *Moreana* 25 (1970): 5-16.

After he considers the question of genre(s) in which to place *Richard III*, Reiter decides the work is best read as a biography, but contrary to Tudor practice, its biographical passages contain an infrequently used kind of panegyric--one that does not praise but blames, one that does not commend but condemns. Read as an inverted panegyric, the work's purpose is not to provide verifiable historical data but to convince readers of Richard's evil nature.

Q047 Ross, Charles. *Richard III*. Berkeley: U of California P, 1981. xxvi-xxxi.

Ross points out the differences between More and Polydore Vergil's treatment of Richard and emphasizes many result from the extent to which More embellishes history with invention beyond what Vergil had already added and from More's "constant hostility" to Richard's character. Hence, Ross regards More's *History* as a moral treatise against tyranny and claims More is not concerned with objectivity or modern historiographical method. He also believes Vergil's *Historia* is a more objective source of information than More's, and that neither More nor Vergil invented the Tudor myth but instead improved upon a view already in place.

Q048 Rowan, D.F. "Shore's Wife." *SEL* 6 (1966): 447-64.

As background to Nicholas Rowe's *Tragedy of Jane Shore*, Rowan traces the popular history of Shore and discusses her appearance in More, Churchyard, Drayton, Shakespeare, and Nashe's works. More's *Richard* is called a most historical document, because it is filled with details, most of which Cardinal Morton, an eyewitness to many events described, supplied.

Q049 Rowse, A.L. *Bosworth Field*. Garden City, NY: Doubleday, 1966.

Although Rowse acknowledges More's *Richard III* is filled with gaps and inaccuracies and is unfinished, he trusts in its historical value and bases his study upon it.

Q050 Rubio, Gerald John. "St. Thomas More's *Richard III* in the Tudor Chronicles." Diss. U of Illinois-Urbana, 1971.

Rubio demonstrates *Richard III* incorporates and emphasizes errors and bias about its subject by design. As a literary construct, it is a travesty of historical narrative by intent, and More expected readers to evaluate it as such. Rubio highlights the unique aspects of More's *Richard* by comparing them with those texts of the work published after More's death in the Tudor chronicles.

Q051 Rudnytsky, Peter L. "More's *History of King Richard III* as an Uncanny Text." *Contending Kingdoms: Historical, Psychological, and Feminist Approaches to the Literature of Sixteenth-Century England and France.* Eds. Marie-Rose Logan, and Peter L. Rudnytsky. Detroit: Wayne State UP, 1991. 149-72.

Rudnytsky invokes the concept of the "uncanny" to examine the motifs of doubling and repetition--centering in the Hastings episode--in More's text itself and in the relation of the first English work of humanist historiography to its political context. He suggests More left it unfinished and unpublished in his lifetime because he saw the past being re-enacted in the present, particularly in the circumstances surrounding the king's "great matter."

Q052 Saccio, Peter. "Richard III: The Last Plantagenet." *Shakespeare's English Kings: History, Chronicle, and Drama.* New York: Oxford UP, 1977. 157-86.

Saccio supplies background for the ten history plays and clarifies dynastic quarrels. The test-piece is this chapter on *Richard III*, which is a model of historical exposition, and notes the More-Hall-Holinshed-Shakespeare monster is indestructible.

Q053 Schulte-Herbrüggen, Hubertus. "A Forgotten Stage in the Tradition of *Richard III* between Thomas More and Shakespeare: Giles Fletcher's *The Rising to the Crown of Richard III*, 1593." *Miscellanea Moreana: Essays for Germain Marc'hadour. Moreana* 100. 209-29.

Published in 1593, at a time of interest in More (as is witnessed by Rowland Lockey's copy of Holbein's More family portrait and the play *The Booke of Sir Thomas Moore*), *The Rising* by Giles Fletcher the Elder (1549?-1611) appeared as an appendix to his volume of love lyrics, *Licia*, and was probably overlooked by both More and Shakespeare scholars for that very reason. Drawing his material from More and Holinshed (via Hardying, Hall, and Grafton), Fletcher, like other Tudor historiographers, makes Richard a Machiavellian villain.

Q054 Schuster, Mary Faith. "Philosophy of Life and Prose Style in Thomas More's *Richard III* and Francis Bacon's *Henry VII*." *PMLA* 70 (1955): 474-87.

Schuster believes More's predominant use of ordered periodic sentences in *Richard III* reflects his own ordered, traditional view of reality; whereas Bacon's dependence on fragmented, curt, loosely organized, anti-Ciceronian sentences in *Henry VII* illustrates his fragmented, skeptical attitude toward reality. In essence, the authors choose the prose styles that "best help teach what they had to say."

Q055 Schuster, Mary Faith. "A Study of the Prose Styles of Thomas More's *History of Richard III* and Francis Bacon's *History of Henry VII* as They Reveal the Philosophies of Life of the Two Authors." Diss. St. Louis U, 1953.

Schuster condensed her study into an article previously cited (Q054).

Q056 Shepard, Alan Clarke. "'Female Perversity,' Male Entitlement: The Agency of Gender in More's *The History of Richard III*." *SCJ* 26 (1995): 311-28.

Most literary critics who study the treatment of women in *Richard* emphasize its portrait of Jane Shore as a woman debauched and conclude the text endorses a narrow view of the agency--political, sexual, and rhetorical--of upper-class women. Shepard reconsiders how the three female principals in *Richard* are represented and emphasizes More's strategy of privileging the voice of Queen Elizabeth Woodville Gray, who battles her late husband's brother, Richard, for the throne. She is created as a rhetorician who ably resists fictions of male entitlement, especially in her courtship by King Edward IV and in her struggle against Richard in Westminster. Through her resistance to the Yorks, More also resists some of the conventions of Petrarchan desire, altruistic motherhood, dynastic marriage, and Satanic congresses as political fictions.

Q057 Sullivan, Patrick J. "The 'Painted Processe': A Literary Study of Sir Thomas More's *History of Richard the Third*." Diss. U of California-Berkeley, 1967.

More's *History* has never suffered from a lack of admirers, though they have more often acknowledged rather than assessed the work's literary achievement. Primarily concerned with the English version of the *History*, Sullivan fills this void with a literary analysis of the text and other related narratives.

Q058 Tey, Josephine [Elizabeth McIntosh]. *The Daughter of Time*. London: MacMillan, 1951.

This novel features Alan Grant who, while he is recovering from a broken leg, attempts to read all he can on the mystery of Richard and the Little Princes.

Because he clears Richard of the deed and incriminates Henry VII, he rejects the view More's *History* projects.

Q059 Thompson, James Westfall. "Historiography in Tudor England." *A History of Historical Writing*. Vol. 1. New York: MacMillan, 1942. 2 vols.

In chapter twenty-five, Thompson praises More's *Richard III* for the literary value of its portrait of Richard, though he warns readers about its Lancastrian bias.

Q060 Warnicke, Retha M. "More's *Richard III* and the Mystery Plays." *Historical Journal* 35 (1992): 761-78.

Warnicke's analysis of the English version of *Richard III* indicates the popular mystery plays with their themes of tyranny and sacrifice influenced its composition--a theory reinforcing speculation More wrote the English version first and then, with the classics in mind, wrote a separate Latin text, for the two versions display different images, word choices, and structures.

Q061 Warnicke, Retha M. "Tyranny and Sacrifice in More's *Richard III*." *Perspective as a Problem in the Art, History and Literature of Early Modern England*. Eds. Mark Lussier, and S.K. Heninger. Lewiston, NY: Edwin Mellen P, 1992. 75-80.

Abundant evidence in *Richard III* "strongly supports the suggestion...More adapted to his history the mysteries' themes of tyranny and sacrifice, and even some of their language and dramatic conventions."

Q062 Womersley, David. "Sir Thomas More's *History of King Richard III*: A New Theory of the English Texts." *RenSt* 7.3 (1993): 272-90.

Womersley proposes the variants between the "H" texts and Rastell's 1557 edition of *Richard III* result from Grafton's conscious rewriting of More's history in the light of his own religious convictions, and he speculates upon his investigation's implications for understanding the nature, purpose, and interest of Tudor historiography.

Q063 Yost, Carlson Ward. "The Researched Novel: Definition, Explication of Five Examples, and Theoretical Discussion of Research in Fiction (Thomas More, Michael Crichton, George M. Fraser, William Golding, Josephine Tey)." Diss. Texas A&M U, 1982.

Yost fits More's *Richard III* and Tey's *Daughter of Time* into his definition of the "researched novel"--a work of fiction founded upon a "particular area of information that...explores a particular 'truth'...usually unrecognized or misunderstood." He declares *Richard III* not only the first novel but the first researched novel in English.

Q064 Zeevald, W. Gordon. "A Tudor Defense of Richard III." *PMLA* 55 (1940): 946-57.

On the basis of evidence in early Tudor defense of Richard III and more evidence in George Buc's *History of Richard III*, Zeevald argues Cardinal Morton was the author of the *History* usually attributed to More.

Utopia

R001   Abrash, Merritt. "Missing the Point in More's *Utopia*." *Extrapolation* 19 (1977): 27-38.

Although there can never be a "final word" on *Utopia*, "awkward" facts must be confronted: the "diversions" have odd implications, there is much in *Utopia* of which More could not have approved, and the Utopians frequently miss the point about matters important to both Christians and humanists. Interpreters of *Utopia*, in turn, have missed the point a utopia so marred could not have been intended as "a place of ideal perfection."

R002   Adams, Robert M. "Paradise a la Mode." *Sir Thomas More*, Utopia: *A Revised Translation, Backgrounds, Criticism*. 2nd ed. 211-16.

Adams discusses More's *Utopia* within the context of other utopian/dystopian fictions and emphasizes the elements that make one person's paradise another's hell.

R003   Adams, Robert M. "The Prince and the Phalanx." *Sir Thomas More*, Utopia. *A New Translation, Backgrounds, Criticism*. 1st ed. 192-203.

Adams contrasts the political setting of Machiavelli's *Prince* with that of More's *Utopia* to speculate upon the authors' notions of rulers, the ruled, and power. More simplified the politics of Utopia and minimized temptations so as to concentrate on the morality of the state and its citizens; Machiavelli neglected the morality of his prince because he concentrates "on using to maximum advantage all the human energies of the community."

R004   Adams, Robert P. "Designs by More and Erasmus for a New Social Order." *SP* 42 (1945): 131-45.

Adams posits, although their ideas for a new "golden age" were mainly set forth in the decade following Henry VIII's accession in 1509, they thought of this new culture-to-be not as an isolated English creation, but as an essential part of the loosely unified civilization of Christian Europe. For inspiration they went largely to the Stoic doctrine of life according to reason, as expounded by Cicero, Seneca, and Plutarch, in which the ancients came closest to the true Christian way of life. Adams illustrates these notions in Erasmus' publications against war, especially *Bellum Erasmi*, which anticipates some features of *Utopia*. In *Utopia*, Adams finds a philosophic unity, with the Stoic doctrine as its basis, but modified by the concession the Utopians may pursue not only virtue, but also pleasure, provided it is not the anti-social kind.

R005 Adams, Robert P. "The Philosophic Unity of More's *Utopia*." *SP* 38 (1941): 45-65.

This essay discovers a unified interpretation of *Utopia* in terms of the philosophic ideas underlying its satire. Adams elaborates upon its Epicurean and Stoical elements and contrasts that philosophical basis with that of sixteenth-century Europe, for the central purpose of the book is shown by the fact the good life in Utopia is achieved by man's wisdom and energy alone, whereas the wretched conditions of Europe were the accomplishments of Christians who had divine revelation.

R006 Adams, Robert P. "The Social Responsibilities of Science in *Utopia*, *New Atlantis*, and After." *JHI* 10 (1949): 374-98.

Adams compares the utopianism found in these so-called commonwealths and suggests a few typical attitudes of scientists and their critics toward the prospect for utopian social advances through science. After three-hundred years based on Bacon's theory scientific knowledge is power and good in itself and leads to sensual luxury and greater material comfort, Adams urges the world to awaken from Bacon's dream and turn back to that of More's *Utopia* in which scientific knowledge is applied to the practical solution of social problems and the benefit of all the commonwealth.

R007 Ainger, Alfred. "Sir Thomas More's *Utopia*." *Moreana* 23 (1969): 71-76.

Ainger emphasizes the humor persona More displays in hoping rather than expecting certain Utopian activities and suggestions Hythloday makes will be adopted.

R008 Allen, John William. "A Sad and Witty Book." *Sir Thomas More*, Utopia. *A New Translation, Backgrounds, Criticism*. 1st ed. 220-24.

Originally published in Allen's *A History of Political Thought in the Sixteenth Century* (London: Methuen, 1928, 153-56), this essay considers the fiction of Utopia from the perspective of More's skeptical inability to believe in humankind's capacity for reform and lack of faith in the genuine possibility of change. (Rpt. in part as "The Saddest of Fairy Tales" in *Twentieth-Century Interpretations of* Utopia: *A Collection of Critical Essays*, 104-06.)

R009 Allen, Peter R. "*Utopia* and European Humanism: The Function of the Prefatory Letters and Verses." *SRen* 10 (1963): 91-107.

Allen considers the complicated machinery of the parerga, the prefatory letters and verses of *Utopia*, not merely to be a blurb, but specifically designed to ensure interpretation of the ensuing work as a document of northern European humanism.

R010 Allen, Ward. "Hythloday and the Root of all Evil." *Moreana* 31-32 (1971): 51-59.

Allen argues Hythloday is an inflexible zealot whose cynical attitude towards man's capacity to make sensible use of nature's precious metals is unlikely to have been shared by More.

R011 Allen, Ward. "St. John Chrysostom: A Footnote to *Utopia*." *Moreana* 78 (1983): 21-22.

Allen comments on the two references to one of More's favorite Church Fathers, Chrysostom, which are listed in the Yale *Utopia* (B019)--one on deception, the other on seating men and women in the temple.

R012 Allen, Ward. "Some Remarks on Gold." *Moreana* 18 (1968): 5-6.

Allen believes More's attitude toward gold as to other subjects in *Utopia* is ambiguous, depending upon whether the reader accepts the More speaking as the real More, persona More, or Hythloday.

R013 Allen, Ward. "Speculations on St. Thomas More's Use of Hesychius." *PQ* 46 (1967): 155-66.

This article directs attention to Hythloday's statement Utopians "have no dictionaries except those of Hesychius and Dioscorides," and suggests More used Hesychius to invent words, puns, and features savoring of Mithraism and Gnosticism in pre-Utopian Abraxa.

R014 Allen, Ward. "The Tone of More's Personal Farewell in *Utopia*: A Reply to J.H. Hexter." *Moreana* 51 (1976): 108-18.

According to Hexter, More's defense of private property in *Utopia* is ironic, for neither More nor his contemporaries thought what "mattered in a commonwealth were splendor, magnificence, and majesty." In refutation, Allen points out More's contemporaries did respect magnificence and that it is dangerous to read the "most secret part of More's being." Allen also refutes the findings of Hexter's contextual analysis of Hythloday's use of the words "*nobilitas*," "*magnificentia*," and "*maiestas*," and further points out Hythloday and More are not one and the same in *Utopia*. Though More does offer unironic statements in *Utopia*, for Allen literary devices encourage ambivalence rather than conceal an argument as Hexter believes. (See Hexter's, "Intention, Words, and Meaning: The Case of More's *Utopia*" [R190], and *More's* Utopia: *The Biography of an Idea* [R192].)

R015 Altman, Joel B. *The Tudor Play of Mind: Rhetorical Inquiry and the Development of Elizabethan Drama.* Berkeley: U of California P, 1978. 79-87, 126-29.

Altman explores the intellectual tradition centered on Erasmus and More which sought to teach by question, debate, exploration of topics through rhetorical development of thesis and counter-thesis--an activity requiring participants to make up their minds through an educative process of serious play. He believes *Utopia* creates a narrative from a series of questions with their own independent existence and that persona More and Hythloday represent the various approaches taken to those questions.

R016 Ames, Russell. *Citizen More and His Utopia.* 1949. New York: Russell & Russell, 1969.

Ames approaches *Utopia* not as a theologian or humanist, but as a middle-class social reformer and holds that even under Tudor absolutism the power of feudalism was far from extinct and the middle class still subordinate. In *Utopia*, More spoke on behalf of this class, and Ames uses sections from the book to support this idea. He claims such views would be censored in England and that this was why the work was written in Latin and published abroad. The constitution of Utopia was modeled on that of classical and contemporary city-states, but with significant differences. Land-owning nobility are completely eliminated; while merchants, priests, and scholars remain, and peasants and citizens are merged into one city-country class. Ames discusses the functions of these various social units in More's imaginary commonwealth against the existing background in his own day, not only in England but on the Continent, and concludes More does not find the causes of human misery in the mind or soul but "in material conditions. Human beings do wrong under social compulsion." (Complete introduction is rpt. in *More's* Utopia *and Its Critics*, 135-47; and in part under the titles "The Bourgeois Point of View," *Twentieth-Century Interpretations of* Utopia: *A Collection of Critical Essays*, 53-57, and "More the Social Critic." Utopia. *A New Translation, Backgrounds, Criticism*, 1st ed., 160-70.)

R017 Astell, Ann W. "Rhetorical Strategy and the Fiction of Audience in More's *Utopia*." *CentR* 29 (1985): 302-19.

Astell believes the parerga, which according to More's wishes should accompany his *Utopia*, provide ways for readers to recover the rhetorical context within which the book's symbols are to be understood, and that artifact and audience, structure and rhetorical strategy, must be considered together if readers are to gain an idea of how More's audience reacted.

R018 Avineri, Shlomo. "War and Slavery in More's Utopia." *International Review of Social History* 7 (1962): 260-90.

Avineri relates Utopian attitudes toward war and slavery to the belief the Utopians must banish any evil or imperfection from the ideal state. Although Avineri excuses the Utopian criminal code because of More's times, he finds the section "On Warfare" worthy of Machiavelli, if not Treitschke.

R019 Baker, David. "First Among Equals: The Utopian *Princeps*." *Moreana* 115-116 (1993): 33-45.

The existence of a *princeps* in the "republic" of Utopia is not accidental; on the contrary, his presence serves a complex artistic purpose. As part of More's political satire, *princeps* cuts in two directions: on the one hand, this elected municipal official provides a standard against which the tyranny and incessant desire for power of European *principes* can be measured and critiqued; on the other, *princeps* also indicates that even Utopia is infected by a human desire to be "first" in authority. Ultimately, the problem raised by the concept *princeps* is the inescapability of fallen human nature and the sin of pride.

R020 Baker, David. "'To Divulgate or Set Forth': Humanism and Heresy in Sir Thomas Elyot's *The Book Named the Governor*." *SP* 90 (1993): 46-57.

Elyot's choice of English over Latin in *The Governor* contrasts strikingly with More's *Utopia* which did not reach an "English vernacular readership until the Robinson translation of 1551"; Baker believes *The Governor*, more than a repudiation of Utopian ideas, attempts to control the interpretation of those ideas--especially that of communal property--by manipulating a reading public into whose hands Elyot tries to put *Utopia* in a "way...they all respond 'with one voice.'"

R021 Baker, David. "Topical Utopias: Radicalizing Humanism in Sixteenth-Century England." *ELH* 36 (1996): 1-30.

Baker uses the first English translations of More's *Utopia* and Erasmus' *Moriae Encomium* to argue radical humanism in England was often a matter of reception, timing, and topicality rather than a tradition with an inherent politics, that More's nowhere "provided...a way of both articulating radical sentiments and expressing profound anxieties concerning the possible overlap between high humanist culture and low Protestant sectarians."

R022 Baker-Smith, Dominic. "The Escape from the Cave: Thomas More and the Vision of *Utopia*." *DQR* 15 (1985): 148-61.

Baker-Smith reviews Plato's myth, which is concerned not only with ascent to true vision but also with the problem of return, to explain exactly what disturbs Hythloday: the total failure of ideal vision to penetrate the conventional world. (Rpt. in *Between Dream and Nature: Essays on Utopia and Dystopia*, Eds. Dominic Baker-Smith, and C.C. Barfoot. Costerus. ns 61. Dutch Quarterly Review Studies in Literature. 2 [Amsterdam: Rodopi, 1987], 5-19.)

R023   Baker-Smith, Dominic.   *More's* Utopia.   Unwin Critical Library. London: Harper, 1991.

Baker-Smith sees a *Utopia* in which literary questions are of the essence. More's book, being a work of literature rather than a treatise, does not "propose a course of action but rather seeks to induce a new attitude or quality of mind." The reader "is continuously subjected to rhetorical controls which complicate response and work against any easy identification with a single view," and neither of the principal characters in More's dialogue should be regarded as the author's mouthpiece. Baker-Smith begins his study with four chapters on the biographical, intellectual, and literary contexts of *Utopia*, and he devotes the remainder to detailed exegesis, which assimilates the vast collection of parallels between *Utopia* and previous works, the book and European political life, and More and his humanistic interpreters.

R024   Baker-Smith, Dominic. "Utopia and the Franciscans." *More's* Utopia *and the Utopian Inheritance*. 37-52.

Baker-Smith discusses one component of "More's social world which can heighten" reading *Utopia*, the significance of the Franciscan habit in More's imagination and its connection to the Utopians' "moneyless society."

R025   Ball, Martha Charlene. "Menippean Satire in More's *Utopia* and Erasmus' *Praise of Folly*." Diss. U of Georgia, 1979.

More and Erasmus adapt the Menippean form to their own needs and those of their age and create works that reflect the Christian humanism of the Renaissance, combining as they do both classical and Christian elements. Both *Utopia* and *Praise of Folly* are works of Renaissance humanism which utilize and renew the tradition of Menippean satire.

R026   Baptiste, Victor N.   *Bartolomé de Las Casas and Thomas More's* Utopia: *Connections and Similarities. A Translation and Study*. Culver City, CA: Labyrinthos, 1990.

Baptiste posits a New World source for *Utopia*--the earliest of Las Casas' proposals for the abolition of the murderous *encomienda* system (in which Spanish colonists were granted lands and consignments of Indians to work them) and its replacement by a humane paternalism. Baptiste believes *Utopia* was inspired by Las Casas' *Memorial de Remedios para las Indias* (1516).

Little can be found to support Baptiste's hypothesis.

R027 Barker, Arthur E. "*Clavis Moreana*: The Yale Edition of Thomas More." *JEGP* 65 (1966): 318-30.

In his review of the Yale edition of *Utopia* (B019), Barker stresses the relation and priority between successive Latin and English versions, emphasizing the authorial weight, against editorial and compositorial manipulation, of the 1517 edition.

R028 Barker, Ernest. "*Utopia* and Plato's *Republic*." *Twentieth-Century Interpretations of* Utopia: *A Collection of Critical Essays*. 100-02.

Parts of Barker's "The Later History of the *Republic*" (Appendix B, *The Political Thought of Plato and Aristotle* [London: Methuen, 1906], 525-30) are rpt. in this consideration of the differences between ideas of communism as presented in *Utopia* and *Republic*.

R029 Barnes, Harry Elmer, and Howard Becker. "Thomas More and the Details of His *Utopia*." *Social Thought from Lore to Science*. Vol. 1. *A History and Interpretation of Man's Ideas About Life with His Fellows*. Boston: Heath, 1938. 314-19.

The authors find Plato, the apostles, Church Fathers, and Scholastics strong influences upon *Utopia*'s social theory; see the work as More's reaction to growing commercialization in England; discuss its plans for social rehabilitation in Book II; disagree with claims More is the father of modern socialism; and rank Machiavelli, not More, as a great social thinker.

R030 Barnes, W.J. "Irony and the English Apprehension of Renewal." *QQ* 73 (1966): 357-76.

Irony is one of the stylistic strategies of *Utopia*. The opinions of Hythloday and the More figure taken together result in what More the author wanted to promote--a reasonable reform of the Church and a combination of the best of Christianity and pagan antiquity. Taken apart, neither Hythloday nor the More figure can speak with authority, and this accounts for the peculiar composition of *Utopia*, in which Book I and an appendix to Book II were written after Book II to facilitate an ironic commentary.

R031 Baumann, Uwe. "Herodotus, Aulus Gellius, and More's *Utopia*." *Moreana* 77 (1983): 5-10.

Baumann develops earlier considerations of Herodotus as a source for *Utopia*, comparing the unfortunate gold-bearing Anemolians with Cambyses II's envoys to the Ethiopians and the Utopians' Mithraism with that of the Persians. Hythloday's proposed treatment of criminals may derive from Aulus Gellius.

R032 Beer, Max. "English Utopians." *The General History of Socialism and Social Struggles.* New York: Russell and Russell, 1957. II, 147-80.

Beer devotes a portion of this section to More's life and its inevitable conflict with Henry VIII and discusses *Utopia*'s use of the ethics and politics of the Church Fathers and humanism to explore secular problems.

R033 Bejczy, István. "More's Utopia: The City of God on Earth?" *Saeculum* 46 (1995): 17-30.

Bejczy demonstrates Hythloday's presentation of Utopia as a perfect community fails, because the efforts by which he tries to set Utopia apart from evil, both in time and space, prove to be counter-effective. His failure, however, does not imply *Utopia* fails as a literary work; in fact, showing that failure is precisely the aim of More's work. In so doing, *Utopia* confirms Augustine's teachings, and Hythloday's Utopian adventure can be seen as a radicalized version of the humanist civilizing project. Hythloday's failure ironically depicts the endeavors of humanism to depose the Middle Ages and to put a splendid Renaissance civilization in their place.

R034 Bejczy, István. *Pape Jansland en Utopia: De verbeelding van de beschaving can middleleeuwen en renaissance.* Nijmegen: Universitair Publikatiebureau, 1994.

Bejczy compares the views of Erasmus and More on classical antiquity, the Middle Ages, and the Renaissance; and then focuses on More's vision of historical development and the relationship of the Renaissance to the past as expressed in *Utopia.*

R035 Bejczy, István. "L'*Utopie* et le moyen âge: la purgation de l'histoire." *Moreana* 118-119 (1994): 29-42.

This article concerns itself with the Utopians' attitude toward the cultural tradition of the Middle Ages. Hythloday is supposed to share the humanist contempt of medieval culture, in particular, of Scholasticism. His description of Utopia can likewise be read as an effort to escape this culture. Twelve-hundred years before Hythloday's arrival, the island underwent the influence of classical culture, without knowing medieval decadence afterwards. Hythloday offers Greek literature and Christian revelation to Utopians, making sure medieval culture is kept out; he remains silent on Latin, the language shared with the Middle Ages, as well as on the ecclesiastical and doctrinal history of western Christendom. In achieving his mission, he perfects Utopian culture and realizes his own cultural ideal at the same time.

R036 Berger, Harry, Jr. "The Renaissance Imagination: Second World and Green World." *CentR* 9 (1965): 36-78.

Berger reads *Utopia* in terms of levels of fiction and stresses the relationship between the "second world" of the author's imagination, the book *Utopia*, and the "green world" within the context of Renaissance fiction, the utopian state. He sees More drawing readers into Hythloday's idealized, womblike, inner world, and then forcing them to reconsider. This pattern of withdrawal and return controls the book's structure and meaning. Berger argues Hythloday is depicted ironically and the self-enclosed spatiality of Hythloday's green world is a retreat protected from the outside world. (In part rpt. as "*Utopia*: Game, Chart, or Prayer?" *Sir Thomas More*, Utopia. *A New Translation, Backgrounds, Criticism*, 1st ed., 203-12.)

R037 Berger, Harry, Jr. "Utopian Folly: Erasmus and More on the Perils of Misanthropy." *ELR* 12 (1982): 271-90.

Berger claims the perils of misanthropy in both *Praise of Folly* and *Utopia* dramatize the same vitiated attitude toward life. Plato's Anaxagoras provides the model of the high-minded misanthrope. More's Hythloday and Hythloday's Utopia are in the same spirit; here, ethical reform is replaced by institutional reform or authoritarian repression. Berger analyzes the Utopians' attitudes to home and family, sexual and personal relationships, war, religion, and money to reveal a suspicious, aggressive culture, repressive of the humane and fundamentally negative.

R038 Berneri, Marie Louise. "Sir Thomas More: *Utopia*." *Journey Through Utopia*. 1950. New York: Schocken, 1971. 58-88.

Berneri critiques positive and negative attributes of More's Utopian system--maintaining the positive side includes abolishing private property and wages, exchanging occupations, reducing working hours, and encouraging study; strict control of daily life, marriage laws, slavery and attitudes toward war and imperialism compose the dark side.

R039 Bevington, David M. "The Dialogue in *Utopia*: Two Sides to the Question." *SP* 58 (1961): 496-509.

Bevington examines More's use of dialogue in Book I as a means of presenting a balanced, middle view of the topics under discussion by allowing the speakers to express conflicting opinions on current problems, which are deliberately left unsolved. Similarly, the account of Utopia is an impartial survey of problems which preoccupied More's inquiring mind concerning the ideal form of political and social organization. (Rpt. in *More's* Utopia *and Its Critics*, 160-70; and under the title "The Divided Mind." *Twentieth-Century Interpretations of* Utopia: *A Collection of Critical Essays*, 76-87.)

R040 Bierman, Judah. "Science and Society in the *New Atlantis* and Other Renaissance Utopias." *PMLA* 78 (1963): 492-500.

Bacon's book not only presents a view of science not shown in his other works, but also contrasts strikingly with the view of science in other Renaissance utopias, such as More's.

R041 Billingsley, Dale B. "Halfhearted Busleyden." *Moreana* 122 (1995): 49-55.

Busleyden's two letters, one written for publication, one sent privately to Erasmus, demonstrate the difficulties presented to writers of the *Utopia* parerga, and can be used as a means to think again about the difficulties of *Utopia*. The relationship among More, Erasmus, and the parergists is thus highly complex, and that complexity is partly reflected in the circumstances of anyone who undertakes to write about *Utopia*.

R042 Billingsley, Dale B. "A Mare's Nest: Pliny, Mandeville, and Hythloday on the Incubation of Eggs." *Moreana* 67 (1980): 80.

If More is looking toward Mandeville as well as Pliny, Hythloday's silence about the means of producing a "uniform heat" can be explained by *Utopia*'s next sentence: "They rear very few horses."

R043 Binder, James. "More's *Utopia* in English: A Note on Translation." *MLN* 62 (1947): 370-76.

Binder declares the often elaborate descriptions added by Robinson alter (usually in the direction of gorgeousness) what More intended in *Utopia*, and he surmises Robinson's translation may affect the work's interpretation. Since Robinson was not a careful student of More's ideas, some implications of what More said in *Utopia* may have escaped him. (Rpt. in *Essential Articles for the Study of Thomas More*, 229-33.)

R044 Blaim, Artur. "The Genre Structure of More's *Utopia* and the Tradition of Carnivalized Literature." *RCEI* 6 (1983): 1-14.

Blaim demonstrates that, in all its major structural characteristics, among which "genre polymorphism" appears most prominent, *Utopia* conforms to the general pattern of carnivalized literature, especially its most complex variety, the *menippea*; and that one of the book's organizing principles, the idea of the world upside down, goes back to the very roots of the carnival.

R045 Blaim, Artur. "More's *Utopia*: Persuasion or Polyphony?" *Moreana* 73 (1982): 5-20.

Blaim counters the notion the book is a straightforward treatise advocating communism or demonstrating arguments against it--persuasion--and advances the idea that, as a complex literary work affirming no single ideology, it is open to many contradictory interpretations--polyphony.

R046 Bleich, David. "More's *Utopia*: Confessional Modes." *AI* 28 (1971):

24-52.

Bleich proposes *Utopia* gave More the opportunity to express his deep desire for ultimate paternalistic authority and to transform frustrations engendered by the repression of sexuality and acquisitiveness into a pleasing work of art.

R047   Bloom, Nicolas van der. "2 x unus=?" *Moreana* 36 (1972): 39-46.

Blom argues More's allusion to an anonymous "*vir pius*" in the prefatory letter to *Utopia*, a cleric wishing to visit Utopia to further the Christian conversion of the islanders and to be created bishop of Utopia to facilitate his work, is a jesting suggestion by or to Erasmus, who in 1516 was himself proposed for nomination as a bishop. Bloom also attempts to identify a certain statesman ("*unum*") referred to in More's letter to Erasmus of 20 September 1516, who wished the publication of the book delayed, concluding that here is another private joke, More referring to his own reluctance to publish the work.

R048   Boesky, Amy Diane. "The Rhetoric of Reform: English Utopian Narrative, 1516-1667." Diss. Harvard U, 1989.

Boesky studies the sociology of utopia in More's *Utopia*, Bacon's *New Atlantis*, Cavendish's *The Blazing World*, and Milton's *Paradise Lost* as examples of a literary genre in Renaissance England, which encode within them contradictions about the nature of reform and the concealed political agenda of improvement. Chapter one compares the establishment of St. Paul's School (1509) with the aspirations of More's fictitious island.

R049   Boewe, Charles. "Human Nature in More's *Utopia*." *Personalist* 41 (1960): 303-09.

Although good men should inhabit a perfect society, More did not believe eliminating vice would necessarily or rapidly result in good men. More was concerned with man's environment and capabilities, which he believed could be improved by education, but not be transmitted biologically.

R050   Bolchazy, Ladislaus J., Gregory Cichan, and Frederick Theobald. *A Concordance to the* Utopia *of St. Thomas More and A Frequency Word List*. Hildesheim, Ger.: George Olms, 1978.

The editors provide an invaluable concordance based on and keyed to the Yale edition of *Utopia* (B019). A word frequency list arranges words in descending order of frequency and supplies counts for each one listed.

R051   Bony, Alain. "Fabula, Tabula: *L'Utopie* de More et l'Image du Monde." *EA* 30 (1977): 1-19.

Bony explores illustrations of early editions of *Utopia* and compares the awkwardness of illustration in the 1516 edition to that of the 1518 edition, due in part to its attempt to be faithful to More's text and in part to the notion it would be impossible to capture any utopia because of its nature in any illustration.

R052 Bourlès, Charles. "La Place De L'Utopie dans la Litterature de Science Fiction." *Moreana* 83-84 (1984): 197-203.

Bourlès compares the forms, contents, and themes of some works of utopian/dystopian literature with those of science fiction.

R053 Boyle, Anthony Thomas. "The Epistemological Evolution of Renaissance Utopian Literature, 1516-1657." Diss. New York U, 1983.

Boyle provides a unified vision of this period's utopian tradition from More's *Utopia* to Harrington's *Oceana* and explains the influential forces behind them by examining them as part of an epistemological evolution.

R054 Bradshaw, Brendan. "More on *Utopia*." *Historical Journal* 24 (1981): 1-27.

Bradshaw reviews the views of Hexter, Surtz, and Skinner as he discusses the debate about the meaning of *Utopia* which comes down essentially to the question of what is made of Book II in which the fictitious narrator, Hythloday, gives an account of the island of *Utopia*. The problem of interpretation is twofold: what does More intend to describe and what is his purpose in describing it.

R055 Branham, R. Bracht. "Utopian Laughter: Lucian and Thomas More." *Moreana* 86 (1985): 23-43.

By retracing the shifting rhetorical boundaries along which More's "jest-earnest" discourse confronts or converges with Lucian, Branham emphasizes More's adaptation of Lucianic themes and techniques "carefully purged of qualities unsuited" to his purposes in *Utopia*.

R056 Brann, Eva. "'An Exquisite Platform': *Utopia*." *IJPP* 3 (1972): 1-26.

Brann deals with utopias in general and *Utopia* specifically as imaginative "political poetry," and focuses on More's work as a "reflection of the political imagination," which proposes a community without pride through which readers might imagine what human nature might achieve.

R057 Bronowski, Jacob, and Bruce Mazlish. "Thomas More." *The Western Intellectual Tradition: From Leonardo to Hegel*. New York: Harper, 1960. 44-60.

Chapter four compares *Utopia* to Machiavelli's *Prince*, examines More's life and how it relates to that work, and emphasizes More's versatility and excellence. The authors believe *Utopia*'s communal vision revises and expands upon *The Rule of St. Benedict*, criticizes as much of the medieval world as it does that of the sixteenth century, and presents a synthesis of many conflicts between the old and the new of More's times.

R058 Bruce, Susan. "Reason, Belief and Morality in Thomas More's *Utopia*." *PQ* 75 (1996): 267-86.

Utopia's "discourse on the problem of death," when read in conjunction with its philosophical observations about the nature of belief, creates ethical, political, and epistemological difficulties the text can neither contain nor resolve.

R059 Brückmann, Patricia. "*In familiari colloquio*: An Intervention in *Utopia*." *Familiar Colloquy: Essays Presented to Arthur Edward Barker*. Ed. Patricia Brückmann. Ottawa, Can.: Oberon P, 1978. 9-14.

Brückmann demonstrates that, apart from the uncertainties generated by the very look of Utopia itself, some important interventions move the work from a "Hythlodaian" monologue to something like a dialogue, in addition to the simple fact not often regarded, More begins and ends the entire performance.

R060 Brugmans, Henri. "Thomas More." *RN* 44 (1966): 3-20.

Brugmans finds at the roots of *Utopia* the spiritual crisis of a generation and claims More was the wisest, noblest, and often most generally indignant representative of that generation.

R061 Campbell, W.E. *More's* Utopia *and His Social Teachings*. 1930. New York: Russell and Russell, 1973.

In his extended meditation on the links between More's religious and social thinking, Campbell writes as a Christian examining the ideas of another Christian in whom strong belief in natural reason was accompanied by equally strong faith in the supernatural. *Utopia* admits the claims of man's natural life but also asserts the higher claims of supernatural life; thus, while More and Hythloday unite in attacking political, social inequalities, only More believes God's grace may change men's hearts to eradicate injustice.

R062 Campbell, W.E. "The *Utopia* of Sir Thomas More." *The King's Good Servant*. Papers Read to the Thomas More Society of London. Ed. Richard O'Sullivan. Oxford: Basil Blackwell, 1948. 26-39.

It is wrong to assume Hythloday rather than persona More represents the author's views. Because persona More has the last word on what Hythloday says about communal ownership in Book II, Campbell says it is safe to assume the author rejects communism. Campbell also rejects the opinion More's own beliefs and actions contradict ideas on religious toleration in *Utopia*.

R063 Carlson, Cindy Laurel. "Imagining Justice in Late Medieval and Tudor Literature." Diss. Columbia U, 1989.

Carlson examines the *Ludus Coventriae*, More's *Utopia*, and Book V of Spenser's *Fairie Queene* and how they consider the relationship of law and procedure in promoting justice. *Utopia*, though it takes up legal procedure, concentrates on finding social justice through the rule of law which, for More, offers an external restraint to the ruler tempted to govern tyrannically.

R064 Carpenter, Nan C. "St. Thomas More and Music: Busleiden's Organ." *CLS* 15 (1978): 17-22.

Carpenter delineates why More's visit to Busleiden's home and enjoyment of the organ music he heard there are significant in illuminating the famous passage in *Utopia*. Carpenter goes on to say *Utopia* was launched on music as it begins with persona More coming from Church service.

R065 Caspari, Fritz. "Humanism as Utopia's Central Principle." *Thomas Morus Jahrbuch 1995*. 46-52.

Caspari contends More's aim in writing *Utopia* is "to show, on his imaginary island, a humanistic state ruled by good, wise...men educated according to the classical principles of the humanists."

R066 Caspari, Fritz. "Sir Thomas More and *Justum Bellum*." Ethics 56 (1946): 303-08.

Caspari believes the conditions *Utopia* advances to justify war were not original and can be found in Aristotle and Aquinas; More does not foresee British colonization and support "just war" in order to rationalize imperialism.

R067 Cassirer, Ernst. *The Platonic Renaissance in England*. Trans. James P. Pettegrove. Austin: U of Texas P, 1953. 22-24, 107-11, 119-20, 172-73, 186-87.

Cassirer gives an estimate of More's thought and character, sees the hedonism of *Utopia* as an expression of its pervasive Platonism, notices a debt to Plato's *Philebus*, and finds in *Utopia* the outline of a religion based on "the purest and best worship of the divine being" rather than on dogmatic theology. (Rpt. as "Religion without Dogma" in *Twentieth-Century Interpretations of Utopia: A Collection of Critical Essays*, 106-08.)

R068 Cavanaugh, John R. "*Utopia*: Sound from Nowhere." *Moreana* 35 (1972): 27-38.

Subsisting on "sayable" material preserved in commonplaces, classical and medieval rhetoric, even when written, operated in a predominantly oral-aural milieu. Analysis of *Utopia* discloses a high incidence of *sententiae*, adages, formulaic expressions characteristic of an oral rather than a chirographic frame of reference. The prefatory letter to Peter Giles explicitly aligns the work with traditional rhetoric--invention, disposition, eloquence, memory, delivery. Within the larger context of More's "discourse" reporting a dialogue, readers hear (or overhear) conversations, voices from the actual past and from the hypothetical future. There are abrupt shifts from speaker to speaker and a minimum of expository writing. The pervasiveness of oral rhetorical attitudes and practices is attested in the response of Erasmus and Giles who added marginal comments. Their voices resonate with those inside the text contributing to and echoing the book's polyphonic quality.

R069 Chené, Adèle. "La proximité et la distance dans l'*Utopie* de Thomas More." *Ren&R* 10 (1986): 277-88.

Chené analyzes the treatment of distance and its relationship to time and space in *Utopia*.

R070 Chirpaz, Par François. "Plaidoyer pour l'Utopie." *Esprit* 42 (1974): 567-84.

Chirpaz examines ideas of the social, economic, and religious institutions of the utopian/dystopian works of Plato, More, Campanella, Bacon, Rousseau, Huxley, and Orwell.

R071 Chomarat, Jacques. "*Superstitio, Religio, et Impietas.*" *Moreana* 83-84 (1984): 151-56.

Chomarat uses a linguistic approach to compare More's treatment of superstition (especially in *Utopia*) to that of Erasmus.

R072 Coles, Paul. "The Interpretation of More's *Utopia*." *Hibbert Journal* 56 (1958): 365-70.

Coles rejects recent British comment *Utopia* is a "fantasia, a *jeu d'esprit*," and suggests reasons for accepting the work as a serious exercise in political thought. He thinks Book II could have stood alone without Book I which was subsequently added partly to provide a more leisurely, interesting introduction to More's powerful statement about the felicity and stability of life in Utopia without private property and a money economy and partly to add to this picture of an idealized society a description and castigation of the social, economic, and political evils of Europe and England.

R073 Coogan, Robert. "'Nunc Vivo et Volo.'" *Moreana* 31-32 (1971): 29-45.

Coogan discusses rival interpretations of Hythloday and the relationship between More and his character, arguing that, far from repudiating Hythloday's views, More admired the independent, freedom-loving mariner and intended his readers to do so, also.

R074 Corrigan, Kevin. "The Function of the Ideal in Plato's *Republic* and St. Thomas More's *Utopia*." *Moreana* 104 (1990): 27-49.

Corrigan argues against abstract, idealistic interpretations of the *Republic* and *Utopia* according to which the essence of the former is the preservation of the static ideal and that of the latter the delineation of the perfect ideal "proof against change." Book II of *Utopia* presents not *the* ideal, but *an* ideal, albeit flawed--a counter-example to the corrupt forms of Book I, which, however fictional, reveals a truth about human nature. As a whole, *Utopia* is constructed according to a complex form of opposition in which fact and fiction, the real and illusory, interpenetrate each other, and yet remain opposed. More presents a dilemma for critical discernment in a manner which catches, and yet transforms, one of the most profound motifs in the Platonic dialogues, and the *Republic* in particular--namely, that in and through perplexity and consequent discernment the ideal be recognized concretely both in nature itself and in the heart of man.

R075 Cox, Virginia. *The Renaissance Dialogue: Literary dialogue in its social and political contexts, Castiglione to Galileo.* Cambridge Studies in Renaissance Literature and Culture 2. Cambridge: Cambridge UP, 1992. 10, 118, 134.

Cox observes "the distinction between real and fictional characters is by no means clear-cut" in More's *Utopia*.

R076 Crosset, John. "More and Lucian." *MLN* 72 (1957): 169-70.

Lucian's dialogue, *Charon 12*, in which Solon proves to Croesus iron is more valuable than gold, affords an analogue to the passage on gold in *Utopia*. Though the moral is the same, its tone varies considerably: Lucian is quick and merry, and his morality is implicit in his wit; More is didactic and speaks openly of *stultitin hominum*.

R077 Crossett, John. "More and Seneca." *PQ* 40 (1961): 577-80.

Crossett discusses an allusion by persona More in his conversation with Hythloday to Seneca's disputation with Nero in *Octavia*. Because that passage voices some of the central ideas in *Utopia* and in Hythloday's comments, particularly with respect to the advantages of retirement from civic duties and the virtues of the Golden Age, More must have been impressed with it.

R078 Crossett, John. "Two Notes on More's *Utopia*." *N&Q* ns 7.10 (Oct. 1960): 366-67.

A passage from Herodotus (II, 172) in which the gold foot pan of an Egyptian king is to be melted to form the image of a god and worshipped may have been the source for More's statement in which the Utopians use gold for chamber pots. The second note has nothing to do with sources and comments on the textual problem of the omission of one sentence in Robinson's translation.

R079 D'Amico, Jack. "The Garden of King Utopus." *MQ* 26 (1985): 499-509.

D'Amico argues the garden of King Utopus allows its citizens to experience a sense of human measure which justifies and transcends society. Without that humanity society becomes chaotic; that sense of measure is, as King Utopus knew, something that cannot be legislated, and the highest objective of the state can only be fulfilled in that space and time set aside for play.

R080 Daniel-Rops, Henri. "Thomas More, Planiste de l'*Utopie*." *Moreana* 6 (1965): 5-8.

Of all the Utopian writers of the Renaissance, More is the most relevant today. The problems of *Utopia*, materialism and impersonality, are ours.

R081 Davis, J.C. "More, Morton, and the Politics of Accommodation." *Journal of British Studies* 9 (1970): 27-49.

Davis defines "the place of accommodation in More's thinking" when he wrote *Utopia*. Was he seriously advocating the approach to politics of the fictional "More" in Book I and, if so, how can this be related to the ideal state of Book II? The two parts were written at different dates and in different environments, Book II (1515) in the Netherlands and Book I (1516) in London. In the latter, throughout a long debate, "More" urges upon Hythloday the claims of state service in the public interest. Hythloday's final counter-argument is that philosophy and the philosopher are impeded not by the essential nature of kings and their courts, but by the malfunctioning structure of society in contemporary western Europe as contrasted with that of Utopia. The case "More" puts forward in the debate reflects the influence of the ambivalent Morton and his entourage, "a society of flatterers and hangers-on," such as More already depicted in his enigmatic and unfinished *Richard III*. Viewed within this context, "the trimmer's prescription" seems crucial to understanding *Utopia* and appreciating its value, as Davis sees the polarization of idealism and accommodation as an "unresolved examination of means."

R082 Davis, J.C. "The Re-emergence of Utopia: Sir Thomas More." *Utopia and the Ideal Society: A Study of English Utopian Writing 1516-1700*. Cambridge: Cambridge UP, 1981. 41-61.

In chapter two, Davis believes *Utopia* is More's answer to the question, "how a good social order can be arrived at and maintained," and that Book II responds to the social-political reality of sixteenth-century Europe depicted in Book I "in the direction of goodness" achieved by loss of privacy, autonomy, and freedom.

R083 Davis, J.C. *Utopia and the Ideal Society.* Cambridge: Cambridge UP, 1981.

Davis distinguishes utopia from the millennium, cockaygne, arcadia, and perfect moral commonwealth, defining it by its concern to "project a total social environment," its recognition of human failings, and its willingness to control the consequent problems through institutional discipline, rather than promote individual happiness. He reviews a range of English and European texts in chronological order; *Utopia* itself does not receive a very penetrating analysis (arguments against it being intended by More as a picture of a perfect society need more consideration).

R084 Davis, Walter. "Thomas More's *Utopia* as Fiction." *CentR* 24 (1980): 249-68.

Davis designates Book I as a dialogue about the sort of thing fiction is about and Book II as the fiction itself. He views the work as an exposition and explanation of the new humanist concept of how fiction could be used to make readers' lives better, if not perfect, by causing them to respond to the image of a possible ideal of society.

R085 Delcourt, Marie. "Le Pouvoir du Roi dans *l'Utopie*." *Mélanges Offerts a M. Abel Lefranc.* Paris: Droz, 1936. 101-12.

Delcourt discusses the purpose and duties of the prince in *Utopia*, the constitution of the utopian state, and the ideas of Rabelais, Erasmus, and More on those subjects.

R086 Demenier, Hubert. "La propriété en utopie: réflexions d'un juriste." *Moreana* 118-119 (1994): 85-101.

Demenier explores the field of reflection More's *Utopia* opens up about the relationship between social institutions and the harmonious development of the individual.

R087 Dennis, Norman, and A.H. Halsey. "A Practical Utopia, Thomas More (1478-1535)." *English Ethical Socialism: Thomas More to R.H. Tawney.* Oxford: Clarendon P, 1988. 13-25.

While focusing largely on Tawney, the authors find his predecessors in More, Corbett, Hothouse, Orwell, and Marshall. They regard ethical socialism, based on classical sociology, as the liberal reply to Marxism, and consider More as one of its founding fathers, for he is an "exceptionally distinguished early son of the tradition and his Utopians are ethical socialists."

R088 Dermauw, Gerard. "Retrospective sur Bruges et Thomas More." *Moreana* 36 (1972): 103-04.

Dermauw finds a possible reason for More making his fool in *Utopia* a native of Bruges in a popular anecdote concerning Charles Count of Flanders (later Charles V) and the burghers of the town.

R089 Derrett, J. Duncan M. "Gemistus Plethon, the Essenes, and More's *Utopia*." *BHR* 27 (1965): 579-606.

Derrett traces parallels between these works and notes the similarity between More's ideal commonwealth, with respect to political and social organization and religion, and Plethon's "Vision of the Peloponnesus," as well as with accounts of the Essenes by Josephus and Philo.

R090 Derrett, J. Duncan M. "More's *Utopia* and Indians in Europe." *Moreana* 5 (1965): 17-18.

References to Indians in *Utopia* may have been inspired by their actual presence in Europe and not by literary sources.

R091 Derrett, J. Duncan M. "Thomas More and Joseph the Indian." *Journal of the Royal Asiatic Society of Great Britain and Ireland*, Pts. 1 & 2 (1962): 18-34.

Derrett believes parts of Hythloday's description of Utopia so "clearly" represent India that More must have drawn directly from "genuine Indian ideas." He is especially interested in parallels between Utopian and Hindu religious practices, and he relates Utopians' attitude toward and uses of gold to some Indian beliefs. He claims More's information about India and Hinduism came from travel literature written by Joseph the Indian.

R092 Derrett, J. Duncan M. "The Utopian Alphabet." *Moreana* 12 (1966): 61-66.

Derrett thinks More and Peter Giles devised the Utopian alphabet from ideas they derived from a printed work by Bernhard von Breitenbach and a work circulated in ms. by Arnold von Harff, both of which contain the alphabets of many Asian nations, especially the Arabic.

R093 Derrett, J. Duncan M. "The Utopians' Stoic Chamber-Pots." *Moreana* 73 (1982): 75-76.

Derrett declares the "true" source of the Utopians' golden chamber pots is located in Plutarch's lengthy attack of the Stoics in the *Moralia*, to which More had access in the Aldine edition of 1509.

R094 Desroches, Rosny. "L'Utopie, Evasion ou Anticipation?" *France and North America: Utopias and Utopians*. Proceedings of the Third Symposium of French-American Studies, March 4-8, 1974. Ed. Mathe Allain. Lafayette, LA: U of Southwest Louisiana, 1978. 83-92.

Desroches places More's *Utopia* and its treatment of key issues within the context of Plato, Bacon, Fénelon, Auguste Comte, Renan, Wells, Huxley, and Bertrand Russell.

R095 Di Luca, Adolfo. "Inventio and Fabula in More, Hall and Swift." *Per una definizione dell'utopia: Metodologie e discipline a confronto*. Atti del Convengo Internazionale di Bagni di Lucca, 12-14 settembre 1990. Ed. Nadia Minerva. Ravenna: Longo, 1992. 81-88.

Di Luca investigates the role of fictionality and its relationship to reader in *Utopia* and compares it to that of Hall's *Mundus Alter et Idem* and Swift's *Gulliver's Travels*.

R096 Di Luca, Adolfo. "La retorica della persuasione nell'*Utopia* di Thomas More." *LdProv* 23.81 (1991): 75-93.

Di Luca analyzes the rhetorical strategies More utilizes in *Utopia*.

R097 Di Scipio, Guiseppe C. "*De Re Militari i*n Machiavelli's *Prince* and More's *Utopia*." *Moreana* 77 (1983): 11-22.

This study shows the similarity of thought in the *Prince* and *Utopia* as it regards armies, war, and the security of the state. At first glance the works may seem to be at opposite poles; yet they have much in common, for both authors advocate basically a self-reliance, strength, and independence that can only be obtained by having an army of citizens who will fight for their good and the good of the commonweal with a spirit of love, sacrifice, and valor.

R098 Domenach, Jean-Marie. Introduction to special edition of *Esprit*, "L'*Utopie* ou La Raison dans l'Imaginaire." *Esprit* 42 (1974): 545-56.

Domenach examines the significance of the word, utopia, and its many contradictions and paradoxes.

R099 Donnelly, Dorothy F. "Temporal and Cosmic Order: The Making of a New Vision in Thomas More's *Utopia*." *PPMRC* 9 (1984): 103-16.

Donnelly analyzes the social, political infrastructure of the Utopian system to show More abandons classical and medieval conceptions of order (systems wherein a world outside the temporal world gives order to it) and develops the notion humankind (independent of systems that transcend time) can, by using reason and intelligence, create an ordered world. This theme of order, not political philosophy or religion, unites *Utopia*.

R100 Donnelly, Dorothy F. "*Utopia* and *Gulliver's Travels*: Another Perspective." *Moreana* 97 (1988): 115-24.

Donnelly shows with respect to two main themes in *Utopia* and *Gulliver's Travels*--the nature of reason and the concept of order--that *Travels* is more anti-utopian in outlook than is generally acknowledged, and this anti-utopianism derives in part from Swift's strongly negative attitude toward human reason, and in part from his inability to offer a conception of order which would give meaning to existence.

R101 Donner, H.W. "The Interpretation of *Utopia*." *SN* 15 (1942-43): 43-48.

Donner believes if the first book, which was written after the second, had not been added, *Utopia* would not have been regarded as anything but a "*jeu d'esprit*." That the first book is critical of the actual conditions of Europe has led critics to conclude the second book must be constructive. Donner claims the opposite is true. The first book offers practical suggestions for reforms; the second is ironic. The virtues of the pagan Utopians show up by contrast the vices of Christian Europe, but their society is not ideal because it is enlightened only by reason, not revealed religion.

R102 Donner, H.W. *Introduction to* Utopia. 1946. Freeport, NY: Books for Libraries P, 1969.

This is not a long book, but it is an important critical work written to counter both communist and imperialist (capitalist) theories about *Utopia*. It stresses the original Latin form, which to More, was a living language; analyzes the Robinson translation; comments on the work's sources; and agrees with R.W. Chambers that *Utopia* presents a picture of the best state humans can attain without revelation. He concludes More would be surprised to find his insights have been translated into practical projects. The book is complete with valuable notes and references. (Part is rpt. as "A Moral Fable" in *Twentieth-Century Interpretation of* Utopia: *A Collection of Critical Essays*, 33-39.)

R103 Donskis, Leonidas. "The End of Utopia?" *SCUL* 79 (1996): 197-219.

Donskis explores More's *Utopia* and its "ideological framework of Reformation England" (along with other utopian/dystopian works) to reassess the place and purposes of utopianism in past and current life and thought.

R104 Dooley, Patrick K. "More's *Utopia*: An Ecosystem at Climax Stage." *Moreana* 101-102 (1990): 37-46.

Dooley finds it worthwhile to consider the goals and accomplishments of the communal society in *Utopia* in the light of "traits characteristic of mature ecosystems." While he observes such examination provides valuable insights into *Utopia* (and the notion of utopian living generally), it also raises questions about the Utopians' ability (and that of others who strive for such goals) to maintain such ecological perfection.

R105 Dooley, Patrick K. "More's *Utopia* and the New World Utopias: Is the Good Life an Easy Life?" *Thought* 60 (1985): 31-48.

Dooley posits More's *Utopia* as a theoretical blueprint for a perfect society against which the actual practices of "real" nineteenth-century New World utopian communities are measured. Specifically, More's views on communism, work, and leisure are compared with the arrangements in New World counterparts.

R106 Dooley, Patrick K. "Theory in *Utopia* Vs. Practice in Utopias: An Invitation to *Thought*." *Moreana* 87-88 (1985): 57-60.

Dooley calls attention to an opportunity for a "straightforward empirical comparison": More's *Utopia* depicted a perfect society and between 1800 and 1900 more than fifty communitarian societies sought to achieve perfect societies in America. When More's theory is compared against the New World practices, it is clear some of More's ideas are soundly affirmed, while others are seriously questioned.

R107 Dorsch, T.S. "Sir Thomas More and Lucian: An Interpretation of *Utopia*." *Archiv* 203 (1967): 345-63.

Dorsch summarizes Lucian's career, works, and techniques; presents *Utopia*'s main points; and argues More turns *Utopia* into a dystopia through the use of Lucianic irony. He concludes *Utopia* and *Gulliver's Travels* are the "two most beautifully developed and most consistently sustained works of Lucianic irony in English literature." (Part of this essay is rpt. as "A Detestable State" in *Twentieth-Century Interpretations of* Utopia: *A Collection of Critical Essays*, 88-99.)

R108 D'Ottavi, Stefania D'Agata. "Tra due utopie." *Per una definizione dell'utopie: Metodologie e discipline a confronto*. Atti del Convengo Internazionale di Bagni di Lucca, 12-14 settembre 1990. Ed. Nadia Minerva. Ravenna: Longo, 1992. 71-80.

D'Ottavi compares *Utopia* to Bacon's *New Atlantis*.

R109 Doyle, Charles Clay. "Ambassadors in China: A Pun in *Utopia*." *Moreana* 59-60 (1978): 90.

Doyle suggests a pun in *Utopia* on *legatus/ligatus*, making the ambassadors' chains signs of servitude.

R110 Doyle, Charles Clay. "Baring Some Facts." *Moreana* 95-96 (1987): 17-18.

Doyle adds more prototypes and analogues to the Utopians' custom of presenting prospective marital partners naked for one another's scrutiny.

R111 Doyle, Charles Clay. "The Mysterious Malady of Pieter Gillis." *Moreana* 110 (1992): 35-37.

Doyle speculates about the nature of Giles' sickness of which Erasmus writes More in a letter of May 1517.

R112 Doyle, Charles Clay. "Poggio and the Anemolian Ambassadors." *Moreana* 15 (1978): 61-63.

Although Doyle finds that parallels between Poggio Bracciolini's *Facetiae* (published posthumously in 1470 and the source of innumerable epigrams) and the Anemolian ambassadors are not especially close, certain passages share emphasis on ostentation and the play on chains as ornaments about the neck and as implements of bondage.

R113 Doyle, Charles Clay. "*Utopia* and the Proper Place of Gold: Classical Sources and Renaissance Analogues." *Moreana* 31 (1971): 47-49.

Doyle examines classical writers--Ovid, Horace, Boethius--on the subject of gold which "for the ancients and for the humanists was a paradox. Its name designated the world's first and most perfect age; yet it was the root of all evil." He also finds analogues to More's perception of gold in Spenser, Milton, and Phineas Fletcher. (Ward Allen responds to Doyle in "Hythloday and the Root of All Evil" [R010].)

R114 Doyle, Charles Clay. "The Utopians' Therapeutic Chamber-Pots." *Moreana* 73 (1982): 75.

Doyle touches on the deep-seated connection between gold and excrement, as in ancient Levantine tales, popular jest books (*Tales and Quicke Answeres*, c. 1532), Jonson's *Alchemist*, and Freudian psychology.

R115 Doyon, Jacques. "La Loi dans L'*Utopie* de More." *Moreana* 103 (1990): 95-99.

Doyon considers the relationship between the laws of Utopian institutions and religious and moral laws of More's time and other times.

R116 Duhamel, P. Albert. "Medievalism of More's *Utopia*." *SP* 52 (1955): 99-126.

Duhamel claims scholarly concentration almost exclusively on the political content of *Utopia* as an anticipation of modern liberal thinking has resulted in the paradox that probably the most medieval of More's works is commonly interpreted as the most Renaissance. *Utopia* comes into true focus when viewed as the product of the Scholastic method, revealing the limitations of the method and the society responsible for it. *Utopia* is all of a piece, marking the end of the Middle Ages and their methods, and the beginnings of a Renaissance which was to rely on different methods of investigation and interpretation. (Rpt. in *Essential Articles for the Study of Thomas More*, 234-50.)

R117 Dujardin, Philippe. "Régime de la Loi, Régime des Images: Le Temple Vide de L'île d'Utopie." *Impressions d'îles*. Ed. Françoise Létoublon. Toulouse: Presses Universitaires du Mirail, 1996. 231-45.

Dujardin studies Utopian beliefs about pleasure, leisure, and other topics to analyze how they affect the design and use of certain spaces, for instance religious edifices, in More's work.

R118 Dupré, Louis. *Passage to Modernity: An Essay in the Hermeneutics of Nature and Culture*. New Haven: Yale UP, 1993. 151-52, 193-94.

Dupré mentions More's *Utopia* and its Utopians who "uninhibitedly embrace the principle of pleasure," and compares the work to *New Atlantis* and *City of the Sun*.

R119 Dust, Philip. "Alberico Gentili's Commentaries on Utopian War." *Moreana* 37 (1973): 31-40.

Gentili is a legal casuist, More a literary humanist. Although Gentili's *De Iure Belli* and More's *Utopia* follow the same pattern in treating war, its motives and justifications, procedures and policies, and formal conclusions; Gentili does not distinguish between Hythloday's contradictions, inadequate proposals, and ambiguities, and the reactions of persona More. He cites passages from *Utopia* "as instances of previous legal judgment" rather than as "an ironic account" of such judgment and fails to notice persona More's suggestion Hythloday's account requires further discussion and that persona More's objection to Utopian war practice is similar to his own. (Rpt. in Dust's *Three Renaissance Pacifists: Essays in the Theories of Erasmus, More, and Vives* [G022].)

R120 Dust, Philip. "Two Allusions to the *Iliad* in the *Utopia*." *Moreana* 98-99 (1988): 213-14.

Dust notes strategy in Homer's *Iliad* becomes strategy for More's *Utopia*. Wise old Nestor, the Greek, is really the model for the Utopians who have supposedly achieved a culture superior to that of Europe without European aid.

R121 Egan, Willis J. "Thomas More: Other-Worldling and Prophet of Secularity." *Moreana* 51 (1976): 102-07.

As a man of his times, More, unable to transcend the perspectives of medieval Christianity, did not espouse the world, but his imagination allowed him to create a philosophy for Utopians which affirms and embraces the world. According to this philosophy, the institutions of secularized society exist and develop autonomously from consciously religious thought, and its members instead of disdaining the world accept it and human nature because both are God-given. *Utopia* echoes these beliefs, for Utopians exult in the satisfaction of being human, receive the world as God's gift, and rationally pursue the good life in large part through their autonomous institutions.

R122 El-Gabalawy, Saad. "The *Ars Moriendi* in More's *Utopia*." *Mosaic* 11 (1978): 115-26.

El-Gabalawy explores the issue of death in *Utopia* against its classical and Christian backgrounds, with special reference to relevant works of the *ars moriendi* in the sixteenth and early seventeenth centuries.

R123 El-Gabalawy, Saad. "Christian Communism in *Utopia, King Lear*, and *Comus*." *UTQ* 47 (1978): 228-38.

In *Utopia* and his early writing, More is critical of private property, which is associated with the sin of *superbia*, and favors the ideals of community and common ownership. King Lear and Gloucester advocate "redistributive justice," and Milton's Lady argues for *sobrietas*. In all three writers, the purpose of Christian communism is the preparation of men on earth for the city of God.

R124 Eliav-Feldon, Miriam. "Thomas More (1477-1535)." *Realistic Utopias: The Ideal Imaginary Societies of the Renaissance, 1516-1630*. Oxford History Monographs. 146. Oxford: Clarendon P, 1982. 15-16.

References to More and *Utopia* abound throughout this study, which estimates More's impact on subsequent utopias and calls it "a baseline for our comparative study."

R125 Elliott, Robert C. "The Shape of *Utopia*." *ELH* 30 (1963): 317-34.

Elliott discusses the satiric element of *Utopia* in relation to More's apparent inconsistencies and heterodox views on communism, toleration, euthanasia, and other disputable topics. *Utopia* can be considered a prose variation on types of satire represented in Horace, Juvenal, and Persius, as well as Lucian and Augustine. The satiric intention is both positive and negative, realistic and idealistic. "*Utopia*, like many formal verse satires, is 'framed' by an encounter between a satirist and an adversary." Both More and Hythloday are expert in their roles, and the former does not necessarily speak in his own person, but rather as a mercurial character after the manner of traditional satire. Hythloday likewise "can use the technique lightly,...or with bitter, driving, daring intensity," with the result "the shape of *Utopia* is finished off, enigmatically but firmly, in the terms Hythloday provides." (Rpt. as Chapter 2 of Elliott's *The Shape of Utopia: Studies in a Literary Genre* [R126], 25-49; and in *Sir Thomas More*, Utopia: *A New Translation, Backgrounds, Criticism*, 1st ed., 177-92.)

R126 Elliott, Robert C. *The Shape of Utopia: Studies in a Literary Genre*. Chicago: U of Chicago P, 1970.

Elliott's collection of essays includes studies of individual utopias and the utopian genre. A central connecting theme is the "relation of utopian literature to satire: the use of the utopia as a strategy of satire, the distribution of positive and negative elements in the two genres." More's *Utopia*, discussed in the second essay (25-49), is assessed as both original and traditional, in one sense "creating its own genre," in another hardly new at all, having much in common with well-established satiric conventions, as Lucian and Latin satirists employed. The Utopians are a "peace-loving people, but their land is born to controversy." In keeping with Elliott's main argument, he devotes more space to Book I of *Utopia* than Book II, the former demonstrating the dramatic roles of Hythloday and "More" as protagonist and antagonist, More's function being "to draw out and to oppose on certain issues Hythloday's defence of communism."

R127 Elton, G.R. *Reform and Renewal: England, 1509-1558*. Cambridge, MA: Harvard UP, 1977. 42-47, 51-52, 75-77, 89-90, 116-17, 126-30, 185-86, 193-95.

Among references to More (his connection with the Hunne case and the Nun of Kent; character; relation with Henry VIII, Wolsey, and Cromwell; attitude toward communism), Elton discusses *Utopia* and finds that, despite its playfulness, it constitutes a serious "programme of reform," some of which Elton finds striking and "rather horrifying."

R128 Erasmus, Charles J. "Utopia: Millenial Man in Fiction." *In Search of the Common Good: Utopian Experiments Past and Future*. New York: Free P, 1977. 197-231.

Erasmus' seventh chapter claims the authors of More's *Utopia*, Plato's *Republic*, Cabet's *A Voyage to Icaria*, Bellamy's *Looking Backward*, and Skinner's *Walden Two* are all behaviorists, because they all suggest "ways of engineering society to reduce behavior they dislike"; he examines their specific dislikes, compares their views of human nature, and describes their behaviorist methods.

R129 Ersgräber, Willi. "Thomas Morus: *Utopia* (1516)." *Literarische Utopien von Morus bis zur Gegenwart*. Eds. Klaus L. Berghahn, and Hans Ulrich Seeber. Königstein/Ts.: Athenäum, 1983. 25-43.

Ersgräber's study of issues in *Utopia* and how scholars have treated them concludes with a bibliography of secondary sources.

R130 Evans, John X. "The Kingdom within More's *Utopia*." *Moreana* 55-56 (1977): 5-21.

Evans argues *Utopia* is less concerned with an ideal political state than with the kingdom of God in the "good and genuinely Christian heart"; thus, many of the practices in Utopia are defensible, the limitations of reason without grace are apparent, and the work looks for spiritual reformation rather than political revolution.

R131 Farnell, James E. "The Governmental Structure of Utopia." *Moreana* 130 (1977): 11-26.

After Farnell shows how Amaurot's government was closely modeled upon that of the City of London, how the Utopian federation was probably patterned on the Netherlands' constitutional tradition, and how the senate incorporated features of the English Parliament; he speculates about the ways More's use of contemporary governments may affect the interpretation of *Utopia*.

R132 Fenlon, D.B. "England and Europe: *Utopia* and Its Aftermath." *Transactions of the Royal Historical Society*. 5th ser. 25 (1975): 115-35.

Fenlon poses answers to four interrelated, frequently overlooked questions in *Utopia* studies: What was the significance of *Utopia* for More himself? What was its significance for its original humanist audience? Were the issues explored in *Utopia* and those that gave rise to the Reformation related? How can scholars explain More's transition from *Utopia* to religious polemics?

R133 Ferguson, Arthur B. *Utter Antiquity: Perceptions of Prehistory in Renaissance England*. Durham: Duke UP, 1993. 88, 90, 117, 118, 122.

Ferguson cites "the ironical mind-set of the More of *Utopia*," as a possible humanist contribution to satiric views of "patriotic pretensions inherent in the Brutus story."

R134 Field, P.J.C. "*Utopia*, the Emperor Constantine, and Pythagorus." *Moreana* 47-48 (1975): 21-23.

The Utopians' initial contact with European civilization occurred 1200 years before Hythloday's visit, or 312 A.D., the year Constantine won the battle of the Milvian Bridge. Utopians could thus acquire classical wisdom at its fullest moment before the triumph of Christianity. This date also establishes a direct cause for the numerous parallels between the Utopian and classical worlds.

R135 Fleisher, Martin. *Radical Reform and Political Persuasion in the Life and Writing of Thomas More*. Travaux d'Humanisme et Renaissance. 132. Geneva: Librairie Droz, 1973.

Fleisher argues More, as a dedicated Christian humanist, was pledged to the reform and perfecting of the European community to which he belonged. More's insistence in *Utopia* on viewing human follies and social disorders as originating in social institutions and political practices thus led him to advance social and political remedies. More diagnosed the evils of warfare, English criminal law, social injustices and political corruption, and above all, money and private property, and in his second book set about creating the harmonious state of Utopia in which social order prevailed and evils were eliminated. But Fleisher not only believes More conceived of Utopia as a perfect state, but that he regarded his vision as a practical blueprint for reform, and was confronted with the task of persuading others to accept and institute his radical system. Fleisher finds it inconsistent that, when More entered practical politics, he should have abandoned his program of radical reform, fearful of challenging authority and failing to encourage the commons to do so.

R136 Fox, Alistair. "English Humanism and the Body Politic." *Reassessing the Henrician Age: Humanism, Politics and Reform 1500-1550*. Essays by Alistair Fox and John Guy. Oxford: Basil Blackwell, 1986. 34-51.

Fox speculates More may have written *Utopia* in response to Erasmus' *Institutio principis christiani*, argues *Utopia* puts Erasmus' ideals about what ought to be realized in an actual state to a test, and concludes there is a "great gap" between the Erasmian sense of what ought to be and the reality of what can be.

R137 Fox, Alistair. "In Search of the Real Thomas More: An Approach to *Utopia*." *Thomas More: The Rhetoric of Character*. 17-34.

Fox answers questions about the consistency of More's thought throughout his career, which he believes can be found in the view of the human condition and its providential frustrations and possibilities embodied in More's writings. Although this consistency is explicit in his controversial works, the fiction of *Utopia* expresses it implicitly, and its purpose and meaning reveal the essential More, who is not an Erasmian optimistic, humanist idealist, but "one who thought reform should be sought and achieved within the ineradicable facts of an imperfect situation...one which is providentially imperfect."

R138 Fox, Alistair. "Paradoxical Equivocation: The Self-subversiveness of Thomas More's *Utopia*." *Politics and Literature in the Reigns of Henry VII and Henry VIII*. Oxford: Basil Blackwell, 1989. 92-107.

In chapter six, Fox relates *Utopia* to *Praise of Folly* as "companion works in a far deeper sense than has yet been realized, for the mode of imagination represented in each work led its author to admit doubts that he would have preferred to keep concealed." He then explains the complexity of *Utopia* and its author's doubts about the "unstable foundations" of humanism by retracing the stages in which More composed it and watching the shifting nature of that fiction with changes in More's circumstances.

R139 Fox, Alistair. Utopia: *An Elusive Vision*. Twayne's Masterwork Studies No. 103. New York: Twayne, 1993.

Fox not only develops a vision of the work and its author that owes much to other scholars, but also reaches further to add his own insights. The book is divided into two parts: "Literary and Historical Context" and "A Reading." The first gives the impression of an introduction for undergraduate students (to whom Twayne is directing this series). The second distinguishes two possible approaches to *Utopia*: reading the work as it was eventually published, moving from the parerga through Books I and II, or reading it as it was composed--Book II, Book I, the parerga. Because Fox is interested mainly in More's mental process, he chooses the second approach, and his reading may be seen as an attempt to reconstruct the "biography of an idea" in an even more comprehensive way than did J.H. Hexter (R192). Fox hypothesizes More, when he started to write, intended to invent an ideal community. In the course of his writing, however, he lost faith in his Utopian vision and therefore mixed his discourse with dystopian elements. To distance himself from the discourse on Utopia, he next invented Hythloday as a narrator and embedded his monologue in the dialogue of Book I. To complicate the interpretation of *Utopia* still further, he and his fellow humanists added the parerga. The result was a work fully exploring all More's personal and political doubts, without ever arriving at a solution.

R140 Fracjowiak, Marian. *Poglady Economiczne Thomas More*. Poznan: Praca Wydana z Zasilku Polskiej Akademii Nauk., 1967.

Because More lived in an age of transition from feudalism to capitalism, he perceived the ill effects of undue emphasis on the profit motive with the dynamic growth of market economy, unjust distribution of wealth, the rapacity and extravagance of courts and magnates, wars waged by the ruling classes entailing ruinous taxation and fines. With clear-sighted vision, More realized the reforms touched upon in Book I would not of themselves remove the source of evils or prevent them from recurring, so Book II sets forth "his maximum programme of reform"--a social and an economic system based on public ownership.

R141 Francis, Kevin. "Democracy, Citizenship and Utopia." Diss. U of Glasgow (UK), 1988.

In his study of a misconception of democracy, Francis analyzes *Utopia* within the context of More's life and identifies the "utopian project" as the attempt to stimulate desire for political reform by extending the bounds of political possibilities.

R142 Freeman, John. "Discourse in More's *Utopia*: Alibi/Pretext/Postscript." *ELH* 59 (1992): 289-311.

Freeman believes Book I encloses Book II, makes it participate in the historical process, places and determines Utopia and its values, and opposes them. All of this becomes more complex when he considers the order of composition of the books, and he argues the two books demonstrate the way an actual historical process shapes and governs a text that evolves "through a three-part process of alibi, pretext, and postscript [which] reenacts the transactions and negotiations that the author undergoes at each stage of the text's composition."

R143 Freeman, John. "'Island of Improvement': More's Utopian Enclosure." Diss. Wayne State U, 1995.

Freeman investigates the role of enclosure in *Utopia* both in the internal structure of the text and its relationship to history to demonstrate *Utopia* is "essentially a topographical text which lies along the fault line of the violently shifting agrarian discourse of More's day."

R144 Freeman, John. "A Model Territory: Enclosure in More's *Utopia*." *The Territorial Rights of Nations and Peoples*. Ed. John R. Jacobson. New York: Edwin Mellen P, 1989. 241-67.

Freeman employs enclosure to describe the textual transactions at work between the two books of *Utopia* as he looks at the topographical character of the text in the light of his belief history itself provides not only the occasion and crisis for writing *Utopia* but also the form for inscribing the terms of difference between its two books.

R145 Freeman, John. "More's 'Island of Improvement': A Field Theory Approach to Utopia." *Moreana* 118-119 (1994): 61-84.

Recent critics have argued there is little connection between More's island of Utopia and historical England. Agrarian field systems like enclosure and the open field play critical roles both in the formation of the island and regulation of its social structure and economy. The field theory approach shows the improvement gained by enclosing Utopia is a conservative value, linking England's present with its past. Open fields and enclosure arrangements are comparable to the "tunable" mathematical landscapes complexity theorists use to model real world variables in evolving systems. Complexity theory helps determine just how fully More's island participates in the agrarian and social evolution of early sixteenth-century England. Far from being a fabulation, Utopia seeks to preserve what one modern agrarian calls "the world we have lost."

R146 Freeman, John. "More's Place in 'No Place': The Self-Fashioning Transition in *Utopia*." *TSLL* 34 (1992): 197-217.

Freeman argues the "created world" of *Utopia* corresponds closely to the world in which More had to find his place. One problem for *Utopia* centers around "how one authors oneself, how one authorizes oneself to speak." Freeman believes *Utopia* is far from being situated nowhere and that it represents a transition of values linking the formation of social identity to the agrarian crisis of More's day. Persona More, Hythloday, and the two books can be read as a "convertibility formula" for working out social identity in private, communal, and state domains.

R147 Frye, Northrop. "Varieties of Literary Utopias." *Daedalus* 94 (1965):

323-47.

An analysis of the Utopian impulse in literature from the *Republic* through More's *Utopia*, Sidney's *Arcadia*, Swift's *Gulliver's Travels*, Thoreau's *Walden*, and many late nineteenth-century utopian satires, to the "Luddite pastoralism" of contemporary protest writers reveals this form of fiction can usually be described as a speculative myth about society. The utopian author, moreover, is writing to communicate a personal vision to his audience rather than simply to share a fantasy with them.

R148 Frye, Northrop. "Varieties of Literary Utopias." *The Stubborn Structure: Essays on Criticism and Society*. Ithaca, NY: Cornell UP, 1970. 109-34.

Although Frye provides considerable information about the Utopian impulse in literature (especially the ways in which technological advances have affected literary utopias), it is perhaps a bit surprising to find him accepting More's *Utopia* as an ideal of which More approved, thus contradicting the notion the work is a *jeu d'esprit*.

R149 Galibois, Roland. "L'*Utopie*: Éloge du plaisiri?" *Moreana* 98-99 (1988): 171-87.

The Utopians maintain all human actions have pleasure and happiness as their end, but the thesis of equating happiness with pleasure needs to be interpreted in a double context--dialectical and existential. Thorough examination of both arguments brought forth in its favor and the daily life of the Utopians reveal (1) the pleasure that is their ultimate end is of a superior nature and results from contemplation of truth; and (2) they take pleasure in a concrete sense, never distinguishing it formally from the activity it accompanies or follows. This thesis is at conscious and deliberate issue with the Stoic position. Hythloday, the spokesman for the Utopians and More (to a certain extent), replaces one antonomasia with another. Pleasure is bad, says the Stoic, for whom the word designates sensual pleasure with no concern for utility and honesty. Pleasure, says Hythloday-More, is good even as a final end, if it is truly human, that is, if sought *natura duce*, with nature as the guide.

R150 Garanderie, Marie-Madeleine de la. "Guillaume Budé lecteur de l'*Utopie*." *Miscellanea Moreana: Essays for Germain Marc'hadour*. *Moreana* 100. 327-38.

The author analyzes Budé's letter to Thomas Lupset (31 July 1517) which prefaced the Paris edition of *Utopia*. More's work has thrown the French humanist into a tumult of thoughts and feelings, triggering a riot of pondering about justice, wealth, Christianity. He seems to have particularly enjoyed More's verbal inventions and subtle use of symbolism, and he himself enters into the game. Thus, the preface reveals affinities between the minds of the two humanists, which will be confirmed by their subsequent encounter (1520) and by the tone of their correspondence.

R151 Gatto, Louis C. "Suicide and Utopian Philosophy." *BSUF* 9 (1968): 33-38.

Sanctioning suicide and euthanasia in *Utopia* is completely inconsistent with orthodox Christian ethics and More's attitude in *Dialogue of Comfort*. Gatto forgets Hythloday is not a mouthpiece for More and that Utopia is a fictional, rationalistic, pagan state which lacks Christian revelation.

R152 Gee, John Archer. "Cuthbert Tunstall's Copy of the First Edition of *Utopia*." *YULG* 15 (1941): 77-83.

The Yale Library acquired for the Albert H. Child collection a copy of the first edition of *Utopia*, and the book's earliest owner was Tunstall, the distinguished ecclesiastic, scholar, and statesman More accompanied on the embassy to Flanders. In addition, the article comments on Yale's collection of other works and mss. by More.

R153 Gentili, Augusto. "La concezione utopistica dello Stato tre Mediaevo Italiano e Rinascimento inglese." *JMRS* 2 (1972): 93-130.

This essay traces the origins and dissemination of the Utopian ideal from More and Machiavelli to Hobbes and Harrington, mentioning along the way Plato's *Republic*, Bacon's *New Atlantis*, some Italian utopian literature, Burton's *Anatomy of Melancholy*, and Shakespeare's *Tempest*. Gentili's Marxist outlook and terminology, however, restrict the value of his analysis.

R154 Giard, Luce. "Voyageuse raison." *Esprit* 42 (1974): 557-66.

Giard traces the origin of *Utopia*, explains its main ideas, and compares it to the *Republic, City of the Sun, Gulliver's Travels, Robinson Crusoe, Candide, Cyrano, Erewhon,* and *Brave New World*.

R155 Gillespie, Gerald. "Education in *Utopia*." *Europäische Lehrdichtung: Festschrift für Walter Naumann zum 70. Geburtstag*. Eds. Hans Gerd Rötzer, and Herbert Walz. Darmstadt: Wissenschaftliche Buchgesellschaft, 1981. 119-31.

Gillespie compares the ideas on education in *Utopia* with didactic treatises of the time on the subject, such as Ascham's *The Schoolmaster* and Lyly's *Euphues*. He also describes and compares the role of education in *Utopia* with other contemporary utopian works.

R156 Glaze, Walter Stephen. "Patronage and *Otium* in Two Renaissance Dialogues: A Comparative Approach." Diss. Emory U, 1995.

Glaze traces the meaning of patronage as conveyed by the word *otium* from classical times to the Renaissance and shows how Conversino and More utilize its ambiguities in two dialogues. *Utopia* imaginatively removes the conditions of patronage by making *otium* the purpose of the Utopian system of government and the goal of reading the book.

R157 Gleason, John B. "Sun Worship in More's *Utopia.*" *Le soliel à la renaissance*. Institute pour l'etude d'humanisme et renaissance 2 (1965): 433-45.

Gleason suggests More seeks to represent the faith of weaker spirits, who cannot rise to the sublime idea of one invisible, eternal God. The religion of Utopia is solidly based upon the Bible and Christian commentaries, and More's acquaintance with standard authorities on both theology and philosophy would have given him some notion of sun worship, which readers would readily accept as a form of worship suited to worshippers in his ideal commonweal.

R158 Goodey, Brian R. "Mapping *Utopia*: A Comment on the Geography of Sir Thomas More." *Geographical Review* 60 (1970): 15-30.

Goodey considers the geographic description of the island, its urban-rural land distribution, and city planning, especially that of its capital city. He finds it intriguing Utopia, a "nowhere" incapable of being mapped, is mapped.

R159 Gordon, Walter M. "Dialogue, Myth and More's Utopian Drama." *Cithara* 25 (1985): 19-34.

There are three ways to interpret Book II of *Utopia*: as a political blueprint, as an upside-down land existing in the interest of satire, or as a combination of both to obtain what Stanley Fish calls a dialectical reading because it "exists to inhabit the mind" and "disrupt the reader's complacency." McCutcheon (R265, R266) delineates the "yes-no" tendency that affirms through the negation of opposites so that the reader experiences the intrinsic relationship between the *mythos* (fable) of Book II and *logos* (rational discussion) presented in Book I. This approach allows for the development of the two sides of the author's mind, the dreamer and the politician, by counterbalancing absurdity with practicality.

R160 Gordon, Walter M. "The Monastic Achievement and More's Utopian Dream." *M&H* ns 9 (1979): 199-214.

Gordon believes the organization of life in medieval monasteries influenced More's plan for Utopia, and following such a pattern that really existed (and still exists) may invite readers to take his fiction literally as a model for life. Gordon speculates upon how seriously More himself took the way of life Hythloday envisions and posits Hythloday may be a parody and mockery of More.

R161 Grace, Damian. "*Utopia*: A Dialectical Interpretation." *Miscellanea*

Moreana: Essays for Germain Marc'hadour. Moreana 100. 273-302.

Grace argues *Utopia* is a rhetorical model rather than a social-political blueprint, and identifies the basic problem More confronts as ideological, "a covering term for the distorted judgment and corrupt communication which protects the interests of the wealthy and the powerful." Grace examines the ways the book engages readers through an ensemble of dialectical strategies as rehabilitative measures for such impaired communication as More invites his audience to assess the dialogue between persona More and Raphael.

R162 Grace, William J. "The Conception of Society in More's *Utopia*." *Thought* 22 (1947): 282-96.

Utopia remains an important book, not because of its creativity, but because of its political and social thought, and Grace unfolds More's conception of society, placing special emphasis on the individual's duty to authority, religious tolerance, and contemporary laws about sedition.

R163 Graziani, René. "Non-Utopian Euthanasia: An Italian Report, c. 1554." *RenQ* 22 (1969): 329-33.

This article concerns a report by Giulio Raviglio Rosso, a Ferrarese diplomat, corroborated by a reference in a sketch of English institutions preserved in a BM ms., stating unequivocally euthanasia was customary among some people in England. Comparison of the two accounts by More and Rosso shows the former as "an *improved* version--more humane, ethical and voluntary and more conscious of the need for safeguards--but drawing on the cruder fact recorded in the Italian account." Rosso's report may be attributed to deliberate leg-pulling by a reader of *Utopia*.

R164 Greenblatt, Stephen. "More, Role-Playing, and *Utopia*." *YR* 67 (1978): 517-36.

Greenblatt views *Utopia* as the "perfect expression" of More's self-conscious role-playing, and thinks More's intense meditation on its limits is embodied in the character of Hythloday and his relation to the "More" who appears as presenter (or recorder) and character. Because Hythloday represents all More deliberately excluded from the personality he created and played, Hythloday is the sign of More's awareness of his own self-creation, "hence his own incompleteness." Greenblatt also sees role-playing and the plays as metaphors central to More's response to the absurd spectacle of life. In *Utopia* the character More performs the world's play, while Hythloday presents directness and "authenticity"; Utopia's abolition of private property also abolishes private, self-conscious individuality, and the role-playing central to More's actual life.

R165 Greenblatt, Stephen. "Utopian Desire." *LittPrag* 2.4 (1992): 30-41.

Greenblatt proposes the depiction of marital relations and sexual pleasure in *Utopia* is More's attempt to imagine an alternative "not to his career but to his sexual psychology."

R166 Greiff, Ursula. "Traces of Stoicism and Neo-Stoicism in Neo-Latin Utopias." *Acta Conventus Neo-Latini Hafniensis*. Proceedings of the Eighth International Congress of Neo-Latin Studies, Copenhagen, 12 August to 17 August 1991. Gen ed. Rhoda Schnur. Eds. Ann Moss, Philip Dust, Paul Gerhard Schmidt, Jacques Chomarat, and Francesco Tateo. MRTS. 120. MRTS, Binghamton, NY: 1994. 445-52.

Greiff cites two passages from More's *Utopia* that refer to the Stoics in her study of five utopian works with traces of Stoic or neo-Stoic thought in them.

R167 Griffin, Robert. "Charting More's *Utopia*." *SFS* 9.2 [27] (1982): 215-16.

Griffin's review of Judith P. Jones' *Thomas More* (G048) comments on the "excellent chart" her book provides for locating *Utopia* "centrally in More's life and literary production."

R168 Gueguen, John A. "Reading More's *Utopia* as a Criticism of Plato." *Quincentennial Essays on St. Thomas More*. 43-54.

Gueguen sees *Utopia* as performing on Plato the kind of criticism Aquinas had performed on Aristotle 250 years earlier by employing the dialectic conversation of Raphael as a "medium" for entering into a dialogue to correct Plato.

R169 Gueguen, John A. "Why Is There No University in *Utopia*?" *Moreana* 77 (1983): 31-34.

Gueguen provides a close reading of More's letters in which he discusses his ideas about the nature and purpose of a university education.

R170 Gundersheimer, Werner L. "Patronage in the Renaissance: An Exploratory Approach." *Patronage in the Renaissance*. Eds. Guy Fitch Lytle, and Stephen Orgel. Princeton: Princeton UP, 1981. 3-23.

Gundersheimer notes one major effect of the distribution of wealth in Utopia is the eradication of patronage by eliminating both its social and material basis.

R171 Gury, Jacques. "Libres Citoyens d'Utopie." *Moreana* 69 (1981): 119-26.

Gury speculates upon the nature and degree of restraint and freedom in the institutions, regulations, customs of Utopia.

R172 Gury, Jacques. "Nouvelles Lectures de l'*Utopie*." *Moreana* 95-96 (1987): 125-30.

Gury examines several recent publications for new readings of *Utopia*, usually as a complex work about "polity" in the light of a long cultural tradition of political fiction.

R173 Gury, Jacques. "Sequentia Utopica. 1. About the Maps of Utopia. 2. Similitudo Concordiam Facit. 3. Une Utopie chrétienne au siècle des lumières." *Moreana* 42 (1974): 99-103.

Both the Louvain edition of *Utopia* in 1516 and the Basle edition in 1518 are illustrated with maps. Though the first one is a rather crude woodcut and the second an elaborate print, their similarity leads Gury to think Ambrosius Holbein could have designed both. Nowadays one longs for diversity and criticizes the Utopian commonweal as too uniform and orderly, but in the sixteenth century, Europe was an untidy patchwork of warring states, and More saw similarity as a unifying factor.

R174 Gury, Jacques. "Thomas More en France à la Fin du XVIIIe Siecle." *Moreana* 70 (1981): 53-54.

Gury details the reception of *Utopia* in eighteenth-century France by giving attention to its presentation in the *Encyclopédie methodique* and *Administration théorique*.

R175 Gury, Jacques. "L'*Utopie* Tous Azimuts" [and] "The Abolition of Rural Work in *Utopia*." *Moreana* 43-44 (1974): 65-66, 67-69.

The second half of chapter 1 of *Utopia* Book II is devoted to rural problems. More puts forward the principles of a radical revolution: he does away with the countryman and leaves the countryside deserted but for a few food-production units around the city. In the days when England was mostly a rural country, More suppresses traditional farming and the village--a revolution justified in Utopia not only for political, economical reasons but also for social, ethical reasons: man can live to the full and blossom only in an urban environment and in a congenial and convivial community, freed from rural bondage and the mirage of Arcadian bliss.

R176 Guy, Alain. "Vivès socialiste et *L'Utopie* de More." *Moreana* 31-32 (1971): 263-79.

Guy investigates the connection between the Spanish humanist's communistic tendencies and the influence of *Utopia* upon them.

R177 Guy, John. "The King's Council and Political Participation." *Reassessing the Henrician Age: Humanism, Politics and Reform 1500-1550*. Essays by Alistair Fox and John Guy. Oxford: Basil Blackwell, 1986. 121-47.

Guy compares attitudes expressed toward the King's Council in John Fortescue, Christopher St. German, Thomas Elyot, Thomas Starkey, and More;

in More's case, Guy concentrates on the dialogue on counsel in Book I of *Utopia* and the Utopian government Hythloday describes in Book II.

R178 Halpern, Richard. "Rational Kernal, Mystical Shell: Reification and Desire in Thomas More's *Utopia*." *The Poetics of Primitive Accumulation: English Renaissance Culture and the Genealogy of Capital*. Ithaca: Cornell UP, 1991. 136-75.

Halpern's thesis--which threads together chapters on Tudor schools, John Skelton's poetry, *Utopia*, Spenser's *Shepheardes Calender*, and *King Lear*--is the claim that "the rhetorical and literary culture of the Renaissance can be usefully situated within, if not quite 'explained' by, the transition from feudalism to capitalism." Influenced by Louis Marin's *Utopiques: Jeux d'espaces* (R255), Halpern's chapter on *Utopia* locates the primary significance of the work in contradictions within the text. Halpern's particular focus is not on spatial (as is the case with Marin) but on logical contradictions which reveal that "whereas *Utopia*'s finished form depicts a utopian-socialist society, this surface conceals an 'interior' realm whose primal fantasy and pleasurable substance turn out to be--the logic of capitalism itself."

R179 Hamilton, Robert. "More's *Utopia*." *Hibbert Journal* 44 (1946): 242-47.

Hamilton contends the totalitarian, socialistic ideas in *Utopia* might not have been so disturbing to Tudor England which was not as free as England and other countries today. He points out how More's state differs from atheistic socialistic-totalitarian states and concludes such states today are doomed because they lack God.

R180 Hammond, Eugene R. "Hythloday's Questions: Clues to His Character? Or Provokers of Thought?" *Moreana* 70 (1981): 25-27.

By discussing More's strategy in having Hythloday question the Utopian attitudes toward pleasure, Hammond further substantiates Surtz' position (R403) that More, in inventing the Utopian pleasure philosophy, "wished to provoke Christians to some serious thought about the nature and object of human happiness."

R181 Hammond, Eugene R. "Nature--Reason--Justice in *Utopia* and *Gulliver's Travels*." *SEL* 22 (1982): 445-68.

The reason governing More's Utopians and Swift's Houyhnhnms has made readers uncomfortable. In earlier centuries, readers often attacked More or Swift for believing in rational solutions to social problems, but this century's increasing interest in personae and irony has allowed critics to distinguish more sharply between the authors and the spokesmen for their utopian societies, Hythloday and Gulliver. Each time new weaknesses are discovered in either

Hythloday or Gulliver, the possibilities increase that the societies they champion were also conceived ironically. Readers, while recognizing More and Swift are playful in their portraits of Utopians and Houyhnhnms, locate crucial values in Utopian and Houyhnhnm reason. In both books, reason is intimately linked with the virtue of justice, and in each the institutional injustice of contemporary society is satirized through comparison with the impressive, if not perfect, justice of an imaginary, rational society.

R182 Hansot, Elisabeth. "The *Utopia* of Thomas More." *Perfection and Progress: Two Modes of Utopian Thought*. Cambridge, MA: MIT P, 1974. 59-78.

Hansot's fourth chapter presents a Christian interpretation which maintains More intends the "true Christianity" of the Utopians to cause readers to examine the "nominal Christianity" many Europeans depicted in the work practice. The Utopians' "true Christianity" results in eradication of pride, enjoyment of pleasure, social unity, happiness, and virtue.

R183 Harbison, E. Harris. "Machiavelli's *Prince* and More's *Utopia*." *Facets of the Renaissance*. Ed. William K. Werkmeister. New York: Harper, 1959. 41-71.

Harbison compares the *Prince* and *Utopia* as two contemporary pictures of an ideal sovereign state, each of which has given a new word to the vocabulary, and which together "have come to personify the beginnings of modern political thinking." Both Machiavelli and More were saved from the dilettantism of many other humanists through strong practical interests reflected in their common awareness of a changing society and in simplicity of style. Differences in status and temperament conditioned the contrast between them. Machiavelli, reacting against the traditional "Mirror of Princes," missed the "moral dimension" of power; More, on the other hand, viewed the key sins of English society with the eyes of a city dweller or clergyman, finding unexploited resources in Christian humanism compounded of the classic and Christian ethic.

R184 Hastings, Margaret. "More and Fortescue." *Moreana* 36 (1972): 61-63.

More and Fortescue attribute the problem of larceny to the poverty that afflicted Renaissance England. Medieval in spirit, Fortescue in *Governance of England* recognizes a strong king will be weakened by poor subjects likely to rebel or rob. Influenced by other humanists, More's *Utopia* stresses the people's welfare rather than the ruler's power and illustrates the poor commit larceny because they are unable to earn a living. The lawyer in Book I of *Utopia* may have been modeled on Fortescue.

R185 Heiserman, A.R. "Satire in the *Utopia*." *PMLA* 78 (1963): 163-74.

Heiserman argues More has his own concept of satire, distinct from that of Erasmus, and that this may be deduced from the preface to his translations from Lucian and from the letter to Giles concerning the nature of fiction in *Utopia*. As shown throughout *Utopia*, More pays close attention to satiric objects and techniques as a means of inducing satiric verisimilitude and of creating a *via diversa* after the manner of the *Republic*, but the fusion of elements in his satire is organic, not mechanical. (Rpt. in *Die Englische Satire*, Wolfgang Weiss, ed. [Darmstadt: Wissenschaftliche Buchges, 1982], 172-200.)

R186 Helgerson, Richard. "Inventing Noplace, or the Power of Negative Thinking." *Genre* 15 (1982): 101-21.

Helgerson compares *Utopia* to Rabelais' *Gargantua and Pantagruel* as he considers the secular thrust of negation in both works, and *Utopia* undertakes a global analysis that finds, in private property, a cause for all abuse. Given this generating point, More creates a "no place" and negates private property in a "thought...game...that erupts from the confines of its own playfulness to become a powerful force in another larger game, coextensive with culture itself."

R187 Hertzler, Joyce Oramel. *The History of Utopian Thought*. 1923. New York: Cooper Square Pub., 1965. 127-46.

Chapter 4, "The Early Modern Utopias," includes a section on More's *Utopia*.

R188 Hester, M. Thomas. "'The Letter Killeth, but the Spirit Giveth Life': Raphael Hythlodaeus and the Law of Love." *ScSat* 6 (1980): 3-8.

Analysis of Hythloday's initial speech illuminates More's rich paradox in *Utopia*. Through an interplay of classical and biblical references, More undercuts the speaker's philosophic credentials and narrative credibility. Alerted by this emblematic introduction, readers perceive that the Utopians, like their advocate, fail to comprehend the fundamental Christian values informing More's "learned joke."

R189 Hexter, J.H. "Claude de Seyssel and Normal Politics in the Age of Machiavelli." *Art, Science, and History in the Renaissance*. Ed. Charles S. Singleton. Baltimore: Johns Hopkins UP, 1967. 389-415.

Hexter compares three ways of thinking about politics that were printed between 1513 and 1516--Machiavelli's *Prince*, More's *Utopia*, and Seyssel's *La Monarchie*--and describes what they share without neglecting their differences. He believes Machiavelli and More's works deviate radically from normal views of politics in the early sixteenth century, whereas Seyssel's book is closer to "the normal look of politics" at that time. (Rpt. as "The Predatory, the Utopian, and the Constitutional Vision: Machiavelli, More, and Claude de Seyssel. *La*

Monarchie de France and Normal Politics on the Eve of the Reformation" in Hexter's *The Vision of Politics on the Eve of the Reformation: More, Machiavelli, and Seyssel* [R196], 204-30.)

R190 Hexter, J.H. "Intention, Words, and Meaning: The Case for More's *Utopia.*" *NLH* 6 (1975): 529-41.

Hexter examines persona More's final speech to defend his contention the author, like Hythloday, took seriously the idea of community life and property. Here Hexter reacts against Ward Allen's "Hythloday and the Root of All Evil" (R010).

R191 Hexter, J.H. "The Loom of Language and the Fabric of Imperatives: The Case of *Il Principe* and *Utopia.*" *American Historical Review* 69 (1964): 945-68.

Hexter, writing as an historian and confessing ignorance of linguistics, suggests both Machiavelli and More use words in relation to the men and communities they know best, regardless of aesthetic or moral values. *Il Principe* and *Utopia* pose the question whether their authors really believe in the systems they present. What concerned Machiavelli was not *"lo stato,"* but *"status reipublicae."* In More's use of *"majestas," "nobilis,"* and *"generosus,"* which represent specific concepts in the chain of being, there are pejorative overtones Robinson's version fails to convey. In sum, both Machiavelli and More "wreaked strange havoc on the fabric of imperatives." (Rpt. as "The Predatory and the Utopian Vision: Machiavelli and More. The Loom of Language and the Fabric of Imperatives: The Case of *Il Principe* and *Utopia*" in Hexter's *The Vision of Politics on the Eve of the Reformation: More, Machiavelli, and Seyssel* [R196], 179-203.)

R192 Hexter, J.H. *More's* Utopia: *The Biography of an Idea.* The History of Ideas Ser. 5. 1952. Westport, CT: Greenwood, 1976.

Hexter relates the composition and ideas of *Utopia* to More's political activities and personal problems between summer 1515 and autumn 1516. Parts composed in the Netherlands and others after More's return to England may be summarized as Book I: Preface (England), Introduction (Netherlands), Dialogue and End Link (England) and Book II: Discourse (Netherlands), Conclusion (England). Hexter contends that as the religion and philosophy of Utopia are products of natural reason, not Christianity, they can be regarded as More's own, though he believes More approved of communal property because he had first-hand knowledge of the economic evils of his time and thought they resulted from sloth, greed, and pride. Quoting opinions More's fellow humanists, Erasmus, Budé, and Busleyden expressed, Hexter argues they too approved of Utopian communism. He also points out curious resemblances between More's Utopia and Calvin's Geneva. After his return from the Netherlands, More had to decide whether he would enter a king's service, a dilemma inspiring the debate on counsel in *Utopia*. (Part of this book, "The Roots of *Utopia* and All Evil" is rpt. in *Sir Thomas More*, Utopia. *A New Translation, Backgrounds, Criticism*, 1st ed., 170-77; it also appears as "A Sermon on Pride" in *Twentieth-Century Interpretations of* Utopia: *A Collection of Critical Essays*, 58-65.)

R193 Hexter, J.H. "Thomas More and the Problem of Counsel." *Quincentennial Essays on St. Thomas More.* 55-66.

Hexter reiterates his thesis counsel is important because it embodies a stance toward *Utopia*, proclaiming it a serious, even philosophical, book written in response to the question--what would be *optimus status republicae*?

R194 Hexter, J.H. "Thomas More: On the Margins of Modernity." *JBS* 1 (1961): 20-37.

After reviewing the views of Lord Acton, Bishop Creighton, Sidney Lee, R.W. Chambers, and others on what More and his *Utopia* owe to medievalism, Hexter argues More's philosophical position in *Utopia* is more modern than medieval, for *Utopia* is the first modern attempt to address the condition of a decently ordered civil life and More the first radical. Hexter revised this essay and incorporated it in his "*Utopia* and Its Historical Milieu" in the introduction to the Yale edition (B019).

R195 Hexter, J.H. "Utopia and Geneva." *Action and Conviction in Early Modern Europe: Essays in Memory of E.H. Harbison.* Eds. Theodore K. Rabb, and Jerrold E. Seigel. Princeton: Princeton UP, 1969. 77-89.

In spite of their differences, Hexter argues similarities between More's Utopia and Calvin's Geneva in detail and spirit are significant; the Calvinistic capital at Geneva even achieved some of More's dreams for an ideal Christian commonwealth, although some of the means through which Calvin achieved Utopian ends were quite dystopian. (Part of this essay is rpt. as chapter 2 of Hexter's *The Vision of Politics on the Eve of the Reformation: More, Machiavelli, and Seyssel* [R196], 107-17.)

R196 Hexter, J.H. *The Vision of Politics on the Eve of the Reformation: More, Machiavelli, and Seyssel.* New York: Basic Books, 1973.

Hexter studies the visions of politics three seminal writers set forth in the middle years of the second decade of the sixteenth-century--the utopian vision of More, the predatory vision of Machiavelli, and the constitutional vision of Seyssel. Over half of the book reproduces and enlarges on Hexter's views of *Utopia* found in the Yale edition and other publications. Hexter's idea of More's political vision focuses on Utopian communism--the political equality of the citizens, common duty to labor, abolition of private ownership, markets, and money.

R197 Holquist, Michael. "How to Play Utopia: Some Brief Notes on the Distinctiveness of Utopian Fiction." *YFS* 41 (1968): 106-23.

Holquist refers to *Utopia* to demonstrate the relationship between chess and battle can be likened to that of utopia and real life. Although it is important to know how to play utopia, just as "you cannot order real battles according to the logic of chess, so you cannot erect actual communities based on the logic of utopia." (Rpt. in *Game, Play, Literature*, Ed. Jacques Ehrmann [Boston: Beacon, 1971], 106-23.)

R198 Hosington, Brenda. "Early French Translations of More's *Utopia*: 1550-1730." *HumLov* 33 (1984): 116-34.

Hosington compares one partial and four complete translations of *Utopia* into French from 1550 to 1730 and assesses the degree to which they represent translation practices of the times.

R199 Hosington, Brenda, and Elizabeth McCutcheon. "Thomas More and the *Utopia*: Notes from Chengdu." *Moreana* 83-84 (1984): 39-43.

Hosington follows the format of McCutcheon's "Thomas More and the *Utopia*: Notes from Beijing" (R272) and, like its model, describes the experience of lecturing on More and his book in the People's Republic of China. McCutcheon comments on Hosington's experience in a postscript.

R200 Huebert, Ronald. "Privacy: The Early Social History of a Word." *SR* 105 (1997): 21-38.

Huebert studies contrasting attitudes toward privacy in early modern England by examining its treatment in More's *Utopia*.

R201 Hunt, Lydia. "The First Spanish Translation of *Utopia*." *Moreana* 105 (1991): 21-41.

Gerónimo Antonio de Medinilla y Porres translated *Utopia* into Spanish in 1637, urged by his friend Francisco de Quevedo y Villegas, who wrote the preface to the work which includes a prologue by the translator, testimonials, epigraphic poems, and other preliminary writings. Those documents, added to the list of publications placed at the end, constitute an informative metatext to be related to the historical context of the work. Compared to the Latin original, this version presents many omissions (starting with that of Book I) and relevant discrepancies with other translations.

R202 Hutchinson, Steven. "Mapping Utopias." *MP* 85 (1987): 70-85.

Hutchinson explores the etymology of the term "utopia," as Louis Marin (R255) uses it to include both "eutopia" and "dystopia," in order to reground that meaning in his investigation of the creative principles and processes involved in making imaginary worlds.

R203 Itkonen-Kaila, Marja. "Translating *Utopia*." *Moreana* 34 (1972): 39-45.

More's prose is plain, forceful, looser than the more ornate classical norm. Robinson's famous English translation is free-wheeling--a fine, ingenious Tudor "Englishing." New translations, echoing new times, are always needed. Surtz' 1964 Yale translation (B019) is closer to the Latin, yet more formal. Marshall's version (C033) is as simple as possible in English. Turner's 1965 Penguin translation (C034) is founded on modern English structure, idiom, and vocabulary; it is vigorous, freely "correct." Translators should state their principles.

R204 Jameson, Fredric. "Of Islands and Trenches: Naturalization and the Production of Utopian Discourse." *Diacritics* 7 (1977): 2-21.

Jameson discusses how Book I, with its debate between Hythloday and the courtiers about conditions in England, supplies the raw materials and sketches the fundamental social contradictions upon which Book II must perform its work of transformation, neutralization, and Utopian production.

R205 Jevons, H. Stanley. "Contemporary Models of Sir Thomas More: *Utopia* and the Socialist Inca Empire." *TLS* 2 Nov. 1935: 692.

Jevons argues the picture of the Utopian commonwealth was influenced by reports of the socialist Inca Empire that reached More during his residence in Flanders in 1515. He enumerates ten similarities between Utopia and the Inca system; the problem, however, is there is no proof any European had visited Peru before 1515.

R206 Johnson, Robbin S. "The Argument for Reform in More's *Utopia*." *Moreana* 31-32 (1971): 123-34.

Johnson explores the "contrast between the vision of a utopian reformer and the image of a Europe trapped in, yet struggling to escape from, the skin of debilitating institutions." He believes More is not suggesting Utopia is an ideal model, but the proper attitude toward ideals and illusions, not specific institutions and reforms, but a way of thinking and being. Hythloday offers an idealist's solution to society's problems by way of paradigms; when persona More, Giles, and Cardinal Morton add to this the perspective of religion and morality, the Utopian solution becomes more complete than that of either the idealist or realist.

R207 Johnson, Robbin S. *More's* Utopia: *Ideal and Illusion*. New Haven: Yale UP, 1969.

Johnson interprets *Utopia* as a discussion between the real, practical demands of public life and the private illusions of an idealist, balancing the vision of the prophet with the awareness of the politician. The island state figures the "coherent outlines of a *telos* myth," described by the visionary Hythloday to an audience of learned men, willing to be enchanted by the Utopian fiction, but aware it is a fiction, conceived not as end in itself, but as a means whereby man may confront the real world with true ideals rather than illusory hopes. The argument evolves through phases, defining the Utopian poet and his auditors, self-consciousness in each character being reflected through dialogue. Hythloday's account of Utopia depicts a "world of mixed blessings," founded on a negative ideal, which More attempts to make real and positive, a totalitarian state which is also *Eutopia*, "the happy place, a garden of illusory pleasures, gained without struggle or sacrifice."

R208 Jones, Emrys. "Commoners and Kings: Book One of More's *Utopia*." *Medieval Studies for J.A.W. Bennett, Aetatis LXX*. Eds. P.L. Heyworth, and Dan Davin. Oxford: Clarendon, 1981. 255-72.

Jones investigates the story Raphael tells during the Cardinal Morton episode in Book I and relates it not only to Raphael's oration on greed and private property in Book II but also to the work's questions about the efficacy of becoming a king's counselor.

R209 Jones, Judith P. "The *Philebus* and the Philosophy of Pleasure in Thomas More's *Utopia*." *Moreana* 31-32 (1971): 61-69.

Only Cassirer (R067) notes the similarity between Utopia's pleasure philosophy and that of Plato's *Philebus*. More and Plato begin with the paradox pleasure may be the supreme good, then rigorously include wisdom and reason with pleasure, with Socrates showing wisdom as the most important. Both rank the pleasures. Plato argues measure is essential; More, similarly, reason. Both recognize and eschew a false view of pleasure. Plato, unlike the Utopians, excludes health as a pleasure--although other dialogues count health good. Health is the highest of physical pleasures in Utopia.

R210 Jordan, Winthrop. "Voyaging--New World as Utopia." *In Search of the American Dream*. San Diego: U of California P, 1974. Unit II, Art. 2, n.p.

Jordan speculates that the New World inspired More to write *Utopia*, for the new lands provided a contrast to the stale ways of the Old World. He elaborates upon this point by referring to the effects of *Utopia* on Sir Humphrey Gilbert and Vasco de Quiroga.

R211 Kaufman, Peter Iver. "Humanist Spirituality and Ecclesial Reaction: Thomas More's *Monstra*." *Church History* 56 (1987): 25-38.

Because of Hythloday's encomium on Cardinal Morton, resemblances of Utopian society to monastic life, and civic duties of Utopian priests; Kaufman sees *Utopia* as an "ecclesial reaction" to the Erasmian-humanist plan for spiritual reform, some of which reveals More's sympathy for the kind of religious ceremony some of his fellow humanists detested. "Given its ecclesial elements," *Utopia* foreshadows More's defense of ecclesiastical hierarchy and ceremony in his *Responsio ad Lutherum*.

R212 Kautsky, Karl. *Thomas More and His Utopia*. Foreword by Russell Ames. Trans. H.J. Stenning. 1927. New York: Russell & Russell, 1959.

Kautsky's 1888 classic Marxist interpretation of *Utopia* places the three major social systems--feudalism, capitalism, socialism--side by side and shows how *Utopia* encompasses More's medieval background, his life experience as spokesman for powerful merchants, and his insight into future human possibilities.

R213 Kendrick, Christopher. "More's *Utopia* and Uneven Development." *BoundaryII* 13 (1985): 233-66.

Kendrick describes how readers are caught by the play of dislocation within Utopia "which comes to stand as the very sign of uneven development," and "it is in this structural play...the Utopian genre makes the text open most fully upon the real movement, the real concrete, that is history."

R214 Kennedy, William J. "The Style of Ironic Discourse." *Rhetorical Norms in Renaissance Literature*. New Haven: Yale UP, 1978. 94-105.

Chapter two analyzes the styles of Erasmus' *Praise of Folly*, *Utopia*, and Rabelais' *Gargantua and Pantagruel* and argues all three take part in an ironic discourse neither completely narrative nor dramatic but mixed in its use of "dialogue, monologue, and narrative interchange." The unresolved positions on various subjects of Hythloday and persona More create multiple irony, inviting readers to ponder those questions. Although *Utopia*'s surface is seemingly uncomplicated, its complex rhetorical strategies complicate any one-sided interpretation.

R215 Kenyon, Timothy. "The Problem of Freedom and Moral Behavior in Thomas More's *Utopia*." *Journal of the History of Philosophy* 21 (1983): 349-73.

According to More's perception of the human condition, man exercising reason and free will, as an autonomous being, independent of divine grace, is potentially capable of achieving a good, but this good is an artefact--the civil society described in Book II--and the means of obtaining an ulterior end, the supernatural good of salvation. To Kenyon, More emerges as a positive libertarian for whom the alternative of the autonomous moral actor is simply unrealistic.

R216 Kenyon, Timothy. *Utopian Communism and Political Thought in Early Modern England*. London: Pinter, 1989. 39-117.

Kenyon's book consists of a methodological introduction, followed by discrete studies of *Utopia* and of the utopian thought of Gerrard Winstanley, and rounded off with a conclusion focusing on the ways More and Winstanley's views reflect the intellectual milieus of the early-sixteenth and mid-seventeenth centuries. Conceding More was not a systematic thinker in the sense of being a philosopher engaged upon a discernible project, Kenyon reconstructs More's theology and political philosophy, putting these views into the context of the traditions of speculative thought to which they relate and illuminating many passages of *Utopia* by placing them in their contexts. Kenyon's concern comprises More's understanding of the Fall and its consequences, the relation of these views to Augustinianism and Scholastic theology, and their bearing on *Utopia*. Kenyon analyzes Book II as essentially a structure of institutions designed to frustrate or rechannel evil--especially prideful--impulses. More's response to this understanding of the human condition is to create in Utopia an institutional structure and a strict moral code. Utopian communism is the manifestation of this principle of design, and many details of Book II are explicable in terms of it.

R217 Khanna, Lee C. "More's *Utopia*: A Literary Perspective on Social Reform." Diss. Columbia, 1969.

Khanna contends the dramatic emphasis of *Utopia* does not depend upon any single philosophical or political system. Instead the two books form a self-contained literary unit with the consistent theme of the importance of open-mindedness for improvement of the social order. The ability to experiment, learn, and change is more important to *Utopia* than any particular new institution or custom presented.

R218 Khanna, Lee C. "*Utopia*: The Case for Open-mindedness in the Commonwealth." *Moreana* 31-32 (1971): 91-105.

Utopia's theme is open-mindedness to improving society. No prescription is presented, but readers are urged to participate in betterment. Erasmus and Giles admire *Utopia*, not as paradigm, but for its expansion of consciousness. Flexibility, the foremost Utopian trait, appears as Utopians thank God for their truest of religions. Utopia's founder urged ideological freedom, believing that truth would eventuate. *Utopia*'s communism encourages non-attachment, thus freedom, non-belligerence. Humor and excess in Utopia create a tolerant climate. Pride, by glorifying the status quo, barring change, deafening men and nations against good counsel, mainly prevents social improvement.

R219 Kinney, Arthur F. *Rhetoric and Poetic in Thomas More's* Utopia. Humana Civilitas: Sources and Studies Relating to the Middle Ages and the Renaissance. 5. Malibu: Undena P (Center for Medieval and Renaissance Studies, U of California, Los Angeles), 1979.

Kinney sets *Utopia* in the context of Renaissance rhetorical exercises as carried out in the Henrician Inns of Court and by contemporary tutors to discover notions about the composition of persuasive speeches by opposed imaginary characters in order to prove legal points, all of which provide clues and tell readers "where to stand" when exploring *Utopia*. Kinney illustrates how More employs prevalent models for writing, such as *suasoria* and *controversiae*, and stresses how More's audience was predisposed to approach subjects presented through these forms--ideas present readers need to bear in mind.

R220 Kinney, Arthur F. "Rhetoric as Poetic: Humanist Fiction in the Renaissance." *ELH* 43 (1976): 413-43.

Kinney discusses the implications and effects of a subtle fusion of *declamation* and *disputation*, in Erasmus' *Moriae Encomium*, *Utopia*, and Gascoigne's *The Adventures of Master F.J.* The authors' skills are such as to convert rhetorical sophistry into a poetic. Kinney is interested in the relationship between the prefatory letters to the works themselves, which he finds illuminates the subtleties of their structures and arguments. With *Utopia*, he insists upon the unreliability of Hythloday's account of that island and claims the latter's inconsistencies and contradictions are neither the product of carelessness on the part of the author nor a demonstration of his indifference toward what Shaw once described as "the small change of verisimilitude" but rather calculated and deliberate. What is more, "Hythlodaeus' view is not what we expected," and finally dystopian.

R221 Knapp, Jeffrey. *An Empire Nowhere: England, America, and Literature from* Utopia *to* The Tempest. The New Historicism: Studies in Cultural Poetics. 16. Berkeley: U of California P, 1992.

Knapp explains the English literary Renaissance which was largely the consequence of a "perceived identity of interest" on the part of English poets between their enterprise and the English nation itself. This perception was rooted in the common notions of the triflingness of poetry and the weakness and isolation of England; for these disadvantages there was, according to English writers, the compensatory advantage of a spiritual superiority. Among the "New World" texts marshalled in support of this new historicist thesis, the role of *Utopia* is to be the first work in a tradition of English "colonialist propaganda." From the outset, however, *Utopia* strongly resists this role.

R222 Koppenfels, Werner von. "Thomas Morus und die humanistische Utopie der Renaissance." *Alternative Welten.* Ed. Manfred Pfister. Münchener Universitäts-Schriften: Philosophische. Texte und Untersuchungen zur Englischen Philologie. 12. Munich: Wilhelm Fink Verlag, 1982. 96-113.

Koppenfels' study of the symbolism, structure, and sources of More's work begins by noting *Utopia*'s influence on Shakespeare's *Tempest*.

R223 Kreyssig, Jenny. *Die* Utopia *des Thomas Morus: Studien zur Rezeptionsgeschichte und zum Bedeutungskontext.* Europaische Hochschulschriften. Ser. 3. Vol. 374. Frankfurt: Peter Lang, 1988.

Kreyssig outlines the history of *Utopia*'s reception, summarizes major ways it has been interpreted as a humanist work, and provides sections on both reception and interpretation of subjects the book treats, such as marriage, family, war, gold.

R224 Kristeller, Paul Oskar. "Thomas More als Humanist." *Thomas More als Humanist: Zwei Essays.* Ed. Dieter Wuttke. Bamberg: H. Kaiser, 1982. 9-37.

Kristeller links *Utopia* to More's life as a humanist.

R225 Lacombe, M.M. "La sagesse d'epicure dans *L'Utopie* de More." *Moreana* 31-32 (1971): 169-82.

Erasmus calls the idea of existence "Epicurean." Pre-Reformation Christian humanism is ubiquitous, and Erasmus' friend More weaves Epicureanism through *Utopia*, which is worth study for the confrontation of Christianity with materialistic wisdom. More learned from Lucian, Lucretius, and Cicero, whose *De Finibus* popularized Epicurean morality. More reconciles the Epicurean search for pleasure with Platonic hope for a beyond by reason, which defines pleasure, affirms the soul's immortality, conforms to nature, and often means Epicurean prudence.

R226 Lange, Bernd-Peter. "Thomas More: *Utopia* (1516)." *Die Utopie in der Angloamerikanischen Literatur: Interpretationen.* Eds. Hartmut Heuermann, and Bernd-Peter Lange. Düsseldorf: Bagel, 1984. 11-31.

Lange concerns himself with the social-economic relations depicted in *Utopia* and provides a thorough bibliography.

R227 Lantham, Richard A. "More, Castiglione, and the Humanist Choice of Utopias." *Acts of Interpretation: The Text in Its Contexts, 700-1600: Essays on Medieval and Renaissance Literature in Honor of E. Talbot Donaldson.* Eds. Mary J. Carruthers, and Elizabeth D. Kirk. Norman, OK: Pilgrim, 1982. 327-43.

Lantham compares More's treatment of freedom in *Utopia* to Castiglione's and shows how "*Utopia*'s literary form allows More to suggest and get credit for an open society." "The greatest artist of this con game is Plato, but More is not far behind." (With slight changes, rpt. as Chapter 3 in Lantham's *Literacy and the Survival of Humanism* [New Haven: Yale UP, 1983], 24-40.)

R228 Lecler, Joseph. "Saint Thomas More (1478-1535): The *Utopia*." *Toleration and the Reformation.* Trans. (from the French version of 1955) by T.L.

Westow. Vol. 1. New York: Association P, 1960. 134-42.

After analyzing Utopian attitudes about religious toleration, Lecler claims More's attitude there is not inconsistent with his approval in theory of the persecution of heretics, because Utopus does not tolerate complete religious freedom, Utopia is not a Catholic country, and *Utopia* is a fiction, not a polemic tract.

R229 Lederer, Dietrich. "Thomas Morus' *Utopia*: Weltbild, Menschenbild, and Literatur." *WB* 31.7 (1985): 1150-60.

Lederer focuses on *Utopia*'s relationship to humanism and the work's treatment of the concepts of utopia and secularity.

R230 Le Doeuff, Michèle. "La reverie dans *Utopia*." *RMM* 78 (1973): 480-86.

In stressing *Utopia* is a dream, Le Doeuff analyzes the imagery More employs in Book II where features of the island's geography are just as important as study of the institutions. Le Doeuff emphasizes the enclosed and insulated nature of the island and argues this imaginary geography affirms that the Utopian state, while aware of its own internal harmony and stability, is blind to all else, and contemplates only itself, like Narcissus in the myth. But if More's work is a dream centered on a conception of happiness that excludes the outside world, it becomes a political work simply because the individual cannot be totally self-sufficient, and institutions are unjust; thus, More moves on to express his political concern in Book I.

R231 Leslie, Marina Ann. "Patterns for Perfecting: Utopian Method in Thomas More and Francis Bacon." Diss. Yale U, 1991.

Leslie examines *Utopia* and *New Atlantis* to describe how More and Bacon's narrative methodologies construct and negotiate the threshold between fiction and reform.

R232 Liljegren, S.B. "*Utopia*." *Studies on the Origin and Early Tradition of English Utopian Fiction*. Essays and Studies on English Language and Literature. 23. Uppsala: Lundequistska Bokhandeln, 1961. 71-91.

Liljegren presents *Utopia* against the background of earlier travel literature, classical and medieval, and as an analogue to the ideal commonwealths of Bacon, Hartlib, and Harington. Believing earlier treatments of the subject to be unsatisfactory, Liljegren distinguishes "between definite influence, and the inspiration occasioned by the existence of events, books, and ideas obvious to More and his contemporaries" and covers the Utopians' attitude toward gold and their notions about slavery, similarities between Plutarch and Utopia, and the location of Utopia, for instance.

R233 Löffler, Arno. "Die Figur des Hythlodaeus in Thomas More's *Utopia*." *GRM* 24 (1974): 168-82.

Löffler insists the Utopian polity is not to be regarded as the blueprint for a perfect society, as Hythloday conceives it, but as a faulty example of human endeavor concerning ordering the state and society. Hythloday's name, profession, and account of Utopia should alert readers to his paradoxical function, and the reader who recognizes the contradictions in the Utopian polity and is able to distance himself sufficiently to understand the satire and jokes and enjoy them will find the key to such a stance lies in the figure of Hythloday.

R234 Logan, George M. "The Argument of *Utopia*." *Interpreting Thomas More's* Utopia. 7-35.

The "strategy of argument" More uses throughout *Utopia* has its origins in rhetorical theory, and the work exploits rhetorical categories to probe the relationship between *honestas* and *utilitas*--honor and expediency--in the political realm. Logan examines the dialogue in Book I and the representation of an ideal commonwealth in Book II from this perspective; asserts the debates about Europe in Book I are juxtaposed to the description of Utopia in Book II so as to throw into relief what is wrong in Europe and what is right in Utopia, which is the burden of the peroration of both books; and scrutinizes the amount of attention Book I pays to the compatibility of the useful and the moral and claims another point the work makes, in relation to Plato's *Republic* and Aristotle's *Politics*, is that the moral is not always the same as the expedient.

R235 Logan, George M. *The Meaning of More's* Utopia. Princeton, NJ: Princeton UP, 1983.

In response to criticism which commits, Logan maintains, "the unpardonable sin of trivializing More's impassioned, profoundly reflective, and enormously learned book as a *jeu d'esprit*," this consideration of the intellectual sources and analogues of *Utopia* sees the work as an object lesson in the methodology of Greek theory (Platonic as well as Aristotelian), which it significantly refines, and as an attempt to bring that methodology to bear in a critique of the substantive conclusions of both Stoic and Greek philosophy. Ultimately, Logan views *Utopia* as a "thought-experiment," a kind of model developed to test notions of the best commonwealth, as a serious work on polished views expressed by More elsewhere and other humanists, and as a "kind of fictionalized party manifesto, the literarily sophisticated party plank in the platform of Erasmian humanism."

R236 Logan, George M. "*Utopia* and Deliberative Rhetoric." *Moreana* 118-119 (1994): 103-20.

The prefatory letter to Giles implies More approached writing *Utopia* in a way prescribed by rhetorical theory, which analyzes composition under the headings of *inventio, dispositio,* and *elocutio.* More's application of this scheme suggests the usefulness of applying it to the interpretation of his book. Logan analyzes *Utopia* in terms of its relation to two of the standard rhetorical genres and More's application of standard views on the *topoi* that stimulate invention in these genres and on the principles that should be applied to disposition in them.

R237 López Estrada, Francisco. *"Fuegos bajo el agua,* de Isaac J. Pardo: Un ensayo general sobre el pasado y el presente de la Utopía." *Moreana* 91-92 (1986): 103-10.

This article summarizes *Fuegos bajo el agua (Fires under water)* which Pardo dedicates to the Utopian genre form from its beginnings to 1516, and then discusses the Utopian genre in five sections: (1) Antiquity, (2) the Old Testament, (3) the New Testament and the early Church, (4) the Middle Ages, and (5) More's work, considered mainly as science-fiction.

R238 López Estrada, Francisco. "Una temprana traducción española de la *Utopía* de Tomás Moro." *Hispanic Studies in Honour of Geoffrey Ribbans.* Eds. Ann L. Mackenzie, and Dorothy S. Severin. Liverpool: Liverpool UP, 1992. 43-45.

López Estrada discusses a translation of *Utopia* into Spanish in the Biblioteca del Palacio Real, MS 1087.

R239 López Estrada, Francisco. "Une traduction espagnole précoce de l'*Utopie* de Thomas More." *Moreana* 111-112 (1992): 15-18.

Medinilla's translation of *Utopia* into Spanish (Córdoba, 1637) was considered the first of its kind, until a sixteenth-century version was recently discovered in the Library of the Royal Palace (Madrid). This article describes and samples the ms., pending its publication.

R240 Ludacer, Kenneth. "The Heaven and Hell of More's *Utopia.*" *CEA* 57 (1995): 66-73.

Ludacer speculates More wrote *Utopia* from both perspectives of the self and the other "as he searches his soul to position himself in relation to those hells [hell as oneself, hell as other people], simultaneously discovering and losing his sense of Self."

R241 Ludwig, Hans-Werner. "Thomas More's *Utopia*: Historical Setting and Literary Effectiveness." *Intellectuals and Writers in Fourteenth-Century Europe.* The J.A.W. Bennett Memorial Lectures. Perugia, 1984. Eds. Piero Boitani, and Anna Torti. Cambridge: Brewer, 1986. 244-64.

Ludwig points out one-sided, reductionist readings of *Utopia* often result from failure to recognize the work's literary character and to realize that, although Book II responds to real social, political, economic needs of More's day, its vision should not be viewed as a practical blueprint for an ideal state.

R242 Luzio, Juan Duran. "Sobre Tomas More en el Inca Garcilaso." *RI* 42 (1976): 349-61.

Although *Utopia* was written before much was known of Peru in Europe, many have noticed similarities between the civilizations of the Incas and the Utopians. In spite of the differences in dates of composition, Luzio discusses the similarities between *Utopia* and Garcilaso de la Vega's *Commentarios de los Incas* (1609, 1617). What More could have known about the Incas must have come from Vespucci.

R243 Mackie, J.D. "The Planner and the Planned-For." *Twentieth-Century Interpretations of* Utopia: *A Collection of Critical Essays*. 109-12.

Though Mackie acknowledges what he values in *Utopia*, he uses it to assess weaknesses in More's ideas of what is wrong with England (Book I) and to evaluate the Utopian state (Book II), in which citizens are restricted in ways resembling Hitler's Germany. He also points out inconsistencies between *Utopia* and More's life. (Parts are rpt. in *The Oxford History of England*, Ed. Sir George Clark, Vol. 7, *The Earlier Tudors, 1485-1558* [Oxford: Clarendon, 1952], 246-48, 258-66, 361-63.)

R244 Manley, Lawrence. "The city and humanism." *Literature and culture in early modern London*. Cambridge: Cambridge UP, 1995. 23-62.

Manley elaborates on how the City of London played a central role not only in shaping More's identity but also the plot of *Utopia*, and what brings its urban bias and inspiration into focus "is the contrastive technique of the work itself, its power of keeping the known, familiar world so much in view while exploring the furthest reaches of a fictional realm."

R245 Manuel, Frank E., and Fritzie P. Manuel. "The Passion of Thomas More." *Utopian Thought in the Western World*. Cambridge, MA: Belknap P of Harvard UP, 1979. 116-49.

This survey of Utopian writing includes a discussion, divided into sections, of More's *Utopia*, the shift in More's later public life away from the playful sensibility of *Utopia*, the enigma of More's character and personality, the historical impact of *Utopia*, and major tendencies in modern scholarship on the work. (It also includes information from Frank E. Manuel's "Reconsideration: Thomas More," *New Republic* 24 [1978], 37-411.)

R246 Manzalaoui, Mahmoud. "More's Reference to the Syrians in *Utopia*, Book I." *N&Q* ns 10.8 (Aug. 1963): 290-92.

Manzalaoui supports Lupton's suggestion More's mention of the Syrians may refer to the Mamelukes on the additional ground that it may be a topical allusion to the defeat of the Mameluke troops by the Ottoman army in August 1516, in which case *Utopia*, Book I, at least in its final form, should be dated somewhat later than generally supposed.

R247 Marc'hadour, Germain. "Father Surtz' *Utopia* in the Wake of G.C. Richards." *Moreana* 118-119 (1994): 155-68.

Marc'hadour focuses on the English version of *Utopia* by the classicist G.C. Richards (Oxford, 1923) and on Surtz' choosing to revise it instead of producing a new translation. The author samples Surtz' many changes, usually made for the sake of greater fidelity to More's Latin, with also a concern for modern readers. Comparing the Richards' text prepared by Surtz for the More Project and the texts published by Yale (B019, C032) reveals there was a second wave of revision, whether by Surtz himself or at the bidding of the Yale edition's Executive Editor.

R248 Marc'hadour, Germain. "M for Map: Maps of Utopia." *Moreana* 73 (1982): 103-6.

Marc'hadour reviews studies of the map of Utopia and provides reproductions of some of them.

R249 Marc'hadour, Germain. "The Meaning of 'Pontifex' in More's *Utopia*." *Acta Conventus Neo-Latini Hafniensis*. Proceedings of the Eighth International Congress of Neo-Latin Studies, Copenhagen, 12 August to 17 August 1991. Gen. Ed. Rhoda Schnur. Eds. Ann Moss, Philip Dust, Paul Gerhard Schmidt, Jacques Chomarat, and Francesco Tateo. MRTS. 120. Binghamton, NY: MRTS, 1994. 607-18.

Marc'hadour examines the meanings of the word, "*pontifex*," to untie the knot surrounding its use in Book II; he also considers how More employs the word in other works.

R250 Marc'hadour, Germain. "Un sillage lumineux: Edward Louis Surtz (1909-1973)." *Moreana* 77 (1983): 121-34.

This assessment of and tribute to Surtz' scholarship focuses on his abilities as one of *Utopia*'s translators.

R251 Marc'hadour, Germain. "*Utopia* and Martyrdom." *Interpreting Thomas More's* Utopia. 61-76.

Marc'hadour deals with the concept of martyrdom within the context of the attitudes and behavior of the religious group in Utopia known as the *Buthrescae*. Because they are self-centered and have not chosen that way of life, Marc'hadour concludes they are not properly called martyrs and "seem to be a near-caricature."

R252 Marc'hadour, Germain, and Henri Gibaud. "Election ou Ordination? Tentation utopienne et tentative coréenne." *Moreana* 87-88 (1985): 167-71.

The authors explore ways editors and scholars have treated the passage in Book II of *Utopia* in which Hythloday relates the problems concerning the administration of certain sacraments to those Utopians who have embraced Catholicism.

R253 Margolin, Jean-Claude. "*Sur l'insularité d'*Utopia: *Entre l'érudition et la rêverie.*" *Miscellanea Moreana: Essays for Germain Marc'hadour*. *Moreana* 100. 303-21.

Margolin speculates upon the significance of space and topography in Utopia in the context of mythical and historical time.

R254 Marin, Louis. "Toward a Semiotic of Utopia: Political and Fictional Discourse in Thomas More's *Utopia*." *Structure, Consciousness, and History*. Eds. Richard Harvey Brown, and Stanford M. Lyman. Cambridge: Cambridge UP, 1978. 261-82.

Marin examines two of the work's principal levels of discourse, the "ought" and the "is," the fictional or utopian discourse outside of time and the historical-political-economic analysis within More's time. Marin's point centers on how More attempts to link these two forms of discourse through the stylistic continuity of the dialogue form and the subject of how to advise a prince.

R255 Marin, Louis. *Utopics: Spatial Play*. Trans. Robert A. Vollrath. Contemporary Studies in Philosophy and the Human Sciences. Atlantic Highlands, NJ: Humanities P, 1984. (Trans. of *Utopics: Jeux d'espaces* [Paris: Minuit, 1973].)

Marin insists on the discontinuity, supplementarity, indeterminacy, otherness, and emptiness of utopia; develops analogues on names with negative prefixes in the book of Hosea; and thinks of all these terms within the conceptual framework of the "neuter"--in senses borrowed from grammar, chemistry, politics, and philosophy--where utopia would be understood as the zero-degree term located between and outside pairs of contraries. More's *Utopia* is neither England nor America, neither the Old nor the New World; it is the in-between of the contradiction at the beginning of the sixteenth century of the Old and New World.

R256 Marin, Louis. "Voyages en utopie." *ECr* 25.3 (1985): 42-51.

Marin investigates the notion of utopia and its relationship to travel.

R257 Maroto Camino, Mercedes. "Mapping *Terra Incognita*: The Reification of America in the Works of Hernán Cortés, Amerigo Vespucci and Thomas More." *Travellers' Tales, Real and Imaginary, in the Hispanic World and*

Its Literature. Ed. Alun Kenwood. Melbourne: Voz Hispánica, 1993. 7-22.

Maroto Camino compares the ways these authors represented America from their vantage points, with More summing "up in *Utopia* how discovery reflected, and was reflected by, the political and ontological changes which took place throughout the Western world."

R258 Marsh, T.N. "The First Bishop of *Utopia*: An Attempt at Identification." *N&Q* ns 4.1 (Jan. 1957): 30-32.

Although some have argued the professor of divinity who wanted to travel to Utopia to become its first bishop was Rowland Phillips, Marsh demonstrates this person is still unidentified or just another figment of imagination devised to add to the Utopian fiction.

R259 Martínez López, Miguel. "The Idea of a Commonwealth According to the Essenes and St. Thomas More's *The Best State of a Commonwealth and the New Island of Utopia*." *More's* Utopia *and the Utopian Inheritance*. 53-68.

Martínez contends the community of the Judaic sect of the Essenes "stands as the major single religious influence on More's shaping of the commonwealth of *Utopia*."

R260 Martínez López, Miguel. "The Life of the Essenes and the Life of the Utopians: A Case Study." *Moreana* 118-119 (1994): 43-59.

This article presents the main sources for the study of the Essenes (Philo, Josephus, Pliny); sums up the main customs, beliefs, and institutions of the Essenes, comparing and contrasting them with those of More's Utopians; and highlights the numerous parallels that exist between these two utopian communities. Whether More knew about the life of the Essenes or used the Essenes as background to his Utopia, these startling concurrences in customs, beliefs, and institutions stress the religious foundations that lie at the core of that function of the imagination that "creates" utopian societies.

R261 Maxey, Chester C. "Strange Interlude." *Political Philosophies*. Rev. ed. New York: Macmillan, 1948. 125-53.

Chapter nine uses Machiavelli's *Prince* and *Discourses on Livy* and More's *Utopia* to exemplify "political literature of materialism" and "literature of political idealism." For *Utopia*, he identifies major influences in its composition, defects in European politics Hythloday describes in Book I, and some elements of Utopian society presented in Book II. He also discusses differences between *Utopia* and Plato's *Republic*.

R262 McCabe, Richard A. "'Ut Publica Est Opinio': An Utopian Irony." *Neophil* 72 (1988): 633-39.

Toward the end of *Utopia*, "*uero*" can ironically qualify "*opinio*," thereby illustrating that in Renaissance Europe public opinion can militate against public interest.

R263 McClung, William A. "Designing Utopia." *Moreana* 118-119 (1994): 9-28.

The design of More's *Utopia* is not only constitutional but also material, setting the precedent for subsequent "utopia" architectural projects. His text constitutes a program--a set of requirements for the built environment of the ideal society. This program is, however, qualified by the ambiguities and contradictions inherent in More's language. Illustrations to editions of *Utopia*, scholarly efforts to rationalize More's prescriptions, and recent student projects testify both to the advantages of rendering the text into architectural designs and to the losses sustained when the inevitable choices are made.

R264 McClung, William A.; trans. Dídia Marques Reckert. "Projectar Utopia." *A Simbólica do Espaço: Cidades, Ilhas, Jardins.* Eds. Yvette Kace Centeno, and Lima de Freitas. Lisbon: Estampa, 1991. 87-105.

McClung notes how illustrations in some editions of *Utopia* depict the island, its cities, and the Utopians' clothing and some customs in order to comment on the diverse interpretations More's text inspires.

R265 McCutcheon, Elizabeth. "Denying the Contrary: More's Use of Litotes in the *Utopia.*" *Moreana* 31-32 (1971): 107-21.

McCutcheon comments on the frequency with which the work employs litotes and the range and variety of its effects. "The figure becomes, ultimately, a paradigm of the structure and method of the book as a whole, echoing, often in the briefest syntactical units, the larger, paradoxical and double vision which will discover the best state of the commonwealth in an island called Noplace." The ambiguity thus created cannot be resolved and probably was not intended to be. (Rpt. in *Essential Articles for the Study of Thomas More*, 263-74, and in *Sir Thomas More*, Utopia: *A New Translation, Backgrounds, Criticism*, 1st ed., 224-30.)

R266 McCutcheon, Elizabeth. "The Language of Utopian Negation: Book II of More's *Utopia.*" *Acta Conventus Neo-Latini Bononiensis.* Proceedings of the Fourth International Congress of Neo-Latin Studies. Bologna, 26 August to 1 September 1979. Ed. R.J. Schoeck. MRTS. 37. Binghamton: MRTS. 1985. 510-19.

McCutcheon continues the kind of investigation which characterizes her essay "Denying the Contrary: More's Use of Litotes in the *Utopia*" (R265). In More's verbal dexterity, she finds "much of the lawyer, as well as the comic story-teller, the satirist, the visionary, the explorer of conscience and consciousness, and the humanist maintaining a 'precarious balance.'" In Book II, the reader surely sees "the poet behind the consummate creation and description of Utopia, a speaking mental picture built by contraries."

R267 McCutcheon, Elizabeth. "*Mendacium Dicere* and *Mentiri*: A Utopian Crux." *Acta Conventus Neo-Latini Sanctandreani*. Proceedings of the Fifth International Congress of Neo-Latin Studies. University of St. Andrews, Scotland, 24 August to 1 September 1982. Ed. I.D. McFarlane. MRTS. 38. Binghamton: MRTS. 1986. 449-57.

McCutcheon explores More's distinction in *Utopia* between "to tell a lie" and "to lie," considering the "style and aesthetic of honest deception" in writing whose equivocations provoke the reader and protect the author.

R268 McCutcheon, Elizabeth. "More's *Utopia* and Cicero's *Paradoxa Stoicorum*." *Moreana* 86 (1985): 3-22.

McCutcheon analyzes the indebtedness of Hythloday's monologue to Cicero to illustrate how More's use of *Paradoxa* illuminates his thought, artistry, and values.

R269 McCutcheon, Elizabeth. "More's Utopia, Callenbach's Ecotopia, and Biosphere 2." *More's* Utopia *and the Utopian Inheritance*. 69-88.

McCutcheon considers "to what degree each of these utopias" represents a society in which social structure is based upon an ecological philosophy of nature.

R270 McCutcheon, Elizabeth. *My Dear Peter: The Ars Poetica and Hermeneutics for More's* Utopia. Angers, Fr.: *Moreana*, 1983.

McCutcheon's monograph on the letter to Giles is both an inventive, syncretic, and summary description of the amazing variety of mental acts More shows readers that language enables him to perform (to create and to think and comprehend, understand and interpret and re-interpret) and a replication itself, leading readers from one certain category to its opposite only to strike a moderating middle position, looping its way line by line through the letter in which there are three separate parts all interlacing.

R271 McCutcheon, Elizabeth. "Puns, Paradoxes, and Heuristic Inquiry: The 'De Servis' Section of More's *Utopia*." *Acta Conventus Neo-Latini Torontonensis*. Proceedings of the Seventh International Congress of Neo-Latin Studies, Toronto, 8 August to 13 August 1988. Eds. Alexander Dalzell, Charles Fantazzi, and R.J. Schoeck. MRTS. 86. Binghamton, NY: MRTS, 1991. 91-99.

McCutcheon provides a close analysis of the significance of the literary effects "implicit in and created by the puns and paradoxes" of "*De Servis*" section, "which adumbrate large concerns about bonding and binding and initiate the heuristic inquiry in which readers are invited to participate."

R272 McCutcheon, Elizabeth. "Thomas More and the *Utopia*: Notes from Beijing." *Moreana* 77 (1983): 23-28.

McCutcheon discusses the lectures she gave on More in Beijing and how students and faculty at the Beijing Institute of Foreign Languages view *Utopia*.

R273 McCutcheon, Elizabeth. "Thomas More, Raphael Hythlodaeus, and the Angel Raphael." *SEL* 9 (1969): 21-38.

McCutcheon traces, in Hythloday's character and role, the influence of a complex "angelic" tradition, figuring the Angel Raphael as spiritual *medicus*, the curer of souls and guide to travellers. Hythloday is also a prophetic messenger, *medicus salutis*, denouncing pride and avarice that mislead martial nations into following the wrong road. McCutcheon is more sympathetic to Hythloday's message than most advocates of the satiric approach, and she shows how the connotations of Hythloday's name call to mind a "speaker of nonsense" as well as the enlightening physician and guiding angel. For her ironically, the book ends with persona More leading the angelic guide.

R274 McCutcheon, Elizabeth. "Time in More's *Utopia*." *Acta Conventus Neo-Latini Turonensis*. Troisième Congrès International D'Études Néo-Latines, Tours. Université Francis-Rabelais, 6-10 Septembre 1976. Ed. Jean-Claude Margolin. 2. Paris: Vrin, 1980. 697-707.

McCutcheon describes how Utopians both use time well in the Pauline sense and enjoy the pleasures of leisure and free time as More's means of clarifying man's understanding of self and relationships with family, commonwealth, and God, and of exploring the delicate balance between the temporal and eternal.

R275 McCutcheon, Elizabeth. "The *Utopia* in Taiwan: An Addendum." *Moreana* 77 (1983): 29-30.

McCutcheon summarizes and comments on the reception and study of *Utopia* in Taiwan.

R276 McCutcheon, Elizabeth. "*William Bullein's* Dialogue Against the Fever Pestilence: *A Sixteenth-Century Anatomy*." *Miscellanea Moreana: Essays for Germain Marc'hadour. Moreana* 100. 341-59.

McCutcheon analyzes Bullein's work closely and concludes by comparing Bullein's work and ideas to those of More and his *Utopia*, noting "like the *Utopia*,...*Dialogue Against the Fever Pestilence* is simultaneously philosophical and 'foolosophical.'"

R277 McKinnon, Dana G. "The Marginal Glosses in More's *Utopia*: The

Character of the Commentator." *RenP* (1970): 11-19.

The 194 marginal glosses in the first three printings of *Utopia* were written by More's friends, Giles and Erasmus, with More's approval, hence making them an integral part of the total work, and they create a fictitious commentator whose "character is consistent throughout the work," although a different facet of his personality dominates each book. In Book I, he evolves as a pedantic humanist-scholar appreciating the details of a new world; in Book II, the commentator's main function is to relate Utopian customs to contemporary European ones and thereby point up the satire More intends. Throughout the glosses serve as section headings.

R278 McLean, Andrew. "A Note on Thomas More and Thomas Starkey." *Moreana* 41 (1974): 31-36.

By stressing the immediate and practicable, Starkey's *Dialogue Between Reginald Pole and Thomas Lupset* contrasts with More's *Utopia*, an idealistic model rather than a workable program for reform. More and Starkey encourage public service and condemn enclosure, unjust laws, and the idle multitudes in England, but Starkey asserts the "real possibility" of reform.

R279 McLean, Andrew. "Thomas More's *Utopia* as Dialogue and City Encomium." *Acta Conventus Neo-Latini Guelpherbytani*. Proceedings of the Sixth International Congress of Neo-Latin Studies. Woffenbüttel, 12 August to 16 August 1985. Eds. Stella P. Revard, Fidel Rädle, and Mario A. Di Cesare. MRTS. 53. Binghamton: MRTS, 1988. 91-97.

McLean examines how *Utopia* blends together "two literary genres dear to Renaissance humanists"--the dialogue and the city encomium; comments on Raphael's *declamatio* as dialogue *manqué*, the first book's more conventional dialogue, and the introductory letters' suggestion of continuing public dialogue; and concludes awareness of More's subtle mixture of these genres "creates a special context in which to read and understand *Utopia*."

R280 Meerse, Peggy Currey. "The Ideal of Order and the Process of Experience in More's *Utopia*." Diss. U of Illinois-Urbana, 1972.

Meerse interprets *Utopia* as a work in which the Erasmian philosophy of men, experience, and social reform is ironically but sympathetically contrasted with More's philosophy both to assess Erasmian principles and ideals and to represent More's ideal of spiritual development.

R281 Metscher, Thomas. "The Ideal Irony of Thomas More." *ShJE* 118 (1982): 120-30.

After assessing irony in *Utopia* and the work's themes, Metscher evaluates its "fundamental ideological status" in order to place it in the tradition of radical literature. Because of its ironic, dialectical, experimental approaches to societal problems, Metscher insists it leaves the question of how to organize an ideal commonweal open.

R282   Mezciems, Jenny. "*Utopia* and 'the Thing which is not': More, Swift, and Other Lying Idealists." *UTQ* 52 (1982): 40-62.

Mezciems discusses various utopias, particularly More's and *Gulliver's Travels*, that depend upon exploiting the interplay between ideal fiction and reality, where fiction is set within half-fiction within reality, and literary convention and rhetoric unsettle the reader.

R283   Miething, Christoph. "Politeia und Utopia: Zur Epistemologie der literarischen Utopie." *GRM* 37.3 (1987): 247-63.

Miething compares More's treatment of utopia to that of Plato (in the *Republic*) and Dante (in *De Monarchia*).

R284   Miles, Leland. "The Platonic Source of Utopia's Minimum Religion." *RN* 9 (1956): 83-90.

Miles notes the similarities between what he calls "minimum religion" in Plato's *Republic* and *Utopia*--belief in the soul's immortality, in one god, in divine providence, and in punishment of evil.

R285   Miller, Clarence H. "The English Translation in the Yale *Utopia*: Some Corrections." *Moreana* 9 (1966): 57-64.

Miller offers a list of corrections to the translation of *Utopia*'s Latin text in the definitive edition (B019).

R286   Miller, Clarence H. "Style and Meaning in More's *Utopia*: Hythloday's Sentences and Diction." *Acta Conventus Neo-Latini Hafniensis*. Proceedings of the Eighth International Congress of Neo-Latin Studies, Copenhagen, 12 August to 17 August 1991. Gen. ed. Rhoda Schnur. Eds. Ann Moss, Philip Dust, Paul Gerhard Schmidt, Jacques Chomarat, and Francesco Tateo. MRTS. 120. Binghamton, NY: MRTS, 1994. 675-83.

Miller examines how Hythloday says what he says, how his speech changes when he speaks about various subjects, and how his speech resembles that of More himself in *Utopia* and his other Latin works in order to determine the closeness and distance between the author-More and his character Hythloday.

R287   Minattur, Joseph. "More's *Utopia* and Kerala." *Moreana* 22 (1969): 39-43.

Minattur claims More "had the people of Kerala in mind" when he composed Utopia, because of many similarities between not only the shape of the island of Utopia and Malabar but also the societal organization, military training, and religion of Utopia and Kerala. He believes More may have learned about India and Kerala through the writings of Father Joseph of Cranganore (Josephus Indus).

R288 Mölk, Ulrich. "Philologische Bermerkungen zu Thomas Morus' *Utopia*." *Anglia* 82 (1964): 309-20.

Mölk's argument hinges on the background to *Utopia* in the *Republic*, the *Timaeus*, the *Somnium Scipionis*, and the work of Lucian. He finds correspondences between the occasion of *Utopia* and that of the *Republic* as well as in the relation between the two parts into which each work is divided. The etymology of Utopian names has Platonic analogues and enforces More's message. Both in the name of the island and in his foreword to the reader, he intimates the unreality of his world of "nowhere," a motive paralleled in both Plato and Lucian and emphasized by Ficino. Hythloday's Christian name figures his angelic nature and origin, and in the end, he returns to *Utopia*, as one not of this world.

R289 Monsuez, R. "Le Latin de Thomas More dans *Utopia*." *Annales publiées par la Faculté des Lettres et Sciences Humaines de Toulouse, Hommage á Paul Dottin. Caliban* ns 2 (1966): 35-78.

Monsuez measures More's Latin style against classical standards and finds More flexible and informal as he analyzes and classifies More's Latin into "*usuelle*," "*savante*," and "*vivante*." Common language employs a large proportion of concrete words, some rarities like "*urbici*," "*ribaldus*," and banalities of current usage. "Learned" language uses Latinisms, ancient and modern, poetic words and usages, and free adaptation of Ciceronian Latin. More's Latin is the "living" language of a creative humanist, who develops and enriches it in a process of adapting it to a work designed primarily for entertainment, which, nonetheless, will satisfy the most erudite readers.

R290 Morgan, Alice B. "Philosophic Reality and Human Construction in More's *Utopia*." *Moreana* 39 (1973): 15-23.

In contrast to the outside world, human constructions in Utopia reinforce nature. True pleasure in More's model world is defined according to the "natural qualities of the 'thing itself.'" In Utopia, use determines an item's value rather than an imaginary one; nobility, wealth, and extravagant clothing, causes of envy in the outside world, are derided because their value is based on imaginary and vicious human constructs. Utopian laws advance rather than impede justice and exemplify human constructions supporting the "Natural and hence the Good."

R291 Morgan, Arthur E. "Nowhere Was Somewhere." *Nowhere Was Somewhere: How History Makes Utopias and How Utopias Make History*. Chapel Hill: U of North Carolina P, 1946. 15-88.

Morgan presents arguments to prove More based *Utopia* upon his knowledge of Peru's civilization. (Part of this study is rpt. as "Is *Utopia* an Account of the Inca Empire?" in *Sir Thomas More*, Utopia: *A New Translation, Backgrounds, Criticism,* 1st ed., 230-33.)

R292 Morgan, Nicole S. "Negotium, Otium et Specula L'*Utopie* de Thomas More ou la Decouverte d'un Nouveau Continent Epistemologique." Diss. U of Ottawa (Can.), 1993.

Morgan analyzes Hythloday's epistemology that opens a new way of thinking contrasting with humanist thought in general and Erasmian ideas in particular. Instead of seeking answers to questions in classical texts, Hythloday reduces and replaces those texts with the idea knowledge comes from experience.

R293 Morgan, Nicole S. "Le petit singe cercopithèque mangeur de bibliothèque." *Moreana* 118-119 (1994): 141-54.

Hythloday's discourse opens a new way of thinking that contrasts strongly with humanist thought in general and Erasmian themes in particular. Even if Hythloday's topics seem all-too-familiar, he is pursuing a consistent, fundamental epistemological reflection unrecognized in the convoluted text. Unlike his contemporaries, Hythloday does not try to find an answer to the political and ethical chaos of his times in classical texts. A mischievous little monkey nibbles away part of one of them which thereby loses the status of authority the humanist movement accorded them. Hythloday reduces them to a complementary accessory if not simply to a source of entertainment or pleasure. The monkey and the spatial voyage to the island of Utopia are metaphors for the foundations of knowledge, and knowledge is born from experience in space.

R294 Mortimer, Anthony. "Hythlodaeus and Persona More: The Narrative Voices of *Utopia*." *CahiersE* 28 (1985): 23-35.

To neglect the complexities of these voices and to identify either Hythloday or persona More with the author is to force answers to questions about the basic tensions inherent in Christian humanism, such as the difficulty of reconciling a stable view of man as fallen with the renewed emphasis on man's capacity to shape his own world, questions which the book leaves open.

R295 Morton, A.L. "The Island of the Saints." *The English Utopia*. 1952. London: Lawrence and Wishart, 1969. 46-77.

Morton places *Utopia* within the context of economic conditions related to the break of the medieval village commune and the growth of "merchant capital, of trade and of urban industry" and maintains More's conception of a just society "looks at once backward and forward."

R296 Mueller, Janel. "'The Whole Island like a Single Family': Positioning Women in Utopian Patriarchy." *Rethinking the Henrician Era: Essays on Early Tudor Texts and Contexts.* Ed. Peter C. Herman. Urbana: U of Illinois P, 1994. 93-122.

Mueller explores how gender roles are constructed--more specifically how women are positioned--in *Utopia*. Although she acknowledges "possibilities" for irony in More's text, she aims to read it "unironically, taking its representations, its rhetoric, and its value judgments at face value, positing a basic correspondence between the authorial More and Morus the reporter of Hythlodaeus." She finds *Utopia*, minus its patriarchal construction, voids "maleness," though the remainder is not generic humanity, but recognizably feminine against the backdrop of a patriarchy in full force elsewhere in that society.

R297 Müllenbrock, Heinz-Joachim. "La position de Wells dans le développement de l'Utopie anglaise moderne sous l'aspect sociologique." *Moreana* 34 (1972): 25-38.

Müllenbrock contrasts and compares the utopian visions of More and Wells.

R298 Mumford, Lewis. "Utopia, the City and the Machine." *Utopia and Utopian Thought.* Ed. Frank E. Manuel. Boston: Beacon P, 1965, 1966. 3-24.

Mumford answers the question why the city is so often the nucleus of utopias by pointing out classical Greek culture influenced More's *Utopia* and that to the Greeks the commonwealth was a city. (This article also appears in *Daedalus*, 94 [1965], 271-92.)

R299 Murphy, Clare M. "Ottoman Analogs to *Utopia*." *Moreana* 69 (1981): 65-75.

Murphy shows that, while *Utopia* makes no direct references to Ottomans, many incidents it relates and many issues it raises may be read in light of the history of the Ottoman Empire or Turkish-European relations--particularly in the way Utopian society is structured on two necessities: maintaining peace and its corollary, avoiding war.

R300 Murphy, Clare M. "The Turkish Threat and Thomas More's *Utopia*." *Acta Conventus Neo-Latini Bononiensis.* Proceedings of the Fourth International Congress of Neo-Latin Studies. Bologna, 26 August to 1 September 1979. Ed. R.J. Schoeck. MRTS. 37. Binghamton: MRTS, 1985. 158-71.

Murphy writes that, "if the fall of Constantinople and its antecedents created the recent Ottoman past to the writing of *Utopia*, the reign of Selim, begun in 1512, served as its immediate historical setting." Read in the light of this threat to Christendom, *Utopia* is a foray into the discord--both religious and political--before which Europe trembled.

R301 Nagel, Alan F. "Lies and the Limitable Inane: Contradictions in More's *Utopia*." *RenQ* 26 (1973): 173-80.

Nagel locates the precedent for More's verbal irony in Plato's *Republic*, although "if the *Republic* initiates the ideal, More's book dwells more upon the criticism of the actual." The "no place" of Utopia is closely related to England, "whereas the critical dimension of More's text depends upon its difference and on the impossibility of any identity." Nagel points out the contradictions contained in More's account of the island, demonstrating that it exists in a topological as well as an etymological "nowhere." More's emphasis on the nothing and nowhere of Utopia reminds the reader that, however close to England it may be, this literary place is not England.

R302 Neumann, Harry. "On the Platonism of More's *Utopia*." *Social Research* 33 (1966): 495-521.

Neumann sees a radical difference in authorial stance between *Utopia* and the *Republic* because More uses two opposed spokesmen, and believes More intended the final dissenting statement of persona More to refute the Platonic ideal society upon which Hythloday expounded.

R303 New, Peter. *Fiction and Purpose in* Utopia, Rasselas, The Mill on the Floss, *and* Women in Love. New York: St. Martin's, 1985. 12-82.

New compares purpose in these fictions and considers whether and how the authors' (or protagonists') fantasies are checked by a sense of external reality of resistance. Chapters two to five cover *Utopia*, written by a Christian and realist, as a subtle and through-going demolition of the Epicurean-utilitarian philosophy (or "felicific calculus" of Jeremy Bentham) espoused by Hythloday and the Utopians.

R304 Norbrook, David. "The *Utopia* and Radical Humanism." *Poetry and Politics in the English Renaissance*. London: Routledge & Kegan Paul, 1984. 18-31.

Norbrook's neo-Marxist's approach emphasizes the split between the ideas embodied in *Utopia* and the realities of Henry VIII's court. In discussing *Utopia*, he rejects "the narrowly literary approach" less concerned with political ideas than with literary subtleties and ironies and shows how verbal games and paradoxes reinforce political satire. He reminds readers of the humanists' rhetoricism and how humanism provided an ideological rationale for economic individualism and the connection between political and rhetorical experimentation.

R305 O'Brien, Brian. "J.H. Hexter and the Text of *Utopia*: A Reappraisal." *Moreana* 110 (1992): 19-32.

Close examination of Hexter's theories (*More's* Utopia: *The Biography of an Idea* [R192]) about the genesis of the text of *Utopia* throws light on the debate as to whether the book is a prescriptive political document or a work of fiction. Study of the process of the work's composition shows More introduced the figure of Hythloday at a late stage and surrounded the work with parerga which made its literary status ambiguous. As part of the process of revision, More introduced the figure of Hythloday, inserted new material into his account of Utopia, and revised the original text to increase its ambiguity. As a result of these changes, More made *Utopia* increasingly less a political and social statement and correspondingly more a complex, ironic work of fiction.

R306 O'Grady, Walter. "A Note on Busleyden's Letter to Thomas More." *Moreana* 11 (1966): 33-38.

O'Grady explores the placement of Busleyden's letter to More in early editions of *Utopia*, with special attention to how Busleyden concentrates on the civic and social values of the Utopian republic.

R307 Olin, John C. "Erasmus' *Adagia* and More's *Utopia*." *Miscellanea Moreana: Essays for Germain Marc'hadour*. *Moreana* 100. 127-36.

Olin discusses the friendship of Erasmus and More and its influence upon *Adagia* and *Utopia*, in which communal property and Christian charity are presented as millenial ideals dependent for their realization upon moral reformation in European Christians.

R308 Olin, John C. *Erasmus, Utopia, and the Jesuits: Essays on the Outreach of Humanism*. New York: Fordham UP, 1994.

In this collection of six brief essays, Olin goes beyond the basic treatment of humanism as the revival of antiquity to highlight its reform thrust--moral, religious, intellectual, social--that guided both the Renaissance and the Reformation. The fourth and fifth essays present the social dimension of humanism's reform thrust and focus on the concept of utopia. Olin links the proverb *Amicorum communia omnium* found in Erasmus' *Adagia* with the theme of More's *Utopia*. In the former essay, Olin contends both Erasmus and More present and develop the same basic idea that "the best social order is one in which all possessions are held in common and a close community of living and sharing prevails." The latter essay compares the utopian vision of More to the utopias found in the literary works of Rabelais, Montaigne, Swift, Voltaire, and Arnold.

R309 Olin, John C. "The Idea of Utopia from Hesiod to John Paul II." *Interpreting Thomas More's* Utopia. 77-98.

Olin explores the concept of utopia and the utopian vision to offer an historical outline extending from antiquity to modern times and inquiring into its character and history. Olin opens his essay by stating what he believes to be a fundamental element of utopian thought--"its religious manifestation or dimension."

R310 Olin, John C. "More, Montaigne, Voltaire and Matthew Arnold: Thoughts on the Utopian Vision." *More's* Utopia *and the Utopian Inheritance*. 99-107.

Olin relates the utopian ideas of Rabelais, Montaigne, Voltaire, and Arnold to More's *Utopia* and Plato's *Republic*.

R311 O'Sullivan, Richard. "The Social Life and Theories of St. Thomas More." *Dublin Review* 199 (1936): 46-62.

O'Sullivan calls attention to the influence of More's legal training and his familiarity with English Common Law and Aquinas upon his works. He refers extensively to *Utopia* to discuss More's social philosophy about the family, the education of children, sexual equality, and religion. (Rpt. in *More's* Utopia *and Its Critics*, 123-34.)

R312 Palmer, William G. "Still More on *Utopia*: A Revival of the Catholic Interpretation? A Review Essay." *SHR* 19 (1985): 347-58.

Palmer evaluates major scholarship on *Utopia*, including that of Chambers, Hexter, Skinner, Fenlon, Duhamel, Surtz, Bradshaw, Fox, and Marius.

R313 Papazu, Monica. "La Tentation Utopique." *Moreana* 87-88 (1985): 157-66.

Papazu discusses Hythloday's treatment of Christian doctrine in *Utopia*.

R314 Park, James W. "The Utopian Economics of Sir Thomas More." *American Journal of Economics and Sociology* 30 (1971): 123-34.

Park considers Book I as a description of economic problems--unemployment, the value of money, and distribution of wealth--and sees Book II as their hypothetical solutions. He also uses the economic theories of Karl Polanyi to analyze production and distribution and trade and commerce in Utopia.

R315 Parker, Thomas M. "Sir Thomas More's *Utopia*." *Essays in Modern Church History in Memory of Norman Sykes*. Eds. G.V. Bennett, and J.D. Walsh. London: Adam & Charles Black, 1966. 1-17.

Because More's membership in the Flemish embassy provided an "inside" look at politics, Parker thinks it may have inspired the composition of *Utopia* and its juxtaposition of European social ills with Utopian practices. He also claims the older, basically medieval, belief in natural law (natural reason) inspired More's work, and that More intends readers to compare their practice of Christianity founded upon revelation with that of the Utopian who practices a religion grounded upon natural law and reason--a view which, in part, agrees with that of Chambers (F040).

R316 Parks, George B. "More's *Utopia* and Geography." *JEGP* 37 (1938): 224-36.

Parks traces Hythloday's probable route from Utopia to Brazil and contends the former would today roughly correspond with Tasmania. He sets forth the view "More developed from established geographical doctrine a new theory which we may call the theory of climatic symmetry." He then gives his ideas on possible meanings of *Utopia*.

R317 Patrick, J. Max, and Glenn Negley. "*Utopia*, 1516: Sir Thomas More, Lord Chancellor of England, Saint and Martyr." *The Quest for Utopia*. New York: Henry Schuman, 1952. 261-84.

The authors believe *Utopia* is a literary exercise, a playful work intended to amuse humanist scholars, a social criticism; and that Hythloday is More's mouthpiece for his own ideas advocating a type of communism.

R318 Pavkovic, Aleksandar. "Propensity and Intellectual Needs: The Credibility and Coherence of More's *Utopia*." *UtopSt* 4.1 (1993): 26-37.

Pavkovic divides his essay into four parts; three are devoted to the credibility of prosperity and intellectual needs as related in Utopia, while the fourth relates credibility and coherence in More's book. There are "two very general, almost trivial, conditions for a credible utopian picture": (1) a utopia "should indicate how the societal goals of the ideal society in question are attained"; (2) it should indicate "what motivates the members of this imaginary society to perform the tasks considered essential for the maintenance of that society." More's work satisfies both of those conditions.

R319 Pavkovic, Aleksandar. "Prosperity, Equality and Intellectual Needs in More's Utopia." *More's* Utopia *and the Utopian Inheritance*. 23-35.

Pavkovic shows *Utopia* satisfies both conditions he stipulates for a "credible utopia," because its "alternative and morally superior society requires a restriction on the scope and variety of human needs."

R320 Peggram, Reed Edwin. "The First French and English Translations of Sir Thomas More's *Utopia*." *MLR* 35 (1940): 330-40.

Peggram compares these two editions and concludes the French composed a translation of the Latin work that was as faithful to the original text as possible, while the first English translation by Robinson takes all sorts of liberties, leaving out entire lines at times and occasionally rearranging entire sentences. Peggram concedes, however, Robinson's alterations have some merit.

R321 Perlette, John M. "Irresolution as Solution: Rhetoric and the

Unresolved Debate in Book I of More's *Utopia*." *TSLL* 29 (1987): 28-53.

Perlette pursues implications of a recognition the clash between rhetoric and philosophy is at the core of the debate in the book and suggests that, after all, there is a kind of "resolution" to the apparently stalemated debate, an implicit decision by default.

R322 Perlette, John M. "Of Sites and Parasites: The Centrality of the Marginal Anecdote of Book I of More's *Utopia*." *ELH* 54 (1987): 231-52.

Perlette looks at "The Merry Dialogue between a Friar and a Hanger-on," which even has its own marginal label that serves as a title suggesting its autonomy, and examines how such labeling provides another way for this parasite story to imitate or "double" the narrative that precedes it as it pursues the same subjects--thieves, vagabonds, and the poor.

R323 Peters, Robert. "*Utopia* and More's Orthodoxy." *Moreana* 31-32 (1971): 147-55.

Peters assesses More's doctrinal orthodoxy in light of his most famous work and relates views expressed therein to the theological issues of the day.

R324 Pineas, Rainer. "Thomas More's *Utopia* and Protestant Polemics." *RN* 17 (1964): 197-201.

References to *Utopia* by Protestant reformers William Tyndale, John Frith, William Roy, and the anonymous author of "The Image of Ipocrysy" usually use More's book to illustrate the warning that as More once passed off falsehood as truth (in *Utopia*), he is quite capable of doing it again (in polemical treatises).

R325 Polak, Frederik L. *The Image of the Future, Enlightening the Past, Orienting the Present, Forecasting the Future.* Trans. (from Dutch) Elsie Boulding. Vol. 1. The Promised Land, Source of Living Culture. European Aspects. Ser. A: Culture. No. 1. Leyden: Sythoff, 1961. 220-25.

Polak compares and contrasts ideas from *Utopia*, Campanella's *City of the Sun*, and Bacon's *New Atlantis* as concrete images of the future. In *Utopia*, while More draws from classical models for ideal commonwealths from the past, he (like Pico) also looks to the future. In spite of *Utopia*'s witty facade and its contradictions, it is "profoundly serious."

R326 Pound, John. *Poverty and Vagrancy in Tudor England.* Seminar Studies in History. New York: Longman, 1986.

Pound casts light on social, economic aspects of *Utopia* and other Tudor literature. The causes of poverty are summarized, and the extent of the problem conveyed; while the legislative, judicial, and philanthropic measures evolved to remedy the situation are clearly set forth. A full bibliography follows a selection of contemporary documents.

R327 Prévost, André. "L'*Utopie*: Le genre littéraire." *Moreana* 31-32 (1971): 161-68.

Utopia is historical-fictional, plausible-implausible, dialectical by its seeming contradictions (verbal and thematic), poetic in its "dream-like aesthetic," and unified through its novelistic form. More contrasts Utopia with Europe to present his solution for man's demeaning, demoralizing loss of land--the community lands worked by all. *Utopia*'s perfect institutions point to man's flawed mind, heart, and will, which are corrigible upon moral reflection, the real key to institutional self-reform. Hythloday, his trip over, has become purified of pride and is now ready to accept the finality of existence, to love work, to cultivate his mind and sense of the holy for these will bring him serenity. The final level of this genre, responsible for its universality and permanence, is its power to galvanize compassion for the oppressed and antipathy to unjust institutions.

R328 Prévost, André. "Une Rétrospective: Le Facsimilé de L'*Utopie* Éditée par Marie Delcourt." *Moreana* 85 (1985): 67-82.

Prévost comments upon Delcourt's textual editing and translation of *Utopia* into French (C026).

R329 Quarta, Cosimo. "L'*Utopia* come generatrice di 'nuovi mondi.'" *Moreana* 118-119 (1994): 121-40.

Utopian projects cannot be identified with the literary invention of individual writers; they are created essentially as a response to concrete human needs. Such needs are the expression of a "lack of being," of a sense of difficulty in the face of conditions that are seen as insufficient, limiting, oppressive--hence, the insistence upon the concepts "new" and "better." In this connection "new" does not mean anything new whatsoever; rather, it implies the idea of "goodness" or of a "better state."

R330 Quattrocki, Ed. "Injustice, Not Councilorship: The Theme of Book One of *Utopia*." *Moreana* 31-32 (1971): 19-28.

Injustice in Book I and justice in Book II are unifying themes. Hythloday blames European injustice on corrupt rulers; More states that from the ruler springs "a stream of all that is good or evil over the whole nation." In England, the rich legally terrorize the poor, driving them to beg and steal. Hythloday's favorite concern is injustice. More's persona urges him to lessen injustice, if he cannot eliminate it entirely. More, unlike Hythloday, could not evade the philosophically distasteful duty of trying to counsel a ruler for justice's sake.

R331 Raitiere, Martin N. "More's *Utopia* and *The City of God*." *SRen* 20

(1973): 144-68.

Raitiere discusses the relevance of Augustine's work to that of More by elucidating More's concern in *Utopia* with the differences between Christian imperatives and those of the *vita socialis*. More learned from Augustine and his own experiences to view the state as beyond the reach of natural law and thus was able to consider with detachment Utopia. Raitiere views this gap between religious ideal and political possibility as the occasion for *Utopia*'s paradoxical structure. (Rpt. in The City of God: *A Collection of Critical Essays*, Ed. Dorothy F. Donnelly [New York: Peter Lang, 1995], 253-76.)

R332 Rebhorn, Wayne A. "Thomas More's Enclosed Garden: *Utopia* and Renaissance Humanism." *ELR* 6 (1976): 140-55.

Rebhorn examines the central image of a Utopian garden cultivated in a fallen world and associates agriculture in Utopia with the humanist faith in education as a tool for domesticating and taming "man's potentially wild and bestial nature."

R333 Reilley, Joseph J. "War and More's *Utopia*." *CW* 154 (1941): 151-59.

After describing the Utopian attitude toward war, the circumstances necessary to make them go to war, their ways of waging war or avoiding it (all of which are related to their disdain for warfare), Reilley concludes More is pointing a finger at the warring and treaty-breaking Europeans through his depiction of the peace-loving Utopians.

R334 Reiss, Timothy J. "From the Middle Ages to the (W)Hole of *Utopia*." *The Discourses of Modernism*. Ithaca: Cornell UP, 1982. 108-39.

In chapter three, because of the appearance of a new form of discourse, the "analytico-referential," More's *Utopia* "writes itself into an insoluble conflict...when the contradiction between the visible and the occulted becomes insuperable," and a hole gapes open where neither meaning nor practice seems possible. The chapter also suggests *Utopia* was not only the first discourse of this kind, but also a *unique* one of this kind. (Reiss refers to More and his works throughout; see also 25, 41, 92, 101, 153, 168, 171, 175-76, 180, 197-98, 214-15, 355-56.)

R335 Reiss, Timothy J. "*Utopia* and Process: Text and Anti-Text." *Substance* 8 (1974): 101-25.

Utopian writing is seen as a product by the Euclidean mind seeking to "mathematize" at once history and the insertion into history of an antihistoric Golden Age. This process from the finite to the infinite, from the temporal to the eternal, is a logical impossibility that forces the utopian text to strive to deny its own textuality. In *Utopia*, both the self-referential literary discourse and that of polity are broken between the mathematical base and its product.

The notion of *becoming*, of *process*, is absent. The text is torn between its service in the text-production of the humanists and its desire to express a pre-textual condition. All the codes which compose Utopian society share their use/non-use of money, their search for a language of direct apprehension, the urge to primitivity of its social system. Utopia is thus a no-place, an anti-text which denies More the writing of it.

R336 Renna, Thomas. "More's *Utopia* and English Medieval Traditions." *Utopia E Modernità: Teorie e prassi utopichè nell'età moderna e postmoderna.* Eds. Giuseppa Saccaro Del Buffa, and Arthur O. Lewis. Vol. 1. Rome: Gangemi editore, 1989. 739-47.

Renna argues *Utopia* integrates two late medieval semi-utopian traditions--the historical perspective "mixed with quasi-nationalist, millenarian, and apocalyptic tendencies" and the reform efforts of the Lollards and Wycliffites.

R337 Reynolds, E.E. "Three Views of *Utopia*." *Moreana* 31-32 (1971): 209-14.

Reynolds examines three views in the nineteenth century (those of Frederic Seebohm, J.R. Green, and Sir Sidney Lee), suspecting "they were puzzled by the same question we all have to try to answer--When was More writing with his tongue in his cheek?"

R338 Rielly, Edward J. "Irony in *Gulliver's Travels* and *Utopia*." *UtopSt* 3.1 (1992): 70-83.

Rielly examines how irony in both books "circulates about and gains impetus (as well as complexity) from the main characters"--Gulliver and "co-protagonists" persona More and Hythloday.

R339 Rimmer, Robert H. "Alternate Lifestyles on the Road to Utopia." *France and North America: Utopias and Utopians.* Proceedings of the Third Symposium of French-American Studies, March 4-8, 1974. Ed. Mathe Allain. Lafayette, LA: U of Southwest Louisiana, 1978. 149-63.

In his consideration of alternatives to the monogamous nuclear family in numerous utopian/dystopian works, Rimmer believes *Utopia* avoids the problems of families, "evidently assuming that they could survive a communal economy."

R340 Romm, James. "More's Strategy of Naming in the *Utopia*." *SCJ* 22 (1991): 173-83.

Although attempts have been made before to find a system for the names in *Utopia*, all have run into difficulties. Some names seem to be clearly from Greek, some translations from Greek, and some complete inventions. Worse still, some combine these schemes. It was More's purpose to thwart any system of interpretation to illustrate the philosophical and semiotic problems of interpreting language generally.

R341 Rops, Daniel. "Thomas More, Planiste de l'Utopie." *Moreana* 6 (1965): 5-8.

Rops contrasts More's ideal commonwealth, based on the moral principles of Christianity, with sixteenth-century Europe, ridden by injustice and ferocity, and the modern communist state.

R342 Ross, Harry. "The Birth of Modern Utopianism: Sir Thomas More." *Utopias Old and New*. The University Extension Library. London: Nicholson and Watson, 1938. 54-63.

Ross believes *Utopia* was not intended to be a serious discourse, although it does attack social, economic conditions in England at that time, and that More's work is neither socialist nor democratic. Ross also traces the work's influence upon other writers of Utopian fiction.

R343 Rossetti, Lorenzo. "Les Paradoxes d'*Utopia*." *Moreana* 103 (1990): 41-48.

Paradox is a constant feature of *Utopia*. The book is simultaneously therapy (*salutaris*) and comedy (*festiuus*); it presents both utopia and dystopia. The narrator is a messenger of salvation (Raphael) and a purveyor of nonsense (Hythloday). More criticizes the perversions of a society in crisis and exhorts readers to awaken their moral consciousness. The community of Utopia, offered as an antidote, which attains the perfection dreamed of by Plato by conforming *naturaliter* to Christian ethics, is chimerical. Where on earth can the devil, the inspirer of pride, be reduced to powerlessness, if it is not in the Church? The basic paradox lies in this: Utopia is society Christianized without Christianity.

R344 Rousseau, Marie-Claude. "Ex non insula...insulam: L'île, fil d'Ariane de l'utopie." *Moreana* 69 (1981): 129-36.

Rousseau explores the symbolic meaning of the island of Utopia.

R345 Rudat, Wolfgang E.H. "More's Raphael Hythloday: Missing the Point in *Utopia* Once More?" *Moreana* 69 (1981): 41-64.

Rudat argues More sets traps for readers, yet at the same time, builds in devices that might warn perceptive readers as to his true, unfavorable opinion of Hythloday. Raphael is initially introduced as a sailor like Palinurus (an unsuccessful steersman, who however mistrusted the calm--unlike Raphael's preference for the quiet life), Ulysses (a notorious nonsense peddler whose stay on Calypso's island was escapist, like Raphael's in womb-like Utopia), and Plato (who traveled to Syracuse to put his *Republic* into practice, with ill success).

Rudat offers close verbal analysis and other deployment of *Utopia*'s use of classical analogues.

R346 Rudat, Wolfgang E.H. "Thomas More and Hythloday: Some Speculations on *Utopia*." *BHR* 43 (1981): 123-27.

Using the etymology of the possible Greek derivation of "syphogrant" and "tranibor" and their replacement by the Utopians with "phylarch" and "protophylarch," Rudat thinks More depicts Utopia as a totalitarian, police state, like that of the Polyerites, and he believes replacing those terms is a type of "newspeak." He also speculates on the meaning of Peter Giles' comparison of Hythloday to Odysseus.

R347 Rudat, Wolfgang E.H. "Thomas More, Hythloday, and Odysseus: An Anatomy of *Utopia*." *AI* 37 (1980): 38-48.

Rudat speculates upon the bearing *Utopia*'s reference to Palinurus and Odysseus as sailors has on the assessment of Hythloday as an advocate of the Utopian system and what that assessment tells readers about More himself.

R348 Ruppert, Peter. *Reader in a Strange Land: The Activity of Reading Literary Utopias.* Athens: U of Georgia P, 1986.

This application of reader-response theory to utopian works from More to this century is useful for its summaries of earlier criticism. Its main point in utopian "open-ended" writing provides a defamiliarizing critique of the established that provokes readers into liberating fantasy and speculation.

R349 Ruyer, Raymond. *L'Utopie et les Utopistes.* Paris: Presses Universitaires de France, 1950.

Ruyer discusses all utopian literature and ideas--spiritual utopias, characteristics of utopias, the utopias of antiquity (especially the *Republic*), and utopian works from the seventeenth century to the present. He treats More's *Utopia* most extensively in the second chapter, "Le Monde Utopique."

R350 Samaan, Angele Botros. "Death and the Death-Penalty in More's *Utopia* and Some Utopian Novels." *Moreana* 90 (1986): 5-15.

Samaan investigates the themes of death and the death-penalty in More's *Utopia* and, by way of comparison, briefly explores those themes in some modern utopian novels--Butler's *Erewhon*, Lytton's *The Coming Race*, Trollope's *The Fixed Period*, Morris' *News From Nowhere*, Huxley's *Brave New World*, and Orwell's *1984*.

R351 Sanderlin, George. "The Meaning of Thomas More's *Utopia*." *CE* 12 (1950): 74-77.

The statement, "Certainly *Utopia* is a work of ideas. But what gives it its rich simplicity, its fascination for the ages since More and for today, is its indirect, imaginative presentation of those ideas," provides Sanderlin's way into his analysis of the work.

R352 Sargent, Lyman Tower. "More's *Utopia*: An Interpretation of Its Social Theory." *History of Political Thought* 5 (1984): 195-210.

Through an analysis of Utopian institutions, Sargent demonstrates Utopian society is "authoritarian, hierarchical and patriarchal," although what is depicted is more economically equal and egalitarian than much of the society in which More lived. He also shows how More adopted and adapted his Utopian organizations from patterns in monastic life modified by ideas from the Renaissance and the discovery of New World.

R353 Sawada, Paul A. "*Laus Potentiae* or the Praise of Realpolitik? Hermann Oncken and More's *Utopia*." *Moreana* 15-16 (1967): 145-64.

Although Sawada concedes Oncken (whose scholarship appeared in German in the 1920s and 1930s) studied *Utopia* carefully, he disagrees with his interpretation of *Utopia* as a tract on imperialism and *realpolitik* and his idea More was another Machiavelli, because Sawada claims Oncken read too many of the problems of his own times into the text.

R354 Sawada, Paul A. "Toward a Definition of *Utopia*." *Moreana* 31-32 (1971): 135-46.

"Utopian" has many meanings, some of them conflicting. *Utopia* is a fiction in which place and society dominate deeds and persons. Necessarily isolated, the society (and genre) selects values, presents itself as ideal. More's utopian idealization came from his theological hope of eternal felicity, the sharing of which led to the happiness of pagan natives, whose island prefigured the "heavenly reality in hope."

R355 Schaeffer, John D. "Socratic Method in More's *Utopia*." *Moreana* 69 (1981): 5-20.

Schaeffer places *Utopia* in the context of the dialogue genre, which includes the Lucianic use of "lacerating folly" to compel a return to common sense, Cicero's attempt to convince through authoritative demonstration, and the Socratic dialogue's method of provoking the active engagement of participants and reader. The account of Utopia grows out of the dialogue on counsel; persona More asks Socratic, testing questions of Hythloday, whose inflexible Ciceronian answers assert his authority and whose limitations make him a Lucianic combination of wisdom and folly. Utopia is his character writ large--rational, authoritarian, and uncivilized, while More's irony is Socratic, provoking commitment to continuous effort. Schaeffer regards the irony of the work as focusing on the paradoxes involved in changing individuals and society for the better and as playing on the relationship of rhetoric and dialogue, Cicero and Socrates, Hythloday and More.

R356 Schoeck, R.J. "The Fifth Lateran Council: Its Partial Successes and Its Larger Failures." *Reform and Authority in the Medieval and Reformation Church*. Ed. Guy Fitch Lytle. Washington, D.C.: Catholic U of America P, 1981. 99-126.

Utopia was written and published during this most neglected of councils, lasting from May 1512 to March 1517. The soul's immortality, a tenet of Utopia's natural theology, was defined in the eighth session of it (19 Dec. 1513). The threat of the Turks was never entirely lost sight of "while the threat from within [the Reformation] was rarely faced." Twenty years later, in *Dialogue of Comfort*, More would structure his consolation around this bitter irony and would contrast the inner and external threats. Against the "closed mind" of Western man, *Utopia* "was in 1516 a last-ditch appeal for the use of reason towards the solution of urgent problems in Christendom."

R357 Schoeck, R.J. "The Intellectual Milieu of More's *Utopia*: Some Notes." *Moreana* 1 (1963): 40-46.

Much is to be learned about the intellectual milieu of *Utopia*; for example, the historical background, academic scene, theological controversies, function of the island, legal procedures, and more.

R358 Schoeck, R.J. "The Ironic and the Prophetic: Towards Reading More's *Utopia* as a Multidisciplinary Work." *Quincentennial Essays on St. Thomas More*. 124-34.

Schoeck suggests *Utopia* cannot be read only as a literary, political, educational, polemical treatise, or as a *jeu d'esprit*, but may be read holistically as a multidisciplinary work; and he amplifies his plea for seeing a structure of relationships in *Utopia* by calling for further study of More's control and employment of traditional logic and rhetoric, especially irony.

R359 Schoeck, R.J. "Levels of Word-play and Figurative Signification in More's *Utopia*." *N&Q* ns 1 (1954): 512-13.

Schoeck notes *Utopia* was originally called "Abraxa" and argues this word implied either the superstitious character of the original inhabitants or the lack of God's grace. He adds More uses word-play frequently in *Utopia*.

R360 Schoeck, R.J. "More, Plutarch, and King Agis: Spartan History and the Meaning of *Utopia*." *PQ* 35 (1956): 366-75.

Though Schoeck acknowledges many ideas for *Utopia* are taken from Plato's *Republic*, he points out that inspiration for some of Plato's (or Socrates') ideas can be traced to Spartan institutions. Some notions which appear in both works include public meals, discarding the use of precious metals for money, garrison life for men, gymnastic training for women, severe discipline for children, and other ideas. Schoeck maintains More may have learned some of these ideas from Plutarch's *Life of Agis*, then popular and highly valued. (Rpt. in *Essential Articles for the Study of Thomas More*, 275-80.)

R361 Schoeck, R.J. "More's *Utopia* and Intertextuality." *Intertextuality and Renaissance Texts*. Gratia: Bamberger Schriften zur Renaissanceforschung. 12. Renaissanceforschung: H. Kaiser-Verlag, 1984. 83-110.

Schoeck believes it is necessary to identify some traditions into which *Utopia* places itself, as well as to generate a sense of context, and to consider the work as a text which cultivates several kinds of intertextuality. (This chapter revises and expands "The Ironic and the Prophetic: Towards Reading More's *Utopia* as a Multidisciplinary Work" [R358].)

R362 Schoeck, R.J. "'A Nursery of Correct and Useful Institutions': On Reading More's *Utopia* as Dialogue." *Moreana* 22 (1969): 19-32.

Schoeck regards *Utopia* as having a serious purpose but one argued through an ironic structure and as inviting a response both engaged and detached. He analyzes the effects of dialogue, calls *Utopia* a bifocal book, and concludes it is a rhetorical *declamatio* which attempts to convince the audience the imaginary is real. (Rpt. in *Essential Articles for the Study of Thomas More*, 281-89.)

R363 Schoeck, R.J. "Renaissance Guides to Renaissance Learning." *Acta Conventus Neo-Latini Turonensis*. Troisième Congrès International D'Études Neó-Latines, Tours. Université Francis-Rabelais, 6-10 Septembre 1976. Ed. Jean-Claude Margolin. 2. Paris: Vrin, 1980. 239-62.

Schoeck presents lists of books given to students as guides to studying, such as those found in the statutes of many universities at the time. The first list of books he discusses is that given in *Utopia* in Book II when Hythloday, after remarking upon the extraordinary "teachableness" of the Utopians, speaks of the books he carried back to Utopia on his fourth voyage.

R364 Schoeck, R.J. "*Utopia*: A Humanistic Masterpiece Revisited." *Thomas Morus Jahrbuch 1989*. 139-51.

Schoeck welcomes the opportunity to talk about *Utopia* as a whole and in the context of humanism. His reading, taking into account the "shifting currents of critical theory in our own age," provides a thorough overview of his own scholarship and that of others.

R365 Schulte-Herbrüggen, Hubertus. "More's *Utopia* as a Paradigm." *Essential Articles for the Study of Thomas More*. 251-62.

Schulte-Herbrüggen maintains the work's structure and meaning center not only on the contrast between the Utopian ideality found in its citizens' ethics and the shortcomings and abuses of the present but also in the contrast between the ideal politics of Hythloday and the realistic politics of persona-More. (This article is translated and revised from *Utopie und Anti-Utopie: Von der Strukturanalyse sur Strukturtypologie* [Beiträge zur englischen Philogie. 43. Bochum-Langendreer: Pöppinghaus, 1960], 16-37.)

R366 Schulte-Herbrüggen, Hubertus. "*Utopia* and After." *Moreana* 62 (1979): 121-32.

Schulte-Herbrüggen places *Utopia* within the genre of utopian fiction (noting five stages in that genre's development and the appearance of dystopias) and examines the connection between Book I with its "English realism" and II with its continental idealism as it reflects More's life.

R367 Schwartz, Peter. "Imagining Socialism: Karl Kautsky and Thomas More." *International Journal of Comparative Sociology* 30 (1989): 44-56.

Schwartz discusses the confrontation in Kautsky's *Thomas More and His Utopia* (R212) between Kautsky's historical materialism and More's providential view of history. Kautsky has trouble addressing providence and history in More's thought because of his concern with comprehending More and his *Utopia* in terms of historical materialism, and he does not take seriously More's religiosity. However, he identifies it, not with the orthodox Catholic Church, but with the popular religious feeling of the Middle Ages. In the process, Kautsky betrays his nostalgia for a lost age of primal innocence and simplicity.

R368 Seeber, Hans Ulrich. "Hythloday as Preacher and a Possible Debt to Macrobius." *Moreana* 31-32 (1971): 71-86.

Seeber illustrates how Hythloday voices complaints which were the stock in trade of medieval and Renaissance preachers and how Macrobius' commentary on *Somnium Scipionis* influenced More in using fiction to teach virtue.

R369 Seeber, Hans Ulrich. "Thomas Morus' *Utopia* (1516) und Edward Bellamy's *Looking Backward* (1888): Ein funktionsgeschichtlicher Vergleich." *Utopieforschung: Interdisziplinäre Studien zur neuzeitlichen Utopie*. III. Ed. Wilhelm Vosskamp. Stuttgart: Metzler, 1982. 357-77.

Seeber compares More's treatment of key issues to that of Bellamy.

R370 Servier, Jean. *Histoire de l'Utopie*. Paris: Gallimard, 1967.

Servier gives a chronological and critical account of successive concepts and portrayals of the ideal state, in particular Plato's *Republic*, the Jewish vision of a promised land, Augustine's *City of God*, *Utopia* and other Renaissance works inspired by scientific and geographical discovery; and Faustian,

Marxist, and post-Marxist schemes of the nineteenth and twentieth centuries. Servier discusses the fantasy of More's *Utopia* within a threefold context-- retrospective, contemporary, and prospective.

R371 Shephard, Robert. "Utopia, Utopia's Neighbors, *Utopia*, and Europe." *SCJ* 26 (1995): 843-56.

The interactions of the Utopians with their neighbors provide a model for the impact More intended *Utopia* to have on Europe. While the Utopians have involvements with the countries around them, they never try to impose their own values or institutions on other societies. Indeed, sometimes they intervene to maintain the non-Utopian status quo. By analogy, readers of *Utopia* are being urged to take an active role in Europe, not as revolutionaries, but as guardians and honest administrators of the already established system. Hythloday argues against the value of such service, and the inconclusive nature of the debate in Book I indicates the historical More's divided mind. But More's eventual decision to become a councilor to Henry VIII is foreshadowed in Hythloday's descriptions of the Utopians' interactions with non-Utopian societies, which subvert his arguments in Book I.

R372 Simmonds, James D. "More's Use of Names in Book II of *Utopia*." *NS* (1961): 282-84.

More uses paradoxical names to intensify the metaphysical unreality of *Utopia* by means of verbal unreality. To people he gives fictitious but literally appropriate names.

R373 Simon, Elliott P. "Thomas More's *Utopia*: Creating an Image of the Soul." *Moreana* 69 (1981): 21-40.

Simon assumes More's argument focuses on barriers to the individual's redemption in a secular culture, because *Utopia* is designed on the common humanist principle the moral improvement of man's fallen condition could be achieved through transformation of social institutions.

R374 Skinner, Quentin. *The Foundations of Modern Political Thought.* Vol. 1. *The Renaissance.* Cambridge: Cambridge UP, 1978. 215-18, 246-47, 255-62.

Skinner disagrees with the idea *Utopia* should be read as a medieval rather than a Renaissance view of politics and develops the notion the work places More in the heart of northern humanist political thought, some of which is critiqued in *Utopia*.

R375 Skinner, Quentin. "More's *Utopia*." *Past and Present: A Journal of Historical Studies* 38 (1967): 153-68.

Skinner provides a detailed critique of the text and critical apparatus of the

Yale edition (B019). He is especially concerned with Surtz and Hexter's interpretations of *Utopia* and their ideas about what influenced More at the time More composed the work. He labels Surtz' reading as "Catholic" and one that sees *Utopia* as the work of a "new man"; whereas Hexter rejects both of these interpretations and places *Utopia* within the movement of Erasmian humanism and the Christian revival. Skinner favors Hexter's reading and discussion of influences.

R376 Skinner, Quentin. "Sir Thomas More's *Utopia* and the Language of Renaissance Humanism." *The Language of Political Theory in Early-Modern Europe*. Ed. Anthony Pagden. Ideas in Context Ser. Cambridge: Cambridge UP, 1987. 122-57.

Although Skinner concedes scholarship emphasizing doubts and equivocations in *Utopia* has added significantly to its understanding, he states such readings embody an unacceptable view of More's basic purposes, and he proposes More's main aim was to challenge readers to consider seriously whether Utopia may not represent the best state of the commonwealth. Skinner also argues Hythloday's Platonic commitment to the contemplative life (*otium*) is brought into conflict with a Ciceronian defense of the active life (*negotium*).

R377 Slavin, Arthur J. "The American Principle from More to Locke." *First Images of America: The Impact of the New World on the Old*. Eds. Fredi Chiappelli, Michael J.B. Allen, and Robert L. Benson. Vol. 1. Berkeley: U of California P, 1976. 139-64.

Slavin devotes half of his essay to *Utopia*, including the facts More knew Peter Martyr's *De Orbe Novo*, was brother-in-law to John Rastell who attempted a voyage to the New World in 1517, and created Hythloday who supposedly accompanied Vespucci on his voyages. Slavin traces many political and economic ideas about the role of the New World to *Utopia* and discusses them in relation to ideas in Montaigne's essays, Shakespeare's *Tempest*, Hobbes' *Leviathan*, and Locke's *Two Treatises of Government*.

R378 Slavin, Arthur J. "*Consilium et timor mortis*: On Speaking, Writing and Silence in *Utopia*." *Ren&R* 16.3 (1992): 17-30.

Slavin reexamines Hythloday's stance against political life, emphasizing the dramatic and angry exchanges between persona More and Hythloday in which honesty (*honestas*) and utility (*utilitas*) are as much in conflict as the speakers are.

R379 Slavin, Arthur J. "'Tis far off, And rather like a dream': Common Weal, Common Woe and Commonwealth." *Explorations in Renaissance Culture* 14 (1988): 1-27.

In order to focus upon the dilemma of self-interest vs. common good in civic humanism, Slavin compares More's ideas of the best commonwealth to those of Richard Morison's *A Lamentation* and *The Remedy for Sedition*, and he discovers the authors disagree about the rights of property and dominion, on one hand, and poverty and sedition, on the other. Morison negates Hythloday's connection between poverty and sedition and defends the right of unlimited acquisition as he likewise reverses Hythloday's condemnation of private property.

R380 Sørensen, Knud. "Notes on the First English Translation of More's *Utopia*." *A Literary Miscellany Presented to Eric Jacobsen*. Eds. Graham D. Caie, and Holger Nørgaard. Publications of the Department of English (U of Copenhagen). 16. Copenhagen: Publications of the Department of English, U of Copenhagen, 1988. 326-37.

Although Sørensen finds Robinson's English translation expands upon More's reservations and is more blunt than the original, he praises it for its vigor and vividness and views it as a compromise between readability and More's Latin text.

R381 Southall, Raymond. "More's *Utopia*: The Case for a Palace Revolution." *Literature and the Rise of Capitalism: Critical Essays Mainly on the Sixteenth and Seventeenth Centuries*. London: Lawrence & Wishart, 1973. 11-20.

Noting the diversity of critical opinion on More's personality, Southall examines his attack on mercantilism and a money economy as embodiments of the sin of pride and the source of social evils. More is concerned with the reformation of society, but his reaction is to formulate the best solution he can conceive of and then leave the matter open for further discussion. He assumes social change can only be effected from above, and that the only effective political force is the establishment.

R382 Sowards, J.K. "Some Factors in the Re-evaluation of Thomas More's *Utopia*." *Northwest Missouri State College Studies* 16 (1952): 29-58.

Sowards stresses ideas that might guide re-evaluation of *Utopia*, such as More's reaction to the rich commerce of Antwerp, his "trenchant wit," the distinction between More's views as the author and a persona in the work, the nature of Utopian religion and the Catholicism of More's time, and the "pervading influence" of Erasmus on the book.

R383 Spradley, Dana Lloyd. "Rewriting the *Respublica*: The Politics of Literary Figuration in More's *Utopia*, Shakespeare's *Pericles*, and Milton's 'Areopagitica.'" Diss. Yale, 1989.

Spradley examines the use of literary figuration to promote social criticism and to project the possibility of political reform and argues each text examined does not merely "re-present," but in effect "rewrites" the figurative logic involved in the reproduction of monarchical power into a broader context of social reproduction and political struggle. Each aims to "rewrite" the "public entity"--the *respublica*--itself into a more strategically resistant political character.

R384 Starnes, Colin. *The New Republic: A Commentary on Book I of More's* Utopia *Showing Its Relation to Plato's* Republic. Waterloo, Ontario, Can.: Wilfrid Laurier UP, 1990.

This book's central thesis was born in a flash of semantic insight about the intended reference of "Traniborus" and "Syphograntus" in *Utopia*. These playful names refer to the "city of pigs" briefly depicted by Socrates in Book II of the *Republic*. Syphogranti are rulers of a pigsty and therefore rulers in this city of pigs; for the purposes of eating, the inhabitants of this city have to use the couches or benches referred to in the name of the second ranking Utopian officials, Tranibori, or bencheaters. Guided by this insight, Starnes comes to believe that Book II of *Utopia* portrays "the rational expansion and development of that first Arcadian city--the 'true and healthy state' or, in Glaucon's scornful version, the 'city of pigs' from which Plato began." Not only Book II but the whole of *Utopia* is "the *Republic* recast in a new mold applicable to the demands of contemporary Christianity as these were understood by More and his circle of reforming friends."

R385 Steintrager, James. "Plato and More's *Utopia*." *Social Research* 36 (1969): 357-72.

Although More models *Utopia* after the *Republic*, the works differ markedly in regard to morality, family, and practical human needs. A "natural morality" in *Utopia*, which emphasizes pleasure and happiness, makes it "much more hedonistic" than the *Republic*, and *Utopia* treats matters--"the body, its needs...and demands"--not receiving much attention in the *Republic*. Steintrager also notices More retains the family rather than abolishing it as Plato.

R386 Stevens, Irma N. "Aesthetic Distance in *Utopia*." *Moreana* 43-44 (1974): 13-24.

More's use of aesthetic distance in *Utopia* is effective because his satiric observer is usually at least twice removed from the author. More switches satiric spokesmen frequently. Hythloday is usually the satiric observer, but occasionally the arguments of both Hythloday and More are equally convincing. More also detaches himself by using inappropriate or paradoxical names, like "Hythloday," the nonsense babbler who speaks truth, and "Utopia," no place or every place. More also juxtaposes European values with their Utopian counterparts to reveal European folly as opposed to Utopian reason. Denunciation is expressed not by More but by the Utopians or Hythloday in a traditional satiric mask--the upright, angry citizen.

R387 Stevens, Richard G. "The New Republic in More's *Utopia*." *Political Science Quarterly* 84 (1969): 387-411.

Utopia is an important part of the long theoretical preparation leading to the restoration of republican institutions in the West, because it establishes religious tolerance as a constitutional principle.

R388 Stevens, Richard G. "On the Practicality of More's *Utopia*." *Social Research* 33 (1966): 30-46.

Stevens discusses four main points of *Utopia*--form of government, type of philosophy, conduct of war, and distribution of property, and focuses upon the last and the question of communism, choosing to believe More never actually expected property to be held in common but proposed Utopian communism as a means of presenting a proper understanding of ownership controlled neither by greed nor the "dialectics of...production."

R389 Still, Judith. "Dreams of the End of Markets: The Model of Women's Work in Plato, More, and Rousseau." *Paragraph* 15 (1992): 248-60.

After examining how Plato's *Republic* serves as a "precursor text" for both More and Rousseau and tackles "certain issues concerning sexual difference which arise from the restriction of private property," Still focuses upon how *Utopia* and *The Social Contract* treat these ideas. She concludes *Utopia* is less egalitarian than *Republic* and its family hierarchy is more reminiscent of Plato's *Laws*.

R390 Stobbart, Lorainne. Utopia: *Fact or Fiction? The Evidence from the Americas*. Stroud, Gloucestershire, Eng.: Alan Sutton, 1992.

In the geography of Utopian criticism, Stobbart's book lies in the region antipodal to humanistic interpretation--that sparsely-populated domain of those who have understood More's commonwealth not as an imaginative construct built on classical foundations but as an essentially factual account of an existing state. Stobbart's claim is *Utopia* is based on some real-but-unknown first-hand account of Mayan civilization. To make a plausible case for this thesis, it would be necessary both to establish the likelihood More had access to information about the Mayans at the time he wrote *Utopia* and to show there are parallels between Utopian and Mayan civilization for which there is no good explanation other than a direct link. Stobbart is unable to do either.

R391 Strosetzki, Christoph. "L'*Utopie* de Thomas More: Une Résponse au debát sur le Nouveau Monde?" *Moreana* 101-102 (1990): 5-24.

Strosetzki elaborates upon how the problematics of the New World--the law of taking possession, grounds for just war, cohabitation, myths of the Golden Age and noble savage--cannot have failed to inspire More in writing *Utopia*, especially as he had spent some time in Flanders where the New World was much spoken of in diplomatic and political circles.

R392 Sulfridge, Cynthia Waugh. "Intimate Narrative: Narrator-Reader Relationship in Three Renaissance Precursors of *Tristram Shandy*." Diss. Johns Hopkins U, 1978.

Tristram Shandy is usually considered a striking narration; but, during the Renaissance, there appeared texts whose narrative approach was similarly distinctive. Sulfridge studies *Utopia*, Nashe's *Unfortunate Traveller*, and Burton's *Anatomy of Melancholy*. Chapter 2 discusses *Utopia* in which More, structuring his book on levels of dialogue between figures who range from the presumably fictive to the obviously real, leads his reader into a debate over political and social ideas for which he makes a resolution impossible. The reader is led to internalize the dialogue and to carry on the debate himself, for, in More's view, the Christian must involve himself in an open-ended dialogue, pursuing the path to truth however uncertain the quest.

R393 Sullivan, E.D.S. "Place in No Place: Examples of the Ordered Society in Literature." *The Utopian Vision: Seven Essays on the Quincentennial of Sir Thomas More*. 29-49.

Sullivan compares the view of ordered societies in More's *Utopia*, Skinner's *Walden Two*, Huxley's *Brave New World*, and Orwell's *1984*.

R394 Surtz, Edward. "Aspects of More's Latin Style in *Utopia*." *SRen* 14 (1967): 93-109.

This article supplements material in the Yale edition (B019) with an analysis of the selection and arrangement of words and phrases, which betray the author's intellectual, emotional, and artistic cast. Surtz suggests the style imitates dialogue with the length and character of sentences reflecting the ebb and flow of thought and feeling.

R395 Surtz, Edward. "The Defense of Pleasure in More's *Utopia*." *SP* 46 (1949): 99-112.

Surtz claims when More asserts the chief felicity of man rests in "*voluptas*," he is engaged in a "*declamatio*," of which the object is not truth but the writer's skill in argument. Surtz shows, from the many synonyms More uses for "*voluptas*," the loose, generic way in which he employs the word. More, in the best traditions of "*declamatio*," astonishingly makes religion and virtue serve as two sources of arguments from the supremacy of pleasure. Careful analysis, however, reveals the object of Utopian happiness is delight in God's presence in the next life. (Chapters two and three of Surtz' *The Praise of Pleasure* [R403] incorporate and add to this essay.)

R396 Surtz, Edward. "Epicurus in *Utopia*." *ELH* 16 (1949): 89-103.

Surtz considers More's adaptations of Epicurus' ideas in *Utopia*. Although both More and Epicurus call the highest pleasures ethical and intellectual, More differs from Epicurus' denial of God's providence, the soul's immortality, and future retribution. More is a Christianized Epicurean. (Rpt., with changes and additions, as chapter four of Surtz' *The Praise of Pleasure* [R403].)

R397 Surtz, Edward. "The Illustrations in the Yale *Utopia*." *Moreana* 10 (1966): 55-73.

Surtz stresses the immensity of the task of obtaining the illustrations, the "incredible degree of patience and unconscionable extent of time expended." He concludes, however, without a doubt the illustrations add interest to the edition (B019) and were worth the effort required.

R398 Surtz, Edward. "Interpretations of *Utopia*." *Catholic Historical Review* 38 (1952): 156-74.

Utopia is a pre-Reformation humanistic document with an eye to all phases and departments of Christian style. If an ideal pagan state like Utopia, based solely upon nature and philosophy, can attain such glory and triumph, what a paradise on earth could not a Christian nation create, which has, besides the finest products of reason and antiquity, the surpassing treasures of revelation and the grace to aid and sustain it.

R399 Surtz, Edward. Elizabeth McCutcheon, ed. "'Like a Fountain Stirred.'" *Moreana* 77 (1983): 53-65.

On the tenth anniversary of Surtz' death, McCutcheon reprints a portion of his 1967 typescript for a "substantial" work to be called *A Guide Through Utopia: A Critique of Structure and Idea in the Best State of a Commonwealth by Thomas More*. "Like a Fountain Stirred," originally the work's conclusion, contains sections on the "role of Hythlodaeus," the "symbol of the council," and the "art of drama," in which Surtz encourages readers to become engaged with both his texts and More's.

R400 Surtz, Edward. "The Link between Pleasure and Communism in *Utopia*." *MLN* 70 (1955): 90-93.

Surtz demonstrates how communism in *Utopia* insures a true commonwealth which looks to the interests of the many, not the few, and which secures a just distribution of the commodities of life. The link between pleasure and communism is the equal, just distribution of material things Hythloday thinks such a system can accomplish. (Surtz incorporates and modifies this essay in chapter thirteen of *The Praise of Pleasure* [R403].)

R401 Surtz, Edward. "Logic in *Utopia*." *PQ* 29 (1950): 389-401.

More states that in logic the Utopians have learned all the ancient philosophers have taught. By this remark, More meant they were versed in the logical treatises of Aristotle and probably Porphyry's *Isagoge*. On the other hand, they cared nothing for all those rules of restrictions, amplifications, and suppositions, invented in the "small Logycalles," because they were contemptuous of the complications the medieval commentators added to Aristotle's scheme of logic. More also attacks other subtle inventions of the Schoolmen, such as "second inventions" and "universals." (With changes and additions, this article is rpt. in chapter nine in Surtz' *The Praise of Pleasure*, [R403].)

R402 Surtz, Edward. "More's *Apologia pro Utopia Sua*." *MLQ* 19 (1958): 319-24.

Surtz refers to the second letter of More to Peter Giles, which has been ignored and overlooked for years, and claims it is important. First, it records one type of common reaction to *Utopia* within one year of its publication. Next, it discloses the literary principles according to which More composed it. Finally, it constitutes a sort of good-natured apology for *Utopia*'s tone and technique.

R403 Surtz, Edward. *The Praise of Pleasure: Philosophy, Education, and Communism in More's* Utopia. Cambridge, MA: Harvard UP, 1957.

This, together with Surtz' *The Praise of Wisdom* (R404) and R.W. Chambers' views, presents the traditional Roman Catholic view of *Utopia*. For Surtz and Chambers, *Utopia* is permeated with the spirit of medieval monasticism and is inherently a criticism of a Christian world which conducts itself much worse than More's pagan one guided only by laws of reason. Surtz sets the ideas in *Utopia* against those found in the wide range of literature and philosophy the humanists studied and interprets More's real views by supplementing the opinions expressed in *Utopia* with those More and his friends expressed in other writings. He then discusses the sources of the thoughts on philosophy, education, and communism the work embodies and maintains the institutions in Utopia are not More's ideal plan for society; instead they are merely a set of points from which readers may examine the institutions and accomplishments of their own society. Thus, Surtz regards *Utopia* as a "cry of distress over the exploited poor and a call to reform in every department of human endeavor in England and Europe." (Chapter 5 is rpt. as "Utopian Felicity" in *Twentieth-Century Interpretations of* Utopia: *A Collection of Critical Essays*, 70-75; chapter 15, "Thomas More and Communism: The Solution," is rpt. in *More's* Utopia *and Its Critics*, 148-59.)

R404 Surtz, Edward. *The Praise of Wisdom: A Commentary on the Religious and Moral Problems and Backgrounds of St. Thomas More's* Utopia. Jesuit Studies. Chicago: Loyola UP, 1957.

Surtz comments on the section on religion in Book II to determine the relationship of specific religious and moral aspects of Utopia to Catholic teaching of the fifteenth and sixteenth centuries. He posits this section advances ideas about using reason to construct an "intellectually satisfying religion and morality" which Christianity could adopt with a few changes, and he believes More would have recommended some Utopian laws and customs as a means to reform and renew the Church.

R405 Surtz, Edward. "St. Thomas More and His Utopian Embassy of 1515." *Catholic Historical Review* 39 (1953): 272-97.

Surtz outlines the commercial negotiations More participated in at Bruges in 1515; identifies the English commissioners; and discusses experiences which may have prompted More's dialogue on counsel, remarks on foreign policy, and references to mercenary troops in *Utopia*.

R406 Surtz, Edward. "The Setting for More's Plea for Greek in *Utopia*." *PQ* 35 (1956): 353-65.

More designed Hythloday's statements in *Utopia* to support his ideas about education, particularly classical Greek learning. Surtz claims the work is More's plea for England and Europe to adopt the study of Greek language and learning with the same willingness with which the Utopians welcome them. (Rpt., with changes and additions, as chapter 11 in Surtz' *The Praise of Pleasure* [R403].)

R407 Surtz, Edward. "Sources, Parallels, and Influences: Supplement to the Yale *Utopia*." *Moreana* 9 (1966): 5-11.

Earlier documents containing ideas which appear in *Utopia* (B019) are pointed out, as well as illusions to Italian political events. Erasmus may be the model for Hythloday, and More himself resembles the portrait of Cardinal Morton.

R408 Surtz, Edward. "Thomas More and the Great Books." *PQ* 32 (1953): 43-57.

Surtz maintains the list of Greek works Hythloday recommends to Utopians is the same list More and Erasmus thought of as being suited to the "peculiar need and taste of their generation." (This article, with changes and additions, is rpt. in Surtz' *The Praise of Pleasure* [R403].)

R409 Süssmuth, Hans. *Studien zur* Utopia *des Thomas Morus: Ein Beitrag zur Geitesgeschichte des 16 Jahrhunderts*. Münster: Aschendorffsche Verlagsbuchhandlung, 1967.

Süssmuth surveys *Utopia*, with critical analyses of its literary features, contemporary political and sociological context, sources and analogues, the impact upon More's fable of Christian humanism (most specifically as reflected in

Pico, Erasmus, and Colet), Utopian political and social theories, and detailed comparison with *L'Institution du Prince* of Budé and *Encomium Morae* of Erasmus. Because it is too complicated for oversimplification, Süssmuth concludes *Utopia* does not allow simple, consistent interpretation either as a spiritual study or as a portrayal of an ideal state.

R410 Suvin, Darko. "The Time Machine versus *Utopia* as a Structural Model for Science Fiction." *CLS* 10 (1973): 334-52.

Time Machine and *Utopia* are proclaimed basic historical models for structuring subsequent science fiction, and Suvin outlines a genealogy beginning with *Utopia* and proceeding to *Gulliver's Travels* to the present in what is called a devolutionary process.

R411 Sylvester, R.S. "Images of the City in Thomas More's *Utopia*." *Les Cités au temps de la Renaissance*. Ed. M.T. Jones-Davies. Paris: Université de Paris-Sorbonne, Institut de recherches sur les Civilisations de l'Occident moderne, 1977. 191-205.

Because *Utopia* presents many images of the city, Sylvester believes More encourages readers to contemplate all those alternatives. He also provides the background from which More drew those images--the Middle-Eastern prototype for Greek city-states, the Greek city-state of Plato and Aristotle, Augustine's City of God and the city of the world, the monastery, and the English rural community.

R412 Sylvester, R.S. "'Si Hythlodaeo Credimus': Vision and Revision in Thomas More's *Utopia*." *Soundings* 51 (1968): 271-89.

Sylvester points out that although Hythloday and persona More disagree on means, they agree on ends, and the book pleads for application of both the former's detachment and the latter's engagement. He also considers the parerga to *Utopia* and the ways in which More sustains the work's ambiguity. (Rpt. in *Essential Articles for the Study of Thomas More*, 290-310.)

R413 Tinkler, John F. "Praise and Advice: Rhetorical Approaches in More's *Utopia* and Machiavelli's *The Prince*." *SCJ* 19 (1988): 187-207.

Tinkler contrasts their use of the demonstrative mode of praise and the deliberative mode of advice: *Utopia* follows the deliberative mode in Book I with the demonstrative in Book II (providing an unusual illustrative *imago*, a panegyric unusual in its plain style, elision of expediency and virtue, and flouting of reader assumptions), while Machiavelli unsettlingly approaches the mirror-for-princes demonstrative tradition with the attitudes of deliberative rhetoric.

R414 Tod, Ian, and Michael Wheeler. *Utopia*. New York: Harmony Books, 1978.

This attractively illustrated book discusses *Utopia*'s place in utopian/dystopian thought in a section entitled "The Renaissance City State" (29-34).

R415 Traugott, John. "A Voyage to Nowhere with Thomas More and Jonathan Swift: *Utopia* and The Voyage to the Houyhnhnms." *SR* 69 (1961): 534-65.

Traugott compares the views and literary manners of the two writers, seeing them both as politicians forced to compromise but "maintaining a utopia in the back of the head as a measure of those compromises." He decides the evidence Swift drew heavily from More is overwhelming, and he emphasizes the concluding sense of alienation in the two books which leaves the reader to bridge the gap between the ideal and the actual. Ultimately, Utopia exists only as a mental state for measuring the present against an "unchangeable ideal." (Rpt. in *Swift: A Collection of Critical Essays*, Ed. Ernest Tuveson [Englewood Cliffs, NJ: Prentice-Hall, 1965], 143-69; a brief excerpt entitled "The Alienated: Gulliver and Hythloday" appears in *Twentieth-Century Interpretations of* Utopia: *A Collection of Critical Essays*, 113-14.)

R416 Trevor-Roper, Hugh. "Sir Thomas More and *Utopia*." *Renaissance Essays*. Chicago: U of Chicago P, 1985. 24-58.

Trevor-Roper puts the work in its intellectual and political contexts (early Platonism and Erasmus, the anti-tyrannical *Richard III*) and emphasizes the illiberality of Utopia and Platonic-communist societies.

R417 Truchet, Sybil. "The Eutopians." *CahiersE* 28 (1985): 17-22.

The real heroes and models are not the Utopians and Utopia--mere imperfect provocations to better thinking and activity--but the "Prime Movers of More's Universe," the Eutopians, his Christian humanist friends and colleagues.

R418 Vickers, Brian. "*Utopia* and Plutarch's *Moralia*." *N&Q* ns 40.2 (June 1993): 152.

Vickers claims Hythloday's attack on pride near the end of *Utopia* recalls a passage from Plutarch's "On Tranquility of Mind" in his *Moralia*.

R419 Volgin, Vyacheslav. "Sir Thomas More." *News, A Review of World Events* 39 (15 Feb. 1953): 14-15.

Volgin sees *Utopia* as an unequivocal blueprint for communism.

R420 Walsh, Chad. *From Utopia to Nightmare*. Westport, CT: Greenwood P, 1962. 40-45.

Walsh compares *Utopia* to Plato's *Republic*, disparaging their regimentation and lack of personal freedom, but preferring More's work to Plato's and conceding Utopia is more desirable than the real world.

R421 Wegemer, Gerard. "Ciceronian Humanism in More's *Utopia*." *Moreana* 104 (1990): 5-26.

Throughout *Utopia*, More creates a subtext of allusions to Cicero, thus providing one measure by which to weigh the arguments of Hythloday and persona More. More defends the philosophy and practice of Ciceronian humanism, while Hythloday argues from a perspective directly opposed to Cicero's views on good government and the best way of life.

R422 Wegemer, Gerard. "*The City of God* in Thomas More's *Utopia*." *Renascence* 44 (1992): 115-35.

To appreciate the depth of *Utopia*, as well as its wit and humor, readers must recognize how More incorporates Augustinian elements that formed his political philosophy and determined his own best way of life.

R423 Wegemer, Gerard B. "The Literary and Philosophic Design of More's *Utopia*." Diss. Notre Dame, 1986.

This study demonstrates the relationship between the literary design and philosophic dimensions of *Utopia*, showing how *Utopia* serves as a witty palimpsest to Plato, Cicero, and especially Augustine. The full humor and depth of *Utopia* depends on a careful weighing and comparison with Plato's *Republic* and Cicero, but especially with Augustine's *City of God*.

R424 Wegemer, Gerard. "The Rhetoric of Opposition in Thomas More's *Utopia*: Giving Form to Competing Philosophies." *P&R* 23 (1990): 288-306.

Wegemer claims contradictory responses to Hythloday and persona More demonstrate "masterful use of a rhetoric based on prosopopoeia," for both characters embody two contrasting philosophies--Hythloday, the Gnostic sophist, rejects the world; persona More, the Christian humanist, favors civic involvement. In addition, the roles shape their rhetoric--Hythloday is "direct, abrupt, and passionate"; persona More is friendly and seeks to build "civil rapport."

R425 Weiner, Andrew D. "Erasmus, More, and the Shape of Persuasion." *Moreana* 65-66 (1980): 87-98.

In his investigation of their participation in the continuing debate on the side of humanistic methodology, Weiner cites examples from their works "of their belief in the transforming power of eloquence." He also compares the techniques of Erasmus in *Encomia Moriae* and More in *Utopia*, in which both authors work to unsettle the reader's preconceptions: Erasmus entertainingly exposes the limitations of man's attempts at wisdom, turning the readers to trust in Christ; in *Utopia*, the attitudes of the characters More and Raphael are inadequate, Utopia's own internal contradictions become apparent, pride replaces money as the root of evil, and Christ replaces communism as humankind's savior.

R426 Weiner, Andrew D. "Raphael's Eutopia and More's *Utopia*: Christian Humanism and the Limits of Reason." *HLQ* 39 (1975): 1-27.

When More changed his title from *Nusquama* to *Utopia*, he added the possibility his new island was not only "no where" (*outopia*) but also a "happy place" (*eutopia*). Although More tried in both of his letters "to" Giles and in the additions he made to Book I to prevent a "philosophic" reading of his work, the history of *Utopia*'s criticism suggests he did not always succeed. By devoting the prefatory letter and much of Book I to developing contrasting *ethoi* for Raphael and "More," the "Distinguished and Eloquent Author" has given readers the means they need to explore Utopia on their own without depending upon the "school" philosopher who would lead them in the manner not of Palinurus or Ulysses but of Plato. By reading "rhetorically," readers are able to discover the way to erect the "best state of a commonwealth" much closer to home.

R427 White, Helen C. "The *Utopia* and Commonwealth Tradition." *Social Criticism in the Popular Religious Literature of the Sixteenth Century*. 1944. New York: Octagon, 1973. 41-81.

Chapter two discusses *Utopia* as an example of the commonwealth tradition of social criticism and contrasts it to Langland's *Piers Plowman*, which is directed toward practical, individual, and social reform unlike More's speculative inquiry which enjoys a moral, intellectual detachment. The works, however, share similarities, such as those embodied in Hythloday's approach to social problems, intense interest in the poor, and eloquent defense of those who are socially and economically deprived. White also discusses *Utopia*'s social hierarchy, communism, relation to issues of More's day, and the degree to which More shared Hythloday's ideas; she concludes by placing *Utopia* in the context of other commonwealth treatises of its period.

R428 White, Thomas I. "Aristotle and *Utopia*." *RenQ* 29 (1976): 635-75.

White emphasizes More's skillful eclecticism and proposes More's knowledge of Aristotle and the influence of Aristotle on *Utopia* have been slighted.

R429 White, Thomas I. "*Festivitas, Utilitas, et Opes*: The Concluding Irony and Philosophical Purpose of Thomas More's *Utopia*." *Quincentennial Essays on St. Thomas More*. 135-50.

White discusses the work's conclusion, addresses the question whether More seriously intended the reservations persona More expresses about Utopian communism, argues for an ironic interpretation by references to both *Utopia* and humanistic works written during this time in More's life, and contends that, at this point in life, More's attitudes about wealth make it impossible for him to intend the criticism of persona More seriously.

R430 White, Thomas I. "An Index Verborum to the Yale *Utopia*." *Moreana* 52 (1976): 5-17.

This index is intended to assist scholars working with the Latin text of *Utopia* and interested in particular themes and concepts or simply More's use of Latin. It includes those words most significant to the philosophical, theological, and social themes of *Utopia*, and is designed to be used in conjunction with the index already in the Yale edition (B019).

R431 White, Thomas I. "The Key to Nowhere: Pride and *Utopia*." *Interpreting Thomas More's* Utopia. 37-60.

The sin of pride is the controlling theme of the work, the concept that serves to bridge the gap between seemingly opposite readings of the text. After acknowledging the well-grounded basis of various approaches to reading *Utopia*, White argues that even dramatically different interpretations of the work "can at least be partially mitigated and *Utopia*'s fundamental unity discovered through the concept of pride." For More, all social and political values are linked to ethics and, in turn, to religion. Hence, More's preoccupation in *Utopia* is two-fold: first, to analyze the essence of pride, and second, to show that pride is the source of social evil.

R432 White, Thomas I. "Pride and the Public Good: Thomas More's Use of Plato in *Utopia*." *Journal of the History of Philosophy* 20 (1982): 329-54.

White clarifies the role of ancient philosophy in *Utopia* and pinpoints parallels between *Utopia* and Platonic writings in which More shows the usefulness of Plato's ideas for advancing the common good by preventing the destructive effects of pride. He also suggests communism alone can secure the public good, since only under communism are avarice and material ostentation wholly impossible. In this regard at least, Hythloday was speaking with the true voice of More, and he concludes that Plato and More were in strategic agreement, holding it more effective to reform institutions than to advise rulers and seeking a form of government in which public good is independent of the personal characteristics of those who wield power.

R433 Williams, Franklin B. "Utopia's Chickens Come Home to Roost." *Moreana* 69 (1981): 76-78.

Williams prints Rudolf Gottfried's discovery of a source for the Utopians' incubation of chickens in Bernard von Breydenbach's *Peregrinatio in Terram Sanctam* (1486).

R434 Wilson, John T. "Is Utopia Possible?" *English* 20 (1971): 51-55.

Wilson surveys the notion of utopia, "the attempt to give concrete expression to man's aspirations to the Good Life," and lists four main types of utopian vision: fantasy, escapism, social criticism (to which category he assigns More's book), and the pure or ideal type (which reaches its apotheosis in Skinner's *Walden Two*).

R435 Wilson, Katharina M. "An Affront to Gold and Silver: Tertullian's *De Cultu Feminarum* and More's *Utopia*." *Moreana* 73 (1982): 69-74.

In addition to the possible sources for the Utopians' use of chamber pots made of gold as a means of deflating its value (which have been found in Martial, Anghiera, Tacitus, Patrizi, and Herodotus), Wilson suggests another analogue in a Patristic writer of the third century, Tertullian, whose *De Cultu Feminarum*, an exhortation addressed to Christian women, has a section resembling the entire passage concerning gold and silver in *Utopia*.

R436 Wilson, Katharina M. "More and Theophrastus: An Idea Put to Work." *Moreana* 67-68 (1980): 35-38.

Wilson suggests the source of the Utopian practice of exposing intended husbands and wives to each other naked is in Theophrastus' *Aureolus Liber de nuptiis*, known through a medieval tradition of philosophical misogamy; More inverts the usual argument to provide comment on both the Utopians and contemporary practice.

R437 Wilson, N.G. "The Name Hythlodaeus." *Moreana* 110 (1992): 33-34.

Wilson accepts previous explanations about the first element of the name, *hythlos*, which means "nonsense," but claims the second element, *daios*, is harder to interpret.

R438 Wilson, Norman Bateham. "Four Paradigms of Utopian Fiction: The Exemplar of Atomism." Diss. U of Michigan, 1980.

Utopian writing has been categorized on the basis of such descriptions as escape vs. reconstruction, authoritarian vs. anti-authoritarian, the degree of centralization, or the positions of upward, outward, and inward. While these categories raise helpful questions, the central question of how a utopia is organized goes unanswered. The method of analyzing utopian fiction in this study is based on the language of symbolic interactionism. Paradigms are seen to comprehend both models of and models for reality. This distinction parallels that which Kenneth Burke makes in noting the differences between planning a picnic and going on a picnic: it is the difference between an analysis or a description and a program. Wilson follows Burke by employing the ratios of his pentad in a "dramatistic" reading of two utopian works to find the locus of motivation, particularly with respect to the shift from analysis to program. Exemplar of such a shift is the movement from Book I to Book II in More's *Utopia*.

R439 Winkler, Gerhard B. "Cönobium, Religion und Toleranz, oder: Wie christlich sind Thomas Mores Utopier?" *A Yearbook of Studies in English Language and Literature 1985/86.* Ed. Otto Rauchbauer. Vienna: Braumüller, 1986. 277-86.

Winkler focuses on *Utopia*'s similarities to religious communities, with special attention on its cenobitical arrangements.

R440 Woll, Mari Anne. "Om kvindens placering i Thomas Mores *Utopia*." *Kvindestudier* 5: *Utopi og subkultur.* Ed. Nynne Koch. Copenhagen: Delta, 1981. 32-71.

Woll provides an overview examining issues central to *Utopia* and placing it in the context of More's career, connections, and times.

R441 Wooden, Warren W. "Anti-Scholastic Satire in Sir Thomas More's *Utopia*." *SCJ* 8 (1977): 29-45.

Wooden traces More's involvement in the humanistic-Scholastic controversy and views Hythloday as both the serious spokesman for European reform and the object of anti-Scholastic satire intended mainly for More's humanist audience.

R442 Wooden, Warren W. "A Reconsideration of the Parerga of Thomas More's *Utopia*." *Quincentennial Essays on St. Thomas More.* 151-60.

Wooden discusses *Utopia*'s apparatus--letters, poems, alphabet, verses, and maps--and even argues that the differences between the Louvain and Basel maps deliberately throw doubt on Hythloday's reliability (though one wonders about the extent of More's control over earlier editions).

R443 Wooden, Warren W. "Satiric Strategy in More's *Utopia*: The Case of Raphael Hythloday." *RenP* (1977): 1-9.

All of the Scholastic argumentative vices More castigates in his 1515 letter to Dorp are found in Hythloday's discourses. The tendency to refer all questions to a universal which itself remains above critical examination, the refusal to accommodate this theory and its subdivisions and corollaries to experience, the circularity of argument, the misuse of common words and misunderstanding or misrepresentation of concepts, and the damaging habit of self-contradiction which flows from this specious dialectic--all these Scholastic vices Hythloday exhibits. However, More changes the frame of reference in which such speculation normally flourished--that is, from the realm of metaphysical speculation to that of state and its proper constitution.

R444 Wooden, Warren W. "Sir Thomas More, Satirist: A Study of the *Utopia* as Menippean Satire." Diss. Vanderbilt U, 1971.

Wooden argues the "most plausible and profitable approach" to *Utopia* is to view it mainly as a work of satire rather than a "predominantly serious sociological or philosophical treatise only tinged occasionally, if at all, with satire."

R445 Wooden, Warren W. "Thomas More and Lucian: A Study of Satiric Influence and Technique." *UMSE* 13 (1972): 43-57.

The satiric strategy employed in *Utopia* is analyzed through the perspective afforded by More's study of the Greek satirist Lucian of Samosata. A survey of More's admiration for and translations from Lucian's work leads into an analysis of satiric devices in *Utopia* and a comparison of these with the satiric stance and methodology of Lucian. More's Utopian narrator, Hythloday, bears strong affinities to the Menippean *Philosophus gloriosus* of Lucianic satire. Examination of Hythloday as a complex satiric tool in turn illuminates a series of juxtapositions between the theoretical and the practical in the narrative which point to a comprehensive satiric design in *Utopia*. In light of the pervasive indebtedness to the techniques of Lucianic satire, *Utopia* should most plausibly be viewed as a work belonging to the genre of Lucianic or Menippean satire.

R446 Wooden, Warren W. "Utopia and Arcadia: An Approach to More's *Utopia*." *CollL* 6 (1979-80): 30-40.

Wooden bases his approach to *Utopia* on a phrase in Budé's preface to the Paris edition--once avarice gone, *aureum saeculum Saturniumque rediret*. He shows Renaissance poets adapting the Golden Age myth to the pastoral framework and thereby focusing "upon the philosophical and satiric dimensions inherent in the pastoral form itself." Despite a greater degree of surface realism, the communistic state of Utopia seems metaphoric in a manner analogous to the shepherd society, and both point not to realistic, practicable alternatives to civilization as Renaissance man knew it, but to states of mind, to sets of human values, which were too often corrupted, sublimated, or ignored in the real world. Neither seeks to create a detailed sociological or institutional ideal nor is either escapist. As interludes, imaginative oases, in the humdrum or hectic course of everyday human existence, both afford an educative, revivifying experience of paramount importance to the life of the mind. The fictional More never loses sight of these qualifications, and he, like the reader of the Renaissance pastoral, disengages himself when the Utopian tale is told and turns his attention again to the real world.

R447 Wooden, Warren W. "Utopia and Dystopia: The Paradigm of Thomas More's *Utopia*." *SHR* 14 (1980): 97-110.

Wooden believes the imaginary island embodies both utopia and dystopia within a single description and paradoxically fuses opposites, which is, in large part, responsible for the work's complexity and its capacity for teasing readers.

R448 Wooden, Warren W. "The Wit of Thomas More's *Utopia*." *StHum* 7 (1979): 43-51.

This work need not be treated solemnly as it traditionally is; it contains a great deal of humor. The genius of More's masterpiece lies less perhaps in its humanistic message than in its imaginative technique. Especially significant are the dialogue format and the fantastic voyage or new world *topoi*. Sixteenth-century critics recognized More for his "incomparable and almost superhuman wit"; modern readers would do well to search for it.

R449 Wooden, Warren W., and John N. Wall, Jr. "Thomas More and the Painter's Eye: Visual Perspective and Artistic Purpose in More's *Utopia*." *JMRS* 15 (1985): 231-63.

The authors believe the multiplicity of perspectives engendered by *Utopia* in the years since 1516 testifies to More's success in forcing readers to examine it over and over again from differing points of view.

R450 Zell, Rosemarie. "Dialogue as Way to Peace in the Utopia of Thomas More." *HEI* 20 (1995): 899-905.

Zell believes More's vision of Utopian life as a dialogue to peace "rests on the active participation of...everyone in developing one's full...potential."

Polemical Works

S001 Anderegg, Michael A. "Nicholas Harpsfield, Thomas More, and William Roper's Lapse into Heresy." *N&Q* ns 23.5-6 (May-June 1976): 225-26.
   In mentioning Roper's flirtation with Lutheranism in his *Life*, Harpsfield uses language similar to that of a passage in More's *Dialogue Concerning Heresies*, in which More may actually have had Roper in mind. Harpsfield knew More's writings well, especially the literary ones, and gave them sympathetic attention, and More's style and tone influenced him in producing this "first scholarly biography extant in English."

S002 Anderson, Marvin W. "William Tyndale (d. 1536): A Martyr for All Seasons." *SCJ* 17 (1986): 331-52.
   Anderson demonstrates how Tyndale brought together elements of Lollardy with the theologies of Luther and other continental theologians. His strongly evangelical understanding of Scripture is reflected in his replies to the harsh attacks upon him and Protestantism in general from More's pen.

S003 Baird-Smith, David. "One Shrewd Wife in All the World." *Moreana* 83-84 (1984): 93-94.
   Baird-Smith compares the use and treatment of the proverb "about one shrewd wife" in Book III, ch. 13, of the *Dialogue Concerning Heresies* with that of Cervantes in Book 2, ch. 22, of *Don Quixote*.

S004 Baker-Smith, Dominic. "The Crisis of Religious Humanism in the Face of the Reformation." *Thomas Morus Jahrbuch 1995*. 37-43.
   Baker-Smith offers "specific evidence of the human complexity" of the Reformation to arrive at a greater sense of its contingency and a better understanding of More's stance in the 1530s. To unravel what More was saying about heresy, Baker-Smith reconstructs the audience he addressed.

S005 Baumann, Uwe. "Logische Exempla und ihre Funktion in der *Responsio ad Lutherum* des Thomas Morus." *Acta Conventus Neo-Latini Guelpherbytani*. Proceedings of the Sixth International Congress of Neo-Latin Studies. Wolfenbüttel 12 August to 16 August 1985. Eds. Stella P. Revard, Fidel Rädle, and Mario A. Di Cesare. MRTS. 53. Binghamton: MRTS, 1988. 563-72.

Baumann explores the uses of logic in the rhetoric of More's *Responsio ad Lutherum*.

S006 Billingsley, Dale B. "The Messenger and the Reader in Thomas More's *Dialogue Concerning Heresies*." *SEL* 24 (1984): 5-22.

Billingsley answers questions about the relationship between the book's interlocutors, the bearing that relationship has on More's attitude toward his readers, and the configuration of these separate but complimentary relationships in the large doctrinal issues of the *Dialogue*. He argues More's concern with interpretation is central not only to the problem of heresy but also to the reader in the process of interpreting the text; that one of the interlocutors, the Messenger, bears a parallel relationship with the reader; and that when the Master Chauncellour rehearses the proper interpretation of Scripture with the Messenger, More is instructing the reader in the same process. Thus, beyond the refutation of certain heretical ideas, the *Dialogue* teaches the reader about methods of interpretation which may be applied to other heretical texts, Scripture, and works other than Scripture.

S007 Birch, David. "Statistical Rank and the Friedman Test as an Indication of Significance in the Preliminary Stages of a Multi-Variable Analysis of Literary Texts." *SN* 55 (1983): 129-41.

Birch uses More's English polemical works to suggest a method of making preliminary judgments about the significance of a full-scale stylistic and linguistic analysis of a major corpus of literary texts, and he presents his findings on More's polemical texts, which contain twenty-one style variables, such as clause type, independent clause variables, and dependent clause variables.

S008 Blackburn, Elizabeth Brooke. "John More's 'A Sermon of the sacrament of the aulter.'" *Moreana* 2 (1964): 5-36.

Both father and son defended the literal interpretation of the Lord's Supper, and Blackburn points to parallels in subject matter and tone between Thomas More's *Letter against Frith* (1533) and John More's English translation from the Latin of Frederick Nausea's *A Sermon of the sacrament of the aulter* (printed and bound with the *Letter against Frith*). She also gives a biographical sketch of Nausea and presents John More's translation of his *Sermon*.

S009 Bradshaw, Brendan. "The Controversial Sir Thomas More." *Journal* *of Ecclesiastical History* 36 (1985): 535-69.

Bradshaw reviews publications on More's life from 1979 to 1982 to provide the basis for countering revisionist theories originally proposed by Geoffrey Elton and taken up by John Guy (F097), J.B. Trapp (B003), and Alistair Fox (G027). Contrary to their claims, Bradshaw argues More's career as a controversialist lies not in his betrayal, but in his "continuing commitment to Christian humanism," and he employs detailed analysis of the literary form and content of *Dialogue Concerning Heresies* and the *Apology* to support his contention. Both works exhibit complex structures developed by the "strategic requirements of argument"; they are not, as the revisionists claim, the "products of a mentally unbalanced...personality." The content of both tracts does not support the revisionist view that More's polemical works show him to be authoritarian and completely opposed to the Reformation; Bradshaw states the works project "a cautious reformer" instead of "a reactionary ultra-conservative."

S010   Campbell, W.E. "More's *Supplication of Souls*." *Dublin Review* 216 (1945): 1-8.

Campbell claims *Supplication* gives insight into the quality and range of More's religious faith, particularly with respect to the doctrine of purgatory.

S011   Clebsch, William. "Thomas More, *Defensor Fidei*." *England's Earliest Protestants, 1520-1535*. Yale Publications in Religion. II. New Haven: Yale UP, 1964. 277-304.

In chapter fifteen, Clebsch examines More's life and thought and assesses his polemical writing. He describes More as a "hunter of heretics" who, before and during his chancellorship, persecuted heretics and seized Protestant books. More was not cruel by nature, but viewed heresy as a "gross offense" against nature, man, God, and the unity of not only England but also Europe. Because of their humor and literary form, the *Dialogue Concerning Heresies* and *Supplication of Souls* are the only polemical works Clebsch credits. He also contrasts More's polemical treatises with his Tower works.

S012   Crawford, Charles W. "Thomas Stapleton and More's *Letter to Bugenhagen*." *Moreana* 19 (1968): 101-07.

Crawford presents events leading to More's *Letter to Bugenhagen*; summarizes Bugenhagen's life, works, and religious activities; parallels events in More's life with the composition and content of the *Letter*; provides a sketch of Stapleton's life; and comments on Stapleton's interest in More's works and his life (published in Stapleton's *Tres Thomae*). Crawford continues this article (*Moreana* 26 [1970], 5-13) and supplies notes to the complete text and a facsimile of Stapleton's annotations to the first published version of More's *Letter*. Marc'hadour comments on Crawford's articles (*Moreana* 26 [1970],

14-16) and presents further information on Stapleton and his relationship with More.

S013 Daniell, David. "Sir Thomas More." *William Tyndale: A Biography*. New Haven: Yale UP, 1994. 250-80.

Chapter ten provides an overview of More's role in religious controversy before it considers his confrontations with Tyndale in detail.

S014 Davis, John F. "The Trials of Thomas Bylney and the English Reformation." *Historical Journal* 24 (1981): 775-90.

Davis discusses More's part in Bilney's trial of 1527 and analyzes More's interpretation of it, along with other Reformation issues linked to it, in *Dialogue Concerning Heresies*.

S015 Devereux, E.J. "Thomas More's Textual Changes in the *Dialogue Concerning Heresies*." *Library* 5th ser. 27 (1972): 233-35.

In discussing textual changes in the *Dialogue*, Devereux observes John Rastell printed little for his brother-in-law More. Rastell's first book was probably More's life of Pico, but More sought an established continental printer for *Utopia* probably because of his desire to secure a wider circulation for the book. It was 1529 before Rastell printed again for More, but the *Dialogue Concerning Heresies* shows More made difficulties for his printer, freely expanding the text as the book was in press. Evidence suggests the work was originally relatively brief, and then expanded, Rastell being forced to hand over much of the printing to Peter Treveris. A further addition of about fifty lines seems to have been set in Rastell's own shop during the course of the actual printing, eight pages being canceled to allow insertion of this new material.

S016 Dillon, William Patrick. "Sir Thomas More: A Descriptive Analysis and Critical Assessment of His Controversial Writings of 1528-1533." Diss. Union Theological Seminary, 1976.

Dillon describes More's controversial career from 7 March 1528 when Tunstall appointed him to compose treatises in the vernacular against English Protestants to 1533, examines major reasons More received this task, and explains why More chose the idea of devotion as one focus of these works.

S017 Doyle, Charles Clay. "Lenten Fare and the Language of Falsehood: Pig and Pike, Fish and Fowl." *Quincentennial Essays on St. Thomas More*. 27-34.

Doyle makes use of literary and psychological analysis to widen understanding of More's wit, polemical technique, and his interest in food and sex as they are revealed in condensed versions of two popular jests in his *Confutation of Tyndale's Answer*. More's treatment of the tales reveals their derivation from coarse popular jokes mixing the sacred and profane, and Doyle thinks More employs them to satirize the "hocus pocus" of Tyndale's handling of language and truth, the marriage of Lutheran clergy, and Lutheran disregard for fast days.

S018 Doyle, Charles Clay. "Looking Behind Two Proverbs of More." *Moreana* 91-92 (1986): 33-35.

Doyle explores the sources and analogues of two proverbs More uses--"out of the frying pan and into the fire" and "all is good that helpeth"--the first of which is found in *Confutation of Tyndale's Answer* and *Dialogue Concerning Heresies*, the second in *Dialogue Concerning Heresies*.

S019 Egan, Willis J. *The Rule of Faith in St. Thomas More's Controversy with William Tyndale, 1528-1533.* Los Angeles: Kellaway Ide, 1960.

Egan analyzes More's debate with Tyndale over the Rule of Faith by examining More's theological background and qualifications for theological debate, providing an overview of More's controversy with Tyndale, and presenting an account of Tyndale's career, character, and works. He next treats the Rule of Faith issue in *Dialogue Concerning Heresies* and the *Confutation of Tyndale's Answer* and examines More's arguments defending the authority of the Church as the "divinely constituted teacher of Christian belief," thereby refuting the reformers' contention Scripture alone is the Christian Rule of Faith.

S020 Fines, John. "An Unnoticed Tract in the Tyndale-More Dispute?" *Bulletin of the Institute of Historical Research* 42 (1969): 220-30.

Fines examines the BM ms. of "A commyssion sent to the bloudy bysshop of London...By the high and mighty Kyng, lord Sathanas the deuill of hell," printed by Thomas Purfoot in 1586. The tract is an example of a medieval convention, to which Foxe refers, reappearing in the sixteenth century. From the evidence of differences in format, content, and spelling between the ms. and printed versions, Fines assigns the former a much earlier date than the latter, and on the strength of details paralleled in Tyndale's polemical writings, attributes the tract to Tyndale or possibly one of his circle. He also considers the tract in relation to Tyndale's *Practice of Prelates* and More's *Dialogue Concerning Heresies*.

S021 Fleissner, Robert F. "*Hamlet* and *The Supplication of Souls* Reconvened." *N&Q* 32.1 (Mar. 1985): 49-51.

Theobald's reading of *Hamlet* (1.5.10-13--"confined fast in fires"), which he later retracted, does not accord with the ghost's leaving purgatory to visit earth. Shakespeare's words are those of More in *Supplication*. The 1603 quarto has "Confinde in flaming fire," again suggesting More's work. Theobald's emendation, "Confined to fast in fire," is odd, in that it implies a spirit's ability to eat.

S022 Flesseman-Van Leer, E. "The Controversy about Ecclesiology between Thomas More and William Tyndale." *Nederlands Archief voor Kerkgeschiedenis* 44 (1960): 65-86.

The author covers the usually conflicting positions of More and Tyndale on the authority of the Church; the Church's ideas of infallibility, composition, traditions, unity, and divergence of opinions within it; the sources of the Christian faith, the ministry, the authority of general councils, papal primacy, and the question of faith. For More the unity and authority of the Church take precedence over the Scripture and papal power, and "his final argument and proof of truth is always the general practice and belief of the Church now and as it always has been." For Tyndale, the authority of Scripture was central as the source of faith and the traditions of the Church were subject to Scripture.

S023 Flesseman-Van Leer, E. "The Controversy about Scripture and Tradition between Thomas More and William Tyndale." *Nederlands Archief voor Kerkgeschiedenis* 43 (1959): 143-64.

The author argues Tyndale's doctrine of the Holy Spirit brings him to belief in the Scripture; whereas, for More, in the *Confutation of Tyndale's Answer*, the Holy Spirit brings man to belief in the Church. After examining Tyndale's convictions about the role of Scripture in matters of faith and the Church's doctrine and tradition, Flesseman-Van Leer turns to More and discusses the four major arguments in his *Answer* in which he attacks the sufficiency of Scripture by defending Church traditions, showing the Church and Christian faith are older than Scripture, claiming only the Church can judge what is truly Scripture, and asserting only the Church can interpret its meaning.

S024 Fox, Alistair. "Thomas More's Controversial Writings and His View of the Renaissance." *Parergon* 11 (1975): 41-48.

Fox believes while More's polemical writings respond to the possibilities of ethical, educational, aesthetic, and religious renewal, they reject the view of the Renaissance as "a sudden new departure from an unmitigated history of tribulation and disaster," one seen in Erasmus and reformers like Tyndale, Fish, and Frith. Thus, More saw tribulation as an inescapable part of the fallen human condition and as a manifestation of the role of providence in shaping human history, and More's polemical writings are "largely an attempt to defend his particular sense of historical renewal against views...he considered...based upon dangerous or despairing assumptions."

S025 Fox, Alistair. "Thomas More's *Dialogue* and the *Book of the Tales of Caunterbury*: 'Good Mother Wit' and Creative Imitation." *Familiar Colloquy:*

Essays Presented to Arthur Edward Barker. Ed. Patricia Brückmann. Ottawa, Can.: Oberon P, 1978. 15-24.

Within a few chapters of *Dialogue Concerning Heresies*, More considers the power of poetry to assist judgment and alludes many times to the *Tales of Caunterbury*, especially the sections dealing with pilgrimages and miracles. In the *Dialogue*, More represents himself as attempting to guide the similarly nervous, faith-shaken Messenger to the same discovery by exposing him, at a crucial moment, to the influence of Chaucer's poetry.

S026 Fox, Alistair. "Thomas More's View of English Historical Experience in the Controversial Writings." Diss. U of Western Ontario, 1974.

Fox believes More's appeals to English historical experience in his controversial works illustrate his conviction the tributary realities of historical experience not only reflect the consequences of "postlapsarian perversity" but also a "divinely creative inducement to humility, faith, and human regenerative effort in cooperation with sustaining grace."

S027 Gabrieli, Vittorio. "*Hamlet* and *The Supplication of Souls*." *N&Q* ns 26.2 (Apr. 1979): 120-21.

The possibility exists Shakespeare preserved a more accurate recollection of a crucial passage in *Supplication*. May he, instead of writing "confin'd to fast," have actually meant to write as Theobald conjectured in his *Shakespeare Restored*, although he later withdrew his conjecture, "confined fast in fires," thus keeping closer to More's primary adverbial sense of fast and totally ignoring the notion of fasting? (See also S021.)

S028 Gairdner, James. *Lollardy and the Reformation in England: An Historical Survey.* Vol. 1. 1908. New York: Burt Franklin, 1968. 307-11, 386-89, 414-15, 437-38, 456-60, 463-67, 469-79, 481-84, 489-504, 505-78.

Gairdner discusses background to and major controversial and doctrinal points in More's polemical writings, especially *Dialogue Concerning Heresies*, *Supplication of Souls*, and *Confutation of Tyndale's Answer*. He defends the Catholic martyrs and More and attempts to resolve the contradiction between More's liberalism exhibited in *Utopia* and his treatment of heretics by referring to the times' social and religious conditions. He also looks at the "whole substance" of *Dialogue Concerning Heresies* as a means of understanding More's ideas and the times during which he wrote his polemical works. Volume two of Gairdner's *Lollardy and the Reformation in England* contains further references to More.

S029 Ginsberg, David. "Ploughboys versus Prelates: Tyndale and More and the Politics of Biblical Translation." *SCJ* 19 (1988): 45-61.

Ginsberg maintains Tyndale made deft political use of his vernacular

English translations of the Bible to win over the common people of Renaissance England to the Protestant cause. Comparison of Tyndale's translation of the Old Testament Book of Jonah and More's favored Douay-Rheims translation of the same with the original Hebrew text shows how these translations reflect their adherents' respective religious, political views.

S030 Gogan, Brian. *The Common Corps of Christendom: Ecclesiological Themes in the Writings of Sir Thomas More*. Studies in the History of Christian Thought. 26. Leiden: E.J. Brill, 1982.

Gogan declares ecclesiology is the most significant subject in the controversial writings. Limited to the *Responsio, Dialogue Concerning Heresies, Confutation*, and materials drawn from the period of the trial, the study focuses on ideas about the nature of the Church, the Church's role in mediating revelation, the importance of tradition and consensus, the role and power of the papacy, the nature of Church councils, and the relationship between the papacy and councils. Gogan outlines the shapes these concepts take in each of the three works and depicts the development of More's thought on them over the time span of their composition.

S031 Gordon, Walter M. "The Argument of Comedy in Thomas More's *Dialogue Concerning Heresies*." *Ren&R* ns 4 (1980): 13-32.

Gordon attends to the relevancy of the work's humorous stories by analyzing their contribution to their particular literary genre and connecting their comedy to both the main issue under discussion (the identity of the true Church) and the *Dialogue's* central objectives. The colloquial diction and controversial tone of the tales not only contribute to the drama and art of the dialogue form, they also meet the needs of the popular reading audience. If some of the tales should be seen as digressions from the central debate, they have relevancy "in the very act of being irrelevant," for by diverting the audience from the serious argument with their humor, the merry tales produce sympathy and understanding, the ultimate objectives of the *Dialogue*.

S032 Gordon, Walter M. "In Defense of More's Merry Tales." *Moreana* 38 (1973): 5-12.

More's merry tales have come under attack in an essay by G.R. Elton who insinuates More's comic spirit was tainted with an unsavory preoccupation with sex and that his imagination readily warmed to topics of a crude nature ("Thomas More, Councillor" [F071]). Elton fails to understand More's metaphorical use of the term "virginity" which has precedents reaching back to Old Testament literature. The stories in *Dialogue Concerning Heresies* deal with subjects of a raw, unvarnished nature. Potentially crude material is treated in the tale of St. Walery where pilgrims' devotions resemble the phallic ritualism of pagan antiquity. However, More's straight-faced approach to the absurd goings-on and his dramatic expertise in dialogue and character elevate the story to a level of hilarious comedy worthy of Rabelais.

S033   Gordon, Walter M. "A Needle in a Meadow: A Missing Reference in the More-Frith Controversy." *Moreana* 52 (1976): 19-23.

In the controversy over the bodily presence of Christ in the Eucharist, Frith's refers to Augustine's familiar dictum that even the risen body of Christ is restricted to one place in support of a key argument in his case about the impossibility for Christ's body to be "in divers places at once." More, who soon secured a copy of Frith's tract and replied to it, was quick to point out Frith could offer no reference to validate his source. More wrote "to seek out one line" in Augustine "were to go look [for] a needle in a meadow."

S034   Gordon, Walter M. "A Scholastic Problem in Thomas More's Controversy with John Frith." *HTR* 69 (1976): 131-49.

Gordon explores More's controversy with Frith and emphasizes Frith's denial and More's defense of the doctrine of "multilocation." In More's defense of the Eucharist in the *Letter against Frith*, an awareness of his popular audience causes him to avoid Scholastic terms and arguments that might confuse readers and to depend on "simple catechism," parable, and analogy.

S035   Gow, Elizabeth. "Thomas Bilney and His Relations with Sir Thomas More." *Norfolk Archaeology* 32 (1961): 292-310.

Gow discusses More's account of Bilney's first trial (November 1527) in the *Dialogue Concerning Heresies* and More's report of his second trial and subsequent execution in the *Confutation of Tyndale's Answer* to demonstrate More is capable of bias.

S036   Gregory, T.S. "The Controversies of St. Thomas More." *Under God and the Law*. Papers Read to The Thomas More Society of London. 2nd ser. Ed. Richard O'Sullivan. Oxford: Basil Blackwell, 1949. 40-58.

Gregory surveys More's religious controversies, with emphasis on those with Tyndale, Fish, and St. German. For each tract covered, he provides background and explains the main theological or doctrinal issues debated.

S037   Guy, John A. "Thomas More and Christopher St. German: The Battle of the Books." *Moreana* 83-84 (1984): 5-25.

Guy uses the *Apology* and *Debellation*, which comprised More's side of his polemical feud with St. German, to illuminate a major historical problem concerning More's last years of life and to identify what Henry VIII probably believed to have been a breach of trust following More's resignation of the chancellorship. Nowhere was the juridical aspect of the Henrician schism better defended than in those books of St. German printed by Berthelet. Since St.

German's *Division* and *Salem* were components of the king's secondary line of propaganda, More's *Apology* and *Debellation* gain political significance. However More perceived his position in law and morality during 1533, Henry VIII believed his ex-chancellor had broken his trust. Within the "volcanic recesses of the king's consciousness," More's mere existence came to pose an intolerable threat.

S038 Haas, Steven W. "Lutheran Emendations to the Latin text of Simon Fish's *Supplication for the Beggars*." *Moreana* 37 (1973): 25-30.

Haas finds traces of Lutheran sentiment and phraseology in the Latin translation of Fish's pamphlet, which may well be the work of the author himself. "One may conjecture that Fish toned down his Protestant enthusiasm in his English version...but felt less compelled to do so for the more learned and possibly sympathetic circles in which the Latin version of the *Supplication* would have circulated."

S039 Haas, Steven W. "Simon Fish, William Tyndale, and Sir Thomas More's 'Lutheran Conspiracy.'" *Journal of Ecclesiastical History* 23 (1972): 125-36.

Haas describes how Fish's *A Supplication for the Beggars* in the autumn of 1529 provoked More's *Supplycayon of soulys* which regards Fish's pamphlet as part of a Lutheran strategy to debase the clergy to the point they could no longer defend the Catholicism.

S040 Hardin, Richard F. "Caricature in More's *Confutation*." *Moreana* 93 (1987): 41-52.

Hardin refers to the two types of humor found in the polemical works (as Walter M. Gordon describes them in "The Argument of Comedy in Thomas More's *Dialogue Concerning Heresies*" [S031]) and believes the *Confutation*, through the technique of literary caricature, which obliquely assaults the "incorporeal theology" of Tyndale and his followers, displays more hostile, aggressive humor than does the *Dialogue Concerning Heresies*.

S041 Headley, John M. "More Against Luther: On Laws and the Magistrate." *Moreana* 15-16 (1967): 211-23.

Headley analyzes the two controversialists' positions on the relationship between the law and the magistrate to illustrate their views on equity. He discovers sometimes when they seem most opposed, they agree upon the problem of "achieving unity and unanimity" in the Church.

S042 Headley, John. "On More and the Papacy." *Moreana* 41 (1974): 5-10.

Headley criticizes Marius' view of More's attitude to the papacy as expressed in the Yale edition of the *Confutation of Tyndale's Answer* (B004) and his misconception of Headley's own treatment in the Yale edition of *Responsio ad Lutherum* (B015). On the basis of a passage in the *Responsio*, Marius claims More as a conciliarist, but Headley argues "whatever conciliarist strains may lurk in the *Responsio*, the full weight of More's ecclesiological view lies elsewhere," More believing "that *consensus* is not enough, for if the church is to know itself and to maintain that community and universality, it must have a recognizable touchstone in the papal primacy, divinely founded." More was never able to expand his affirmation of papal primacy, but "there persists in a muted undertone the vital adherence to Rome," and from 1523 to his death, the "fact of papal primacy runs as a continuing thread through More's thinking on the church."

S043 Headley, John M. "Thomas More and Luther's Revolt." *Archiv fur Reformationsgeschichte* 60 (1969): 145-60.

Headley traces More's reactions to Luther in the 1520s by presenting in chronological order his first impression of Luther, his involvement in Henry VIII's *Assertio septem sacramentorum*, the two versions of More's *Responsio ad Lutherum*, his epistle to Bugenhagen (1526), and his *Dialogue Concerning Heresies* (its last four books treat Luther and Lutherans almost exclusively). Headley also finds More's friendship with those who shared his passionate opposition to Luther--Thomas Murner, Johann Eck, and Johann Cochlaeus--important. Three central and related issues revealed in More's polemical work define his opposition to Luther--the problems of authority, the Church, and the will.

S044 Headley, John M. "Thomas Murner, Thomas More, and the First Expression of More's Ecclesiology." *SRen* 14 (1967): 73-92.

Although Headley speculates Murner could have served as a catalyst in More's recognition that denying papal authority could lead to social revolution, he acknowledges there is not a single notion in the *Responsio ad Lutherum* that could not have come from another source. In spite of the inability to prove the case for the influence of Murner on More, Headley sees "the existence of common circumstances and common tradition" between them.

S045 Hecht, Jamey. "Limitations of Textuality in Thomas More's *Confutation of Tyndale's Answer*." *SCJ* 26 (1995): 823-28.

Hecht explores the ways a crucial debate of the English Reformation was the product of paradoxes and ironies each side deployed but neither could entirely assimilate. The relatively new medium of the printed book frustrated the ends of both More and Tyndale, because the textuality of the printed debate unwittingly ironized both the banned books it discussed and the illiterate consensus More valorized. The More-Tyndale debate, with its ancient underlying themes, exemplified the process of religious evolution this essay calls Judeo-Christianity's "metabolism."

S046 Hitchcock, James. "More and Tyndale's Controversy Over Revelation: A Test of the McLuhan Hypothesis." *JAAR* 39 (1971): 448-66.

Hitchcock believes More and Tyndale's controversy over revelation anticipates Marshall McLuhan's ideas of oral and print culture. He thinks More, during his debate with Tyndale, downplays the authoritative role of Scripture and the importance of the printed word and advances the notion the ultimate source of revelation is the "common consensus of all members of the believing community, who inherit their belief primarily through an oral and manuscript tradition." Tyndale, on the other hand, argues the printed Bible is not only the main source of revelation but also the means through which one "liberates himself from the tyranny and falsehood implicit in the community."

S047 Hitchcock, James. "Thomas More and the *Sensus Fidelium*." *Theological Studies* 36 (1975): 145-54.

Hitchcock contends More's conception of consensus was the "most extreme in the entire history of the Church," and he discusses More's understanding and treatment of *sensus fidelium* in his controversial works. For More, consensus is connected to tradition, and "popular will" is not revolutionary but inherited from the past. He also considers More's uncertainty about the "precise locus of authority" in the Church, his doubts about the authority of Scripture, and his preference for oral over print culture.

S048 Horst, Irvin Buckwalter. *The Radical Brethren: Anabaptism and the English Reformation to 1558*. Bibliotheca Humanistica et Reformatorica. Vol. 2. Nieuwkoop: B. de Graaf, 1972. 37, 40-43, 46, 48, 53, 57, 59, 63, 65, 97, 104, 143, 161, 169.

Many leading English religious controversialists appear in Horst's study of anabaptism during the period when "the radical forces released by the Reformation made their first impact." In the course of his discussion, Horst shows how More, in contrast to Erasmus who was not without sympathy for the anabaptists, could never bring himself "to commend any form of modern devotion or scriptural obedience not under the rule of Rome," because "he honestly hated all heretics and was fearful of what the world would endure at their hands."

S049 Keen, Ralph. "A Correction by Hand in More's *Supplication*, 1529." *Moreana* 77 (1983): 100.

The five known copies of the first of the two editions of *Supplication* (printed by William Rastell, 1529) contain a "glaring" error that was overlooked when the errata was compiled that was so egregious Rastell was willing to expend the effort of correcting all his copies by hand.

S050 Keen, Ralph. "Humanism and Reformation in Controversy." *Thomas Morus Jahrbuch 1995*. 84-91.

Keen sees the apologetic theology to which More, Tyndale, and Cochlaeus "gave their energy...not [as] a renunciation of...humanism" but rather as a "renewal of it in synthesis with the inherited theological tradition."

S051 Keen, Ralph. "More Bibliographical Notes." *Moreana* 25 (1988): 141-43.

Keen explains the different dates given on the second publication of *Dialogue Concerning Heresies*.

S052 Keen, Ralph. "Thomas More and Geometry." *Moreana* 86 (1985): 151-66.

Keen maintains More's long-standing interest in geometry, especially Euclid's axioms, influenced his polemical method, so frequently based on the assumed infallibility of Scripture and Patristic tradition. Thus, geometry's presupposition of absolute, if unprovable truths and its method of presentation were "indisputably attractive" to More; and to refute heretical errors, it was a given More would "embrace the attitude there are absolute truths proven through exegetic 'deduction.'" Keen also sees differences between More and Luther in geometric terms, comments on annotations in a copy of Euclid's *Elements* (with More's signature and hence probably his own), and speculates upon the extent of More's education in mathematics.

S053 Kernan, Gerald. "Saint Thomas More, Theologian." *Thought* 17 (1942): 281-302.

Through an examination of chapters ten to twelve in Book IV of *Dialogue Concerning Heresies*, Kernan determines More's background and reading in theology and his capacities as a theologian. He finds More's position, popularity, and ability to write clear, convincing English prose depended on the fact he could support all his serious thoughts "with solid learning in the Sacred Scriptures, the Fathers, and traditional Christian theology."

S054 Knox, David Broughton. *The Doctrine of Faith in the Reign of Henry VIII*. London: James Clarke, 1961. 121-29, 132-37.

Knox surveys the doctrine of justification by faith as expounded by English writers during the earliest phases of the Reformation. Beginning with the controversial glosses and pamphlets of Tyndale, he deals with the works of Roye, Frith, Joye, Barnes, and Coverdale, taking into account the views of these writers on election, the sacraments, predestination, and clerical celibacy. In this context, Knox elaborates on More's role as the "foremost opponent" of these writers, deals mainly with More's controversy with Tyndale in the *Dialogue Concerning Heresies* and *Confutation of Tyndale's Answer*, and focuses on points of contention that divided the reformers and their opponents.

S055 Levin, Carole. "From Beggars to Souls: Thomas More's Response to Simon Fish's *Supplication*." *LJHum* 16 (1990): 5-22.

Levin focuses upon literary and historical strategies of More's response to Fish in his *Supplication* to comment on the Protestant-Catholic debate in the 1520s in England. She is interested in how both dealt with the historical character of King John, whom Protestants recast as a hero. Since King John had great problems with the Church, his story was an ideal place to situate this argument, and divergent interpretations of John mark the whole question of kingly rights versus the Church, a critical issue for Henry VIII. Fish charges clergy provoked sedition and took power away from the king; More's tract counters this charge.

S056 Marc'hadour, Germain. "The Devil and the Lombards: Two Merry Tales by Thomas More." *Cithara* 19 (1980): 5-19.

Marc'hadour scrutinizes the social, political, literary, and religious significance of these "gems of Morean wit" that feature the devil in Book II of the *Dialogue Concerning Heresies*, comments on More's involvement with and understanding of Italian affairs, and describes the strong presence of Lombardy in England at the time. *Dialogue Concerning Heresies*, "the first of More's seven works of controversy in English...is no doubt the best, at least from a literary standpoint."

S057 Marc'hadour, Germain. "Thomas More et les Conciles Oecuméniques." *Moreana* 121 (1995): 33-52.

Although the reconciliation between the Greek Orthodox and the Roman Church (brought about by the *Decree of Union*, 6 July 1439) was short-lived, the Greek delegates found the Catholic dogma of purgatory constant with their own immemorial practice of praying for the dead. On this count More is indebted to them in his *Supplication of Souls*. Unlike John Fisher, who quotes verbatim from conciliar texts and duly identifies his source, More is content to invoke the "general councils" in bulk, only naming those of Nicea (once) and of Constance (twice).

S058 Marius, Richard. "The Pseudonymous Patristic Text in Thomas More's *Confutation*." *Moreana* 15 (1967): 253-66.

Marius considers the role of Patristic authority in Reformation writing and discusses two erroneous citations in *Confutation*. Marius concedes More was occasionally taken in by spurious texts, but asserts his reliance on such false texts is not that significant in the *Confutation*, in which More touches upon St. Cyprian, a Dionysius possibly the Areopagite, and Origen. Marius generalizes about how More's hesitant treatment of the issue of the use (or misuse) of the pseudonymous Patristic text in the *Confutation* reflects some of the concerns the humanists had about authentic texts and other textual problems.

S059 Marius, Richard. "Thomas More and the Early Church Fathers." *Traditio* 24 (1968): 379-407.

Marius stresses More's lifelong devotion to these writers as authoritative interpreters of the Bible in this study of their pervasive influence on More's theology. In the *Confutation of Tyndale's Answer* and other polemical writings, the Fathers are constantly cited as witnesses for Catholic dogmas rejected by Protestants, and in this faith readers "are brought back to a fundamental trait of his personality--his sober melancholy awareness of the coming of death."

S060 Marius, Richard. "Thomas More and the Heretics." Diss. Yale, 1962.

Marius studies the bases of More's religious thought, with particular attention to religious ideas in his works before the Reformation (the most important of which is *Utopia*), in this analysis of More's polemical works.

S061 Marsh, T.N. "Humor and Invective in Early Tudor Polemic Prose." *Rice Institute Pamphlet* 44 (1957): 79-89.

Marsh notes the frequent use, in the controversial writings of the sixteenth century, of proverbial and colloquial turns of phrase, and even downright slang, of puns and jokes, and of open scurrility. Prominent already in More and Tyndale, these forms of expression persist in the prose of Nashe, Dekker, Donne, and Milton.

S062 Martz, Louis L. "More as Author: The Virtues of Digression." *Moreana* 62 (1979): 105-19.

Martz provides defense of More's *Confutation of Tyndale's Answer*. The work's enormous length results from More's concern each chapter, while countering one of Tyndale's arguments, should be representative of or epitomize the whole. Thus, repetition is intended to have a cumulative, unifying effect. Tyndale's logical and eloquent progress is countered not only by argument but by repetition, digression, emotionalism, and innuendo, often of a rather deplorable kind. More, who probably never expected readers to read the entire polemic, uses what seems repetitive or digressive because he composed a compendium of essays in confutation, each intended to have its own certain completeness.

S063 Maveety, Stanley R. "Doctrine in Tyndale's New Testament: Translation as a Tendentious Art." *SEL* 6 (1966): 151-58.

Maveety explains Tyndale's deliberate transformation of traditional words, such as "priest" to "elder," "confess" to "acknowledge," and others, under the influence of Luther's New Testament, one of the grounds of More's attack on Tyndale's translation.

S064 McCutcheon, R.R. "Heresy and Dialogue: The Humanist Approaches of Erasmus and More." *Viator: Medieval and Renaissance Studies* 24 (1993): 357-84.

McCutcheon compares the way More and Erasmus use the dialogue form in response to the Lutheran "threat" of the early sixteenth century--Erasmus with the *Inquisitio de fide* (in the 1524 edition of his *Colloquies*) and More with his 1529 *Dialogue Concerning Heresies*.

S065 McCutcheon, R.R. "The *Responsio ad Lutherum*: Thomas More's Inchoate Dialogue with Heresy." *SCJ* 22 (1991): 77-90.

Literary dialogue seems the natural medium of religious debate. However, as a genre dialogue presents the Christian apologist not only advantages but also hazards. To enter into an exchange with heresy is to concede it some standing and to imply matters of faith can be arrived at by reason. Even so, in the 1529 *Dialogue Concerning Heresies*, More adopted the form. The 1523 *Responsio ad Lutherum* appears as a sort of embryonic dialogue, adumbrating the role of orality in literary dialogue More could enlist against what he saw as Luther's theological literalism. (See also, R.R. McCutcheon, "Thomas More and the Limits of Dialogue," Diss. Stanford U, 1991.)

S066 McLean, Andrew M. "'Detestynge Thabomynacyon': William Barlow, Thomas More and the Anglican Episcopacy." *Moreana* 49 (1976): 67-77.

McLean discusses the relationship between Barlow's *A Dyaloge Descrybyng the Orygynall Ground of these Lutheran Faccyons* and More's *Confutation of Tyndale's Answer*, which he advises is more illuminating and interesting than simply using Barlow's work as a gloss to More's.

S067 McLean, Andrew M., ed. *The Work of William Barlowe Including "Bishop Barlowe's Dialogue on the Lutheran Factions."* The Courtenay Library of Reformation Classics. 15. Appleford, Berkshire, Eng.: Sutton Courtenay, 1981.

In an essay appended to this edition, "Authorship of the Dialogue," McLean defends Barlow's authorship of the *Dialogue Against the Lutheran Factions* and discusses "a previously unnoticed connection" between More and Barlow (Barlow's conveyance of writings by John Bugenhagen to More in 1525-26 which More mentions in his *Letter to Bugenhagen*). In another essay, "Authorship: An Alternative View," G.E. Duffield argues Barlow wrote the *Dialogue* under duress from More to escape persecution for his alleged Protestant sympathies and concludes that, although Barlow's name appears on the title page, it was "common knowledge" More was the true author, whoever actually wrote it. He also reviews More's career as a religious controversialist and his methods in the treatment of heresy.

S068 Meyer, Carl S. "Thomas More and the Wittenberg Lutherans." *Concordia Theological Monthly* 39 (1968): 245-56.

Meyer examines More's controversies with Luther and Bugenhagen, notes that in none of his attacks against Wittenberg Lutherans does he write against Wittenberg humanist Philipp Melanchthon, and believes this silence is deliberate and due to More's respect and affinity for Melanchthon. He treats More's part in the action taken in early 1526 against the merchants of the Hanseatic League residing in the Steelyard in London and posits that, despite More's milder attitude toward Lutherans in the *Dialogue of Comfort* and in other earlier controversial works, More did not understand Lutheranism. He also looks at the attitudes of the Wittenberg Lutherans toward More and Luther and Melanchthon's reactions to More and Fisher's executions.

S069 Miles, Leland. "John Colet: An Appreciation." *Moreana* 22 (1969): 5-11.

To assess Colet's orthodoxy from the vantage point of sixteenth-century Catholicism, Miles places Colet's doctrinal and theological views against those of More, whom he regards as a reliable criterion of Catholic orthodoxy. Miles notes Colet never attacked heretical works he apparently read as did More and discovers striking contrasts between their views on pilgrimages, holy relics, sainthood, sacraments, scriptural exegesis, prayer, and mystical union. When placed side by side, Colet is far to the left of More on "almost every point of Catholic doctrine and practice."

S070 Miles, Leland. *John Colet and the Platonic Tradition*. London: Allen and Unwin, 1961. 174-79, 185-86, 203-06, 208-09, 213-16.

In this study intended to be the first of three volumes examining the relation of the Platonic tradition to Oxford reformers Colet, More, and Erasmus, Miles contrasts Colet and More's positions on various ecclesiastical and theological matters. He notices Colet condemned clerical immorality and Church abuses more severely than More, that More defended veneration of relics, prayers to saints, the efficacy of sacraments--all of which Colet denied or condemned, that in comparison to More Colet rarely mentions purgatory, that Colet unlike More did not quote Church authorities in interpreting Scripture, and that opposed to Colet's Neoplatonic approach to exegesis of Scripture, More defended the medieval "Four Senses" method. He also points to More's condemnation of Colet's "spiritual religion" in *Dialogue Concerning Heresies* and his active persecution of heretics during his chancellorship.

S071 Miles, Leland. "Protestant Colet and Catholic More: A Study of Contrast in the Use of Platonism." *Anglican Theological Review* 33 (1951): 30-42.

Miles explains the "considerable doctrinal cleavage" between Colet and More, demonstrated in "unique and startling fashion" in *Dialogue Concerning*

Heresies in which More implicitly rejects the "Platonic Religion of the Spirit" Colet endorses, by studying the contrasts between their positions on the nature and significance of the sacraments, the relation of the individual to the Church, and what is necessary to earn salvation. More defended the orthodox "justification by faith and works," whereas Colet advocated the Platonic "justification by love."

S072 Milward, Peter. "A Judgment Judged: C.S. Lewis on the More-Tyndale Controversy." *Moreana* 64 (1980): 28-36.

Milward takes issue with Lewis' view (G054) of the More-Tyndale controversy, asserting that the literary quality of More's polemical writings is not inferior to that of *Utopia* as Lewis claimed, that Lewis did not understand the seriousness of More's intentions as he subjected his opponents to comic abuse, and that More did not misunderstand the ideas of Tyndale and other reformers.

S073 Minns, Denis P. "Thomas More's Use of Scripture in the *Dialogue Concerning Heresies*." *Thomas More: Essays on the Icon.* 71-88.

Minns draws attention to the peculiarities of More's use of Scripture in the *Dialogue* and points out More "does not consistently use Scripture in accordance with any theory of the way it may be legitimately used."

S074 Mozley, J.F. "*The Supper of the Lord*: Tyndale or Joye?" *Moreana* 10 (1966): 11-16.

Mozley discusses the authorship of the anonymous *Supper of the Lord*, an answer to a controversial letter on the sacrament addressed by More to Frith. From internal and external evidence, he attributes it to Tyndale and not, as some, to George Joye.

S075 Mozley, J.F. "Tyndale and More." *William Tyndale*. London: Society for Promoting Christian Knowledge, 1937. 212-38.

In chapter ten, Mozley studies doctrinal, theological, and personal points in the More-Tyndale controversy and focuses on *Dialogue Concerning Heresies* and *Confutation of Tyndale's Answer*. From a literary vantage, *Dialogue* exhibits "much of the charm of the real More," whereas *Confutation* is "hackwork" controversy. From a controversial stance, Mozley finds little to recommend in either tract and objects to More's defense of Church authority and failure to condemn abuses within the Church. Although More had a "nobler side," he never showed it to reformers, and he accuses More, as a religious controversialist, of having sold his liberal and humanist principles for power and wealth.

S076 Murray, Francis. "The Holy Spirit in St. Thomas More's *Confutation to Tyndale's Answer*." *Clergy Review* 42 (1977): 388-92.

Murray explains More's use of the Holy Spirit in the *Confutation* by referring to Paul's first letter to the Corinthians in which he says no one can say and confess Our Lord except by the Holy Spirit.

S077   Muse, Philip John. "Sir Thomas More's *Dialogue Concerning Heresies* and the Shifting of Christian Consciousness in the Early Reformation." Diss. U of Georgia, 1977.

This study concerns the polemical controversy between More and Tyndale as it reflects a basic difference in the perception of religious truth. More was an iconophile and defender of the inherited medieval/Catholic tradition, Tyndale an iconoclast and assailant of that tradition. Further, More saw the individual Christian as capable of participating in the work of his own salvation, with the essential aid of grace and the centuries-old teachings of the Church; Tyndale, on the other hand, like Luther, distrusted mundane institutions and placed his reliance on divine predestination and the concept of justification by faith alone. To More, such a view involved moral blindness, a mistaken belief in one's invulnerability to sin, and even damnation.

S078   Oakley, Francis. "More, St. German, Gerson and Pseudo-Chrysostom on Matthew XXI, 12." *N&Q* ns 10.8 (Aug. 1963): 292-93.

More cites a passage whose authorship is questioned in a letter to St. German in 1532-33.

S079   Ogle, Arthur. "Murder or Suicide? Sir Thomas More in the *Dialogue*." *The Tragedy of the Lollards' Tower. The Case of Richard Hunne and Its Aftermath in the Reformation Parliament, 1529-1533*. Oxford: Pen-in-Hand, 1949. 37-47, 88-112, 278-85, 370-73.

Ogle scrutinizes More's treatment, fourteen years after it occurred, of the Richard Hunne case in his *Dialogue Concerning Heresies* and shows that, while More is absolute in his statement Hunne was a heretic, he is evasive about the suspicious nature of Hunne's death. For Ogle, such evasiveness demonstrates More's attempt to defend Church authority by softening the evil impression the Hunne case created and fourteen years "had in no way lessened." Ogle also looks at More's defense of the clergy in *Dialogue*, his treatment of heretics, and his trial.

S080   Partridge, A.C. *English Biblical Translation*. The Language Library. London: Andre Deutsch, 1973. 5, 34, 37, 40-43, 45-46, 99, 103, 131, 214.

Partridge examines examples from a wide range of English biblical translations, setting analysis within the context of a general discussion of problems besetting the potential translator. Chapters on the sources of the Bible and its texts, and on the English Bible up to Wyclif, lead into an examination of the work of Erasmus and Tyndale. More's case against Tyndale's version of certain fundamental terms as set forth in the *Dialogue Concerning Heresies* is examined, and scholarly justification found for the reformer's renderings.

S081 Pineas, Rainer. "George Joye's Controversy with Thomas More." *Moreana* 38 (1973): 27-36.

In his dispute with More concerning Church authority and the real presence doctrine, the radical Protestant Joye resorts to "various rhetorical devices" and strange accusations and uses contemporary politics rather broadly. Ironic refrains and polemical exemplum are Joye's favorite rhetorical techniques. He charges More with supporting the Roman position only because he is paid to and accuses him of "wholesale forgery," claiming More should not be believed because he is both "poet" and "jester." Joye exploits More's tenuous association with Elizabeth Barton, the Nun of Kent, to reassert Tyndale's theory Catholicism and treason go "hand in hand."

S082 Pineas, Rainer. "George Joye's Polemical Use of Persona." *Forum* 12.2 (1975): 15-21.

More's use of persona (notably in the 1529 *Dialogue*) and "the pose of self-confidence" he maintains (instinctively rather than to obey Quintilian) provide obvious parallels to Joye's technique.

S083 Pineas, Rainer. "George Joye's Use of Rhetoric and Logic as Weapons of Religious Controversy." *ELWIU* 2 (1975): 10-23.

Joye places Fisher and More in hell-fire along with Wolsey "for burning gods worde and the professours thereof." When Joye's charges become more specific, Pineas demonstrates, through quotes and references, that "Joye was here deliberately attempting to vilify More by what we know to be distortions of the truth."

S084 Pineas, Rainer. "More versus Tyndale: A Study of Controversial Technique." *MLQ* 24 (1963): 144-50.

Pineas particularizes the polemic devices which More habitually employs, such as appeal to the Church and the Fathers, the testimony of miracles wrought by God through the Church, the appeal to custom and Scripture, the use of Colet's method of biblical exegesis, logical reasoning, changing his terms within an argument, and innuendo at the opponent's expense. In Tyndale, Pineas notes the frequent use of irony with a humorous by-play distinct from the straight humor of More, quotation from the Bible, and the reduction to absurdity of the opponent's arguments.

S085 Pineas, Rainer. "Polemical *Exemplum* in Sixteenth-Century Religious Controversy." *BHR* 28 (1966): 393-96.

Pineas discusses uses of this device by Tyndale and More against one another in, for instance, the pretense of clarifying discussion, More's attack on

Tyndale's failure to discriminate between "no" and "nay," and Tyndale's irony through indirect attack on the clergy. Pineas attributes the popularity of exemplum to the dual precedent of classical and medieval usage.

S086 Pineas, Rainer. "Polemical Technique in Thomas More's *The Answere to...the Poysened Booke.*" *Miscellanea Moreana: Essays for Germain Marc'hadour. Moreana* 100. 385-93.

Rainer focuses on the polemical devices which derive from More's real or assumed attitude toward his opponent, his opponent's anonymity, and tactics common to all More's polemics; he concludes the historical circumstances in which More wrote the *Answere*, together with his perception of events, combined to rob that work of the acumen displayed in his earlier polemics.

S087 Pineas, Rainer. "Sir Thomas More's Controversy with Christopher Saint-German." *SEL* 1 (1961): 49-62.

Pineas discusses the background to More's *Apologie* and a probable influence upon his technique as a controversialist. St. German's *Diuision...betwyxte the spiritualitie and the temporalitie* (1532), against which much of the *Apologie* is directed, seems to have struck More as especially dangerous on account of its ostensibly mild and impartial spirit. His reply to More's criticism, entitled *A dialogue betwyxte...Salem and...Bizance*, was countered by More in *The Debellacyon of Salem and Bizance*, both works relating to the rival priorities of canon and civil law. Through illustration from the pamphlets of both writers, Pineas demonstrates how palpably and deliberately More adopts St. German's controversial devices, such as the generalization "they say," left-handed compliment, and the complaints of his opponent's inconsistencies, More's object being to tear down St. German's facade of impartiality in the conviction that behind it lay a ruthless desire to destroy the Church and discredit the clergy. If More was, in fact, thus paying back his opponent in the latter's own coin, this was probably intentional.

S088 Pineas, Rainer. *Thomas More and Tudor Polemics*. Bloomington: Indiana UP, 1968.

The historical context of the controversial writings interchanged between More and protagonists of Protestantism from Luther to St. German is linked with analysis of the polemical techniques More and each of his adversaries employ in support of their cases. More's polemical strategy reveals itself as one of defense, his opponents' one of attack. The chapter on More and Tyndale, comprising nearly one-third of the book, examines the main lines of Tyndale's attack, his insistence on the absolute authority of Scripture; appeal to history, especially English chronicles, as evidence of papal aggression; and a method of argumentation revealing "a strong pragmatic, rather than a theoretical, approach." In replying, More defends the authority of the Catholic Church and the papacy as divinely inspired and confirmed by the evidence of history, reason, and logic; he reinforces his arguments with the aid of dramatic dialogue, enlivened by "merry tales," irony, and *reductio ad absurdum* of his opponent's case. His replies to other Protestant apologists demonstrate his dexterity in adapting his methods of argumentation to the case he is answering, his use of vituperative satire, and ironic character-drawing, particularly through mock-assumption of the role and character of his opponent. Pineas shows the progression in the vernacular polemical books of More's involvement in religious controversy and also points to the role it played in the development of the language.

S089 Pineas, Rainer. "Thomas More's Controversy with Simon Fish." *SEL* 7 (1967): 15-28.

Pineas discusses Fish's *A Supplycacioun for Beggars* and More's answer *The Supplicacioun of Soules.* In attacking clergy for allegedly subversive activities, Fish employs "reportial technique" similar to that of Skelton and St. German; More, in replying, uses his opponent's technique together with others, including the appeal to history and the device, popular with contemporary polemicists, of "remolding the record of past events to suit his needs."

S090 Pineas, Rainer. "Thomas More's Use of Humor as a Weapon of Religious Controversy." *SP* 58 (1961): 97-114.

After having illustrated uses of humor as a popular weapon for theological disputation from the works of Erasmus, Luther, Tyndale, and others, Pineas examines modes and features of More's humor as exemplified in his replies to Simon Fish and Tyndale, as well as St. German. One of his favorite artifices, employed to rebut Fish's statistics of clerical and monastic wealth, is to invert his opponent's argument by means of *reductio ad absurdum*. More subtle than this is the introduction, in the *Dialogue*, of a messenger, ostensibly arguing against More on behalf of the reformers, a device clearly allowing unlimited scope for the use of dramatic irony. Another artifice, exploited both in the *Dialogue* and the *Confutacion*, is the introduction of a "merry tale," which serves both to relieve monotony and divert attention from the point at issue. In short, throughout More's controversial works, humor frequently takes the place of direct refutation, with irony and *reductio ad absurdum* doing service for argument. In common with other writers, More deemed it necessary to defend his use of humor in religious controversy.

S091 Pineas, Rainer. "Thomas More's Use of the Dialogue Form as a Weapon of Religious Controversy." *SRen* 7 (1960): 193-206.

In an analysis of More's use of the dialogue form as a weapon of religious controversy, Pineas compares the *Dialogue concernynge heresyes* with contemporary controversial works, religious and secular, noting particularly its dramatic character as conversation between gracious host and guest, enlivened by wit, irony, and incidental narrative, which combine to give an effect of easy disorder contrasting to the scholastic method Fisher employs.

S092 Pineas, Rainer. "Tyndale's Accusation of Forgery against More." *AN&Q* 3 (1965): 68-69.

William Barlow had been a reformer and returned to Catholicism while Tyndale was on the Continent and did not know about his conversion. When Barlow published a book in 1531 describing Lutheran factions and abuses, Tyndale thought Barlow could not have written it and accused More of being its author, especially because William Rastell (More's nephew) printed it.

S093 Pineas, Rainer. "William Tyndale: Controversialist." *SP* 60 (1963): 117-32.

Economy was the chief stylistic principle governing Tyndale's controversy with the Catholic Church. Tyndale's language depends primarily on sarcasm, with infrequent irony and slips of the tongue; he also shows almost no sense of humor. Likewise Tyndale shows little concern for sixteenth-century rules of rhetoric. He understands logic and uses analogy, illustration, appeal to authority (especially Erasmus), and emphasis on the factual, but he is guilty of sophistical and specious reasoning and of such fallacies as *reductio ad absurdum*, begging the question, non sequitur, and misrepresentation out of context. He generally employs the straight treatise or point-by-point answers, usually answering More at his weakest points, but he also invented a "modified dialogue" form characterized by brevity and simplicity, thus making his own writing considerably more popular than More's.

S094 Raban, Sandra. *Mortmain Legislation and the English Church (1279-1500)*. Cambridge Studies in Medieval Life and Thought. 3rd ser. Vol. 17. Cambridge: Cambridge UP, 1982.

The controversy which surrounded mortmain was rendered moot only a year after More's death by the summary confiscation of Church property. However, it remained a partisan issue as late as 1529 when More wrote *Supplication of Souls* in response to Simon Fish's *Supplication for Beggars*. *Souls*, of course, includes a greater range of subjects than mortmain legislation, but Raban's study of it from the first law to 1500 supports the arguments More makes in the *Supplication*.

S095 Rashkow, Ilona Nemesnyik. "Upon the Dark Places: English Renaissance Biblical Translation." Diss. U of Maryland-College Park, 1988.

Rashkow studies differences in and functions of poetic principles between the Hebrew Bible and major versions of the English Renaissance; chapter two discusses the power of the translator to interpret as reflected in the controversy between More and Tyndale.

S096 Rockett, William. "More and St. German: *Ex Officio* and Lay-Clerical Division." *Moreana* 129 (1997): 21-43.

In his dispute with St. German in *Debellatior of Salem and Bizance*, More places unusual importance upon the use of *ex officio* suits to defend practices employed in canon law courts, particularly in heresy trials.

S097 Rogan, Marie Joseph. "More, Fisher, and Rastell and the Dispute Concerning Purgatory with an Edition of John Frith's *Disputacion*." Diss. Fordham U, 1951.

Rogan's introduction and notes provide information about the purgatory controversy in general and details about More, Fisher, Rastell, and Frith's roles in it.

S098 Rogers, Elizabeth Frances. "Sir Thomas More's Letter to Bugenhagen." *Modern Churchman* 35 (1946): 350-60.

Rogers explains why More wrote the *Letter*, describes its method and style, establishes its date of composition as sometime in 1526, and probes key points it presents. Rogers also notes the *Letter*, which was not published until 1568, reached a small audience in More's time and was not even mentioned by Bugenhagen's biographer. Although it failed to convince Bugenhagen and other Lutherans, Church leaders, especially Tunstall (who licensed More to read and refute heretical books in 1528), respected More's *Letter*. (Rpt. in *Essential Articles for the Study of Thomas More*, 447-54.)

S099 Schaeffer, John D. "Dialogue and Faith in More's Humanism: Voice and Belief in the Structure of the *Dialogue Concerning Tyndale*." Diss. St. Louis U, 1971.

Schaeffer investigates the relation of the dialogue form and Patristic theology to the content and purpose of the *Dialogue Concerning Tyndale* to show how More structures the work so readers, identifying with More's antagonist, feel they have shared existentially in More's own faith.

S100 Schoeck, R.J. "Common Law and Canon Law in the Writings of Thomas More: The Affair of Richard Hunne." *Proceedings of the Third International Congress of Medieval Canon Law. Strasbourg, 3-6 September 1968.* Ed. Stephan Kuttner. Monumenta Juris Canonici. Ser. C: Subsidia. Vol. 4. City of the Vatican: Biblioteca Apostolica, 1971. 237-54.

After an account of the Hunne affair and the related debate of Kidderminster and Standish about the jurisdictional prerogatives of the ecclesiastical courts, Schoeck probes how the Hunne affair influenced not only More's career and thought but also his treatment of the affair in several of his polemical works. Although More was careful never to present his complete view of the affair, More was convinced Hunne was a heretic who had committed suicide (and not been murdered as some assumed), and that in the conflict between common and canon law, More probably rejected the idea Parliament could solve "disputed points of canon law."

S101 Schoeck, R.J. "The Most Erudite of Christian Lawyers, Christopher St. German." *JRMMRA* 4 (1983): 107-24.

Schoeck notices how the writings of John Guy (F097), J.B. Trapp (B003), and others have begun to clarify the significant contribution St. German made to the strategies of Henry VIII and Cromwell after about 1530. Perhaps because More knew St. German had the ear of the king himself, More hesitated to name St. German in the *Apology* and *Debellation*, though as yet scholars cannot be certain More did not know the author of the *Doctor and Student* and other controversial writings by name.

S102 Schoeck, R.J. "The Use of St. John Chrysostom in Sixteenth-Century Controversy: Christopher St. German and Sir Thomas More in 1533." *HTR* 54 (1961): 21-27.

In the theological controversies between More and St. German which also involved the conflict between common law and Roman law in England, a quotation, first used by St. German, is then accepted and repeated by More as coming from Chrysostom's commentary on Matthew. Schoeck discovers this quote is not from Chrysostom, but he is undecided as to whether More knew this. Though More refers to the work and to the quote in his *Confutation*, in this treatise he claims the quote is not from Chrysostom.

S103 Schuster, Louis A. "Reformation Polemic and Renaissance Values." *Moreana* 43-44 (1974): 47-54.

The Reformation debate between More and Tyndale was supported by two systems that seem opposed and mutually exclusive, but from the deeper level of today's perspective often prove complementary. One of the main reasons for this disjunction in creed and cult that characterized Reformation polemic lay in the nature of the polemical process. Since the polemical mode is committed to a problematic of exclusiveness, it follows almost inevitably that each opponent would preempt a series of positions advocating only a partial view of his complete vision and the value system that nurtured it. Beneath the preoccupations with faith and works, the true Church, authority, and conscience lay the fundamental critical issue of the Reformation debate between More and Tyndale; namely, the question of certitude in salvation.

S104 Schuster, Louis A. "Sir Thomas More, Polemicist of Christendom." *ForumH* 9 (1971): 42-45.

Controversy between More and Tyndale illustrates the dynamics of the polemical mode, which operates on a problematic of exclusiveness and proceeds by a series of either-or propositions. It usually begins in the order of action with one polemicist preempting a position, which tends to polarize an antithetical position which in turn is relegated to the opposing party. After the preemption-polarization process is effected, both positions of protagonist and antagonist crystallize. As either party becomes more solidly entrenched in his viewpoint, attempts at dialogue and resolution of differences become increasingly futile. The sundering and fragmentation of Christendom was conducted in such a divisive mode and process.

S105 Sinclair, Malcolm. "Saint Thomas More's 'Good Scottish Frere.'" *Moreana* 14 (1977): 53-54.

The Scottish friar mentioned in *Dialogue Concerning Heresies* may have been Donald Gilbert. Until a better alternative candidate is proposed, he seems the most likely.

S106 Smelser, Marshall. "The Political Philosophy of Sir Thomas More As Expressed in His Theological Controversies." *St. Louis University Studies in Honor of St. Thomas Aquinas* 1 (1943): 12-32.

After an introduction to the continental and English backgrounds against which More lived, Smelser explores More's polemical works for their political ideas on the problem of toleration, the proper relation between Church and state, the nature and source of royal authority, international relations; and the nature, sanction, classification, and true variety of the law. Smelser finds More's political philosophy makes him a "medieval theorist in a national state protecting Christian unity with his life against the disintegration of the European civilization into which he had been born."

S107 Sodeman, Nancy R. "More's Use of Amplification in Two Dialogues." Diss. Georgia State U, 1976.

Sodeman shows rhetorical devices of amplification strengthen the arguments in *Dialogue Concerning Heresies* and *Dialogue of Comfort* by being used in fallacies, topics of arguments, and figures, including schemes, tropes, and figures of thought. More's handling of these devices ultimately is responsible for his development of a more original, personal dialogue form centered less on the procedure of debate and focused more on the process of meditation through dialogue.

S108 Sodeman, Nancy R. "Rhetoric in More's English Dialogues." *Moreana* 59-60 (1978): 13-18.

Sodeman compares *Dialogue Concerning Heresies* with *Dialogue of Comfort*, with respect to the devices of amplification--use of fallacies, topics of argument, and figures of thought--as they are employed within three modes of persuasion (appeals to reason, to emotion, and to the speaker's personality) and notes the progress to a more exploratory, meditative, and personal effect.

S109   Sylvester, R.S. "Thomas More and 'The Further I Go, The More Behind.'" *N&Q* ns 9 (1962): 370-71.

Sylvester comments on More's citation of these lines from a popular ballad at the close of the *Dialogue Concerning Heresies* and, four years later, in his *Confutation of Tyndale's Answer*. Whereas in the former, More makes use of the tag in defense of the Church's authority; in the latter, he reverses his tactics by applying it to Tyndale's faulty method of argument.

S110   Walker, Greg. "The Image of Dissent: John Skelton, Thomas More, and the 'Lost' History of the Early Reformation in England." *Persuasive Fictions: Factions, Faith and Political Culture in the Reign of Henry VIII*. Aldershot, Hants, Eng.: Scolar P, 1996. 166-77.

Chapter seven considers how More attacks the trial for heresy of young scholar Thomas Bilney in *Dialogue Concerning Heresies*, although More does not name him "outright."

Devotional Works

T001 Billingsley, Dale B. "'Imagination' in *A Dialogue of Comfort.*" *Moreana* 74 (1982): 57-63.

Billingsley describes how More turns again, in that work, to the problem of the disciplined imagination, and solves it not by renouncing the images of the world, but by replacing them with a single image--the suffering and crucified Christ--which allows More to place his suffering in the proper framework.

T002 Billingsley, Dale B. "'Resources of Kind' in *A Dialogue of Comfort.*" *Moreana* 74 (1982): 64-68.

Billingsley maintains that while the number of kinds in *A Dialogue*--digression, excursus, and the imitation of other kinds, whether literary, subliterary or extraliterary--is great, each of the three books takes one kind as its keynote, and Anthony governs the change from one kind to another. More shows throughout the *Dialogue* that he is willing to exploit any device to remedy the weakness of human nature, "shifting kindly from one means to another to secure his end."

T003 Birchenough, Edwyn. "The Book of Hours." *Moreana* 6 (1965): 65-67.

Birchenough enlarges upon Marc'hadour's "A Godly Meditation" (T029) by providing a bibliographical description of the Book of Hours (More wrote "A Godly Meditation" on its margins) and by discussing the typical spiritual uses and arrangement of such books of prayer during More's times.

T004 Byron, Brian. "From Essence to Presence: A Shift in Eucharistic Expression Illustrated from the Apologetics of St. Thomas More." *Miscellanea Moreana: Essays for Germain Marc'hadour. Moreana* 100. 429-41.

Byron maintains More's Patristic texts, especially *Treatise Upon the*

Passion, illustrate a shift in expression between the Church Fathers and the age of the Scholastics. That shift was from expressions of *what the Eucharist is* (the Body and Blood of Christ) to *what is in the Eucharist* (the Body and Blood of Christ are present in the Eucharist), and Byron cites the texts More used in his own translation.

T005 Celestine, Sr. "Thomas More and Dialogue." *WisSL* 2 (1965): 1-10.

More's *Dialogue of Comfort* synthesizes the best in the Platonic-Augustinian tradition of dialogue. It displays a Socratic informality and flexibility of structure and a tolerance of opposing views as well as an Augustinian purpose to advance the soul to perfection and to view human experience in the light of Divine Providence. Vincent's three visits to his eighty-year old Uncle Anthony provide the fictional framework for and the three-book division of the *Dialogue*, and the problem of whether it is possible to derive comfort in tribulation is pursued through the interplay of free discussion in which rhetorical devices are used admirably to serve functional purposes.

T006 Clark, James Arthur. "More and Tyndale as Prose Stylists: Finding Directions in *A Dialogue of Comfort* and *The Practice of Prelates*." *Moreana* 82 (1984): 5-17.

Clark adds to C.S. Lewis' observations (G054) about More's "lively humor" and Tyndale's "powerful intensity" by tracing stylistic differences in their word choices, rhythms, and rhetorical strategies to their sources in their convictions and methods. Paradox and an evocative, leisurely, subtle indirection characterize More's prose style; whereas bluntness, immediacy, and directness mark Tyndale's.

T007 Domingo Malvadi, Arantxa. "Un Noveau Manuscrit de More en Espagne." *Moreana* 127-28 (1996): 57-60.

Domingo Malvadi describes a ms. of More's *Dialogue of Comfort* (translated from Latin to French and from French to English) in the Bibliothèque Royale de Madrid.

T008 Donner, H.W. "St. Thomas More's Treatise on the Four Last Things and the Gothicism of the Transalpine Renaissance." *EM* 3 (1952): 25-48.

Donner speculates on the influence which may have inspired More's unfinished *Four Last Things* in about or in 1521--fear of death by political broil, pestilence, famine, or war; "fear of being taken unawares, of dying without the chance of repentance and so being condemned to eternal torment." Because of the work's Gothic naturalism and highly visual details and images that align it with the Gothicism of the transalpine Renaissance, Donner rejects claims classical sources, mainly Plato's *Phaedo*, influence the treatise; the *Valdo Mori* poems, *Memento Mori* verses, *specula hominis*, *Everyman*, the *Three Living and* the *Three Dead*, the *ars moriendi*, and the *Dance of Death* provide inspiration for *Four Last Things*. (Rpt. in *Essential Articles for the Study of Thomas More*, 343-55.)

T009 Finan, Thomas. "Some More Comforts: More and the Consolatory Tradition." *Irish Theological Quarterly* 45 (1978): 205-16.

Finan discusses the theme of "the just man's tribulation and his quest for comforting" in the *Dialogue of Comfort* and its relationship to the "consolatory tradition." He finds More is ultimately less interested in attempting to justify God's ways to man and more concerned with explaining "the great psychological temptations that threaten to deflect understanding from the solution and resolution provided by faith, hope, and charity" which are the "successive foci" of the three books of the *Dialogue*. Finan also describes the relationship between More's treatment of the theme of tribulation and his use of humor and paradox.

T010 Fisher, Bernard. "English Spiritual Writers: St. Thomas More." *Clergy Review* ns 45 (1960): 1-10.

In a discussion of "A Godly Meditation" (1534) and "A Devout Prayer" (1535) as a means of understanding More's spirituality, Fisher examines their theological accuracy, the influence of Walter Hinton, the Carthusian roots of More's spirituality, his devotion to the dogma of the mystical Body, and the chance for prayer and meditation his imprisonment provided. Fisher reminds readers three-fourths of More's writings are either ascetical or theological and that his devotional works are deeply influenced by the English mystics, though couched in the careful language of the lawyer. The rhythm of More's life was founded upon faith; therefore, "the only way to understand More's spirituality is to start from the prayers, and to use his ascetical and theological works as a commentary...upon them."

T011 Foord, Bede. "Thomas More and the *Rule of St. Benedict*." *Moreana* 16 (1979): ii, 45-47.

Foord likens the prayers of petition written in the margins of More's prayer book to chapter four of the *Rule*.

T012 Gest, John B. "Thomas More's Prayer Book." *Catholic Lawyer* 16 (1970): 274.

Gest praises Martz and Sylvester's edition of the Prayer Book (B016).

T013 Gibson, R.W. "St. Thomas More's Book of Hours." *BC* 9 (1960): 202.

Gibson describes More's Book of Hours.

T014 Gordon, Walter M. "Suicide in Thomas More's *Dialogue of Comfort*." *ABR* 29 (1978): 358-70.

Gordon argues the lengthy section on suicide in Book II of the *Dialogue* is "best explained" within the literary framework of the work as a whole. Given the "perilous atmosphere" within which the *Dialogue* was written and is set, it is apparent why the topic of suicide fits within its logical, thematic plan, for it forms one possible consideration of the central conflict--the question of how to deal with the soul's struggle against evil and temptation.

T015 Gordon, Walter M. "Tragic Perspective in Thomas More's Dialogue with Margaret in the Tower." *Cithara* 17 (1978): 3-12.

Gordon stresses how the Tower dialogue (transcribed in a letter by Margaret Roper to Alice Alington) captures a trying moment in the lives of father and daughter and develops their meeting in a manner suggestive of tragedy. This final exchange reduces to essence the actual concerns of each. What Margaret fears most is her father will hold to a position which he, in turn, begs God for the strength to maintain. More regards change as outright defection; Margaret only sees it as a means to avoid the worst--her father's execution.

T016 Gruffyd, R. Geraint. "A Prayer of St. Thomas More's in Welsh, 1587." *Moreana* 13 (1967): 45-52.

Gruffyd writes More's prayer, "Give me thy grace, good Lord, to despise the world," appears in a Catholic devotional book printed on a secret press in a cave, Little Orme's Head, near Llandudno, Caernarvonshire, between 1586 and 1587.

T017 Hanna, Ralph III. "Two New Texts of More's *Dialogue of Comfort*." *Moreana* 74 (1982): 5-11.

Hanna examines the "at least two further" sixteenth-century ms. texts that the editors of the Yale edition of *Dialogue* (B009) overlooked and argues that the variants of H, together with those of G, may offer helpful information on the transmission of More's work in the years down to 1555.

T018 Haupt, Garry E. "The Personal and the Impersonal in the Late Works of Sir Thomas More." *Interpretations: Studies in Language and Literature* 6 (1974): 14-23.

In his later works, especially the Latin and English treatises on the Passion, More fuses the personal and impersonal (as exhibited by tradition and the Church and state) which, Haupt posits, is typical of northern humanism. In doing so, More heals the dissociation of head and heart characteristic of late medieval Scholasticism and achieves a "psychic balance" between the personal contents of the mind and impersonal forces outside the mind.

T019 Himelick, Raymond. "Walter Ralegh and Thomas More: The Uses of Decapitation." *Moreana* 42 (1974): 59-64.

Himelick finds More anticipates Ralegh's image of decapitation in "The Passionate Man's Pilgrimage" in *Dialogue of Comfort Against Tribulation*: "Ralegh is graphic and circumstantial where More...is laconic; but the conceit is the same."

T020 Hosington, Brenda. "'Quid dormitis?': More's Use of Sleep As a Motif in *De Tristitia*." *Miscellanea Moreana: Essays for Germain Marc'hadour. Moreana* 100. 55-69.

Hosington provides a stylistic examination in which she claims the work's references to sleep fulfill a triple function: structurally, they develop the discussion of the events of the agony in the garden and their significance; thematically, they convey two main ideas about martyrdom and prayer; and, rhetorically, they take form through More's sense of drama and his use of irony, digression, repetition, and rhetorical question.

T021 Hutchinson, F.E. "Sir Thomas More as a Translator of the Bible." *RES* 17 (1942): 1-10.

Hutchinson comments on the more than 200 biblical citations contained in *Dialogue of Comfort* and *The Four Last Things* and says they illustrate More's competence as a translator and sense of rhythm and diction. He also praises More's ability to use the English idiom in his translations rather than the Latin or Greek words some translators try to preserve.

T022 Jones, Judith P. "The Polemical Nature of Thomas More's *A Dialogue of Comfort*." Diss. Auburn U, 1975.

Jones analyzes the structure of *Dialogue* and compares it to the polemical treatises to show More's purpose in this *Dialogue* was both polemical and meditative and that the polemical theme joins with the meditative one to produce unified treatment of the comforts in tribulation.

T023 Jones, Judith P. "The Structure of Thomas More's *A Dialogue of Comfort*." *SPWVSRA* 2 (1978): 20-29.

Jones demonstrates More's conscious, skillful construction of the *Dialogue* by examining the internal structure of each of the three books and their complex structural relationships, which More achieves through his fusion of disparate elements, "intertwining" of themes, use of foreshadowing, and repetition throughout of the dependence of comfort and instruction. She shows how the comfort theme of Book I and the tribulation and temptation themes of Book II meet in the meditation of martyrdom in Book III, how the earlier themes look forward to the meditation theme, and how the figure of the Turk (introduced in

Book I, used throughout, and dominant in Book III) is an allegorical representation of the Lutheran threat and a way to tie the tribulation theme of Book I to the temptation theme of Books II and III.

T024 Khanna, Lee Cullen. "Truth and Fiction in *A Dialogue of Comfort*." *Moreana* 65-66 (1980): 57-66.

Khanna traces connections between a central theme--the nature of truth--and the literary devices expressing it and concludes the quest for truth in the troubled times in which More found himself during his imprisonment is assisted, paradoxically enough, by fictions: an exotic setting, imaginative characters who experiment with different roles, a complex use of figurative language. For Khanna, Book I marks the difference between limited human understanding and the divine knowledge and truth, to which man must submit. Book II, however, presents man not as passive but as active participant in the game of life; the book contains a crucial discussion of the difficulty of distinguishing between reality and dream, revelation and illusion: in this world, truth can be apprehended only indirectly through metaphor, paradox, fiction, and role-playing. In Book III, the metaphor of the prison is introduced, questioned, and confirmed: "fantasy" is "very plain truth."

T025 Kuhn, Joaquin. "The Function of Psalm 90 in Thomas More's *A Dialogue of Comfort*." *Moreana* 22 (1969): 61-67.

Kuhn describes Psalm 90's structural and thematic importance in the *Dialogue*. Because it is traditionally the main psalm of the liturgical hour of compline and is recited before sleep to free the mind from the devil's tricks, its rich associations suit the *Dialogue* well, for in it More is praying for help and comfort against the many enemies to his faith.

T026 Manzalaoui, Mahmoud. "'Syria' in the *Dialogue of Comfort*." *Moreana* 8 (1965): 21-27.

More, who had referred to Syria earlier in *Utopia*, refers to it three times in the *Dialogue*, eighteen years later. The defeat of Syria More evidently is alluding to is the collapse of the Mameluke kingdom of Egypt and Syria. On the basis of these references, Manzalaoui calculates the two Hungarian interlocutors (Anthony and Vincent) are about eighty and twenty years of age respectively and thus represent old age and youth "meeting together to discuss a problem of faith and conscience" so the younger man may learn through the older of comfort against and through suffering. Because More's age at the time he wrote *Dialogue* is just about halfway between those of Anthony and Vincent, Manzalaoui suggests they may represent two aspects of More himself, a kind of symbolic splitting of his personality, which may present the debate going on within him.

T027 Marc'hadour, Germain. "For the Winning of Christ." *Westminster Cathedral Chronicle* 59 (1965): 84-86.

Although Marc'hadour is mainly concerned with More's prayers in the Tower (especially those written in the margins of his *Book of Hours*), he discusses his prayer-like writings throughout his life.

T028 Marc'hadour, Germain. "Le *Dialogue de Réconfort* au péril des interprètes." *Moreana* 113 (1993): 27-54.

More's *Dialogue of Comfort against Tribulation* (1534) was not printed until 1553, and the next edition (1557) stems from a different ms. The initial "peril" thus lies in establishing More's text by arbitrating between the handwritten and printed copies: the Yale edition (B009) differs significantly from the Everyman (C038). A worse peril of betrayal besets "modernizers"; even if they alter only the spelling, they are apt to read "own" as "one," "whither" as "whether," and so on. Translation began with Stapleton's Latin excerpts (1588) and flowered in a succession of vernaculars--French (1959), Italian (1970), Spanish and German (both 1988). The last two are here reviewed with special care. The words of the title provide choice samples for gauging their fidelity. Other specimens take into account the theological virtues which underlie the work's three-book structure, stylistic traits of More's prose, and his "merry" spirit.

T029 Marc'hadour, Germain. "'A Godly Meditation.'" *Moreana* 5 (1965): 53-72.

Marc'hadour provides a description of how this prayer is written in the margins of thirty-seven entries spread over nineteen pages of More's Prayer Book and shows it was probably composed in 1534 rather than 1535. By comparing the handwriting of the prayer to that in the autograph copy of More's *Expositio Passionis* (*De Tristita*), Marc'hadour proves it is written in More's own hand; he also uses this comparison (complete with reproductions from the prayer and *Expositio*) as a way to discuss some of the distinctive features of More's handwriting.

T030 Marc'hadour, Germain. "More's Book of Hours." *Moreana* 7 (1965): 101-06.

Marc'hadour describes the Latin Primer in which More wrote "A Godly Meditation," gives information about the Book's publication, discusses the condition of More's copy, and lists the Book's sections and their contents.

T031 Marc'hadour, Germain. "St. Thomas More." *Month* ns 29 (1963): 69-84.

Marc'hadour considers More's spiritual attitudes and principles in his works, especially his letters and devotional writings; singles out More's "intense devotion" to the mystical Body of Christ as their most striking feature, the "central piece of his doctrinal construction"; detects a connection between his thoughts on the mystical Body and the unity of the Church, consensus, the Eucharistic mystery, the doctrine of purgatory, and meaning of companionship and community in life; and discusses More's devotion to the Passion of Christ, his attitude toward death, the beneficial role he gives to suffering and tribulation, and his ideas about how to meet temptation.

T032 Marc'hadour, Germain. "Three Tudor Editors of Thomas More." *Editing Sixteenth-Century Texts*. Papers Given at the Editorial Conference, University of Toronto, October 1965. Ed. R.J. Schoeck. Toronto: U of Toronto P, 1966. 59-71.

The three editors of More Marc'hadour assesses are Richard Tottel, whose *editio princeps* of the *Dialogue of Comfort* (1553) is characterized by poor paper and typing and crude misspelling of Latin quotations; William Rastell, editor of More's *English Works* (1557); and John Fowler, a Bristol recusant, who reprinted the *Dialogue* at Antwerp in 1573, possibly from a ms. other than that used by Tottel, adding many glosses and grammatical emendations. Collation of the three texts of the *Dialogue* shows tampering with the original text, giving an impression of haste, and leading to the conclusion, "Not only for scripture, but in other sentences internal evidence will often reveal the superiority of the drab, unprepossessing Tottel."

T033 Marc'hadour, Germain. "With a Coal?" *Moreana* 13 (1967): 107-08.

Marc'hadour disagrees with the sequence of events and books Miles describes in his "With a Coal?" (T046) and believes More's *English History of the Passion* belongs to the time between his *Answer to a Poisoned Book* (finished no later than 1 December 1533) and his imprisonment (April 1534) and that *How to receive the blessed body* may also belong to that period. He asserts there is "no need to ascribe a deadline" to when the *Dialogue of Comfort* was finished and no reason to place the interruption of the *Expositio Passionis* before June 1535.

T034 Martz, Louis L. "The Design of More's *Dialogue of Comfort*." *Moreana* 15-16 (1967): 331-46.

Contrary to the assumption of readers who believe the *Dialogue* is "rough and uncorrected," Martz asserts it possesses "all the signs of More's finest literary skill"--detailed language, complete development, careful planning and writing. Martz analyzes the "broader aspects of design" within and between the work's three books to demonstrate its logical development and unity and sees a movement from moral theory (Book I) to practical experience and the inadequacy of human reason to cope with temptation (Book II) to meditation as the best way to overcome tribulation (Book III).

T035 Martz, Louis L. "Thomas More: The Sacramental Life." *Thought* 52 (1977): 300-18.

Martz focuses on the style, tone, and content of the Tower Works and draws similarities and differences among them to present key ideas in More's spirituality and to trace his movement from the world of affairs to the inner world of private devotion. He spends the most time on More's Latin treatise on the Passion, *De Tristitia*, and wonders why More, who had written an earlier English treatise on the Passion, changed from English to Latin for his treatment of Christ's capture and agony; he also points to the Erasmian influences in the work and analyzes the humanistic mode in which it is written. In addition, Martz considers More's final polemical book, *Answer to the Poisoned Book*, in relation to his late devotional writing and maintains both More's later polemics and the Tower Works reflect a central spiritual concern--to prevent a breach between flesh and spirit--and he stresses the Eucharist as central in More's spirituality.

T036 Martz, Louis L. "Thomas More: The Tower Works." *St. Thomas More: Action and Contemplation*. 57-83.

Martz uses internal and external evidence to prove the order of composition and to stress thematic unity in More's last writing. The *Dialogue of Comfort*, the brief *Treatise to Receive the Blessed Body of our Lord* (which Martz believes to be a missing part of the *Treatise on the Passion*), the meditations and prayers, and the last letters provide "our best account of More's conduct during his interrogations and imprisonment, our best account of his state of mind, and, it is not perhaps too much to say, some of his finest works of art." More's art of improvisation and exploration "allows for long digressions, excursions, and familiar asides, but in the end it reveals, lying under and within all its apparent wandering, a firm and central line, a teleological structure, based on a goal never forgotten."

T037 Martz, Louis and R.S. Sylvester. "Thomas More's Prayer Book." *YULG* 43 (1968): 53-80.

This article includes a lengthy bibliographical description of More's Prayer Book which is actually composed of two printed books--a Latin Book of Hours and a Latin Psalter. The authors also comment on how its marginalia reflect More's thoughts.

T038 McNabb, Vincent. "More's *History of the Passion*." *Blackfriars* 22 (1941): 338-48.

McNabb assesses More's Latin *Treatise on the Passion* (*De Tristita*) and discusses the circumstances of its composition, its English translation by Mary Basset (More's granddaughter), the publication of Basset's translation in Rastell's 1557 edition of More's *English Works*, and the work's significance as a dialogue between More and Christ. He also relates the Latin *Treatise* to *Utopia* and the *Dialogue of Comfort*.

T039 Miles, Leland. "Boethius and More's *Dialogue of Comfort*." *ELN* 3 (1965): 97-101.

Comparing the *Dialogue* with *De Consolatione Philosophiae*, Miles traces parallelism between three chapters of the former and the rationale Boethius employs to justify the notion misfortunes are blessings in disguise. In listing the main types of material pleasures, More follows the same order as Boethius, to whom he refers favorably in a letter, and whose book is included in the Nostell painting of the More family. Furthermore, Anthony, in the *Dialogue*, speaks "as a sort of Boethian Lady Philosopher."

T040 Miles, Leland. "The *Dialogue of Comfort* and More's Execution: Some Comments on Literary Purpose." *MLR* 61 (1966): 556-60.

Although More may have written the *Dialogue* either as a means of preparing Tudor Catholics for future persecution or as a comfort to his family, it is more likely it served as a source of strength for himself. Tortured by fear of a terrible death by disembowelment or beheading, More sought to prepare himself for the worst through constant references to painful death.

T041 Miles, Leland. "The Literary Artistry of Thomas More: The *Dialogue of Comfort*." *SEL* 6 (1966): 7-33.

Miles reviews the book's structure, sources, allegory, autobiographical elements, dramatic and rhetorical techniques, and poetic devices to illustrate More's effective use of characterization, suspense, climax, and anecdote, and mastery of argumentation, all of which were quickened by literary gifts denied expression in other works.

T042 Miles, Leland. "More's *Dialogue of Comfort* as a First Draft." *SP* 63 (1966): 126-34.

Unnecessary repetition, eccentric chapter division, intermittent dismissal of the technique of dialogue, structural false starts, disruptive and irrelevant digressions, and contradictions in thought from one part of the treatise to another all suggest the *Dialogue* is a first draft, a classic that might have been, not a finished masterpiece.

T043 Miles, Leland. "Patristic Comforters in More's *Dialogue of Comfort*." *Moreana* 8 (1965): 9-20.

The Patristic fathers, More's "old holy doctors," were a source of comfort second only to the Bible during his imprisonment. Although Augustine was the most important of the fathers for More, in the final chapter of *Dialogue*, he understandably turns to the theme of the courage of the early martyrs.

T044 Miles, Leland. "Persecution and the *Dialogue of Comfort*: A Fresh Look at the Charges Against Thomas More." *Journal of British Studies* 5 (1965): 19-30.

More's own later action against heretics contradicts his doctrine of religious toleration in *Utopia*; he stands guilty of persecution according to his own definition in the *Dialogue of Comfort*. Miles "takes a fresh look" at these charges leveled against More occasioned by his attitude about persecution and concludes the argument over his alleged inconsistency is irrelevant, because More simply changed his mind on the subject during his life.

T045 Miles, Leland. "Thomas More's Sources." *N&Q* ns 11.10 (Oct. 1964): 388.

Miles lists quotations from the *Dialogue of Comfort* and asks if readers can identify their sources.

T046 Miles, Leland. "With a Coal? The Composition of Thomas More's *Dialogue of Comfort*." *PQ* 45 (1966): 437-42.

Miles pursues More's reported statement the *Dialogue* was "for the most part written with no other pen than a coal," thereby confirming evidence that for a time, during his imprisonment, he was without conventional writing materials.

T047 Miller, Clarence H. "Another Eye-Witness (c. 1690) of the Valencia Holograph." *Moreana* 61 (1979): 5-7.

Sometime between 1688 and 1697, the Spanish priest Pedro Caber o Sebastian saw the holograph of More's *De Tristitia Christi* in the reliquary closet of the Patriarca (Royal College and Seminary of Corpus Christi) at Valencia. Mention of this holograph supplies one more bit of information to fill out the history of this most valuable ms.

T048 Miller, Clarence H. "The Heart of the Final Struggle: More's Commentary on the Agony in the Garden." *Quincentennial Essays on St. Thomas More*. 108-23.

Miller traces the history and transmission of the holograph copy of *De Tristitia*, describes More's exegetical method, and provides three reasons why the ms. of More's Latin treatise is especially valuable. He speculates upon More's identification of his own ordeal, in *De Tristitia*, with Christ's agony in the garden, and argues More, a reluctant and fearful martyr, and one profoundly in touch with the Church throughout the ages, found the ultimate ground of his witnessing in loyalty to the person of Christ.

T049 Miller, Clarence H. "The Holograph of More's *Expositio Passionis*, a Brief History." *Moreana* 15-16 (1967): 372-79.

Miller discusses the rediscovery of the holograph of the *Expositio* (*De Tristitia*) at the Royal College of Corpus Christi (Valencia) and explains its transmission and how it wound up in Valencia.

T050 Norland, Howard B. "Comfort Through Dialogue: More's Response to Tribulation." *Moreana* 93 (1987): 53-66.

Norland explores how More chooses the dialogue form for his last English work written in the Tower, but draws upon a tradition far different from those utilized in his previous writing. Lucianic irony and religious controversy are put aside as More in *Dialogue of Comfort* focuses upon the spiritual crisis he perceived both in his world and in himself. More's method is closer to the Ciceronian dialogue form, which typically focuses upon a principal speaker, and that, like Petrarch and Augustine before him, More uses the dialogue form to examine his vulnerable self and find a higher truth in reaffirming his commitment to God.

T051 O'Donnell, Anne M. "Cicero, Gregory the Great, and Thomas More: Three Dialogues of Comfort." *Miscellanea Moreana: Essays for Germain Marc'hadour. Moreana* 100. 169-97.

O'Donnell compares the uses of dialogue, a favorite classical and humanist form, in Cicero's *Tusculan Disputations*, Gregory's *Dialogues*, and More's *Dialogue of Comfort*, by focusing on their authors, the dialogue form, the settings, the times, the double speakers (both mentors and disciples), major themes and moral exempla, and general resemblances.

T052 O'Malley, John W. "Thomas More's Spirituality Compared." *Thought* 52 (1977): 319-23.

O'Malley believes More's spirituality combines Gothic detail with humanist breadth of theme, invests the Passion and real presence with a significance about the unity of heaven and earth, and cultivates inner devotion while expanding himself as the king's good servant. The convergence of these elements in More's spirituality, as expressed in his last writings, precludes that spirituality's being falsely identified with either late-medieval or Italian-Renaissance piety, though the affinities with the former seem stronger.

T053 Polansky, Janet Michaelle. "The Dialogue of Redemptive History in More's *Dialogue of Comfort against Tribulation*." Diss. Tulane U, 1980.

More's discourse is apologetic, perceiving an alteration in the progress of redemptive history which demands legitimizing fundamental values. The background of Suleiman's victory at Mohacz portends the decline of Christendom and the rise of apostasy, as More's image of the Turk comments on the Henrician policy. The controlling image of the Mystical Body shows an *ecclesia* fragmented, diseased, and in need of consolation and transformation. Contemporary events are placed in the context of individual and communal redemption. Dialogue structure recapitulates redemptive history, capturing the dialectic between temporal and eternal within a synthesis subsuming contradictory imperatives in a closing apocalyptic exhortation.

T054 Pujals, Esteban. "Tomás Moro y su *Diálogo de la Fortaleza contra la Tribulación.*" *Moreana* 105 (1991): 81-83.

Pujals provides an interpretation and appreciation of *Dialogue of Comfort* within the context of some of More's other devotional works.

T055 Purcell, Maureen. "Dialogue of Comfort for Whom?" *Thomas More: Essays on the Icon.* 89-108.

In dealing with the *Dialogue of Comfort*, Purcell proposes this answer to the question her article's title poses: "not for every man, unless he cast off the devil, leave aside his pusillanimity, his self-deception; not for the gamblers with salvation." She also compares More's treatment of the subject with Juliana of Norwich's *Revelations of Divine Love.* The "comfort" in question is expensive; those who can afford it have their treasury in heaven.

T056 Russell, J. Stephen. "More's *Dialogue* and the Dynamics of Comfort." *Moreana* 65-66 (1980): 41-55.

Russell takes issue with the notion its three-part division precludes association within a unified structure; searches for the form, tactic, or dynamic within which all parts operate; and specifically examines the work as a reading experience. Book I displays a failure of rhetoric, where Anthony imparts theologically sound matter in an unpersuasive, uncomforting manner; Book II shows a conscious reaction, proceeding by relaxed humor and anecdote, enabling Vincent to cope and to see absurd humanity sheltered beneath God's wings; Book III reconciles the matter and manner of the first two books when Vincent is taught to laugh at all earthly life, to turn to a comforting *contemptus mundi* and to return to God.

T057 Santinello, Giovanni. "Thomas More's *Expositio Passionis.*" *Studi sull'Umanesimo Europeo.* Padua: Editrice Antenore, 1969. 116-28.

Santinello relates More's *Expositio Pasionis* (*De Tristitia*) to the debate between Erasmus and Colet (thirty-five years earlier) over the meaning of Christ's agony in the garden and contends More's exposition is free of the controversial tone of the Erasmus-Colet exchange, because it was written for the purpose of meditation, comfort, and devotion. He also writes that More resolves the Erasmus-Colet opposition, and he examines the *Expositio* in terms of More's personal situation. (Rpt. in *Essential Articles for the Study of Thomas More*, 455-61.)

T058 Schoeck, R.J. "Thomas More's *Dialogue of Comfort* and the Problem of the Real Grand Turk." *EM* 20 (1969): 23-35. (Appendix: "Thomas More and the Turks, 1528-1534," 35-37).

In discussions of the *Dialogue*, critics have long lost sight of the dread of Turkish invasion and possible conquest of Europe prevalent in the 1520s and 30s. With Turks rumored as marching westward in Hungary (where the *Dialogue* is set), various writers were then urging each Christian king not to be the Grand Turk and war on other Christian kings in such a time of peril, but to write against the common enemy. This current concern is an element of the *Dialogue*, which rises above any single such inspiration.

T059 Schulte-Herbrüggen, Hubertus. "A Prayer-Book of Sir Thomas More." *TLS* 15 Jan. 1970: 64.

Schulte-Herbrüggen traces the records of the book's survival in the possession of the Drüffel family of Münster during the eighteenth century, its disappearance and subsequent recovery, and adds comments on biographical entries recording the births of the children of More's son, John. Schulte-Herbrüggen corrects some comments he made in "More's Genealogy" (F305).

T060 Schuster, Louis A. "The Tower of London: More's Gethsemane." *Moreana* 74 (1982): 39-45.

Schuster gathers biographical information to delineate how the characteristics of More's fear of pain and death and his responses to them surface repeatedly through the final book of *Dialogue of Comfort* and the *De Tristitia*. If *Dialogue* depicts More's inner struggle, if it can be read as a debate between his cognitive faculty (Anthony) and his sensitive nature (Vincent), readers can understand how More's problem of pain is exposed. Although More "in his best secular manner" makes Anthony diagnose fear as the result of melancholia and has him prescribe a change of diet, medicines, and purgatives, later in the *Tristitia* readers find him viewing this theory from a transcendental perspective. *Tristitia* shows More's imagination translating the Garden of Olives into the Tower of London and transforming his own cell into Gethsemane.

T061 Sims, James H. "Psalm 90 and the Pattern of Temptation in *A Dialogue of Comfort* and *Paradise Regained*: From 'Solicitations' to 'Furiose Force.'" *Moreana* 74 (1982): 27-37.

Although the force/fraud dichotomy in temptation was central to the exegetical tradition on Psalm 90 from Augustine onward, Sims maintains it takes on special significance in the development of More and Milton's narratives. Anthony's subdivision of the temptations of Psalm 90: 5-6 into three "wily temptacion[s]" and one of "furiose force" anticipates the Father's prophecy in *Paradise Regained* that His Son will overcome all the "solicitations" and all the "vast force" of Satan.

T062 Sylvester, R.S. "Conscience and Consciousness: Thomas More." *The Author in His Work: Essays on a Problem in Criticism.* Eds. Louis L. Martz, and Aubrey Williams. New Haven: Yale UP, 1978. 163-74.

Sylvester observes More's lifelong tendency toward role-playing is evident in the Tower Works and especially in the letter from Margaret Roper to Alice Alington, in which More plays himself on this occasion and casts his daughter in the role of the temptress Eve who "might persuade the man she loves most to forsake the principles by which he has lived." Sylvester believes More's strategy in this letter and others written in the Tower is to get his family, particularly Margaret, to understand what his conscience meant to him, and he argues More's creation of the fictional role of Eve for his daughter is designed to bring her to that understanding. More's consciousness of artifice and the integrity of his conscience are one.

T063 Thelca, Mary. "New Corn from an Old Field: St. Thomas More's *Treatise Upon the Passion*." *CW* 164 (1947): 344-50.

Thelca covers how More wrote *Treatise* as an apologia and consolation, and includes ideas on Tudor customs, the observance of Maundy Thursday, More's reluctance to seek martyrdom, and his placing love of God above love of family.

T064 Thelca, Mary. "St. Thomas More and the *Catena Aurea*." *MLN* 61 (1946): 523-29.

Though More nowhere acknowledges his use of *Catena Aurea* (except for a rather incidental mention in an earlier work), this well-known collection of excerpts from some eighty Greek and Latin commentators on the New Testament would have been a likely choice for the limited library of a prison cell. That More may have used *Catena Aurea* frequently in his Tower works is indicated not only by several parallel arrangements of excerpts but also by two ostensibly quoted passages.

T065 Trapp, J.B. "The Holograph of More's *Expositio Passionis*: A Postscript." *Moreana* 18 (1968): 59-63.

Trapp draws attention to a previously unpublished account, in the ms. diary of Cassiano dal Pozzo, of the holograph ms. of More's *Expositio* (*De Tristitia*) in the Royal College of Corpus Christi (Valencia) in 1626 and claims the account clearly demonstrates that in 1626 the ms. was venerated as a relic as part of the cult of More on the Continent. Trapp reproduces parts of the account in an appendix.

T066 Wegemer, Gerard. "Thomas More's *Dialogue of Comfort*: A Platonic Treatment of Statesmanship." *Moreana* 101-102 (1990): 55-64.

Wegemer argues *Dialogue of Comfort* imitates in both form and content

Plato's treatment of the statesman. Plato's trilogy on statesmanship holds the statesman must possess true knowledge and virtue himself and be able to bring others to attain them as well. More presents and dramatizes just such a statesman in Anthony. Anthony uses the same dialectical and rhetorical approach as Plato's Socrates and also aims at leading his interlocutor to knowledge and virtue through a doctrine of recollection similar to Plato's.

T067 Wilson, K.J. "More and Holbein: The Imagination of Death." *SCJ* 7 (1976): 51-58.

Wilson suggests Hans Holbein's woodcut "Dance of Death" may have inspired More's image of death in the *Dialogue of Comfort*.

T068 Yee, Nancy. "An Analysis of the Prose Style of Thomas More's *Dialogue of Comfort*." Diss. Boston U, 1975.

This stylistic analysis of *Dialogue* discusses More's knowledge of classical rhetoric and use of rhetorical devices and considers the whole work's design and its individual components of meaning.

T069 Yee, Nancy. "Thomas More: In Defense of Tribulation." *Moreana* 74 (1982): 13-26.

Yee believes *Dialogue of Comfort* has "the argumentative thrust of forensic oratory and displays the formal divisions of classical oration including exordium, narration, proof/refutation, and formal peroration." She not only analyzes the work's larger structures, but also examines the effects achieved by manipulation of pronouns, paradox, and rhetorical figures. She maintains that through the exordium and narration More "establishes the basic conflict between worldly wit and divine wisdom" that underpins his argument, through the proof/reputation he works out the paradox of comfort, and through the concluding peroration he summarizes all the issues Book I raises.

T070 Yee, Nancy. "Thomas More's *Moriae Encomium*: The Perfect Fool in *A Dialogue of Comfort Against Tribulation*." *Moreana* 101-102 (1990): 65-74.

After examining the sources of the tradition of the fool, Yee writes that recognizing More's use of the "fool of Christ" clarifies unresolved enigmas in Anthony's character as well as seemingly abrupt shifts in tone in the work's three parts.

Personal Correspondence

U001   Fulham, Mary Vianney. "Some Aspects of the Prose Style of Thomas More in His English Letters." Diss. Catholic U of America, 1962.

Fulham examines More's English letters to bring into prominence some aspects of his style--for instance, his use of concrete nouns and transitive active verbs, his exact narration and description, his lively diction--heretofore obscured by the attention given to his early literary works and by the length of his controversial writings.

U002   Galibois, Roland. "Lettres de Thomas More à Frans van Cranevelt." *Moreana* 117 (1994): 67-84.

Galibois provides French translations of More's letters to van Cranevelt (that Clarence H. Miller presents in his article in the same issue of *Moreana* [U005]).

U003   Mann-Phillips, Margaret.   "The Correspondence of Erasmus and Thomas More." *Thomas More, 1477-1977*. Colloque international tenu en novembre 1977. Travaux de l'Institut Interuniversitaire pour l'étude de la Renaissance et de l'Humanisme. 6. Ed. Alois Gerlo. Bruxelles: Éditions de l'Université de Bruxelles, 1980. 27-37.

Mann-Phillips searches the correspondence between Erasmus and More, particularly More's letters of December 1526, his next to the last of 1532, and his final one in 1533, for insights into their similarities and differences, affection, shared interests and friends, appreciation of each other's jokes, and essential unity of mind, in spite of their divergent views on Luther and the Reformation.

U004   McCutcheon, Elizabeth.   "'The Apple of My Eye': Thomas More to

Antonio Bonvisi: A Reading and a Translation." *Moreana* 71-72 (1981): 37-56.

McCutcheon offers biographical information about More's connections with Bonvisi and uses More's letter to Bonvisi to show how important it was and continues to be for the image it presents of More's values, ideals, and "sense of self...when...imprisoned in the Tower." She also publishes her translation of the letter.

U005 Miller, Clarence H. "Thomas More's Letters to Frans van Cranevelt Including Seven Recently Discovered Autographs: Latin Text, English Translation, and Facsimiles of the Originals." *Moreana* 117 (1994): 3-66.

After a biographical sketch of van Cranevelt and an explanation of More's connection with him, Miller presents the Latin text of More's letters, English translations of each letter, facsimiles of the originals, and copious notes.

U006 Schulte-Herbrüggen, Hubertus. "Artes dictandi und erasmische Theorie in More's lateinischen Briefen." *Acta Conventus Neo-Latini Guelpherbytani*. Proceedings of the Sixth International Congress of Neo-Latin Studies. Wolfenbüttel 12 August to 16 August 1985. Eds. Stella P. Revard, Fidel Rädle, and Mario A. Di Cesare. MRTS. 53. Binghamton: MRTS, 1988. 503-12.

Schulte-Herbrüggen examines the rhetorical principles of More's Latin correspondence.

U007 Schulte-Herbrüggen, Hubertus. "Ein unbekannter Brief an St. Thomas More." *Moreana* 15-16 (1967): 241-47.

Schulte-Herbrüggen argues, from internal and external evidence, More was the addressee of a letter generally assumed to be addressed to Wolsey.

U008 Schulte-Herbrüggen, Hubertus. "A Letter of Dr. Johann Eck to Thomas More." *Moreana* 8 (1965): 51-58.

Schulte-Herbrüggen duplicates and discusses the letter of Eck to More (February 1516) which is not printed in Rogers' *The Correspondence of Sir Thomas More* (B005).

U009 Schulte-Herbrüggen, Hubertus. "Seven New Letters from Thomas More." *Moreana* 103 (1990): 49-66.

Schulte-Herbrüggen discusses the authenticity of seven letters from More to Frans van Cranevelt. He also examines the letters' handwriting, contents, style, and includes a summary evaluation, along with illustrations of the letters' features.

U010 Schulte-Herbrüggen, Hubertus, ed. *Sir Thomas More. Neue Briefe.*

Neue Beiträge zur Englischen Philologie. 5. Münster: Verlag Aschendorff, 1966.

Schulte-Herbrüggen prints letters not in the Rogers' collection, including one to More from John Eck, thanking him for the gift of a copy of "Rosseus" and in return sending him one of Eck's *Enchiridon*. This letter is printed to introduce a collection of about twenty letters of More's correspondence hitherto unpublished. The volume also includes a bibliography of primary and secondary sources, index, and introduction about the letters' biographical-historical context and their sources and models.

U011 Schulte-Herbrüggen, Hubertus. "Three Additions to More's Correspondence." *Moreana* 79-80 (1983): 35-41.

Schulte-Herbrüggen reprints and comments on the three letters J.A. Guy found at the Public Record Office--two of which shed light on More's life in 1521, the third of which "is of particular importance as it is one of the few extant *holograph* letters by More."

Other Topics

V001 Anderegg, Michael. *"The Booke of Sir Thomas More* and Its Sources." *Moreana* 53 (1977): 57-62.

Anderegg discusses how this play's authors could have employed materials from More's early biographers--Roper, Harpsfield, Stapleton, even Ro:Ba.

V002 Billingsley, Dale B. "An Iconographical Note on the Seal of St. Anthony's Hospital." *Moreana* 58 (1978): 39.

Billingsley replies to E.E. Reynolds' "St. Anthony's" (*Moreana* 57 [1978]: 5-8) and argues the central figures (a crutch, bell, and pig) on the seal of St. Anthony's Hospital probably represent not the Master of the Hospital, but the patron, St. Anthony.

V003 Blayney, Peter W.M. *"The Booke of Sir Thomas Moore* Re-Examined." *SP* 69 (1972): 167-91.

Blayney reconstructs the probable history of the ms. during the process of writing and revision. The present state of the ms. is examined and found to provide evidence suggesting two distinct stages of censorship by the Revels Office. On this basis, Blayney formulates a hypothesis, which goes into detail about Fol. 6, 7, the Shakespeare addition, and another possible Shakespearean addition.

V004 Boventer, Hermann. "By day as a cloud, by night as a pillar of fire: Thomas More, a model for our times." *Thomas Morus Jahrbuch 1989.* 106-17.

Boventer examines the "message" in More's courage, wit, sense of civic duty, and steadfast religious faith that makes him a model for our times.

V005 Chesterton, G.K. "A Turning Point in History." *The Fame of Blessed*

Thomas More. Being Addresses Delivered in His Honour in Chelsea, July 1929. 1929. *Essential Articles for the Study of Thomas More.* 501.

Chesterton pays tribute to More as humanist, mystic, martyr, and Englishman.

V006 Chillington, Carol A. "Playwrights at Work: Henslowe's, Not Shakespeare's, *Book of Sir Thomas More.*" *ELR* 10 (1980): 439-79.

Chillington's detailed investigation of the practice of playwrights working for Henslowe makes a strong case for challenging Shakespeare's hand in writing the play.

V007 Compton, Piers. "St. Thomas More, Martyred Chancellor." *Priest* 14 (1952): 318-20.

Compton sees More's martyrdom as his way of bearing witness to the truth of Catholicism.

V008 Devereux, E.J. "English Translations of Erasmus, 1522-1557." *Editing Sixteenth-Century Texts: Papers Given at the Editorial Conference, University of Toronto, October 1965.* Ed. R.J. Schoeck. Toronto: Toronto UP, 1966. 43-58.

From among the forty odd translations made before 1550, Margaret Roper's version of *Precatio Dominica* is noted as "a family concern," with a preface by Richard Hyrde, the More family tutor, and an experiment in double translation. Affinity between Erasmian ideas and those of English Protestants is illustrated in translations by Richard Taverner and other reformers, and patronage of their work, though Edmund Becke's version of two colloquies, in Devereux's opinion the most interesting Edwardian translation, satirizes the more radical and vehement reformers.

V009 Devereux, E.J. "John Rastell's Press in the English Reformation." *Moreana* 49 (1976): 29-47.

Rastell's career suggests a Reformation printer's life "could be as dangerous financially as it was physically or spiritually." Influenced by More's *Utopia*, particularly its stress on reason, Rastell's *A new boke of Purgatory* attempts to prove the purgatory's existence solely by unimpeded reason, without reference to Scripture. When John Frith refuted his position, Rastell was converted and devoted his energies to reforming the English Church. After switching positions and not always understanding either one, Rastell lost his orthodox friends' support and never gained the reformers' esteem. He suffered financially when his commitment to the new religion caused frequent absences from his printing business.

V010 Devereux, E.J. "John Rastell's Utopian Voyage." *Moreana* 51

(1976): 119-23.

That More shows in *Utopia* a good knowledge of contemporary voyages as well as classical, with what looks very like indifference to the implications of discovery, can partly be explained by the interests of his brother-in-law Rastell, who was planning a voyage of exploration of the American coast the year More began his book.

V011   Forker, Charles R., and Joseph Candido. "Wit, Wisdom, and Theatricality in *The Book of Sir Thomas More.*" *ShStud* 13 (1980): 85-104.

While the usual stage biography of the time gave prominence to "the political or religious significance" of its hero's actions, this play's singularity lies in its revelation of the inner life of its hero, in its focus on "those unique features of More's mind and personality which set him apart from ordinary men."

V012   Geritz, Albert J. "The Dramas and Prose Works of John Rastell." Diss. U of Missouri-Columbia, 1976.

Geritz reevaluates and adds insights to the literary career of More's brother-in-law and examines Rastell's debts to More and his Circle.

V013   Geritz, Albert J., and Amos Lee Laine. *John Rastell.* TEAS 363. Boston: Twayne Publishers, 1983.

More and his Circle are central to this study of the life and writings of More's energetic, eclectic brother-in-law.

V014   Gerwing, Alphons. *"Real learning is its own greatest reward." Thomas Morus Jahrbuch 1989.* 100-05.

Gerwing pays tribute to More's dedication to learning in his life and works.

V015   Ho, Koon-ki T. "Utopianism: A Unique Theme in Western Literature? A Short Survey on Chinese Utopianism." *Tamkang Review: A Quarterly of Comparative Studies between Chinese and Foreign Literatures* 13.1 (1982): 87-108.

Ho surveys utopianism in Chinese classical literature.

V016   Jenkins, Harold. "Readings in the Manuscript of *Sir Thomas More.*" *MLR* 43 (1948): 512-14.

Jenkins suggests an emendation in the play, which he bases upon its ms.

V017   Kurtz, Martha Anne. "'Present Laughter': Comedy in the Elizabethan History Play." Diss. U of Toronto (Can.), 1988.

Kurtz suggests political attitudes among playwrights and audiences were more complex and heterogeneous than usually assumed; among the plays she employs to demonstrate this thesis is *Sir Thomas More*.

V018 Laine, Amos Lee. "John Rastell: An Active Citizen of the English Commonwealth." Diss. Duke U, 1972.

Laine examines the career and thought of More's brother-in-law.

V019 Latz, Dorothy L. "Neglected Writings by Recusant Women: *Part I*-Poetry: 17th Century Metaphysical Poetesses Gertrude More, Clementina Cary, Gertrude Aston Thimelby and Katherine Thimelby Aston; *Part II*-Prose: English Recusants Elizabeth Shirley, Winifred Thimelby and Catherine Holland: Building on Medieval Mystics in the 17th Century." *Neglected English Literature: Recusant Writings of the 16th-17th Centuries.* Ed. Dorothy L. Latz. Salzburg, Aus.: Institut für Anglistik und Amerikanistik, Universität Salzburg, 1997.

Latz sketches the life of More's great-great-granddaughter Dame Gertrude More and provides a copy and an interpretation of her poem on More, "Magnes Amoris Amor."

V020 Lauvergnat-Gagnière, Christiane. *Lucien de Samosate et le lucianisme en France au XVIe siècle: Athéisme et polémique.* Genève: Librairie Droz, 1988.

In her aim to determine Lucian's role in the controversies over religion and free thought in sixteenth-century France and thereby clarify the long-obscured meanings of terms such as "lucianiste" and "lucianisme," Lauvergnat-Gagnière argues the height of Lucian's popularity coincided with humanism's peak and that the translations of Erasmus and More established his reputation as a satirist.

V021 Maber, R.G. "Une Machabée Moderne: Margaret Roper, vue par le Père Pierre Le Moyne (1647)." *Moreana* 82 (1984): 33-40.

Maber discusses and reprints the account of Margaret Roper by the French Jesuit Pierre le Moyne in *La Gallerie des femmes fortes* (1647), as part of the French feminist movement of the time.

V022 Maber, R.G. "Pierre Le Moyne's *Encomium of Margaret Roper*, Translated by John Paulet, Marquis of Winchester (1652)." *Moreana* 90 (1986): 47-52.

Maber reprints the text of Paulet's translation of Moyne's work, along with some commentary.

V023 Marc'hadour, Germain. "E.E. Reynolds: A Sampling of His Books." *Moreana* 71-72 (1981): 63-87.

Marc'hadour pays tribute to Reynolds in this survey of Reynolds' scholar-

OTHER TOPICS 363

ship on More and other figures.

V024 Marc'hadour, Germain. "Erasmus Englished by Margaret More." *Clergy Review* 43 (1957): 76-91.

Marc'hadour speculates upon Margaret Roper's translation of Erasmus' treatise on the Pater Noster published by Richard Hyrde.

V025 Marc'hadour, Germain. "A Man for All Seasons." *Drama Critique* 4 (1961): 18-26.

Bolt's play superimposes a historical parallel on a contemporary problem and, in doing so, makes it difficult for spectators to be gripped and shaken by the man and his tragedy. Part of the difficulty is in the production, part in Bolt's incomplete portrait of More. Its mixed critical reception results from incomplete and erroneous conceptions of More.

V026 Marc'hadour, Germain. "St. Thomas More: Patron des librespenseus? Reflexions sur la pièce de Bolt." *Moreana* 8 (1965): 29-42.

Bolt's characterization of More in *A Man for All Seasons*, though retaining a semblance of verisimilitude, misunderstands More's martyrdom. Bolt's More champions the individual, the self as opposed to external institutions. More was no modern man in this sense; he died in and for the Catholic Church.

V027 McCutcheon, Elizabeth. "Margaret More Roper's Translation of Erasmus' *Precatio Dominica*." *Acta Conventus Neo-Latini Guelpherbytani*. Proceedings of the Sixth International Congress of Neo-Latin Studies. Wolfenbüttel 12 August to 16 August 1985. Eds. Stella P. Revard, Fidel Rädle, and Mario A. Di Cesare. MRTS. 53. Binghamton: MRTS, 1988. 659-66.

McCutcheon believes Margaret Roper's translation was mainly published to advance the cause of the new learning for women.

V028 McDermott, C. Logan. "Sir Thomas More Plays." *N&Q* 194 (1949): 305.

McDermott asks if anyone knows of or possesses a copy of James Hurdis' *Sir Thomas More* (published in 1792) and also expresses interest in any other plays about More.

V029 McMillin, Scott. "*The Book of Sir Thomas More*: A Theatrical View." *MP* 68 (1970): 10-24.

McMillin examines this play's ms. as it is intended for performance.

V030 McMillin, Scott. *The Elizabethan Theatre and* The Book of Sir Thomas More. Ithaca: Cornell UP, 1987.

From this study More *amici* will learn little of More, while students of

Elizabethan theatre will find an intriguing compilation of detailed research and cogent argument.

V031 McNamara, Robert F. "Who Was Theodore Maynard?" *Moreana* 39 (1973): 5-13.

McNamara discusses the life, work, and influences of Maynard (1890-1956), a prominent American Catholic poet, critic, biographer of More, and historian.

V032 Merriam, Thomas. "Chettle, Munday, Shakespeare, and *Sir Thomas More*." *N&Q* ns 39.3 (Sept. 1992): 336-41.

Merriam uses stylometric ratios concerning authorship of different scenes in *Sir Thomas More*.

V033 Merriam, Thomas. "Did Munday Compose *Sir Thomas More*?" *N&Q* ns 37.2 (June 1990): 175-78.

Gary Taylor has underestimated the stylometric argument against Munday's authorship. Four stylometric habits distinguish Shakespeare's plays in the First Folio from four of Munday's. Only when the basic question of Munday's authorship is settled can that of Shakespeare's or Chettle's role in writing the play be considered properly.

V034 Merriam, Thomas. "Lord Say, *Sir Thomas More*, and Good Friday." *Moreana* 109 (1992): 47-52.

The two accounts of Lord Say's being brought before Jack Cade in the *Quarto* and *Folio* versions of *Henry VI, Part 2* differ. The *Folio* presents Say as a humanist scholar, who resembles More in several respects, with overtones of Christ condemned to death. Verbal echoes link Shakespeare's phrases with *Sir Thomas More* and the Latin words of the Good Friday Reproaches. Other scholars have detected echoes of the Easter hymn *Exsultet* in *The Merchant of Venice*, *Romeo and Juliet*, and *The Tempest*.

V035 Merriam, Thomas. "*Sir Thomas More* without Stylometry." *N&Q* ns 44.1 (Mar. 1997): 67-72.

Merriam argues in favor of the "place for...reassessment of *Sir Thomas More's* authorship, free of statistics."

V036 Metz, Harold. "The Play of *Sir Thomas More*: The Problem of the Primary Source." *Moreana* 82 (1984): 41-48.

Although Michael A. Anderegg's impression that Munday originated the idea of a play on More as a result of having come upon one of the lives may be correct, Metz proposes to describe another explanation more in accord with some bits of evidence not taken into account in Anderegg's "*The Book of Sir

Thomas More and Its Sources" (V001) and which recognizes the realities of theatrical conditions of the 1580s and 1590s.

V037 Moss, Ann. *Printed Commonplace-Books and the Structuring of Renaissance Thought.* Oxford: Clarendon P, 1996. 114-15, 209.

Moss notes although the commonplace book became a "ubiquitous learning tool," it may not have been everywhere "Erasmus could have watched it employed so fetchingly as by the daughter of Thomas More."

V038 Murphy, Robert T. "Thomas More, Abraham Lincoln and the Natural Law." *Moreana* 12 (1966): 53-56.

Murphy compares these two heroes as models for lawyers devoted to natural law.

V039 Pacholski, Richard Allen. "The Humanist Drama of the Sir Thomas More Circle." Diss. U of Wisconsin, 1969.

Pacholski stresses the dramatic qualities of *Nature, Fulgens and Lucre, Four Elements, Gentylnes and Nobylyte,* and *Calisto and Melebea* in addition to their humanistic origins and themes as part of More's Circle.

V040 Pajardi, Piero. "In Comunione con Marialisa Bertagnoni nel ricordo di Tommaso Moro." *Moreana* 104 (1990): 53-59.

Pajardi, President of the Milan Court of Appeals, had the privilege of Bertagnoni's cooperation as reader of the manuscript of his book *Utopia avverata*, and writer of the preface, her last published composition. He evokes her gratefully and then comments on the title of his book--*Utopia Come True, Nowhere Realized Somewhere.*

V041 Pitard, Derrick G. "An Undescribed Manuscript of St. Thomas More's 'A Devoute Prayer' and Its Relation to Mid-Sixteenth Century Devotional Practice." *Neglected English Literature: Recusant Writings of the 16th-17th Centuries.* Ed. Dorothy L. Latz. Salzburg, Aus.: Institut für Anglistik und Amerikanistik, Universität Salzburg, 1997. 107-30.

Pitard describes the form and content of a prayer-roll (Folger MS X.d 532) which contains a previously unknown copy of one of More's last written works ("A Devoute Prayer") and discusses the milieu in which it was composed.

V042 Prescott, Anne Lake. "Humanism in the Tudor Jestbook." *Moreana* 95-96 (1987): 5-16.

Prescott retells some very old jokes from John Rastell's *A Hundred Merry Tales* and Thomas Berthelet's *Tales and Quick Answers,* as evidence of the humanist interest in mental flexibility and the use and abuse of logic and language.

V043 Reynolds, E.E. "The Significance of *A Man for All Seasons*." *Moreana* 23 (1969): 34-39.

Reynolds praises the admirable characteristics of More that Bolt's play develops, but faults some of the playwright's portrayal of the Tudor Age.

V044 Samaan, Angele B. "Butler's *Erewhon*: A Centenary Tribute." *Moreana* 36 (1972): 97-102.

Samaan stresses the immediate popular and critical success of Butler's work.

V045 Scarisbrick, J.J. "Thomas More: A Model for Us All." *Moreana* 87-88 (1985): 85-90.

This article reprints an address Scarisbrick delivered at Chelsea Old Church on Sunday, 21 July 1985.

V046 Schoeck, R.J. "Moreans from Chambers to Marc'hadour: Some Recollections and Reflections." *Miscellanea Moreana: Essays for Germain Marc'hadour. Moreana* 100. 223-31.

Schoeck describes and connects some scholars who have devoted their lives to the study of More in the last half century, and he focuses upon the Yale Thomas More project as a center of research and mutual support.

V047 Schoeck, R.J. "William Rastell and the Prothonotaries: A Link in the Story of the Rastells, Ropers, and Heywoods." *N&Q* 197.19 (13 Sept. 1952): 398-99.

Schoeck proves Rastell received aid in compiling his book of Entries from three other legal experts who were members of More's Circle.

V048 Smith, Christopher. "A Drama for All Times? *A Man for All Seasons* Revived and Reviewed." *Moreana* 25 (1988): 51-58.

Recent revivals on stage at Chichester and London and Charlton Heston's portrayal of More in the latter production lead the author to survey critical reactions and ponder the play's depth of characterization and future on the stage.

V049 Smith, M.W.A. "Shakespeare, Stylometry and *Sir Thomas More*." *SP* 89 (1992): 434-44.

Smith examines the stylometric evidence, arguments, and assumptions upon which previous scholars have based their findings on the authorship of *Sir Thomas More*, without recourse to the mathematics of statistical theory, to demonstrate the question of who wrote the play "remains exactly as it was before any...stylometric studies were undertaken."

V050 Smith, M.W.A. "*Sir Thomas More, Pericles*, and Stylometry." *N&Q*

ns 41.1 (Mar. 1994): 55-58.

In response to Thomas Merriam's "Chettle, Munday, Shakespeare, and *Sir Thomas More*" (V032) and *"Pericles* I-II Revisited and Considerations Concerning Literary Medium as a Systematic Factor in Stylometry" (*N&Q* ns 39.3 [Sept. 1992], 341-45), Smith argues "much needs to be corrected and reworked before a serious literary reassessment" of the authorship of *Sir Thomas More* "would be warranted."

V051 Spikes, Judith D. *"The Book of Sir Thomas More*: Structure and Meaning." *Moreana* 43-44 (1974): 25-39.

Munday's structural principle is to repeat similar or contrasting patterns and themes in various contexts. The play's theme is responsibility: the first part deals with social and political responsibility, as the title character More, the prototype of the virtuous man, acts in the private and political spheres; the second illustrates a moral responsibility that supersedes law. The two halves pivot on the central section, which abstractly states the conflict between the world's claims and a higher claim in More's soliloquy; it presents the conflict in terms of a moral allegory in an interpolated play. The play's emphasis on conscience is true to its source, Roper's *Life*, and also stresses its own artistic unity.

V052 Strong, Roy. *Holbein and Henry VIII*. The Paul Mellon Foundation for British Art. London: Routledge & Kegan Paul, 1967.

Strong strikes a new line of approach to the political, religious revolution of the 1530s by demonstrating the force and significance of imperial propaganda, in Henry's patronage of art, which, like most of his policies, was directed primarily to promoting and publicizing the Tudor myth. Against this background of portrayals of Henry and the Tudor dynasty, Strong advises readers to reconsider Holbein's work as court artist during his second visit, in contrast to the first, when he was moving in the tranquil, pious More Circle.

V053 *Thomas More Through Many Eyes*. London: Leighton Thomas, 1978.

This volume collects twenty-five memorial and eulogistic sermons about More preached at Chelsea Old Church from 1954 to 1978.

V054 Trapp, J.B. "'Suavius oblet': A Bronze Medal of Thomas More and Its Motto." *Moreana* 4 (1964): 31-45.

On the obverse side of the medal, More is shown in profile in a portrait of less than three-quarter face, with the legend, "Thomas Morvs Angliae Cancellarius." On the reverse side is a design of a felled tree, an axe embedded in the stump, and the trunk and foliage curved so as to follow the line of the rim, lying in the foreground. The motto, "Suavius Oblet," appears above this. Trapp is uncertain of the date the medal was cast.

V055 Urbain, Olivier. "L'Intertextualite dans le Theatre de Jean Anouilh: Les Dix Dernieres Annees." Diss. U of Southern California, 1990.

In showing how a reading of Anouilh's plays published in the last ten years of his life based on "intertextuality" (the relationship between one work and another or between parts of the same work) adds to their originality, Urbain discusses Anouilh's last published play, *Thomas More ou l'homme libre*.

V056 Valk, J.M.M. de. "More: A Man for Our Times." *Moreana* 97 (1988): 41-46.

With minor alterations, this sermon was delivered at Chelsea Old Church on 15 July 1984 for the annual commemoration of More.

V057 Walker, Greg. *Plays of Persuasion: Drama and Politics at the Court of Henry VIII*. Cambridge: Cambridge UP, 1991. 112, 155-58, 162, 165, 168, 187, 216, 224.

More receives mention in connection with the political significance of *Godly Queene Hester*, Heywood's *Play of the Weather*, and Bale's *King Johan*.

V058 Warner, James Christopher. "Representing Henry VIII: Humanist Discourse in the Years of the Reformation Parliament." Diss. U of Washington, 1994.

Warner studies uses of fiction during the years Henry sought to divorce Catherine to show how official publications from the press of Thomas Berthelet (the king's printer) depicted Henry as humanistic scholar or philosopher-king and how this campaign was answered with plays and dialogues John and William Rastell, More's kinsmen, printed.

V059 Wheeler, Jeffrey Matthew. "Palpable Fictions: Religious Relics, Populist Rhetoric and the English Reformation." Diss. U of Southern California, 1996.

Wheeler examines how and why the illusion of a debate about relics was created and the implication of this phenomenon for understanding Renaissance discourse. Because relics inspired a peculiar general interest many early Protestant writers (as well as those writing against Protestantism, including More and Erasmus) exploited, such writings constitute a "widespread experiment to create a rhetoric appropriate to general tastes."

V060 Zapatka, Francis E. "'My Strong House': The Tower and Its Use in *Sir Thomas More*." *Moreana* 108 (1991): 41-50.

Reference to prisons (Newgate and the Tower) is made some thirty times in *Sir Thomas More*, and the Tower serves as the setting for four of the play's seventeen scenes. The Tower itself is treated at times as a kind of character; it also enables the playwright(s) to characterize More very tellingly through his paradoxically positive comments on his place of confinement. The treatment of prisons in the play, moreover, provides some appropriate historical ironies in connection with More and Fisher. Finally, numerous parallels between *Sir Thomas More* and *King Lear*, *Richard III*, and *Henry VIII* are seen within the context of the play's prison references.

Index

Abraham, F163
Abrash, Merritt, R001
Abyngdon, Henry, N008, N009, N023
Acton, Lord, I098
Adams, Robert M., xv, B020, C021, C037, R002, R003
Adams, Robert P., G001-G003, J001, R004-R006
Aesop, N013, N016
Agricola, Rudolf, K002, P003
Ainger, Alfred, R007
Albanese, Denise, I001
Albery, Peter, I002
Albin, Hugh O., I003
Alciati, Andrea, N003
Alington, Alice, F130, F201, F261, T015, T062
Allain, Mathe, R094, R339
Allen, DeWitt Clinton, F001
Allen, Don Cameron, N020
Allen, H.M., B001
Allen, John William, R008
Allen, Michael J.B., R377
Allen, P.S., A026, B001, C021
Allen, Peter R., R009
Allen, Ward, I004, J002, R010-R014, R113, R190

Alston, R.C., C035
Altman, Joel B., R015
Ames, Russell, A024, C021, R016, R212
Ammonius, Andreas, F089, N032
Anderegg, Michael A., B002, F002-F005, I005, I102, S001, V001, V036
Anderson, Judith H., Q001
Anderson, Marvin W., S002
André, Bernard, N006
Aneau, Barthelémy, I013
Anouilh, Jean, I085, V055
Aquinas, Thomas, B008, P008, R066, R168, R311
Argent, Joseph Edward, I006
Aristotle, K001, R066, R168, R234, R235, R401, R411, R428
Armstrong, C.A.J., Q002
Arnold, Matthew, R308, R310
Ascham, Roger, C012, G026, G071, K011, K014, R155
Astell, Ann W., R017
Aubrey, John, F087
Audley, Thomas, F165
Aveling, J.C.H., F006
Avineri, Shlomo, R018

Bacon, Francis, D006, F120, F292, I001, J031, K001, Q001, Q040, Q054, Q055, R006, R048, R070, R094, R108, R153, R231, R325
Baines, Barbara J., F023
Baird-Smith, David, S003
Baker, David, R019-R021
Baker, Howard, F007
Baker, Thomas, C003
Baker-Smith, Dominic, I007, R022-R024, S004
Baldwin, T.W., N020
Baldwin, William, G071
Bale, John, H005
Ball, Martha Charlene, R025
Bancroft, Thomas, A030
Baptiste, Victor N., R026
Barfoot, C.C., R022
Barker, Arthur E., R027, R059, S025
Barker, Ernest, R028
Barker, Nicolas, F008, F160, F213
Barlow, William, S066, S067, S092
Barnes, Harry Elmer, R029
Barnes, Robert, B004, F244, S054
Barnes, W.J., R030
Barnet, Mary Jane, G004
Barnstable, Robert, F317
Barton, Elizabeth (the "Nun of Kent"), F061, F127, F140, F216, S081
Basset, Bernard, A026, F009
Basset, Mary, B007, C020, T038
Bataillon, Marcel, I008
Batmanson, John, P005
Batson, F.W., A027
Baumann, Eduard H.L., J003
Baumann, Uwe, G005, L001, L002, R031, S005
Bayne, Diane Valeri, J004
Bebel, August, N016
Beck, Egerton, F010

Beck, George Andrew, G070
Becke, Edmund, V008
Becker, Howard, R029
Becket, Thomas, F046, F091, F162
Beer, Max, R032
Beith-Halahmi, Esther Yael, Q003
Bejczy, István, R033-R035
Bek, Lise, F011
Bell, Philip Ingress, F012, F013
Bellamy, Edward, R128, R369
Belloc, Hilaire, F014
Bennett, G.V., R315
Bennett, J.A.W., R208, R241
Benson, Robert L., R377
Bentham, Jeremy, R303
Bentley, Catherine, F142, F189
Berger, Harry, Jr., C021, R036, R037
Berghahn, Klaus L., R129
Beringause, Arthur F., G006
Berneri, Marie Louise, R038
Berners, Lord, K014
Berrigan, J.R., I009
Berrong, Richard M., I010
Bertagoni, Marialisa, A001-A003, G007, I011, V040
Berthelet, Thomas, V042, V058
Beuchot, Mauricio, I012
Bevington, David M., R039
Biernan, Judah, R040
Bietenholz, Peter G., F015-F017
Billingsley, Dale B., D001, R041, R042, S006, T001, T002, V002
Billon, Francois de, N028
Bilney, Thomas, S014, S035, S110
Binder, James, R043
Biondi, Lawrence, F115
Biot, Brigette, I013
Birch, David, S007
Birchenough, Edwyn, F018, F019, T003
Birchenough, Josephine, F019
Bishop, R.J., F020

Black, Ben W., I014
Black, J.B., D002
Blackburn, Elizabeth Brooke, F021
Blaim, Artur, R044, R045
Blanchard, André, I015, I016, N001
Blayney, Peter W.M., V003
Bleich, David, R046
Blom, Nicolas van der, R047
Boardman, Brigid M., I017
Bodin, Jean, J018
Boesky, Amy Diane, R048
Boethius, M004, T039
Boewe, Charles, R049
Boitani, Piero, R241
Boker, George Henry, I105
Bolchazy, Ladislaus J., R050
Boleyn, Anne, F097, F098, F118, F310, I002, I039, I105
Bolt, Robert, A026, F022, F033, F332, F339, G040, I005, I018, I066, I079, V025, V026, V043
Bonvisi, Anthony, F284, H021, U004
Bony, Alain, R051
Bork, Robert H., J005
Boswell, Jackson Campbell, A004, F023
Botero, Giovanni, I095
Bouchet, Jean, I019
Boulding, Elsie, R325
Bourbon, Nicolas, N014
Bourlès, Charles, R052
Boventer, Hermann, xv, V004
Bowers, Fredson, O001
Boyer, Abel, A009
Boyle, Anthony Thomas, R053
Bracciolini, Poggio, L018
Bradner, Leicester, B013, C014, C018, I064, N002
Bradshaw, Brendan, F024, R054, R312, S009
Bradshaw, David, L003

Bradshaw, Jack R., F025
Brandsma, Titus, I067
Branham, R. Bracht, R055
Brann, Eva, R056
Bregis, John, F320
Breitenbach, Bernhard von, R092, R433
Brémond, Henri, F026
Bridgett, Thomas E., A024, A026, F050, F263, G009
Britnell, Jennifer, I019
Brixius, Germanus, B005, B013, C014, N010, N026
Bronowski, Jacob, R057
Brooks, Peter Newman, F069
Brouwer, Piet, A005, H001, I020
Brown, Barbara, Q004
Brown, Brendan F., F027
Brown, Dorothy Harrell, I021
Brown, Richard Harvey, R254
Bruce, Susan, R058
Brückmann, Patricia, R059, S025
Brugmans, Henri, J006, R060
Buc, George, Q064
Buchanan, George, I007, K002
Buck, August, F302
Budé, Guillaume, F052, F084, F153, F162, R150, R192, R446
Bugenhagen, John, B005, B014, S012, S067, S098
Bullein, William, R276
Bullough, Geoffrey, D003
Bulwer-Lytton, Edward, R350
Burnet, Gilbert, C030, I060, I096
Burns, John Lanier, G010
Burton, Robert, R153, R392
Bush, Douglas, F028
Busleyden, Jerome, F301, R041, R064, R192, R306
Butkie, Joseph, E001
Butler, Brian, F029
Butler, Johanna M., H002

Butler, Mary Basil, G011
Butler, Samuel, R350, V044
Byron, Brian, xv, F030-F032, G063, T004
Byron, Lord, I081

Cabet, Etienne, I027, R128
Cahn, Edmond, F033
Caie, Graham D., R380
Callahan, Virginia Woods, N003
Calvin, John, N012, R192, R195
Cameron, Alan, L019, N004
Campanella, Tommaso, R070, R325
Campbell, W.E., A024, A026, D010, F034, G070, R061, R062, S010
Candido, Joseph, Q005
Canfield, Benedict, G078, G079
Carey, John, G012
Carlson, Cindy Laurel, R063
Carlson, David R., N006
Caron, Antoine, F105, F106
Carpenter, Nan C., G013, N007-N009, R064
Carpinelli, Frank, F036
Carruthers, Mary J., R227
Carver, George, H003, Q006
Caspari, Fritz, G014, R065, R066
Cassirer, Ernst, R067, R209
Castelli, Alberto, G015
Castiglione, Balthasar, G056, G071
Catherine of Aragon, F140, F239, G020, I002, N025, V058
Catherine of Siena, J017
Cavanaugh, John R., J007, R068
Cavendish, George, C012, F328, G042, K014, Q001, R048
Caxton, William, G071
Cecil, Algernon, F037
Celestine, Sr., T005
Centeno, Yvette Kace, R264

Cervantes, Miguel de, I042, I061, I100, S003
Chambers, R.W., A024, A026, A042, A044, C021, C039, F028, F038-F040, F043, F050, F051, F116, F180, F218, F225, F240, F261, F339, I022, R102, R194, R312, R315, R403
Champion, Larry S., Q007
Chapuys, Eustace, F351
Charles I, F212
Charles V, F042, F068, F138
Chaucer, Geoffrey, L022, S025
Checksfield, Muriel May, G016
Cheke, Sir John, G050
Chené, Adèle, R069
Chesterton, G.K., V005
Chettle, Henry, V032, V033
Chevallier, R., L016
Chevreau, Urbain, I101
Chiappelli, Fredi, R377
Child, Albert H., R152
Chillington, Carol A., V006
Chirpaz, Par François, R070
Chomarat, Jacques, L004, R071, R166, R249, R286
Churchyard, Thomas, Q004, Q009, Q048
Cicero, G083, R225, R268, R355, R421, R423, T051
Cichan, Gregory, R050
Clark, James Arthur, T006
Clark, Sir George, R243
Clebsch, W.A., G077, S011
Clement, John, F198, F347
Clement, Margaret Giggs, F198, F215, F299, F347
Clifford, Rosamond, Q009
Cline, James Mason, F274
Cochlaeus, Johannes, B008, B015, F352, S043, S050
Cock, Alfred, D004
Coles, Paul, R072

Colet, John, C019, F166, F217, F296, G001, G003, G020, G025, G035, G064, G077, J001, J010, J029, J032, L010, R409, S069-S071, T057
Colley, Dorothy, F060
Collins, Daniel G., F033
Colt, Jane. *See* More, Jane Colt.
Compton, Piers, V007
Comte, Auguste, R094
Condren, A.C., L005
Condren, Conal, F041, I023, L005, Q008
Conrad, F.W., F042
Constable, John, I106
Constantine, R134
Coogan, Robert, L006, M001, M002, R073
Cooper, M. Scholastica, P001
Corbett, Elizabeth Burgoyne, R087
Cornell, Christine Anne, Q009
Cornwallis, William, Q008
Corrigan, Beatrice, I024
Corrigan, Kevin, R074
Cortés, Hernán, R257
Cossiga, Francesco, A001
Costain, Thomas, Q010
Coulton, G.G., F043
Cousins, A.C., M003
Cousins, A.D., xv, M004
Coverdale, Miles, S054
Cowie, L.W., F044
Cox, Virginia, R075
Crane, Mary Thomas, K001
Cranevelt, Frans van, U002, U005, U009
Cranmer, Thomas, C006, F064
Craven, William G., O002
Crawford, Charles W., S012
Creeth, Edmund, C012
Creighton, Bishop, R194
Cresacre, Anne, F006
Crewe, Jonathan V., F045

Crichton, Michael, Q063
Cro, Stelio, A023, I025
Cromwell, Thomas, C019, F064, F065, F070, F072, F098, F118, F135, F270, F306, F312, F348, G064, I079, R127
Cross, Gustav, Q011
Crossett, John, R076-R078
Cunningham, J.V., I032
Curzon, Lord, I083

Dalzell, Alexander, B001, F173, F288, R271
D'Amico, Jack, R079
Daniel-Rops, Henri, R080
Daniell, David, S013
Dannenfeldt, Karl H., J008
Dante, R283
Darcy, Thomas, F351
Dart, J.L.C., F046
Dauglish, A.F., D004
Daunce, William, F036
Davin, Dan, R208
Davis, Herbert, I026
Davis, J.C., R081-R083
Davis, John F., S014
Davis, Walter, R084
Day, R. Morris, N010
De Graaf, Bob, N012
Deakins, Roger Lee, F047, K002
Dean, Leonard F., Q012
Dean, Paul, Q013
Dean, William, N011
degli Azzi, Faustina, I068
Dekker, Thomas, S061
Del Buffa, Giuseppa Saccaro, R336
Delany, Selden P., F048
Delcourt, Marie, A006, C026, F053, R085, R328
Delcourt, Joseph, F049-F052, F218, G017
Delendick, Patricia, A007
Demenier, Hubert, R086

Demetz, Peter, G038
Dennis, Norman, R087
Dermauw, Gerard, R088
Derrett, J. Duncan M., A024, F054-F063, R089-R093
Desroche, Henri, A008, I027
Desroches, Rosny, R094
Dethloff, Uwe, H004
Deutscher, Thomas B., F017
Devereux, E.J., D005, F064, S015, V008-V010
Di Cesare, Mario A., xvi, F011, I117, O014, R279, S005, U006, V027
Di Luca, Adolfo, R095, R096
Di Scipio, Guiseppe C., R097
Diamond, Jeff Barja, G018
Dickens, A.G., E002, F065, F069, G077
Digges, Sir Dudley, I073
Dillon, William Patrick, S016
Doherty, Felix, I085
Dolan, John P., C007, C039
Dolan, Patrick Anthony, Jr., G019
Dolet, Etienne, I046, I112
Domenach, Jean-Marie, R098
Domenichi, Lodovico, N028
Domingo Malvadi, Arantxa, T007
Donaldson, E. Talbot, R227
Donne, John, F081, Q008, S061
Donne, John (the younger), A009
Donnelly, Dorothy, F066, F067, R099, R100, R331
Donnelly, Gertrude Joseph, C028
Donnelly, John P., C036
Donner, H.W., A024, A027, F068, R101, R102, T008
Donno, Elizabeth Story, I028, Q014
Donskis, Leonidas, R103
Dooley, Patrick K., R104-R105
Dorp, Martin, B005, F112, P001, R443

Dorsch, T.S., R107
D'Ottavi, Stefania D'Agata, R108
Dowling, Maria, G020
Doyle, Charles C., xv, A004, A009-A012, B013, I029-I033, N013-N017, R109-R114, S017, S018
Doyle-Davidson, W.A.G., G021, K003
Doyon, Jacques, R115
Drayton, Michael, Q048
Duffy, Robert A., M005
Duhamel, P. Albert, R116, R312
Dujardin, Philippe, R117
Duncan, Douglas, L007
Dupré, Louis, R118
Durant, Jack M., Q007
Dust, Philip C., G022, I034, N018, R119, R120, R166, R249, R286

Ebert, Kenneth Bryan, J009
Eck, Johann, B008, S043, U008, U010
Edward IV, G042, Q033, Q035, Q056
Edward VI, G064
Edwards, Anthony S.G., B010, M006, O003-O005
Edwards, J.G., Q043
Egan, Willis J., R121, S019
Egerton, Sir Thomas, I074
Egretier, Noëlle-Marie, I035
Ehrmann, Jacques, R197
Eldridge, Laurence, N019
El-Gabalawy, Saad, R122, R123
Eliav-Feldon, Miriam, R124
Elliott, Robert C., C021, R125, R126
Ellsworth, J.D., F192
Elton, G.R., A024, F069-F072, F111, F260, G029, I092, R127, S009, S032
Elvira, Doña, F239

INDEX 377

Elyot, Sir Thomas, C012, F042,
F068, F113, F138, F182, F292,
F348, G014, G055, G071, K002,
K005, K014, R020, R177
Emden, A.B., F073
Emerson, Kathy Lynn, F074
Epicurus, R396
Erasmus, Charles J., R128
Erasmus, Desiderius, B012, B013,
B015, B017, B019, C014, C019,
C025, C026, C039, C040, F009,
F011, F015, F017, F019, F026,
F034, F037, F040, F045, F053,
F084, F089, F112, F130, F134,
F143, F148, F155, F157, F162,
F166, F169, F171, F174, F180,
F182, F188, F190, F194, F202,
F238, F240, F242, F243, F245,
F248, F261, F264, F280, F287,
F292, F294, F301, F303, F313,
F322, F329, F330, F338, F340,
F345, G001, G003, G004, G014,
G016, G018, G020, G022,
G025, G026, G031, G033,
G035, G038, G044, G056,
G067, G077, H009, H010, H019,
J001, J010, J018, J023, J024,
J029, J031, J032, J034, K006,
K011, K012, K015, K022, L004,
L010, L020, L026, N018, N019,
P002, P005, P009, R015, R034,
R041, R047, R068, R071, R085,
R111, R185, R192, R218, R225,
R277, R307, R308, R382, R407,
R416, S064, T057, U003, V024,
V027
  Adages, L021
  Bellum Erasme, R004
  Christian Prince, G002
  Collected Works of Erasmus,
    B001
  *The Correspondence of
    Erasmus*, B001
  Praise of Folly (*Encomium
    Moriae*), A001, F034, F045,
    G015, G060, G061, G083,
    I078, I079, J013, P001,
    R021, R025, R037,
    R138, R214, R220, R409,
    R425
  Precatio dominica, J004
Ersgräber, Willi, R129
Esmonde, Margaret Powell, O006
Estep, William R., F075
Evans, John X., I036, R130
Evans, Robert C., I037
Evans, Scott D., I038
Everaerts, Jan (Johannes
  Secundus), I068

Fabyan, Robert, L024
Fantazzi, Charles, F173, F288,
  R271
Farnell, James E., R131
Farrow, John, F076
Fasan, Vada Belshaw, J010
Fcho, Door, F077
Fellheimer, J., I039
Fénelon, François de Salignac de
  la Mothe, R094
Fenlon, D.B., G023, R132, R312
Ferguson, Arthur B., G024-G026,
  G077, R133
Ficino, Marsilio, R288
Field, P.J.C., R134
Finan, Thomas, T009
Fines, John, S020
Fineux, Sir John, M011
Fish, Simon, B014, C022, C023,
  G077, S024, S038, S039, S055,
  S089, S094
Fish, Stanley, R159
Fisher, Bernard, F078, T010
Fisher, John, B007, C019, F050,
  F064, F065, F116, F126, F140,
  F166, F172, F216, F239, F272,

F311, F321, F341, F352, G020,
G064, G077, G078, G079, I016,
I019, I035, I099, J024, K014,
S057, S097
Flaherty, P.A., D005
Flegel, Kenneth M., F079
Fleisher, Martin, R135
Fleissner, Robert F., I040, S021
Flesseman-Van Leer, E., S022,
S023
Fletcher, Anthony, F080
Fletcher, Giles, Q053
Fletcher, Harris, N020
Fletcher, Phineas, R113
Flower, Barbara, B001
Flynn, Dennis, F081
Foley, Stephen Merriam, B002,
B013
Foord, Bede, C001, T011
Forker, Charles R., V011
Fortescue, John, R177, R184
Foster, Thomas, I102
Fox, Alistair, xv, F193, G027,
J019, Q015, Q016, R136-R139,
R177, S009, S024-S026
Fox, Richard, F132, G020
Foxe, John, B014, C012, F188,
F272, H005, H024, I124
Fracjowiak, Marian, R140
Francis, Kevin, R141
Fraser, George M., Q063
Frasnay, Daniel, F092
Fredericks, Daniel David, G028
Freeman, John, R142-R146
Freemantle, Anne, F082
Freitas, Lima de, R264
Freud, Sigmund, J016
Fressanges, G.A., F083
Friederich, Werner P., H005
Frijhoff, W. Th. M., F169
Frith, John, B005, B014, F272,
L024, R324, S024, S033, S034,
S054, S097, V009

Fritze, Ronald H., G029
Frye, Northrop, R147, R148
Fulham, Mary Vianney, U001
Fuller, Thomas, I054
Fussner, F. Smith, Q017

Gabel, John Butler, I041
Gabrieli, Vittorio, G030, I042,
I043, O007, S027
Gaguin, Robert, O011
Gairdner, James, S028
Galbraith, V.H., Q043
Galibois, Roland, R149, U002
Gallagher, Ligeia, xv, C015
Garanderie, M.M. de la, F084,
R150
Garavaglia, Gian Paolo, F085,
I044
Garretson, Albert H., F033
Garrod, H.W., B001
Garvin, Katharine, F039
Gascoigne, George, R220
Gatto, Louis C., R151
Gee, John Archer, R152
Gellius, Aulus, L025, R031
Gelman, Richard, F086
Gentili, Alberico, R119
Gentili, Augusto, R153
Gentrup, William Frederick, G031
Geritz, Albert J., A013, F087-
F089, I045, V012, V013
Gerwing, Alphons, V014
Gest, John B., T012
Giard, Luce, R154
Gibaud, Henri, xvi, I046, R252
Gibson, R.W., A004, A010-A012,
A014, A021, A024, A036,
A038-A040, A042, D006, T013
Giggs, Margaret. *See* Clement,
Margaret Giggs.
Gilbert, Donald, S105
Gilbert, George, I099
Gilbert, Sir Humphrey, I056, R210

INDEX

Giles, Peter, F011, F330, H019, I053, R068, R092, R111, R185, R206, R218, R236, R270, R277, R346, R402
Gillespie, Gerald, R155
Gilmore, Myron, O008, Q018
Ginsberg, David, S029
Glaze, Walter Stephen, R156
Gleason, John B., I047
Gleckman, Jason, G032
Glunz, Hans Hermann, G033
Goethe, I097
Gogan, Brian, S030
Golding, William, Q063
Goodey, Brian R., R158
Goodier, Alban, F090
Gordon, Walter M., G034, G035, K004, L008, Q019, R159, R160, S031-S034, S040, T014, T015
Gottfried, Rudolf B., F091, R433
Goulder, Laurance, F092
Gouveia, Antonio, I007
Gow, Elizabeth, S035
Gracc, Damian, xv, G036, J011, N021, N022, Q020, Q021, R161
Grace, William J., R162
Grafton, Richard, Q053, Q062
Graham, Hugh, F093
Grant, Alan, Q058
Grant, Patrick, Q022
Graziani, Antonio Maria, F283
Graziani, René, R163
Green, J.R., R337
Green, Paul D., F094
Greenblatt, Stephen, G037, K006, R164, R165
Greene, James J., C007, C039, F005, F095, F096
Greene, Robert, K006
Greene, Thomas, G038
Gregory, T.S., S036
Greiff, Ursula, R166
Gresham, Stephen, Q023

Griffin, Robert, R167
Grocyn, William, F166, F218, J032
Gross, Janet Sussman, C041
Gruffyd, R. Geraint, T016
Gueguen, John A., R168, R169
Guerlac, Rita, P002
Guildford, Sir Edward, Q038
Gundersheimer, Werner L., R170
Gury, Jacques, H006, I048, R171-R175
Guth, Delloyd J., I092
Guy, Alain, R176
Guy, John A., B006, F097-F099, F144, F193, G063, R136, R177, S009, S037, S101, U011
Gygges, Thomas, F295

Haas, Steven W., S038, S039
Hadlich, Roger L., F192
Hageman, Elizabeth H., viii
Hales, John, G050
Haley, Martin, C024
Hall, Anne Drury, Q024
Hall, Edward, B011, G042, H024, I120, Q005, Q032, Q052, Q053, R095
Hall, Noeline, F100
Hallett, Philip Edward, C002, C003, C006, C021, C029, F271, F314, F315
Halpern, Richard, R178
Halsey, A.H., R087
Hamilton, Robert, R179
Hamlet, G059
Hamm, V. Michael, O009
Hammond, Eugene R., R180, R181
Hanham, Alison, Q020, Q025-Q027,
Hankins, James, F345
Hanna, Ralph III, T017
Hansot, Elisabeth, R182
Harbison, E. Harris, L009, R183,

R195
Hardin, Richard F., S040
Harding, David P., F328
Hardinge, George, H019
Hardyng, John, B011, Q053
Harff, Arnold von, R092
Harner, James L., Q028
Harpsfield, Nicholas, F004, F005, F041, F116, F267, F292, F319, F339, G033, H003, H010, S001, V001
Harrington, James, R053, R153
Harris, Muriel Sheila, Q029
Harrison, Maurice E., F101
Harvey, F. Brompton, G039
Haschak, Paul G., A015
Hastings, Cecily, F136
Hastings, Margaret, F102-F104, R184
Hastings, William, Q019, Q051
Hauerwas, Stanley, G040, G066
Haupt, Garry E., B018, C017, C027, T018
Haussy, Nathalie, F105, F106
Hawes, Stephen, N032
Hawkins, John, E004, E005, G070
Hay, Denys, F107, G047
Haynes, Robert William, K005
Headley, John M., B015, F108-F110, F179, F222, S041-S044
Heath, T.G., Q030
Hecht, Jamey, S045
Heckscher, William S., G041
Heffernan, Thomas J., F111
Heilen, Hans, A016, F112
Heinrich, Hans P., C009, G005, Q031
Heiserman, A.R., R185
Helgerson, Richard, R186
Helm, P.J., G042
Helmstaedter, Gerhard, F113
Heninger, S.K., Q061
Henry VI, O004

Henry VII, Q016, Q045, Q054, Q055, Q058, R138
Henry VIII, B014, B038, C019, D002, E001, F022, F027, F028, F030, F031, F037, F040, F043, F057, F059, F061-F064, F068, F070, F071, F086, F094, F098, F108, F127, F135, F143, F144, F155, F175, F177, F186, F187, F193, F197, F216, F219, F232, F244, F252, F263, F266, F268, F279-F282, F306, F318, F323, F324, F331, F332, F339, F352, G007, G020, G022, G064, H006, H022, I022, I019, I035, I079, N032, P007, Q016, R032, R127, R138, S037, S043, V052, V057, V058
Henslowe, Philip, V006
Herman, Peter C., R296
Hermes Trismegistus, J008
Hernandez Conesa, Salvador, F114
Herodotus, L004, R031, R078, R435
Herrero, Javier, F115
Herrick, Robert, K001
Hertzler, Joyce Oramel, R187
Hesiod, J016, R309
Hester, M. Thomas, Q007, R188
Heuermann, Hartmut, R226
Hewitt, Janice L., I049
Hexter, J.H., A024, B019, C021, C033, G043, R014, R054, R139, R189-R196, R305, R312, R375
Heylyn, Peter, I051
Heywood, Ellis, F047, F081, F238, K002
Heywood, Jasper, F081
Heywood, John, F047, G011, G050
Heywood, Richard, F284
Heyworth, P.L., R208
Hibbard, G.R., G044
Hibbert, Eleanor, I050

INDEX   381

Hildegard, St., J017
Hiller, Wendy, I066
Himelick, Raymond, T019
Hitchcock, Elsie V., C012, F116,
    F271, F273, F274
Hitchcock, James, S046, S047
Hitler, Adolf, R243
Ho, Koon-ki T., V015
Hobbes, Thomas, R153, R377
Hoby, Sir Thomas, G071
Hoeniger, F. David, I051
Hogrefe, Pearl, F117, F118, G045
Holahan, Susan L., N023
Holbein, Ambrosius, R173
Holbein, Hans, F008, F038, F124,
    F126, F139, F183, F184, F202,
    F213, F214, F220, F223, F246,
    F248, F343, I052, I110, Q038,
    Q053, T067, V052
Holden, W.H., F119
Holdsworth, William, F120
Holinshed, Raphael, H024, Q005,
    Q040, Q052
Holland, Philemon, I034
Hollis, Christopher, F121, F122
Holquist, Michael, R197
Holst, Henriette Roland, I020
Holt, John, F218, F257, N020
Holt, Nicholas, F225, F226, F293
Homer, R120
Honigmann, E.A.J., I052
Hooker, Richard, I104
Hopkins, G.M., M007
Horace, M005, R113, R125
Horst, Irvin Buckwalter, S048
Hosington, Brenda, R198, R199,
    T020
House, Seymour Baker, F123,
    F144, G046
Howard, Thomas, F332, F333
Howorth, R.G., M007
Hoyle, Richard, F144
Hsia, Po-Chia R., A017

Huddleston, Rt. Rev. Trevor, C001
Hudson, Hoyt Hopewell, N024
Huebert, Ronald, R200
Hulse, Clark, F124
Hunne, Richard, F037, F285,
    F298, G077, J021, S079, S100
Hunt, Lydia, R201
Hunter, David G., A018
Hunter, Joseph, F209
Hurdis, James, I045, V028
Hurstfield, Joel, G047
Husbands, H.W., A027
Hutchinson, F.E., T021
Hutchinson, Steven, R202
Hutten, Ulrich von, C039, F134,
    F171, F322, G033
Hutton, James, N025
Huxley, Aldous, R070, R094,
    R350, R393
Hyrde, Richard, J004, V008, V024

Indus, Josephus (Joseph the
    Indian), R287
Itkonen-Kaila, Marja, R203
Ives, Eric, F144

Jacob, E.F., Q043
Jacobsen, Eric, R380
Jacobson, John R., R144
Jacques, J., F125
Jameson, Frederic, R204
Janelle, Pierre, F126
Jansen, Sharon L., F127
Jarrott, Catherine, F128, L010
Jenkins, Claude, F129
Jenkins, Harold, V016
Jevons, H. Stanley, R205
John Paul II, R309
Johnson, Robbin S., R206, R207
Jones, Emrys, R208
Jones, Emyr Wyn, Q032
Jones, John, H015
Jones, Judith P., viii, A013, A019,

G048, G049, J012, R167, R209, T022, T023
Jones, Rayston, I053
Jones, Whitney R.D., G050
Jones-Davies, Marie-Thérèse, F276, K009, R411
Jones-Hugh, Lloyd, F190
Jonson, Ben, I037, K001, L007, Q008, R114
Jordon, Winthrop, R210
Joye, George, F244, S054, S074, S081, S082
Julian of Norwich, J010
Julius II, N018
Juvenal, R125

Kaiser, Walter Jacob, J013
Kant, Immanuel, I055
Kapótsy, Béla, A020
Kaufman, Peter Iver, F130, R211
Kautsky, Karl, A024, C021, I020, R212, R367
Keen, Ralph, xv, A021, B006, D007, S049-S052
Kelley, Donald R., F131
Kendall, Paul Murray, Q033-Q035
Kendall, Timothe, N011
Kendell, Angela J., F132
Kendrick, Christopher, R213
Kennedy, James L., F209
Kennedy, Richard F., I054
Kennedy, William J., R214
Kenny, Anthony, F133
Kenwood, Alun, R257
Kenyon, Timothy, R215, R216
Kernan, Gerald, S053
Khanna, Lee Cullen, G051, G052, R217, R218, T024
Kincaid, Arthur Noel, Q036
Kinney, Arthur F., viii, H012, K006, R219, R220
Kinney, Daniel, xv, B012, B013, C025, D008, G061, N026, P003, Q037
Kirk, Elizabeth D., R227
Klawiter, Randolph, F134
Knafla, Louis, J014
Knapp, Jeffrey, R221
Knowles, David, F135
Knox, David Broughton, S054
Knox, John, H005
Koch, Nynne, R440
Konecsni, Johnemery, I055, I056
Koppenfels, Werner von, R222
Kozikowski, Stanley J., M008
Krapp, George Philip, G053
Kreyssig, Jenny, R223
Kristeller, Paul Oskan, J015, N004, O012, R224
Kuhn, Joaquin, T025
Küng, Hans, F136
Kurtz, Martha Anne, V017
Kuttner, Stephen, S100

Lacas, M.M., I057
Lacombe, M.M., R225
Laine, Amos Lee, V013, V018
Lakowski, Romuald Ian, K007
Lane, John, F165
Lange, Bernd-Peter, R226
Langland, William, R427
Lantham, Richard A., R227
Larkin, James F., A022
Larkin, Michael J., F137
Latimer, Hugh, F159, G077
Latz, Dorothy L., V019, V041
Lauvergnat-Gagnière, Christiane, V020
Lawler, Thomas M.C., B008
Lawson, George, I023
Le Doeuff, Michèle, R230
Leblond, Jean, I013
Lecler, Joseph, R228
Lederer, Dietrich, R229
Lee, Edward, B005
Lee, Sidney, R194, R337

Leech, Peter, xv
Lefevre, Jacques, F157
Lehmberg, Stanford E., F138, O010
Leicester, Jane, F104
Leigh, Joyce, O008, O012
Leslau, Jack, Q038
Leslie, Marina Ann, R231
Létoublon, Françoise, R117
Levin, Carole, S055
Levin, Harry, J016
Levy, F.J., Q039
Lewi, Angela, F139
Lewis, Arthur O., R336
Lewis, C. S., C021, G054, S072, T006
Lietz, Paul S., I058
Lievsay, John L., I024
Liljegren, S.B., R232
Lily, William, F218, F257, F330, I106
Linacre, Thomas, F113, F146, F147, F166, F218, J032
Lincoln, Abraham, V038
Lindt, Gillian, N004
Littleton, Taylor, Q040
Livy, L004
Llanos y Torriglia, Felix de, F140
Lloyd-Jones, Kenneth, I059
Loades, David, F141
Locke, John, R377
Lockey, Rowland, F074, F124, F139, F246, Q053
Lodge, Edmund, I110
Lodge, Thomas, K006
Loeb version, B017
Löffler, Arno, R233
Logan, George M., B020, C037, R234-R236
Logan, John Frederick, I060
Logan, Marie-Rose, Q051
Logan, Terence P., vii
Loomie, Albert, F142, F189

López Estrada, Francisco, A023, I025, I061-I063, R237-R239
Lovera di Castiglione, Carlo, F143
Lowell, Robert, I125
Lucian, A014, B017, C034, F191, G010, G061, G069, G080, G084, I012, J013, L015, L020, R055, R076, R107, R125, R185, R225, R288, R445, V020
Lucretius, R225
Ludacer, Kenneth, R240
Ludwig, Hans-Werner, R241
Lumby, J. Rawson, C031
Lupset, Thomas, K005, R150, R278
Lupton, Thomas, I092, R246
Lusardi, James P., B004
Lussier, Mark, Q061
Luther, Martin, B015, C028, F279, G020, G058, G059, G062, J024, P008, S041, S043, S064, S065
Luzio, Juan Duran, R242
Lydgate, John, M008
Lyly, John, I092, K006, K012, R155
Lyman, Stanford M., R254
Lynch, Arthur, I064
Lynch, Charles A., B013, C014, C018
Lytle, Guy Fitch, P004, R170, R356

Maber, R.G., V021, V022
MacCulloch, Diarmid, F144
MacDonald, A.A., D005
MacDonald, William, A024
Machiavelli, G018, G074, J018, J031, L009, M008, Q008, Q031, R003, R018, R029, R057, R097, R153, R183, R189, R191, R195, R196, R261
Mackenzie, Ann L., R238
Mackey, John, F145

Mackie, J.D., R243
Mackintosh, Sir James, I091
MacNalty, Arthur S., F146, F147, I065
Macrobius, R368
Maguire, John, F148, F149
Mahoney, Edward P., O012
Maier, Hans, F150
Major, John M., G055
Malhomme, Florence, G056
Malpass, E. Deanne, N010
Mancini, Dominic, Q002, Q003
Mandeville, Scholastica, B015
Manley, Frank, B009, B014, C005
Manley, Lawrence, R244
Mann-Phillips, Margaret, U003
Manning, Anne, I020
Manningham, John, I102
Manuel, Frank E., R245, R298
Manuel, Fritzie P., R245
Manzalaoui, Mahmoud, R246, T026
Manzone, Alessandro, I011
Marc'hadour, Germain, xv, xvi, A021, A025, A026, B008, B014, C001, D009, F087, F151-F175, F259, G057, G058, G063, H007, I003, I067-I069, J017, K008, K009, L011-L017, O013, Q053, R247-R252, R276, R307, S056, S057, T027-T033, V023-V026
Margolin, Jean-Claude, F176, P005, R253, R274, R363
Marin, Louis, R202, R254-R256
Maritain, Jacques, G070
Marius, Richard C., B004, B008, B014, C038, F040, F109, F177-F181, F222, F228, G059, R312, S058-S060
Marlowe, Christopher, G037
Marmion, John P., A026, F182
Maroto Camino, Mercedes, R257
Marsh, T.N., R258, S061

Marshall, Peter K., C033, R203
Martial, R435
Martínez, López Miguel, R259, R260
Martins, Jose V. de Pina, H008
Martyn, John R.C., I070
Martyr, Peter, R377
Martz, Louis L., B009, B016, C005, F183, F184, S062, T012, T034-T037, T062
Marullus, C014
Mary of France, F239
Maskell, David, O011
Mason, H.A., G060, G061
Massaut, Jean Pierre, L017
Massingham, K.R., F185
Maveety, Stanley R., S063
Maxcey, Carl E., G062
Maxey, Chester C., R261
Mayer, Thomas, F042
Maynard, Theodore, F186, F187, V031
Mazlish, Bruce, R057
McAleer, John, F188
McCabe, Richard A., R262
McCann, Timothy J., F189
McCarthy, John, G063
McClung, William A., R263, R264
McConica, James K., A024, A027, F190, F191, G064, G077, H009, H010
McCutcheon, Elizabeth, xvi, C021, F192-F194, G065, I071-I074, M009, R199, R265-R276, R399, U004, V027
McCutcheon, James M., I075
McCutcheon, R.R., K010, S064, S065
McDermott, C. Logan, V028
McDonald, Miles, F195
McFarlane, I.D., F155, F348, R267
McGregor, Frank, Q021
McKenna, John W., I092

INDEX 385

McKinnon, Dana G., R277
McLean, Andrew, R278, R279, S066, S067
McMillin, Scott, V029, V030
McNabb, Vincent, T038
McNamara, Robert F., V031
McNamee, M.B., A028
Meagher, R.W., F196
Meany, John W., I076
Medinilla y Porres, Gerónimo Antonio, I053, R201
Medwall, Henry, G011
Meerse, Peggy Currey, R280
Meijer, Marianne S., N027, N028
Melanchthon, Philipp, S068
Melander, Dyonisius, N012
Melander, Otto, N012
Meller, Horst, M012
Mercanti, G.C., L018
Mermel, Jerry, F197
Merriam, Thomas, F198, I077, V032-V035, V050
Mesnard, Pierre, J018
Metellus, F054
Metscher, Thomas, R281
Metsys, Quentin, F011, H019
Metz, Harold, V036
Metzner, Patricia, G066
Meulon, Henri, E003, F199-F206
Meyer, Carl S., S068
Mezciems, Jenny, I078, R282
Miething, Christoph, R283
Miles, Leland, C003, F207, R284, S069-S071, T039-T046
Miller, Clarence H., viii, xvi, B002, B006, B007, B010, B013, B014, B019, B020, C017, C027, F208, I079, L019, R285, R286, T047-T049, U002, U005
Miller, David Lee, F124
Miller, Joe, H023
Milton, John, R048, R383, S061, T061

Milward, Peter, I080, S072
Minattur, Joseph, R287
Minerva, Nadia, H011, R108
Minns, Denis P., S073
Mölk, Ulrich, R288
Monfasani, John, F345, G067
Monsuez, R., R289
Montaigne, Michel de, R308, R310, R377
Moore, Michael J., xvi
More, Agnes Graunger, F154
More, Alice Middleton, F012, F023, F041, F055, F089, F165, F215, F221, F227, F338, F339
More, Cresacre, F002-F005, F209, F210, F212, F308
More, David, F211
More, Elizabeth, F088
More, Gertrude, V019
More, Jane Colt, F161, F215, F340, N002
More, John (father of Thomas More), F038, F102, F145, F262, I110
More, John (son of Thomas More), E002, F006, F117, I110, S008, T059
More, Margaret. *See* Roper, Margaret More.
More, Mary, F167
More, Thomas
  Act of Succession and, F054, F236, F265
  Act of Supremacy and, F013, F022, F062, F091, F135, F234, F235, F265
  Act of Treason and, F234, F265, F281
  afterlife, attitude toward, G059, G075, G078
  Alington, Alice, and, T015, T062
  amplification, use of, K016

More, Thomas (*continued*)
  ancestry of, F081, F102, F104, F119, F142, F167, F189, F305, F308, F309, V019
  anecdotal tradition of, F002
  angina pectoris and, F079
  antihumanism and, F069
  aphorisms, use of, K001
  Ascham, Roger, and, K011
  Attainder Bill and, F064
  Aubrey, John, and, F087
  Augustine and, J002, L023
  authority of Church, G076
  Bacon, Francis, and, J031
  Barton, Elizabeth (Nun of Kent), and, F061, F127, F140, F216
  Basle sketch of, F086
  Becket, compared to, F046
  Bible, use of, L011, L015, L017
  bibliographies, A001-A056; Belgium, Netherlands, A005, A016; exhibition, A035, A050; general, A006, A013, A019, A021, A022, A024, A026, A027, A039, A040, A042, A044-A048, A051, A054, G005, G015, G073, G075, G077; Hungary, A020; Italy, A001-A003; Japan, A033, A034; Margaret More Roper, A055; New Rochelle, A041; Russia, A049; St. John's U, A053; St. Louis U, A028; Slovenia, A056; Spain, Latin America, A023; Tudor, A043; United States, A025, A038; Washington, D.C., A018
  Biography, studies of, F001-F352
  birth, date of, F171
  body and execution, in works of, G019
  Boethius and, M004
  Boleyn, Anne, and, F097, F310
  Bonvisi, Anthony, and, F284
  Bracciolini, Poggio, use of, L018
  bronze medal of, V054
  Bruges and, F167
  Budé and, F084, F153
  Busleyden, Jerome, and, F301
  Canon, E001-E006
    "Vision," attribution of, E001, E004, E005
    "New Prayer," E002
  canonization of, F035, F048, F049, F143, F341
  canon law and, F118, F229-F232, F247, F285, J021
  capital punishment, view of, G062
  Caron, Antoine, and, F106
  Catherine of Aragon and, F140, F239
  Catholic as, F049, G057, V007
  celibacy and, F069, F136
  cervical disc of, F114
  chancellorship of, F018, F037, F069, F070, F097, F133, F141, F175, F191, F232, F255, F280, F282, F290, F304
  change, attitude toward, G047
  character of, F022, F037, F121, F186, F187, F200, F219, F259, F265, F322, F327, F336, G040, G083
  Chaucer, use of, L022
  Chelsea and, F044, F092
  chivalry, view of, G026
  Christian, as, F020, F033, F158, G072
  Christian unity and, F083, F090, F122, G072
  Church patron, as, F123
  Chrysostom, St. John, and, S102
  Cicero, use of, L010

INDEX 387

citizen, as, F205, F234
citizenship, view of, G024
City of London and, F224, F232, F254
civil authority and, F101
classics and, F093, F182, G025, G031, G057
Clement, John, and, F198, F347
Clement, Margaret Giggs, F215, F295, F299, F347
Colet, John, and, F217, F296, G001, J001, J010, J029, J032, L010, S069-S071
comic tone of, F129, F162, F322, G030, G054, G081, G084
common law and, F120, F229-F232, F247, F298, J014, J021
compared to
 Luther, G062
 Machiavelli, G074, L009
 St. Maximus, L003
 Socrates, L005
communism and, F033, J026
complexes of, F172, F279
conciliarist, as, F107, F109, F110, F179, F222
conscience of, F033, F054, F131, F164, F180, F251, F253, F286
controversialist, as, F026, F280
conveyance of lands and, F056
courts of equity and, F099, F247
Cranmer and, F064
creation of self, G048
Cromwell, Thomas, and, F064, F065, F072, F270, F306
"Cronica Cronicarum," reference to, L024
Crosby Place and, F284
Darcy, Thomas, and, F351
daughters of, F238, J009
Daunce family and, F036
death, attitudes toward, F318, G057, G075, G078
detachment of, F125
Devotional Works, T001-T070
 general critical studies, C027, G006, G012, G016, G027, G048, G069, G073, G075, G080, K018, T010, T018, T022, T031, T035, T036, T052-T054, T062, T064
 individual works
  De Tristitia Christi
   agony in the garden and, T048, T057, T060
   autograph copy of, T029, T065
   Colet-Erasmus debate, relation to, T057
   Basset's translation of, B007, C021, T038
   content of, T035
   date and composition, B007, T038
   Dialogue of Comfort, relation to, T038, T060
   martyrdom and, T048
   More's situation, relation to, T057
   other editions, C021, C027
   sacramental life and, T035
   sleep motif in, T020
   standard edition, B007
   style of, T035
   textual history, B007, C021, T038,

More, Thomas (*continued*)
  Devotional Works (*continued*)
    individual works (continued)
      De Tristitia (continued)
        textual history (*continued*), T047, T049, T065
        tone of, T035
        Tower of London and, T060
        Treatise on the Passion, relation to, B007, T038
        Valencia ms., B007, D003, T047, T049, T065
        Utopia, relation to, T038
      Dialogue of Comfort against Tribulation
        agony in the garden and, T060
        allegory, use of, T041
        amplification, use of, K016, S107, S108
        apologetic, as, T053
        argument of, C003, T041, T069
        art of improvisation in, B009
        audience of, B009, T040
        Augustinism and, T005, T043, T050
        autobiographical elements of, T041
        biblical translation in, T021
        Boethius, influence of, T039
        Christ's Passion, as meditation of, B009
        Church Fathers, use of, T043
        Cicero and, T051
        classical oration and, T069
        comfort, theme of, T009, T055
        communism and, J026
        composition of, B009, C002, T046
        connection with last letters, C002
        consolatory tradition, place in, T009
        "Dance of Death" and, T067
        date of, T033, T036
        decapitation and, T019, T040
        design of, C005, T034
        De Tristitia Christi, relation to, T060
        dialogue form, use of, B009, K007-K009, K019, K020, L020, T005, T050, T051, T053, T055
        digression in, B009, T002
        dramatization in, G080, T041, T066
        excursus in, T002
        faith, hope, charity in, B009, C005
        facsimile edition, C004
        first draft, as, T042
        general critical studies of, G015, G078, T053, T054
        Gregory the Great and, T051
        heresy and heretics, relation to, T044
        Holbein's influence, T067
        humanism in, J015
        humor in, G084

INDEX 389

images of women in, G052
imagination in, T001
imitation in, T002
influence on, I108
Juliana of Norwich and, T055
levels of address in, C005
Lucian's influence, L020
medieval devotional handbook, as, G079
More's execution, relation to, T040
musica reservata in, G013
mystical body, image of, T053
nature of truth in, T024
other editions, C002, C003, C005, C038
Paradise Regained, relation to, T061
perfect fool in, T070
persecution and, T044
persccution litcraturc, tradition of, G079
Petrarch and, T050
Platonic dramaturgy of, K004, T005, T066
Plutarch, use of, L008
poetic devices in, T041
polemical nature of, T022
polemical works, relation to, T022
prison metaphor in, G065
Psalm 90 in, T025, T061
Ralegh and, T019
redemptive history and, T053
rhetorical techniques of, T041
role of fiction in, T024
role-playing in, G080
self-fashioning in, G037

Scripture, use of, B009, C002, C003, C005
sources, C003, T041, T045
spirituality of, G058, T050
standard edition, B009
statesmanship and, T066
structure of, T023, T041, T056, T069
style, B009, C002, T006, T068
suicide in, T014
Syria in, T026
temptation and, T061
textual history, B009, C002, C003, D008, T007, T017, T028, T032
Tower of London and, T060
tribulation, theme of, T009, T069
Turkish aggression, response to, B009, G067, T053, T058
tyranny in, G023
Utopia, relation to, T044
Four Last Things
  ars moriendi in, B010
  biblical translation in, T021
  composition, B010
  date, B010
  fear of death and, T008
  gothicism, influence on, T008
  medieval traditions in, B010
  mysticism in, J012
  seven deadly sins in, B010
  sources of, T008
  standard edition, B010

More, Thomas (*continued*)
  Devotional Works (*continued*)
    individual works (continued)
      Four Last Things (continued)
        style, B010, K003
        textual history, B010
      Instructions and Prayers
        "A Devout Prayer," T010, V041
        other editions, C006, C016, C017, C027
        standard edition, B018
        textual history, B018
      Prayer Book
        bibliographical description, T037
        critique of Yale edition, T013
        Dialogue of Comfort, relation to, B016
        facsimile edition, B016
        "Godly Meditation," B016, T003, T010, T016, T029, T030
        Latin Book of Hours, B016, T003, T013, T027, T030
        Latin Psalter, B016
        marginalia in, B016, T027, T029
        mysticism in, J012
        Rule of St. Benedict, relation to, T011
        standard edition, B016
        textual history, B016, T029, T059
        "Thy Grace to Set the World at Nought," J012
      Treatise on the Blessed Body
        date of, T033, T036
        other editions, C006, C016, C017, C027
        standard edition, B018
        textual history, B018
      Treatise on the Passion
        apologia, as, T063
        Church Fathers and, T004
        composition, T038
        consolation and, T063
        date of, T033, T036
        De Tristitia Christi, relation to, B018, T038
        eucharistic expression in, T004
        love of God and, T063
        martyrdom and, T063
        other editions, C016, C017, C021, C027
        Scholasticism and, T004
        standard edition, B018
        textual history, B018, D008
        Valencia ms., relation to, B018
  dialogue form, use of, G007, G069, K002, K004, K005, K007-K010, K019, K020, K022
  diplomatic service of, F204, F282
  disillusionment of, F207, F331
  divine providence and, G027
  divorce questions and, F022, F039, F090, F140, F143, F187, F280, F323, G020
  Doctors' Commons and, F118, F185, F197, F285, F300
  Dorp, Martin, and, F112, F169
  "double vision" of, F327
  drama and, F291, G013, G028, G045, G057, G068, G069, V039
  duty, sense of, V004
  early biographies of, F004, F005, F039, F095, F096, F111,

F148, F149, F283, F288
early training of, F093, F190
Editorial Critiques and Questions, D001-D014
printers and More, D005
Yale edition, D011-D013
education of, F121, F143, F225, F226, F293
education, views of, F009, F080, F093, F126, F176, F182, F192, F194, F215, F238, F259, F261, F263, F277, G055, J004, J009, J023, J034
Egypt and, J008
Eltham, connections to, F019
Elyot, Thomas, and, F042, F068, F113, F138, F182, F348, G055, K014
English characteristics of, F223, G054
English clergy, view of, G046
English language, regard for, J033
English law and, F103, F120, F131, F229-F232
English Poems, M001-M014
English works of, G021
equity, view of, F120, F230, F247
Erasmus and, F015, F026, F034, F040, F053, F084, F134, F143, F157, F169, F174, F180, F182, F190, F202, F240, F242, F243, F245, F264, F280, F287, F294, F301, F302, F313, F329, F330, F345, G001-G003, G004, G015, G016, G022, G031, G038, G044, G060, G061, G067, G077, J001, J013, J023, J024, J029, J031, J032, J034, K012, L004, L010, L020, L021, L026,

V008, V024, V027, V037
etymology of More (name), F162
Evil May Day riots and, F127
execution of, F037, F065, F067, F097, F101, F105, F143, F232, F255, F280, F306, F335, F344, F352
faith of, F043, F191, F265, G083, G084, V004
familial life of, F009, F026, F048, F077, F078, F121, F125, F136, F183, F184, F191, F223, F280, G016
fear of death, G059
feminist, views of, F084, F215, G002, G049
fiction, view of, G008, K006
final years of, F014
Fisher, John, and, F050, F064, F065, F272, F311, F321, F341, F352, J024, S083, S091, S097
folly and, J013
France and, F052
friendship, F009, F125, F169, F217, F264, F277, F294, F313, F321, F332, F333, F345, F348, G001, G031, G057, L026
Gellius, Aulus, use of, L025
General Critical Studies, G001-G084
German *Life* of, F208
Giles, Peter, and, F330
grammarian, as, F218
Greek Anthology, use of, L019
Greek studies and, J008, J032
Grocyn, William, and, J032
hagiographies of, F148, F260
Harpsfield, Nicholas, and, F116, F267
heresy/heretics and, F031, F037, F098, F180, F183, F184,

More, Thomas (*continued*)
  heresy/heretics and (*continued*),
    F186, F188, F191, F265,
    F269, G055
  hermeneutics and, G004
  Hermes Trismegistus and, J008
  hermetic philosophy, interest in,
    G038
  Herodotus, use of, L004
  Hesiod and, J016
  Heywood, Ellis, and, F047
  Heywood, John, and, V057
  hierarchy of authority and, F031
  History of King Richard III,
    Q001-Q064
  history, perspective on, G026
  Holbein's portrait of, F008,
    F139, F183, F184, F202,
    F213, F214, F220, F223,
    F246, F248, V052
  holiness of, F009, F258, F289,
    F342
  Holy Orders, view of, G046
  hope of, G040, G066, G078
  Horace, influence of, M005
  household, F126, F220, F259,
    F263
  household school, F009, F083,
    F176, F192, F194, F259, F261
  Howard, Thomas and, F332,
    F333
  humanist, as, F048, F083, F093,
    F121, F133, F150, F182,
    F186, F190, F218, F245,
    F251, F253, F263, F277,
    F292, F294, F296, G001,
    G002, G004, G005, G014,
    G020, G022, G024, G025,
    G027, G038, G047, G054-
    G057, G060, G061, G064,
    G072, G073, G075, G077,
    G081-G083, J006, J015, J018,
    J022, J029-J031, V005, V039,
    V042, V058
  Humanist Letter-Treatises,
    P001-P009
  humanist poetics and, K006
  Humanist Works
    general critical studies, G005,
      G012, G016, G027, G048,
      G069, G073, G075, G080,
      K018
    individual works
      English Poems
        Boethius and, M004
        critical response to, B010
        date, B010
        form, B010
        Fortune, treatment of,
          M007, M008, M011,
          M012
        genre, B010
        general critical studies,
          M014
        Horace, use of, M005
        More as poet, M003
        images of women, in,
          G051
        number symbolism of,
          M009
        occasion of, B010
        other editions, C013,
          C018, C024, C026
        "Pageant Verses," G080,
          M001, M005, M006,
          M009
        Petrarch, use of, M001,
          M002, M005
        rhythms of, M010
        role of counselor in, G028
        role-playing in, G080
        "A Ruful Lamentacion,"
          M013
        Sallust, use of, M011
        sources, B010, M007
        standard edition, B010

INDEX

Stoicism in, M004
textual history, B010
traditions, literary and iconographic, B010
History of King Richard III, The
  authorship, B011, B012, Q031, Q043, Q045, Q064
  Bacon's *Henry VII*, compared to, Q054, Q055
  biography as, Q001, Q039, Q045, Q046
  bibliographies, G005
  Chaucer, use of, L022
  Churchyard's *Shore's Wife*, relation to, Q004, Q009, Q048
  classical history and, Q012, Q031, Q039
  classical tyrant, sources of, L002
  comic elements in, Q026
  composition, B011, B012, Q014, Q027, Q031, Q042
  Cornwallis' work, relation to, Q008
  date of composition, B011, B012, Q014, Q027, Q031, Q043
  denunciation, as, Q014
  design of, Q050
  doubling/repetition motif in, Q051
  drama in, G069, Q026, Q036
  English past in, Q013
  exemplum, history as, B011, Q019, Q022
  fall-of-princes pattern and, Q012, Q022
  fiction as, Q001, Q025
  Fletcher's play, relation to, Q053
  Gellius, Aulus, use of, L025
  genre of, Q014, Q037, Q046
  "generic misrule" in, Q037
  general critical studies, G005, G075, Q014, Q031, Q033, Q040, Q043-Q045, Q049, Q057, Q059
  Hastings in, Q019
  historical context of, Q016, Q035
  historical method and purpose of, Q021, Q029, Q031, Q039, Q050, Q062
  historical truth as, Q001, Q017, Q025, Q045, Q049, Q050, Q052
  humanism in, J015, Q007, Q014, Q022, Q029, Q031
  images of women in, G052
  inhumanity in, C009
  inverted panegyric, as, Q046
  irony in, Q007, Q012, Q021, Q024
  irrationality in, C009
  Jonson, Ben, influence on, I037
  kingship, notion of, Q016
  Lancastrian bias in, Q059
  Latin version (*Historia Richardi Tertii*) relation to, B011, B012, Q006, Q027, Q030, Q031,

More, Thomas (*continued*)
  Humanist Works (*continued*)
    individual works (continued)
      History of King Richard III
        (continued)
        Latin version (*continued*), Q037, Q039, Q043
        literary method of, B011
        literary quality of, Q017
        Little Princes in, Q038
        Lucianic vein of, Q026
        Lust's Dominion, relation to, Q011
        Machiavelli's views, compared to, Q031
        "male entitlement" in, Q056
        Mancini's account, relation to, Q002
        moral treatise, as, Q007
        morality plays and, Q041, Q060, Q061
        Morton and, Q006, Q043, Q064
        natural order in, Q036
        other editions, C009, C011-C013, C018, C026
        parody, as, Q026, Q027
        Petrarch, use of, L006
        Plutarch, use of, L008, Q003
        political theory of, J011, Q031
        power, idea of, Q006
        psychological determinism and, Q018
        "researched novel," as, Q063
        role of counselor in, G028
        Richard's character, Q018, Q030, Q041, Q047, Q059
        Richard's disfigurement, Q032
        Roman historians and, Q013
        Roman past in, Q013
        Sackville's *Complaint*, relation to, Q023
        sacrifice in, Q060, Q061
        Sallust, use of, Q022
        sanctuary in, G035
        satirical drama, as, Q020, Q026, Q027
        Shakespeare's *Richard III*, relation to, G033, Q005, Q015, Q048, Q052
        Shore, Jane, in, Q003, Q009, Q019, Q028, Q035, Q048, Q056
        sources, B011, Q005, Q039, Q043, Q045
        stage metaphor in, Q036
        standard editions, B011, B012
        structure of, Q012, Q030, Q031, Q036, Q051
        style of, K003, K012, Q024, Q031, Q042, Q045, Q054, Q055
        Suetonius, use of, Q022
        Tacitus, use of, Q022
        textual history, B011, B012, Q045, Q062
        Tey's novel, Q058
        themes of, B011
        tone of, Q007, Q014, Q024
        treatment of women in, Q056
        Tudor historiography and, Q016
        Tudor myth and, Q026, Q059

INDEX 395

  tyranny in, G023, Q006,
    Q016, Q023, Q060,
    Q061
  unfinished state of, Q006,
    Q010, Q049
  Utopia, relation to, C009,
    Q006, Q025, Q031
  Vergil, Polydore, and,
    Q003, Q010, Q026,
    Q047
  vice figure and, Q041
  vituperatio, as, Q014
  Walpole's account,
    relation to, Q034
Humanist Letter-Treatises
  authority of Church in,
    G076
  biblical translation and,
    P001
  Christian wisdom in,
    B012, C025
  epistolary conventions
    and, P006
  Erasmus, as defense of,
    P001, P002, P005,
    P008, P009
  Erasmian reforms,
    relation to, B012, C025,
    P001
  general critical studies,
    G075, P006, P009
  historical context, B012,
    C025
  humor and faith in, G084
  "humanist in action," as,
    P009
  Letter to Brixius, B005,
    C025
  Letter to Edward Lee,
    B012
    Erasmus, defense of,
      P005
  Letter to Martin Dorp,
    B012, C019
    academic skepticism in,
      G036
    Church Fathers and,
      P008
    defense of humanism,
      as, P003
    Dorp's background,
      P001
    medieval logic in, P002
    positive theology in,
      P008
    rhetorical features,
      P003
    tone of, P001
  Letter to a Monk, B012
    Batmanson, John, and,
      P005
    communism in, J026
    date of composition,
      P005
    Erasmus, defense of,
      P005
    occasion of, P005
    publication
      circumstances, P005
    spirituality of, G058
  *Letter to the University of
    Oxford*, B012
    biblical languages and,
      P004
    Church Fathers and,
      P004
    defense of humanism,
      as, P007
    humanist reform and,
      P004
  More's readers, B012,
    C025
  other editions, C025
  positive theology in,
    B012, C025, P008
  rhetoric of, P006

More, Thomas (*continued*)
  Humanist Works (*continued*)
    individual works (continued)
      Humanist Letter-Treatises (*continued*)
        secular learning in, B012, C025
        standard edition, B012
        structure, B012, C025, P006
        style, B012, C025, P006
        textual history, B012
      Latin Poems
        Abyngdon, Henry, and, N008, N009, N023
        Aesopic background of, N013, N016
        analogues to, B013
        Aphrodite in, N003
        astrology in, N016, N030
        beggars in, N003, N030
        Bourbon's *Nugae*, relation to, N014
        Brixius, Germanus, B013, N010, N026
        "But no Starres," N027
        Catherine of Aragon and, N025
        "Choice" poems, B013
        "citizens" or "subjects," in, N021
        classical sources of, L001
        cuckoldry in, N016
        composition, B013
        coronation verses, N032
        date, B013
        Domenichi, Lodovico, and, N028
        Epigrammata
          classical tyrant, sources of, L002
          death, theme of, N002
          political theory and, J011
          duplicity and, N006
          Erasmus, role of, in, B013
          folk literature and, N017
          general critical studies, N001, N019, N024, N033
          German edition of, N012
          Holt, John, and, N020
          images of women, in, G051
          influence on Erasmus, N018
          jestbooks and, N017
          "Jesting Poem to a Faithless Mistress," N007
          "Joke About a Helpful Fellow," N007
          Kendall, Timothe, and, N011
          Martial, influence of, N029
          More's Latinity, B013
          music and, N008, N009
          other editions, C013, C014, C018, C024, C026, N031
          Planudean Anthology (Greek Anthology), use of, N003, N004, N033
          political theory in, N022
          Progymnasmata, B013
          publication of, N005
          reputation and, N006
          Richard III, relation to, N022
          role-playing in, G080
          Sanford, James, and, N011
          16th and 17th-century reputation of, N015
          sources, B013, N016,

N024, N033, N034
standard edition, B013
style, B013, N033
subjects of, B013, C014,
  N002, N003, N008-
  N010, N016, N020,
  N024, N033
textual history, B013,
  N034, N036
themes of, B013, N024
"To thee thou arie Prophet
  all," N027
tone of, N033
translation of, N011,
  N027, N035
translator, More as, B013,
  C014
Utopia, relation to, N022
versification in, B013
Life of Pico
  asceticism of, O009
  bibliographies, G005
  changes in, O007
  Collectarium's influence
    on, O004
  date, B010, O012
  Dialogue of Comfort,
    relation to, O007
  Four Last Things, relation
    to, O007
  general critical studies,
    G005, G075, O006,
    O010, O012
  genre, B010, O006
  Leigh, Joyce, dedication
    to, O008, O012
  medieval sermons and,
    O006
  mysticism in, J012
  More's interest in, O002
  More's translation of
    Pico's "Twelve Rules,"
    O014

More's vocational crisis
  and, O008, O010, O012
occasion of, B010
oral tradition and, O006
Parkyn, Robert, and,
  O005
Pico's influence on More,
  O007
reception of, B010
role-playing in, G080
St. Francis of Assisi, use
  of, L014
saints' lives, relation to,
  O006
Scripture, use of, L015
17th-century reaction to,
  O003
sources, B010
spiritual elements of,
  G058, O013
standard edition, B010
style, K003, O006, O012
textual history, B010,
  O001, O005
themes of, O006
translation compared to
  Gaguin's, O011
Worde, Wynkyn de
  (edition of), O001
Translations of Lucian
  context of, B017
  drama of, G069
  Erasmus, role in, B017,
    G060
  humor and faith in, G084
  Lucian, response to, B017
  role-playing in, G080
  Ruthall, Thomas,
    dedication to, B017
  spirituality of, G058, S010
  standard edition, B017
  style, L015
  textual history, B017

More, Thomas (*continued*)
  Humanist Works (*continued*)
    individual works (continued)
      Translations of Lucian
        (*continued*)
        translator, More as, B017
      Utopia
        "Abraxa" and, R359
        academic skepticism in, G036
        active life (*negotium*) in, R076
        adages, use of, R068
        aesthetic distance in, R386
        agrarian crisis in, R146, R175
        agriculture and, R143,-R145, R175, R332
        allusions in, R047, R120
        alternate lifestyles and, R339
        ambiguities of, R265, R266, R376, R412
        analogues, B019, R409
        Anemolian ambassadors in, R112
        Angel Raphael and, R273
        anti-text, as, R335
        apocalyptic tendencies, in, R336
        apostles, influence on, R029
        Aquinas, influence of, R311
        architectural designs and, R263
        argumentative strategy of, R234
        Aristotle and, R235, R428
        Arnold, Matthew, and, R308, R310
        ars moriendi in, R122
        Ascham and, R155
        audience, humanist, C032, R132, R207, R317, R417
        authorial stance of, R302
        authority in, R046
        Augustine's influence on, R033, R125, R216, R331, R422, R423
        Bacon and, R040, R048, R108, R153, R231, R325
        behavioralism and, R128
        Bellamy and, R369
        biblical references in, R188, R255
        bibliographies, A007, A008, A015, A017, A029, A031, A032, A036, A037, G005, R129, R226, R326
        bifocal book, as, R362
        biographical context, R023
        Books I and II, relationship of, B019, C032, C037, R030, R072, R084, R101, R126, R135, R139, R140, R142, R144, R146, R159, R192, R208, R234, R305, R413
        Boethius and, R113
        book list, as, R363, R408
        Bracciolini, Poggio, and, R112
        Budé and, R150, R192, R409
        Bullein and, R276
        Burnet's translation of, C030
        Busleyden and, R041,

INDEX

R064, R192, R306
Buthrescae in, R252
Campanella and, R118, R154, R325
capitalism in, R102, R140, R178, R295, R381
capital punishment in, R350
"carnivalized" literature and, R044
Castiglione and, R227
Catholic interpretation, C029, C033, R312, R375, R398, R403, R404
Catholic sacraments in, R252
cenobitical arrangements in, R439
chamber pots in, R078, R093, R114
change, attitude toward, R008
chess and, R197
chickens, incubation of, R433
Chinese reaction to, R199, R272, R275
Christianity and, R030, R061, R135, R180, R182, R225, R307, R308, R312, R315, R331, R341, R343, R367, R382, R403
Chrysostom, St. John, reference to, R011
Church Fathers, use of, R011, R029, R032
Cicero, use of, R004, R225, R268, R355, R376, R421, R423
city encomium as, R279

city in, R298, R411
City of London, effect on, R244
city planning and, R244, R263
classical allusions in, C029, G025, R134, R188, R345
classical antiquity and, R030, R034, R134, R298, R401, R403, R406
classical Greek learning and, R403, R406
classical tyrant, sources of, L002
colonialist propaganda, as, R221
commercialism, reaction to, R029, R140, R381, R382
comic elements in, B019, C032, R007, R055, R343, R382, R448
common law and, R311
commonwealth literature, as, R427
communal vision of, R057, R104, R123, R176, R190, R216, R307, R308, R317, R341, R343, R400, R403, R416, R432
communism in, J026, R028, R045, R062, R102, R105, R123, R176, R216, R317, R341, R400, R403, R416, R419, R429, R432
composition, B019, C029, C033, R192, R305
conclusion of, R429

More, Thomas *(continued)*
  Humanist Works *(continued)*
    individual works (continued)
      Utopia (continued)
        concordance to, R050
        connections to
          Adagia, R307, R308
          The Adventures of Master F.J., R220
          Anatomy of Melancholy, R153, R392
          Arcadia, R147
          Areopagitica, R383
          Aureolus Liber de nuptiis, R436
          The Blazing World, R048
          Brave New World, R154, R350, R393
          Candide, R154
          City of God, R331, R422, R423
          City of the Sun, R118, R154, R325
          The Coming Race, R350, R350
          Comus, R123
          The Courtier, G056, R227
          Cyrano, R154
          De Cultu feminarum, R435
          De Finibus, R225
          De Iure Belli, R119
          De Monarchia, R283
          De Orbe Novo, R377
          Dialogue against the Fever Pestilence, R276
          Dialogue between Reginald Pole and Thomas Lupset, R278
          Discourses on Livy, R261
          Erewhon, R154, R350
          Euphues, R155
          Faerie Queene, R063
          The Fixed Period, R350
          Gargantua and Pantagruel, R085, R186, R214
          Governance of England, R184
          The Governor, G055, R020
          Gulliver's Travels, R095, R100, R107, R147, R154, R181, R282, R338, R410, R415
          Institutio principis christiani, R136
          King Lear, R123
          A Lamentation, R379
          Leviathan, R377
          Looking Backward, R128, R369
          Ludus Coventriae, R063
          The Mill on the Floss, R303
          La Monarchie, R189
          Moralia, R418
          Mundus Alter et Idem, R095
          New Atlantis, R040, R048, R108, R118, R153, R231, R325
          1984, R393
          Odyssey, R345-R347
          Paradise Lost, R048
          Paradoxa, R268
          Pericles, R383
          Philebus, R067, R209
          Piers Plowman, R427

INDEX 401

Praise of Folly, R138, R214, R220, R425
The Prince, R003, R057, R097, R183, R191, R261, R413
Rasselas, R303
The Remedy for Sedition, R379
The Republic, R028, R074, R128, R153, R185, R234, R283, R284, R288, R301, R302, R345, R360, R384, R385, R389, R420, R423
Robinson Crusoe, R154
Rule of St. Benedict, R057
The Schoolmaster, R155
Somnium Scipionis, R288, R368
The Tempest, R153, R221, R222, R377
Timaeus, R288
Time Machine, R410
Two Treatises of Government, R377
Tristram Shandy, R392
The Unfortunate Traveler, R392
A Voyage to Icaria, R128
Walden, R147
Walden Two, R128, R393, R434
Women in Love, R303
contemplative life (*otium*) in, R376
context, C032
contraries in, R265, R266
controversiae in, R219
Cortés and, R257

counsel, dialogue of, R177, R192, R193, R254, R371, R378, R399, R405
credibility of, R318, R319
crux in, R276
Dante and, R283
death in, R058, R350
debate, as, R321
declamation as, R220, R279, R362, R395
De Servis section, R271, R378, R399
dialectical interpretation of, R161
dialogue form, use of, K002, K004, K005, K007-K009, K019, K020, L020, R015, R039, R059, R159, R214, R234, R254, R279, R355, R362, R448, R450
Dialogue of Comfort, relation to, R356
diction of, R286
diplomacy in, R371, R405
discontinuity of, R255
discourse in, R142, R254, R334
dislocation within, R213, R255
disputation in, R220, R236
distance, treatment of, R069
doctrinal orthodoxy of, R323
double vision of, R265, R322
dramatic elements in, B019, G069, G080, R015, R214, R399

More, Thomas *(continued)*
  Humanist Works *(continued)*
    individual works (continued)
      Utopia (continued)
        dream, as, R230, R327
        dystopia, R202, R447
        early editions, illustrations in, R051, R173
        early French translations of, R198
        early modern England and, R216, R371
        ecclesial reaction, as, R211
        economics and, R175, R226, R241, R254, R295, R314, R326
        ecosystem of, R104, R269
        editions of, B019
        education, ideas of, C033, R155, R311, R403
        18th-century France, reception of, R174
        electio and, R236
        Eliot, George, and, R303
        emptiness of, R255
        enclosure and, R143-R145
        English ethical socialism and, R087
        Epicurean ideas in, R005, R225, R303, R396
        epistemology of, R292, R293
        equivocation in, R267, R376
        Erasmus' influence upon, G044, L021, R004, R025, R034, R037, R041, R047, R071, R085, R136-R138, R185, R192, R211, R214, R225, R277, R280, R292, R307, R308, R375, R382, R407-R409, R416, R425
        Essenes, influence on, R089, R259, R260
        etymology and, R346
        euthanasia and, R151, R163
        eutopia, meaning of, R202, R207, R426
        Eutopians and, R417
        exchanging occupations in, R038
        exploration and, R377
        expression of humanist ideals, as, G060, G075
        facsimile edition (Louvain), C035
        facsimile edition (Robinson trans.), C008
        faith in, R061
        family, attitudes toward, R037, R223, R311, R389
        fantasy, as, C034, R072, R303, R327, R370, R448
        feminism in, G049, R296
        festivus in, B019, R343
        festivitas in, C030, R429
        feudalism and, R178, R292
        Ficino, influence of, R288
        fiction, R036, R075, R084, R095, R254, R282, R327
        fictitious commentator, R277
        Fifth Lateran Council and, R356
        first bishop of, R258
        first edition of, R152
        first Spanish translation

of, R201, R238, R239
Flemish embassy, influence of, R315, R405
fool, source of, R088
foreign policy and, R405
Fortescue, John, and, R184
Franciscans' influence on, R024
freedom in, R171, R215, R227, R420
French translations of, H011, R320
"Friar and Hanger-on" section, of, R322
fusion of opposites, as, R447
garden as, R332
Gellius, Aulus, as source, R031
general critical studies, G005, G016, G042, G048, G075, R023, R054, R056, R070, R072, R102, R125, R126, R129, R132, R135, R139, R147, R148, R153, R159, R167, R178, R187, R192, R207, R217, R221, R222, R235, R241, R245, R255, R270, R329, R348, R349, R351, R354, R357, R358, R366, R370, R386, R388, R398, R409, R438, R440
generosus, meaning of, R191
Geneva, similarities to, R195
gender roles in, R296
genre of, R044, R213, R279, R327
geography and, R158, R230, R253, R316, R390
Gilbert, effect on, R210
Giles, Peter, R111, R185, R277, R402, R426
gold, attitude toward, R012, R076, R078, R113, R223, R232, R435
governmental structure of, R131, R388
great books and, R408
green world of, R036
happiness in, R149, R180, R182, R209
health, value of, R209
hedonism in, R067
Herodotus, influence of, R031, R078
Hesychius, use of, R013
heuristic inquiry of, R271
Hinduism and, R091
historical context of, B019, R254, R357
historical materialism and, R367
historical perspective, R335
Hobbes and, R377
home, attitudes toward, R037
honestas, meaning of, R234, R378
Horace and, R113, R125
human nature, concept of, R181
humanism in, C029, J015, J030, R032, R065, R211, R224, R229,

More, Thomas (*continued*)
  Humanist Works (*continued*)
    individual works (continued)
      Utopia (continued)
        humanism in (*continued*), R279, R292, R308, R317, R332, R357, R364, R372, R375, R376, R398, R403, R406, R409, R421, R425, R426, R429
        humanist poetics and, K006
        humanistic masterpiece, as, R364
        humanitas in, G071, J003
        human nature in, R049
        humor and faith in, G084, R007
        Hythloday, C032, F091, I078, I081, R010, R012-R015, R022, R030, R033, R035-R037, R042, R054, R061, R062, R073, R075, R077, R081, R091, R113, R119, R125, R126, R134, R146, R149, R151, R160, R161, R164, R168, R177, R180, R188, R190, R204, R206-R208, R211, R214, R220, R233, R252, R261, R268, R273, R286, R288, R292-R294, R302, R303, R305, R313, R316, R317, R327, R330, R338, R343, R345-R347, R355, R363, R365, R368, R371, R376-R379, R386, R399, R400, R406-R408, R412, R418, R421, R424, R426, R427, R432, R437, R441-R43, R445
        ideals and illusions in, R207
        Iliad and, R120
        illustrations in editions, R264
        images of women, in, G052
        immorality in, R225
        imperialism and, R353
        Inca Empire and, R205, R242, R291
        index verborum to, R430
        Indians, influence on, R090, R091, R287
        individual's development in, R086
        influence on, B019; Bacon's *New Atlantis*, I001; Burnet, Gilbert, I060; Byron, I081; Cervantes' *Don Quixote*, I042, I061, I100; Curzon (Lord), I083; Digges, Dudley, I073; Donne, John, I047; East Central Europe, I108; Egerton, Thomas, I074; English Civil War, I044; Foxe, John, I124; Gilbert, Humphrey, I056; Hall, Joseph, I120; Hooker, Richard, I004, I104; Lawson, George, I023; Lupton, Thomas, I092; Manzoni's *I promessi sposi*, I011; missionary endeavors, I075;

INDEX 405

Orwell, George, I049;
Percy's *Love in the Ruins*, I009;
Philonomous, I096;
Plat, Hugh, I084; Poca, Andrés de, I008;
Pudsey, Edward, I072;
Quiroga, Don Vasco de, I012, I057, I058, I122, I127-I130; Rabelais, I010, I082; Rouseau, I094; Sand, George, I093; Scève, Maurice, I059; 17th-century England, I109; Shakespeare, I036, I040, I086; Sidney, Philip, I038; Spain, I053, I061-I063, I126-I130; Spanish colonization, I025, I126-I130; Swift's *Gulliver's Travels*, I006, I078, I118; utopian tradition, I103; Voltaire, I082; Whittington, Robert, I041, I107; Williams, Roger, I113
injustice in, R330, R341
intellectual context of, R023, R357, R416
intellectual needs in, R318, R319
intellectuals in, G047
intertextuality of, R361
inventio and, R236
irresolution as solution in, R321
iron, attitude toward, R076
irony in, R030, R107, R133, R214, R281, R301, R302, R358, R361, R362, R429
island, as, G074, R230, R344, R357
jeu d'esprit, as, G054, R072, R101, R235, R342
Johnson, Samuel, and, R303
Josephus as source, R260, R287
justum bellum, notion of, R066, R119
Juvenal and, R125
justice in, J018, R061, R063, R181, R330
Kautsky and, appraisal, R367
Kerala, influence on, R287
lack of revelation in, R102
lack of university in, R169
Langland, William, R427
larceny and, R184, R322
Las Casas, influence of, R026
Latin, choice of, R020
Latin style of, C029, C032, R286, R289, R394
laws of, R115
Lawrence, D.H., and, R303
legal procedures and, R357
leisure in, R105, R117
letter to Giles, R270
Letter to Martin Dorp, relation to, R443
literary character, B019, R241
literary context of, R023, R139

More, Thomas (*continued*)
  Humanist Works (*continued*)
    individual works (continued)
      Utopia (continued)
        literary design of, R423
        literary exercise, as, R317
        litotes, use of, R265
        Locke and, R377
        logic in, R401
        Lucian, use of, L007, L020, R055, R076, R107, R125, R185, R225, R288, R345, R355
        Lucretius, use of, R225
        Lyly, John, and R155
        Machiavelli, and, R003, R029, R097, R183, R189, R191, R196, R261, R353, R413
        Macrobius, influence on, R368
        magnificentia, meaning of, R014
        maiestas, meaning of, R014, R191
        Mandeville, as source, R042
        mapping of, R158, R248
        marginal glosses in, R277
        marriage in, R038, R165, R223
        Martyr and, R377
        martyrdom in, R251
        Marxist interpretation of, C033, R212, R367
        materialism, problem of, R080
        Mayan civilization, as source, R390
        medieval Christianity in, C029, R034, R035, R367
        medicus, meaning of, R273
        Menippean satire and, R025, R044, R444, R445
        Middle Ages and, R034, R035, R116, R194, R292, R315, R334, R336, R374
        "minimum religion" of, R284
        misanthropy in, R037
        "missing the point" in, R001
        modernity and, G043, R194, R334
        monasticism, influence upon, R160, R352
        money, attitudes toward, R037, R314
        monkey in, R293
        monologue, as, R059, R214
        Montaigne and, R308, R310
        morality, problem of, R215, R372, R404
        More's decision on royal service and, C030, R192, R371
        More's polemical works, relation to, R132
        Morison, Richard, and, R379
        Morton, in, R081, R206, R208, R211, R407
        multidisciplinary work, as, R358, R361
        multiple perspectives of, R449
        music and, G056, R064
        musica reservata in, G013
        mysticism of, J019

myth of Golden Age and, J016, R346, R391
naked spouse selection in, R110, R436
names in, significance of, R340, R373
narrative method of, R231, R294, R392
natural law in, R315
nature in, R290
neo-Marxist approach to, R304
new attitude, development of, R023
new republic of, R387
New World and, R210, R257, R377, R391
negative attributes of, R037, R038, R186
19th-century criticism of, R337
nobilitas, meaning of, R014, R191
no placc in, R186
northern European humanism and, R009, R374
ontological change and, R257
open-mindedness, case for, R217, R218
oral-aural techniques of, R068
order, theme of, R099, R100, R280
other editions, C007, C015, C021, C026, C029-C039
other, from perspective of, R240, R255
otium, meaning of, R156
outopia, meaning of, R426
paideia in, G071
Palinurus, reference to, R345-R347, R426
paradigm, as, R365
paradigms of utopian fiction, R438
paradoxical nature of, R233, R265, R271, R343
parerga, function of, R009, R017, R041, R139, R150, R270, R305, R306, R426, R442
parody of travel literature, as, G032
pastoral myth and, R446
patriarchy in, R296, R352, R389
patronage and, R156, R170
peace, ideas about, R004, R119, R299, R300, R333, R388
perfect community, as, R033
Persius and, R125
persona "More" in, R007, R012, R015, R030, R062, R073, R075, R125, R126, R146, R164, R190, R206, R214, R286, R292, R302, R330, R338, R355, R365, R371, R378, R382, R412, R421, R424, R426, R429
personal relationships, attitudes toward, R037
Petrarch, use of, L006
Philo as source, R260
philosophia christiana, J003

More, Thomas (*continued*)
  Humanist Works (*continued*)
    individual works (continued)
      Utopia (continued)
        philosophic unity of, R005, R121, R235, R388, R403, R423, R432
        philosophy and rhetoric in, R321
        Pico's influence on, R325, R409
        pietas in, J003
        Plato's influence on, R029, R037, R067, R074, R168, R209, R225, R234, R235, R283, R284, R288, R301, R302, R345, R360, R376, R384, R385, R389, R416, R423, R426, R432
        Platonic dramaturgy of, K004
        Plato's myth of the cave and, R022
        playful spirit of, R245
        pleasure in, R118, R149, R165, R182, R209, R225, R290, R395, R400, R403
        Plethon, Gemistus, parallels to, R089
        Pliny as source, R042, R260
        Plutarch, use of, R004, R093, R360, R418
        political document, as, R305, R371
        political theory of, J011, J018, J020, R032, R039, R099, R100, R135, R141, R183, R189, R196, R206, R216, R217, R241, R254, R257, R365, R371, R374, R381, R383
        politics of accommodation in, R081
        politics of literary figuration in, R383
        pontifex, meaning of, R249
        positive attributes of, R038
        poverty in, R322, R326, R379
        power in, G074, R003
        preachers and, R368
        precious metals, attitude toward, R010
        pride, C030, R418, R431, R432
        priest, idea of, J003, R211
        princeps, concept of, R019, R085
        privacy, attitudes about, R200
        process of becoming in, R335
        process of experience and, R280
        property, attitude toward, R014, R038, R123, R186, R190, R379, R388
        prosperity in, R318, R319
        Protestant polemicists' use of, R324
        providence, role of, R137, R367, R396
        public interest, concept of, R262
        public opinion, concept of, R262

puns in, R013, R109, R271, R359
purpose of, R054
quality of mind, inducement of, R023
Quiroga, effect on, R210
Rabelais and, R214, R310
"radical humanism," as, R021, R304
radical literature, as, R281
Rastell, John, and, R377
reader-response theory and, R348
reason in, R004, R061, R099, R100, R181, R215, R315, R356, R426
reception, general, R223; Italy, H021; Poland, H020; Portugal, H008; Russia, H014; 17th century, H016; Slovenia, H026
recreation, attitude toward, R079, R117
reform and, R336, R404
Reformation, relation to, R228, R308
regimentation in, R038
relationship of ruler and ruled in, R003
religious communities in, R439
religious edifices in, R117
religious toleration in, J003, R228, R311, R387
Renaissance, view of, R034, R035
Responsio ad Lutherum, relation to, R211
restrictions in, R171
rhetoric of opposition and, R424
rhetoric of reform and, R048
rhetorical strategy of, R017, R048, R096, R219, R220, R236, R265, R266, R355
Richard III, relation to, R416
Richards' translation of, R247
Robinson's translation of, C030, C041, C043, R078, R320, R380
role of counselor in, G028
role-playing in, G037, G080, R164
St. Francis of Assisi, use of, L014
satire, as, G054, R125, R126, R133, R159, R185, R441, R443-R445
Scholasticism, reaction to, R029, R401, R441
science and, R006, R040
science fiction, relation to, R052, R237, R410
"second world" of, R036
secularity, concept of, R229
self-fashioning in, G037
self, from perspective of, R240
self-subversiveness in, R138
Seneca, use of, R004, R077
sententiae, use of, R068
serious program of reform, as, R127, R235
sexual relationships, attitudes toward, R037,

More, Thomas (*continued*)
  Humanist Works (*continued*)
    individual works (continued)
      Utopia (continued)
        sexual relationships, attitudes toward (*continued*), R046, R165, R311
        Seyssel, and, R189, R196
        16th-century Europe, reaction to, R082
        skepticism in, R008
        slavery in, R018, R038, R232
        social classes in, R016
        social order in, R004, R006, R016, R029, R039, R048, R061, R079, R082, R086, R097, R099, R135, R161, R179, R182, R183, R204, R206, R217, R226, R241, R269, R307, R308, R317, R343, R352, R372, R381, R383, R393, R427
        socialism in, R179
        Socrates and, R209, R355
        soul's immortality, tenet of, R356, R396
        sources, B019, C029, C037, R031, R042, R088, R089, R107, R112, R113, R125, R131, R134, R160, R222, R259, R260, R268, R273, R287, R288, R298, R301, R302, R311, R315, R331, R360, R368, R384, R385, R389, R390, R396, R407, R409, R411, R422, R423, R428, R432, R433, R435, R436
        space, treatment of, R069, R117, R253, R255
        spiritual elements of, G058, R060, R130, R211, R280
        standard editions, B019, B020
        Starkey and, R278
        Stoicism and, R004, R005, R093, R166, R235
        straightforward treatise, as, R045, R072, R193, R235, R376
        structure of, R222
        stylistic continuity, R254
        suasoria in, R219
        suicide and, R151
        superstition, treatment of, R071
        Surtz' translation of, R247, R250
        Swift and, R095, R100, R107, R147, R154, R181, R282, R308, R310, R338, R415
        symbolism of, R222
        Syrians, response to, R246
        text, as, R335
        textual history, B019, C032, R027, R051
        theological controversies and, R357
        Theophrastus and, R436
        thought experiment, as, R235
        time, treatment of, R069, R253, R254, R274
        tone of, R014, R030
        topoi, use of, R236

totalitarianism in, R179
translation of, R043, R203, R238, R247, R285, R320, R328
travel literature, relation to, R232
travel, relation to, R256
Turkish aggression, response to, G067, R299, R300, R356
tyranny in, G023
unemployment, problem of, R314
uneven development of, R213
uniformity in, R173
universal appeal of, C032, R327
urban life, view of, R175, R244
utilitas, R234, R378
utilitarianism of, R303
utopia, meaning of, R098, R202, R229, R329, R354
Utopian alphabet, origins of, R092
Utopian religion, C030, R037, R121, R157, R356, R404
Utopian tradition, place in, C036, R002, R048, R053, R056, R070, R083, R094, R103, R105, R106, R124, R126, R147, R148, R153, R154, R166, R172, R187, R232, R237, R282, R298, R309, R310, R325, R329, R339, R342, R348, R349, R366, R370, R393, R410, R414, R434, R438, V015
Utopian values, R290
utopian vision, R434, R450
Utopians and Christianity, R047
vagrancy in, R326
verbal dexterity of, R266
Vespucci and, R257, R377
vir pius in, R047
virtue in, R182
Vives' influence on, R176
Voltaire and, R308, R310
war, ideas about, R004, R018, R037, R038, R066, R097, R119, R299, R300, R333, R388
way of thinking, as, R206, R217, R218
weaknesses of, R243
wealth, distribution of, R313, R322
Wells and, R297, R410
Winstanley and, R216
wisdom, value of, R209
wit of, R382, R448
women's work in, R389
word play in, R013, R359
work in, R038, R105, R204
work of fiction, as, R305
Yale edition, critique of, R027, R375, R397
Hunne case and, F298, G077, S100
Hutten, Ulrich von, and, F134
Hyrde, Richard, and, J004, V008
iconography of, F105, F160, F213, F214, F248, F343, V054
imprisonment of, F037, F065,

More, Thomas (*continued*)
  imprisonment of (*continued*),
    F067, F072, F097, F143,
    F191, F204, F232, F255, F265
  indictment of, F030, F229, F232,
    F234, F236, F265
  Influence on, I001-I130; Acton
    (Lord), I098; Albery's *Anne
    Boleyn*, I002; Aneau,
    Barthelémy, I013; Anouilh,
    Jean, V055; Bacon's *New
    Atlantis*, I001; Bolt's *Man for
    All Seasons*, I005, I018, I066,
    I079, V025, V026, V043,
    V048; *Booke of Sir Thomas
    More*, I014, I022, I043, I052,
    I065, V001, V003, V006,
    V011, V016, V017, V029,
    V030, V032-V036, V049-
    V051, V060; Botero,
    Giovanni, I095; Bouchet, Jean,
    I019; Brandsma, Titus, I067;
    Burnet, Gilbert, I060; Butler,
    Samuel, V044; Byron, I081;
    Cabet, Etienne, I027, I046;
    Cervantes, I042, I061, I100;
    Chevreau, Urbain, I101;
    Constable, John, I106; Curzon
    (Lord), I083; Digges, Dudley,
    I073; Dinot, Richard, I111;
    Dolet, Etienne, I112; Donne,
    John, I047; drama, I115;
    Dutch drama, I116, I117; early
    American drama, I105; early
    epitaph, I064; East Central
    Europe, I108; Egerton,
    Thomas, I074; English Civil
    War, I044; English morality
    plays, I021; Foxe, John, I124;
    general, I114; Gilbert, George,
    I099; Gilbert, Humphrey,
    I056; Goethe, I097; Gouveia,
    Antonio, I007; Hall, Joseph,
    I120; Heylyn, Peter, I051;
    Hibbert, Eleanor, I050; Holst's
    Thomas More, I020; Hooker,
    Richard, I004, I104; Hurdis'
    Sir Thomas More, I045, V028;
    Italian stage, I024; Jonson,
    Ben, I037; Kant, Immanuel,
    I055; Lawson, George, I023;
    Lodge, Edmund, I110; Lowell,
    Robert, I125; Lupton, Thomas,
    I092; Mackintosh, James,
    I091; Manningham, John,
    I102; Manzoni's *I promessi
    sposi*, I011; Maynard,
    Theodore, V031; missionary
    endeavors, I075; More,
    William, I071; Nash, Thomas,
    I089; Orwell, George, I049;
    Owen, John, I070; Pajardi,
    Piero, V040; Pellico's *Thomas
    More*, I039; Percy's *Love in
    the Ruins*, I009; Philonomous,
    I096; Plat, Hugh, I084; Poca,
    Andrés de, I008; poems, I068;
    Pole, Reginald, I035;
    Protestant polemics, I087;
    Pudsey, Edward, I072;
    Quiroga, Don Vasco de, I012,
    I057, I058, I076, I122, I127-
    I130; Rabelais, I010, I082;
    Renaissance England, I054,
    I121; Reynolds, E.E., I090;
    Rousseau, I094; St. Dunstan's
    Church, I003; Sand, George,
    I093; Scève, Maurice, I059;
    Second, Jean, I015; 17th-
    century England, I109;
    Shakespeare, I036, I040, I065,
    I069, I077, I080, I086, V034,
    V060; Sidney, Philip, I038;
    16th-century, I016; Smith,
    Walter, I088; Spain, I053,
    I061-I063, I126-I129; Spanish

INDEX 413

colonization, I025, I126-I129; Swift's *Gulliver Travels*, I006, I078, I118; Swift, Jonathan (in general), I026; Thompson, Francis, I017; Thomson, James, I048; 20th-century drama, I085; utopian tradition, I103; Vallembert, Simon, I007; Vogel's *Meg*, I119; Voltaire, I082; White, Olive B., I123; Whittington, Robert, I041, I107; Williams, Roger, I113; Zinnemann, Fred, I005, I066
interludes and, G013, G045, G068, G069, V039
interrogation of, F072
Inns of Court and, F029, F231, F292
jestbooks, interest in, V042
justice, concept of, G010, G062
Language and Style, K001-K022
Latimer, Hugh, and, F159
Latin historians, use of, L004
Latin language, study of, K011
Latin Poems, N001-N036
Latin, use of, G041
lawyer, as, F027, F066, F137, F168, F195, F211, F229-F332, F255, F256, F286, F290, F292, F298, F350, G063, G066, G075, J005
layman, as, F048, F101, F137, F170, F253, F258, J021
legal training of, F010, F093, F121, F168, F197, F211, F232, F255, F257
Life of Pico, O001-O014
Linacre, Thomas, and, F113, F146, F147, F166, J032
Lincoln, Abraham, and, V038
Lincoln's Inn and, F092, F168, F231, F291
literary personality of, G080
Livy, use of, L004
Lockey's portrait of, F074, F139, F246
London and, F092
London Charterhouse, at, F037
loyalty of, F031, F251
Lucian, use of, G061, L020, V020
Lutheranism, views of, F122
luxury, views of, F125
Machiavelli and, J031
magic, view of, G038
maiestas in thought of, G034
Mannerist portrait of, F024
marriages of, F012, F023, F041, F055, F089, F115, F161, F215, F221, F227, F338-F340
Martial, influence of, N029
martyrdom, F077, F094, F133, F311, G032, V005, V007
medieval romances, views of, G002, G026
medieval saint, as, F001
Mercers' Company and, F254
merry tales of, G030
metamorphosis, concept of, G038
Middle Ages and, G054
modernity of, G043
More, Agnes Graunger (mother), F154
More, Alice Middleton, F012, F023, F041, F055, F089, F165, F215, F221, F227, F338-F340
More Circle and, F021, F051, F074, F113, F138, F174, G004, G045, G050, V039
More, Cresacre, and, F085, F209, F210, F212
More, Elizabeth, and, F088

More, Thomas (*continued*)
  More family and Yorkshire,
    F006
  More, Jane Colt, F161, F215
  More, John (father), F038, F102,
    F145, F262
  More, John (son), F117
  More, Mary, F167
  Morton, John, and, F145, K015
  Moses, use of, J008
  music and, G056
  musica reservata, use of, G013
  mystic, as, F078, J010, J019,
    V005
  myth of Golden Age and, J016
  name devices and, K015
  natural law and, V038
  new Tudor aristocracy and, J022
  noun phrase structures of, K013
  obedience of, F163
  Oedipus complex and, F172,
    F279
  Other Editions of his works,
    C001-C041
  Other Topics, related to, V001-
    V060
  Ovid and, J016
  Oxford, at, F007, F025, F073,
    F197, G015
  Oxford reformers and, F040,
    G064, J025
  Pace, Richard, and, F322
  papal supremacy and, F107,
    F109, F110, F177, F196
  parents of, F077
  Patenson, Henry, and, F100
  patronage of, F126
  peace, views of, F039, F090,
    G001, G003, G022, J001
  Personal Correspondence of,
    U001-U011
    addressee, as, U007
    bibliography of, U010
    Bonvisi, Antonio, with, U004
    Cranevelt, Frans van, with,
      U002, U005, U009
    Eck, Johann, and, U008, U010
    Erasmus, with, B001, U003
    historical context of, U010
    holograph of, U010
    Margaret More Roper, with,
      C001
    models of, U010
    other editions, C019
    prose style of, U001
    rhetorical principles of, U006
    sources of, U010
    standard edition, B005
  personality of, F039, F187,
    F259, F327, F336, G057
  perjury, view of, F325
  Petrarch and, J031, L006, M001,
    M002, M005
  philosophia christiana, J003
  physicians and, F113, F146,
    F147
  Pico, influence on, F083, F145,
    F296
  place in university curriculum,
    H018
  Plato and, J032
  Plutarch, use of, L004, L008
  Polemical Works, S001-S110
    general critical studies, G006,
      G012, G016, G027, G048,
      G053, G069, G073, G075,
      G076, G080, G084, K018,
      S004, S007, S009, S011,
      S013, S016, S024, S026,
      S028, S029, S036, S040-
      S043, S046-S048, S050,
      S052, S054, S059-S061,
      S063, S064, S068-S072,
      S075, S080, S083-S085,
      S088, S090, S092-S095,
      S097, S100-S104, S106,

INDEX 415

S110, T022, T035
individual works
  Answer to a Poisoned Book
    argument of, B002
    date of, T033
    De Tristitia Christi,
      compared to, T035
    eucharistic controversy in,
      B002
    polemical devices in,
      S086
    real presence in, B002
    Souper of the Lorde,
      response to, B002
    standard edition, B002
    textual history, B002
    theology of, B002
  *Apology of Sir Thomas
    More*
    argument of, B003
    battle of the books, as,
      S037
    content of, S009
    literary form of, S009
    rhetoric in, B003
    St. German, Christopher,
      as opponent, B003,
      S037, S087, S101
    standard edition, B003
    textual history, B003
  *Confutation of Tyndale's
    Answer*
    argument of, B004
    authority of Church and,
      S019, S022, S030, S075
    Barlow, William, and,
      S066
    Barnes, Robert, as
      opponent, B004
    caricature, use of, S040
    content of, S054
    digression, defense of,
      S062

    ecclesiology and, S022,
      S023, S030, S075
    "hack-work," as, S075
    Holy Spirit, use of, S076
    humor, use of, S090
    merry tales, use of, S090
    More's citation in, S109
    Patristic authority, role of,
      S058, S059
    popular jests and, S017,
      S018
    prose style, G053
    rule of faith and, S019
    Scripture and tradition,
      conflict in, S023
    standard edition, B004
    textual history, B004,
      D008
    textuality and, S045
    view of Church in, B004
    view of papacy in, B004,
      S042
    wit of, S017, S018
  *Debellation of Salem and
    Bizance*
    battle of the books, as,
      S037
    ex officio suits and, S096
    Gellius, Aulus, use of,
      L025
    St. German, Christopher,
      response to, B006,
      S037, S087, S101
    standard edition, B006
    textual history, B006,
      D008
  *Dialogue Concerning
    Heresies*
    amplification, use of,
      K016, S107, S108
    Aquinas, in, B008
    authority of Church,
      defense of, S019, S022,

More, Thomas (*continued*)
  Polemical Works (*continued*)
    individual works (continued)
      Dialogue Concerning Heresies (continued)
        authority of Church, defense of (*continued*), S030, S075
        biblical translation and, S080
        Bilney's trials and, S014, S035, S110
        "busyness," motif in, B008
        Cervantes, compared to, S003
        Chaucer's influence on, S025
        Church Fathers, use of, S053, S099
        Colet and, S069–S071
        comic elements of, S031, S032, S056, S090
        content of, S009, S054
        dialogue form, use of, K007–K009, K019, K020, S064, S065, S091, S099
        dramatization in, G080
        ecclesiology and, S022, S030, S075
        Harpsfield, Nicholas, and, S001
        historical context, B008
        Hunne case and, S079
        Joye, George, influence of, S082
        literary form of, S009
        Luther, reaction to, S043
        merry tales, use of, S056, S090
        Messenger in, B008, S006, S025
        More's citation in, S109
        More's theological capacity in, S053
        persona, use of, S082
        Platonic dramaturgy of, K004
        prose style, G053
        proverbs and, S018
        Rastell, John, and, S015
        religious truth and, S077
        Roper, William, and, S001
        rule of faith in, S019
        Scottish friar in, S105
        Scripture, knowledge and use of, S053, S073
        sources, B008
        speaker "More," in, B008
        standard edition, B008
        structure of, S099
        textual history, B008, D007, D008, S015, S051
        theological context, B008
        Treveris, Peter, and, S015
        Turkish aggression, response to, G067
        unnoticed tract, effect on, S020
        wit of, S018
      Letter against Frith
        consensus fidelium in, B014
        controversial letter, S074
        Frith, John, as opponent, B014, S033
        Joye, George, and, S074, S081
        More, John, and, S008
        Nausea, Frederick, and, S008
        real presence, defense of, B014, S034, S081

INDEX 417

    Scholasticism and, S034
    standard edition, B014
    textual history, B014
    Tyndale and, S074
Letter to Bugenhagen
    audience of, S098
    Barlow and, S067
    Bugenhagen, as response to, B014
    Bugenhagen's life and works, S012
    composition, B014, S098
    Luther, reaction to, S043
    method of, B014, S098
    quotation-response in, B014
    Responsio ad Lutherum, relation to, B014
    rhetorical strategies of, B014
    standard edition, B014
    Stapleton, Thomas, and, S012
    style of, S098
    textual history, B014
Responsio ad Lutherum
    allusions in, B015
    argumentative tactics in, B015
    authority of Church and, S030
    "Baravellus" version, B015, C028
    communism in, J026
    dialogue, use of, C028, S065
    ecclesiology and, S030
    form, B015
    logic, use of, S005
    Luther, reaction to, S043
    Murner, Thomas, influence of, S044
    northern humanism in, B015
    other editions, C028
    reception of, B015
    rhetoric of, S005
    "Rosseus" version, B015
    Ross, William, identity of, C028
    Scholasticism in, B015
    standard edition, B015
    style, B015, C028
    textual history, B015
    theological competence of, C028
    view of papacy in, S042, S044
Supplication of Souls
    economic context, B014
    Fish, Simon, response to, B014, C022, S038, S039, S055, S089, S094
    Hamlet and, S021, S027
    indulgences in, B014
    mortmain legislation and, S094
    Newman's *Apologia*, compared to, C023
    other editions, C022, C023
    political context, B014
    prayers for the dead in, B014
    purgatory in, B014, S010, S021, S027, S057, S097
    religious faith of, S010
    standard edition, B014
    textual history, B014, S049
polemicist, as, F133, V059
politics, vision of, F131, F195, F324, F331, G018, G023, G034, G055, G057, G072, J011, J018, J020, J028
portrayal in Bolt's play, F033,

More, Thomas (*continued*)
portrayal in Bolt's play (*continued*), G040
position, views of, F125
poverty, attitude to, F158
power, view of, F071, G040, G066, G074
printing, views of, F297
prison metaphor, use of, G065
pronunciation of, G017
property, attitudes about, F132
prose rhythms of, K017
prose style of, G012, G053, K012, K018
Protestant presentation of, F016, F307
proverbs, use of, K001
public figure, as, F026, F037, F039, F077, F078, F097, F121, F191, F197, F211, F249, F253, F255, F256, F258, F277, F278, F280, F290, F320, F324, F331, F350, G057, G066, J028
public health reformer, as, F146, F147
Rastell, John, and, F088, V009, V010, V012, V013, V018, V042
Rastell, William, and, V047
reading, views of, G007
realist, as, J018, J020
Reception and Reputation, H001-H026; Belgium and Netherlands, H001; 18th century, H019, H023; France, 1550-1789, H011; French literature, H006; Harpsfield's *Life* and, H003; Italy, H021; legacy of, H012; martyr, as, H022; 19th-century England, H025; Poland, H020; Portugal, H008, H013; Protestant hands, in, H024; recusant, as, H009, H010; Renaissance France, H004; Renaissance Switzerland, H005; Russia, H014; 17th century, H016; 16th and 17th century, H017; 16th-century France, H002; Slovenia, H026; Tudor England, H015; United States, H007
recusants, relation to, V019
Reference, A001-A056; English Renaissance, A004; Renaissance, A030; to 1750, A014; 17th and 18th century, A009-A011; 16th and 17th century, A052; Tudor, A012
Reformation and, F043, G077
Reformation Parliament and, F070
relative constructions of, K014
relevance of, F082
relics of, F049, F124, F302
religion, views on, F039
Religious and Philosophical Backgrounds, J001-J034
religious edifice (symbolism of), G035
rhetorical prowess of, F033
Rich, Richard, and, F266
Ro:Ba: and, F271, F317
role-playing and, F180, G028, G080
Roper, Margaret More, and, C001, F119, F130, F156, F182, F192, F194, F201, F261, F276, G015, T015, T062, V008, V021, V022, V024, V027, V037
Roper, William, and, F039, F042, F045, F267, F273-F275, F326, F328, F346, F349
royal service and, F071, F091,

F109, F128, F133, F145,
F155, F185, F191, F197,
F232, F277, F280, F282
  saint, as, F078, F137, G016,
G039
St. Basil, use of, L012
St. Francis of Assisi, use of,
L014
St. German, Christopher, and,
S087, S088, S096, S101
St. Jerome, use of, L013
St. Stephen, and, J007
Sallust, use of, L004, M011
satire, use of, G010, G011
scholar, as, F040, F048, F083,
F186, F249, G039, G081,
V014
Scholasticism and, J024, J025
secular world, and, F101
sentencing of, F072
sexual desire, and, F180
silence of, F057, F135, F229,
F265, F310
Skelton, John, and, F333
social order, view of, G014,
G055, G062, G072, J027
Socrates and, F319, J008
spirituality of, F033, F078, F183,
F184, F199, F200, F204,
F215, F289, F342, G057,
G058, T031, T052, V004
spiritual writers and, J017
Standard Editions of his works,
B001-B020
Stapleton, Thomas, and, F157,
F173, F314-F316
statesman, as, F077, F136, F269,
G039
suffering of, F205
suicide, views of, F060, F094
syntax of, G017, K021
Temple Guyting case, and, F132
theological abilities of, F078,

F243
Tower of London and, F092
tradition, view of, G047, G072
translation, art of, G060
traumas of, F172, F279
treason and, F091, F310
trial of, F014, F033, F057-F059,
F062, F063, F065, F067,
F072, F097, F101, F135,
F191, F232, F255, F256,
F265, F280, F281, F298,
F306, F335, F344
tributes to, V045, V053, V056
Tudor humanism and, F028
Turkish aggression, response to,
G067
20th-century scholarship on,
V046
Tyndale, William, and, F034,
F075, S002, S013, S093
tyranny, view of, G023
Use of Classical and Christian Sources, L001-L026
Utopia, R001-R450
Valla, Lorenzo, and, J031
Vives and, F115, F182, G001,
G022, G067, J001, J004, J009,
J034
Virgil, influence on, L016
vocational crisis of, F009, F037,
F069, F091, F097, F128,
F145, F191
war, views of, F039, F090,
G001, G003, G022, J001
wealth and, F032, F158
Wentworth, Anne, and F127
Wentworths and, F334
Wilson, Woodrow, and, F178
wit of, F129, F162, G009, G030,
G061, G081, G084, V004
Wolsey and, F097, F099, F181,
F269, F337
women, views of, F084, F215,

More, Thomas (*continued*)
  women, views of (*continued*),
    G002
  world of, F174
  world vision of, F090, G072
  Wyclif, John, and, J002
  youth of, F077, F190, F257,
    F277, G057
  Zoraster and, J008
More, Thomas II, I052
More, Thomas, S.J., F006, F209,
  F308
More, William, F104, I071
Morgan, Alice B., R290
Morgan, Arthur E., R291
Morgan, Nicole S., R292, R293
Morison, Richard, F352
Morison, Stanley, A026, F213,
  F214, F160
Morris, Eileen, C023
Morris, Joseph A., H012
Morris, William, R350
Mortimer, Anthony, R294
Morton, A.L., R295
Morton, John (Cardinal), F037,
  F145, K015, Q006, Q010, Q043,
  Q048, Q064, R206, R208, R211,
  R407
Morwen, John, F021
Moser, Fernando de Mello, H013,
  I081
Moss, Ann, R166, R249, R286,
  V037
Mozley, J.F., S074, S075
Mueller, Janel, R296
Müllenbrock, Heinz-Joachim,
  R297
Mumford, Lewis, R298
Munday, Anthony, V032, V033,
  V036, V051
Murner, Thomas, S043, S044
Murphy, Clare M., viii, xvi, I082,
  P005, R299, R300

Murphy, Robert T., V038
Murphy, Virginia, F144, F323
Murray, Francis G., F215, S076
Muse, Philip John, S077
Musto, Ronald C., G067
Myers, A.R., Q041, Q042
Mynors, R.A.B., B001

Nagel, Alan F., R301
Nash, Thomas, I089
Nashe, Thomas, K006, Q048,
  R392, S061
Nausea, Frederick, S008
Neame, Alan, F216
Negley, Glenn, A029, R317
Nelson, Lowry, Jr., G038
Nelson, William, xvi, F217, F218
Nenniger, J.E., A042
Neumann, Harry, R302
New, Peter, R303
Newman, Bertram, C011
Nichols, Fred J., N029
Noakes, Aubrey, I083
Nolan, Feergal, F219
Noonan, John, Jr., F033
Norbrook, David, R304
Nørgaard, Holger, R380
Norland, Howard B., G068, G069,
  T050
Norrington, Ruth, F220, F221,
  F227
Nugent, Donald Christopher, J019

Oakley, Francis, F109, F179,
  F222, S078
O'Brien, Brian, R305
O'Connell, John R., F223, F224
O'Dair, Sharon, F124
O'Donnell, Anne M., T051
Ogden, H.V.S., C021, C030
Ogle, Arthur, S079
O'Grady, Walter, R306
O'Leary, John, F225, F226

INDEX 421

Olin, John C., xvi, R307-R310
Oliver, Revilo P., B013
O'Malley, John W., T052
Oncken, Hermann, R353
O'Neill, Mary, F227, F228
Ong, Walter, K011, K012
Orgel, Stephen, R170
Orwell, George, A001, I049, R070, R087, R350, R393
Ossinovsky, Igor N., A049, H014
O'Sullivan, Richard, A026, F229-F232, F257, G070, R062, R311, S036
Ovid, C021, J016, R113
Owen, John, I030, I033, I070
Ozment, Steven, F233

Pace, Richard, F322
Pacholski, Richard Allen, V039
Pagden, Anthony, R376
Pajardi, Piero, V040
Palmer, William G., R312
Panofsky, Richard J., I084
Papazu, Monica, R313
Pardo, Isaac J., I126
Park, James W., R314
Parker, Thomas M., R315
Parkins, John, F298
Parks, George B., O012, R316
Parkyn, Robert, E002, O005
Parmiter, Geoffrey de C., F234-F237
Parr, Catherine, G064
Partridge, A.C., S080
Patenson, Henry, F100
Patrick, J. Max, A014, R317
Patrides, C.A., L020
Patrizi, Francesco, R435
Paul, Frances, F238
Paul, John E., F239
Paul, Leslie, F225, F240
Paulet, John, V022
Pavkovic, Aleksandar, R318, R319

Pearl, Valerie, F190
Peggram, Reed Edwin, R320
Pellico, Silvio, I039
Percy, Walker, I009
Perez, Demetrio Ramos, I126
Perlette, John M., R321, R322
Perry, Kathleen, N030
Persius, R125
Peters, Christoph, I085
Peters, Robert, R323
Petrarch, Francesco, J031, L006, M001, M002, M005, T050
Petrilli, Giuseppe, F241
Pettegrove, James P., R067
Pfister, Manfred, R222
Phillimore, J.S., F028
Phillip III of Spain, F142
Phillips, Elias H., G071
Phillips, Margaret Mann, F242, L021
Phillips, Rowland, R258
Pico della Mirandola, F009, F037, F083, F145, F207, F296, G038, M001, O001-O014, R409
Pineas, Rainer, F243, F244, I086, I087, R324, S081-S093
Pinnard, Pierre, F245
Piper, David, F246
Pitard, Derrick G., V041
Plant, Raymond M., F247
Plat, Hugh, I084
Plato, C020, F068, G083, J016, J032, R022, R028, R029, R067, R070, R074, R094, R128, R153, R168, R209, R227, R234, R235, R283, R284, R288, R302, R310, R343, R345, R360, R370, R384, R385, R389, R411, R416, R420, R423, R432, T066
Plethon, Gemistus, R089
Plutarch, L004, L008, Q003, R093, R232, R360, R418
Poca, Andrés de, I008

Polak, Frederik L., R325
Polansky, Janet Michaelle, T053
Polanyi, Karl, R314
Pole, Margaret, F239, I099
Pole, Reginald (Cardinal), I035, J034, R278
Pollard, A.F., Q043, Q044
Pontanus, Joannes Jovianus, C014
Pope-Hennessy, John, F248
Porphyry, R401
Potter, David, F144
Potter, George Richard, F249
Potter, Jeremy, Q045
Potter, Marguerite, N010
Pound, John, R326
Prada, Andres Vasquez de, F250
Prescott, Anne Lake, A004, A030, E004, I088, I089, V042
Prévost, André, F251, G072, R327, R328
Privat, Edmond, F252
Pudsey, Edward, I072
Pujals, Esteban, T054
Purcell, Maureen, T055
Purfoot, Thomas, S020
Purnell, Frederick, Jr., F345
Pyle, Fitzroy, M010
Pythagorus, R134

Quarta, Cosimo, R329
Quattrocki, Ed, R330
Quenneville, Jean-Guy, F253
Quevedo y Villegas, Francisco de, R201
Quiroga, Vasco de, I012, I057, I058, I076, I112, I128-I130, R210

Raban, Sandra, S094
Rabb, Theodore K., R195
Rabelais, François, F052, I010, I078, I082, J013, R085, R186, R214, R308, S032

Rädle, Fidel, F011, I117, O014, R279, S005, U006, V027
Raitiere, Martin N., R331
Ralegh, Walter, T019
Ramsey, G.D., F254
Randall, Dale B.J., I024
Rashkow, Ilona Nemesnyik, S095
Rastell, John, viii, D005, F088, O005, R377, S015, V009, V010, V012, V013, V018, V042, V058
Rastell, William, B003, B011, C013, D005, F004, F081, F116, F117, F130, F284, G011, I090, O005, Q062, S049, V047, V058
  English Works, B004, B007, B016, B018, C002, C003, C006, C010, C012, C021, C039, C040, D001, D002, D007, D009, D010, F161, F173, F252, G021
  Life of More, D010, F116
Rauchbauer, Otto, R439
Raumolin-Brunberg, Helena, K013
Rawlinson, of Ewell, Lord (Peter), F255, F256
Rawson, Claude, I078
Rea, Robert P., Q040
Rebhorn, Wayne A., R332
Reckert, Dídia Marques, R264
Redgrave, Vanessa, I066
Reed, A.W., A024, A026, A027, D010, F218, F257, F271
Regau, Thomas, I085
Reilley, Joseph J., R333
Reiss, Timothy, R334, R335
Reiter, Robert E., Q046
Renna, Thomas, R336
Revard, Stella P., F011, I117, O014, R279, S005, U006, V027
Rex, Richard, F258
Reynolds, Anthony, G063
Reynolds, E.E., C010, F059, F259-

INDEX 423

F268, F314, G073, I090, I091, R337, V002, V023, V043
Rice, Eugene F., Jr., G067
Rich, Sir Richard, F030, F059, F259, F266, I079
Richards, G.C., B019, C032, R247
Ricks, Christopher, G012
Ridley, Jasper, F193, F269
Rielly, Edward J., R338
Rimmel, Lesley A., F270
Rimmer, Robert H., R339
Ritter, Gerhard, G074
Rizzi, Marius, N031
Ro:Ba:, F004, F161, F271, F293, F317, H010, V001
Robinson, Ralph, C008, C015, C020, C029-C031, C041, R043, R078, R102, R191, R203, R320
Robles, Mercedes M., F115
Rochet, Abbe, I093
Rockett, William, S096
Rodgers, Katherine Gardiner, B010
Roe, Bartholomew, F317
Rogan, Marie Joseph, S097
Rogers, Elizabeth Frances, A024, A026, B005, C019, S098, U008, U010
Roig, Arturo A., I126
Romm, James, R340
Rope, H.E.G., F272
Roper, Margaret More, A055, C001, F019, F119, F130, F156, F182, F192, F194, F201, F215, F261, F264, F265, F276, F284, G015, I119, J004, T015, T062, V008, V021, V022, V024, V027
Roper, William, A044, C016, E005, F004, F005, F019, F021, F039, F041, F064, F156, F252, F266, F284, F293, F336, F339, F346, G033, G080, H010, S001
    The Lyfe of Sir Thomas More,

Knighte, C010, C012, C031, F001, F042, F045, F068, F138, F149, F199, F267, F273-F275, F286, F326, F328, F349, I020, Q001, V001, V051
Rops, Daniel, R341
Rose, Elliot, I092
Rosenbaum, Elisabeth, B001
Ross, Charles, Q047
Ross, Harry, R342
Ross, William, C028
Rossetti, Lorenzo, R343
Rosso, Giulio Raviglio, R163
Rötzer, Hans Gerd, R155
Rousseau, Jean-Jacques, R070, R389
Rousseau, Marie-Claude, A007, F276, R344
Roussel, Jean, I093, I094
Routh, E.M.G., F277
Rowan, D.F., Q048
Rowse, A.L., Q049
Roy, William, R324
Rubio, Gerald John, Q050
Rudat, Wolfgang E.H., R345-R347
Rude, Donald W., H015-H017, I095
Rudnytsky, Peter L., Q051
Rundle, David, N032
Rupp, Gordon, F278
Ruppert, Peter, R348
Russell, Bertrand, R094
Russell, J. Stephen, T056
Russell, of Killowen, Lord, C029
Ruthall, Thomas, B017
Ruyer, Raymond, R349
Ryan, Francis X., L022
Ryan, Lawrence, N033
Rydén, Mats, K014

Sabal, Andrew J., N034
Saccio, Peter, Q052

Sackville, Thomas, Q023
Saffady, William, F172, F279
St. Anthony, V002
St. Augustine, F205, G010, J002, L012, L023, O013, R033, R125, R331, R370, R411, R422, R423, S033, T043, T050
St. Basil, L012
St. Bonaventure, J017
St. Francis of Assisi, F158, L014
St. German, Christopher, B003, B006, F120, F298, J014, R177, S037, S078, S087, S096, S101, S102
St. Gregory the Great, L012
St. Jerome, L012, L013, P001
St. John Chrysostom, R011, S102
St. Maximus, L003
St. Peter, F163
St. Stephen, J007
Sallust, L004, M011, Q022
Samaan, Angele Botros, A031, R350, V044
Samaan, Neil, F144
Sand, George, I093
Sanderlin, George, R351
Sander-Regier, Raymond, I096
Sanford, James, N011
Sandgathe, Mechtild, I097
Sankaran, Sabita, E001
Santinello, Giovanni, T057
Sargent, Daniel, F280, F281
Sargent, Lyman Tower, A032, R352
Sawada, Paul A., A033, A034, J020, R353, R354
Scarisbrick, John J., F282, V045
Scève, Maurice, H002, I059
Schaeffer, John D., R355, S099
Schmidt, Mary T., L023
Schmidt, Paul Gerhard, R166, R249, R286
Schnur, Rhoda, R166, R249, R286

Schoeck, Richard J., B004, F173, F283-F300, G075, H018, I098, J014, J021, K015, L024, L025, M011, N003, N035, P004, P006, R265, R271, R300, R356-R364, S100-S102, T058, V008, V046, V047
Schroeder, Karl G., F301, I099
Schulte-Herbrüggen, Hubertus, A035, A050, D011, F259, F302-F306, G005, M012, Q053, R365, R366, T059, U006-U011
Schuster, Louis A., B004, S103, S104, T060
Schuster, Mary Faith, Q054, Q055
Schütt, Marie, F307
Schwartz, Peter, R367
Schwoebel, Robert, F249
Scofield, Paul, I066
Scombargo, Nicolo (Cardinal), F344
Scott, John Anthony, C033
Scott-Craig, T.S.K., P007
Searle, William, I100
Seary, Edgar Ronald, D005
Seeber, Hans Ulrich, R129, R368, R369
Seebohm, Frederic, C021, G064, R337
Seigel, Jerrold E., R195
Selden, John, J014
Selig, Karl-Ludwig, N004
Seneca, G083
Servier, Jean, R370
Severin, Dorothy S., R238
Seyssel, Claude de, R189, R191, R195, R196
Shaffer, Thomas L., G040, G066
Shakespeare, William, A001, C040, F090, F161, G033, G037, G044, I022, I036, I040, I065, I069, I077, I079, I080, I086, I105, J013, K003, Q001, Q005,

INDEX 425

Q015, Q032, Q040, Q048,
Q052, Q053, R153, R178, R222,
R377, R383, S021, S027, V006,
V032-V034, V049
Shanahan, D., F308, F309
Shaw, Robert, I066
Sheehan, John, C036
Sheldrake, Philip, G076
Shenstone, William, A009
Shepard, Alan Clarke, Q056
Shephard, Robert, R371
Shore, Jane, Q003, Q004, Q009,
Q019, Q028, Q035, Q048, Q056
Sidney, Sir Philip, G014, G026,
I038, K006, R147
Siegel, Paul N., J022
Sigonio, Carlo, K002
Silva, Álvaro de, P008
Simmonds, James D., R372
Simon, Elliott P., R373
Sims, James H., T061
Sinclair, Malcolm, S105
Singer, Charles, F147
Singleton, Charles S., R189
Skelton, John, F333, F334, F337,
G050, M008, N032, R178, S110
Skinner, B.F., R054, R128, R393,
R434
Skinner, Quentin, R312, R374-
R376
Slavin, Arthur, G077, R377-R379
Slote, Bernice, F207
Smelser, Marshall, S106
Smith, C.N., H019
Smith, Christopher, I101, V048
Smith, Constance, A021, A036-
A039, E005
Smith, Denzel S., vii
Smith, Lacey Baldwin, F310
Smith, M.W.A., V049, V050
Smith, Malcolm C., A040
Smith, Richard Lawrence, F311
Smith, Thomas, I092

Smith, Walter, I088
Socrates, F041, F319, J008, L005,
R355
Sodeman, Nancy Ruthford, K016,
S107, S108
Somerville, Robert, N004
Sørensen, Knud, R380
Sorlien, Robert P., F002, F312,
I102
Soto, Pedro de, B007
Southall, Raymond, R381
Southwell, Robert, G078, G079
Sowards, J.K., F313, J023, L026,
R382
Spenser, Edmund, E005, G014,
G026, G037, K003, R063, R113,
R178
Spikes, Judith Doolin, A041, V051
Spradley, Dana Lloyd, R383
Stamm, Rudolf, A042
Standish, Henry, F063, F298
Standley, Fred, I103
Stanier, R.S., F226
Stanwood, P.G., I104
Stanyhurst, Richard, N008
Stapleton, Thomas, F004, F005,
F156, F173, F208, F293, F314-
F316, F339, G071, G077, H010,
S012, V001
Starkey, Thomas, C012, G014,
G025, G050, J014, K002, K005,
R177, R278
Starnes, Colin, R384
Starrett, Agnes Lynch, G081
Steintrager, James, R385
Stenning, H.J., R212
Stevens, Irma N., R386
Stevens, Richard G., R387, R388
Stewart, Patricia L., I105
Still, Judith, R389
Stobbart, Lorainne, R390
Story, G.M., D005
Strauss, Paul E., G078, G079

Strong, Roy, V052
Strosetzki, Christoph, R391
Strype, John, F060
Stuart, Morna, I085
Suetonius, Q022
Sühnel, Rudolf, M012
Sulfridge, Cynthia Waugh, R392
Sullivan, E.D.S., xvi, R393
Sullivan, Frank, viii, A004, A022, A024, A043-A045, E006, F317-F320, H025, N036
Sullivan, M. Rosenda, K017
Sullivan, Majie Padberg, A004, A022, A024, A044-A048, H025
Sullivan, Patrick J., Q057
Surtz, Edward, xvi, A024, B019, C020, C032, F321-F323, J024-J026, R054, R203, R247, R250, R312, R375, R394-R408,
Süssmuth, Hans, R409
Sutton, Walter, G029
Suvin, Darko, R410
Suzuki, Yoshinori, F324, J027, J028
Swift, Jonathan, I006, I026, I078, I118, R100, R107, R147, R181, R282, R308, R415
Sylvester, R.S., xv, xvi, A002, B011, B016, C009, C013, C018, D012, F154, F325-F328, G080, I106, I107, K018, K019, P009, R411, R412, S109, T012, T062
Szendrey, Thomas, I108

Tacitus, Cornelius, Q022, R435
Tait, James, Q043
Tamura, Hideo, A049, I109
Tateo, Francisco, R166, R247, R286
Taverner, Richard, V008
Tawney, R.H., R087
Taylor, Gary, V033
Telle, Emile V., I110-I112

Tertullian, R435
Teunissen, John J., I113
Tey, Josephine (Elizabeth McIntosh), Q058, Q063
Thelca, Mary, C022, G081, T063, T064
Theobald, Frederick, R050
Theobald, Lewis, S021
Theophrastus, R436
Thomas, Ivo, G070
Thompson, Craig R., B017, F329, G082, J029, J030
Thompson, D.F.S., B001
Thompson, Francis, I017
Thompson, James Westfall, Q059
Thomson, James, I048
Thoreau, Henry David, R147
Tinkler, John F., J031, R413
Tod, Ian, R414
Tokarczyk, Roman A., H020
Torre, Fray Alonso de la, I062
Torti, Anna, R241
Toups, Noel Joseph, I114
Tournoy, Gilbert, F330
Trapp, J.B., A035, A050, B003, S009, S101, T065, V054
Traugott, John, R415
Treveris, Peter, S015
Trevor-Roper, Hugh, J032, R416
Trinkaus, Charles, G083
Trollope, Anthony, R350
Tromly, Frederic B., M013
Truchet, Sybil, R417
Tsukada, Tomiharu, F331
Tucker, M.J., F332-F334
Tudor, Mary (Queen), J034
Tunstall, Cuthbert, C019, F166, F203, R152, S016
Turner, Paul, C034, R203
Tyndale, William, B004, C012, D008, F034, F039, F069, F075, F109, F243, G037, G050, G077, K014, R324, S002, S013, S017,

S019, S020, S022-S024, S029,
S039, S040, S045, S046, S050,
S054, S061-S063, S072, S074,
S075, S077, S080, S081, S084,
S085, S093, S103, S104, T006

Ugrinsky, Alexej, I049
Underwood, E. Ashworth, F147
Unterweg, Friedrich-K., I115-I117
Urbain, Olivier, V055

Valcke, Louis, O013
Valk, J.M.M. de, V056
Valla, Lorenzo, J031, P003
Vallembert, Simon, I007
Vecchiolla, Donald, E001
Vega, Garcilaso de la, R242
Verdier, Antoine de, N035
Vergil, Polydore, G042, H024,
 L024, Q003, Q005, Q010, Q026,
 Q032, Q040, Q041, Q047
Vespucci, Amerigo, R257
Vickers, Brian, I118
Virgil, L016
Visser, F.Th., K020
Vives, Juan Luis, F115, F162,
 F175, F182, F239, F261, G001,
 G002, G022, G025, G067, J001,
 J009, J034, P002, P003, R176
Vocht, Henry de, F335
Vogel, Paula A., I119
Volgin, Vyacheslav, R419
Vollrath, Robert A., R255
Voltaire, François Marie Arouet
 de, R308, R310
Vrljicak, Kazimir, F336

Wall, John N., Jr., R449
Walker, Greg, F337, S110, V057
Walpole, Horace, Q034
Walsh, Chad, R420
Walsh, J.D., R315
Walton, Izaak, Q001

Walz, Herbert, R155
Wands, John M., I120
Warner, James Christopher, V058
Warnicke, Retha, F338-F340,
 I121, Q060, Q061
Warren, Fintan B., I122
Warren, James Perrin, F341
Watkins, David R., D013
Watson, George, A027
Watt, Lewis, G070
Webb, John, F284
Weber, Harold, F124
Webster, John, I031
Weever, John, F154
Wegemer, Gerard, C017, F342,
 R421-R424, T066
Weiland, J. Sperna, F169
Weinberg, Carole, J033
Weiner, Andrew D., R425, R426
Welles, Orson, I066
Wells, H.G., R094, R297
Wells, Kathleen, F343
Wells, Stanley, I052
Welti, Manfred E., D014
Wemyss, Courtney T., I049
Wentworth, Anne, F127
Wentworth, Laura, F334
Wentworth, Margaret, F334
Wentworth, Michael D., viii, A051
Wentworth, Sir Roger, F334
Werkmeister, William K., R183
Westow, T.L., R228
Wheeler, Jeffrey Matthew, V059
Wheeler, Michael, R414
Wheeler, Thomas, F344, H021
White, Helen C., H022
White, Olive B., I123
White, Robert P., Jr., Q007
White, Thomas I., F345, R428-
 R432
Whitford, Richard, F257, J017
Whiting, M.B., F346
Whiting, Robert, F144

Whittingham, William, H005
Whittington, Robert, I041, I079, I106, I107
Wilby, Noel McDonald, F347
Willeke, Caspar, I085
Williams, Aubrey, T062
Williams, Franklin B., Jr., A052, H023, R433
Williams, George Walton, F023, I024
Williams, Roger, I113
Willow, Mary Edith, M014
Wilson, Florence, I007
Wilson, John T., R434
Wilson, K.J., A021, C040, F348, K021, T067
Wilson, Katharina M., F194, R435, R436
Wilson, N.G., R437
Wilson, Norman Bateham, R438
Winkler, Gerhard, J003, R439
Winstanley, Gerrard, R216
Woll, Marie Anne, R440
Wolsey, Thomas, C019, F037, F097, F099, F155, F181, F193, F211, F269, F280, F328, F337, G020, G042, I079, R127, U007
Womersley, David, Q062
Wooden, Warren W., F349, H024, I124, J034, R441-R449

Woodville, Elizabeth, Q038, Q056
Woolf, D.R., F042
Worde, Wynkyn de, O001, O005
Worden, Blair, F190
Wortley, B.A., F232
Wright, John, F350
Wright, Nicholas, Q021
Wright, Thomas, F275
Wuttke, Dieter, F150
Wyatt, Sir Thomas, G037, K001
Wyclif, John, J002, S080
Wyland, Russell M., H025

Yeandle, Laetitia, I104
Yee, Nancy, T068-T070
York, Elizabeth (Queen), M013
Yost, Carlson Ward, Q063
Young, Archibald Morrison, K022

Zajac, Hal, A053, A054
Zapatka, F.E., I125, V060
Zavala, Silvio, A023, I126-I130
Zeevald, W. Gordon, Q064
Zell, Rosemarie, R450
Ziegler, Georgianna M., A055
Ziemer, Penny Benson, G084
Zimmerman, Hans-Joachim, M012
Zinneman, Fred, I005, I066
Znidarsic, Lilijana, A056, H026
Zumarraga, Bishop, I076

About the Compiler

ALBERT J. GERITZ is Professor of English at Fort Hays State University. He is the coauthor of *John Rastell* (1983) and the editor of *A Critical Edition of John Rastell's* The Pastyme of People *and* A New Boke of Purgatory (1985). His articles on More, Rastell, John Cheke, Samuel Daniel, and other subjects have appeared in journals such as *Moreana* and *English Literary Renaissance*. He also edited *Kansas English* and organizes special sessions on Thomas More and his circle every year at the International Congress on Medieval Studies.